Fifth Edition

Manual of FORENSIC ODONTOLOGY

Fifth Edition

Manual of FORENSIC ODONTOLOGY

Edited by

David R. Senn

Richard A. Weems

A Publication of the
American Society of Forensic Odontology

CRC Press
Taylor & Francis Group
Boca Raton London New York

CRC Press is an imprint of the
Taylor & Francis Group, an **informa** business

CRC Press
Taylor & Francis Group
6000 Broken Sound Parkway NW, Suite 300
Boca Raton, FL 33487-2742

First issued in paperback 2021

ISBN 13: 978-0-367-77851-4 (pbk)
ISBN 13: 978-1-4398-5133-3 (hbk)

Library of Congress Cataloging-in-Publication Data

Manual of forensic odontology. -- 5th ed. / editors, David R. Senn and Richard A. Weems.
p. ; cm.
Includes bibliographical references and index.
ISBN 978-1-4398-5133-3 (alk. paper)
I. Senn, David R. II. Weems, Richard A.
[DNLM: 1. Forensic Dentistry--United States. 2. Jurisprudence--United States. W 705]

614'.18--dc23 2012030322

Visit the Taylor & Francis Web site at
http://www.taylorandfrancis.com

and the CRC Press Web site at
http://www.crcpress.com

Contents

Foreword vii
Preface ix
Editors xi
Contributors xiii

1 History of Forensic Odontology 1
BARRY E. LIPTON, DENISE C. MURMANN, AND EDWARD J. PAVLIK

2 Forensic Pathology 41
GARY T. SIMMONS

3 Science and Forensic Odontology 61
MARY A. BUSH AND VERONIQUE F. DELATTRE

4 Dental Identification 75
GARY M. BERMAN, MARY A. BUSH, PETER J. BUSH, ADAM J. FREEMAN, PETER W. LOOMIS, AND RAYMOND G. MILLER

5 Dental, Oral, and Maxillofacial Radiographic Features of Forensic Interest 129
ROBERT A. DANFORTH, EDWARD E. HERSCHAFT, AND RICHARD A. WEEMS

6 Disaster Victim Identification 159
GARY M. BERMAN, BRYAN CHRZ, LILLIAN A. NAWROCKI, KENNETH P. HERMSEN, RAYMOND G. MILLER, AND RICHARD A. WEEMS

7 Missing and Unidentified Persons 193
STEPHANIE A. KAVANAUGH AND JOHN E. FILIPPI

8 Dental Age Estimation 211
JAMES M. LEWIS AND DAVID R. SENN

9 Bitemarks 257

JON CURTIS DAILEY, GREGORY S. GOLDEN, DAVID R. SENN, AND FRANKLIN D. WRIGHT

10 Animal Bitemarks 325

KENNETH F. COHRN

11 Abuse and Violence 355

JOHN P. KENNEY, JOHN D. MCDOWELL, AND DUANE E. SPENCER

12 Jurisprudence and Expert Witness Testimony 377

ROBERT E. BARSLEY, THOMAS J. DAVID, AND ROGER D. METCALF

13 Organized Forensic Dentistry 397

ADAM J. FREEMAN AND BRUCE A. SCHRADER

14 Becoming Involved in Forensic Odontology 405

KATHLEEN A. KASPER AND DENISE C. MURMANN

Appendix A: Educational Outcomes and Objectives 423

EDWARD E. HERSCHAFT

Appendix B: Presidents: American Society of Forensic Odontology 431

Index 433

Foreword

In 1980, the *Forensic Odontology Workbook* was published as a three-hole punched, loose leaf binder. Dr. Bob Siegel and I created this workbook in the spirit of sharing our collective knowledge with the emerging forensic community. The book covered procedures in bitemark analysis, preservation of the chain of evidence, and courtroom procedures, as well as the identification of individuals through forensic odontology, age determination, mass disaster procedures, dental disaster teams, and dental photography and radiography procedures.

The stimulus for writing the workbook came from our involvement in the crash of Pacific Southwest Airlines after a mid air collision with a private plane over San Diego in 1978. At the time, it was the worst air disaster in the United States. Of the 144 passengers and crew who perished, most were identified by dental comparison.

Since those early years, I have had the pleasure of contributing to each subsequent manual edition. With each new edition, procedures and practices have been updated as forensic odontology has grown and developed. The second edition (renamed the *Manual of Forensic Odontology*) was published as a bound book in 1991. The third edition followed in 1997 and the fourth edition in 2006. Credit is due to the editors of those books, Drs. Marden Alder, David Averill, Gary Bell, Michael Bowers, Edward Herschaft, David Ord, Raymond Rawson, and Steven Smith.

Much has transpired in the 32 years since that first edition. This new edition provides updates to the knowledge and procedures that were discussed in the preceding editions and is a compilation of the current state of the science. It is written by some of the most knowledgeable and experienced contributors in the field of odontology who bring years of practical experience to the project.

As a past-president of the American Society of Forensic Odontology, it has been a pleasure to have been involved from the beginning. Many other past-presidents have now passed on and we all miss them. The opportunity to write this foreword for the *Manual of Forensic Odontology, Fifth Edition*, is not only a pleasure but an honor. I sincerely thank the editors for the opportunity to reflect and to summarize from whence we came!

Norman D. (Skip) Sperber, DDS, D-ABFO

Preface

Since its genesis in 1970, the American Society of Forensic Odontology (ASFO) has welcomed all who have an interest in forensic dentistry. This inclusive attitude has contributed to the improvement of forensic odontology, fostered continued learning, and facilitated the development of valued long-term relationships.

In 1980, Drs. Robert Siegel and Norman Sperber coedited the *Forensic Odontology Workbook*, the first manual. This work was well received and in 1991, Dr. David Averill edited the *Manual of Forensic Odontology, Second Edition*. The third edition of the manual was published in 1995 and was edited by Drs. Michael Bowers and Gary Bell. The 2006 publication of the fourth edition included Drs. Edward Herschaft, Marden Alder, David Ord, Raymond Rawson, and Steven Smith as editors. The first four editions of the manual were published and printed by the ASFO. These manuals have been read, studied, and valued by many and are considered among the best sources for information about forensic odontology.

In 2009, the National Academy of Sciences (NAS) published a report titled "*Strengthening forensic science in the United States: A path forward*"; this publication was critical of many forensic disciplines. The report was released two days after I became president of the ASFO. The impetus for the development of the fifth edition was partly a response to the NAS report. I believed it was essential for members of the forensic odontology community to create a text accurately communicating the current state of the science and technology of forensic odontology. The quality of the information in previous manuals was excellent. The time had come to select a respected company, experienced in the production of forensic works, to publish the next edition. The board of governors agreed, and a contract with Taylor & Francis Group/CRC Press was unanimously approved. Drs. David Senn and Richard Weems were selected as editors for the fifth edition.

I am confident all who read this new book will find the information useful. Hopefully, they will add the book to their forensic odontology libraries. The editors, for whom I have the utmost respect, are among those forensic dentists I consider my mentors and friends. They have assembled a cadre of authors whose numbers include the best and brightest in their field.

I am humbly honored to have been invited to write this preface to the *Manual of Forensic Odontology, Fifth Edition*. I hope the information on these pages will be useful and valuable to you. My associations with the people involved in organized forensic odontology have meant a great deal to me; the relationships are among the most gratifying of my professional life.

If you are a grizzled veteran of forensic odontology, you will find useful information on these pages. If you are new to the discipline, welcome to forensic odontology and to a lifetime voyage of learning. My experiences tell me there are many who will help you along your journey.

Adam J. Freeman

Editors

David R. Senn, DDS, attended the University of Texas in Austin and earned his dental degree from the University of Texas Dental Branch at Houston. He practiced general dentistry from 1969 until 1992 and has practiced and taught forensic odontology exclusively since 1992. He is board certified by the American Board of Forensic Odontology (ABFO).

Dr. Senn is clinical assistant professor in the Department of Comprehensive Dentistry at the University of Texas Health Science Center at San Antonio (UTHSCSA) Dental School. He is the director of the Center for Education and Research in Forensics, the two-year fellowship in forensic odontology, and has directed the 15th through 20th iterations of the Southwest Symposium on Forensic Dentistry. He has authored books, book chapters, and papers in refereed journals on forensic odontology topics.

As a forensic odontologist for DMORT, he worked in victim recovery and identification in New York following the World Trade Center attacks, in East Texas after the Shuttle Columbia crash, and in Louisiana following Hurricanes Katrina and Rita. He is the chief forensic odontologist for the Bexar County (Texas) Medical Examiner's Office.

Dr. Senn serves on the board of editors for *The American Journal of Forensic Medicine and Pathology* and is an editorial consultant for *Forensic Science International.* He is a fellow in the Odontology Section of the American Academy of Forensic Sciences (AAFS). He also serves on the board of governors for the American Society of Forensic Odontology (ASFO). Dr. Senn is secretary and a director for the Forensic Specialties Accreditation Board (FSAB), serves on the board of directors for the Scientific Working Group on Disaster Victim Identification (SWGDVI), and is past-president (2009–2010) of the ABFO.

Richard A. Weems, DMD, MS, earned his dental degree from the School of Dentistry, University of Alabama at Birmingham (UAB), in 1977. He then served for two years as a dental officer in the United States Army at Fort Jackson, South Carolina, and received the Army Commendation Medal. He received his MS in oral radiology from UAB in 1984.

Dr. Weems' first teaching position was in 1984 at the College of Dental Medicine, Medical University of South Carolina in Charleston. In 1987, he returned as a faculty member in the UAB School of Dentistry. He has served as director of Student Affairs, director of Clinical Operations, and head of Oral Radiology. Currently, he is an associate professor and is director of the UAB Maxillofacial CBCT Imaging Center.

In 1988, he became a forensic dental consultant to the Alabama Department of Forensic Sciences (ADFS) and continues in that capacity. In addition, he currently serves as the chief forensic dentist for the Jefferson County (Alabama) Coroner/Medical Examiner Office. Dr. Weems has also served as a volunteer advisor to the Alabama Office of Emergency Preparedness related to its mass disaster response planning group.

Dr. Weems is a member of the Disaster Mortuary Operational Response Team (DMORT) and participated in DMORT's response to the World Trade Center disaster in 2001. He also participated in DMORT's response to Hurricane Katrina in both Gulfport, Mississippi, and Saint Gabriel, Louisiana, in 2005. In 2008, he was deployed by DMORT in the aftermath of Hurricane Ike, which struck Galveston, Texas. Currently, he is the Dental Section Leader for DMORT's Region IV and has conducted DMORT and NDMS (National Disaster Medical System) training at several regional and national conferences. He has also served as a member of the NDMS Conference Executive Working Group.

In 2005, Dr. Weems received certification by the American Board of Forensic Odontology (ABFO) and developed the board's "curricular guidelines in forensic odontology." Additionally, he has participated in the activities of the ABFO Credentialing and Examination Committee for the last five years. He has also served on the Board of Governors of the American Society of Forensic Odontology and recently completed six years of service to the Odontology Section of the American Academy of Forensic Sciences, culminating in the position of Section Chair.

Nationally and internationally, Dr. Weems has published numerous chapters in textbooks relating to dental radiology, forensic odontology, and forensic medicine.

Contributors

Robert E. Barsley, DDS, JD, D-ABFO
Department of Dental Health Resources
LSUHSC School of Dentistry
and
Chief Forensic Odontologist
Jefferson Parish Coroner
New Orleans Forensic Center
Orleans Parish Coroner
New Orleans, Louisiana

Gary M. Berman, DDS, D-ABFO
Forensic Odontology Consultant
Sparrow Forensic Pathology Services
Lansing, Michigan
and
Forensic Odontology Consultant
Wayne County Medical Examiner's Office
Detroit, Michigan

Mary A. Bush, DDS
Department of Restorative Dentistry
SUNY at Buffalo School of Dental Medicine
and
Department of Chemistry: Forensic Chemistry
Buffalo State College
Buffalo, New York

Peter J. Bush, BS
South Campus Instrumentation Center
SUNY at Buffalo School of Dental Medicine
and
Department of Art Conservation,
Buffalo State College
Buffalo, New York
and
Department of Chemistry: Forensic Chemistry
Buffalo State College
Buffalo, New York

Bryan Chrz, DDS, D-ABFO
Forensic Odontology Consultant
Office of the Chief Medical Examiner
State of Oklahoma
Perry, Oklahoma

Kenneth F. Cohrn, DDS, D-ABFO
Department Pathology, Immunology and Laboratory Medicine
School of Medicine
University of Florida
Gainesville, Florida
and
Chief Forensic Odontologist
Office of the Florida Medical Examiner
5th and 9th Judicial Districts
Lady Lake, Florida

Jon Curtis Dailey, DDS, D-ABFO, D-ABP
Forensic Odontology Consultant
and
Prosthodontics and Forensic Odontology Residency Program
Penobscot Community Health Center
Bangor, Maine

Robert A. Danforth, DDS, D-ABOMP
Clinical Sciences and Radiology
UNLV School of Dental Medicine
Las Vegas, Nevada

Thomas J. David, DDS, D-ABFO
Forensic Odontology Consultant
Division of Forensic Sciences
Georgia Bureau of Investigation
Decatur, Georgia

Veronique F. Delattre, DDS, D-ABFO
Department of General Practice and Public Health
University of Texas Health Science Center
School of Dentistry
Houston, Texas
and
Forensic Odontology Consultant
Harris County Institute of Forensic Science
Houston, Texas

John E. Filippi, DDS, D-ABFO
Forensic Odontology Consultant
Douglas County Nebraska Coroner's Office
Omaha, Nebraska

Adam J. Freeman, DDS, D-ABFO
Columbia University
College of Dental Medicine
New York City, New York
and
Forensic Odontology Consultant
Office of the Chief Medical Examiner
Farmington, Connecticut
and
Forensic Odontology Consultant
State Police Major Crimes Division
Meriden, Connecticut

Gregory S. Golden, DDS, D-ABFO
Deputy Coroner
Chief Forensic Odontologist
County of San Bernardino
San Bernardino, California

Kenneth P. Hermsen, DDS, MS, FACD
Department of General Dentistry
Creighton University School of Dentistry
Omaha, Nebraska
and
Forensic Odontology Consultant
State of Nebraska
Lincoln, Nebraska
and
Sarpy County Nebraska Coroner's Office
Bellevue, Nebraska

Edward E. Herschaft, DDS, MA, D-ABFO, D-ABOM
Department of Biomedical Sciences
UNLV School of Dental Medicine
Las Vegas, Nevada
and
Oral and Maxillofacial Pathology College of Dental Medicine
Medical University of South Carolina
Charleston, South Carolina
and
Forensic Odontology Consultant
Clark County Coroner's Office
Las Vegas, Nevada

Kathleen A. Kasper, DDS, D-ABFO
Forensic Odontology Consultant
Tarrant County Medical Examiner's District
Fort Worth, Texas

Stephanie A. Kavanaugh, DMD, MSD, D-ABFO
Forensic Odontology Consultant
Snohomish County Medical Examiner's Office
Everett, Washington
and
Washington State Patrol
Missing/Unidentified Person Unit
Olympia, Washington

John P. Kenney, DDS, MS, D-ABFO
Deputy Coroner
Identification Services
DuPage County Coroner's Office
Wheaton, Illinois
and
Forensic Odontology Consultant
US Joint POW/MIA Accounting Command
Central Identification Laboratory
Hickham AFB, Hawaii

James M. Lewis, DMD, D-ABFO
Forensic Odontology Consultant
Alabama Department of Forensic Sciences
Madison, Alabama

Barry E. Lipton, DDS, D-ABFO
Department of Justice Studies
Florida Gulf Coast University
Fort Myers, Florida
and
Chief Forensic Odontologist
Office of the Medical Examiner
6th, 10th and 13th Judicial Districts

Peter W. Loomis, DDS, D-ABFO
Department of Pathology
University of New Mexico School of Medicine
and
Forensic Odontology Consultant
Office of the Medical Investigator
Albuquerque, New Mexico

John D. McDowell, DDS, MS, D-ABFO
Department of Diagnostic and Biological Sciences
Oral Diagnosis, Oral Medicine and Forensic Sciences
University of Colorado School of Dental Medicine
Aurora, Colorado

Roger D. Metcalf, DDS, JD, D-ABFO
Chief Forensic Odontologist
Human Identification Laboratory
Tarrant County Medical Examiner's District
Fort Worth, Texas
and
Center for Education and Research in Forensics
Dental School
The University of Texas Health Science Center at San Antonio
San Antonio, Texas

Raymond G. Miller, DDS
Department of Oral Diagnostic Sciences
SUNY at Buffalo School of Dental Medicine
Buffalo, New York
and
Chief Forensic Odontologist
Erie County Medical Examiner's Office
Buffalo, New York

Denise C. Murmann, DDS, D-ABFO
Forensic Odontology Consultant
Naperville, Illinois

Lillian A. Nawrocki, DDS, MA, D-ABFO
Chief of Forensic Odontology
Office of the Medical Examiner, Suffolk County
Hauppauge, New York

Edward J. Pavlik, DDS, MS, D-ABFO, D-ABO
Chief Forensic Sciences
Cook County Sheriff's Police
Chief Consultant
Forensic Odontology
Will County Coroner's Office
Forensic Odontologist
Will County Sheriff's Police
Cook and Will Counties, Illinois

Bruce A. Schrader, DDS, D-ABFO
Forensic Odontology Consultant
Lubbock County Medical Examiner's Office
Lubbock, Texas
and
Center for Education and Research in Forensics
Dental School
The University of Texas Health Science Center at San Antonio
San Antonio, Texas

David R. Senn, DDS, D-ABFO
Center for Education and Research in Forensics
Dental School
The University of Texas Health Science Center at San Antonio
San Antonio, Texas
and
Chief Forensic Odontologist
Bexar County Medical Examiner's Office
San Antonio, Texas

Gary T. Simmons, MD
Department of Pathology
University of Alabama at Birmingham
and
Associate Coroner/Medical Examiner
Jefferson County Chief Coroner/Medical Examiner's Office
Birmingham, Alabama

Duane E. Spencer, DDS, D-ABFO
Forensic Odontology Consultant
Alameda, Contra Costa, San Mateo and Solano Counties
and
Forensic Odontology Consultant
California Department of Justice
Walnut Creek, California

Richard A. Weems, DMD, MS, D-ABFO
Department of General Dental Sciences
University of Alabama at Birmingham School of Dentistry
and
Forensic Odontology Consultant
Alabama Department of Forensic Sciences
and
Forensic Odontology Consultant
Jefferson County Chief Coroner/Medical Examiner's Office
Birmingham, Alabama

Franklin D. Wright, DMD, D-ABFO
Forensic Odontology Consultant
Hamilton County Coroner's Office
Cincinnati, Ohio

History of Forensic Odontology 1

BARRY E. LIPTON
DENISE C. MURMANN
EDWARD J. PAVLIK

Contents

1.1 Coroner and Medical Examiner Systems 2
1.1.1 Significant Dates in the Evolution of U.S. Coroner and Medical Examiner Systems 3
1.1.2 Distribution of Medical Examiners and Coroners by State 5
1.2 Dental Identification 5
1.2.1 Agrippina the Younger Identifies Lollia Paulina, AD 49 5
1.2.2 Pliny the Elder Publishes *Natural History*, AD 77 6
1.2.3 First Earl of Shrewsbury Identified by His Herald, 1453 6
1.2.4 Charles the Bold Identified by His Page, 1477 7
1.2.5 Colonel Sir Peter Halket(t), 1758 7
1.2.6 Dr. Joseph Warren Identified by Paul Revere, 1776 8
1.2.7 First British Trial in Which Dentists Were Cited as Expert Witnesses, 1814 13
1.2.8 Caroline Walsh, 1831 14
1.2.9 Homicide at Harvard: Dr. George Parkman and Dr. John Webster, 1849 14
1.2.10 John Wilkes Booth, 1865 and 1869 15
1.2.11 Second Lieutenant Henry M. Harrington, 1885 16
1.2.12 Claudius Beaupied, Victim of the "Killer of the Little Shepherds," 1897 17
1.2.13 Adolf Hitler, 1945 17
1.2.14 Henrietta Durand-Deacon, Final Victim of the "Acid Bath Murderer," 1949 19
1.2.15 Exhumation of Lee Harvey Oswald, 1981 21
1.2.16 Czar Nicholas II, the Last Czar of Russia, 1991 and 2008 21
1.2.17 Ramses I, 2003 22
1.2.18 Queen Hatshepsut, 2007 22
1.3 Disaster Victim Identification 23
1.3.1 Bazar de la Charite, 1897 23
1.3.2 Disaster Relief Act of 1974 (Public Law 93-288) 23
1.3.3 Jonestown, 1978 24
1.3.4 John Wayne Gacy, 1978 24
1.3.5 American Airlines Flight 191, 1979 25
1.3.6 Disaster Mortuary Operational Response Team (DMORT), 1992 26
1.3.7 Waco Siege, 1993 26
1.3.8 Oklahoma City Bombing, 1995 26
1.3.9 World Trade Center, New York; The Pentagon, Virginia, and Shanksville, Pennsylvania, 2001 26
1.3.10 Hurricane Katrina, 2005 26
1.3.11 Haiti Earthquake, 2010 27

1.4 Bitemarks and Bitemark Cases 27
1.4.1 William I of England, 1027–1087 27
1.4.2 George Burroughs and the Salem Witch Trials, 1692 27
1.4.3 Ansil L. Robinson Murder Trial, 1870 27
1.4.4 *Doyle v. Texas*, 1954 28
1.4.5 *Public Prosecutor (Norway) v. Torgersen*, 1958 28
1.4.6 *Crown (Scotland) v. Hay*, 1967 28
1.4.7 *Illinois v. Johnson*, 1972 29
1.4.8 *California v. Marx*, 1975 29
1.4.9 *Illinois v. Milone*, 1976 29
1.4.10 *Florida v. Bundy*, 1979 29
1.4.11 *Florida v. Stewart*, 1979 30
1.4.12 *State of Wisconsin v. Robert Lee Stinson*, 1984 30
1.4.13 *Louisiana v. Willie Jackson*, 1986 30
1.4.14 *Oklahoma v. Wilhoit*, 1987 30
1.4.15 *Commonwealth of Pennsylvania v. Kunco*, 1991 31
1.4.16 *New York v. Roy Brown*, 1992 31
1.4.17 *Arizona v. Krone*, 1992 and 1996 31
1.4.18 *Michigan v. Moldowan and Cristini*, 1991 32
1.4.19 *Illinois v. Young and Hill*, 1992 32
1.4.20 *Mississippi v. Brewer*, 1995, and *Mississippi v. Brooks*, 1992 32
1.4.21 West Memphis Three, 1994, Alford Plea 2011 33
1.4.22 *New Jersey v. Jesse K. Timmendequas*, 1997: Megan's Law 33
1.4.23 *Massachusetts v. Edmund Burke*, 1998 33
1.4.24 *State of New York v. James O'Donnell*, 1998 33
1.5 Age Estimation 34
1.5.1 Louis XVII "The Lost Dauphin," 1894 34
1.5.2 Massler and Shour, 1941 and 1944 34
1.5.3 Moorrees, Fanning and Hunt, 1963 34
1.5.4 Mincer, Harris and Berryman, 1993 34
1.5.5 King Tutankhamen, 2005 35
1.6 Abuse and Neglect 35
1.6.1 Mary Ellen Wilson, 1874 35
1.7 Forensic Odontology; Books and Chapters in Books 36
Acknowledgments 37
References 37

1.1 Coroner and Medical Examiner Systems

Coroners are public officials, usually elected at the county level of government, whose principal duty is to inquire into the cause of any death, but especially those deaths that may not be due to natural causes. Most coroners are not required to have medical training. Medical examiners have replaced coroners in some jurisdictions. Medical examiners usually are physicians and often have training in medicolegal death investigation, pathology, and forensic pathology. Medical examiner requirements vary from state to state (U.S. Department of Labor, 2012). Medical examiners generally have greater expertise in unnatural death investigations than do coroners (Hanzlick and Combs, 1998). The American Board of Pathology certifies physicians who meet the criteria in anatomic and clinical pathology and in the subspecialty of forensic pathology. For some local and state jurisdictions, certification in forensic pathology is required. Some states have mixed medical examiner/coroner systems. At present, there are insufficient numbers of board certified forensic pathologists to serve as medical examiners or coroners at every local level (Hanzlick, 2007).

The first coroner's office was created in England prior to 1194. As documented, in that year in the *Articles of Eyre* the office was charged with keeping the "pleas of the Crown" (Knight, 2012). Keeping those pleas involved recording the details of crimes or legal cases including burglaries, thefts, rapes, and homicides. The coroner also acted as a tax collector and investigated sudden deaths. While the coroner was involved in the legal system, his main duties were ensuring that the Crown received any monies, fines, and taxes owed. The method of dealing with suicide illustrates the pecuniary role of early English coroners (Coroners' Society, 2012). For deaths ruled by coroners to be a result of suicide, the property of that decedent would become the property of the Crown (Wellington, 1905).

The Births and Deaths Registration Act of 1836 was passed partly in response to concerns in England and Wales over homicides being passed off as natural deaths (Coroners' Society, 2012). This Act, and the Coroner's Act of 1887, required the coroner's office to focus more on determining the medical cause and legal circumstances of a sudden death. Autopsies became more common to better investigate these deaths (U.K. National Archives, 2012).

Autopsies have been performed since the time of the ancient Egyptians. They remain important procedures associated with investigations of deaths in both coroner's and medical examiner's offices. Early autopsies were less than optimally recorded and, what records were made, reflected the limitations of early practitioners of medicine. In the seventeenth century, Theophilus Bonetus published a collection of over 3000 autopsy reports (Buess, 1951; Knight and Meehan, 1973). Some of the reports were only a few sentences while others spanned several pages. Some contained the deceased's detailed history while others simply stated gender and age. Standardized autopsy procedures were proposed by German pathologist and anthropologist Rudolf Virchow in the nineteenth century (Ackerknecht, 1953). Many of the procedures he pioneered are still in use today.

1.1.1 Significant Dates in the Evolution of U.S. Coroner and Medical Examiner Systems

1860: In the United States, the State of Maryland took the first step toward converting to a medical examiner system by requiring a physician be present at coroner proceedings. Before this change, the sheriff or another public officer would certify the deaths (Jentzen, 2009).

1877: Massachusetts was the first state to replace coroners with medical examiners who were required to be physicians. This new medical examiner system resulted in a great improvement in death investigations. The Massachusetts Medico-Legal Society was created to assist and educate any physician that wanted to become a medical examiner (Jentzen, 2009).

1884: Following Massachusetts's example, Rhode Island created a medical examiner system in 1884. The Rhode Island system created a "mixed" system of coroners and medical examiners that featured medical examiners appointed for counties and coroners elected by town councils. Medical examiners were required to be physicians (Jentzen, 2009).

1914–1927: Other cities began to replace coroner's offices with the medical examiner system. These cities included Cleveland (1914), New York City (1915), Chicago (1922), and Newark (1927) (Jentzen, 2009).

1915: Dr. Charles Norris became the first chief medical examiner of New York City. He was given the authority to determine when autopsies would be performed (Jentzen, 2009).

1939: Maryland created the first statewide medical examiner and required that the medical examiner be a physician (Jentzen, 2009).

1954: The Model Post-Mortem Examinations Act (also known as the Model Act) was issued by the National Conference of Commissioners on Uniform State Laws. This Act cited that coroners are not required to have training in the field of pathology and recommended that each state create an office with a trained pathologist whose duties would include the investigation of deaths involving potential criminal liability. Many states adopted the guidelines and recommendations set forth in the Model Act (National Research Council, 2009).

1955: The Texas Medical Examiner Act came into effect, which provided that any Texas county with a population of more than 250,000 may change from a Justice of the Peace system to a medical examiner system (Justices of the Peace serve as coroners in many Texas counties).

1960–1979: Twelve additional states converted to a medical examiner system as recommended by the Model Act.

1966: The National Association of Medical Examiners (NAME) was established. NAME is a national organization whose purpose is to improve the field of medicolegal death investigation (National Association of Medical Examiners, 2012).

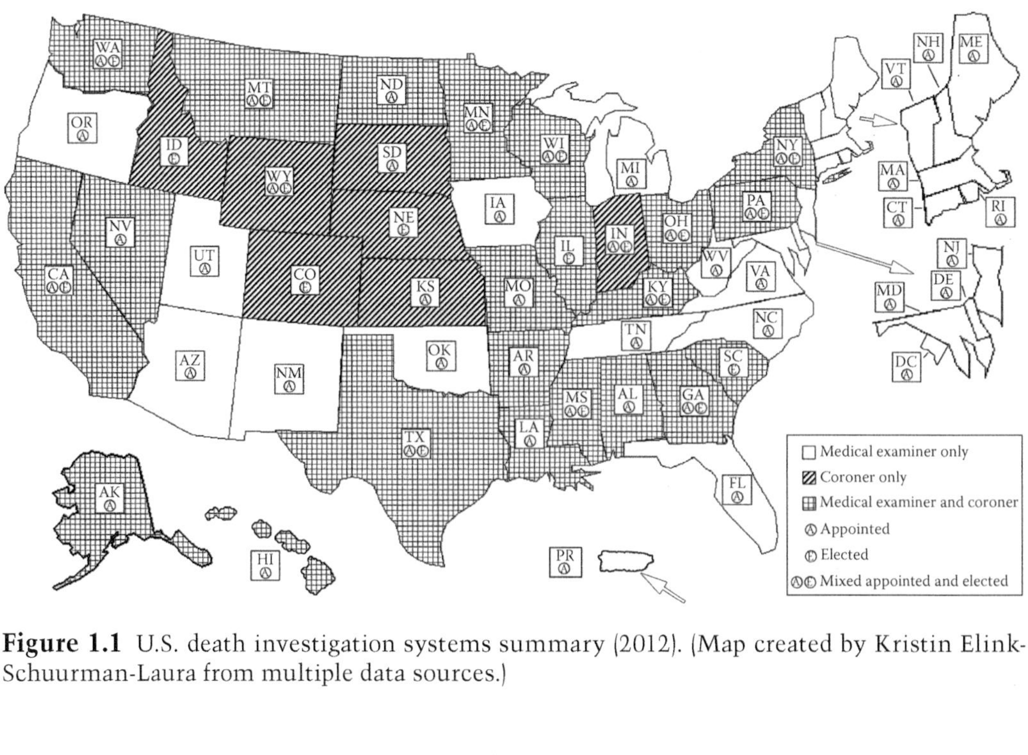

Figure 1.1 U.S. death investigation systems summary (2012). (Map created by Kristin Elink-Schuurman-Laura from multiple data sources.)

1.1.2 Distribution of Medical Examiners and Coroners by State

Currently, 21 states have medical examiners only, 7 states have coroners only, and 21 states have a mixed system. The states with mixed systems may have a medical examiner at the state or local level and coroners at the county level. Chief medical examiners are usually appointed and can select their deputy medical examiners while coroners are usually elected (Figure 1.1) (U.S. Department of Labor, 2012).

1.2 Dental Identification

The distinctiveness of human teeth has facilitated the identification of persons throughout history. The following accounts are examples of both lay and professional dental identifications.

1.2.1 Agrippina the Younger Identifies Lollia Paulina, AD 49

Claudius, emperor of the Roman Empire, sought a new wife. The first three had been dispatched by divorce or death. For the stability of the empire, a fourth wife was needed. Every woman that could conceivably be considered worthy flaunted her nobility, appearance, and wealth. In the end, it came down to a final dispute between two, Lollia Paulina and Julia Agrippina, known as Agrippina the Younger (Tacitus, 2004).

According to Dio, Agrippina "had beauty" (Dio, Project Gutenberg). There is nothing specific written about Lollia's beauty, but she had "bling," and lots of it. As a guest at a simple wedding dinner, she arrived covered in emeralds and pearls in alternating layers. Covered is not hyperbole, they were on her head, hair, ears, neck, wrists, and fingers. All together, the jewels were worth 40 million sesterces, and estimated value of 20–120 million in today's dollars. She produced receipts to prove their value (Pliny the Elder, Perseus Digital Library). Both women were rich, but Lollia enjoyed a distinct advantage.

The two had much in common. They were both noblewomen who had been married before. Agrippina was the sister of Emperor Caligula and Lollia had been married to him (they divorced in AD 38). They both had dental anomalies. Agrippina had two upper right canines, considered a sign of good fortune. Having two upper *left* canines was considered a bad omen (Pliny the Elder, Perseus Digital Library).

In the end, Agrippina's family lines would make her the better political choice. She married Claudius early in AD 49 after the approval of the senate that required a change in a law about incest. Claudius was also Agrippina's paternal uncle. As Empress of the Roman Empire, she thrived and became one of the most powerful women in antiquity. Ancient historians have not been particularly kind to her, writing that she could have only come to so much power by sleeping and murdering her way to the top. However, at least one modern scholar points out that both Claudius and her son Nero reigned more wisely under her influence (Barrett, 1996). But none doubt her involvement in what happened to Lollia Paulina.

Agrippina arranged for an accuser to allege that Lollia had consulted astrologers, magicians, and the idol of Apollo to influence Claudius' choice for a new bride. The case was heard before the senate, and the defendant was not allowed to speak. According to the charge, her plan was to ruin the state. The senate decided to confiscate her property and most of her money (she was left with only 5 million sesterces) and sent her into exile from Italy. For Agrippina, however, that was not enough. A tribune (Roman officer) was sent to Lollia in her exile to "drive her to death," meaning to force her to commit suicide (Tacitus, 2004); then, in accordance with Agrippina's instructions, the head of Lollia Paulina was brought back to Italy for confirmation of her death.

> As she did not recognize the woman's head when it was brought to her, she opened with her own hand the mouth and inspected the teeth, which had certain peculiarities (Dio, Project Gutenberg).

Barrett suggests it was Agrippina's own dental peculiarity that made her mindful of the peculiarities of others (Barrett, 1996).

1.2.2 Pliny the Elder Publishes *Natural History*, AD 77

Gaius Plinius Secundus (AD 23–79), known in English as Pliny the Elder, was a Roman officer and prolific writer. He is best known for his 37-volume encyclopedia, *Natural History*, which covered astronomy, geography, anthropology, physiology, biology, botany, horticulture, medicine, and mineralogy. In Book 7, chapter 15, he wrote what he had observed about teeth. Some of it was correct, some was not:

- "The number of teeth allotted to men… is thirty-two."
- "Those persons who have a greater number are thought to be destined to be long-lived."
- "Women have fewer teeth than men."

Pliny also made observations about the potential value of teeth for identification and the cause of tooth decay:

> The teeth are the only parts of the body which resist the action of fire, and are not consumed along with the rest of it. Still, however, though they are able thus to resist flame, they become corroded by a morbid state of the saliva (Pliny the Elder, Perseus Digital Library).

1.2.3 First Earl of Shrewsbury Identified by His Herald, 1453

John Talbot was England's first Earl of Shrewsbury. In 1429 he was engaged in a battle against the French in the Hundred Years War (actually several wars that were fought over the course of not 100, but 116 years from 1337 to 1453). John was famous for his skill and bravery but the fame of his French opponent would last far longer. It was during the battle of Patay that the French army, led by Joan of Arc, captured the renowned John Talbot. As a part of the negotiations for his release, he promised to never bear arms or wear armor against the French again. Joan of Arc was dead 2 years later, after being captured by the Bergundians and then sold to the English who executed her in 1431.

It was John Talbot who led the English into the Battle of Castillon in 1453. True to his word, he did not wear a full suit of armor, but only a breastplate covered in scarlet velvet. Talbot was killed during the mêlée. After the battle, the French wanted to be sure that John Talbot had really been killed. Talbot's personal herald was asked to identify his master.

> However, the next day, many heralds and weapon officers from the English side came to the battlefield in between, one of which was wearing seigneur Talbot's coat of arms. The officers were requested to search and try to find their respected masters. Talbot's herald was asked if he could look for and identify his master for which he responded happily that he would try (thinking his master had been taken prisoner alive).
>
> He was brought to where it was thought seigneur de Talbot's body to be, lying of a shield. They told him, "Look and tell us if this is your master." His face changed color but he could not yet make any judgment since the body was disfigured from the gashes on his face and his body damaged for having been dead from the previous day and a half. Nevertheless, the officer kneeled and said that he would find the truth. He placed one of his right fingers in the dead man's mouth searching for a left molar that he knew was missing on his master. While still kneeling, he kissed him on the mouth and said "Monseigneur, my master, it is you! I pray God to forgive you of your misdeeds. I have been your herald for over 40 years, it is time that I give this back to you." While lamenting, moaning, and crying, he removed his coat of arms and covered his master's body. That recognition ended the debate on who was that dead man (d'Escouchy, 1863).

John Talbot was famous enough to be included in into one of Shakespeare's plays. Henry VI part 1, Act 4, Scene 7 depicts the victorious French saying:

> "And now to Paris, in this conquering vein: All will be ours, now bloody Talbot's slain" (Shakespeare, 1591).

Indeed they were right; the Battle of Castillon was the last battle of the Hundred Years War.

1.2.4 Charles the Bold Identified by His Page, 1477

Following is the account of the identification of Charles the Bold in 1477:

> Separated from this group by a little space at the very edge of the pool, was another naked body in still more doleful plight. The face was disfigured beyond all semblance of what it might have been in life. One cheek was bitten by wolves; one was imbedded in the frozen slime. Yet there was evidence on the poor forsaken remains that convinced the searchers that this was indeed the mortal part of the great duke. Two wounds from a pick and a blow above the ear… showed how death had been caused. The missing teeth corresponded to those lost by Charles, there was a scar just where he had received his wound at Montl'hery, the finger nails were long like his, a wound on the shoulder, a fistula on the groin, and an ingrowing nail were additional marks of identification,—six definite proofs in all. Among those who gazed at this wretched sight, on that January morning, were men intimately acquainted with the duke's person (Putnam, 1908).

1.2.5 Colonel Sir Peter Halket(t), 1758

The French and Indian War was a 9 year conflict (1754–1763) in North America. This name is that by which it is now known in the United States, but there are several different names for the war in the different countries that played a part. It was not a war between the French and those who were native to North America and referred to as Indians but rather a war between the British and the French while Native Americans fought for both sides.

In 1755, the British wanted control of the French Fort Duquesne located in the area that is now Pittsburg, Pennsylvania. The British commander-in-chief was General

Edward Braddock. One of the two British regiments that fought under him was Colonel Sir Peter Halket's 44th Foot. Braddock had two lieutenant colonels with him that would later become famous opponents in the war for American independence, George Washington and Thomas Gage. The British forces had traveled far and were in need of wagons and supplies from the locals. Another British subject who would later play a part in the revolution, Benjamin Franklin, arranged for both. Daniel Boone and Daniel Morgan were among the wagon drivers. In the ensuing battle, the British were routed. General Edward Braddock was seriously wounded and helped from the battlefield by George Washington. He later died. Col. Sir Peter Halket was also killed in the battle as was his son, Lt. James Halket, who was fatally shot as he went to the aid of his wounded father.

In 1758, Peter Halket's son, Major Francis Halket, returned to the site of the battle to investigate the fate of his father and brother. A Native American reported that he knew where they had been killed and could find the spot again, for it had been under "a remarkable tree." A company of Pennsylvania Rifles and some Native American guides accompanied Halket.

> In a moment two gaunt skeletons were exposed lying together, one upon the other, as they had died. The hand that tore away their scalps had not disturbed their position; but no sign remained to distinguish the relics from the hundred others that strewed the ground. At the moment Sir Peter remembered him of a peculiar artificial tooth which his father bore. The bones were then separated, and an examination of those which lay undermost at once solved all doubts. "It is my father!" exclaimed the unhappy youth, as he sunk into the arms of his scarce less affected friends (Sargent, 1855).

This account is especially important to forensic odontology historians as it chronologically precedes the next one, long believed to be the first reported dental identification in North America.

1.2.6 Dr. Joseph Warren Identified by Paul Revere, 1776

This is a tale of not one, but of two heroes. Dr. Joseph Warren was a Harvard-educated physician and one of the leaders of the revolution in Boston. As chairman of the Committee of Correspondence, he wrote prodigiously about the rights of Americans and abuses of the British monarchy to bolster morale and to inform other colonists. He authored the Suffolk Resolves document endorsed by the Continental Congress in 1774. His home served as one of the safe meeting places for the leaders of the revolution. Like most of the Founding Fathers, Dr. Joseph Warren was part of the upper class, wealthy from inheritance and marriage.

Paul Revere did not share Dr. Warren's social status. He was a middle class workingman and accomplished as an engraver, silversmith, and dentist. As an engraver, he created several engravings and political cartoons; his most famous being of the so-called Boston Massacre in 1770, which helped to stir some colonists' longing for independence (Figure 1.2). It is not widely known that he also produced a second drawing of the Boston Massacre, a crime scene sketch showing the identity and location of the bodies of those who perished that day (Figure 1.3). The drawing was submitted as evidence in the Boston Massacre trials, officially titled *Rex v. Weems et al.* At the trial six British soldiers were acquitted and two found guilty of manslaughter (Linder, 2007). Thus, it seems we can add crime scene investigator to Paul Revere's growing list of occupations. Before the war for

Figure 1.2 Paul Revere's etching "The Bloody Massacre perpetrated in King Street, Boston on March 5th, 1770 by a party of the 29th Regiment" published 3 weeks after the event.

independence, Paul Revere had expanded his business to include dentistry. In September 1768, he advertised his dental business for the first time in the Boston Gazette. Apparently the advertisement worked well because 2 years later, he ran a second advertisement, thanking his customers who employed him as a dentist (Figure 1.4). It was during this time (1768–1775) that Paul Revere wired in a false tooth for Joseph Warren (Davis, 1987).

Paul Revere worked as a spy, and then became a spymaster (Davis, 2008; National Museum of Health, 2012).

Joseph Warren sent Paul Revere on his famous "midnight ride" to warn Samuel Adams and John Hancock that the Regulars were coming to arrest them. (He did not say "The British are coming!" as they were all British at this point.) Revere had been sent previously by Warren on other trips to take letters and news to leaders of the revolution. Worried that he might be caught on his mission of April 18, 1775, Revere and some others came up with the idea of sending signals by lanterns from the Old North Church, the now well-known "One if by land and two if by sea." Warren also sent a second rider, William Dawes, by a different route, in case Revere was captured.

The Battle of Bunker Hill was fought on June 17, 1775. The colonists mistakenly built their defensive works on Breeds Hill, which was just south of Bunker Hill and was shorter, and more difficult to defend. Even though Warren had been appointed a general, his

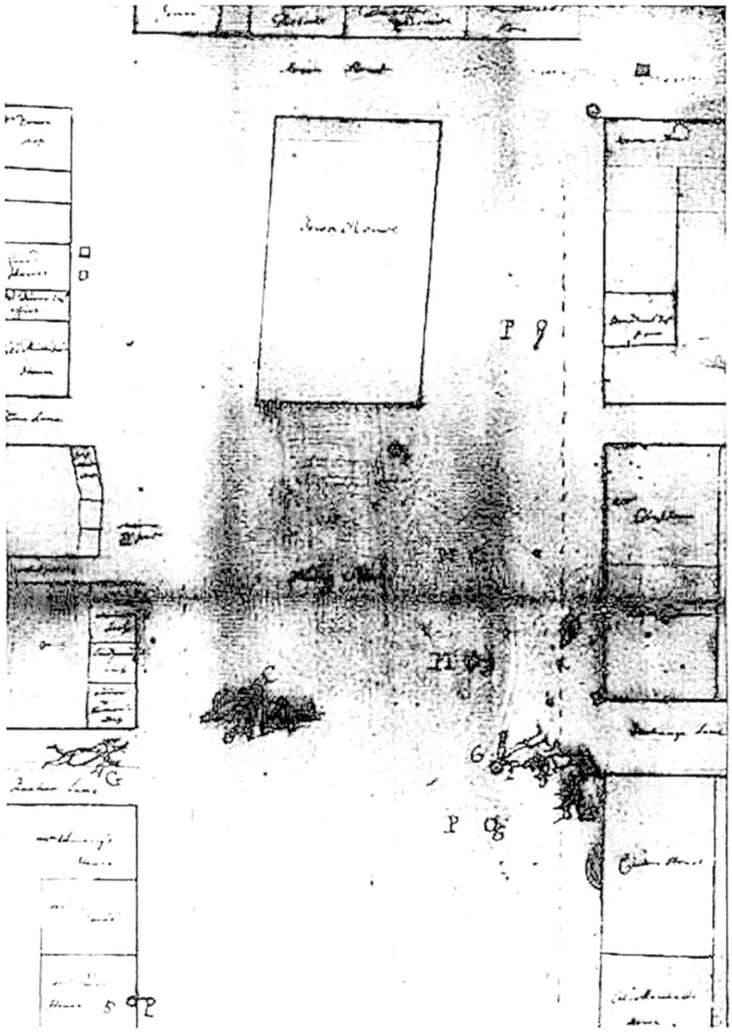

Figure 1.3 Paul Revere's 1770 Boston Massacre scene diagram showing location and identity of bodies.

commission was not yet in effect, and yielding to others with more battlefield experience, he volunteered to fight on the front lines. The patriot militia did well until they ran out of ammunition. A retreat was ordered and during the retreat, Warren was shot and killed.

The British won the battle but at a great cost of lives. On June 23, 1775, Captain Walter Sloan Laurie, a British officer, wrote that he "was employed as the officer commanding the detachment to bury the dead, a most disagreeable piece of duty." Later in the same letter, he reported:

> Doctor Warren, President of the Provincial Congress, and Captain General, in the absence of Hancock and Adams, and next to Adams, in abilities, I found among the slain, and stuffed the scoundrel with another rebel into one hole, and there he, and his seditious Principles may remain (Sloan, 1775).

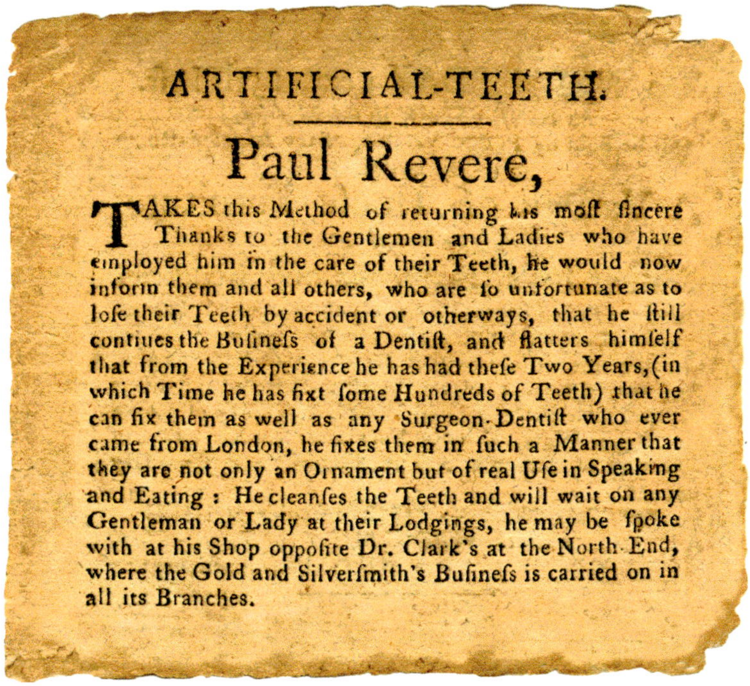

Figure 1.4 Advertisement for the dental practice of American Revolution patriot, Paul Revere, from *The Boston Gazette* of August 13, 1770. (Courtesy of Reynolds Historical Library/ Historical Collections, University of Alabama at Birmingham, Birmingham, AL.)

So, according to Laurie the reported "mass grave" held two bodies, Warren's and that of "another rebel" (Laurie, 1952). The British controlled the area until March 17, 1776 at which time they left Boston. Nine months after the battle, Warren's relatives, along with others, went to the area to look for the grave of Joseph Warren. Fortunately, among them was Warren's friend and dentist, Paul Revere. According to a letter written by Abigail Adams to her husband John, Warren's body was located on April 7. Revere identified Joseph Warren by a false tooth that Revere had constructed for him, as well as by the wire that he had made to hold it in place. Years later, eyewitnesses recalled what they had seen that day.

> "Mr. Clark, above-named (Mr. Jonathan Clark) as well as another soldier whose name I have forgotten, was here on the 17th, who assisted at the exhumation in the presence of the Doctor's two brothers, who were satisfied of the identity of the body, by many circumstances which they detailed. If stronger evidence of its identity were wanting, that afforded by Col. Paul Revere who set the artificial tooth…and who recollected the wire he used in fastening it in, would afford it" (Sumner, 1858).

Although not the first dental identification in North America (see Section 1.2.5) it very likely was the first dental identification by a dentist.

On April 8, 1776, there was a large, stately funeral and his body was laid to rest in the Old Granary Burying Ground. The following was published in *The Pennsylvania Evening Post*, April 25, 1776:

New York, April 24.

Extract of a letter from Boston, dated April 13.

> Last Monday the remains of the brave General Warren were reinterred at Boston… The General's remains were known by two artificial teeth fastened in with gold wire, and by being found under the remains of a person buried in trousers, agreeable to the account given by one who was well acquainted with that circumstance.

On the same date, in *The New England Chronicle*, Warren's teeth were also mentioned:

> Though the Body (which our savage enemies "scarce privileged with earth enough to hide it from the birds of prey") was disfigured, when taken up, yet was sufficiently known by two artificial teeth, which were set for him a short time before his glorious exit.

By the 1800s, the country was stable enough to look back at the moments of its beginning and a monument was planned for Bunker Hill. Dr. John Warren (Joseph Warren's youngest brother and one of the men who went to look for Joseph's grave) had a son, John Collins Warren. This nephew of the hero of Bunker Hill decided to search for his famous uncle's grave. This is the history that he wrote in 1854 about both exhumations:

> The body, which had been deposited at Bunker Hill, and had lain there till March, 1776, was then exhumed, and recognized by his brothers, for the circumstance that the left upper cuspidatus, or eye-tooth, had been secured in its place by a golden wire… In 1825, when the foundation of Bunker Hill Monument was laid, it was thought proper to discover, identify and, preserve them; but, those who were concerned in the ceremonies of 1776 having passed off the stage, the last place of deposit had been forgotten, and was unknown. After a long search… the lost remains were discovered in the Minot Tomb, in the Granary Burying-ground, at the distance of a few steps for the house of the writer. They were recognized by the condition of the eye-tooth above mentioned, and the mark of the fatal bullet behind the left ear; were carefully collected, deposited in a box of hard wood, designated by a silver plate, as placed in the Warren Tomb in St. Paul's Church, Boston" (Warren, 1854).

The family later decided to move his remains yet again from St. Paul's Church to the family plots at Forrest Hills. There, at least for now, is Joseph Warren's final resting place. Jonathan Mason Warren, M.D., the great nephew of Joseph Warren, related some details of the last exhumation.

> The remains of General Joseph Warren were removed from St. Paul's to Forest Hills on Aug. 3, 1855, when my father, John Collins Warren, Sullivan, William Appleton, and myself put them into a stone or earthen urn, like those of John Warren, Mrs. Warren, and my mother. The place was quite moist where they were put, and the hole in the head of General Warren was becoming enlarged by the crumbling of the margin. I had a photograph made of it in three positions—Journal, May 6, 1859 (Warren, 1886).

Those photographs represent another piece of forensic dentistry history. In 1973 forensic odontologist Lester L. Luntz and his wife Phyllys co-authored the first American

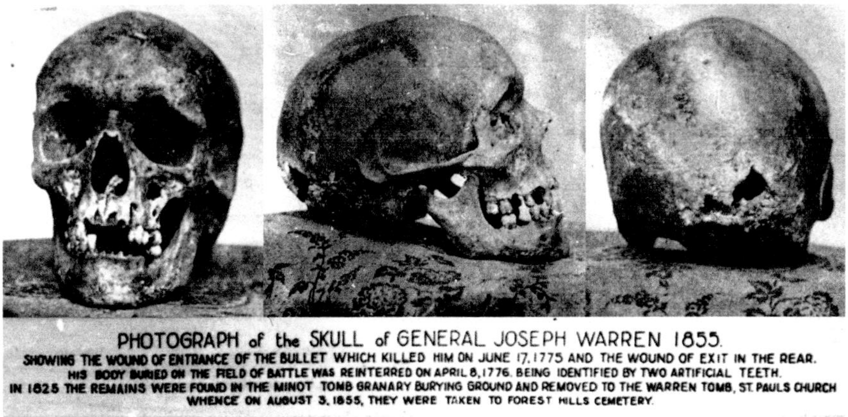

Figure 1.5 Three images of the skull of General Joseph Warren taken by John Warren in 1855. (Adapted from images made and published by Lester Luntz in 1973. With permission of Harvard Medical School.)

textbook on Forensic Dentistry, *The Handbook for Dental Identification*. The first chapter included images that Luntz made from a poster of Jonathan Warren's photographs. Luntz noted:

> Three views of the skull of Joseph Warren, taken by Author (L.L.L.) from a composite print made when Warren was again exhumed in 1865. Original print was traced by the Author to the sub-basement of Old South Meeting House, Boston. (Luntz and Luntz, 1973).

Luntz donated his photographs to Harvard University, where they are archived in the Harvard Medical School Faculty and Staff Portrait Collection (Figure 1.5). The original images that Jonathan Warren made in 1855 have been lost.

Paul Revere left his silversmith business in 1775 to serve in the colonial army during the war. When he returned to private life there is no evidence that he continued practicing dentistry. Paul Revere died in 1818 and was buried in Boston's Granary Burying Ground. He, unlike his friend Joseph Warren, has remained there.

Paul Revere may have been as forgotten were it not for the 1860 Henry Wadsworth Longfellow poem. However beloved, most of the information in the poem is incorrect. America was on the verge of civil war and Longfellow apparently wanted to inspire people to see the difference that one man could make to save the country. Although America took its time memorializing Joseph Warren, Paul Revere honored his friend in his own way. On April 30, 1777, about 2 years after Warren was killed, and 1 year after he identified him, Paul Revere named his newborn son Joseph Warren Revere.

1.2.7 First British Trial in Which Dentists Were Cited as Expert Witnesses, 1814

"It is note worthy that, in Edinburgh in 1814, the *first* British trial took place in which dentists were cited as expert witnesses" (Campbell, 1963, 301). Unfortunately, by order of the court, none of the testimony was transcribed. Campbell found his information about the case from the notes of one of the judges.

The case concerned the body of Mrs. McAlister, buried in Glasgow. Four men were accused of stealing her body for dissection. Two of the men were lecturers and two were students. Granville Sharp Pattison, lecturer in anatomy, was the man on trial.

Mrs. McAlister's dentist, Dr. James Alexander, testified that he had "broken off the natural teeth at the gum margins" (Campbell, 1963). He testified that he made a maxillary denture for her, and that this was shortly before her death. He had been called to the college to see if he could identify the body. He said that he was able to seat the denture into the mouth of the decedent, that it fit properly with the bottom teeth and that a denture made for one mouth would not fit into another mouth.

Two other dentists testified for the defense. The first, Dr. James Scott, disagreed with Dr. Alexander in that he said that the denture did not fit the decedent. He also said that the decedent that he observed not only did not have a denture, but also had loose teeth with cavities.

The final dentist, Dr. Robert Nasmyth, disputed Dr. Alexander's statement that a denture would not fit any other mouths. He testified that he put the denture in four other cadavers and they fit just as well.

While prosecution's evidence was conclusive, the dental testimony shook the case. The verdict was "All in one voice find the accused not guilty, and the libel not proven" (Campbell, 1963).

1.2.8 Caroline Walsh, 1831

In a London murder case, Elizabeth Ross was accused of killing Caroline Walsh, an elderly Irishwoman. Ross' son testified that he had seen his mother suffocate Walsh, that he saw Walsh's body in the cellar the next day, and that in the evening of the same day he saw his mother carrying a heavy sack from the house (Taylor, 1865). The case grew complicated when an old Irishwoman, named Caroline Welsh, was found alive. She died shortly thereafter at a London hospital. Elizabeth Ross claimed that the injured woman was the same one that she had been accused of murdering, thus proving her innocence. Investigations indicated that the two women were from different cities, were of different ages, and most importantly, had different teeth. Walsh, although she was 84, had "very perfect incisor teeth." Welsh had no front teeth. A medical witness testified that for Welsh "the alveolar cavities corresponding to them *had been obliterated for a considerable time*." This, and other evidence moved the court to convict Elizabeth Ross of murder and she was executed.

1.2.9 Homicide at Harvard: Dr. George Parkman and Dr. John Webster, 1849

George Parkman was a Harvard-trained physician, who focused on being a landlord and moneylender thus becoming wealthy and influential. John Webster was an instructor of chemistry at Harvard. With four daughters, Webster had social aspirations and the required parties and fine dresses got him into financial trouble. He had turned to George Parkman, who lent him money but he was clearly living beyond his means and had trouble paying him back. George Parkman mysteriously disappeared. Although one of the last to see him alive, Webster was not initially a suspect. Ephraim Littlefield, janitor of the Medical Building at Harvard, suspected John Webster had murdered George Parkman. Webster had a private privy that he had not opened for the police when they searched the medical building for George Parkman. Littlefield entered the building through a trap door in the floor of the building. Intermittently over the course of 2 days, he dug through a brick

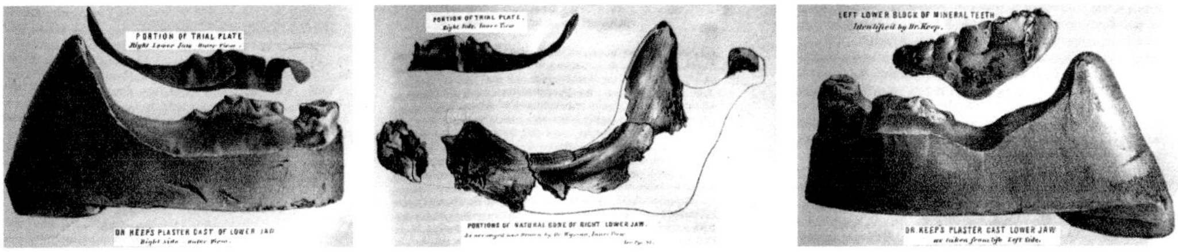

Figure 1.6 The dental evidence from the trial of John W. Webster for the murder of Dr. George Parkman.

wall and looked inside and found dismembered human remains. Alerting other professors, police were called and eventually John Webster was arrested.

In Webster's furnace more human remains were found that included part of a lower jawbone and a partial denture. Dr. Nathan Keep, Parkman's dentist, identified the partial as one he had made for Parkman and provided casts of Parkman's lower jaw that he had retained (Figure 1.6).

Dr. William T. G. Morton (famous for being credited with having discovered the anesthetic use of ether) testified for the defense and said that the jawbone was not distinctive.

Webster maintained his innocence and was astonished that he was found guilty and sentenced to death by hanging. He later asked for a commutation of his sentence, admitting that he had killed Dr. Parkman, but that it was not premeditated. He explained that in the passion of their argument, he had hit Dr. Parkman with a stick of wood, just once.

The Committee of Pardons considered the request and decided that there were "insufficient reasons to justify them in recommending the interposition of Executive clemency." On August 30, 1850, John White Webster was hanged. The case was the first in the United Sates in which dental evidence and testimony played a part in a murder conviction (Bemis, 1850).

1.2.10 John Wilkes Booth, 1865 and 1869

On April 14, 1865, John Wilkes Booth shot President Abraham Lincoln at Ford's Theater. He had planned his escape and had a stable boy holding his horse for him in the alley behind the theatre. After a 12 day manhunt, Booth was cornered in a barn. When he refused to come out, the barn was set afire. Sergeant Boston Corbett fired at Booth, who was still in the barn, hitting him in the neck. Booth was pulled out of the blaze, still alive, but he died a few hours later on April 26.

Booth's body was taken to the USS *Montauk* in Washington on April 27. It was on the *Montauk* that the remains were identified by his physician, the clerk at the hotel where Booth had been staying, and by Booth's dentist, Dr. William Merrill, who recognized two gold fillings that he had placed shortly before he died. Clarence F. Cobb, was quoted in February 26, 1916 in "Dramatic Mirror".

> He (General Barnes) and nine others had identified the body; that Dr. Merrill, the dentist, had filled two teeth for Booth the week before (the murder): that they had forced the mouth open and saw the fillings. So the identification was complete… (Bryan, 1940).

Booth's body was buried in a storage room in the Washington Penitentiary. It was moved to another place in the penitentiary in 1867. In 1869, Mary Ann Booth and Edwin, the mother and brother of John Wilkes Booth asked President Andrew Johnson to release Booth's body to their family for burial. President Johnson consented.

The New York Clipper ran an article on February 27, 1869, on the disinterment of Booth's body. When the body was removed from the ground and able to be viewed, Booth's brother, Joseph Booth, confirmed the identification of the remains, "by a peculiarly plugged tooth."

1.2.11 Second Lieutenant Henry M. Harrington, 1885

Custer's Last Stand was not only unfortunate for Custer, but for all involved. The defeat of Custer and his men was complete and the victory for the Native Americans pyrrhic and short lived; the American Army soon destroyed and very nearly annihilated them. The Sioux had been removed from their ancestral lands, sequestered to territories that were later downsized to smaller reservations. When gold was found by trespassers on their reservation in South Dakota, the Sioux were ordered off that land as well. The Sioux ultimately determined to fight and were joined by other tribes, including the Cheyenne, until they numbered between 2000 and 4000 (Davis, 2011, 259–260). In spite of being warned about the large numbers awaiting him, on June 25, 1876, General George A. Custer led his 250 men in the ill-advised attack in Montana, the Battle of the Little Big Horn. Custer and all the soldiers who fought along with him died, including the commander of Company "C," a Lieutenant Harrington. The victorious combatants stripped and mutilated most of the bodies of the slain. The Army was not able to bury the bodies of their dead until June 28. The combination of battle damage and decomposition made battlefield identification difficult. Harrington was ruled to have been killed, but his remains were not identified. Eight years later, in September, 1884, the *Weekly Yellowstone Journal* reported that five cowboys had found human remains in the area of the battlefield. They removed four teeth from a skull and brought them to a dentist in Miles City, Dr. C. S. Whitney. They included a "right central incisor, right lateral incisor, left bicuspid, and upper canine or eye-tooth." The right central incisor was later described as "the front tooth of the upper jaw," and the canine was later described as being on the left. All four of the teeth were restored with gold fillings. Dr. Whitney determined that they "belonged to a man of mature years, between 35 and 40 years of age." The gold fillings were large, well made, and thus expensive, so the decedent was more likely to be an officer than an enlisted man. Drawings of the teeth and the fillings were included in the article.

Dr. Alfred C. Girard read and retained the article (Girard, 1888). On April 8, 1885 he mailed the article to his friend Dr. William Saunders the U.S. Military Academy's dentist reasoning that Harrington may have been his patient and hoping that Saunders would recognize the drawings in the article. He wrote:

> I had an idea that from the peculiar filling of the teeth in the discovered skull you might recognized Lt. Harrington's fate and thus remove an uncertainty which must be always a load on the mind of his widow and his relatives (Hyson and Whitehorn, 1993, 103–107).

According to the 2007 Walt Cross annotated version of Thompson's Narrative of the Little Big Horn, Harrington's remains were not identified on the battlefield but collected a year after the battle well east of the scene by Army surgeon Lt. Robert W. Shufeldt and later identified in the Smithsonian's anthropology collection in 2003.

There was another set of remains that was found the same month, that was also hoped to be Harrington. Oddly enough, it was noted that there was dental evidence, and that evidence was also submitted for publication so that a dentist could identify the decedent. In July 1885 The Dental Cosmos reported that Dr. Thomas F. Coryell had examined the remains of a man found at the battle site by Dr. E. C. Koons. He described six teeth: Three maxillary teeth (right central, left lateral, and right cuspid—all with gold fillings) and three mandibular teeth (right first and second molars missing, the right third molar had an amalgam filling). Coryell's reported intent for reporting this to the editor was that "who did the work would be likely to read the article."

So was either of the remains Harrington's? Harrington's family did not know. According to Grace Ailene Harrington, Harrington's daughter in 1938 (Taunton, 1987):

> The only thing mother had was a leaf from father's notebook sent her—there were some teeth sent to the dentist at West Point to see if they were father's but he would never tell mother, which has made me think that perhaps they were—but I do not know...

1.2.12 Claudius Beaupied, Victim of the "Killer of the Little Shepherds," 1897

Claudius was the 11th victim of a serial killer who roamed the countryside of France, Joseph Vacher. Vacher was suspected in 25 homicides with similar characteristics, including strangling, throat slitting, mutilation of the body, and sodomy. Beaupied's body had not been found. After Vacher was arrested, the press wrote skeptically about the truth of his exploits. It was important to him to prove his veracity, hoping that by confessing he would be declared insane and not face the death penalty. He told the police about killing a boy and then throwing his body in a well and then gave a description of the area where the well could be found. After 2 days of searching, the well was found and when excavated, contained the bones of a 14 year old boy. No one knew who the boy was. Finally, a woman came forward saying her 14 year old son had been missing. She was shown "the jawbone and asked... if she recognized any dental patterns. Sobbing, she made the identification: Certain teeth were missing, and two were crossed in a particular way" (Starr, 2010).

1.2.13 Adolf Hitler, 1945

In 1945, Soviet Union soldiers located and excavated the bunker where Hitler had reportedly died. The Soviets did not reveal what they found there. In 1968, Lev Bezymenski published *The Death of Adolph Hitler: Unknown Documents from Soviet Archives.* He had served as a member of Marshal Zhukov's staff during the time of the Soviet siege of Berlin.

Thirteen bodies were found in the garden of the Chancellery on May 4, 1945: six children, five adults, and two dogs. For two of the burned adults, visual identification was impossible. Autopsies were performed for all of the bodies found, including the dogs. The *Soviet Document 12* reported on the body, which they determined to be that of Adolf Hitler. (Tooth notations in parentheses converted from Palmer to Universal notation for clarity for American readers.)

> The following objects taken from the corpse were handed over to the SMERSH Section of the 3rd Shock Army on May 8, 1945: a) a maxillary bridge of yellow metal, consisting of 9 teeth; b) a singed lower jaw, consisting of 15 teeth...
>
> In the upper jaw there are nine teeth connected by a bridge of yellow metal. The bridge is anchored by pins on the second left and the second right incisor. This bridge consists of

> 4 upper incisors (#'s 7, 8, 9, and 10), 2 canine teeth (#'s 6 and 11), the first left bicuspid (#12), and the first and second right bicuspids (#'s 4 and 5), as indicated in the sketch. The first left incisor (#9) consists of a white platelet, with cracks and a black spot in the porcelain (enamel) at the bottom. This platelet is inset into the visible side of the metal tooth. The second incisor, the canine tooth, and the left bicuspid, as well as the first and second incisors and the first bicuspid on the right, are the usual porcelain (enamel) dental plates, their posterior parts fastened to the bridge. The right canine tooth is fully capped by yellow metal. The maxillary bridge is vertically sawed off behind the second left bicuspid (#13) *[Note: should be "the first left bicuspid (#12) Sognnaes and Strom later discovered typographical errors in the Bezymenski text]*. The lower jawbone lies loose in the singed oral cavity. The alveolar processes are broken in the back and have ragged edges. The front surface and the lower edge of the mandibular are scorched. On the front surface the charred prongs of the dental roots are recognizable. The lower jaw consists of fifteen teeth, ten of which are recognizable. The incisors (#'s 23, 24, 25, and 26) and the first right bicuspid (#28) are natural, exhibiting considerable wear on the masticating surface and considerably exposed necks. The dental enamel has a bluish shimmer and a dirty yellow coloration around the necks. The teeth to the left (#'s 17, 18, 20, and 21) are artificial, of yellow metal, and consist of a bridge of gold crowns. The bridge is fastened to the third, the fifth (in the bridge, the sixth tooth), and the eighth tooth (in the bridge, the ninth tooth). The second bicuspid to the right (#29) is topped by a crown of yellow metal which is linked to the right canine tooth by an arching plate. Part of the mastication surface and the posterior surface of the right canine tooth is capped by a yellow metal plate as part of the bridge. The first right molar is artificial, white, and secured by a gold clip connected with the bridge of the second bicuspid and the right incisor *[should read "right cuspid" another Bezyenski typo discovered by Sognnaes and Strom]* (Bezymenski, 1968).
>
> The most important anatomical finding for identification of the person are the teeth, with much bridgework, artificial teeth, crowns and fillings (see documents) (Bezymenski, 1968).

On May 9, the Soviets sought Hitler's dentist, Professor Hugo Blaschke. They found his private office, but the dentist had already left Berlin. His assistant, Käthe Heusermann, retrieved, and then gave them Hitler's chart. "The entries gave evidence that the Führer had had very poor teeth in need of frequent repair" (Bezymenski, 1968). The radiographs were not there, Heuserman advised them they would be in Professor Blaschke's office in the Chancellery. There they found, "X-ray photographs of the Führer's teeth and a few gold crowns that had been prepared, but time to put them to use had run out on dentist and patient" (Bezymenski, 1968).

Both Hitler and Eva Braun had extensive fixed restorative dental work. Heusermann advised them that the work was completed by the dental technician, Fritz Echtmann. He was also summoned and they were interrogated separately. Both were able to describe Hitler's teeth and restorations in detail. These descriptions were consistent with the dental chart, and the dental radiographs. They were both individually shown the maxilla and mandible of the unidentified male decedent. They both identified them being Hitler's. The same process was repeated with Eva Braun's dental records and remains.

That cause of death put forth by the Soviet scientists was poisoning with cyanide compounds. This was disputed by the Germans, who insisted he shot himself. In the 1940s, it was considered heroic to commit suicide by shooting oneself, but cowardly to use poison. Some said that both methods were used, to ensure that he was successful.

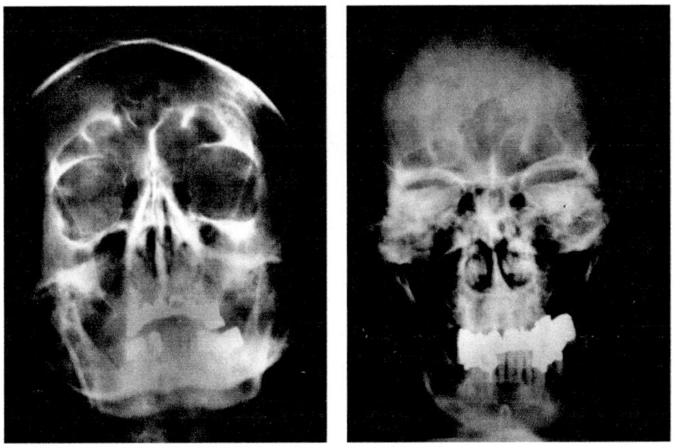

Figure 1.7 Antemortem skull radiographs of Adolf Hitler from September 19, 1944. (With permission from Informa Healthcare, May, 2012.)

Of note in the autopsy report is the single sentence, "Part of the cranium is missing." Bezymenski adds a footnote about it, "At a somewhat later date occipital parts of a cranium were found, quite probably belonging to Hitler's corpse" (Bezymenski, 1968).

That part of the cranium made the news in 2009 when it was examined by an anthropologist, Dr. Nick Bellantoni, who determined that it looked like the bones of a younger (open sutures) female (gracile), 20–40 years of age. Hitler was 56 in 1945. Some small pieces of bone from the skull fragment were tested for DNA and it was confirmed that the skull was from a woman. To date, there has been no DNA testing on the teeth.

In 1972, Drs. Reidar Sognnaes and Ferdinand Strom published a paper describing their work reviewing all of the then available odontological material used in the identification of Adolf Hitler. The materials included information from the interrogation of Hitler's American trained dentist, Hugo Johannes Blaschke, D.D.S., a 1911 graduate of the University of Pennsylvania School of Dental Medicine. Dr. Blaschke was Hitler's dentist from 1934 to 1945. Also examined were newly discovered radiographs of Hitler taken in 1944 following an assassination attempt (Figure 1.7), and information from the Russian autopsy report including the images of the jaws, teeth, and restorations (Figure 1.8). Drs. Sognnaes and Strom produced a graphic summary chart of the condition of Hitler's mouth in 1945 (Figure 1.9). After comparing all of the data they formed the opinion that the person identified from the 1945 Russian autopsy that was not made public until 1968 was, in fact, Adolf Hitler.

1.2.14 Henrietta Durand-Deacon, Final Victim of the "Acid Bath Murderer," 1949

John Haigh did not actually kill anyone with an acid bath. He just used that method to dispose of his victim's bodies. He was under the mistaken impression that if there was no body found, he could never be tried for their murders, and was quite haughty with the police after he was arrested. He blithely told them that the bodies had been dissolved in the old drums filled with sulfuric acid in his workshop. The drums were examined and the bodies were found mostly destroyed. Upon searching through the sludge three gallstones

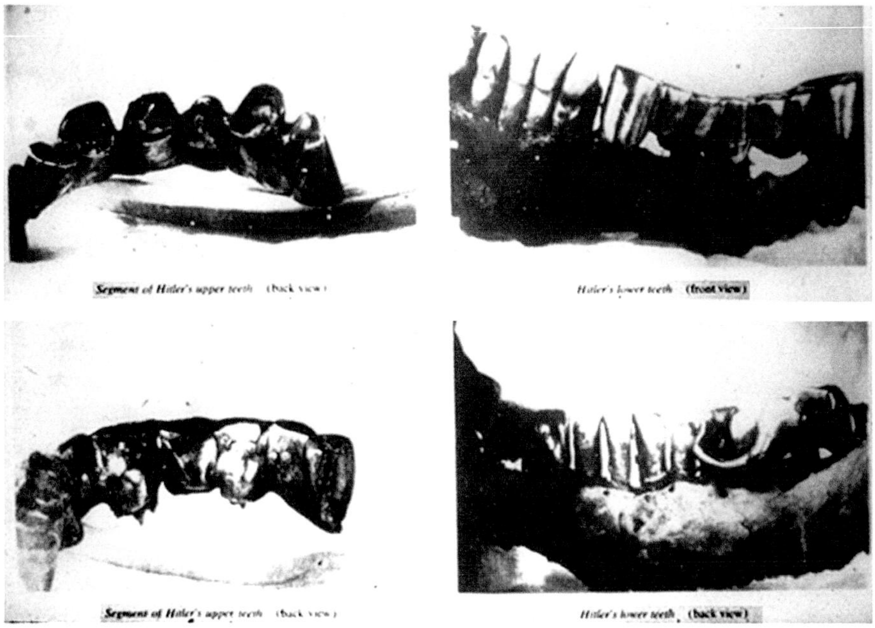

Figure 1.8 The jaws and dental prostheses of Adolf Hitler in 1945. (With permission from Informa Healthcare, May, 2012.)

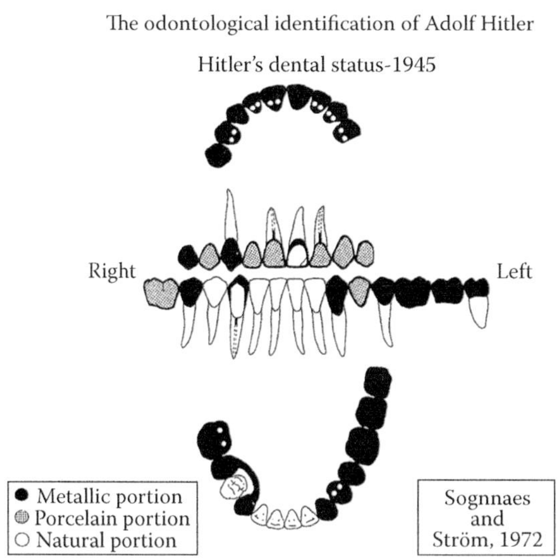

Figure 1.9 Graphic representation of the dental status of Adolf Hitler in 1945 recreated in 1972. (With permission from Informa Healthcare, May, 2012.)

and a complete set of dentures were found. Mrs. Durrand-Deacon's dentist testified at trial that they were hers (Jeffers, 1999).

Haigh then told the police that he had drunk the blood of his victims. It is believed that he fabricated this ruse in an attempt to be found innocent on the grounds of insanity. The police and the prosecutor didn't buy it, but the press loved it and they hailed him the "Vampire of London" (Jenkins, 2010). However, it was the title "Acid Bath Murder" that stuck. John Haigh was hanged in August 1949.

1.2.15 Exhumation of Lee Harvey Oswald, 1981

In 1963, 2 days after President John F. Kennedy was assassinated, Lee Harvey Oswald was shot to death by Jack Ruby. An unauthorized photo was taken of Oswald in his coffin. United Press International reported that when Oswald's wife Marina saw the photo, she stated that the man in the photograph was not her husband.

Starting in the 1970s, Michael Eddowes, English lawyer, investigator, and author, tried to convince the world that there had been a conspiracy and that a Russian assassin had murdered President Kennedy, was subsequently shot, and was buried as Oswald. Dr. Earl Rose had performed the autopsy on Oswald and identified him by his fingerprints. In spite of this, the influential Eddowes pressed for an exhumation of the body in Oswald's grave but met extensive legal opposition. Oswald's widow, Marina Oswald, consented to the exhumation, provided all expenses were paid by Eddowes. Oswald's brother Robert however tried to stop the exhumation with injunctions. Eventually, the exhumation was accomplished and the casket was taken to Baylor Medical Center in Dallas.

Two forensic odontologists, Drs. James Cottone and Irvin Sopher, completed a thorough dental examination, including charting, photographs, radiographs, and impressions of the decedent's teeth. The records were compared to Oswald's military dental records. Forensic pathologist Dr. Linda Norton made the announcement that the remains had been positively identified as Lee Harvey Oswald (New York Times, 1979; Norton et al., 1984).

1.2.16 Czar Nicholas II, the Last Czar of Russia, 1991 and 2008

Tsar Nicolas II, the last Russian czar and his family were brutally executed by the Bolsheviks on the night of July 16–17, 1918. The royal family members, their doctor, the cook, a maid, and the valet, a total of 11 people were shot. The bodies were loaded onto a truck and driven to a mineshaft. Stripped of clothing, the bodies were burned then dumped into the mine. Hand grenades were used to destroy the bodies and collapse the mineshaft. The clandestine mission was accomplished as directed except that the executioners', tongues lubricated and loosened by alcohol, talked about what they had done. The bodies had to be moved. The damaged and decaying bodies were retrieved and loaded first onto carts and later a truck that was prone to becoming stuck in mud. Ultimately, with the truck so badly stuck that they could no longer move they decided to bury the bodies there. Two burned bodies were buried separately; the other nine were placed in a grave six feet deep and eight feet square and doused with sulfuric acid. The bodies were covered with layers of mud and wood.

Geli Ryabov and Dr. Alexander Avdonin found the larger grave in 1979 but the discovery was not publicly reported until 1989. The high-quality dental work found on the skull of Tsarina Alexandra, including two platinum crowns, some porcelain crowns and gold fillings were key findings that helped with the identifications (Maples and Browning, 1994). Three other skulls were found to have "extensive amalgam fillings" (Maples and Browning, 1994). After the analysis of the nine, it was reported that the remains of Prince Alexi and one female, possibly Anastasia, were missing. Many hoped that Anastasia was still somehow alive but there was less hope for Alexi, the heir, as he had hemophilia.

In 1992, an American team evaluated the skeletal remains in Russia. The team included Drs. William Maples (forensic anthropology), Lowell Levine (forensic odontology), Michael Baden (forensic pathology), and criminologist Cathryn Oakes (hair and fiber microscopy).

In 1993, mitochondrial DNA tests were performed on the remains, comparing them to the DNA of Prince Philip (husband of Queen Elizabeth II). They had a common maternal ancestor in Queen Victoria. Labs in both Great Britain and the United States determined that they were from the same family.

In 2008, 90 years after they were murdered, the last two children were found. They were identified as Prince Alexi and Marie. This was based on similar amalgam fillings, similar injuries that were consistent with bullet wounds and mitochondrial DNA tests that showed they also belonged to the same family (Reuters, 2008).

1.2.17 Ramses I, 2003

The Niagara Falls Museum is more of a curio cabinet than a formal museum. At one point, they were able to purchase two Egyptian mummies and placed them on display. They did not receive as much attention as the two-headed calf. One of the two mummies did capture the attention of an archeologist, who imagined that the mummy looked rather royal. She mentioned this to several other of her archeology friends and was soundly mocked. Then one of her friends came to visit and she insisted that he view the mummy at the museum. Oddly enough, he agreed with her. They were both mocked.

When the financially struggling museum was sold, the new owner looked to sell off part of the exhibits, to make ends meet. A sarcophagus or two might be of worth, even if the mummies weren't. Atlanta's Carlos Museum purchased the two mummies and their sarcophagi and went to work to find out about them. More and more evidence pointed toward one mummy being Ramses I. In 1967, Orthodontist James E. Harris, Chairman of the Department of Orthodontics at the University of Michigan, went to Egypt to take lateral cephalometric x-rays of the pharaohs of Egypt. He then traced and digitized the data. He examined the same data from the mummy in the Carlos Museum and compared it data from the Pharaohs of Egypt. Dr. Harris concluded they were in fact related (NOVA, 2006).

Although it is not yet fully accepted that this mummy is Ramses I, the evidence from Dr. Harris and other evidence convinced the Carlos Museum to return the mummy to Egypt. The Egyptian Director of Antiquities has welcomed the return of the ancient pharaoh (BBC News, 2003).

1.2.18 Queen Hatshepsut, 2007

Hatshepsut lived from about 1508 to 1458 BC. When her father, Thutmose I died, she married her half brother, Thutmose II. Because he was ill, they co-ruled until he died in 1479 BC. His successor was his son (but not hers), Thutmose III. Since Thutmose III was too young to rule, Hatshepsut filled the void. In 1473, she had herself crowned as pharaoh and reigned until 1458 when Thutmose III overthrew her. She also died in 1458, causing many historians to theorize she may have been killed by Thutmose III. She had arranged for construction of a magnificent funerary temple, but she was not there. In 1903, Howard Carter found her sarcophagus, but she was also not there. Carter later discovered another tomb that held two female mummies. One thin mummy was in an open sarcophagus and the other more ample mummy was simply lying on the floor. Three years later, a different archeologist removed the mummy in the coffin to the Egyptian Museum and the inscription on the coffin was linked to Hatshepsut's nurse. In 1989, Donald Ryan returned to the tomb excavated, recorded, and reclosed it with the obese mummy still inside. He theorized it could be Hatshepsut, but had little evidence to corroborate.

Zahi Hawass initiated a project to CT scan all royal female mummies from the 18th dynasty and to attempt to determine age and cause of death for each. Both the thin and ample mummies were included in the study. Hawass also recalled that in 1881 a small wooden box was discovered inscribed with Hatshepsut's name. A CT scan of the box revealed that it contained a liver and surprisingly, a tooth, a maxillary molar with part of its root missing (Horswell, 2004). Ashraf Selim, professor of radiology at Cairo University, reexamined the jaw images of the four mummies, and found in the right upper jaw of the ample mummy from KV60, a retained root. Measurements and comparisons indicated that the tooth was consistent with the retained root and the dental space (National Geographic, 2007).

The CT also seemed to dispel theories that Hatshepsut was killed by her stepson. Instead she likely died of either an infection caused by an abscessed tooth, possible complications from advanced bone cancer, or possibly diabetes. The discovery makes Hatshepsut the first ancient Egyptian ruler to be identified since King Tutankhamen was excavated by Howard Carter in 1922 (National Geographic, 2009).

1.3 Disaster Victim Identification

1.3.1 Bazar de la Charite, 1897

This historic and tragic fire occurred at an annual charity event in Paris. In the conflagration 126 lost their lives and another 200 were injured, mostly aristocratic women. The bazaar site was in a large wooden building made of pine, with 22 wooden booths, a tarred roof, and a wooden floor. It was decorated with painted canvas flats, cardboard, lace, ribbons, and paper-mâché. The ceiling was covered with fabric with a gas-filled balloon hanging from the middle.

Moving images projected by a new Lumiere brother's technology using a system of ether and oxygen was said to be the cause of the fire. When it was time to begin, the projectionist asked his assistant for more light. A match was struck, causing an ether lamp to explode. The flames rapidly spread throughout the enclosure.

Many of the bodies were burned so badly that they were identified by only a piece of jewelry or scrap of clothing leading to misidentification. The Duchesse d'Alencon, sister of Empress Sisi of Austria, and other prominent victims were identified by dental comparisons.

The dental identifications in this tragedy initiated the idea for the first textbook on forensic odontology, *L'Art Dentaire en Medicine Legale*, by Dr. Oscar Amoedo published in 1898.

1.3.2 Disaster Relief Act of 1974 (Public Law 93-288)

The Disaster Relief Act of 1974 outlined a presidential disaster declaration process. Congress amended the act in 1988 and renamed it as the Stafford Disaster Relief and Emergency Assistance Act after Robert Stafford, the man who helped pass the law. The Stafford Act details the systematic management of disasters for state and local government agencies. In 1979, President Jimmy Carter signed Executive Order 12148, creating the Federal Emergency Management Agency (FEMA) based partly on the provisions set forth in those acts.

1.3.3 Jonestown, 1978

The Peoples Temple was a cult led by Jim Jones. During the 1970s, he established Jonestown, the informal name for the Peoples Temple Agricultural Project in Guyana. U.S. Congressman Leo Ryan visited Jonestown to investigate rumors that were circulating about the cult. As the California congressman and his entourage were preparing to leave Jonestown, they were attacked at the airstrip by members of the Peoples Temple. In the gunfire that erupted, Congressman Ryan and others were killed. Jones told his followers that there would be retaliation and that they should all commit "revolutionary suicide." The members drank a poisoned punch containing valium, cyanide, Phenergan, and chloral hydrate. A total of 912 people died, including 276 children. Dental records were used to identify some of the bodies (Reiterman, 2008).

1.3.4 John Wayne Gacy, 1978

Cook County includes the City of Chicago and many of its suburban areas. Within a 6 month period in 1978–1979, something approaching a forensic odontologist's nightmare scenario became a reality. In December 1978, John Wayne Gacy was arrested and charged with the murder of 33 individuals, the largest mass murder case attributed to one individual in the history of the United States. On May 25, 1979, American Airlines Flight 191 crashed moments after take-off from Chicago's O'Hare Field, killing 274 individuals, making it the worst commercial air disaster in U.S. history. The probability that two events of this magnitude could occur in one U.S. county in a 6 month period is indeed exceedingly unlikely.

The John Wayne Gacy case involved identifications of individuals of specific population groups within a potentially unlimited population. The Flight 191 crash identification process was different in that the process was made simpler because the potential victim population was limited to passengers, crew, and relatively few ground victims but made more complex because of incineration and fragmentation of the victims.

The John Wayne Gacy murders had occurred between 1972 and 1978. Gacy had been sentenced to a 10 year prison term after a conviction of sodomy in Iowa in 1968. He was released after 18 months for good behavior and for being a model prisoner. Ten years later in December 1978, he was arrested for what was called the most horrible crime of the century. During the time after his release, he had been a contractor, model citizen, loving father, active in community politics, and "Man of the Year" for the Jaycees. He was later called the "Killer Clown" as he had been known to dress as a clown to entertain children.

His mode of operation was to pick up young men and boys on various pretenses including offering them work in his company. He would subdue, torture, and sexually assault his victims prior to killing them. He disposed of 27 bodies nearby, 25 in the crawl space under his home, one under his barbeque pit, and one under his driveway. Many of his victims dug their own graves, thinking they were working on a construction project. All the buried bodies were covered with a caustic powder to decompose the soft tissue. After he ran out of space at home, Gacy dropped the next four victims into the Des Plaines River. An archeological-style site was developed in the crawl space to find and remove the remains. Identification of skeletonized remains was routine if adequate antemortem records were available. Requests through media outlets were made for any antemortem records that could be useful in identification.

While most relatives readily provided the dental records, it is speculated that some were reluctant to produce those records because of the potential homosexual connotations for the relationship between Gacy and his victims. Two hundred dental records were submitted and reviewed.

The final identification count of 25 included 23 dental identifications. Two were identified by skeletal features. In 2011, at the direction of the Cook County Sheriff, the eight remaining bodies were exhumed to procure DNA samples. Since that time, one additional identification was made using DNA and confirmed by dental identification. Of interest, only after the DNA identification did the family provide the antemortem dental information that this victim's maxillary cuspids had been extracted although previous descriptions of postmortem features for this victim had included the unusual finding. The information, combined with other findings, could have produced identification 33 years earlier. The dental identification team consisted of three dentists, two Cook County Sheriff's Police investigators, and the Chief of Forensic Services, Cook County Sheriff's Police, Dr. Edward J. Pavlik. John Wayne Gacy was tried, convicted, and on March 13, 1980 sentenced to death. After 14 years on death row he was executed on May 10, 1994.

1.3.5 American Airlines Flight 191, 1979

American Airlines flight 191 from Chicago O'Hare to Los Angeles, California, a DC-10 airliner, crashed on take-off on May 25, 1979. The deadliest airliner accident to occur at that time on U.S. soil killed 259 passengers, 13 crew, and 2 ground victims.

The port engine of the triengine aircraft fell off on take-off, the cause being attributed to a shortcut in maintenance procedures, which cracked a support brace approximately 2 months previous to the crash. As the engine tore from the wing, hydraulics to the flaps were severed and electrical warning systems became inoperable. The experienced crew could not see the engine from the cockpit and reaction time was not sufficient to upright the aircraft, which became partially inverted to 112°. The impact and subsequent conflagration accelerated by a full load of jet fuel, resulted in fragmentation and incineration of the victims. High-pressure fire hoses further dispersed body parts.

Victim recovery was organized as a gridded site with tagging of parts to specific locations. Three hundred and twenty-five body bags were moved to refrigeration trucks in proximity to the American Airlines hanger, which would become the forensic institute for the next 2 months.

A dental identification team of 19 individuals was in place the day after the crash. Team organization responsibility was undertaken by Edward J. Pavlik, Chief of Forensic Sciences, Cook County, and Sheriff's Police. Some of the team members were actively recruited—three from the John Wayne Gacy case—and some came to the scene to volunteer. Some problems did occur with some of the volunteers as compliance with simple rules about contact with media sources and professional demeanor was ignored. These individuals were asked to leave the scene.

Since the majority of the victim population was on the airplane's manifest, support personnel contacted victim families for antemortem records of all types. Identification efforts were a coordination of dental, anthropological, fingerprint, and personal effects. The American Airlines hanger was set up with exam tables, lights, running water, dental and body x-ray facilities, photographic section, resection and chart areas, as well as a separate room for identification. Two hundred and forty-four were identified, 90% by dental identifications. Thirty of the victims were declared dead by court order as no identifiable body parts were found.

1.3.6 Disaster Mortuary Operational Response Team (DMORT), 1992

Tom Shepardson volunteered to assist the Department of Health and Human Services' Office of Emergency Preparedness to improve America's response to mass disasters in the 1980s. Shepardson outlined a system of using volunteer teams of people who had experience in forensics and mortuary services. His plan became operational in 1992 when the National Disaster Medical System established ten DMORT (Disaster Mortuary Operational Response Team) regions and teams (Hammer et al., 2006). DMORT has assisted in the recovery and identification of decedents in events including the 1995 Oklahoma City Murrah Federal Building Bombing, the 2001 World Trade Center attacks, the 2005 Hurricanes Katrina and Rita, and the 2010 earthquake in Haiti.

1.3.7 Waco Siege, 1993

In 1993, the Bureau of Alcohol, Tobacco, Firearms, and Explosives (ATF) arrived at the Branch Davidian ranch near Waco to carry out a search warrant for illegal weapons. Living at the ranch were members of a religious group lead by David Koresh. Shots were fired and the FBI was brought in an attempt to contain and control the situation. The siege lasted for 3 months and, when over, 82 people were dead. A fire started during the siege meant many of the bodies were very badly damaged. About half of those who perished were identified by dental records, fingerprint records, and forensic pathology findings (Johnson, 2011).

1.3.8 Oklahoma City Bombing, 1995

The bombing of the Alfred P. Murrah Federal Building in Oklahoma City was the worst pre-9/11 terrorist attack in North America. Timothy James McVeigh claimed he targeted the federal building in response to the federal government's role in the Waco Siege. Packing a truck with 4800 lb of volatile materials, McVeigh demolished the building and killed 168 people. Bodies were badly damaged and many had to be removed from the precarious rubble of the building. Once again, dental records were used to help identify some of the remains.

1.3.9 World Trade Center, New York; The Pentagon, Virginia, and Shanksville, Pennsylvania, 2001

The body count from the September 11 terrorist attacks was over 3000. The locations included the World Trade Center in New York, the Pentagon in Washington, DC, and a field near Shanksville, Pennsylvania. At the Pentagon, 124 people were killed on the ground and all 64 people on the plane, including the 5 terrorists. The Pennsylvania crash site was the grave of 40 United Airlines passengers and 4 terrorists. At the World Trade Center 2749 died after both towers burned and collapsed. As of 2010, only 1626 victims have been positively identified. Many remains were badly damaged either from the actual plane crashes or the fires that resulted. Over 500 victim identifications were by dental record comparisons.

1.3.10 Hurricane Katrina, 2005

Hurricane Katrina struck Louisiana and Mississippi on Monday, August 29, 2005. New Orleans, Louisiana, withstood the initial effects of the storm but broken levees later flooded 80% of the city. More than 1200 died in the storm and its aftermath most in Louisiana and Mississippi, making Katrina the third deadliest hurricane in mainland U.S. history. Katrina was a particular challenge for the forensic odontology community because many dental records were destroyed when the dental offices were flooded or washed away.

1.3.11 Haiti Earthquake, 2010

In 2010, an earthquake brought Haiti to its knees. The estimated death toll was in the thousands and many structures were destroyed. Along with sending humanitarian aid, the United States also helped to identify the remains.

1.4 Bitemarks and Bitemark Cases

1.4.1 William I of England, 1027–1087

William I, also known as William the Conqueror, was the King of England during the eleventh century. He was known for biting the wax seals on official documents. Since his teeth were distinctive, it gave English officials a unique way of confirming the documents' authenticity (Dorion, 2011).

1.4.2 George Burroughs and the Salem Witch Trials, 1692

Between 1680 and 1683, George Burroughs was a minister in Salem, Massachusetts. During this time, Burroughs made a dangerous enemy in the Putnam family because of unpaid debts and his suspected Baptist beliefs. This animosity played a part in his being charged with witchcraft in 1692. His accusers, mostly young girls, claimed he would bite them if they didn't sign his book, indicating they supported his beliefs. Burroughs was forced to open his mouth in court to provide evidence that he had bitten his accusers. Despite evidence that he was in jail when the alleged events took place, Burroughs was convicted and executed in 1692 (Dorion, 2011).

1.4.3 Ansil L. Robinson Murder Trial, 1870

In 1870, Robinson was accused of murdering his mistress, Mary Lunsford. Lunsford had multiple bitemarks on her arms. The prosecutor brought in three dentists to give testimony. The three dentists testifying determined that teeth had unique characteristics, each person had unique dental characteristics and bitemarks can be evaluated. Unfortunately, the method used by one of the dentists, Dr. Whitney, was a bit unusual. Soon after the body was found, Dr. Whitney bit the decedent's arm to compare his own bitemark to that of the killer. Robinson was also asked to bite Dr. Whitney's arm so his bitemark could be compared to those found on the victim. Robinson was found not guilty. This is considered one of the first cases in American history in which a dentist testified about bitemark evidence. However, the murder trial wasn't widely or officially reported. The information available today comes primarily from a few newspaper articles from that time period (Dorion, 2011).

The following bitemark cases are important because they are (1) seminal local or national cases that influenced the management and/or adjudication of cases that followed them, (2) cases involving famous or infamous characters, or (3) cases for which convictions were later vacated or reversed and in which forensic odontology or forensic odontologists played a part.

1.4.4 *Doyle v. Texas*, 1954

Doyle was charged with burglary. Part of the evidence against him was a piece of cheese with a bitemark left at the scene. Doyle was made to bite another piece of cheese so that a firearms examiner and Dr. William J. Kemp, a dentist, could compare the two bitemarks. Dr. Kemp and the forensic examiner were able to determine and opine that the bitemarks originated from the same dentition, linking Doyle to the scene of the crime. *Doyle v. Texas* is considered the first reported case in which bitemark evidence was used to convict the suspect in the United States (Dorion, 2011).

1.4.5 *Public Prosecutor (Norway) v. Torgersen*, 1958

The body of Rigmor Johnsen was found by firemen responding to a fire in the basement of her apartment building in December 1957. Investigators determined that she had been sexually assaulted and murdered. There was a bitemark injury on her breast. Professor Ferdinand Strom, a well-known forensic dentist, documented the evidence. The breast was removed and the tissue was preserved in Kaiserling's solution following the autopsy. Professor Strom testified that Torgersen caused the bitemark. Torgersen was convicted, receiving a life sentence. Torgersen maintained his innocence and, when released 16 years later, sought a new trial. While the Norwegian courts did not grant a new trial, they did allow Professor Gisele Bang (Sweden) to review the 1957 evidence in 1975. Professor Bang also determined that the bitemark was Torgersen's. In 1999 and 2000, Professors David Whittaker (Wales) and Gordon MacDonald (Scotland) again reviewed the evidence and concluded that Professors Strom and Bang were correct. In 2001, Dr. David Senn (USA) was engaged to review the case and was allowed access to the remaining evidence including the preserved breast tissue. For the first time since Professor Storm documented it at autopsy in 1957, the actual injury pattern in Johnsen's breast was analyzed. The prior reexaminations had been made on other material but not by direct examination of the preserved, bitten breast. Dr. Senn opened the sealed case and made three-dimensional models of the breast tissue. He documented the bitemark with digital photography and microphotography. After evaluating all of the available evidence, Dr. Senn determined that the evidence indicated that Torgersen could be excluded as the biter. He sought independent and blinded second opinions by sending the evidence to three board-certified forensic odontologists without disclosing to them the details of the case. All three forensic odontologists consulted independently stated that the suspect could not have made the bitemark. Despite these new reports, the Norwegian courts still refuse to grant Torgersen a new trial. As of 2012, Torgersen and his team continue their efforts (Dorion, 2011).

1.4.6 *Crown (Scotland) v. Hay*, 1967

Fifteen-year-old Linda Peacock was found strangled to death in a Biggar, Scotland, cemetery. There was a bitemark pattern on her breast. Dr. Warren Harvey and Professor Keith Simpson investigated 29 potential suspects in Biggar, including the occupants of the Loaningdale School for troubled boys. Five boys from the school were selected for further investigation, including Gordon Hay. Due to features seen in the bitemark corresponding to pits at the tips of his canines, the bitemark was determined to have been caused by Hay.

1.4.7 *Illinois v. Johnson*, 1972

Johnson was accused of rape and aggravated battery. The victim had a bitemark on her breast. Dr. Paul Green, an Illinois dentist, was able to show that the bitemark matched Johnson's dentition. Johnson was convicted of the crime (Dorion, 2011).

1.4.8 *California v. Marx*, 1975

Lovey Benovsky, an elderly woman, was sexually assaulted and strangled. There was a severe bitemark on her nose. At autopsy the pathologist noted the bitemark injury but failed to collect photographs or casts of the injury. Walter Marx was charged with Benovsky's murder and, initially, refused to submit to dental impressions. He was held in contempt of court and ultimately agreed to the dental casts. Benovsky's body was exhumed so the bitemark on her nose could be photographed and a model of the injury could be created. Three dentists worked initially independently and later together to evaluate the bitemark evidence for this case. Dr. Gerald Felando, Dr. Reidar Sognnaes, and Dr. Gerald Vale used three-dimensional models of the nose, overlays, and scanning electron microscopy to compare Marx's dentition to the bitemark. All three testified that Marx made the bitemark on Benovsky's nose. This was this the first time bitemark evidence was used in California court and established the admissibility of bitemark evidence in a court of law in California (Dorion, 2011).

1.4.9 *Illinois v. Milone*, 1976

Sally Kandel was found murdered in 1972. She had a bitemark injury on her inner thigh. Richard Milone was charged with the crime. *Illinois v. Milone* became a battle of the experts with three dental experts testifying for the prosecution and four for the defense. The number of dental experts increased to eleven when Milone appealed his conviction. The courts upheld the conviction and noted that even though forensic odontology was relatively new at the time of the trial, the evidence presented had value and the defense was not hindered in cross-examining witnesses or presenting their own experts (Dorion, 2011).

1.4.10 *Florida v. Bundy*, 1979

Theodore Robert Bundy was a serial killer and rapist who killed an estimated 40 women. One of his victims in Florida had a double bitemark pattern on her buttocks. One photograph included a ruler and because of that ruler, forensic odontologist, Dr. Richard Souviron was able to resize the photograph to better compare the bitemark to Bundy's dentition. Drs. Lowell Levine and Norman Sperber evaluated the bitemark evidence as well and all three forensic odontologists testified to the admissibility of bitemark evidence in Florida's court of law. Drs. Levine, Souviron, and Homer Campbell testified that it was indeed Ted Bundy that created the bitemark pattern on the victim and Bundy was convicted. This trial established the admissibility of bitemark evidence in Florida. Ted Bundy would be charged with another murder in 1980 and for a second time, sentenced to death. In 1989, Bundy was executed in the electric chair for the later crime (Bell, 2008; Dorion, 2011).

1.4.11 *Florida v. Stewart*, 1979

Margaret Hazlipwas found sexually assaulted and murdered. She had a bitemark pattern on her hip. At first, some theorized that Hazlip had bitten her own hip but that theory was later dismissed as the biter profile indicated a gap between the upper two central incisors and Hazlip had no gap. The biter profile was partially developed by studying a piece of partially eaten bologna found at the scene. Roy Allen Stewart was later charged with the murder and brought to trial. Dr. Lowell Levine was asked to examine Stewart and the bitemark evidence for the defense. However, Dr. Levine did not testify because he was testifying at Ted Bundy's trial at the same time as Stewart's trial. Dr. Levine did give the defense tips for cross-examining of Dr. Souviron, the prosecutor's expert. Stewart would later be convicted and executed for this crime. This case, along with others that came before it, indicated that two forensic odontology experts could come to different conclusions from the same evidence (Evans, 2007).

1.4.12 *State of Wisconsin v. Robert Lee Stinson*, 1984

Sixty-three year old Ione Cychosz was found dead in a vacant lot near her Milwaukee, Wisconsin home. Bitemark injuries were found and a forensic odontologist was asked to evaluate the evidence. Robert Lee Stinson was charged with the crime. Two forensic odontology experts reported that Stinson's teeth had created several of the patterned injuries. Robert Earl Stinson, the suspect's fraternal twin brother, was excluded by the one of the experts. Stinson's attorney stated he was unable to find a forensic odontologist to testify for the defense. Robert Lee Stinson was convicted of the murder. In 2005, the Innocence Project engaged a panel of four forensic odontologists to review the bitemark evidence. The panel excluded Stinson as the biter. The Innocence Project also arranged for DNA testing of saliva found on Cychosz's sweater. The DNA comparisons excluded Stinson and later indicated another man already in prison for a different murder. Stinson's conviction was overturned in 2009 after he had served 23 years in prison (Innocence Project, 2012).

1.4.13 *Louisiana v. Willie Jackson*, 1986

Willie Jackson was charged with rape and robbery in 1986. A bank receipt found in the victim's car was from his account. He lived 185 miles from the scene of the crime but his mother and brother lived in the area. While searching his mother's house, police found evidence items consistent with the victim's description. In a photographic lineup the victim identified Jackson as her attacker. A forensic odontologist testified that the bitemarks on the victim were made by Willie Jackson. After Willie Jackson was convicted, his brother, Milton Jackson, confessed to being the rapist. In 2004, a DNA test was run on semen recovered from the victim's pantyhose excluded Willie Jackson and did not exclude Milton Jackson. In 2006, Willie Jackson's conviction was overturned.

1.4.14 *Oklahoma v. Wilhoit*, 1987

Greg Wilhoit was convicted and sentenced to death in 1987 for the 1985 murder of his ex-wife. The testimony of a forensic odontologist stated that not only did Wihoit's dentition match the bitemark found on the victim, but the bitemark also had a rare bacterium that could be linked to Wilhoit. Wilhoit's family had engaged an opposing expert but the defense decided not to put the expert on the stand. After Wilhoit was convicted, his defense expert sent the bitemark evidence to 11 additional board-certified forensic odontologists for evaluation. Each of these eleven also excluded Wilhoit. In 1991, after an evidentiary hearing, Wilhoit was granted a new trial. The state decided to drop the charges and released him in 1992 after he had served 5 years on death row (Wilhiot v. State, 1991).

1.4.15 *Commonwealth of Pennsylvania v. Kunco*, 1991

In 1991, John Kunco was convicted of brutally raping a 55 year old woman. The two pivotal pieces of evidence against him included the victim identifying his lisp and a bitemark on the victim's shoulder. Beyond those two items of evidence, none of the hair, fiber, or blood linked Kunco to the crime. The bitemark on the victim was photographed 5 months after the crime using UV photography. The forensic odontologists stated that the bitemark was made by Kunco. At appeal, the defense team argued that the bitemark testimony should not have been allowed because of statements in a report by the National Academy of Science, indicating bitemark evidence could not positively identify a perpetrator. The Pennsylvania Supreme Court denied Kunco's petition for a retrial. The Innocence Project has submitted other evidence for DNA testing. Those results are pending (Innocence Project, 2012).

1.4.16 *New York v. Roy Brown*, 1992

A social worker was found beaten, stabbed, and strangled. She had been bitten seven times. A prosecution bitemark expert testified that the bitemarks were "entirely consistent" with the teeth of Roy Brown. A defense expert opined that six of the bitemarks were insufficient for analysis and the seventh excluded Brown. Saliva found on the victim's sweater was tested at the time of the trial but the tests were inconclusive. After he was convicted, Brown diligently worked from prison to prove his innocence. By reviewing the testimony and the prosecution records he received through the states Freedom of Information Law, he essentially solved the case for which he had been wrongly convicted. In 2005, with assistance from the Innocence Project, he discovered that there were more samples of the saliva collected from the shirt of the victim. The DNA results from the subsequent testing excluded Brown and strongly included another suspect who had committed suicide after Brown wrote to him from prison accusing him of the crime. Brown was exonerated in 2007 (Innocence Project, 2012).

1.4.17 *Arizona v. Krone*, 1992 and 1996

Kim Ancona was found murdered in the bar where she worked. She had been sexually assaulted and had bitemarks on her neck and breast. There was a variety of biological evidence including blood, semen, and saliva. However, the DNA results at the time were said to be inconclusive. Ray Milton Krone, a postal worker, was charged and convicted of the crime. A bitemark expert stated bitemarks were like fingerprints and that this particular bitemark was a "scientific match" to Krone's dentition.

Krone was convicted and given the death penalty. Krone appealed citing withheld evidence by the prosecution. The same expert testified at the retrail and Krone was convicted a second time in 1996 but the sentence was reduced to life. In 2001, the biological samples were retested using significantly more advanced DNA testing. The results excluded Krone and pointed to another man who had lived in the neighborhood of the crime and was already in prison for another offense. Krone was exonerated in 2002 (Arizona Justice Project, 2012).

1.4.18 *Michigan v. Moldowan and Cristini,* 1991

When Maureen Fournier was kidnapped and sexually assaulted, Michael Cristini and Jeffery Moldowan were charged with the crime. Two forensic odontologists testified that Cristini's and Moldowan's dentition matched the bitemarks that were found on the victim. One of the odontologists stated the match was to a mathematical certainty. There is no scientific basis for claims of mathematical certainty in bitemark analysis. On appeal in 1997, two additional forensic odontologists testified that both Moldowan and Cristini could be excluded. New trials were granted. Cristini was exonerated in 2002 and Moldowan in 2004.

1.4.19 *Illinois v. Young and Hill,* 1992

Kathy Morgan was found murdered in a burning building. Harold Hill and Dan Young were charged with her murder and convicted in 1992. During the investigation, Hill and Young confessed they committed the crime with help from Peter Williams. Further investigation, revealed that Williams was incarcerated when the crime occurred and Young was found to have an IQ of 56. A bitemark expert also associated the bitemarks found on the victim to Hill and Young. In 2004, DNA tests on hairs found at the scene and fingernail scrapings from the victim excluded Young and Hill. They were exonerated in 2005.

1.4.20 *Mississippi v. Brewer,* 1995, and *Mississippi v. Brooks,* 1992

In 1992, 3 year old Christine Jackson was found raped and murdered. Kenny Brewer, the boyfriend of Christine's mother, was charged with the crime. A forensic odontologist claimed that 19 oddly shaped wounds on Jackson's body were bitemarks and they matched Brewer's dentition. Brewer was convicted and sentenced to life in prison. In 1990, there had been a similar murder in the same county. Levon Brooks was charged with the rape and murder of his girlfriend's 3 year old daughter. The child had mysterious wounds that a forensic odontologist linked to Brooks. Both children had been taken from their homes in the middle of the night, assaulted, and then dumped in a body of water near the area.

In 2001, the Innocence Project took an interest in Brewer's case. They engaged two forensic odontologists to independently review the bitemark evidence and had semen that was collected from the crime scene tested for DNA. The bitemark evidence review indicated that none of the marks on Christine Jackson were bitemarks. The DNA results excluded Brewer. Brewer was granted an appeal for a new trial and the prosecutor stated he intended to go for the death penalty. The Innocence Project also agreed to investigate Brooks' case but learned the DNA samples from the 1992 crime were too degraded to test.

Mississippi's Attorney General was asked to step in after the Innocence Project grew concerned due to Noxubee County official's alleged conflict of interest in Brewer's and Brooks' case. The Attorney General appointed a special prosecutor for both cases. The investigation quickly turned toward Albert Johnson, who was originally a suspect in both cases. He lived near each of the victims at the time of the crimes and had a history of sexually assaulting young girls. Johnson's DNA was tested against the biological evidence from Brewer's case.

The results were positive. Confronted with the evidence, Johnson confessed to both murders and stated he acted alone. Brewer and Brooks were both exonerated in 2008. The same odontologist had testified in both cases (Innocence Project, 2012).

1.4.21 West Memphis Three, 1994, Alford Plea 2011

In 1993, three young boys were mutilated and murdered. Damien Echols (18), Jessie Misskelley Jr. (17), and Jason Baldwin (16) were accused of killing the boys in a satanic ritual, and in 1994 the three were convicted. In 1998 Brent Turvey, a Forensic Scientist and Criminal Profiler, reviewed the available autopsy and photographic evidence from the original trial. He theorized that injuries on one of the victim's face were in fact bitemarks and that patterned injuries on the inner thigh of one of the other victims were also bitemarks. A board, certified forensic odontologist reported one of the marks on one victim was a human bitemark and excluded Echols, Misskelley, and Baldwin. The state's expert concluded that there were no bitemarks at all. DNA testing on the biological evidence found at the scene excluded Baldwin, Misskelley, and Echols. Prior to considering a new trial, Judge David Laser held a hearing at which the three defendants entered Alford pleas, maintaining their innocence while acknowledging that the prosecutor likely had enough evidence to convict them. All three were released in 2011 (Northwestern University School of Law, 2012; Innocence Project, 2012).

1.4.22 *New Jersey v. Jesse K. Timmendequas*, 1997: Megan's Law

Megan Kanka was sexually assaulted and murdered. Jesse K. Timmendequas, a sex offender that lived in Kanka's neighborhood was charged with the crime. Timmendequas had a bitemark on his hand. A bitemark expert stated that the mark could have come from Kanka. Megan's parents helped to create what is now known as Megan's Law, a law that requires sex offenders to register with their local law enforcement. In many states, Megan's Law also specifies the residents of a neighborhood and local schools be notified when a sex offender joins their community (Fisher and Lab, 2010).

1.4.23 *Massachusetts v. Edmund Burke*, 1998

Irene Kennedy, a 75 year old woman, was found beaten and stabbed. A bitemark was found on her breast. Edmund Burk, a handyman, was suspected of the crime. A bitemark expert testified that, to a reasonable scientific certainty, Burk was the biter. Burk was arrested but released 6 weeks later when a DNA test was performed on saliva found on the victim indicated that the saliva was not from Burk. When the bitemark expert was questioned about the DNA test, he said the police could have contaminated the sample. The expert also stated another forensic odontologist had looked at the evidence and agreed Burk was the biter. In 2003, the DNA profile was entered into a database and was matched to a convicted murderer.

1.4.24 *State of New York v. James O'Donnell*, 1998

In 1998, James O'Donnell was convicted of attempting to sexually assault a woman. The victim had a bitemark on her hand, which a bitemark expert claimed could only have been caused by O'Donnell. Despite his girlfriend's and son's testimonies that he was home at the time of the crime, O'Donnell was convicted. In 1999, a rape kite that was collected from the crime was tested for DNA, which excluded O'Donnell. O'Donnell was officially exonerated in 2000 (Innocence Project, 2012).

1.5 Age Estimation

1.5.1 Louis XVII "The Lost Dauphin," 1894

King Louis XVI and his wife Queen Marie Antoinette were both beheaded during the "Reign of Terror" during the French Revolution. Their son and heir was not executed, but imprisoned for 2 years. He died at the age of 10 in 1795. He was buried in an unmarked grave so those who wanted to restore the monarchy would have no place to rally support for their cause.

It was thought that he was buried near the church wall in the Sainte-Marguerite cemetery in Paris. The area was excavated and a coffin was found that bore markings leading them to believe it could be the little lost heir.

To determine if it was indeed Louis XVII, Dr. Léonce Manouvrier was summoned, as he had done studies on the lengths of bones to determine age estimation. Dr. Émile Magitot was asked to evaluate the teeth, as 1880 he and Charles Legros had published, "The Origin and Formation of the Dental Follicle: The First Memoir on the Development of Teeth," that included on page 160 a chart showing the age when different parts of the teeth are formed and when they erupt.

Magitot noted that there were no deciduous teeth. The decedent had a missing lower right first molar (#30) and the bone in the socket was completely healed. Moreover, the second molar (#31) had shifted mesially at an angle until it contacted the second premolar (#29). In addition, the wisdom teeth had erupted through the bone, but not through the gums. Therefore, he gave the age estimation range as 18–20 years old, and thus it could not be that of Louis XVII. His findings were published in the *Archives d'Anthropoligie Criminelle* (*Archives of Criminal Anthropology*) that same year.

1.5.2 Massler and Shour, 1941 and 1944

Dr. Maury Massler and Dr. Isaac Shour created a chart to be used for dental age estimations. The chart showed 21 stages of tooth development. In 1944, they updated their chart to include 22 stages of tooth development from before birth to 35 years of age. See Chapter 8 for a more complete description.

1.5.3 Moorrees, Fanning and Hunt, 1963

Moorrees, Fanning, and Hunt developed a system of age estimation based on tooth root formation. The system includes five stages of development and separate age ranges for males and females. See Chapter 8 for a more complete description.

1.5.4 Mincer, Harris, and Berryman, 1993

In 1993, Dr. Harry Mincer, Dr. Edward Harris, and Dr. Hugh Berryman published a modified Demirjian's molar development technique applied specifically to third molars. See Chapter 8 for a more complete description.

1.5.5 King Tutankhamen, 2005

King Tutankhamen reigned from 1341 to 1323 BC. His tomb had been only partly plundered and was truly filled with treasures. In 1922, Howard Carver excavated the tomb of the "boy king." But just how old was he? In 2005, King Tutankhamen's mummy was submitted to a noninvasive medical procedure, a CT scan. Radiographs taken in 1968 and 1978 were used to estimate his age. The report stated:

> Tutankhamen was about 19 years old when he died, based on the following observations, using modern developmental tables:
>
> The fusion of the epiphyseal plates (the parts of the bone that is responsible for growth until a certain age) matches the development of a young man of 18 or more, and 20 or less.
>
> All of the cranial sutures are still at least partly open.
>
> The wisdom teeth are not completely erupted. One of these (upper left) is impacted, and there is a slight thinning of the sinus cavity above. This was not life-threatening, and there are no signs of infection (Zahi Hawass, blog post, March 8, 2005).

1.6 Abuse and Neglect

1.6.1 Mary Ellen Wilson, 1874

Mary Ellen Wilson was born in 1864. Hers is a story that inspired the founding of the first efforts at protecting children from abuse. After her parents died, Mary was placed in the care of the New York Department of Charities who then placed her with Mary McCormack who later married Francis McConnolly. In 1874, when she was 9 years old, someone reported hearing her cries and asked for intervention. Mrs. Etta Angell Wheeler, a Methodist mission worker, promised that she would do what she could. Wheeler went to the New York City authorities. While there were laws in place to remove abused children, most were reluctant to intervene. She had thought about contacting the Society for Prevention of Cruelty to Animals (SPCA), but thought it was silly idea. Finally, her niece urged her to contact Mr. Bergh at SPCA, "You are so troubled over that abused child, why not go to Mr. Bergh? She is a little animal surely." Henry Bergh was the founder of the SPCA and president of NYSPCA. He sent an NYSPCA investigator posing as a census worker to the tenement to investigate the child's condition. Bergh had an NYSPCA attorney file a petition to remove the child from the home. He did this as "a human citizen," and made sure he was "clarifying that he was not acting in his official capacity as president of the NYSPCA." It was later reported that he did this work in his official capacity, but he did not. He knew the process needed to make a good case, he knew people in the legal system, and he brought the case to the press. The child was removed from the home and brought before a judge to investigate the claim of abuse. Ms. Wheeler was present to give her testimony.

> Her body was bruised, her face disfigured, and the woman, as if to make testimony sure against herself, had the day before, struck the child with a pair of shears, cutting a gash through the left eye-brow and down the cheek, fortunately escaping the eye.
>
> The child's appearance was testimony enough, little of mine was needed, and, thus, on Thursday, April 9, 1874, her rescue was accomplished.

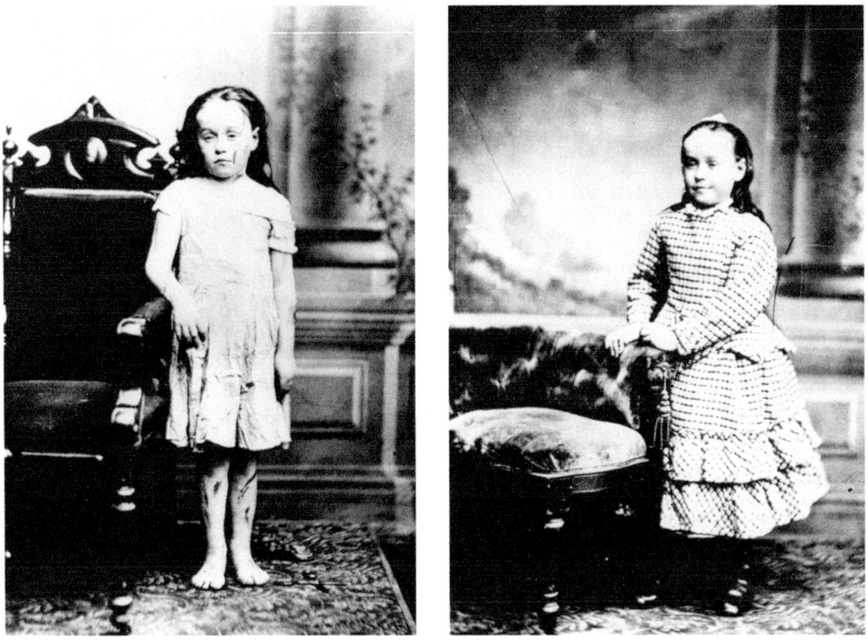

(a) (b)

Figure 1.10 Mary Ellen Wilson just after her "rescue" (a) and following her adoption (b).

Thus, Mr. Bergh had accomplished the rescue within 48 hours after first hearing of the case. The court placed Mary Ellen in home for "grown girls, some of them wayward." A judge later placed her with Sally Angell, Etta Wheeler's mother, and after Angell's death with Etta's youngest sister. Mary Ellen's life was much improved (Figure 1.10), and after she married she named her first child Etta, for Etta Wheeler (American Humane Association; Watkins, 1990).

1.7 Forensic Odontology; Books and Chapters in Books

1898: Amoedo, O. *L'Art Dentaire en Medicine Legale*. Digital edition available (French) http://www.archive.org/details/lartdentaireenm00amo

1966 Gustafson, G. *Forensic Odontology*. London, U.K.: Staples Press.

1973: Luntz, L. and Luntz, P. *Handbook for Dental Identification*. Philadelphia, PA: Lippincott Williams & Wilkins.

1974: Cameron, J. M. and Sims, B. G. *Forensic Dentistry*. Edinburgh, U.K.: Churchill Livingstone.

1975: Gladfelter, I. A. *Dental Evidence: A Handbook for Police*. Springfield, IL: C. C. Thomas Publishers.

1976: Sopher, I. M. *Forensic Dentistry*. Springfield, IL: C. C. Thomas Publishers.

1976: Harvey, W. *Dental Identification and Forensic Odontology*. London, U.K.: Henry Kimpton Publishers.

1980: Seigel, R. and Sperber, N. *Forensic Odontology Workbook—The First Manual of Forensic Odontology.* Saratoga Springs, NY: American Society of Forensic Science.

1980: Spitz, W. U. and Fisher, R. S. *Medicolegal Investigation of Death: Guidelines for the Application of Pathology to Crime Investigation*. Springfield, IL: C. C. Thomas Publishers.

1980: Keiser-Nielsen, S. *Person Identification by Means of the Teeth: A Practical Guide.* Oxford, U.K.: Butterworth-Heinemann Ltd.

1982: Cottone, J. A. and Standish, S. M. *Outline of Forensic Dentistry.* Chicago, IL: Year Book Medical Publishers.

1984: Hill, I. R. *Forensic Odontology: Its Scope and History.* Solihull, UK: Alan Clift Associates.

1989: Whittaker, D. K. and MacDonald, D. G. *A Colour Atlas of Forensic Dentistry.* London, U.K.: Wolfe Medical Publications.

1991: Averill, D. C. *Manual of Forensic Odontology*, 2nd edn. Saratoga Springs, NY: American Society of Forensic Science.

1995: Bowers, C. Michael and Bell, Gary L. *Manual of Forensic Odontology*, 3rd edn. Saratoga Springs, NY: American Society of Forensic Science.

1997: Stimson, P. G. and Mertz, C. A. *Forensic Dentistry.* Boca Raton, FL: CRC Press.

2005: Dorion, R. B. J. *Bitemark Evidence.* New York: Marcel Dekker.

2006: Herschaft, E. E., Alder, M. E., Ord, D. K., Rawson, R. D., and Smith, E. S. *Manual of Forensic Odontology*, 4th edn. Saratoga Springs, NY: American Society of Forensic Science.

2010: Senn, D. R. and Stimson, P. G. *Forensic Dentistry*, 2nd edn. Boca Raton, FL: CRC Press.

2011: Dorion, R. B. J. *Bitemark Evidence*, 2nd edn. Boca Raton, FL: CRC Press.

Acknowledgments

Joanne Ethier, DMD, MS, translated the work by Mathieu d'Escouchy on the identification of the First Earl of Shrewsbury. The task was made even more difficult because it was written in Old French. We are grateful for her valuable assistance.

Kristin Elink-Schuurman-Laura created the map detailing the distribution of medical examiners and coroners in U.S. jurisdictions.

References

Ackerknecht, E. H. 1953. *Rudolf Virchow: Doctor, Statesman, Anthropologist.* Madison, WI: University of Wisconsin Press.

American Humane Association. The story of Mary Ellen. http://www.americanhumane.org/about-us/who-we-are/history/story-of-mary-ellen.html

Arizona Justice Project. Justice project. http://www.azjusticeproject.org/

Barrett, A. A. 1996. *Agrippina: Sex, Power, and Politics in the Early Empire.* London, U.K.: Yale University Press.

BBC News. 2003. Egypt's 'Ramses' mummy returned. http://news.bbc.co.uk/go/pr/fr/-/2/hi/middle_east/3215747.stm

Bell, S. 2008. *Encyclopedia of Forensic Science*. New York: Facts on File, Inc.

Bemis, G. 1850. Report of the case of John W. Webster: Indicted for the murder of George Parkman... before the Supreme Judicial Court of Massachusetts.

Bezymenski, L. 1968. *The Death of Adolph Hitler: Unknown Documents from Soviet Archives*. New York: Harcourt, Brace & World, Inc.

Bryan, G. S. 1940. *The Great American Myth*. New York: Carrick & Evans, Inc.

Buess, H. 1951. Theophil Bonet and the significance of his Sepulchretum in the history of pathologic anatomy. *Gesnerus* 8(1–2): 32–52.

Coroners' Society. A brief history. http://www.coronersociety.org.uk/wfBriefHistory.aspx

Davis, K. C. 2008. *America's Hidden History*. New York: HarperCollins, p. 128.

d'Escouchy, M. 1863. *Chronique de Mathieu D'escouchy*, book 2, Ed. G. Beaucourt. Paris: Société de L'histoire de France.

Dio, C. *Roman History*; translated by H. B. Foster, Vol. 4, Book 60. http://www.gutenberg.org

Dorion, R. B. J. 2011. *Bitemark Evidence: A Color Atlas and Text*, 2nd edn. Boca Raton, FL: CPC Press.

Evans, C. 2007. *The Casebook of Forensic Detection: How Science Solved 100 of the World's Most Baffling Crimes*. New York: Berkley Trade.

Fisher, B. S. and Lab, S. P. 2010. *Encyclopedia of Victimology and Crime Prevention*. Thousand Oaks, CA: SAGE Publications, Inc.

Girard, A. C. RG 404, The US Military Academy. Entry 156, Adjutant General Division, letters received, 1881–1903, No. 1207:1888, NA.

Hammer, R., Moynihan, B., and Pagliaro, E. M. 2006. *Forensic Nursing: A Handbook for Practice*. Sudbury, MA: Jones and Bartlett Publishers.

Hanzlick, R. 2007. The conversion of coroner systems to medical examiner systems in the United States: A lull in the action. *Am J Forensic Med Pathol* 28(4): 279–283.

Hanzlick, R. and Combs, D. 1998. Medical examiner and coroner systems: History and trends. *JAMA* 279(11): 870–874.

Horswell, J. 2004. *The Practice of Crime Scene Investigation*. Boca Raton, FL: CRC Press LLC.

Dr. Hawass, Z. blog, http://www.drhawass.com/blog/press-release-tutankhamun-ct-scan

Hyson, J. M. and Whitehorne, J. W. A. 1993. Dental forensics: The fate of Lieutenant Harrington at the Little Big Horn. *Bull Hist Dent* 41(3): 103–107.

Innocence Project. The innocence project. www.innocenceproject.org

Jeffers, H. P. 1999. *Bloody Business: An Anecdotal History of Scotland Yard*. New York: Barnes & Noble.

Jenkins, M. C. 2010. *Vampire Forensics*. Washington, DC: National Geographic.

Jentzen, J. M. 2009. *Death Investigation in America: Coroners, Medical Examiners, and the Pursuit of Medical Certainty*. Cambridge, MA: The President and Fellows of Harvard College.

Johnson, S. P. 2011. *Trials of the Century: An Encyclopedia of Popular Culture and the Law*. Goleta, CA: ABC-CLIO, LLC.

Knight, B. Crowner: Origins of the office of coroner. http://www.britannia.com/history/coroner1.html

Laurie, W. S. 1952. A letter from Captain Walter Sloan Laurie. Dated Camp on Charles Town Heights, 23 June 1775. Quoted in Sigmund Diamond, "Bunker Hill, Tory Propaganda, and Adam Smith," *The New England Quarterly* 25: 367 [Sept. 1952]. https://www.masshist.org/publications/apde/portia.php?mode=p&id=AFC01p272

Linder, D. 2007. The Boston Massacre trials: An account. Available at: http://ssrn.com/abstract=1021327 or http://dx.doi.org/10.2139/ssrn.1021327

Luntz, L. and Luntz, P. 1973. *Handbook for Dental Identification*. Philadelphia, PA: Lippincott Williams & Wilkins.

Maples, W. and Browning, M. 1994. *Dead Men Do Tell Tales: The Strange and Fascination Cases of a Forensic Anthropologist*. New York: Double Day.

National Association of Medical Examiners. General Information. http://thename.org/index.php?option=com_content&task=view&id=46&Itemid=29

National Geographic. June 2007. Egypt's female pharaoh revealed by chipped tooth, experts say. http://news.nationalgeographic.com/news/2007/06/070627-mummy-tooth.html

National Geographic. April 2009. Hatshepsut. http://ngm.nationalgeographic.com/2009/04/hatshepsut/brown-text/1

National Museum of Health and Medicine. A RESOLVED Case Study: Major General Joseph Warren and Paul Revere. http://nmhm.washingtondc.museum/exhibits/resolved/paul_revere.html

National Research Council. 2009. *Strengthening Forensic Science in the United States: A Path Forward.* Washington, DC: National Academies Press.

Northwestern University School of Law. Center on wrongful convictions. http://www.law.northwestern.edu/wrongfulconvictions/

Norton, L. E., Cottone, J. A. et al. 1984. The exhumation and identification of Lee Harvey Oswald. *J Forensic Sci* 29(1): 19–38.

NOVA Science Programming. Original PBS Broadcast, January 3, 2006. *The Mummy Who Would Be King.* Boston, MA: WGBH Educational Foundation.

Pliny the Elder. Natural History. Book 7, Chapter 15. http://perseus.tufts.edu/hopper

Pliny the Elder. Natural History. Book 9, Chapter 58. http://perseus.tufts.edu/hopper

Putnam, R. 1908. *Charles the Bold, Last Duke of Burgundy, 1433–1477.* New York: G.P. Putnam's Sons.

Reiterman, T. and Jacobs, J. 2008. *Raven: The Untold Story of the Rev. Jim Jones and His People.* New York: J.P. Tarcher/Penguin.

Reuters. July 16, 2008. Russian says remains of last Tsar's son identified. http://www.reuters.com/article/2008/07/16/us-russia-tsar-idUSL1519544820080716

Sargent, W. The History of an expedition against Fort Du Quesne, in 1755; under Major General Edward Braddock, Generalissimo of H.-B. M. Forces in America. Edited from the Original Mss. By Winthrop Sargent, M. A., Member of the Hist. Soc. of Pennsylvania. 8vo. Philadelphia: 1855.

Starr, D. 2010. *The Killer of Little Shepherds: A True Crime Story and the Birth of Forensic Science.* New York: Alfred A. Knopf.

Sumner, W. H. Reminiscences relating to General Warren and Bunker Hill. *New England Historical Genealogical Register and Antiquarian Journal* 12. SG Drake, 1858: Pages 113 and 119. Google eBooks http://books.google.com/

Tacitus, C. 2004. *The Annals/Tacitus*; translated, with introduction and notes by A. J. Woodman. Book 12. Indianapolis, IN: Hackett Publishing Co.

Taylor, A. S. 1865. *The Principles and Practice of Medical Jurisprudence.* London, U.K.: Churchill.

The Pennsylvania Evening Post, April 25, 1776. Photographs of the newspaper can be found on http://teachhistory.com courtesy of the Edwards Collection of Colonial Newspapers. A photo of the newspaper can be seen at the Rag Linen (an educational archive of rare and historic newspapers) web site: http://raglinen.com/collections/1776-collection/

The New York Times, October 29, 1979. Around the Nation; "Pathologist Says Autopsy Verified Oswald Identity"

U.K. National Archives. Coroners act 1988. http://www.legislation.gov.uk/ukpga/1988/13/contents

U.S. Department of Labor. http://www.dol.gov/

Warren, J. C. 1854. *Genealogy of Warren with Some Historical Sketches*, p. 47.

Watkins, S. A. 1990. The Mary Ellen myth: Correcting child welfare history. *Social Work* 35(6): 500–503.

Wellington, R. H. 1905. *The King's Coroner: Being a Complete Collection of the Statutes Relating to the Office Together with a Short History of the Same.* London, U.K.: W. Clowes & Sons.

Forensic Pathology

2

GARY T. SIMMONS

Contents

2.1 Forensic Pathology Defined 41
2.2 Death Investigation 42
2.2.1 History 42
2.2.2 Scene Investigation 43
2.2.3 Evidence Collection 44
2.3 Changes after Death 44
2.3.1 Rigor Mortis 45
2.3.2 Livor Mortis (Hypostasis) 45
2.3.3 Algor Mortis (Postmortem Cooling) 46
2.3.4 Tissue Decomposition 47
2.3.5 Stomach Contents 49
2.4 Time of Death 49
2.5 Cause of Death 50
2.5.1 Natural Deaths 50
2.5.2 Blunt Force Trauma 51
2.5.3 Sharp Force Trauma 52
2.5.4 Gunshot Wounds 53
2.5.5 Asphyxia 56
2.5.6 Fire 56
2.5.7 Drugs 57
2.6 Manner of Death 58
2.7 Autopsy Reports 59
2.8 Death Certificates 59
2.9 Professional Relationships 59
References 60

2.1 Forensic Pathology Defined

Forensic pathology is the scientific examination of human bodies in order to elucidate the cause, manner (e.g., natural, homicide), and circumstances involved with death. The actual examination is normally performed by a forensic pathologist who is a licensed physician. After 4 years of medical school, the typical forensic pathologist has completed an additional 3–4 years of training in an anatomic/clinical pathology residency program, followed by a year of specialized training in a forensic pathology fellowship. After this training and successful completion of the anatomic pathology board examination, the forensic pathologist is eligible to sit for the forensic pathology board examination administered by the American Board of Pathology. If successful, the forensic pathologist is then a "board-certified" forensic pathologist. Unfortunately, in the United States there is a shortage of board-certified forensic pathologists with only an estimated 400 board certified forensic pathologists practicing forensic pathology full time (Hanzlick et al. 2008, 114). Thus, as a practical matter, many forensic examinations are carried out by nonboarded forensic pathologists whose backgrounds can vary considerably.

Although it is commonly believed that a forensic pathologist is only concerned with the cause and manner of death, this view is incomplete. The forensic pathologist is also concerned with what can be scientifically determined concerning the circumstances surrounding an individual's death. This process includes gathering evidentiary materials such as DNA, which might be of immeasurable assistance to the investigation and subsequent adjudication. However, the forensic pathologist should at all times be an independent physician in search of the scientific truth without regard to whether this truth is favorable or not to a particular party in a legal dispute.

Although the postmortem examination itself is typically conducted by a forensic pathologist, the laws governing death investigation and subsequent types of investigative offices in the United States can have significant variations from state to state and sometimes, even within individual states. Some states have statutes covering all death investigation within that state; other states have different individual local laws. Most populous jurisdictions have offices run by appointed forensic pathologists and are generally referred to as medical examiner offices. However, in approximately 69% of the counties in the United States, death investigations are performed by coroners' offices run by elected coroners, the vast majority of whom are not board-certified forensic pathologists and who commonly are not physicians. In a few localities medical examiners need only be physicians, who may not actually perform autopsies, or may not be required to be physicians at all (Hanzlick 2007, 279). As one might expect with these interoffice variables, there are differences in the customs, as well as the laws governing specific individual case investigation. These include factors such as the types of cases that are investigated, who has legal authority to accept or decline cases, whether a full autopsy or an external examination is performed, what records are open to public access, and how much legal standing the next-of-kin has to object to an autopsy. There are also frequently significant variations with regard to the level of monetary support different offices receive from their governing bodies. These differences in approach and funding between different individual offices can result in differences in the resultant quality of the examination process. It would, therefore, behoove the forensic odontologist to be aware of the specifics of the medicolegal system with which they are working and that system's support capabilities.

2.2 Death Investigation

2.2.1 History

The investigation of a death always begins with a history of the involved circumstances. It is a classic error to believe that the autopsy alone will be all-encompassing and all-knowing. Unfortunately, this erroneous belief is not uncommon among the nonmedical public, including law enforcement. An example of this would be a gunshot wound to the right temple in which the autopsy revealed the end of the gun barrel was up against the skin (i.e., a contact wound). This finding could indicate a suicide or an execution-style murder. However, both cases have the same exact autopsy findings. It is therefore incumbent upon the forensic pathologist to impress upon applicable personnel as to the importance of an adequate history. This process begins the moment the coroner/medical examiner office is notified of a death. If, for example, it is a member of law enforcement reporting a death, they should be queried as to all of the available information. This preliminary information should be recorded and carefully assessed in view of the medicolegal requirements for a complete death investigation. Frequently, this active deliberate assessment will result in the discovery of additional issues, which should be pursued. It cannot be assumed that law enforcement will automatically know what information needs to be gathered, especially with regard to medically related issues. In complex cases, such as child abuse where the caregiver is giving potentially self-serving false information, it is frequently helpful to give investigative personnel a detailed list of exactly what questions should be pursued. The forensic pathologist should generally never attempt to personally question any known potential criminal suspects. Criminal investigations need to be done in a coordinated fashion by law enforcement to reduce the likelihood of omissions or inadvertent premature release of information. Furthermore, strict requirements exist concerning the admissibility of evidence in criminal proceedings that experienced police investigators know to follow, of which medical personnel are likely to be much less familiar. The forensic pathologist should keep in mind his or her role as an independent scientist as opposed to a law enforcement investigator.

Although the first notification of a death is frequently made by law enforcement, it is not unusual for medical facilities to contact the coroner/medical examiner office directly. Frequently at this stage the police have not been notified. If there is any reasonable suspicion that a non-natural death has occurred, it is best to notify the police at this time while the body is still at the other medical facility. This enables the police to begin any necessary investigation at an early stage and helps to provide the forensic pathologist with any necessary information.

2.2.2 Scene Investigation

A major difference between a hospital autopsy and a forensic autopsy is the importance of a scene investigation. Ideally a preliminary scene investigation should have been completed at the time of the autopsy. Findings of interest include whether the scene was secure and whether there was evidence of a confrontation or violence. Prescription pill containers provide insight into medical issues of the decedent, as well as, identify the treating physician. In cases where identification is an issue, this can be an important starting point in the quest to find antemortem medical records. An inventory of the contents of such containers against the information on the label can reveal inappropriate amounts of missing medication, as happens in accidental overdoses or suicides. Furthermore, while a typical routine toxicological screen includes most common drugs of abuse, such screening is far from inclusive for all drugs or poisons. Information as to what specific drug(s) the decedent had access to can lead to specific directed screening and the detection of additional drugs, which otherwise might have been missed. The same is true for household chemicals that might have been employed as poisons. As is the case with the autopsy itself, the scene is examined with the consideration of all the available information. A good investigator will constantly be actively correlating all the available information into a single narrative. It is imperative that if some of the information does not "fit" what has been discerned by the medical examiner, that this be recognized and appropriately addressed lest a serious error be made.

2.2.3 Evidence Collection

Evidence of various types is commonly collected at all stages of the investigation, both at the scene and in the autopsy suite. Evidence related to clothing and the body itself may include material in the pockets, foreign material such as fibers or paint chips, fingernail scrapings or clippings, sexual assault kits, foreign biological material and projectiles. Deliberate, thoughtful care must be taken to ensure that not only are the appropriate procedures completed, but they are done in the correct order to ensure that valuable evidence is not compromised. For example, it is inappropriate to allow a body to be washed at the morgue prior to taking swabs of bite marks for DNA samples. Foreign material collection needs to be performed as early as feasible during the investigation with particular care taken to avoid contamination. In a criminal investigation, appropriate evidence collection can be the most important aspect of the autopsy examination. Results from bite mark evidence and DNA from a sexual assault kit can correctly lead authorities to or away from individual suspect(s) in a way that simply determining the cause of death may not. Within reason, it is better to "over-collect" evidence even if subsequent events reveal that it is not pertinent. The case history and/or the available information not uncommonly changes at a later date and the investigation or counsel may subsequently focus on something totally unexpected. Superfluous evidence can always be discarded. If, however, evidence such as a sexual assault kit becomes needed at a later date, it is impossible to be subsequently obtained. In view of the current ubiquitous use of DNA in issues ranging from postmortem paternity testing to criminal investigations, it is wise to retain a dried blood sample or appropriate applicable tissue for possible future DNA testing from every examination, including natural deaths.

During and after collection of evidence, care must be taken to scrupulously maintain a proper chain of custody. This documentation includes a written detailed list of exactly what evidence was collected, where it was collected, who collected it, and the date and time of collection. Evidence must be appropriately securely stored so that it can be honestly testified to that the evidence has not been altered. If evidence is transferred, correct written documentation of the transfer must be maintained by all parties. Typically there is an extended period of time before a case is adjudicated during which memories can fade. This makes correct written record keeping all the more imperative.

2.3 Changes after Death

Beginning at the time of death, changes related to decomposition of the body begin and continue in a predictable sequence. These changes and their sequence generally occur regardless of the specific cause of death. Unfortunately, while the sequence is generally predictable, the time frame over which the sequence unfolds can show considerable variability based on individual case circumstances. Nevertheless, the examiner must be aware of and adequately document these changes. The medicolegal importance of these changes is that they can be useful in approximating the time of death, can mimic or compromise the examination of premortem injuries, and can help determine if a body has been moved at some point after death. To maximize the usefulness of these observations, notation of these changes should be made as soon as reasonably feasible, preferably at the scene. Refrigeration and storage of the body prior to examination adds another layer of complexity to the interpretation of many of these changes.

2.3.1 Rigor Mortis

Rigor mortis or rigor is rigidity of the muscles, "locking" the affected structures (e.g., limbs) in place after death. The effect of rigor is secondary to postmortem chemical changes in muscles with the two major muscle proteins, actin and myosin, forming locking chemical bridges. Although the process begins immediately after death, it is usually not grossly discernible until approximately 1–4 h after death, reaching its maximal extent in approximately 8–12 h in temperate environments. Although this chemical process proceeds in all muscles, it is frequently first discernible grossly in the smaller muscles such as those of the oral-facial complex. Factors that may increase the speed of development of rigor mortis include increased body temperature from any cause including hyperactivity, electrocution, and a hot environmental temperature. Cool environmental temperatures will slow development of rigor mortis. Also, individuals with reduced muscle mass may have less prominent rigor mortis since rigor is caused by the binding of muscle proteins, which are less prevalent in such cases. After the development of maximal rigor mortis, decomposition of the muscle progresses along with protein breakdown. Rigor will therefore begin to diminish and disappear completely by approximately 36 h after death. The timeline for rigor's disappearance is influenced by the same factors that influenced its onset. Unfortunately, because of all of these variables the preceding timeline is only a general outline. If rigor mortis is forcefully broken after maximal development, it will not reappear. However, if rigor mortis is broken before it is fully developed a variable amount of rigidity will reappear (Knight 1996, 60–63; Spitz and Spitz 2006, 101–103).

It should be determined if the rigor mortis observed is appropriate for the position of the body at the scene. Rigor mortis that is antigravitational or otherwise inconsistent with the position of the body at the scene is a strong indication that the body has been moved after death.

2.3.2 Livor Mortis (Hypostasis)

Livor mortis or lividity is a purplish-blue discoloration of the gravitationally dependent (i.e., the lowest) areas of the body. It is caused by blood passively moving along blood vessels because of gravity to dependant areas of the body from nondependent areas. This results in an excessive amount of blood in dependant areas relative to nondependent areas and thus a noticeable color differential. This coloration can be misinterpreted as bruising by the inexperienced observer. Since the blood flow is passive along blood vessels, firm external pressure against the skin will impede this flow and result in an area of color blanching relative to the surrounding livid skin (Figure 2.1). Livor mortis begins immediately after the heart stops beating and becomes more noticeable with the passage of time, usually becoming first discernible by approximately 2 h after death. It generally becomes fully developed approximately 8–12 h after death. With the full development of livor mortis, blood congeals or moves out of the vessels into the tissues and becomes fixed. Once lividity becomes fixed, it will not change position even if the body's position is subsequently altered, thus providing evidence that the body has been moved after death. If a body is moved after lividity becomes visible but before it becomes completely fixed, two different patterns of lividity may develop, again indicating the body has been moved. Lividity, however, can be difficult to discern in dark-skinned individuals. Also, since livor mortis is based on blood movement, conditions such as significant anemia or extensive blood loss can make lividity nondiscernable. Unfortunately, because of the occurrence of significant individual case

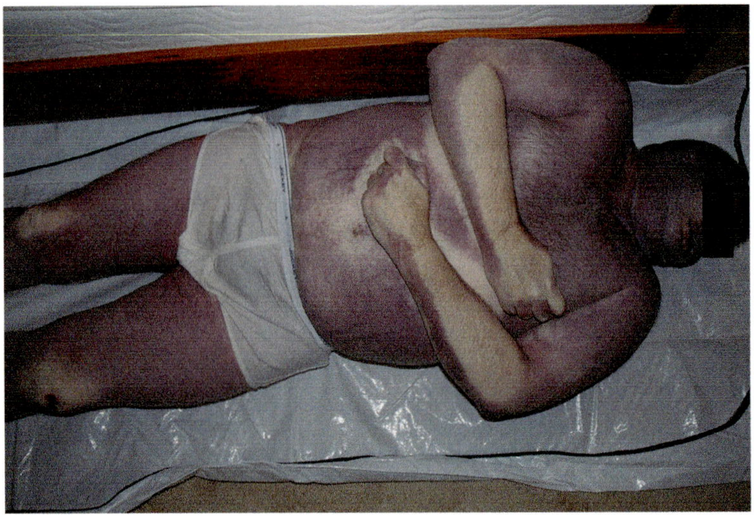

Figure 2.1 Body has been lying prone several hours prior to discovery. Anterior lividity is fixed with color blanching of dependent areas of the body lying directly against supporting structure.

variations from the preceding general timeline, livor mortis is not a precise indicator of the victim's time of death. It can, however, be a useful indicator that a body has been moved since death (DiMaio and DiMaio 2001, 21–25).

2.3.3 Algor Mortis (Postmortem Cooling)

After death the body will begin to assume the environmental temperature. Over the years numerous studies with various published mathematical formulas or nomograms have been conducted to use this phenomenon in order to establish the time of death. It is beyond the scope of this work to discuss the specifics of these different approaches but they can be found in appropriate references. As an alternative to these relatively complex approaches, one can also use the approximation that under average conditions the body loses 1.5°F–2°F/h, on average, during the first 12 h and then 1°F for the next 12–18 h. All of these approaches generally use core body temperatures (such as rectal or liver temperatures) rather than skin temperatures because the skin, being directly exposed to the environment, exhibits more variability in its cooling rate than the core body temperature. Unfortunately, because of multiple variables involved in each individual case, these different approaches are all inexact and therefore of limited usefulness. Any attempt to use body cooling as a determinant of the time since death must take into account these variables, which are subsequently discussed. Even then, the data should be cautiously interpreted and correlated with all of the other available information (Spitz and Spitz 2006, 95–96).

The cooling curve of the body immediately after death with respect to time is not a simple straight line mathematical function. While heat transfer within the body through circulation ceases with death, metabolic heat production in muscles, liver, and the gastrointestinal tract continues for a variable amount of time after death. Additionally, these tissues are poor heat conductors. Thus, while the skin will begin to cool with death, the internal core temperature will generally not register a significant fall for some time, typically several hours. With time, a temperature gradient between the environment and the core tissues will be established. This gradient will then result in a relatively straight or shallow cooling curve with respect to time.

As the body begins to approach environmental temperature, the differential between the environment and the core temperature lessens and the cooling curve will again flatten, resulting in a sigmoid-shaped curve. While the general overall shape of the cooling curve is fairly well defined, variables affect the timeline itself, thus preventing postmortem temperature determinations from doing more than giving a general range of time since death.

One variable to be considered is the decedent's actual body temperature at the time of death. Hyperthermia may be caused by things such as sepsis, physical activity, seizures, heat stroke, various metabolic abnormalities, or drugs such as cocaine. Alternatively, the decedent may have been hypothermic due to environmental conditions, shock, or drug effects. As a body temperature of 98.6°F (37°C) at the time of death is generally assumed for these calculations, deviations from this temperature can potentially induce significant error.

Another consideration is the environment surrounding the body. Heat is normally lost by convection to the adjacent air. However, if the body is in water, heat transfer is by conduction through direct contact. This process is much more efficient than convection and results in much more rapid heat transfer and a resultant steeper (more rapid) cooling curve. If the body is in air, the rate of cooling will vary based on the amount of air moving around the body. Air movement brings fresh cooler air in contact with the body and thus increases the temperature gradient. A larger temperature gradient results in a steeper cooling curve. An additional confounding variable is that the environment may change during the cooling process. This is particularly a concern outdoors where the body can be exposed to changes in temperature, wind conditions, rain, and sunlight. Obviously, if the temperature in the environment is above the body temperature at death the body temperature will actually increase postmortem.

Clothing or other coverings on the body act as insulation and will slow heat loss across the temperature gradient. The effectiveness of this slowing depends upon the amount and nature of the material as well as the percentage of the body that is covered. Wet clothing relative to dry clothing will increase the rate of cooling because of heat loss through the process of evaporation. The dimensions of the body itself will also influence heat loss. Adipose tissue acts as insulation and will retard heat loss. A larger surface area to mass ratio, such as that found in children, will increase the rate of cooling.

The nature of the surface on which the body is lying can also affect heat loss by conduction. For example, a body lying on a metal mortuary tray will cool more rapidly than a body lying on thick vegetation. Furthermore, the amount of skin in contact with the surface can also affect body cooling. A body lying completely flat in a spread-eagle manner will cool faster than a body bent over in a sitting position because heat transfers more rapidly by conduction than by convection through air (Knight 1996, 80–89).

2.3.4 Tissue Decomposition

After death, the biochemical processes that maintained the integrity of the body's cells cease to function and the body begins to disintegrate or decompose. There are in effect two parallel processes at work. One is autolysis, which is the aseptic self-destruction of the body by the enzymes of the body. The other process is putrefaction, which is decomposition leading to liquefaction brought about by the action of bacteria and fermentation. Destruction of the body may also be brought about by anthropophagy, the destruction of the body by various types of predators ranging from insects to larger animals, particularly rodents. However, most unembalmed bodies primarily undergo putrefaction, which is what most individuals are referring to when discussing decomposition and what is primarily considered in the following discussion.

The rate of decomposition after death varies widely. The rate depends to some extent on the condition of the body at the time of death (e.g., sepsis, open wounds), but much more important is the environment affecting the decomposing body. Temperature is the greatest single variable with heat significantly accelerating the decomposition process and vice versa. The temperature of the environment may vary over the time between death and the body being discovered further complicating the timeline of decomposition. Relative to air, a water environment slows the decomposition process, and burial slows it even more. Access to the body by insects and animals with resultant postmortem tissue damage will speed the decomposition process. Also complicating an accurate interpretation is the fact that different parts of the same body may undergo decomposition at different rates. With all of these variables, it is not possible to accurately delineate an exact timeline for all cases of decomposition. However, one can look at the characteristic decomposition pattern of an undisturbed body in a closed temperate environment and from this baseline extrapolate to local conditions in a particular case.

Early decomposition usually becomes evident within the first 24–30 h in the form of greenish discoloration caused by denaturation of hemoglobin by bacteria. This discoloration typically begins in the right lower quadrant of the abdomen due to the close proximity of the cecum to the lower abdominal wall. It extends within 36–48 h to involve the head, chest, and extremities, becoming dark-green, to purple, to black. As this occurs, the putrefactive bacteria tend to spread most easily at first along blood vessels with a resultant "marbling" pattern to the skin. As decomposition progresses, skin vesicles begin to appear and the skin begins to slip off either spontaneously or with minimal manipulation. The skin of the hands, including the nails, may slough off in an intact glove-like pattern. This glove phenomenon can have identification ramifications. Frequently it is possible to actually put the "skin glove" on one's own gloved hand, ink the skin glove, and obtain useful, high-quality fingerprints. During this time, the body also becomes bloated due to postmortem gas formation by bacteria metabolism with generalized bloating becoming prominent after approximately 72 h. This bloating may give the impression of a heavy individual when in fact the body has lost weight due to decomposition. At this stage decompositional fluid will begin to form from tissue breakdown. This breakdown will result in blood-tinged fluid, or purge, coming from the natural orifices of the nose and mouth. The inexperienced frequently misinterpret this fluid as blood and an indication of foul play when in reality it has no predictive value whatsoever with regards to a particular cause of death (Figure 2.2). Decomposition then continues with additional tissue breakdown, leading eventually to skeletonization. Under temperate, closed conditions, the minimal time necessary for complete skeletonization is about 12–18 months. However, the timeline for skeletonization is highly variable, being significantly influenced by temperature and access to the body by insects and scavenging animals. A body outside in the heat of the summer may become completely skeletonized in as little as 10 days (DiMaio and DiMaio 2001, 30–35; Knight 1996, 64–68).

It should be noted that as part of the putrefactive process ethanol is occasionally, but not always, produced endogenously by microbial activity. The blood ethanol level in these cases is typically less than 0.20 g/dL. Since urine and vitreous fluid are relatively sequestered until late in the putrefactive process, these fluids will typically have negative or much lower ethanol levels compared to blood in these cases (Zumwalt et al. 1982, 553–554).

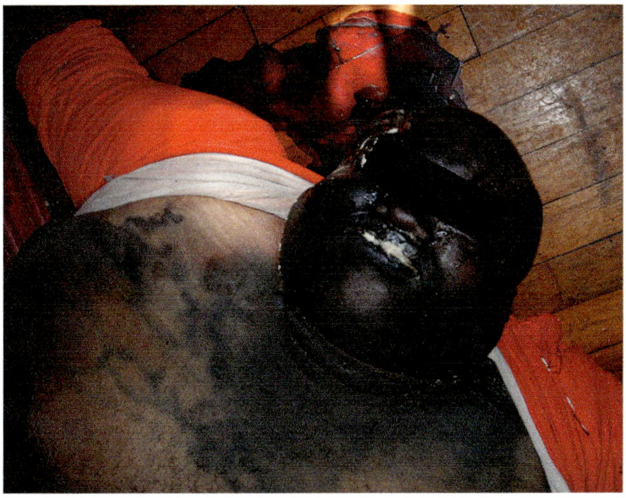

Figure 2.2 Decompositional discoloration, skin marbling, bloating, and red-tinged purge fluid exuding from facial orifices.

2.3.5 Stomach Contents

In the past, attempts have been made to assess the state of digestion and the amount of gastric contents to determine the time between the decedent's last meal and death. Experience and research has shown that the rate of gastric digestion and gastric emptying are subject to numerous variable influences. This precludes using them as a reliable assessment of the time between the last meal and death except for extremely circumscribed exceptions. The state of digestion relative to a timeline is extremely difficult to assess. Variables affecting digestion include the degree of mastication, the type of food, the amount of liquid in the stomach, physical and emotional stress, and the rate of gastric emptying. The factors affecting gastric emptying, and thus, the amount of material remaining in the stomach, include the physical nature of the food and liquid in the stomach, individual variation, and degree of emotional or physical stress. Analysis of gastric contents however can be useful in certain cases where recognizable pieces of food remain. This information may be correlated with reported information concerning the decedent's last meal as evidence that the decedent had not substantially eaten again or as confirmation of the available history (DiMaio and DiMaio 2001, 37–39; Knight 1996, 89–91).

2.4 Time of Death

From the preceding discussion, it is evident that establishing the time of death can be one of the more difficult tasks a forensic pathologist is asked to perform. At best, the pathologist will be able to give a range of time with the general rule that the longer someone has been deceased the greater this range will be. The case history, as related to when the decedent was last seen or spoken to or whether the decedent reported to work and kept appointments, is extremely important. Also helpful are any dated materials found or not found (e.g., newspapers, mail) at the scene. Despite utilizing all of the available information, the wise and experienced examiner will typically be forced to give a fairly large window and not be overly dogmatic. Time of death can be used to include or exclude access to the decedent by suspects and mistakes can have serious consequences. Unfortunately, popular media tends to give the general public unrealistic expectations as to the specificity and degree of certainty one can have based on solid and valid scientific principles.

2.5 Cause of Death

Deaths that result in medicolegal attention generally fall into two broad categories. One category is that of sudden unexpected deaths, which may or may not be under suspicious or unusual circumstances. The other broad category of deaths involves those suspected to be due to various types of trauma, be it physical or chemical (e.g., drugs). These traumatic deaths attract medicolegal involvement even when the cause of death is "obvious" for several reasons. First, unexpected findings do occur and may be missed if the body is not examined. For example, a motor vehicle driver might actually have had a fatal cardiovascular event or been shot, causing the "accident." In the case of criminal homicide, the state has the legal burden of proving that an individual's death was in fact due to homicidal violence. Additionally, the concerns and needs of interested parties not uncommonly extend far past the single question of the immediate cause of death. Interested parties are frequently more concerned with what the forensic pathologist can scientifically determine concerning the circumstances related to the decedent's death so as to confirm or refute the purported case history.

It should be noted that the mechanism of death is sometimes confused with the cause of death. The mechanism of death is the physiologic derangement produced by the cause of death. For example, clinicians occasionally list on death certificates "cardiopulmonary arrest" or similar terminology as the cause of death. However, this term defines the mechanism of death and tells the reader nothing with regard to the actual cause of death or why the decedent's heart and lungs stopped. With this in mind, the more common broad categories of causes of death are subsequently briefly discussed.

2.5.1 Natural Deaths

Natural deaths frequently result in medicolegal attention when they are sudden and unexpected or under suspicious or unusual circumstances. Included within these cases are deaths of individuals without a personal local physician. This is due to the practical consideration that the decedent's family must have a signed death certificate to enable settlement of the decedent's estate and for vital statistics purposes. The medical examiner/coroner thus by default becomes that individual's personal physician. Since signing the required death certificate includes listing the cause of death, decedents may require a full autopsy to make this determination. Because of this and the fact that natural deaths greatly outnumber other types of death, natural deaths are frequently the most common type of death investigated by a coroner/medical examiner office. The majority of these are cardiac in nature. Other sudden and unexpected natural deaths are due to entities such as pulmonary thromboemboli, cerebrovascular disease, asthma, epilepsy, chronic ethanol abuse, undiagnosed infections, and occasionally unrecognized malignancies.

What should not be overlooked is that correctly diagnosing a natural cause of death provides benefits to both society and the decedent's family by providing an accurate diagnosis of the underlying condition that contributed to the events leading to the death. There is also an undeniable public health benefit in terms of disease surveillance. Additionally, it is not unusual for accusations to arise from family members that a sudden, unexplained death may be non-natural, particularly if money or animosity among relatives is involved. The forensic pathologist can not only allay these concerns but can also prevent miscarriages of justice by refuting false allegations about poisoning, strangulation, blunt trauma, etc., in what was a natural death. This critical role in preventing false criminal or civil allegations being placed against innocent individuals is frequently unrecognized by the general public who may mistakenly believe that the forensic pathologist works for the prosecution. If the forensic pathologist rules a death natural or finds evidence to exonerate a suspect, there is usually no public trial and no general appreciation of the medical examiner offering evidence that supported the innocence of a suspect.

2.5.2 Blunt Force Trauma

Blunt force trauma is the most commonly seen physical type of trauma. It can be caused by broad flat surfaces such as a roadway or by other objects such as a baseball bat, gun handle, etc. Blunt force trauma results in three different types of lesions: abrasions, contusions, and lacerations. Additionally, skeletal fractures may occur in cases where the force is sufficient to overload the underlying bone.

Abrasions result from the removal of the epithelial layer of the skin by scraping/friction or by the destruction of epithelium by compression. They can also involve the dermis or, less commonly, the underlying subcutaneous tissues. They may be caused by an object striking the skin or by the skin striking a surface, such as in a fall or being ejected from a vehicle onto a roadway.

A contusion or bruise is caused by blunt trauma rupturing internal blood vessels resulting in hemorrhage into the surrounding soft tissues. They can occur not only in skin but also in internal organs, although deep contusions may not be visible externally. A focal collection of frank blood within a contusion is referred to as a hematoma. The size of the contusion generally varies with the intensity of the impact. Other factors that can influence the size of contusions include the age and physical condition of the victim, as well as the location and type of tissue struck. Individuals with impaired blood clotting ability from any cause will bruise more easily and prominently.

Lacerations are caused by blunt trauma tearing soft tissues as opposed to the cutting of soft tissue, which occurs in sharp force trauma. Since lacerations are caused by the tearing of soft tissues, lacerations typically feature strands of tissue, called tissue bridging, extending across the wound (Figure 2.3). Additionally, since the blunt object causing an injury has width, as opposed to a thin object such as a knife blade, there commonly is an associated abrasion along the wound edge (DiMaio and DiMaio 2001, 91–107).

On occasion, blunt force causes a lesion with a readily apparent pattern, which may allow one to identify the type of implement likely causing the injury. This is illustrated in Figure 2.4, which shows the body of an individual run over by a truck. In this case, pressure by the flat aspect of the tire has displaced the blood from torn vessels under the skin "into" the tread spaces in the tire with resultant patterned tread marks. Even in cases when the causative implement is not immediately discernible, there should be accurate documentation of the size, shape, and location of the external lesion and the resultant internal trauma. Appropriate photographs are extremely helpful in this endeavor. Proper documentation may also exclude specific objects, which at times might be useful to the investigation and

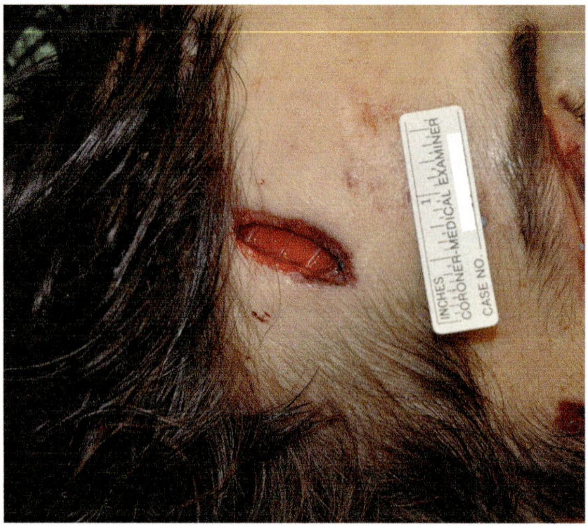

Figure 2.3 Laceration from blunt force trauma with tissue bridging extending across wound and abrasion of wound edges.

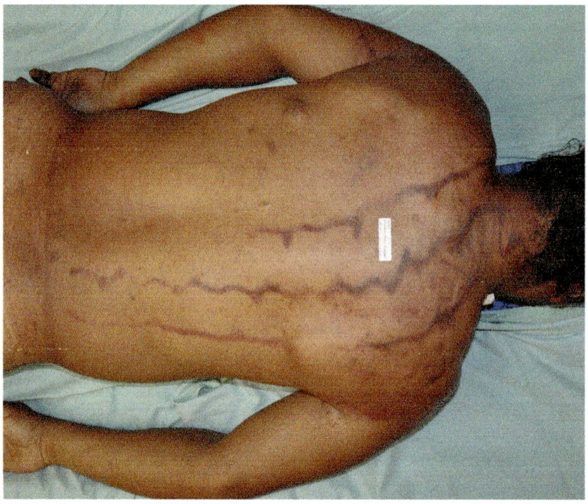

Figure 2.4 Tire tread markings. These may be used to identify a specific tire brand and model.

provide guidance to the police. Also, DNA is an extremely useful tool to include or exclude a particular weapon when biological material is present. In addition to the need to document the mechanism, cause, and manner of death, other questions that frequently arise include what physical activity the decedent would have been capable of before, while, or after the injuries were sustained, pain and suffering, survival interval, and drug use.

2.5.3 Sharp Force Trauma

The majority of fatal sharp force trauma seen by forensic pathologists involve the use of knives as weapons. There are, however, multiple other implements that can cause sharp force trauma such as scissors, ice picks, machetes, axes, and glass. There are two basic types of sharp force

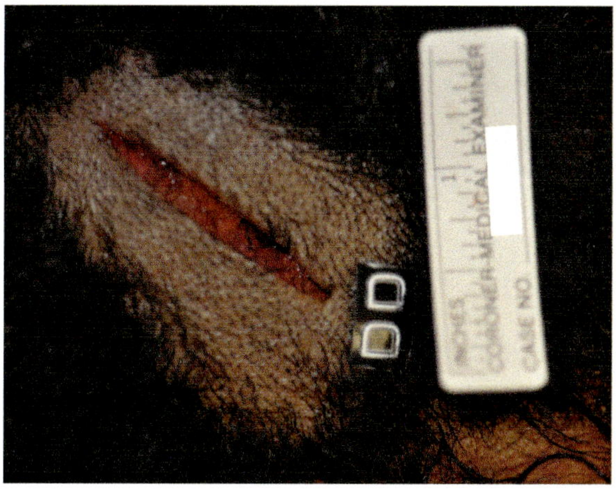

Figure 2.5 Stab wound caused by single cutting edge knife with the sharp cutting edge superiorly and the blunt edge (back of knife) inferiorly.

trauma: incised wounds and stab wounds. Incised wounds are wounds whose skin length is greater than their depth. Stab wounds are the opposite as they are wounds whose depth is greater than their skin length. Sharp force injuries caused by knives tend to be slit-like in appearance. In wounds caused by a single cutting edge knife, it may be possible to appreciate the knife's configuration after examination of the wound (Figure 2.5). When sharp force injuries are caused by thin objects such as knives, they usually do not have an associated skin abrasion from the cutting edge/blade itself. However, the guard or handle of a knife may leave an abrasion, possibly patterned, if the blade is completely inserted so that the guard or handle impacts the skin. Thicker implements, such as screwdrivers or axes, may cause a relatively thin skin abrasion around the edge of the wound. Since these implements cut rather than lacerate tissue, they do not cause tissue bridging in the wound as occurs with blunt force trauma. The skin length and depth of the wound track should be measured, as this can be compared to the dimensions of a suspected weapon to help include or exclude it as the possible weapon. Other considerations with regard to examining and documenting sharp force injuries are otherwise generally the same as those described for blunt force trauma.

2.5.4 Gunshot Wounds

In the United States, gunshot wounds are the most common cause of homicidal and suicidal deaths (CDC, 2008). In addition to documenting the external skin wound(s) and what organ(s) internally are injured, critical questions include range of fire and directionality of the wound track. The range of fire is determined by the presence or absence of soot and gunpowder particles, which are expelled with the bullet from the muzzle of the gun as the burning of gunpowder is not 100% efficient. In the case of a contact wound, the muzzle is against the skin and residue material is deposited around the edges of the entrance defect and/or within the proximal wound track. An additional characteristic of a contact wound is that there may be a prominent circumferential ring of abrasion, or muzzle imprint, around the entrance defect (Figure 2.6). This imprint is a consequence of the gas emitted from the muzzle. Because of the contact nature of the wound this gas is driven into the soft tissue wound track with subsequent expansion of the subcutaneous

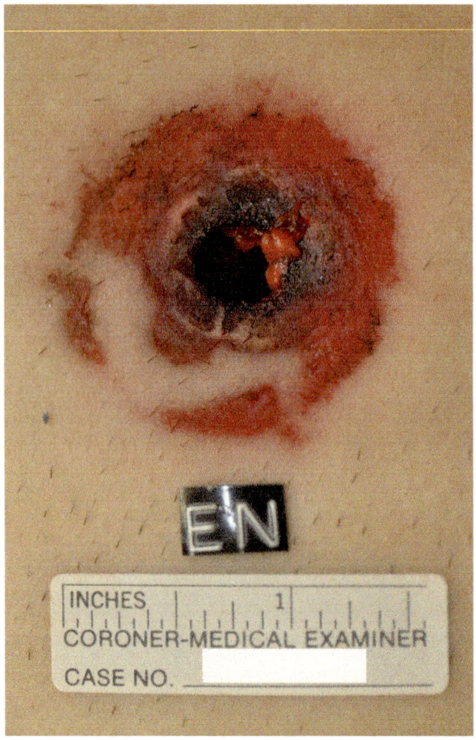

Figure 2.6 Contact gunshot wound with gunpowder residue along edge of defect with surrounding muzzle abrasion.

space causing ballooning-out of the skin against the muzzle of the weapon. This can occur with enough force to abrade the outline of the muzzle onto the skin. As the muzzle distance moves away from the skin, gunpowder residue will be deposited on the skin around the entrance wound. Soot will generally travel up to a maximum range of approximately 1 ft from the muzzle for most handguns. Gunpowder particles will travel a greater distance than soot with individual gunpowder particles being capable of actually abrading the skin, causing punctate lesions called powder tattooing or stippling (Figure 2.7). The presence of powder tattooing by definition means that the wound is of intermediate range. The tattooing pattern becomes larger but less prominent as the range increases and the gunpowder particles begin to disperse. The maximal distance from the muzzle that gunpowder can cause powder tattooing on uncovered skin is roughly three feet for handguns. However, the actual maximal distance from the muzzle for both soot deposition and powder tattooing is dependent upon several factors such as the caliber of the weapon, specific type and amount of gunpowder in the cartridge, length of the gun barrel, and the characteristics of the individual weapon.

Additionally, hair and clothing can filter out soot and gunpowder, making the range of fire seem greater than it actually was (DiMaio 1999, 127–140). Thus, any applicable hair or clothing should be examined when evaluating the range of fire. If the actual weapon is available, it may be test-fired by a firearms examiner with similar ammunition to define specific gunpowder residue patterns at different ranges. These may then be compared to what was found on the body to more specifically estimate the range of fire. Once the range

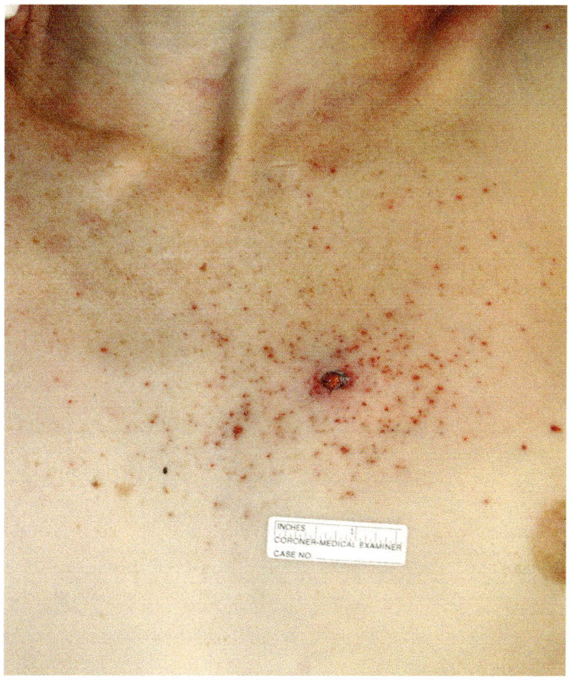

Figure 2.7 Intermediate range gunshot wound with surrounding punctate gunpowder tattooing or stippling.

increases to the point where there is no powder tattooing, the entrance wound will look the same regardless of distance and the wound is classified as a distant gunshot wound.

When considering whether a wound is an entrance or exit wound, if there is gunpowder residue or a retained bullet with no exit, the choice is obvious. Lacking these factors, entrance wounds usually can be recognized by a relatively round, regular appearance with a frequent abrasion collar caused by the bullet abrading the immediately adjacent epithelium as it perforates the skin. The abrasion collar of a distant gunshot wound, however, is typically much less prominent than the abrasion caused by a muzzle imprint from a contact wound. Since bullets typically tumble to some extent as they go through a body, when a bullet exits, it usually is not nose first but rather at an angle. This may result in the presentation of a greater bullet area at the exit site relative to the entrance. Additionally, bullets are commonly deformed as they pass through the body, which also tends to cause them to present a greater area at the site of exit. Because of these factors, the exit wound is typically larger and more irregular than the entrance wound. Exit wounds also do not have an associated abrasion collar unless an outside object is firmly up against the skin, resulting in a shored exit (DiMaio 1999, 92–95). Homicide cases in which the bullet remains in the body demand recovery of the bullet so a determination can potentially be made as to whether the bullet was fired from a specific weapon. Radiographic examination is extremely helpful in this endeavor. All gunshot wounds, including those with apparent exit wounds, should be routinely radiographed to help assure no significant bullet fragments are unwittingly left in the body. This procedure is important because it is not uncommon for bullets to fragment as they progress through the tissues, and the “exit” wound may actually have been created by only a bullet fragment or piece of bone driven out of the body.

Figure 2.8 Partially suspended suicide victim utilizing slip knot with lower extremities bent at knees with feet on the ground.

2.5.5 Asphyxia

Asphyxia is defined as "the lack of oxygen in the blood or the failure of cells to utilize oxygen, and a failure of the body to eliminate carbon dioxide" (Dolinak et al. 2005, 201). It is a broad term and may result from a number of causes. Asphyxial deaths can result from obstruction of the airway, compression of the neck vasculature, compression of the chest, lack of oxygen in the environment, and chemical asphyxia at a cellular level. The resulting spectrum of asphyxial deaths is wide-ranging from the obvious to the inconspicuous. The most common type of asphyxial death is that of suicidal hanging (CDC, 2008). Contrary to common belief, the victim does not have to be completely suspended with victims frequently being found with their feet or other body parts (e.g., knees, buttocks) easily touching the ground (Figure 2.8). This positioning is possible because the actual mechanism of death in most hangings is interference with blood flow. It is said that only 5 or 6 lb of pressure per square inch is sufficient to occlude the carotid arteries and jugular veins while 32 lb of pressure are required to block the airway (Brovardel 2006, 790).

Of the less obvious asphyxial deaths, a special note should be made of carbon monoxide deaths, which are not uncommon. Carbon monoxide is a colorless and odorless byproduct of incomplete combustion that strongly binds to blood hemoglobin, making it unable to carry oxygen. It classically causes the skin, blood, and/or organs to have a cherry-red hue. However, this hue is frequently not easily discernible or distinct and may not be appreciated. While in some cases the scene and/or history is suggestive of carbon monoxide poisoning, other cases such as faulty gas stoves or gas space heaters may have subtle or virtually no signs at the scene. It is important in these cases that there is a high index of suspicion with an appropriate investigation lest the diagnosis be missed, possibly allowing a repeat situation in which another victim unnecessarily succumbs to the same fate.

2.5.6 Fire

Fire deaths due to burning and/or smoke inhalation are frequently obvious at the time of the scene examination. Nevertheless, it is important that the bodies of all such victims be examined. Attempts to incinerate homicide victims are occasionally made to

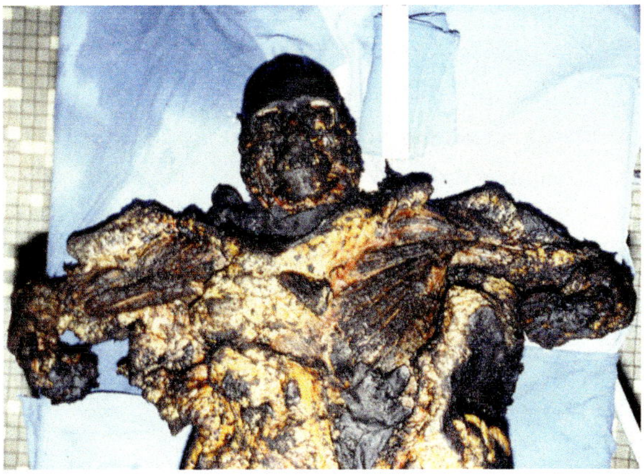

Figure 2.9 Charred fire victim. Although skin and subcutaneous tissues are burned, the internal vital organs were well preserved.

obscure the crime. Extensive charring of the body can easily obscure pre-existing traumatic injuries externally, although internally even badly charred bodies frequently have well-preserved organs (Figure 2.9). This preservation is due in part to 50% or more of the body weight normally being attributed to water (Hall 2011, 286). Blood carbon monoxide levels can only be increased by active respiration and cannot be altered postmortem. Samples should therefore be obtained to help make a determination as to whether the decedent was alive at the time of the fire. Routine complete body radiographs are invaluable for establishing whether retained projectiles are present and as an aid in identification of the victim. The history and scene examination with regard to the origin of the fire are of critical importance. If the fire's origin is determined to be a result of arson, the fire death is a homicide. If the fire was accidental in origin, the fire death is considered as accidental. Additional questions that must always be addressed include whether the decedent was under the influence of drugs and whether there were other physical impediments that hindered escape.

2.5.7 Drugs

Drug related deaths fall into two categories: (1) those in which the death was directly drug related due to a frank overdose or toxic fatal side effect and (2) cases in which drug use was not the mechanism of death but contributed to the circumstances surrounding death. In directly drug-related cases, a full autopsy examination is required to detect and account for any natural disease. Individuals under the influence of drugs may still succumb to totally unrelated natural disease processes (such as a ruptured aneurysm). Additionally, fatal postmortem drug levels can have significant individual variability. Therefore, any attempt to interpret postmortem drug levels without considering any natural disease that might be present invites the risk for error. An additional consideration is that an autopsy permits obtaining and analyzing the amount of drug(s) remaining in the gastric contents, which may be helpful in determining if a death is accidental or deliberate (suicide). Further complicating postmortem drug level interpretation is that for certain classes of drugs, such as opiates, individuals can develop considerable true physical tolerance. Since tolerance usually cannot be assessed postmortem, any history concerning prior drug use and the general circumstances surrounding death are also critical for correct toxicological and case interpretation.

The second category of those in which drug use was contributory but not the direct cause of death also requires careful and thorough investigation. A common example would be traffic deaths in which a driver was under the influence of drugs. In all cases, the need for following scrupulously correct procedures for the collection and preservation of appropriate toxicological samples with proper chain of custody documentation is required.

2.6 Manner of Death

Death certification requires that the manner of death be certified in addition to a cause of death. The categories generally available are natural, accident, homicide, suicide, and undetermined. Some jurisdictions also allow therapeutic complication in applicable cases. Often the manner of death obviously and logically follows the cause of death. In other cases, the history and scene examination are a critical part of the determination. For example, an autopsy by itself cannot determine whether a pedestrian was inadvertently struck and killed by a motor vehicle (an accident) or deliberately run over (a homicide). Because of the complexity of the events surrounding some deaths and the requirement to fit conclusions neatly into a limited number of single-word, predetermined choices, the process may be difficult. Competent death certifiers may and do disagree. For example, drug overdose deaths in depressed individuals with a history of drug abuse can be challenging to evaluate as to whether they are suicidal or accidental in nature. Despite the best efforts of investigators, on occasion a manner of death cannot be clearly defined and the categorical term, undetermined, must be used.

The manner of death certified as indicated on a death certificate is an opinion utilized by the vital statistics bureau as to how the death should be statistically coded. It is also used by other entities such as insurance companies and police departments for administrative purposes. However, the certified manner of death is not binding on the judicial system. For example, individuals under the influence of ethanol who are operating a motor vehicle and are involved in a crash with a fatality may still be legally charged for the death, although the death certificate in many jurisdictions may list the manner of death of the victim as accident. Similarly, certification of a death as a homicide simply means death resulted as a consequence of a volitional act of another. Homicide does not necessarily mean there is criminal culpability. Legitimate cases of self-defense are common examples of unprosecuted homicides.

Manner of death may have practical implications for identification issues involved with decomposed remains. In the case of a natural death, a dental examination, which is "suggestive of" or "consistent with" an individual coupled with the history, a secure scene, personal effects, and/or other general physical characteristics, may be sufficient for identification without resorting to DNA. This can be significant since for many offices DNA testing is very time-consuming and/or an additional expense. In the case of a homicide, no other collaborative evidence may be available or a greater degree of scientific certainty may be required because of potential criminal justice procedures and penalty issues. In these cases, a "suggestive of "or "consistent with" dental identification may not be sufficient, and DNA or other identification procedures will be necessary.

2.7 Autopsy Reports

Upon completion of an examination, a written autopsy report of the findings suitable for dissemination is obviously required. The autopsy report generally has two sections. One is the body of the report itself where the examination findings are objectively recorded. The wise expert will not forget the adage that if it is not recorded, it did not happen. The second is an opinion section where all of the available information is assembled to form an opinion with regard to the cause and manner of death in a fashion that can be readily understood by the general public. Speculation should be absent or minimal. These reports should be prepared with anticipation that the findings and/or conclusions may be challenged by family, legal counsel, or an opposing expert.

In preparing the autopsy report, the medical examiner should always remember that all of the material in the case file is potentially discoverable in legal proceedings. This includes any personal notes, comments, reference materials, etc. A simple rule is to never put anything in the case file that you would not want read back to you in open court.

The autopsy report is used in criminal and civil proceedings. In these proceedings the cause of death many times is not in dispute. What the parties are frequently more interested in is that which can be scientifically discerned about the circumstances around the death. Issues such as time of death, other nonfatal injuries, relative position of the body at the time of injury, ability to move after injury, survival interval, pain and suffering, evidence collection, influence of drugs, and preexisting natural disease are commonly where the main concern of the interested parties lie. The challenge for the medical examiner is to anticipate these issues, which may not be encountered until legal proceedings occur years later, and to conduct his or her investigation accordingly with the appropriate documentation.

2.8 Death Certificates

All deaths are officially recorded through the use of a generally standardized death certificate. The funeral director, with guidance from the family, fills out demographic information while the medical certifier is responsible for the cause and manner of death as well as the circumstances around death in non-natural cases. Individual death certificates are used by various entities such as families and their attorneys settling estates, insurance companies, workman's compensation boards, and genealogists. On a larger scale, the information from individual certificates is compiled into statistical summaries by local governments and forwarded to federal health agencies (Spitz and Spitz 2006, 449–450). These tasks generally cannot occur if it is unknown who the deceased individual is. Even more devastating are the entanglements caused by a mistaken identity.

2.9 Professional Relationships

The special knowledge that subspecialties such as anthropology and odontology bring to death investigation can be invaluable to a medical examiner, particularly in establishing the identity of the decedent. Since these professionals typically have additional expertise that the medical examiner does not possess, they should generally prepare their own separate reports, which are most often referenced in the autopsy report. This may necessitate that these experts subsequently testify in the legal proceedings.

The findings of these different experts should always be considered, compared, and correlated together and with the rest of the available information. For example, an odontological examination of skeletal remains may be consistent with the remains being that of a certain individual. An anthropologic examination may indicate the individual's sex and approximate height and age, as well as, detect evidence of certain degenerative diseases and trauma. The importance of early recognition and reconciliation of discordant findings is self-evident.

Excellent death investigations require the conscious and deliberate synthesis of all available information. The scientific expertise brought to bear during this process by different professionals can be invaluable and is generally well-received. All participants during this process however should always remember to never overstep the boundaries of their actual knowledge or expertise. It is unreasonable to expect any one person, not even a professional expert, to always be knowledgeable about all matters.

References

Brovardel, P. 2006. In *Medicolegal Investigation of Death*. eds. Werner Spitz and Daniel Spitz, 4th edn., p. 790. Springfield, IL: Charles C. Thomas. Originally published in *La pendaison, la strangulation, la suffocation, la submersion*. Paris, France: Bailliere, 1897.

CDC. 2008 Leading causes of death. http://www.cdc.gov/injury/wisqars

DiMaio, VJM. 1999. *Gunshot Wounds*, 2nd edn. Boca Raton, FL: CRC Press.

DiMaio, VJM and DiMaio, DJ. 2001. *Forensic Pathology*, 2nd edn. Boca Raton, FL: CRC Press.

Dolinak, D., Mathesis, E., and Lew, EO. 2005. *Forensic Pathology*. New York: Elsevier Academic Press.

Hall, J. 2011. *Guyton and Hall Textbook of Medical Physiology*, 12th edn. Philadelphia, PA: W. B. Sanders.

Hanzlick, R. 2007. The conversion of coroner systems to medical examiner systems in the United States: A lull in the action. *Am J Forensic Med Path* 28(4): 279–283.

Hanzlick, R., Prahlow, JA., Denton, S., Jentzen, J., Quinton, R., Sathyavagiswaran, L., and Utley. S. 2008. Selecting forensic pathology as a career: A survey of the past with an eye on the future. *Am J Forensic Med Pathol* 29(2): 114–122.

Knight, B. 1996. *Forensic Pathology*, 2nd edn. New York: Oxford University Press.

Spitz, W. and Spitz, D. eds. 2006. *Medicolegal Investigation of Death*, 4th edn. Springfield, IL: Charles C. Thomas.

Zumwalt, RE., Bost, RO., and Sunshine, I. 1982. Evaluation of ethanol concentrations in decomposed bodies. *J Forensic Sci* 27(3): 549–554.

Science and Forensic Odontology

3

MARY A. BUSH
VERONIQUE F. DELATTRE

Contents

3.1 Definition of Science 62
  3.1.1 Perspective on Science 62
  3.1.2 Scientific Method 62
3.2 Experimental Design and Terms of Methodology 63
  3.2.1 Bias 63
  3.2.2 Error 63
  3.2.3 Standard Deviation and Variance 63
  3.2.4 Other Considerations with Regard to Error: Accuracy versus Precision 64
  3.2.5 P Value 64
  3.2.6 Correlation/Nonuniformity 64
3.3 Types of Clinical Studies: Randomized Control Trials 65
  3.3.1 Single Blind Study 65
  3.3.2 Double-Blind Study 65
3.4 Validity: Sensitivity and Specificity 65
  3.4.1 Sensitivity 65
  3.4.2 Specificity 66
3.5 Science in the Courtroom 66
3.6 Landmark Cases for Admissibility of Scientific Evidence in the Courtroom 66
  3.6.1 Frye Test 66
  3.6.2 Daubert Standard 67
3.7 Qualifications of an Expert Witness with Regard to Scientific Basis 67
  3.7.1 Specialty Certification 68
3.8 How Science Is Viewed in the Courtroom—CSI Effect: Expectations of a Jury 69
3.9 Challenges to and Support of Forensic Odontology Science 69
  3.9.1 Challenges 69
  3.9.2 2009 National Research Council Report on Forensic Sciences 69
  3.9.3 Research Funding Sources 70
    3.9.3.1 American Board of Forensic Odontology 70
    3.9.3.2 American Society of Forensic Odontology 70
    3.9.3.3 ASFO, Dr. Gerald Reynolds Research Grant for New Investigators 70
    3.9.3.4 Forensic Science Foundation: Acorn Grants 70
    3.9.3.5 Forensic Science Foundation: Lucas Grants 71
    3.9.3.6 Forensic Science Foundation: Jan Grant Award 71
    3.9.3.7 NIJ/FSF Forensic Science Student Research Grant 71

3.9.3.8 Grants.gov 71
3.9.3.9 National Institute of Justice 71
3.9.3.10 Midwest Forensic Resource Center 72
3.10 Needed Research 72
3.10.1 Bitemark and Patterned Injury Research 72
3.10.2 Identification Research 72
3.10.3 Mass Fatality Incident Management Research 73
3.10.4 Victim Abuse Research 73
3.10.5 Witness Consultation and Testimony Research 73
3.10.6 Age Estimation 73
3.10.7 Facial Approximation Research 73
References 74

3.1 Definition of Science

3.1.1 Perspective on Science

Few would argue that science has not changed our lives. We are surrounded by the products of science; an array of technological tools and discoveries that continue to appear at an ever-increasing rate. For most, the word "science" would seem to encompass these technologies and also extend to the extensive body of knowledge that has been amassed describing the universe and its workings. However, our use of technology or the knowledge we have gained does not necessarily constitute the workings of science. Better defined, science is a process—a means of discovering and verifying facts. In order to gain an understanding of how science relates to forensic odontology and what its implications are, it is first necessary to gain a working knowledge of science and investigation—how it is accomplished and how it is analyzed. The essence of the process of science has been described as the *scientific method*. It is by application of the scientific method that theories regarding explanations about the world are proposed, refined, or corrected through experimentation, thus bringing about the improvements and advances we have come to realize.

3.1.2 Scientific Method

There are many ways of describing the scientific method. In simple terms, the scientific method is a systematic technique for the advancement of knowledge. It consists of development of a theory that, in the end, may or may not be proven true when subjected to testing by empirical methods (Brunette, 1996).

This process involves a presupposition that a particular question can be resolved by collection and analysis of data. Thus, the first step in the sequence is to define a problem, where the problem is usually based on some observation(s). The second step is to formulate a hypothesis, an educated guess that attempts to explain a specific phenomenon. The hypothesis must be testable, meaning that an experiment can be designed to investigate the hypothesis and either prove or disprove. This process may be continued by revision of and retesting the hypothesis with the final outcome being rejection or acceptance of the hypothesis. This testing is accomplished through proper experimental design.

3.2 Experimental Design and Terms of Methodology

An important aspect in the testing of a hypothesis is the designing of an experiment that will yield data that are as objective as possible. Without proper design, the validity of the experiment could be in jeopardy as data derived might give results that could be interpreted ambiguously or erroneously. The proper types and numbers of controls and variables must be chosen in the construction of the experiment. In this regard, there are several major components to experimental design that include choosing of population/samples, allocation of the population/samples, and measures to be made on the population/samples. In addition, the potential for bias and sources of error must be recognized, accounted for, and minimized as an early step.

3.2.1 Bias

A bias is a prejudice, a tendency that prevents impartial consideration and can stem from many sources. In short, the bias can either arise from the researcher, participants of the study, or the samples utilized. For either the researcher or participant, normally, some type of human factor will play a role in the bias such as cognitive bias, where decisions are made on cognitive affects (perception) rather than evidence (Kahneman and Tversky, 1972). In sample bias, the sample is skewed in a way where certain specimens or members of a population are unrepresented or less likely to be included in study than others, or conversely, selected so that a hypothesis might be proven true (Pagano and Gauvreau, 1993). If this issue is not identified, the results from the study can be flawed because results may be attributed to the sampling methods rather than a true outcome of the study.

3.2.2 Error

There is a degree of error in everything humans do. Hence, in research, variability in measurements of objects and observations is unavoidable. Because of accuracy or resolution in the measuring tools utilized, and how an operator uses these tools, slight discrepancies will be seen every time an object is measured even with the same device (Brunette, 1996). In this sense, the use of the term "error" does not define a mistake but rather it describes this variability in measurement in the study. The amount of error must be recognized, delineated, and taken into account in order to give true meaning to the data. This allows the researcher to distinguish whether results are due to true discrepancies in data or are the effects of error. With human operators, the amount of error existing in the data can be defined through interoperator (differences between different operators) and intraoperator (differences performed by the same operator) evaluation. In these circumstances, a certain number of objects are measured multiple times to detect the variation. This value then sets limits as to how accurate the results can be. This variability can then be reported by variance or standard deviation.

3.2.3 Standard Deviation and Variance

Standard deviation and variance are both measures of variability (Brunette, 1996). The variance describes how much each value in the dataset deviates from the mean (describing the spread of responses) and is a squared value. The standard deviation also describes variability and is defined as the square root of the variance (allows for description of variability in the same units as the data). A low-standard deviation indicates that the points of data tend to be close to the mean, and a high-standard deviation indicates that the points of data are spread out over a large range of values. Standard deviation is also used to describe confidence levels in statistical conclusions. This is also known as margin of error and is usually twice the standard deviation, typically described by the 95% confidence level. Normal random error can be distinguished from true variation depending on whether the data lies within the confidence level or not.

3.2.4 Other Considerations with Regard to Error: Accuracy versus Precision

Accuracy of a measurement system is a measure of how close measurements are to the true value. Precision is the degree to which repeated measures will produce the same results; how close the measures are to each other (Brunette, 1996). Results can have low accuracy but high precision and vice versa. For example, if hitting the center of a target with an arrow is the desired outcome and the arrows are all well away from the center, but tightly grouped together, you would have low accuracy but high precision. A mistake is made, but the same mistake is made in each circumstance. In other words, you are pretty good at making the same mistake in a repeated fashion. Conversely, if all arrows are around the center, but are like hands on a clock and not grouped together, then you would have high accuracy but low precision.

3.2.5 P Value

P value helps to determine the amount of evidence required to demonstrate that the result(s) more than likely did not occur by chance (Brunette, 1996). It describes the probability of observing results if the null hypothesis is true (Kahneman and Tversky, 1972). The null hypothesis is the opposite of the stated hypothesis (i.e., there is no relationship found in the data or that a potential treatment has no effect).

P value describes statistical significance of the data, and this significance level is arbitrarily set at a value. These values are typically designated with a cut-off point of around 0.05 (5%) or 0.01 (1%) (Pagano and Gauvreau, 1993). For example, data with a P value of 0.01 mean that there is only a 1% chance of obtaining the same results seen if no real effect exists (a 1% chance the null hypothesis is true). If the null hypothesis can be rejected (P value is less than arbitrary cut-off point), then the test is said to be statistically significant.

A problem with P value is that the term "significant" can be misunderstood to mean "important" with regard to the results. P value describes statistical significance and not biological or test significance.

3.2.6 Correlation/Nonuniformity

In dealing with biological systems, correlation and nonuniformity of the data are important issues and must be recognized when deciding what types of statistical analysis to use. When investigating biological systems, it is important to bear in mind that structures are typically correlated, one influences the other, and results will show a nonuniform distribution. When structures are correlated, variables cannot be viewed independently. If the variables are not independent, statistical tools such as the product rule cannot be used.

The product rule calculates the probability of independent events occurring. Under this rule, the likelihood of one event is multiplied by the likelihood of the other events. So if event A occurs with odds 1/10, B occurs with odds 1/10, and C occurs with odds 1/10, the chance that A, B, and C all occur is 1/10*1/10*1/10 = 1/1000. It can be seen that with more events, this number can become very large very quickly. If one more event that has odds 1/10 is included in the last example, the odds would reach 1/10,000. But, most biological systems have correlations, which means that the events or variables are not independent, and this calculation cannot be used (Bush et al., 2011).

3.3 Types of Clinical Studies: Randomized Control Trials

In randomized control trials, two groups are formed. One is made up of subjects who receive the experimental treatment and the other (control group) of subjects who receive a conventional treatment, a placebo, or no treatment at all.

3.3.1 Single Blind Study

In a single blind study, information that could bias the participant is held back. In clinical trials, the participant will not know if they are assigned to the true experimental group or a control group. The researcher, though, will be privy to all of the information, knowing all of the facts surrounding the experiment. This can jeopardize the study, however, in that it may be possible for the researcher to subconsciously influence the participants' decisions through their own expectations of the experiment. In order to overcome this obstacle, studies can, and should be, double-blinded.

3.3.2 Double-Blind Study

In a double-blind study, neither the researcher nor the participant is aware of the circumstance of the study. In this situation, the participant is randomly assigned to a group with the allocation held confidential by a third party. This information is not made available until the conclusion of the study.

3.4 Validity: Sensitivity and Specificity

3.4.1 Sensitivity

Sensitivity and specificity are used as statistical measures of the performance of a binary classification test and is often used to measure the effectiveness of medical diagnostics. Sensitivity is a measure of the amount of true positives. For example, if a test subject has a disease, this will measure how often a particular diagnostic test will detect that disease when present. It is calculated by true positive/true positive + false negative.

3.4.2 Specificity

Specificity is a measure of the amount of true negatives. For example, if the test subject does not have a disease, how often will a particular test correctly indicate a lack of the disease? It is calculated by true negative/true negative + false positive. Effective diagnostic tests will demonstrate a high level of both sensitivity and specificity.

3.5 Science in the Courtroom

Science seeks to define natural laws, but the word "law" here has a different meaning from the same word that describes the set of rules and punishments that we as humankind have created as our legal system.

Science and the law have goals that may be described as fundamentally different. The goal in the courtroom consists of the resolution of a dispute. The legal process has as its objective the execution of justice. A courtroom verdict indicates truth. However, science attempts to approach truth through testing and modification of a theory via the scientific method. While both seek truth, how truth is derived and what is accepted as proof in either system has distinct differences.

The U.S. court system utilizes an adversarial process. It is the supposition that in this context, faulty scientific evidence will be exposed through cross-examination of experts and presentation of contrary opinions.

In science, this examination is dealt with through the peer review system. Scientists of equal caliber evaluate and scrutinize work submitted for publication for any inaccuracies or research design flaws, making recommendations for correction before publication, or rejecting the work if it is deemed that research protocols were less than adequate.

Admissibility of expert testimony and how the courts have dealt with the scientific basis of testimony is at the crux of the intersection of the two worlds. This is typically based on outcomes of prior court cases.

3.6 Landmark Cases for Admissibility of Scientific Evidence in the Courtroom

3.6.1 Frye Test

This case, which originated in 1923, was based on the admissibility of the systolic blood pressure deception test, a precursor to the polygraph, as evidence. The Frye standard became known commonly as the "general acceptance test" when attempting to determine the admissibility of scientific evidence (*Frye v. United States*, 1923). To satisfy this standard, the evidence must be generally accepted by a meaningful segment of the relevant scientific community. The counsel for Frye stated in their brief to the court, "The rule is that the opinions of experts or skilled witnesses are admissible in evidence in those cases in which the matter of inquiry is such that inexperienced persons are unlikely to prove capable of forming a correct judgment upon it, for the reason that the subject-matter so far partakes of a science, art, or trade as to require a previous habit or experience or study in it, in order to acquire a knowledge of it. When the question involved does not lie within the range of common experience or common knowledge, but requires special experience or special knowledge, then the opinions of witnesses skilled in that particular science, art, or trade to which the question relates are admissible in evidence." (*Frye v. United States*, 1923). More detailed information can be found in Chapter 12.

3.6.2 Daubert Standard

The Daubert standard (*Daubert v. Merrell Dow Pharmaceuticals*, 1995) also addresses admissibility of expert witness testimony but is considered by some to be more rigorous than that posed by Frye (also see Chapter 12). According to Daubert, not only must the evidence be generally accepted, but scientific validity must also be demonstrated. The judge, as gatekeeper, is asked to evaluate the methods by which the conclusions of testimony are reached and may consider the following:

- Has the method been subjected to empirical testing?
- Is the method not only relevant but also reliable? Has it resulted from studies that used the scientific method?
- Has it been subjected to peer review and publication?
- Is there a known error rate and are there standards for applying the method?
- Is there general acceptance by the relevant scientific community?

Specifically, as amended in 2011, Rule 702 of the Federal Rules of Evidence state the following:

A witness who is qualified as an expert by knowledge, skill, experience, training, or education may testify in the form of an opinion or otherwise if

a. The expert's scientific, technical, or other specialized knowledge will help the trier of fact to understand the evidence or to determine a fact in issue
b. The testimony is based on sufficient facts or data
c. The testimony is the product of reliable principles and methods
d. The expert has reliably applied the principles and methods to the facts of the case

3.7 Qualifications of an Expert Witness with Regard to Scientific Basis

An expert witness is someone who is summoned to answer questions under sworn testimony in a court of law in order to provide specialized information relevant to the case being tried. The role of the expert witness in the U.S. Judicial System is to assist the trier of fact (the judge or the jury) to comprehend the evidence presented or to determine a fact in issue. An expert witness should serve as a "friend of the court," that is, as an expert of the evidence, not as an advocate for the defense or prosecution.

In order to present expert testimony, the expert witness must first be qualified as an expert by the court. The expert witness must be familiar with the science of the field and be familiar with what studies have been accomplished and have demonstrated validity and reliability based on the scientific method. Voir Dire is the process by which expert witnesses are questioned about their backgrounds and qualifications before being allowed to present their testimony in court.

There are two primary requirements for qualifying as an "expert witness" under Federal Rule of Evidence 702:

1. The witness must be qualified by knowledge, skill, experience, or education.
2. The expert's specialized knowledge must assist the trier of fact to understand the evidence or determine a fact in issue.

An expert witness will typically be asked a series of qualifying questions during Voir Dire including the following:

- Position, title, professional duties
- Education and degrees
- Current licenses
- Specialties and certifications
- Training in the specialty
- Membership in professional organizations and societies
- Publications produced
- Teaching activities
- Professional accomplishments
- Prior experience as an expert witness

The judge then rules as to whether or not one qualifies to testify as an "expert witness" after hearing responses to the aforementioned questions and after the opportunity for cross-examination by the opposing counsel.

Some general advice for the novice expert witness is to always maintain a professional demeanor. Such a demeanor on the witness stand gains the respect of the jury by not appearing to be arrogant, hostile, or perceived as a "hired-gun" (one who might appear to be there just to gain a fee for their testimony). Restrict testimony to your own area of expertise in order to maintain credibility with the jury. Answer only the questions that are being directly asked and do not volunteer additional information. Prepare thoroughly and present information clearly and directly to the jury. Present your information in layperson's language so that the jury can follow your testimony. Dress appropriately and remember that every word you speak is being recorded in the trial transcript.

3.7.1 Specialty Certification

A forensic odontologist is a dentist who specializes in the proper handling, examination, and evaluation of dental evidence, which may then be presented in the interest of justice in a court of law. In the field of forensic odontology, certification may be attained through the American Board of Forensic Odontology (ABFO) based upon the candidate's personal and professional record of education, training, experience, and achievement as well as the results of a formal examination. The ABFO is recognized by the American Academy of Forensic Sciences and accredited by the Forensic Specialties Accreditation Board. An up-to-date directory of certified diplomates of the ABFO can be found in the ABFO's website (www.abfo.org).

3.8 How Science Is Viewed in the Courtroom—CSI Effect: Expectations of a Jury

Public perception can be influenced by what is seen on television shows. Usually, these programs depict an unrealistic portrayal of how science is used to solve crimes. The public expects that real-life court cases should be comparable to these shows.

It is thought that the CSI effect influences verdicts in two ways, each can either decrease or increase the conviction rate (Schweitzer and Saks, 2007). First, the jury expects forensic evidence that simply may not exist or is not relevant for the case. When the evidence is unavailable, the acquittal rates increase as juries will not convict without it. Second, juries have greater confidence in scientific forensic evidence that is presented, even when the evidence is not warranted. This leads to higher conviction rates.

Though highly theorized and accepted in the legal profession that the CSI effect exists, there is little empirical research to prove that it does (Tyler, 2006).

3.9 Challenges to and Support of Forensic Odontology Science

3.9.1 Challenges

Many forensic odontologists are dental practitioners and not researchers. Involvement of academia is therefore necessary to further the science of forensic odontology. In order to attract researchers, funding must be made available. The National Institute of Justice (NIJ) is the main governmental funding source for substantial forensic research (www.nij.gov). A listing of additional sources that fund smaller amounts for forensic research is addressed further in a subsequent section.

Other agencies that typically fund dental research such as the National Institute of Health, The National Institute for Dental and Craniofacial Research, and the National Science Foundation unfortunately do not fund forensic research, creating a limited source for significant funds.

Furthermore, restrictions posed by Human Subject Institutional Review Boards (HSIRB) limit the types of studies that may be performed on living subjects. If a project is to utilize human volunteer subjects, HSIRB must review the project for ethical considerations of the volunteers. Consent forms must include enough description of the study procedures to obtain informed consent. The study design must also comply with HIPAA. In bitemark studies, for example, inflicting a wound comparable to that seen in an excessively violent attack may not be allowed with HSIRB normal restrictions. In circumstances where live volunteers cannot be used, having an adequate model for study is imperative. No model exactly duplicates real-world events. However, without models, research would be impossible in such restrictive fields. If a field is not grounded on scientific validity, does it belong in the courtroom, especially when life and liberty are at stake? Other challenges to forensic odontology science include the acquisition of large databases and the inclusion of appropriate statistical analysis for the studies.

3.9.2 2009 National Research Council Report on Forensic Sciences

The 2009 National Research Council (NRC) report "Strengthening Forensic Science in the United States: A Path Forward" was published by the NRC. This comprehensive report includes recommendations about what is needed to advance all forensic science disciplines including the need to upgrade forensic organizational structures, advanced training, widespread adoption of uniform and enforceable best practices, and mandatory certification and accreditation programs for the forensic sciences. In regards to forensic odontology, the report is mainly concerned with what it calls "inherent weaknesses involved in bite mark comparisons," although it acknowledges that it is reasonable to assume that the process can reliably exclude suspects.

A summary of the overall goals put forth by the study stated, "With more and better educational programs, accredited laboratories, certified forensic practitioners, sound operational principles and procedures, and serious research to establish the limits and measures of performance in each discipline, forensic science experts will be better able to analyze evidence and coherently report their findings in the courts." More information may be found at: www.ncjrs.gov/pdffiles1/nij/grants/228091.pdf.

Also, the National Science and Technology Council Committee on Science (COS) formed a subcommittee on forensic science in 2009 specifically to address the practical challenges posed in the implementation of recommendations found in the NAS report. The subcommittee's purpose is to advise and assist several coordinating bodies of the executive office of the president, including the COS and the National Science and Technology Council, on policies, procedures, and plans related to forensic science in the national security, criminal justice, and medical examiner/coroner systems at the local, state, and federal levels. More information is available at http://www.forensicscience.gov/.

3.9.3 Research Funding Sources

3.9.3.1 American Board of Forensic Odontology

The goal of the ABFO Research Committee is to encourage and stimulate investigation and research in forensic odontology and related areas. Funding is available for projects requiring budgets up to $1000. For more information, refer to the ABFO's website: www.abfo.org.

3.9.3.2 American Society of Forensic Odontology

The American Society of Forensic Odontology (ASFO) grants $2500 funding to encourage and stimulate investigation and research in forensic odontology and related disciplines. For more information, refer to the ABFO's website: www.asfo.org.

3.9.3.3 ASFO, Dr. Gerald Reynolds Research Grant for New Investigators

Dr. Reynolds was a strong proponent for employing the scientific method in testing new theories in forensic odontology and initiated this grant to encourage members of the ASFO to conduct peer-reviewed research. The $500 grant is available to ASFO members for their first research project in the field of forensic dentistry. For more information, refer to the ASFO's website: www.asfo.org.

3.9.3.4 Forensic Science Foundation: Acorn Grants

The American Academy of Forensic Sciences' Forensic Science Foundation's (FSF) Acorn Grants (up to $500) are intended to help the investigator initiate original problem-oriented research. These grants are open to members and affiliates of the American Academy of

Forensic Sciences. For more information, refer to the FSF Acorn Grants website: http://www.forensicsciencesfoundation.org/grants/acorn_grants.htm.

3.9.3.5 *Forensic Science Foundation: Lucas Grants*

The FSF Lucas Grants ($501–$5000) are intended to help the investigator in original in-depth problem-oriented research. These grants are open to members and affiliates (at any level) of the American Academy of Forensic Sciences. For more information, refer to the FSF Acorn Grants website: http://forensicsciencesfoundation.org/grants/lucas_grants.htm.

3.9.3.6 *Forensic Science Foundation: Jan Grant Award*

The FSF Jan Grant Award ($500 + $1200 travel) is to provide graduate students with financial assistance to complete their thesis or independent research project as required for a graduate degree in Criminalistics/Forensic Sciences. The thesis or research project must be in the field of Criminalistics/Forensic Sciences. The Jan Grant Award is $500, and an additional $1200 is available for travel expenses to attend a future AAFS Annual Meeting where the awardee has an approved platform presentation of the completed research. The funding must be used to complete the research project. For more information, refer to the FSF Jan Grant Award website: http://forensicsciencesfoundation.org/grants/bashinski_grant.htm.

3.9.3.7 *NIJ/FSF Forensic Science Student Research Grant*

The NIJ/FSF Forensic Science Student Research Grant ($7000) is available to eligible undergraduate or graduate students enrolled in a Forensic Science Education Programs Accreditation Commission accredited program. The NIJ partnered with the FSF launched the NIJ/FSF Forensic Science Student Research Program and began a collaborative relationship of shaping the next generation of forensic scientists. For more information, refer to the NIJ/FSF Forensic Science Student Research Grant website: http://forensicsciencesfoundation.org/grants/NIJ-FSF_grant09-10.htm.

3.9.3.8 *Grants.gov*

Grants.gov is a government initiative to streamline the application process for federal grants. It is internet-based and provides a single access point for over 900 grant programs offered by 26 federal grant-making agencies. For more information, refer to Grants.gov website: http://www.grants.gov/.

3.9.3.9 *National Institute of Justice*

The NIJ awards grants and agreements for (1) research, development, and evaluation of criminal justice projects; (2) forensic laboratory enhancement to reduce evidence backlogs and improve the quality and timeliness of forensic science and medical examiner services; and (3) research fellowships.

As stated in the last section, the NIJ is the main governmental granting agency, with funding that reaches a maximum of $250,000/year. The grants can be multiyear proposals. Funding under a government agency also allows for much more latitude in how the money can be spent. These grants will allow for salary recovery and payment of fringe benefits. Solicitations are released on an annual basis.

For more information, refer to NIJ website: http://www.nij.gov/funding/welcome.htm.

3.9.3.10 Midwest Forensic Resource Center

Proposals through this organization must be made be in conjunction with a forensics laboratory located in the Midwest States (www.ameslab.org). The maximum awards are typically $50,000. For more information, refer to Midwest Forensic Resource Center (MFRC) website: www.ameslab.gov/mfrc/.

Thinking outside of the box can also lead to funding sources. Private companies may fund projects and/or donate equipment. Homeland security and the Department of Defense are also places to look for funding.

3.10 Needed Research

There is an ongoing initiative by the ABFO to encourage scientific studies on topics of importance to the forensic dental community. The research page of the ABFO website gives suggestions for needed studies as well as providing information on funding sources available. A study on needed topics was conducted by members of the Research Committee of the ABFO (Delattre et al., 2007). It was carried out in a concerted effort to stimulate the increase in the quantity and quality of research performed in the field of forensic dentistry. Respondents to the survey, members of the ABFO, were asked to rank a list of eight general research topics in their order of importance. The respondents were next asked to list specific research questions that they felt would be important areas to study in each of the eight general topics. Two of the topics stood out as being the most important areas in need of future study. The field of patterned injury/bitemark analysis was ranked as the area most in need of modern research data, with the field of dental identification a very close second. The remaining topics in order of most need for further research were ranked in the following order of importance: mass fatality incident management, person abuse, expert witness consultation and testimony, age determination, dental jurisprudence, and facial approximation.

In conclusion, this survey of experienced, ABFO Board Certified, forensic dentists revealed a wide range of suggestions for research questions that merit exploration through scientific investigation.

3.10.1 Bitemark and Patterned Injury Research

In the field of patterned injuries and bitemarks, respondents felt that the following specific questions would merit further research data: (1) what is a quantitative measure of the individuality of the human dentition; (2) how might pain from a bitemark be measured for legal purposes; (3) studies on three-dimensional analysis of bite injuries; (4) studies on the validity of bitemark analysis; (5) confidence levels in analyzing bruise marks from any source; (6) develop a database of large populations to give statistical relevance of tooth position and dental anomalies; and (7) can techniques such as transillumination and alternate light source be proven valid in a large group of observers?

3.10.2 Identification Research

In the area of dental identification, respondents felt that the following specific questions would merit further research data: (1) tooth morphology in reference to race determination;

(2) degree of certainty of identification of test cases; (3) do computer-aided methods of dental record comparisons really save time in the long run over traditional manual methods; (4) factors other than radiographic that forensic dentists use to perform dental identifications; (5) are individuals truly unique dentally as far as identifications; (6) reliability of dental identifications using only orthodontic models; and (7) value of digital radiography versus traditional dental film.

3.10.3 Mass Fatality Incident Management Research

In the area of mass fatality incident management, respondents felt that the following specific questions would merit further research data: (1) the role of the forensic dentists in incident command management at all levels, (2) development of a psychological test specific to forensic dentists for the impact posttraumatic stress after a mass incident on experienced versus less-experienced dental personnel, and (3) comparison of results of DNA analysis versus dental information during a mass fatality incident.

3.10.4 Victim Abuse Research

In the area of person abuse (child, elder, and spousal), respondents felt that the following specific questions would merit further research data: (1) comparison of issues common to child, elder, and spousal abuse; (2) the incidence of abuse reported in dental offices; (3) current demographics of abusers and those abused; (4) frequency of reporting elder abuse in institutional versus private care facilities.

3.10.5 Witness Consultation and Testimony Research

In the area of expert witness consultation and testimony, respondents felt that the following specific questions would merit further research data: (1) how is an expert witness defined in different jurisdictions; (2) a study on trial aids used during testimony; and (3) data on fees charged by forensic dental consultants in various regions.

3.10.6 Age Estimation

In the area of age estimation, respondents felt that the following specific questions would merit further research data: (1) dental differentiation of age among various races; (2) reliability of occlusal wear in age determination; (3) third molar root development; (4) age of majority among different jurisdictions; (5) use of dental age determination for legal purposes, that is, immigration; (6) reliability of hand/wrist radiographs versus dental radiographs.

3.10.7 Facial Approximation Research

In the area of facial approximation, respondents felt that the following specific questions would merit further research data: (1) data on how forensic artists and forensic anthropologists determine facial approximation and (2) with what frequency does facial approximation result in identification of an individual.

References

Brunette D.M. 1996. *Critical Thinking: Understanding and Evaluating Dental Research*. Carol Stream, IL, Quintessence Publishing.

Bush M.A., P.J. Bush, H.D. Sheets. 2011. Statistical evidence for the similarity of the human dentition. *Journal of Forensic Science* 56(1): 118–123.

Daubert v. Merrell Dow Pharmaceuticals, Inc., 43 F. 3d (9th Cir. 1995)

Delattre V.F., R.E. Wood, R.A. Weems. 2007. Looking to the future-opportunities for research in forensic dentistry. *The Proceedings of the American Academic of Forensic Science* 13:139.

Frye v. United States of America, 293 F. 1013 (D.C. Cir 1923).

Kahneman D., A. Tversky. 1972. Subjective probability: A judgment of representativeness. *Cognitive Psychology* 3(3): 430–454.

Pagano M., K. Gauvreau. 1993. *Principles of Biostatistics*. Belmont CA. Wadsworth Publishing.

Schweitzer N.J., M.J. Saks. 2007. The CSI effect: Popular fiction about forensic science affects public expectations about real forensic science. *Jurimetrics* 47: 357–364.

Tyler T.R. 2006. Viewing CSI and the threshold of guilt: Managing truth and justice in reality and fiction. *The Yale Law Journal* 115: 1051 and 1054.

Dental Identification

4

GARY M. BERMAN
MARY A. BUSH
PETER J. BUSH
ADAM J. FREEMAN
PETER W. LOOMIS
RAYMOND G. MILLER

Contents

4.1 Human Identification 76
4.1.1 Methods of Human Identification 77
4.1.1.1 Visual 77
4.1.1.2 Fingerprints 78
4.1.1.3 Anthropology/Radiology 78
4.1.1.4 DNA 79
4.1.1.5 Dental 80
4.1.2 Postmortem Dental Profiling 81
4.1.3 Burned and Incinerated Remains 85
4.1.4 Cremated Remains 88
4.2 Tooth Numbering Systems (Dental Notation, Dental Nomenclature) 91
4.2.1 Introduction 91
4.2.2 Various Systems 91
4.2.2.1 Universal Numbering System 91
4.2.2.2 FDI (Federation Dentaire Internationale) 93
4.2.2.3 Palmer Notation System 93
4.3 Dental and Nondental Comparison 93
4.3.1 Photographic Facial Superimposition 93
4.3.2 Facial Reconstruction 94
4.3.3 Frontal Sinus Pattern Radiographic Comparisons 95
4.3.4 DNA 95
4.3.5 Rugae 96
4.3.6 Cheiloscopy 96
4.3.7 Dental Appliances 97
4.3.7.1 Denture Labeling Law 97
4.3.7.2 Denture Teeth Molds, Size, Shape, Color 97
4.3.7.3 Orthodontic Fixed Appliances 98
4.3.8 Dental Implants 98
4.4 Postmortem Dental Data 98
4.4.1 Collection of Postmortem Data 99
4.4.1.1 Postmortem Dental Charting Forms 99
4.4.1.2 Examination Procedures 100
4.4.1.3 Photography 103
4.4.1.4 Radiography 104

4.4.1.5 Viewable Remains 106
4.4.1.6 Nonviewable Remains 106
4.4.1.7 Dental Examination 108
4.5 Antemortem Dental Data 109
4.5.1 Presumptive Identification 109
4.5.2 Locating Antemortem Dental Records 110
4.5.2.1 Nontraditional Sources of Antemortem Dental Information 110
4.5.3 What Antemortem Dental Records Should Be Requested 112
4.5.4 Release of Dental Records and Chain of Custody 112
4.5.5 Antemortem Record Form 112
4.6 Comparison 114
4.6.1 Dental Features for Comparison 114
4.6.2 Statistical and Mathematic/Algorithm Methods 116
4.6.3 Dental Identification Guidelines 116
4.6.4 Report Writing 117
4.7 Advanced Methods of Dental Materials Evidence Analysis 117
4.7.1 Challenges to and Limitations of Traditional Methods 117
4.7.1.1 Radiopacity 118
4.7.2 Methods of Detection and Analysis 118
4.7.2.1 Visible Light Fluorescence 118
4.7.2.2 Scanning Electron Microscopy/Energy-Dispersive X-Ray Spectroscopy 119
4.7.2.3 X-Ray Fluorescence 124
References 125

4.1 Human Identification

Dental identification of a deceased individual is a core task in forensic odontology. Along with determining the manner and cause of death, the medical examiner or coroner (ME/C) has the statutory responsibility and authority to identify the deceased and issue a death certificate. The forensic dentist can provide rapid and economical means of victim identifications in this process.

- A positive identification is vital for family members in going through the grieving process, providing closure in knowing that their loved ones have been found.
- A positive identification and subsequent death certificate is necessary in order to settle business and personal affairs. Disbursement of life insurance proceeds, estate transfer, settlement of probate, execution of wills, remarriage, and child custody issues can be delayed for years by legal proceedings if a positive scientific identification cannot be rendered.
- Criminal investigations and potential prosecution in a homicide case may not proceed without a positive identification of the victim.

The ME must determine whether the scientific information available justifies the declaration of a positive identification and issuance of a death certificate. The consequences of a misidentification might well have emotional and legal ramifications well beyond a specific case.

All methods of scientific identification involve comparing postmortem victim evidence with known antemortem data. If a presumed identification has been established by circumstance, then antemortem data of the individual may be compared to the postmortem evidence to establish a positive identification. Fingerprint records can be compared to those taken from the body; DNA evidence, available before death, can be compared to that recovered from postmortem tissues; and dental and medical characteristics can be compared to antemortem records and images. Each method has its advantages and shortcomings but all are dependent on the existence of antemortem material. If there is no presumptive identity of the individual, clues may be observed by careful examination of the remains, which might limit the pool of potential persons, eventually leading to identification.

4.1.1 Methods of Human Identification

Five methods of human identification are commonly employed.

4.1.1.1 Visual

Visual identification is a nonscientific method, but is often used by the ME/C when there is no significant question as to who the individual is, the remains are intact and viewable, and/or the death was witnessed. Changes in appearance from illness (Figure 4.1), the circumstances of death (fire, trauma, disintegration, etc.), and postmortem taphonomic changes (decomposition, mummification, saponification, skeletonization, animal predation) render visual identification unreliable in many instances. Tattoos, scars, piercings, subdermal body modification, and soft-tissue abnormalities are useful for identification if the tissue is intact. Personal effects found with the remains or at the scene (ID cards, jewelry, cell phones etc.) should never be solely used to make an ID, but are important clues that direct the investigation to obtain antemortem data on the individual for comparison to the postmortem evidence.

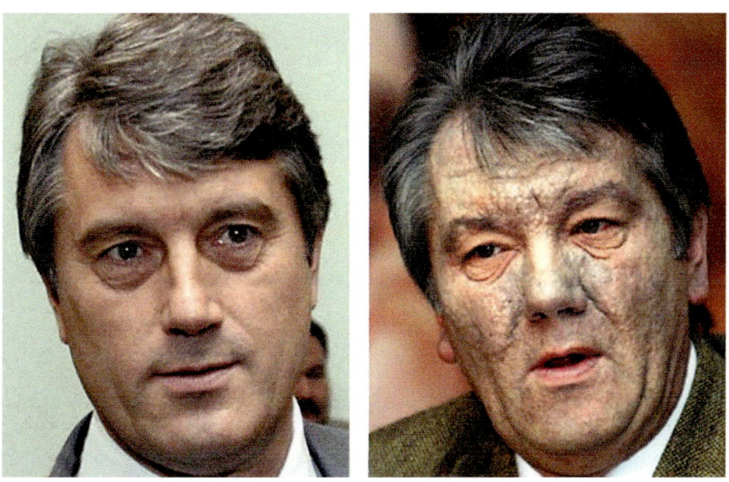

Figure 4.1 Victor Yuschenko before and after dioxin poisoning.

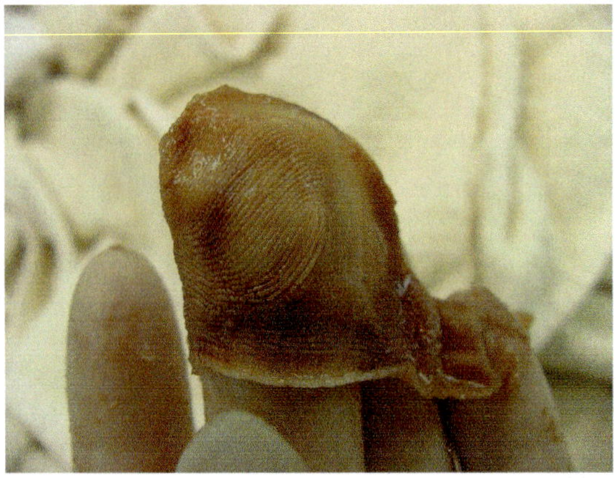

Figure 4.2 Degloved finger epidermis ready to print.

4.1.1.2 *Fingerprints*

An excellent biometric method of human identification if the soft tissue of the fingers is intact, an adequate impression or image of the friction ridges can be obtained, and antemortem fingerprint records are available (Figures 4.2). Obviously burned, decomposed (skin slippage or degloving), skeletonized, and fragmented remains may not readily exhibit fingerprints. The two largest finger print databases in the United States are the FBI Integrated Automated Fingerprint Identification System (IAFIS), with 30 million civil and 60 million criminal fingerprint files, and the Department of Homeland Security (US-VISIT) fingerprint database with over 100 million files. INTERPOL maintains an AFIS system for its 188 member countries of 104,000 files. Although the NAS report, *Strengthening Forensic Science in the United States: A Path Forward*, published in 2009, is critical of fingerprint analysis, it is often the most expedient method for human identification if the fingers can be printed and if antemortem fingerprint records are available (National Research Council, 2009).

4.1.1.3 *Anthropology/Radiology*

Another biometric method of identification that relies on unique characteristics of the skeleton is to compare postmortem radiographs with antemortem medical imaging and written records. Radiographs of bony anomalies, healed fractures, pathological lesions, medical/surgical hardware, or unusual qualities of the skeleton can be used to make a positive identification (Figure 4.3). However, many individuals have never had

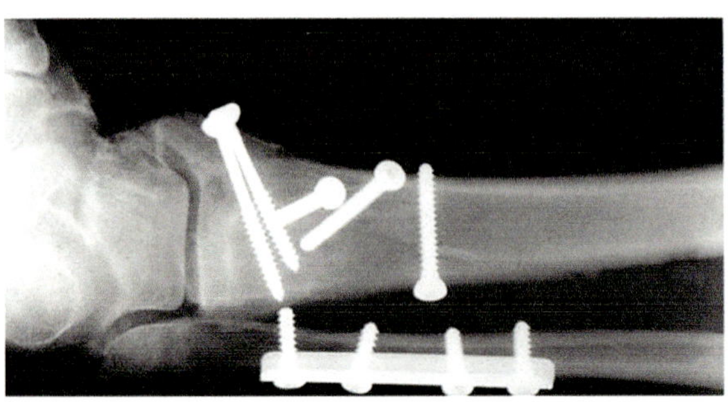

Figure 4.3 Bone fixation plate and screws in lower limb.

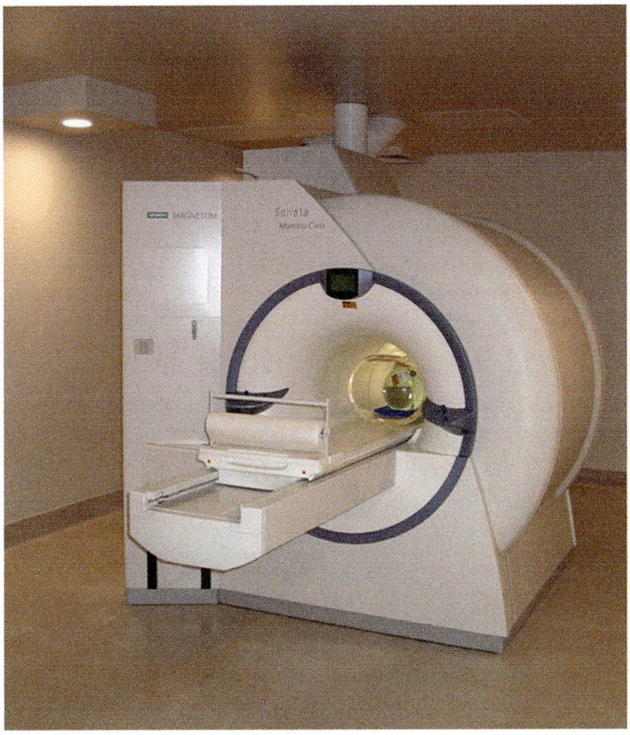

Figure 4.4 MRI scanner.

antemortem skeletal imaging performed, or the images may no longer be available. Some medical examiner offices have recently installed dedicated computed tomography (CT) scanners that can provide images to compare with both conventional and CT antemortem images as well as provide reconstructive images of the skeleton that can be very helpful in comparisons. At least one ME facility in the United States now has its own magnetic resonance imaging (MRI) scanner (Figure 4.4).

4.1.1.4 DNA

Like the previous biometric methods of identification, DNA comparison relies on accessible antemortem data. Direct reference samples from the decedent during life are the best sources. Direct primary DNA sources include blood, a tissue biopsy slide, a pap smear, tooth remnants, and a hair sample (with roots). Direct secondary DNA sources could include a toothbrush, comb, bedding, or clothing (NIJ, 2006). Indirect DNA reference samples are those from biological relatives. DNA testing requires more time, effort, specialized personnel, and higher cost than other identification methods. The degree to which human remains are fragmented or degraded determines the value of DNA analysis in the identification process. Intact, large body parts lend themselves to identification by less costly methods, such as dental examination, radiographic imaging, and fingerprints. However, DNA analysis may be the only viable method for identifying severely fragmented or degraded remains. Even when whole bodies are recovered, DNA analysis may be the best approach when antemortem records that are necessary for other identification modalities are unavailable. The majority of forensic DNA tests are performed on nuclear DNA using polymerase chain reaction (PCR) amplification of the sample with short tandem repeat (STR) typing. Simultaneous analysis of mitochondrial DNA (mtDNA) may be necessary in order to improve the identification process. Human mitochondrial DNA differs from nuclear DNA in that it is a closed and circular (rather than linear) molecule; it is smaller, consisting of approximately 16,569 base pairs, and is only maternally inherited and therefore limited in its specificity. It also does not undergo recombination, and it is present in high copy numbers within the cell.

STRs are particularly informative when using well-preserved soft tissue and bone samples and even on degraded tissue and bone fragments if the DNA extraction process is optimized. However, STRs alone are often not sufficient for identification when samples are severely compromised. When the amount of extracted DNA is very small or degraded (as can be the case in fragmented tissue samples of bone, teeth, and hair), an identification is more likely using mtDNA rather than nuclear DNA. In those situations, mtDNA sequencing or single nucleotide polymorphism is often used.

Forensic DNA analyses for human identification have seen a tremendous upsurge since the President's DNA Initiative Program that began in 2003. The program provided funding, boosted training, and further financial assistance to ensure that forensic DNA would reach its full potential in identifying missing persons (NIJ, 2006). From this program, the National Institute of Justice now provides funding to have DNA analysis performed on unidentified remains by the Center for Human Identification at the University of North Texas or the FBI. Once the analysis is complete, the profiles (if they qualify) are entered into the FBI's CODIS system (Combined DNA Index System) and uploaded into the National DNA Index System.

4.1.1.5 Dental

A dental identification is the most common biometric method for identifying burned, decomposed, skeletonized, and fragmented remains. Why?

1. Teeth survive—Tooth enamel is the hardest biological substance in the human body, and posterior teeth are well protected by soft tissues (the tongue, facial musculature, and adipose tissue). Teeth survive prolonged immersion, decomposition, desiccation, extensive trauma, and direct heat in excess of 1000°F.
2. Tooth morphology, the presence or absence of teeth, tooth position, dental restorations, dental and oral pathology, bony anatomy, periodontium, maxillary and frontal sinus morphology, and many other features of the oral cavity and maxillofacial complex are available for comparison. No two individuals have the exact same dental features (De Villiars and Phillips, 1998).
3. Many people have been to dentist and have a dental chart and radiographs.
4. A postmortem dental examination (clinical and radiographic) can be done quickly and inexpensively.
5. Dental records of missing persons are kept in several national databases to compare with newly discovered remains.
6. Even in mass fatality incidents, it is the most expedient method for identifying burned, fragmented, and decomposed human remains (Pretty and Sweet, 2001; Pretty et al. 2001; Pretty and Addy, 2002).

Since the complete adult human dentition consists of 32 teeth that may be virgin, missing, or restored on one or more of each tooth's five surfaces, a great many combinations of dental patterns exist that are helpful in making a dental identification (Adams, 2003a,b).

In addition, the postmortem radiographic appearance of the victim's teeth, restorations, bone, anomalies, and maxillary and frontal sinuses is essential when determining a dental identification.

4.1.2 Postmortem Dental Profiling

The results of a postmortem dental examination provide not only a comparative dental identification (comparison of the postmortem dental evidence with the known antemortem dental record of the presumed decedent), but also may establish postmortem dental profiling in cases where there is no presumptive identity of the individual. Postmortem dental profiling may help to limit the population pool of possible victims, thus directing the investigator to a presumptive identification of the individual and a potential identification. This profile may provide information on the decedent's age, ancestry, sex, location of origin or residence, occupation, habits, lifestyle behavior, past or present systemic diseases, and socioeconomic status.

With careful clinical and radiographic examination of the teeth and oral structures, the following characteristics may often be inferred:

1. Age estimation (see Chapter 8)
2. Ancestry

   The classification of race includes three distinct populations of heritable phenotypic characteristics; European, African, and Asian. These classifications are also influenced by culture, ethnicity, and socioeconomic status. It is important to note that these traits do not imply that the person is categorically of the group associated with the trait, but rather as an indicator that a more likely probability exists.

   a. European: the Carabelli trait (Carabelli cusp) can range from a slight groove to a full size cusp on the mesiolingual cusp of the maxillary first molar tooth A bilobate chin, undulating mandibular border and deep canine fossae may also be present (Figure 4.5).
   b. African: multicusped and multiple premolars, maxillary midline diastemas, straight mandibular border, prognathism (Figure 4.6).
   c. Asian: shovel-shaped incisors, incisor rotations, buccal pits, extension of the enamel below the general contour of the enamel border on the buccal surface of mandibular molars, often into the furcation (Figure 4.7).

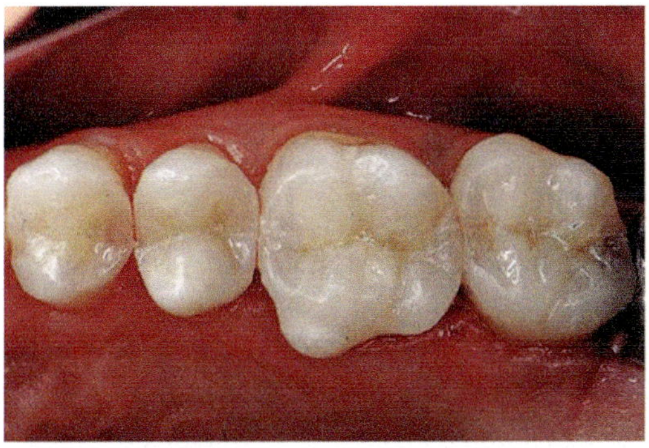

Figure 4.5 Cusp of Carabelli on UL first molar.

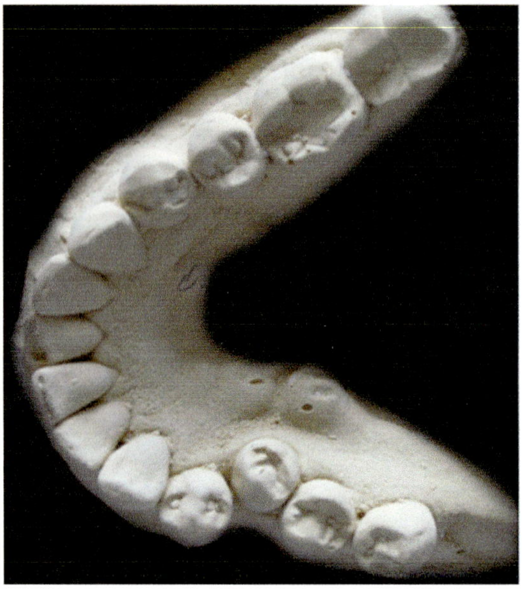

Figure 4.6 Two supernumerary mandibular left premolars.

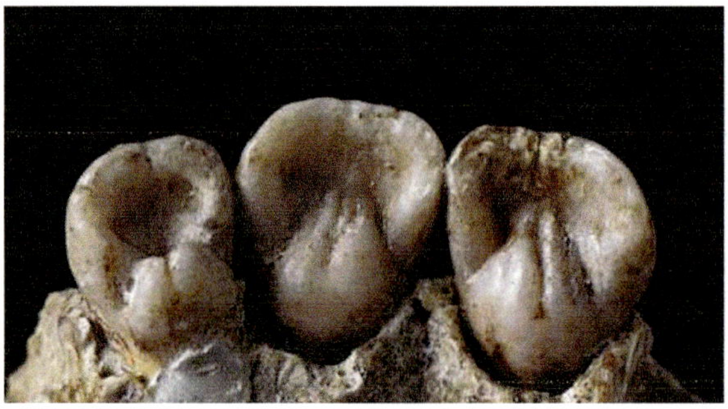

Figure 4.7 Shoveled maxillary incisors.

The odontologist must be aware that dental features related to ancestry are morphological and as such may be obliterated by dental restorations, trauma, and incineration. Also, consultation with the forensic anthropologist is always indicated when attempting to classify ancestry. The cranial and postcranial traits that the anthropologist recognizes may be more accurate in estimating ancestry than the available dental evidence. Also, in today's diverse global society, traits are increasingly blurred across ancestral groups.

3. Sex

While there are many morphological cranial differences between males and females, there is no sexual dimorphism of the teeth. Males may have slightly larger teeth than females, but the morphology of the crown and roots is the same. Sex determination can be accomplished with microscopic examination of the pulp tissue observing the nuclei of somatic cells. Females will exhibit Barr bodies in the nuclei that males do not. DNA examination of pulp tissue using PCR analysis of the amelogenin gene is also a reliable method of sex determination. An anthropological consultation may be of great benefit in determining the victim's sex.

4. Habits
   Habits and customs of individuals and ethnic groups may provide a clue as to their identity. Teeth may be used as tools or weapons and are also subject to stains, chemical erosion, attrition, and mutilation (Table 4.1; Figure 4.21 later in chapter).
5. Past and present systemic disease
   The teeth and oral structures may be affected by systemic disease, hereditable maladies, and medications (Table 4.2) (Figures 4.8 through 4.12).
6. Occupation
   Occupational environmental conditions and using the teeth as tools can adversely affect the teeth and soft tissues of the mouth (Table 4.3).
7. Country or area of origin or residence
   The type of dental restorations present, quality of treatment, and materials used may indicate a country or region where the dentistry was completed. Generalizations should be made with caution but can be useful when trying to determine the identity of an unknown person (Table 4.4).
8. Socioeconomic status
   Dental restorative work may provide an indication of the socioeconomic status of the individual. Lack of or inferior dental restorative quality, materials, and techniques as well as poor oral health may indicate a lower economic status. This inference may not be true in many situations and could be related to an individual's "dental phobia," but it still is a possibility that the prudent forensic dentist should consider.

Table 4.1 Habits and Customs That May Affect the Teeth

Habit	Appearance	Cause
Coffee, tea, red wine drinkers	Brown or black staining of teeth. More obvious when calculus is present on teeth	An extrinsic stain caused from drinking the liquids
Pipe smoking	Unusual tooth wear patterns and staining	Unilateral attrition
Mastication of leather to soften for making garments	Extreme attrition of teeth	Some Native North American habits
Betel leaf and nut chewing	Black or brown stains	Extreme extrinsic stains
Tooth mutilation	Various sharpened or flattened teeth	Some African and Australian tribes
Tooth blackening—Ohaguro	Black teeth	Japan and Southeast Asia custom
Alcoholism	Acidic erosion commonly on the lingual surfaces of teeth	Regurgitation and acid reflux
Drugs of abuse—methamphetamine, cocaine, heroin, methadone	High caries rate, attrition, acidic erosion, tooth fracture advanced periodontal disease	Oral neglect, dry mouth, high sugar consumption, regurgitation, bruxism
Mouth rinses including chlorhexidine, scope, cepacol	Exogenous staining from chlorhexideine and cetylpyridinium chloride	Extrinsic stains from rinsing mouth

Table 4.2 Past and Present Systemic Disease, Hereditable Maladies, and Medications That May Affect the Teeth

Condition	Appearance	Cause
Congenital syphilis	Mulberry molars and Hutchinson's incisors	Enamel defects
Cleidocranial dysplasia	Multiple supernumerary teeth, small or missing clavicles, forehead bossing	Hereditary congenital disorder (syndrome)
Dentinogenisis imperfecta	Endogenous brownish-blue discoloration of dentin. Opalescent appearance; Sclerotic pulps	Hereditary; abnormal development of odontoblasts
Amelogenesis imperfecta	Endogenous brown yellow, white "snow capped" discoloration of enamel	Hereditary; abnormal development of ameloblasts
Ectodermal dysplasia	Congenitally missing teeth, peg teeth, sparse hair	Hereditary x-linked, abnormal development of ectodermally derived structures
Anorexia, bulimia, alcoholism, GERD, hiatal hernia	Erosion of lingual surfaces of maxillary anterior teeth	Acidic erosion of teeth from regurgitation of gastric contents
Generalized enamel hypoplasia	Hypoplastic enamel of multiple teeth, horizontal discoloration, malformations	Febrile illness, malnutrition hypoxia, trauma leading to ameloblast damage during tooth development
Tetracycline staining	Endogenous discoloration of the dentin which appears as yellow/ brown/green bands	Ingestion of tetracycline family of antibiotics during tooth formation

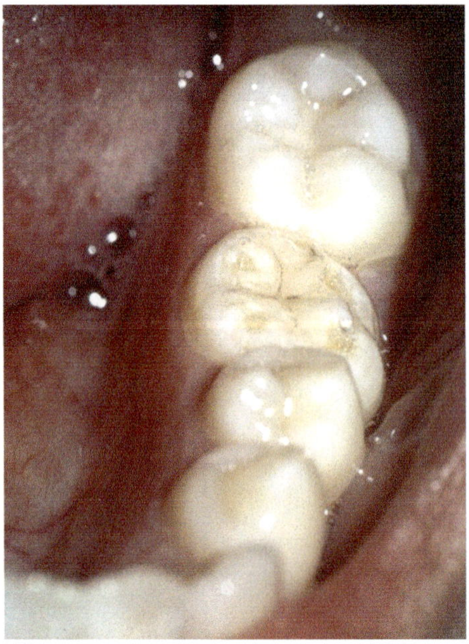

Figure 4.8 Mulberry molar resulting from congenital syphilis.

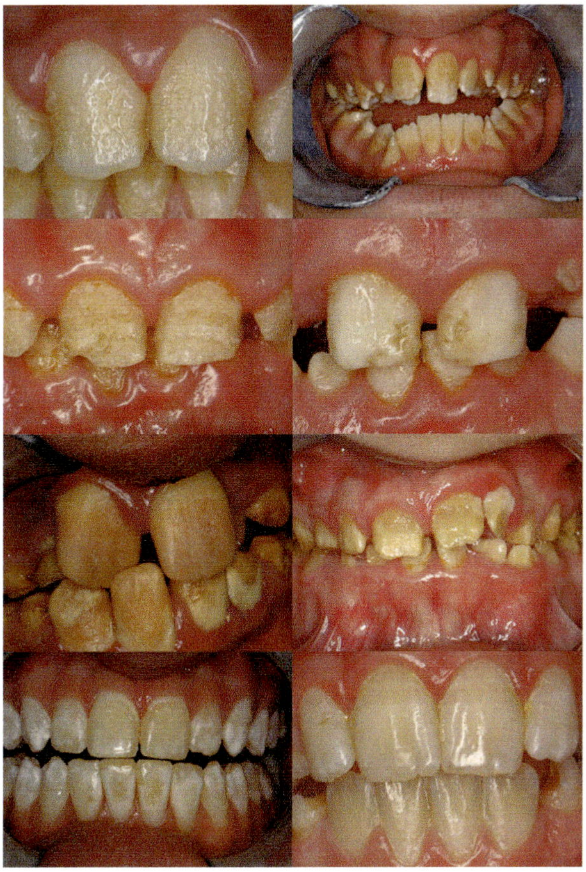

Figure 4.9 Amelogenesis imperfecta.

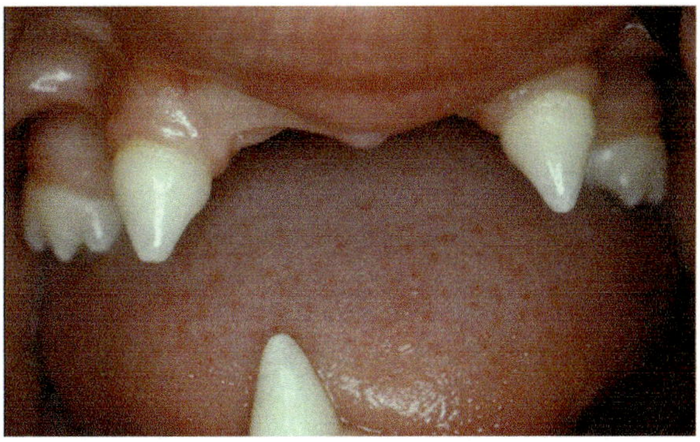

Figure 4.10 Hypodontia as a result of ectodermal dysplasia.

4.1.3 Burned and Incinerated Remains

Burned victims, even those severely burned, often will still have available dental evidence that may lead to a dental identification. Unprotected teeth can survive direct temperatures of 1000°F–1200°F, and the protected posterior teeth in situ may survive

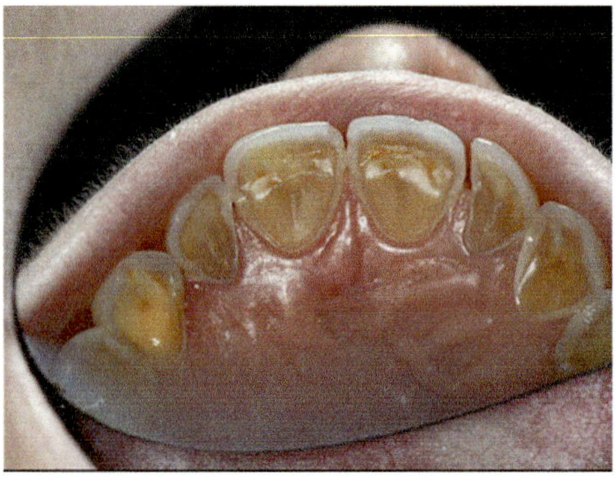

Figure 4.11 Erosion of lingual surfaces of maxillary incisors from acid dissolution.

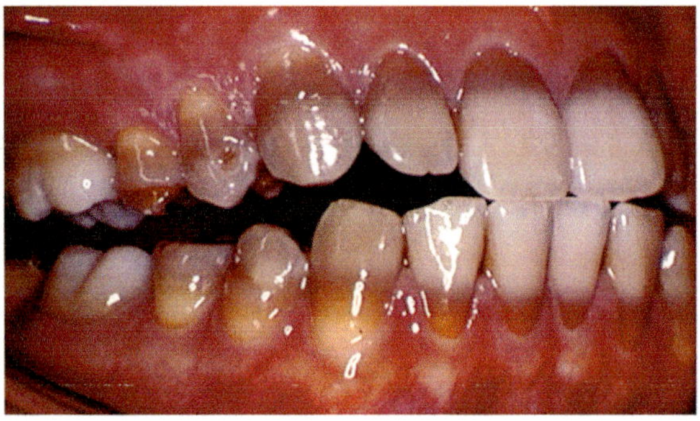

Figure 4.12 Tetracycline staining.

indirect temperatures of over 1800°F. The teeth receive thermal protection from the buccinator, masseter, and pterygoid muscles; parotid gland; and also the tongue (genioglossus), geniohyoid, and mylohyoid muscles. The anterior teeth are not as well protected by the thin obicularis oris muscle and will often exhibit severe thermal damage as they are exposed by retraction of the soft tissues as the muscle protein denatures and the tissue shrinks (Botha, 1986) (Figure 4.13).

As the temperature increases, the tooth undergoes advancing change from dehydration to complete carbonization with concomitant color changes. The amount of time to which the teeth are exposed to a given temperature also greatly affects the destructive changes created. At 400°F, the teeth become dark yellow. As the temperature increases to between 750°F and 1100°F, carbonization occurs as the organic material is vaporized, and the tooth will start to darken, progressing to a dark gray and then finally to black with a highly glossed appearance. The moisture of the pulp and dentin may expand, causing the enamel of the tooth to separate intact, which may mimic a glossy restorative crown in appearance with the remaining body of the tooth falsely mimicking a crown preparation (Figure 4.14). With continued exposure to the heat, the carbon will start to vaporize, and the tooth will begin to lighten in color, fading from black back to gray and finally to white. At this point, the tooth has become calcined, with no organic material present (Muller et al., 1998; Herschaft et al., 2006; Bush et al., 2008). The "typical" house fire burns at approximately 1100°F, and motor vehicle fires can vary over a wide range from 1100°F to over 2400°F.

Table 4.3 Occupational and Environmental Conditions That May Adversely Affect the Teeth and Soft Tissues of the Mouth

Occupation	Appearance	Cause
Musicians, traffic officer Carpenters, electricians Seamstresses, hairdressers Shoe maker/repairer Upholsterer, glassblower	Unusual abrasion or wear patterns on teeth	Stripping wires, holding nails, brads, pins, needles with teeth, biting on reed/mouthpiece, whistle, etc.
Sandblasters, grain mill, saw mill workers Miners, cement and stone cutters, jackhammer operator	Generalized tooth abrasion	Abrasive dust and particulate matter causing abrasion
Chemical, galvanizing and battery workers making or using acids	Eroded labial surfaces of anterior teeth, often smooth	Decalcification of enamel and dentin from acidic fumes
Bakers, candy makers, sugar refinery workers	Dental caries on facial surfaces of teeth	Sucrose exposure
Metal workers using copper, nickel, tin, iron	Green, yellow, black stains	Dust and fumes from exposure to the metals
Wine tasters	Erosion of labial surfaces of maxillary anterior teeth	Wine tasting of more than 20 samples per day
Competitive/professional athletes	Acidic erosion, dental caries	Increased consumption of sports drinks, gels; decreased pH of swimming pool water

Table 4.4 Teeth and Dental Restorations May Provide Specific Indicators as to the Country/Area of Origin, or Residence of an Individual

Area of Origin or Residence	Appearance	Cause
Dental school treatment	Gold foil and cast gold restorations	
SW Texas, SE New Mexico, Rural United States, China, Africa	Dental fluorosis, mottled teeth	Excess fluoride in water wells and municipal water
Mexico, Central America	Silver or gold color metal crowns on anterior teeth	
Eastern Europe	Full cast metal crowns with acrylic facings on anterior teeth; may be inferior quality	

Because of the high degree of fragility of burned teeth, extreme care must be taken during the postmortem examination to prevent additional breakdown (see section on postmortem dental examination) (Maelati et al., 2002, 2004). A recommended technique is to apply a stabilizing adhesive such as cyanoacrylate cement to the fragile teeth to help maintain their anatomical integrity. This commonly used procedure will not chemically contaminate restorative materials that may later be analyzed and identified using x-ray fluorescence (XRF) or scanning electron microscopy with energy-dispersive spectroscopy (SEM/EDS) (Bush et al., 2006, 2007, 2008).

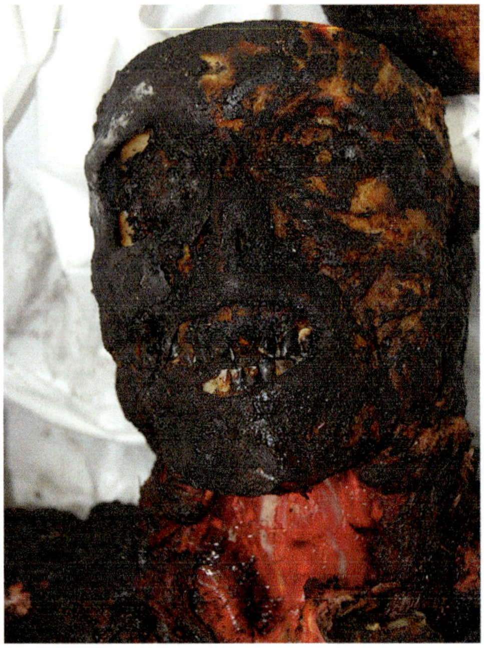

Figure 4.13 Severely burned victim showing damage to anterior teeth.

Figure 4.14 Radiograph showing enamel of the teeth separated but intact.

4.1.4 Cremated Remains

Commercially cremated remains (cremains) may have enough dental evidence to be useful in the determination of identity. During the commercial cremation process, items of value and artificial pacemakers are removed, and the body is placed in a combustible container and into the retort (oven). By law, only one body at a time may be cremated in the retort, and the retort is designed to hold only one body (Figure 4.15). The time/temperature cycle is 1.5–3 h (depending on body mass) at about 1800°F. The cremains consist of 4–8 lb of calcined inorganic material (mainly calcium phosphate other minor minerals) as well as various artifacts (staples, gown snaps, surgical hardware, shoe brads, funerary material, and dental restorations). Tooth fragments and some noncalcined bone

Figure 4.15 Cremation retort lined with refractory brick that may trap cremains.

Figure 4.16 Cremains prior to processing.

fragments may remain. The cremains are swept from the retort and then processed in a cremulator to reduce their particle size (Figures 4.16).

The dental examination of processed cremains is time-consuming and tedious, but can yield abundant information with regard to the existence of dental restorations:

1. A magnet is used to separate out any ferrous material. Often a surprising amount of ferrous material may be recovered, including staples, shoe brads, gown snaps, funerary material, and globules of melted metal (Figure 4.17).

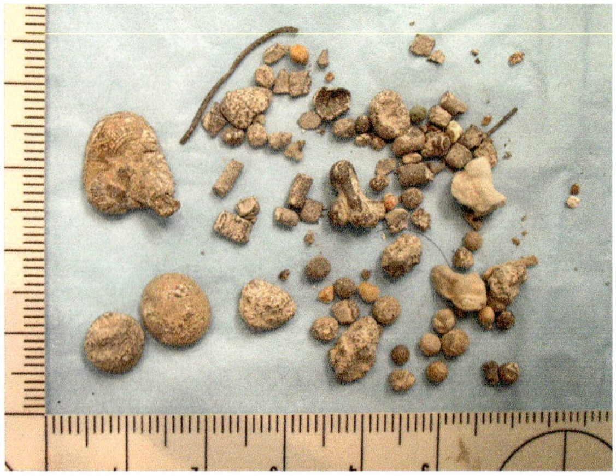

Figure 4.17 Metal artifacts recovered in cremains.

Figure 4.18 Sieves used to separate various particle sizes from cremains.

2. A series of U.S. Standard Testing sieves are used to separate various particle sizes. Usually, 1 mm or less, 2 mm, 4 mm, and >4 mm. (Figure 4.18)
3. Each portion is photographed, radiographed, and examined macroscopically with a stereo microscope to separate out tooth fragments, bone fragments, dental restorations, and other nonferrous metals that may be present.
4. Dental evidence recovered can include porcelain fragments, cast dental restorations including crowns, fixed bridges and partial denture frameworks, endodontic posts, dental implants, porcelain denture teeth, endodontic filling material within root fragments, inorganic components of composite restorations, and globules of melted nonferrous metal (Table 4.5) (Skinner and Phillips, 1967; Robinson et al., 1998) (Figure 4.19).
5. The dental evidence can then be compared to antemortem dental records to make a determination of potential inclusion or exclusion for identification.
6. Keep in mind that all states allow a certain amount of coincidental commingling of cremains due to the physical aspects of the cremation chamber (retort). The chamber, lined with refractory brick, traps particles from a previous cremation that may be commingled when swept out.

Table 4.5 Melting Points of Dental Restorative Materials

Gold crown alloys	1600°F–2000°F
Porcelain/metal alloys	2100°F–2300°F
Porcelain low fusing	1400°F–1800°F
Porcelain medium fusing	2000°F–2370°F
Porcelain high fusing	2370°F–2550°F
Chrome/cobalt alloy (RPD frameworks)	2500°F–2850°F
Silver amalgam	Hg in silver amalgam begins to evaporate at 215°F. The metals of the silver alloy, (Ag, Cu, Zn, and Sn), melt over a wide range from 450°F to 1800°F
Composite restorations	The organic material vaporizes at a relatively low temperature, but the inorganic elemental components can withstand temperatures well over 2000°F and may be analyzed with SEM/EDS to ascertain brand of composite
Polymethylmethacrylate	Begins to melt at 230°F and burns at 1100°F

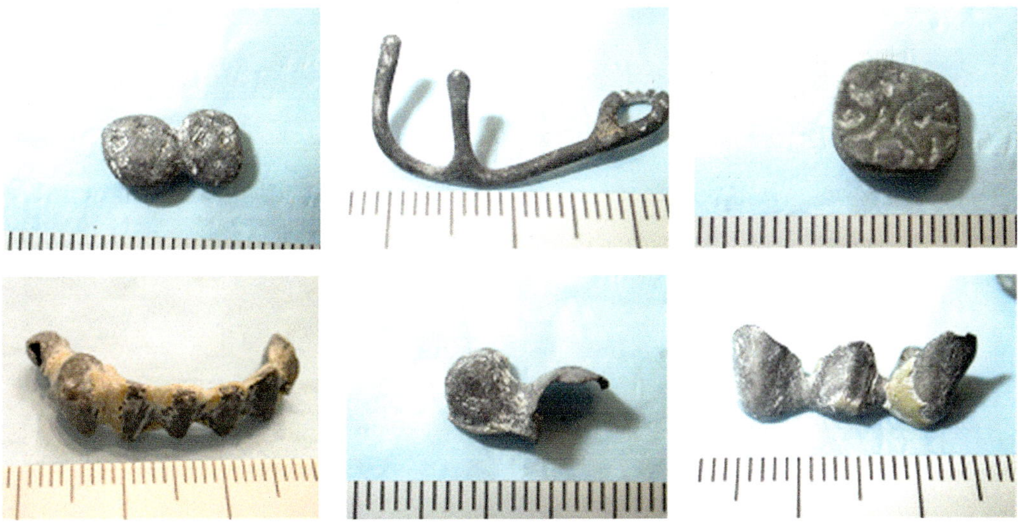

Figure 4.19 Dental restorations recovered in cremains.

4.2 Tooth Numbering Systems (Dental Notation, Dental Nomenclature)

4.2.1 Introduction

Dental notation or numbering systems are used to identify and refer to a specific tooth. Several systems of dental notation have been used over the years and the three most commonly used are presented in Section 4.2.2.

4.2.2 Various Systems

4.2.2.1 Universal Numbering System

This is primarily used in the United States and adopted by the American Dental Association.

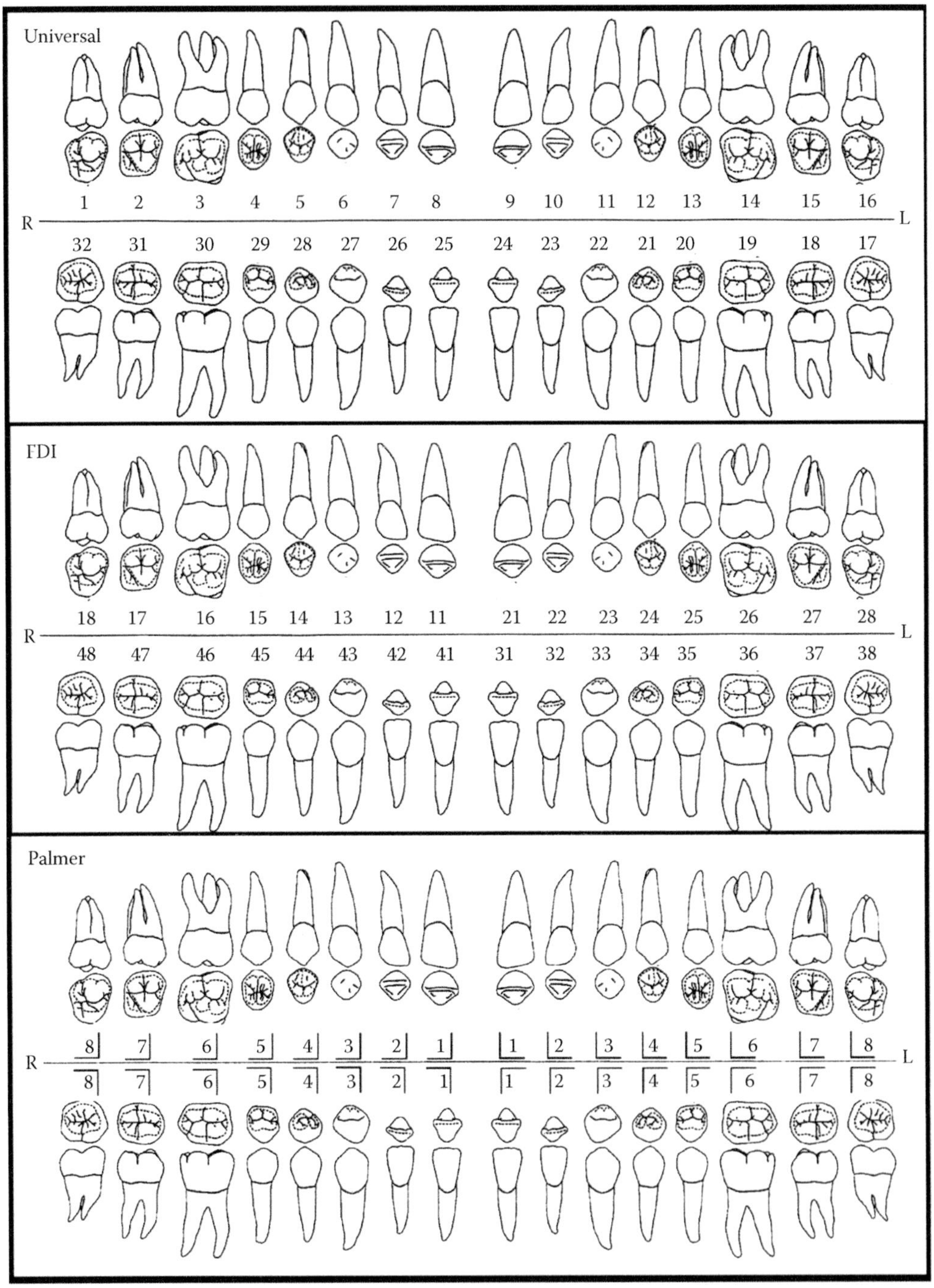

Figure 4.20 Universal, FDI, and Palmer numbering and notation system of permanent teeth.

Permanent teeth: Designated by number 1–32, beginning with the maxillary right third molar as tooth #1 and proceeding to the maxillary left third molar as tooth #16. The mandibular left third molar is #17, proceeding to the mandibular right third molar #32 (Figure 4.20).

Deciduous teeth: Designated by letter A–T, beginning with the maxillary right deciduous second molar as tooth A and proceeding as described earlier to the mandibular right deciduous second molar as tooth T.

4.2.2.2 FDI (Federation Dentaire Internationale)

This notation system is the international system widely used in most countries other than the United States.

Permanent teeth: The four quadrants are identified as 1–4 beginning in the upper right and then progressing clockwise and ending with the lower right quadrant. The individual teeth are numbered 1–8 beginning at the midline with the central incisor, proceeding distally to the third molar for each quadrant. Thus, each tooth has two digits, the first being the quadrant number (1–4) and the second being the tooth number. The upper right third molar's FDI notation is then #18 and the lower right third molar is #48.

Deciduous teeth: The four quadrants are identified as 5–8, and the individual teeth are numbered 1–5 beginning at the midline, proceeding distally for each quadrant as the permanent teeth.

4.2.2.3 Palmer Notation System

This system is used by some United States orthodontists, pedodontists, oral surgeons and dentists in the United Kingdom. This is a graphical system using a bracket to designate the quadrant, originally known as the Zsigmondy system first developed in 1861.

Permanent teeth: The mouth is divided into four quadrants (as in the FDI system). Each quadrant is designated by a bracket in one of four orientations, and the teeth are numbered 1–8 in each quadrant beginning at the midline as tooth #1 for the central incisors, proceeding distally to the third molar designated as tooth #8. Each tooth has only one digit, and its bracket designates the quadrant.

Deciduous teeth: The same bracket designation is used like the permanent teeth, but the teeth are lettered A–E in each quadrant.

4.3 Dental and Nondental Comparison

4.3.1 Photographic Facial Superimposition

Occasions may arise where the examiner is working with skeletal remains and is unable to locate dental records. Identification then may be attempted by the use of photographic facial superimposition. The use of a high-resolution, full-face photograph of the presumed victim that shows the teeth is required. The skull is then photographed in an attempt to match the exact position of the three planes seen in the photograph of the individual. The photograph of the skull is then enlarged until it equals the magnification of the facial antemortem photograph. The examiner will then compare the following common features seen in the superimposed images: the outline of the skull to the soft tissues of the face, the orbit to the eye, the brow ridges to the eyebrows, the zygomatic process to the cheek bones, the nasal aperture to the nose, and, most importantly, the superimposition of the teeth. Often, DNA is done concordantly with this technique.

4.3.2 Facial Reconstruction

When the medical examiner's investigative process toward establishing a presumptive identity for the victim is unsuccessfully complete, an artist's facial reconstruction may be attempted. Facial reconstruction from a skull is a combination of science and art. The forensic artist will consult with many different forensic specialists before beginning the reconstruction. The anthropologist should be able to provide information regarding the estimated age, ancestry, sex, and stature. The forensic dentist provides information related to any racial characteristics seen in the teeth and any unusual dental traits or anomalies. The various law enforcement agencies involved may provide information concerning items found at the recovery scene such as hair color, eye glasses, facial hair, and unusual clothing or jewelry. There are two methods of facial reconstruction. The first is a 2-D method, which is a sketch of the unidentified accomplished upon life size photographs of the skull. The second is the 3-D method, which requires clay to be applied to the actual skull in an attempt to render a sculpture of the unidentified subject. The artist uses known "tissue thickness stops" for each anatomical location of the skull (Figures 4.21 and 4.22).

Both methods have pros and cons. The 2-D technique is less time-consuming but may be dismissed by the media and public as a typical artist's composite sketch. The 3-D version generates much more interest, and attention yet is much more time-consuming and expensive to produce. Obviously, the skull must also be available and in a stable condition in order to support the clay. The 3-D method also allows the inclusion of actual articles found at the scene such as jewelry, eyeglasses, and wigs. When the facial reconstruction is completed, photographs of the finished reconstruction are then submitted to the news media asking for help in identifying the unknown individual (Figure 4.23).

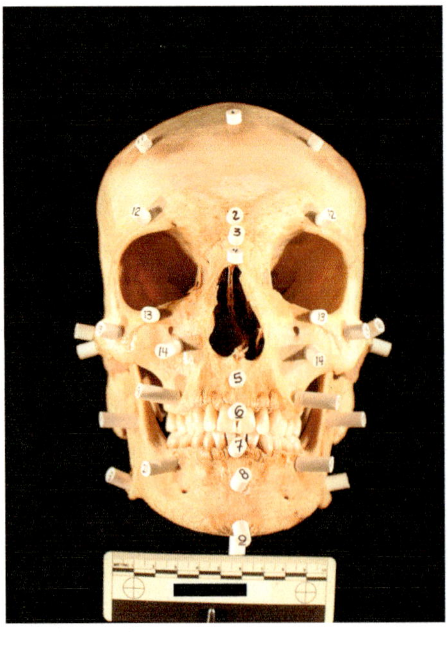

Figure 4.21 Facial reconstruction depth markers.

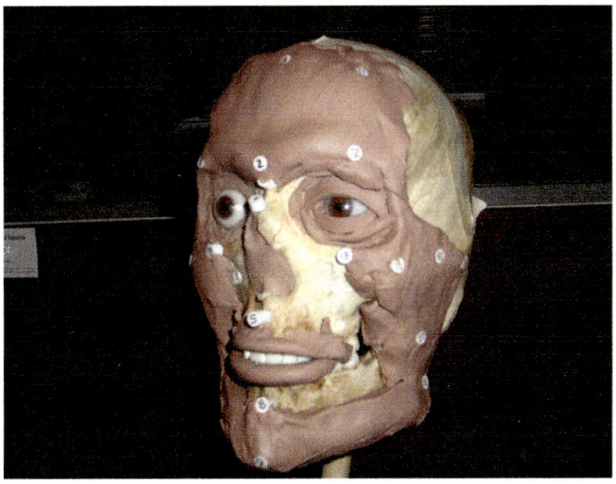

Figure 4.22 Facial reconstruction—clay being applied.

Figure 4.23 Completed facial reconstruction and actual victim.

4.3.3 Frontal Sinus Pattern Radiographic Comparisons

The first case of identification using frontal sinuses was performed by Culbert and Law in 1925. A recent study result supports previous assertions that individuals' frontal sinus pattern and resulting radiographic representations are a reliable means of identification, reporting no incorrect associations in their study (Smith et al., 2010). This method may be extremely helpful in establishing an identity but obviously, antemortem extraoral skull radiographs (e.g., PA Ceph) or maxillofacial CT scan studies of the skull are mandatory.

4.3.4 DNA

This powerful tool with applications in human identification, mass fatality management, and bitemark analysis is becoming more common each year (Dorion, 2005). The process of DNA analysis remains slow, extremely expensive, and must be performed in a limited number of highly specialized laboratories. The time period for this analysis can be as fast as 5–7 days and as slow as nine months depending on the capabilities of the DNA laboratory used by the medical examiner/coroner. Analysis of nuclear DNA is preferred when both optimal antemortem and postmortem samples are available for comparison (Duffy et al., 1991).

mtDNA analysis is substituted for skeletal remains and when soft tissues are desiccated, severely decomposed, or severely degraded. It has been shown that the neurovascular cells of the dental pulp and, to a lesser degree, odontoblasts are embedded in the predentin layer, and dentinal tubules during mineralization can be a valuable source of DNA. mtDNA is used to determine the maternal lineage but is not unique to the individual. All offspring of the same mother will have the same mitochondrial genome and often referred to as establishing a pedigree in the identification process. mtDNA has and is being utilized to identify our country's military unknown. The odontologists at JPAC (Joint POW/MIA Accounting Command) are responsible for sampling the dentin of teeth for the analysis of mtDNA. These samples are sent for analysis to AFDIL (Armed Forces DNA Identification Laboratory) in Rockville, Maryland.

4.3.5 Rugae

Palatal rugae are found on the anterior part of the palatal mucosa on either side of the median palatal raphe and behind the incisive papilla just behind the maxillary central incisor teeth. These ridges consist of anatomical folds or wrinkle in the palatal soft tissue and are composed of fibrous connective tissue. Anatomically, the rugae consist of about three to seven rigid and oblique ridges that radiate out tangentially from the incisive papilla. Palatal rugae have been shown to be highly individualistic and consistent in shape throughout life (Stuart and Leonard, 2005). Studies have shown that the palatal rugae pattern is unique to each human being including identical twins. Once formed, they do not undergo change except in length, due to normal growth (Almeida et al., 1995), and remain in the same position throughout a person's lifetime. Diseases, chemical aggression, or trauma do not seem to change the palatal rugae pattern. Changes that occur from orthodontic movement, extraction, aging, and palatal expansion do not modify the rugae enough to hamper identification (Almeida et al., 1995). In a study, Hemanth et al. (2010) showed less than a 1% error rate when using computer software to compare rugae for a human identification. As seen in Figure 4.24, rugae comparison can result in a positive identification.

4.3.6 Cheiloscopy

Cheiloscopy is the study of the patterns formed by the wrinkles and grooves of the labial mucosa (sulci labiorum) forming a characteristic pattern described as "lip prints" (Sharma et al., 2009; Sivapathasundaram et al., 2001). First, as described by Fisher in 1902, it was first used in criminology in 1932 by Edmond Locard in France. In 1974, Suzuki and Tschihashi confirmed that the lip print was the same following trauma and after healing. Studies have shown that these patterns are unique to each individual, remain stable over time, and that they show gender differences (Caldas et al., 2007; Narang, 2011). Cheiloscopy is applicable mostly in identifying the living since lip prints may be left at crime scenes and can provide a direct link to a suspect. Salivary DNA, if available from the object, may render a more statistically sound identification.

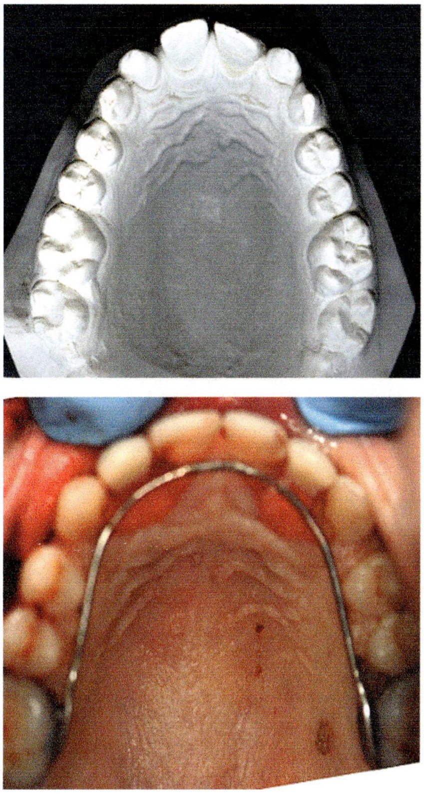

Figure 4.24 Rugae comparison.

4.3.7 Dental Appliances

4.3.7.1 Denture Labeling Law

The American Dental Association policy (1979: 637) states, "Resolved, that the American Dental Association urges constituent societies to actively support the use of uniform methods of marking dental prosthesis for forensic identification purposes."

Labeled dental appliances are important in identifying the owners in case of accident, misplacement in hospitals, and/or nursing homes and in aiding in the identification of the unknown in mass disaster situations. In the United Kingdom, the National Health Services provide payment to the dentist for patients in "care homes." In the United States, only 22 states require denture labeling: AK, AZ, CA, GA, IL, IN, KS, LA, ME, MA, MI, MN, MO, NV, NJ, NY (on patient request), ND, OH, TX, WA, WV, and WI.

4.3.7.2 Denture Teeth Molds, Size, Shape, Color

The fabrication of an individual's dentures involves tooth selection regarding the size, shape, and color of the denture teeth. When these details are properly documented in the dental chart, this information can be useful when there is no "name" labeled in the denture. Different mold charts are available online, which can be compared to the denture if the manufacturer of the denture teeth is known. Acrylic denture teeth have mold numbers on the back of the tooth. This information can be later compared to the actual denture recovered. Although not conclusive enough for a positive identification, this information may form another piece of the puzzle (Marella and Rossi, 1999).

4.3.7.3 Orthodontic Fixed Appliances

The size, shape, and material of fixed orthodontic appliances vary both within a given orthodontic manufacturer's products and among different manufacturers. Whether they are ceramic or stainless steel, whether they attach on the buccal or lingual, and whether they have covers over the arch wire or need to be ligated with elastics can all be helpful information. Contacting the manufacturer of the "braces" seen in an unidentified individual can provide you with the names of dentists/orthodontists that use this company's orthodontic equipment in a given community.

4.3.8 Dental Implants

Although dental implant companies still do not label their dental implants with a serial number, there is much information that can be derived from a dental implant.

As of the time of this publication, there are 32 manufacturers of dental implants that can be purchased in the United States. These dental implants vary significantly in design. When evaluating a dental implant, it is useful to determine both the manufacturer and type of implant so that you can compare this information to the victim's dental chart. Dental implant radiographic comparison charts can be found at www.whatimplantisthat.com. When starting at the coronal aspect of the implant, determine the type of abutment interface and what type of flange and collar is present. At the mid-body, determine the taper, thread design, and presence of a mid-body groove. At the apical aspect, discern the apex shape, and whether the apex is open. Finally, consider whether the implant has a round or oblong hole, chamber shape, and the presence of an apical groove.

4.4 Postmortem Dental Data

As noted earlier, teeth, jaws, and restorative materials are extremely resilient. They can withstand drastic temperature changes and are resistant to decomposition as well as severe trauma (Figure 4.25). The stability of the human dentition allows the process of antemortem/postmortem comparison.

Accurate documentation is the essence of all postmortem examinations. By means of clinical charting, photographs, and postmortem radiographs, the forensic odontologist can precisely document the dental conditions that may lead to a positive identification.

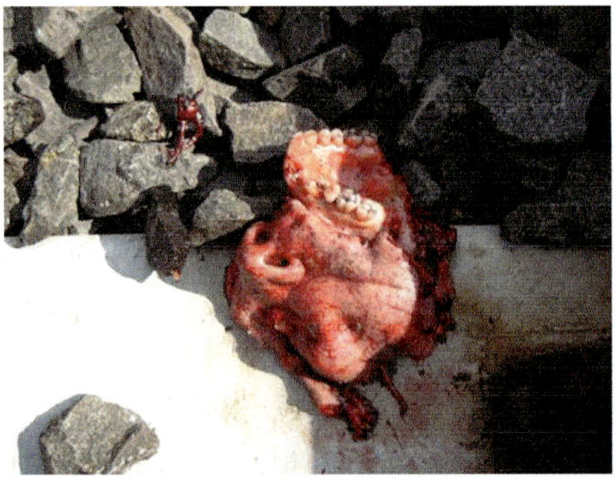

Figure 4.25 Maxilla after train versus person accident.

With increased data collected, there is higher likelihood that a successful identification will be made. The condition of the remains found will influence the ease or difficulty of the process. For example, a body that is fully intact with little to no trauma to the face will be easier to create an accurate postmortem dental record than those remains that have been subject to extreme heat, explosions, or severe trauma to the face. By developing and following a step-by-step checklist, the forensic odontologist will consistently create an accurate complete postmortem dental record (Bowers and Bell, 1996).

4.4.1 Collection of Postmortem Data

4.4.1.1 Postmortem Dental Charting Forms

The use of a postmortem dental charting form simplifies the process and several types of these exist. The Center for Education and Research in Forensics has developed antemortem and postmortem data collection forms, which utilize 11 primary codes and 12 secondary WinID3 codes, which were developed by Dr. James McGivney (Figures 4.26 and 4.27). The FBI's National Crime Information Center (NCIC) has also developed data collection forms using only 10 total codes (Figure 4.28). Developing a consistent protocol for data collection is the key. The odontologists should always record

1. The case number used by the local authority
2. The name of the person requesting your services
3. The date and time you were contacted
4. The date and time that the examination occurred
5. The jurisdiction and the location of the examination
6. The person(s) that was/were present at the time of the examination
7. The name of the medical examiner or coroner assigned to the case
8. The gender, race, and approximate age
9. In some cases, a putative identification may be available, which should also be recorded

Some have suggested a classification of remains:

Class I Fresh

1. Whole
2. Fragmented

Class II Decomposed/Incinerated

1. Whole
2. Fragmented

Class III Skeletal

1. Whole
2. Fragmented

The condition of the remains will influence the exact course and sequence of the examination.

Antemortem Dental Record

Last:______________________First:_______________MI:__ SSN/ID#:____________

Date (this record completed)________ Sex: __________Age/DOB:_______________

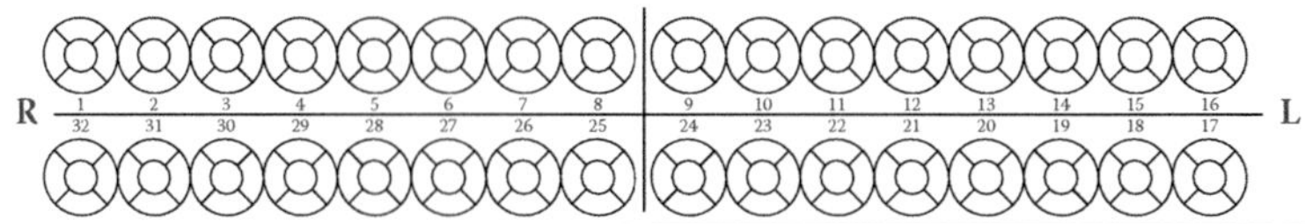

WinID Codes	
Primary Codes	**Secondary Codes**
M–Mesial	A-Annotation
O-Occlusal	B-Deciduous
D–Distal	C-Crown
F–Facial	E-Resin
L–Lingual	G-Gold
I–Incisal	H-Porcelain
U–Unerupted	N-Non-Precious
V–Virgin	P-Pontic
X–Missing	R-Root Canal
J–Missing Cr	S-Silver Amalgam
/-No Data	T-Denture Tooth
	Z-Temporary

Comments___________________________

Univ #		Code	Description	*FDI #*		Univ #
1				*18*		**1**
2				*17*		**2**
3				*16*		**3**
4	*A*			*15*	*55*	**4**
5	*B*			*14*	*54*	**5**
6	*C*			*13*	*53*	**6**
7	*D*			*12*	*52*	**7**
8	*E*			*11*	*51*	**8**
9	*F*			*21*	*61*	**9**
10	*G*			*22*	*62*	**10**
11	*H*			*23*	*63*	**11**
12	*I*			*24*	*64*	**12**
13	*J*			*25*	*65*	**13**
14				*26*		**14**
15				*27*		**15**
16				*28*		**16**
17				*38*		**17**
18				*37*		**18**
19				*36*		**19**
20	*K*			*35*	*75*	**20**
21	*L*			*34*	*74*	**21**
22	*M*			*33*	*73*	**22**
23	*N*			*32*	*72*	**23**
24	*O*			*31*	*71*	**24**
25	*P*			*41*	*81*	**25**
26	*Q*			*42*	*82*	**26**
27	*R*			*43*	*83*	**27**
28	*S*			*44*	*84*	**28**
29	*T*			*45*	*85*	**29**
30				*46*		**30**
31				*47*		**31**
32				*48*		**32**

Figure 4.26 CERF antemortem dental charting form.

4.4.1.2 Examination Procedures

The examination procedures developed by the ABFO are as follows:

1. Visually identifiable body
   a. Photographs
   b. Radiographs
   c. Dental charting
   d. Dental impressions, if applicable
   e. Resection
2. Decomposed/incinerated body
   a. Photographs
   b. Radiographs
   c. Dental charting
   d. Resection and preservation of jaw specimens if indicated

Postmortem Dental Record

ID#: ________________ Agency: ________________________________

Date: ______________ Sex: ______ Race: _____ Estimated Age: _____

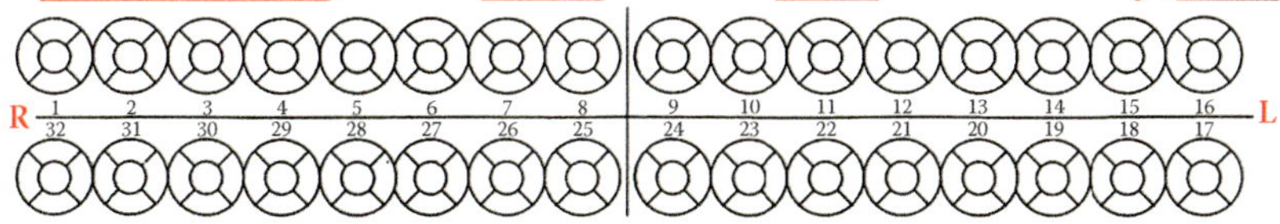

Univ #		Code	Description	FDI #	
1				18	
2				17	
3				16	
4	A			15	55
5	B			14	54
6	C			13	53
7	D			12	52
8	E			11	51
9	F			21	61
10	G			22	62
11	H			23	63
12	I			24	64
13	J			25	65
14				26	
15				27	
16				28	
17				38	
18				37	
19				36	
20	K			35	75
21	L			34	74
22	M			33	73
23	N			32	72
24	O			31	71
25	P			41	81
26	Q			42	82
27	R			43	83
28	S			44	84
29	T			45	85
30				46	
31				47	
32				48	

WinID Codes	
Primary Codes	**Secondary Codes**
M–Mesial	A–Annotation
O–Occlusal	B–Deciduous
D–Distal	C–Crown
F–Facial	E–Resin
L–Lingual	G–Gold
I–Incisal	H–Porcelain
U–Unerupted	N–Non-precious
V–Virgin	P–Pontic
X–Missing	R–Root canal
J–Missing Cr MPM	S–Silver amalgam
I–No data	T–Denture tooth
	Z–Temporary

Comments: ____________________________

Figure 4.27 CERF postmortem dental charting form.

3. Skeletonized remains
   a. Photographs
   b. Radiographs
   c. Dental charting

If the resection of the jaws or a soft-tissue dissection is necessary to gain access to the oral structures, it must be approved by the coroner or medical examiner, and if the body is viewable, an inframandibular technique is suggested. Specific techniques are described later in this chapter.

NCIC Unidentified Person File
Data Collection Entry Guide

Agency Case #: ____________

NCIC Unidentified Person Dental Report

SECTION 1

ME/Coroner Case #: ____________ NCIC #: ____________

Completed by: ____________ Date completed: ____________

Address: ____________

Telephone #: ____________ Email Address: ____________

X-Rays Available? ☒ Yes ☐ No Dental Models Available? ☐ Yes ☐ No Dental Photographs Available? ☒ Yes ☐ No

SECTION 2 ***DENTAL CHARACTERISTICS***

Upper Right			Lower Right	
01 (18) ____			32 (48) ____	
02 (17) ____			31 (47) ____	
03 (16) ____			30 (46) ____	
04 (15) ____	(A)	(Numbers in parentheses represent FDI System.)	29 (45) ____	(T)
05 (14) ____	(B)		28 (44) ____	(S)
06 (13) ____	(C)		27 (43) ____	(R)
07 (12) ____	(D)		26 (42) ____	(Q)
08 (11) ____	(E)		25 (41) ____	(P)
Upper Left			**Lower Left**	
09 (21) ____	(F)	(Letters in parentheses represent deciduous dentition.)	24 (31) ____	(O)
10 (22) ____	(G)		23 (32) ____	(N)
11 (23) ____	(H)		22 (33) ____	(M)
12 (24) ____	(I)		21 (34) ____	(L)
13 (25) ____	(J)		20 (35) ____	(K)
14 (26) ____			19 (36) ____	
15 (27) ____			18 (37) ____	
16 (28) ____			17 (38) ____	

SECTION 3 ***DENTAL CODES***

X = Tooth has been removed or did not develop
V = Tooth is present and unrestored
M = Mesial Surface Restored
O = Occlusal/Incisal Surface Restored
D = Distal Surface Restored
F = Facial or Buccal Surface Restored
L = Lingual Surface Restored
C = Lab Processed or Prefabricated Restoration
R = Endodontic Treatment
/ = Postmortem Missing or Not Recovered (Default Code)

(*The codes V and / are used differently in the Unidentified Person Report than in the Missing Person Dental Report.)

SECTION 4 ***DENTAL REMARKS***

☐ **ALL** (All 32 teeth are present and unrestored) ☐ **UNK** (No dental information available)

Rev 2/06 30

Figure 4.28 NCIC dental charting form.

4.4.1.3 *Photography*

A robust photographic documentation should ideally be obtained using a high quality camera and lens. Most odontologists use digital cameras today although some still use film. High quality images are essential, and many factors influence the digital image including the lens, the camera's megapixel rating, and most importantly proper camera alignment (Figure 4.29). Images taken should include

1. Full face
2. Full-face lips retracted
3. Close-up of anterior teeth in occlusion
4. Lateral views with teeth and in occlusion
5. Occlusal views of maxillary and mandibular teeth
6. Any other photographs should be taken of unique findings (Figure 4.30)

If the remains are fragmented, skeletonized, or burned, the odontologist should capture sufficient photos to document all surfaces of teeth and any areas of special interest. Taking photographs both before and after cleaning of the specimens may help to document the process of identification and may record evidence, which may become useful later in an investigation.

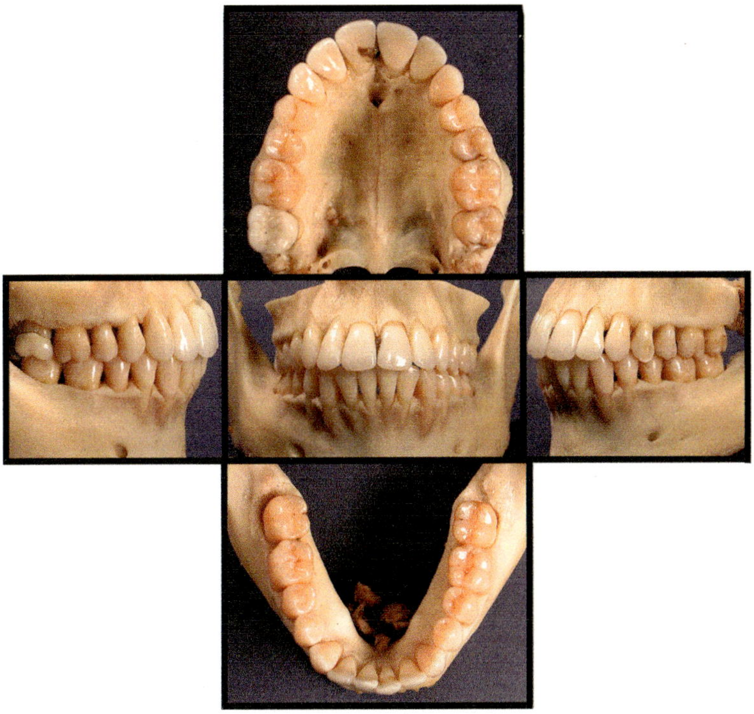

Figure 4.29 Postmortem dental photographic protocol (after specimen cleaning).

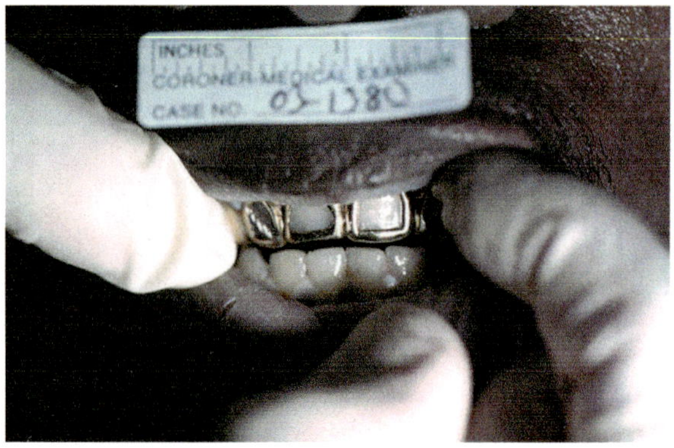

Figure 4.30 Close-up photo of item of interest (grill).

4.4.1.4 Radiography

A full mouth series of radiographs should ideally be taken on all remains (Figure 4.31). When the specimen is skeletonized, resected, or badly burned, the x-ray exposure settings may require a reduction in the beam's energy by as much as 50% (Weems, 2010). Forensic odontologists have devised ways of stabilizing a skull or head in order to create a panoramic radiograph and now with the popularity of cone beam technology, techniques for obtaining this type of image will be developed. Both film and digital radiographs will suffice; however, digital radiographs have some advantages over film. The speed in which one receives the image allows the operator to make sure that they have obtained a properly oriented and angled view of the teeth being captured. It also allows the examiner to attempt to replicate that the antemortem projection geometry antemortem films are available at the time of the examination. Resection of the soft and hard tissue is often necessary to gain proper access to the jaws and will be discussed later in this chapter. The use of a digital x-ray sensor (Figure 4.32), a portable x-ray generator such as the Nomad (Figure 4.33), and a laptop

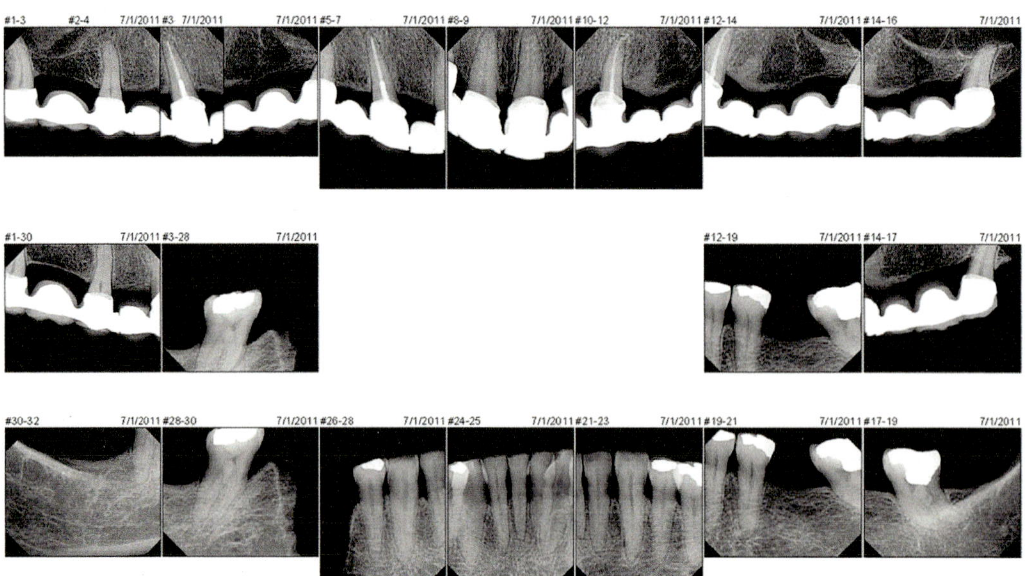

Figure 4.31 FMX taken with Nomad and Dexis sensor.

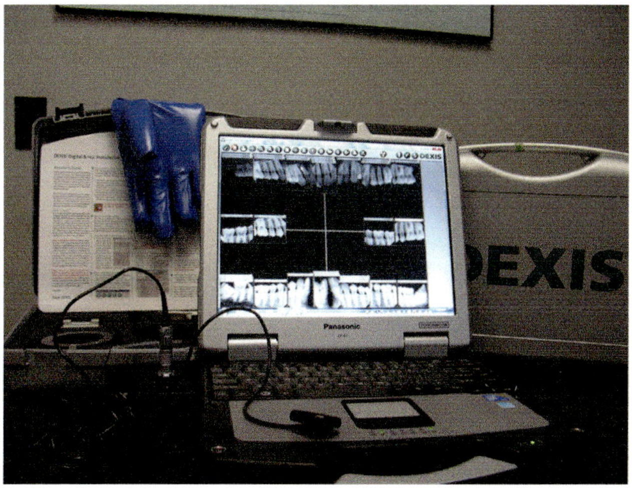

Figure 4.32 Dexis sensor, lead-lined gloves, and Panasonic Toughbook laptop.

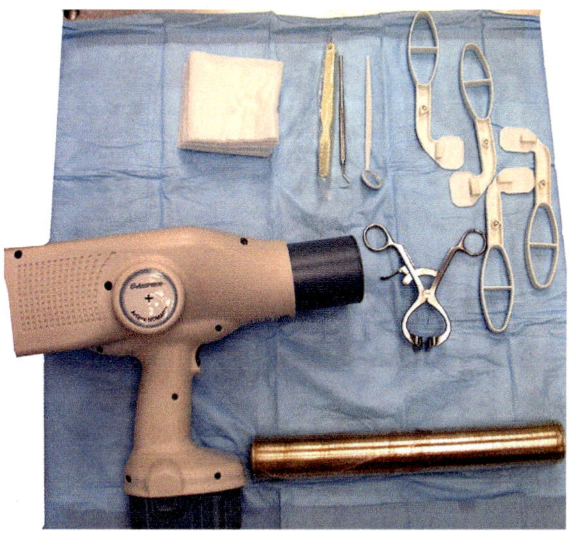

Figure 4.33 Nomad x-ray device and wrap for use as barrier.

computer allows the capture of digital x-rays almost anywhere and under any circumstances. Digital radiography also easily allows integration of all of the images taken into various DVI matching software programs as well as duplicating and remotely transmitting the resultant images electronically.

Several techniques have been developed to hold film and/or digital sensors in place during exposure. In fresh and accessible remains, most commercially available film/sensor positioners will suffice. Some use lead-lined gloves to push the mandible into a "biting" position to hold the positioning device. Another technique is to utilize a paper towel to exert a lateral pressure on the film or sensor and use the bisecting-the-angle technique to obtain the proper angulation. In fragmented or skeletonized remains, the use of soft dental rope wax on the film/sensor may enable the stabilization of the film/sensor so that the proper alignment may be achieved. It is also important to radiograph all dental fragments, dissociated teeth, bone, and restorations. Dental identifications have been made from a single tooth.

4.4.1.5 Viewable Remains

Restricted access to the oral cavity in order to perform an examination with radiographs may often be difficult due to rigor mortis. According to Spitz and Fisher (2006), "rigor becomes apparent within half an hour to an hour, increases progressively to a maximum within twelve hours, remains for about ten to twelve hours, and then progressively disappears within the following twelve hours." There are several options when dealing with rigor in viewable bodies.

1. The massaging of the masseter may occasionally allow sufficient release of rigor and allow enough access for an examination.
2. The breaking of rigor with bilateral downward leverage on the mandible in the retromolar region. In this technique, the application of a lever to the retromolar region is employed to open the jaws. Once enough access is gained, the jaws can be pulled apart. However, caution must be exercised not to break or avulse teeth.
3. Intraoral incision of the masticatory muscles, with or without fracture of the condyles within the cranial cavity. Using a scalpel intraorally, the muscles of mastication—the masseter, internal, and external pterygoids are incised—which will allow access for the examination.
4. Waiting until the rigor subsides
5. Inframandibular dissection. Bilateral incisions are made across the upper anterior neck and extend to points posterior and inferior to the ears. The skin and underlying tissues are then reflected upward over the lower face thereby exposing the mandible.

4.4.1.6 Nonviewable Remains

In visually identifiable remains, it is important not to disrupt the integrity of the face. However, in remains that are not visually identifiable such as decomposed or burned remains, it may be advantageous to surgically reflect the overlying soft tissues in a manner that gains an ease of access that allows for a complete examination. Beginning at the oral commissures and extending posteriorly to the tragus of the ear, this reflection of the soft tissues will allow better access (Figures 4.34 and 4.35). As stated previously, prior to any soft-tissue exposure or excision of the jaws, permission is necessary from the coroner or medical examiner even if the remains are considered nonviewable.

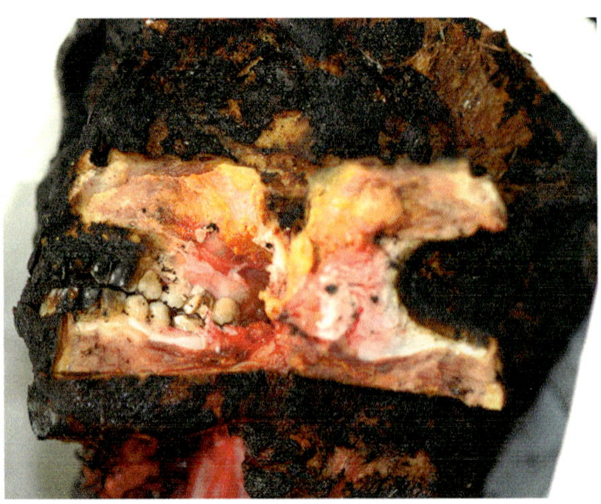

Figure 4.34 Burn victim soft-tissue reflection, lateral view.

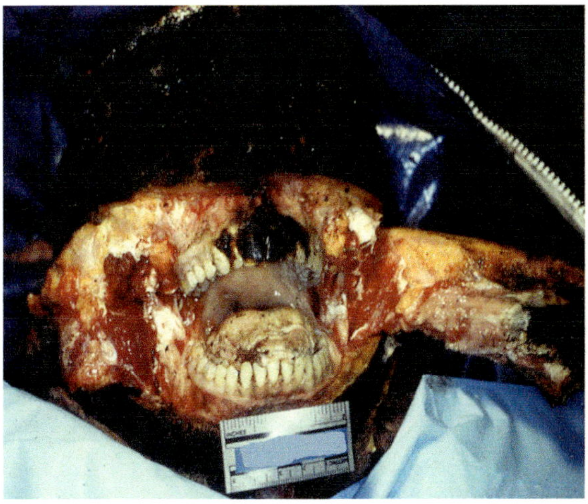

Figure 4.35 Burn victim soft-tissue reflection, facial view.

4.4.1.6.1 Jaw Resection In cases where the remains are badly decomposed, burned, or fragmented, it is sometimes necessary to resect the jaw(s) prior to examination. Careful resection should be employed to preserve fragile dental evidence. There are three methods for removing jaws on nonviewable remains. Regardless of which method is used, it is a common yet avoidable mistake when the operator cuts through the apices of the roots, particularly when removing the maxilla.

4.4.1.6.1.1 The Stryker Saw Method The soft tissue and muscle attachments on the lateral aspect of the mandible are dissected away by incisions, which extend through the muco-buccal fold to the lower border of the mandible. Lingual attachments are similarly incised to include the internal pterygoid attachments to medial aspect of the rami and the masseter attachments on the lateral aspect. On the maxilla, facial attachments are incised high on the malar processes and superior to the anterior nasal spine. Stryker saw cuts are made high on the rami to avoid possible impacted third molars. Alternatively, the mandible may also be removed by disarticulation at the temporomandibular joints. Bony cuts through the maxilla are made high on the malar processes and above the anterior nasal spine to avoid the apices of the maxillary teeth. A surgical mallet and a chisel inserted into the Stryker saw cuts in the malar processes and above the anterior nasal spine are used to complete the separation of the maxilla. Any remaining soft tissue attached to the specimen is then dissected free.

4.4.1.6.2 Pruning Shears Method An alternative technique for the resection of the jaws involves the use of large pruning shears. Shears should be considered when the specimen is extremely brittle, and there is concern regarding the effects of vibration from the Stryker saw (Figure 4.36). The soft tissue/muscle dissections are the same as those for the Stryker saw method. The small blade of the pruning shears is placed within the nares and forced back into the maxillary sinus. A cut is then made along a plane superior to the apices of the maxillary teeth bilaterally. The mandibular bone cuts are performed by inserting the small blade of the shears high on the lingual aspect of the ramus near the coronoid notch bilaterally. A fast sharp closure of the shears works better than slow gradual force.

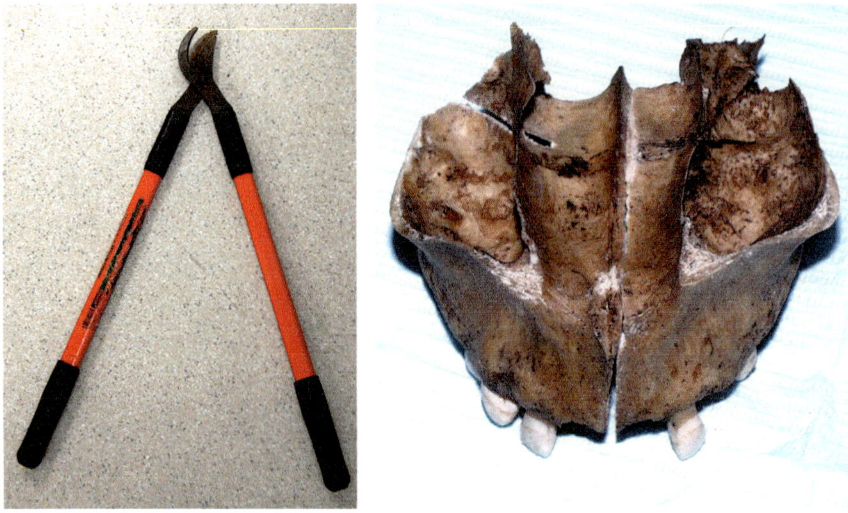

Figure 4.36 Shears used for jaw resection, cut is made above the nasal floor into sinuses.

4.4.1.6.2.1 Mallet and Chisel Method A mallet and chisel can be used to induce a "Le Fort" Type I fracture of the maxilla. The chisel blows are made below the zygomatic arch but as high on the maxillary sinus walls as possible bilaterally. Since it is virtually impossible to fracture the mandibular rami with the mallet and chisel, the mandible should be disarticulated at the temporomandibular joint.

When jaws are removed, it is important to properly preserve the specimens and to maintain a proper chain of custody.

4.4.1.7 Dental Examination

The odontologist should perform a clinical examination of the dentition recording the results on a dental chart. It is this author's suggestion to use WinID3 codes for the purpose of standardization. In the United States, the forensic odontological examinations use the universal numbering system. The odontologist should progress tooth-by-tooth documenting whether each tooth is present or missing: if there are restorations; the surfaces restored; the restorative material used; any prostheses; fractures; malformed teeth such as peg lateral; and implants as well as other findings. Radiographs should confirm the findings and also allow the odontologist to see other nonvisual clues such as root canals, posts, pins, cysts, and other pathology. Often odontologists will work in teams conferring on all findings. The use of a UV flashlight (365–395 nm wavelength) during the postmortem examination aids in the detection of tooth-colored materials as they can either fluoresce or absorb the light, either bright or dark in comparison to other teeth.

There are many schools of thought when it comes to the postmortem charting. Some espouse the charting of every item includes stains, decay, attrition, erosion, rotations, and periodontal evaluation. Others suggest that by just coding teeth that are missing or present, the surfaces restored is sufficient. Adams, in his research, showed significant results charting only 28 teeth (leaving third molars out) and only if the tooth is present, missing, or restored. He found that detailed documentation of restorations does not necessarily increase the uniqueness of dental patterns (Adams, 2003a). Ultimately, it is up to each odontologist along with consultation of the coroner or medical examiner to determine the level of information to be recorded.

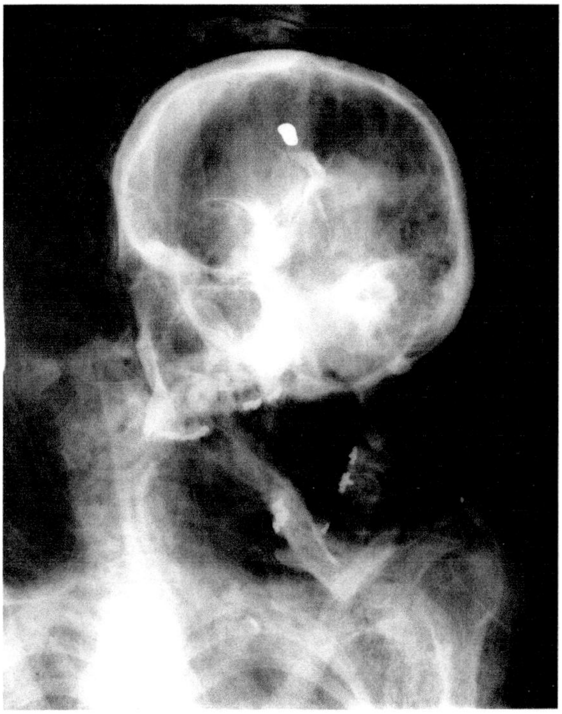

Figure 4.37 Portion of full body x-ray, portion of mandible is located near shoulder.

In situations where the remains have been subjected to deceleration incidents or severe trauma to the head, a full body radiograph may be necessary to locate misplaced dental structures and restorations or prosthesis (Figure 4.37).

In cases where the remains have been exposed to high temperatures for prolonged periods of time, the teeth can become charred and/or calcined, and the specimen can become too fragile to manipulate. As mentioned previously, the teeth can be stabilized using several techniques. Transparent nail polish, hair spray, or cyanoacrylate has been used to stabilize calcined teeth. Research has also shown that teeth and jaws that have been subjected to high temperatures for an extended period can exhibit shrinkage of up to 28%.

4.5 Antemortem Dental Data

4.5.1 Presumptive Identification

A presumptive identification is made most often by the investigating agencies.

This is often based on circumstantial evidence and can assist in the accumulation of medical/dental records to be used in the scientific identification process. The location of the unidentified body may provide useful clues. If a decedent is found in a residence, one can establish a putative identification; similarly, if a decedent is found in a vehicle, the Vehicle Information Number can establish the owner of the vehicle and, therefore, a putative identification. Personal effects found with the body often provide information such as the name on a driver's license, cellular phone, business cards, or laundry labels in clothing. Jewelry can be compared to descriptions or photographs provided by the family, and engraved personal information can often be found in rings and lockets. Body tattoos can also aid in the presumptive identification of an individual. In mass transportation accidents, it is important to obtain a manifest of the presumed individuals listed as passengers. Finally, local missing persons' reports and missing person databases, NCIC and NamUs, can also provide presumptive names to the investigating agency. Once the investigator or investigating agency has a presumptive name for the unidentified individual, they will need to obtain the antemortem dental records.

4.5.2 Locating Antemortem Dental Records

Often, it is as simple as asking a family member for the name of the deceased individual's treating dentist. Unfortunately, with the exception of a spouse, this information is often not known. In such cases, the information may be found in either the individual's personal phone book or in their household financial records.

Job-related insurance companies can also provide the name of the individual's treating dentist and, in some cases, provide a list of dental procedures completed under the policy. Dental insurance carrier information can be obtained from

Council of Dental Care Programs
American Dental Association
211 E Chicago Ave
Chicago, IL 60601

Also, if the deceased was in the military, it is possible that they were treated in the local VA hospital for dental needs upon discharge, and their dental records from their time of service may be obtained from

Military Records Depository
900 Paige Blvd
St. Louis, MO 63115

Other sources for antemortem dental records are the local dental schools, Public Health Department Dental Clinics, and dental records from any prior incarceration, including County, State, and Federal.

The mandated length of time a dentist must retain dental records varies from state to state. Every Forensic Dentist will most likely experience at some point, the disappointing specter of purged dental records (Tables 4.6 and 4.7).

4.5.2.1 Nontraditional Sources of Antemortem Dental Information

Dental structures can be an incidental finding on medical radiographs taken for other diagnostic purposed. Both radiographs of the head and neck area and CT/MRI data often contain excellent antemortem dental information. Likewise, radiographs taken at by a chiropractor for upper regions of the spine may show dental structures. Also, photographs of

Table 4.6 Dental Record Retention Mandates for the United States

Alabama	No mandate	Nebraska	No mandate
Alaska	No mandate	Nevada	5 years
Arizona	6 years	New Hampshire	7 years
Arkansas	No mandate	New Jersey	7 years
California	No mandate	New Mexico	No mandate
Colorado	7 years	New York	6 years
Connecticut	7 years	North Carolina	10 years
Delaware	No mandate	North Dakota	6 years
Florida	4 years	Ohio	No mandate
Georgia	10 years	Oklahoma	3 years
Hawaii	No mandate	Oregon	7 years
Idaho	No mandate	Pennsylvania	5 years
Illinois	10 years	Rhode Island	5 years
Indiana	7 years	South Carolina	5 years
Iowa	6 years	South Dakota	No mandate
Kansas	10 years	Tennessee	7 years
Kentucky	7 years	Texas	5 years
Louisiana	6 years	Utah	No mandate
Maine	7 years	Vermont	7 years
Maryland	5 years	Virginia	3 years
Massachusetts	7 years	Washington	5 years
Michigan	10 years	West Virginia	No mandate
Minnesota	7 years	Wisconsin	No mandate
Mississippi	7 years	Wyoming	No mandate
Missouri	7 years	Washington, D.C.	3 years
Montana	No mandate	USVI	No mandate

Table 4.7 Dental Record Retention Mandates for Canada and the United Kingdom

Alberta	11 years
British Columbia	30 years
Manitoba	No mandate
New Brunswick	No mandate
Newfoundland and Labrador	10 years
Nova Scotia	2 years
Ontario	10 years
Prince Edward Island	20 years
Quebec	5 years
Saskatchewan	6 years
Northwest territories	No mandate
Nunavut	No mandate
Yukon	10 years
United Kingdom	11 years

the individual smiling can be useful for superimposition and when the victim has distinctive crowns involving the anterior teeth.

4.5.3 What Antemortem Dental Records Should Be Requested

All dental records of the decedent should be requested, both written and radiographic. Radiographs must be labeled with patient's name, the date they were taken, and, ideally, the treating Dentist's name. It is also preferable that they should be signed or initialed by the Dentist. Experience has shown that the requested radiographs should be originals to the greatest extent possible. Copies of these radiographs may be made and retained, if desired, by the treating Dentist. The original radiographs may be returned to the treating dentist after completion of the case, but only after being copied or scanned by the Forensic Odontologist.

Copies of the entire dental chart should be requested and sent. Often, dental treatment is completed after a set of radiographs are taken. Without a copy of the dental chart, these changes in the individual dentition will make the identification more difficult.

All dental models and photographs should be requested. Especially in cases of extreme fragmentation, a dental model can be helpful in comparing the coronal portion of fragmented teeth (Figure 4.38).

In summary, the entire dental record and any available lab-work should be requested and received by the medical examiner/coroner's office.

4.5.4 Release of Dental Records and Chain of Custody

The treating dentist maintained status as the "custodian of the dental records" up until the time that the request is made for their release to the investigating agency. It is important that a chain of custody request and receipt is used to establish the location and disposition of the records. This form can be in two parts, with the top portion of the letter requesting all original dental radiographs, photographs, dental models, and a copy of the dental chart. This should be signed by the requesting agency. The lower half should list separately all items received, the treating dentist name, address, and his/her signature. The form may also state whether the treating dentist would like these items returned.

When time is of the essence, FEDEX or next-day UPS are acceptable. Upon opening the envelope containing the dental records, all items present should be listed, and this form is signed by the Forensic Odontologist.

All individual states allow for the right of the investigating agency to obtain Public Health records when needed as part of an ongoing investigation.

The Health Insurance Portability and Accountability Act (HIPAA) provides an exemption for the release of original records for the purpose of identifying the dead. Code of Federal Regulations, 45 CFR 164.512(g)(1) states, "a covered entity may disclose protected health information to a coroner or medical examiner for the purpose of identifying a deceased person…." Most investigative agencies make it a practice to provide the dentist of record with a copy of this HIPAA exemption when patient records are obtained.

4.5.5 Antemortem Record Form

Reconstruction of the antemortem record demands meticulous evaluation of all of the antemortem dental record components received. It is often difficult and may be extremely

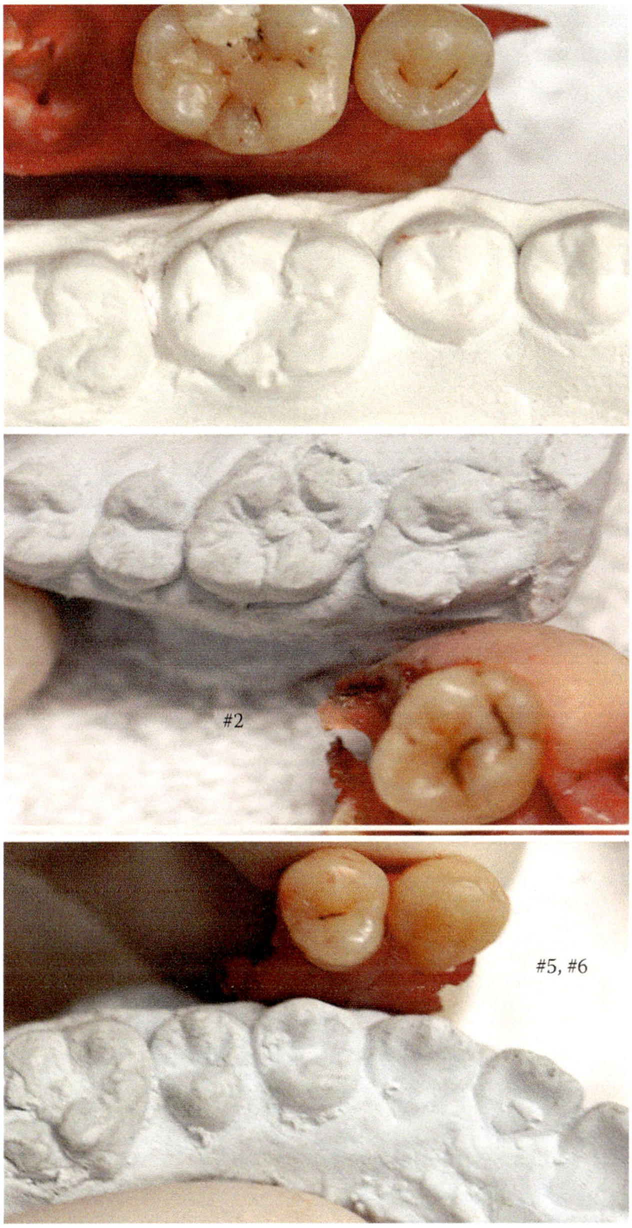

Figure 4.38 Comparison of teeth postmortem to antemortem dental models.

time-consuming. The objective is to recreate what the individual's dentition and oral structures were at the time of his last dental visit. There should be a thorough review of not only all the dental radiographs but also the written dental chart. It is important that the antemortem dental record (charting) is recorded in a format that is easy to understand. No abbreviations should be used, with all words fully spelled out (i.e., "MO Amal" should be spelled "Mesial Occulsal Amalgam"). Also, copied antemortem radiographs are oriented as if the examiner's view is toward the patient's mouth only when the bump (pimple) appears in the lower right or upper left corner of the image when the radiograph is oriented horizontally.

The antemortem dental form should contain the following information: The date of examination, the name of the victim, and any other information including the birth date and address of the deceased. A complete description of all dental findings should be noted and an odontogram should be completed. Any additional comments should be listed, and the form should have the name and signature of the forensic odontologist completing it. This form will eventually be compared to the postmortem dental form and must be verified for accuracy.

4.6 Comparison

4.6.1 Dental Features for Comparison

Once the antemortem record has been compiled and the postmortem data has been collected, a comparison can be made. It is important to stay objective and to compare all of the available information. One irreconcilable difference between antemortem and postmortem records will result in a "nonmatch." Using antemortem and postmortem forms that are mirror images (Figure 4.39) of each allows for an easy comparison once both datasets are recorded (Herschaft et al., 2006). Using a predetermined charting method also simplifies the process. Most forensic odontologists and the Disaster Mortuary Operational Response Team use WinID3 codes for dental charting purposes. The antemortem and postmortem charts and radiographs should be compared tooth-by-tooth, reconciling each feature from the antemortem record to the postmortem record. Some discrepancies can be reconciled. For example, an MO amalgam can become an MOD composite restoration, or a tooth that is present in antemortem data can be lost postmortem. A filling can go from shallow to deep over time. Similar antemortem to postmortem findings can be listed as natural progressions. However, a tooth CANNOT have a filling progress from more extensive in the antemortem records to less-extensive postmortem; teeth do not heal themselves. Extracted teeth CANNOT reappear. Improper comparisons can lead to a "misidentification." Many odontologists work in teams of two or three conferring on all points to come to the same conclusion or discuss and reconcile any differing opinions or chartings.

Additional features may be compared including pulp chamber shapes, crown and root morphology and anomalies, the radiographic shape of the restoration(s) placed, trabecular bone patterns, the lamina dura from extraction sites, or teeth that are missing postmortem. Tori, the relationship of adjacent teeth, the anterior nasal spine, the shape of the incisive foramen, and the size and shape of maxillary sinuses should also be compared. In fact, any maxillofacial feature that is seen antemortem may be compared to postmortem remains, if well documented.

When a decedent is found wearing a denture, it should be examined for any identifying features. As discussed earlier, many states have regulations that mandate that dentures must have some identifier on the denture. One may also remove the teeth from the acrylic and look for mold numbers on the back if they have not been ground down. Shades of denture teeth may also be compared.

Comparisons of antemortem study casts, bleaching trays, night guards, removable partial dentures, and sleep apnea oral devices can be compared to postmortem remains, and these devices can be "tried in" to confirm an identity.

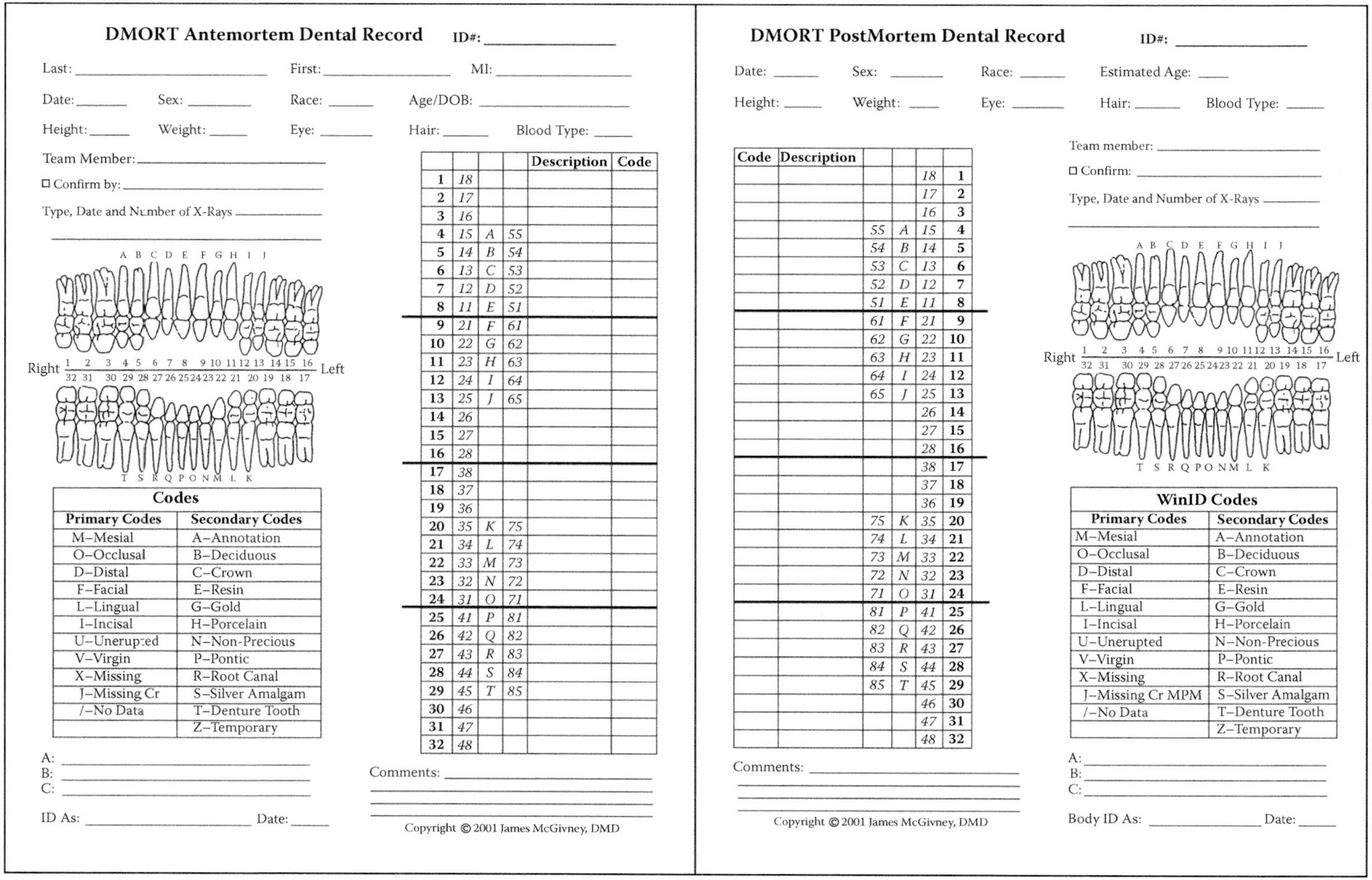

DMORT Antemortem Dental Record ID#: ____

Last: ____ First: ____ MI: ____

Date: ____ Sex: ____ Race: ____ Age/DOB: ____

Height: ____ Weight: ____ Eye: ____ Hair: ____ Blood Type: ____

Team Member: ____

☐ Confirm by: ____

Type, Date and Number of X-Rays ____

A B C D E F G H I J

Right 1 2 3 4 5 6 7 8 9 10 11 12 13 14 15 16 Left

32 31 30 29 28 27 26 25 24 23 22 21 20 19 18 17

T S R Q P O N M L K

				Description	Code
1	18				
2	17				
3	16				
4	15	A	55		
5	14	B	54		
6	13	C	53		
7	12	D	52		
8	11	E	51		
9	21	F	61		
10	22	G	62		
11	23	H	63		
12	24	I	64		
13	25	J	65		
14	26				
15	27				
16	28				
17	38				
18	37				
19	36				
20	35	K	75		
21	34	L	74		
22	33	M	73		
23	32	N	72		
24	31	O	71		
25	41	P	81		
26	42	Q	82		
27	43	R	83		
28	44	S	84		
29	45	T	85		
30	46				
31	47				
32	48				

Codes

Primary Codes	Secondary Codes
M–Mesial	A–Annotation
O–Occlusal	B–Deciduous
D–Distal	C–Crown
F–Facial	E–Resin
L–Lingual	G–Gold
I–Incisal	H–Porcelain
U–Unerupted	N–Non-Precious
V–Virgin	P–Pontic
X–Missing	R–Root Canal
J–Missing Cr	S–Silver Amalgam
/–No Data	T–Denture Tooth
	Z–Temporary

A: ____
B: ____
C: ____

Comments: ____

ID As: ____ Date: ____

DMORT PostMortem Dental Record ID#: ____

Date: ____ Sex: ____ Race: ____ Estimated Age: ____

Height: ____ Weight: ____ Eye: ____ Hair: ____ Blood Type: ____

Code	Description				
				18	1
				17	2
				16	3
		55	A	15	4
		54	B	14	5
		53	C	13	6
		52	D	12	7
		51	E	11	8
		61	F	21	9
		62	G	22	10
		63	H	23	11
		64	I	24	12
		65	J	25	13
				26	14
				27	15
				28	16
				38	17
				37	18
				36	19
		75	K	35	20
		74	L	34	21
		73	M	33	22
		72	N	32	23
		71	O	31	24
		81	P	41	25
		82	Q	42	26
		83	R	43	27
		84	S	44	28
		85	T	45	29
				46	30
				47	31
				48	32

Team member: ____

☐ Confirm: ____

Type, Date and Number of X-Rays ____

A B C D E F G H I J

Right 1 2 3 4 5 6 7 8 9 10 11 12 13 14 15 16 Left

32 31 30 29 28 27 26 25 24 23 22 21 20 19 18 17

T S R Q P O N M L K

WinID Codes

Primary Codes	Secondary Codes
M–Mesial	A–Annotation
O–Occlusal	B–Deciduous
D–Distal	C–Crown
F–Facial	E–Resin
L–Lingual	G–Gold
I–Incisal	H–Porcelain
U–Unerupted	N–Non-Precious
V–Virgin	P–Pontic
X–Missing	R–Root Canal
J–Missing Cr MPM	S–Silver Amalgam
/–No Data	T–Denture Tooth
	Z–Temporary

Comments: ____

A: ____
B: ____
C: ____

Body ID As: ____ Date: ____

Figure 4.39 Side-by-side comparison of mirrored antemortem and postmortem charts.

4.6.2 Statistical and Mathematic/Algorithm Methods

Historically, the recording and matching of multiple antemortem and postmortem dental records via algorithmic models (computers) have been in existence since the 1970s (Kogon, et al., 1974; Siegel and Sperber, 1977; Lorton and Langley, 1986; McGivney and Fixott, 2001). An early statistical model was developed using simply the presence or absence of a tooth as well as whether any of the remaining teeth were restored and was found to be effective in the identification process (Keiser-Nielson, 1980). For example, the possible combinations of a person missing six teeth and having the same five restored teeth are 59,609,309,760, or the probability of another individual having the same combination is 1 in over 59 billion (Senn and Stimson, 2010). As mentioned previously, the WinID dental matching software and dental codes have induced some amount of commonality of "digital charting language" among forensic dentists because this coding system and the WinID matching program have been proven to be effective in successfully identifying very large numbers of victims in numerous mass disasters (also see Chapter 6).

A program developed by Bradley Adams, Ph.D. in cooperation with the Joint POW/MIA Accounting Command (JPAC) called "OdontoSearch 2.0" can be found at www.jpac.pacom.mil/index.php?page = odontosearch. The OdontoSearch program is a database of "dental findings" compiled from 40,108 individuals. The goal of the OdontoSearch 2.0 database is to provide a representative sample of the dental findings and treatment of the adult U.S. population. It allows the user to run searches of specific dental chartings from 1 to 28 teeth (it excludes third molars). For example, if a user searched for a specific dental charting pattern and was observed in only 24 of the individuals, then this would indicate that the pattern would be seen 1 in 1666 individuals and can therefore give the user an empirical probability that can be quantified for use in a report or in a court of law.

4.6.3 Dental Identification Guidelines

The American Board of Forensic Odontology in 1994 established standards and guidelines for dental identifications; available on their website www.abfo.org. They have developed and updated the following conclusions to a dental comparison and subsequent identification (ABFO, 2012).

1. Positive identification
   The antemortem and postmortem data match in sufficient detail to establish that they are from the same individual. In addition, there are no irreconcilable discrepancies.
2. Possible identification
   The antemortem and postmortem data have consistent features, but, due to the quality of either the postmortem remains or the antemortem evidence, it is not possible to positively establish dental identification.
3. Insufficient evidence
   The available information is insufficient to form the basis for a conclusion.
4. Exclusion
   The antemortem and postmortem data are clearly inconsistent. However, it should be understood that identification by exclusion is a valid technique in certain circumstances.

All conclusions are stated to a reasonable dental/medical certainty.

4.6.4 Report Writing

Once an identity has either been established or excluded, the odontologist may be requested to write a report discussing their findings. While there is no standardized report, there are components that the ABFO has established that should be included in every report. These include

1. Your name, address, and contact information
2. The medical examiner/coroner office and case number
3. An introduction that includes who requested your services and the date they contacted you and the name of the putative identification
4. The antemortem examination, what you examined, and where you received the records from
5. The postmortem examination, the date of the examination as well as material you examined, what you did, and the number of radiographs you took and examined
6. A summary of the antemortem and postmortem charting
7. A discussion of the findings
8. A conclusion
9. Signature

When antemortem dental records are not available, there are other methods of comparison that can be made. Dr. Richard Souviron has recommended "the smiling face photograph identification." An antemortem photograph that shows enough detail of the anterior teeth can be compared to the postmortem anterior teeth. Using image processing programs, they can be superimposed over each other making one layer transparent. By then comparing position, size, and rotations edges, one can make an inclusive identification. If sufficient detail such as chipped or missing teeth is seen, some odontologists may feel comfortable making an exclusive identification (Silver and Souviron, 2009).

The comparison process must be performed systematically, and the clinician must stay objective. Often, pressure will be put to bear to "make" identification. However, it is thoroughness and objectivity that must be maintained to arrive at a correct conclusion. When in doubt, always obtain a second opinion from a colleague.

4.7 Advanced Methods of Dental Materials Evidence Analysis

4.7.1 Challenges to and Limitations of Traditional Methods

As described in earlier sections in this chapter, an important aspect of dental identification is noting the presence, shape, and location of restorative materials in the dentition, including composite resins, amalgam fillings, crowns, posts, full and partial dentures, bridges, and implants. Even root canal sealers can play a role in the assemblage of information that the investigator might use to make the identification.

In recent years, there has been an explosion of competing products available to the dental practitioner. A dental chart today might reflect the presence of an array of dental materials that were not available 20 or even 10 years ago. With composite resins alone, there have been well over 100 brands available on the U.S. market in the last decade. Each of these materials has physical and chemical attributes that determine how they appear both visually and radiographically.

However, these attributes bring with them some challenges. For example, the variation in elemental composition of composite resins can play a large role in their radiographic appearance. In addition, as materials are developed that more closely mimic tooth structure, detection for charting purposes becomes more challenging. Fortunately, for the investigator, many of the brands have distinctly different compositions and microstructures that can be used to distinguish products. This section explores how different tools can be used to classify materials based on their physical and chemical properties.

It is a logical extension from noting the presence of a restorative material to determination of brand of that material, potentially adding another level of certainty to the identification. Clearly, the value of this information is dependent on whether detailed records are available in the chart. It can be expected that not all treating clinicians keep records on this level; however, the practice of recording brand is included in contemporary dental education, primarily for the purpose of providing an evidence base for the performance of materials. This section emphasizes the importance of detailed recording of procedures and materials in the dental chart.

4.7.1.1 *Radiopacity*

In dental radiography, the conditions of radiation exposure and detector sensitivity (film or digital) are established to reveal subtle differences in contrast to enamel, dentin, and, by consequence, bone structure. The amount and density of mineral in the radiographic field of view provide contrast to reveal structure and pathology.

Elements with higher atomic number absorb more radiation. Restorative materials such as amalgam, stainless steel posts, and some ceramics appear in radiographs simply as white regions and may be indistinguishable from each other in a typical dental radiograph. However, if exposure and detector conditions are varied sufficiently, differences in contrast between these materials will be apparent.

Manufacturers of dental materials have often (but not always) added radiopacifiers to their products in the form of compounds containing high-atomic number elements. The result is that a contemporary individual who has undergone a number of restorative procedures over the years potentially may have in their dentition a combination of materials with widely differing radiographic properties. Some prefabricated endodontic posts made of composite material and the cements used for their insertion are not radiopaque and are virtually "invisible" in radiographic images (Weems et al., 2004).

Further compounding the ability to distinguish, and chart or record, the presence of restorative resins is the current trend toward minimally invasive preparations, in which small amounts of restorative material might be carefully placed. Such restorations might easily be missed on a routine examination.

4.7.2 Methods of Detection and Analysis

4.7.2.1 *Visible Light Fluorescence*

Enamel and dentin fluoresce when illuminated with light close to the ultraviolet (UV) end of the visible light spectrum. It is principally the organic component in tooth structure that fluoresces, and therefore dentin (with higher organic component) fluoresces with a higher intensity than enamel. Fluorescence can be simply described as the emission of light of a longer wavelength when a subject is illuminated with a shorter wavelength. In the case of tooth structure when illuminated with near-UV light, the emission or visible color is principally in the blue region of the electromagnetic spectrum.

Dental materials vary considerably in their fluorescence properties. In recent years, manufacturers of dental materials have made various claims regarding fluorescent properties, with the result that there exists a range of brightness and color between materials. In composite resins, for example, organic fluorophores may be added to achieve supposed improved esthetic qualities. Similarly, trace amounts of rare earth oxides may be added to porcelain powders to achieve the same effects. Different brands of the same classes of materials (such as composite resins) may have dramatically different fluorescence characteristics.

The result is that an individual may have an assortment of materials in their dentition that show contrast from the tooth structure and from each other when illuminated by near-UV energy, either in brightness or in color.

The recent advent of a new generation of light-emitting diodes (LEDs) has allowed flashlights to be constructed that emit light in narrow spectral ranges. These flashlights are compact and emit with enough intensity to produce contrast for dental inspections. These lights represent an important new tool for forensic odontology (Hermanson et al., 2008).

A significant advantage of dental inspection with a UV LED flashlight is the speed with which one can identify or confirm the location of suspected restorations. The use of this technique is not intended to replace but rather to supplement the traditional radiography and tactile inspection methods.

LED lights are available in a range of wavelengths. It has been the experience of the authors that wavelengths from 365 to 395 nm are most useful in inspecting the dentition. The recommended wavelength of most general utility is 395 nm, and a flashlight with several LEDs is recommended for illumination of a quadrant.

The emission wavelength and intensity of a given material can be measured quantitatively in the laboratory using a spectrophotometer. Studies comparing restorative resins have shown that these properties are not readily diagnostic to brand (Hermanson et al., 2008). Thus, the use of this method is qualitative in nature; the operator is simply looking for contrast differences between tooth structure and restorative materials to detect if restorations are present.

The contrast and color differences can be quite dramatic. Epoxy, for example, can fluoresce with a yellowish color, while most modern composite resins fluoresce blue to green under 365 nm illumination. The porcelain-containing materials have a similar dramatic range of radiance, ranging from dark brown to brilliant white. It should be noted, however, that some materials either fluoresce with the same intensity and wavelength as tooth structure or do not fluoresce at all. Thus, this method must always be considered adjunctive to the traditional inspection protocols (Figure 4.40).

4.7.2.2 Scanning Electron Microscopy/Energy-Dispersive X-Ray Spectroscopy

SEM/EDS is a well-established combination of instrumental techniques that provide information about the microstructure and inorganic elemental composition of a sample. Specifically, SEM/EDS techniques have been employed for the identification and distinction of tooth structure from other materials, verification of the use of restorative procedures, and identification of inorganic restorative materials (Bush et al., 2006). This information is potentially important in victim identification in both nonincinerated and incinerated remains. In the latter case, they may offer the forensic odontologist a last line of approach to obtain evidence. The ability to analyze microscopic evidence by SEM/EDS permits the forensic dentist to obtain results from trace amounts of evidence.

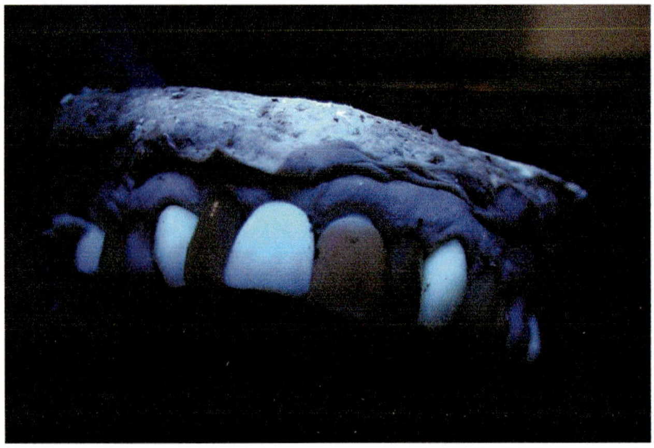

Figure 4.40 Anterior view of maxilla using 395-nm UV LED light.

Evidence taken from a scene may include fragments of material that are questionable as to their nature and as to whether there may be dental information present. Surprisingly, useful information may be obtained by examination of evidence using these methods.

Written documentation in a dental chart of a restorative procedure such as etch and bond technique and verification of that procedure could potentially help identify recovered remains. Marks left as a result of restorative procedures can be recognized microscopically. Ridges left by the use of a bur in cutting a preparation may be seen readily by SEM imaging. Visualization of such artifacts by optical microscopy is difficult due to the lower resolution, poor depth of field, and inherent contrast problems.

Even after cremation, evidence of etch and bond technique can be revealed. Figure 4.41 shows a mandible segment with two teeth recovered from a cremated individual. The enamel has fragmented from the teeth, but inspection showed the possibility of a preparation base still evident in the coronal dentin of tooth #19. Low-magnification SEM clearly revealed the bur marks (Figure 4.42). High magnification shows a dramatic difference in appearance of the dentin in the preparation base (Figure 4.43) as compared to the fractured dentin outside the preparation (Figure 4.44). In the base area, the dentin tubules are demineralized and

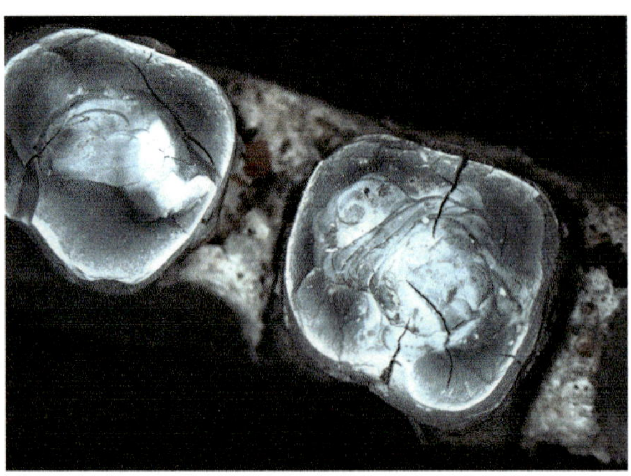

Figure 4.41 Stereomicroscopic view of cremated mandibular fragment.

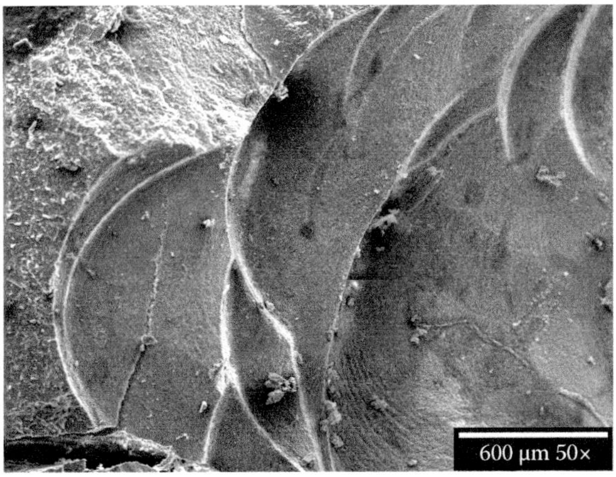

Figure 4.42 SEM view of tooth #19 in Figure 4.41. Note grooves left by bur.

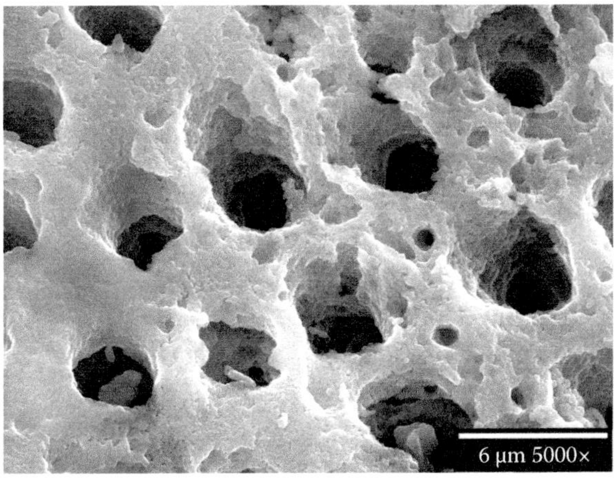

Figure 4.43 SEM image in base of preparation in Figure 4.42. Magnification 5000×. The dentin tubules are wide open. Evidence of use of phosphoric acid in etch and bond procedure.

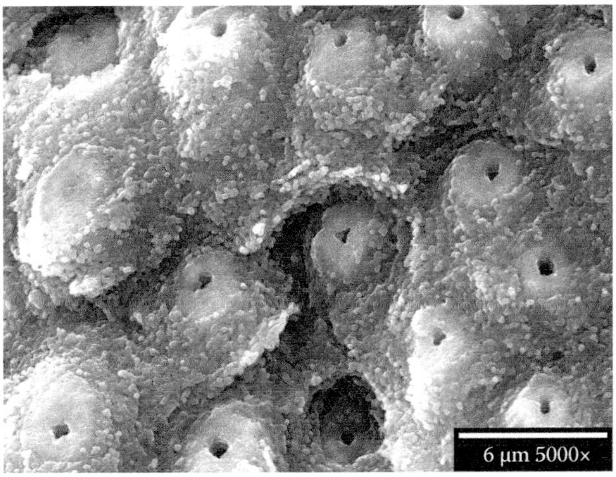

Figure 4.44 SEM image of dentin in fractured area in Figure 4.42. The dentin tubules are much smaller indicating no acid etching. Magnification 5000×.

widely patent, while those in the fractured dentin are shrunken and become dense. This is clear evidence of the use of an etch and bond technique, and this evidence remarkably survived cremation. Dental records in this case confirmed the use of the acid etch technique on tooth #19.

4.7.2.2.1 Analysis of Restorative Materials Tooth-colored (matching) resins used in restorative procedures present the widest variation of all dental materials in terms of microstructure and composition. These are organic resin mixtures that contain inorganic filler particles. This broad description encompasses a variety of product types including hybrids, microhybrids, microfills, nanofills, packables, and flowables. The analytical methods discussed are useful in distinguishing brand or brand group of material based on the microstructure and inorganic filler elemental composition. Spectral databases have been developed that allow identification of brand (Bonavilla et al., 2008; Bush et al., 2008).

In Figures 4.45 through 4.48, the dramatic differences in microstructure between resin brands can be seen. These images are backscattered electron images in which the brightness is related to atomic number. Figure 4.45 shows the resin Quixx (Dentsply, Milford, DE) with inset EDS spectrum. Figure 4.46 shows the resin Gradia Direct (GC America, Alsip, IL) and its elemental constituents. Similarly, Figure 4.47 shows the resin Tetric Ceram (Ivoclar, Amherst, NY). Hence for the product Tetric Ceram, the bright regions in the image correspond to particles of Yb glass, a heavy rare earth element. Likewise, the large particles in the Quixx resin are high in Sr content.

The persistence and existence of restorative materials has been demonstrated after the cremation process. Even after the extreme step of comminution in a mortuary processor (grinder), particles of these materials can be found. Figure 4.48 shows amalgam particles in a field of processed cremains. The usefulness of this type of analysis is demonstrated in that backscattered imaging reveals the location of the high-atomic number amalgam particles. EDS analysis can then be performed on each particle at high magnification to confirm composition.

Figure 4.45 Microstructure and EDS spectrum from resin brand Quixx.

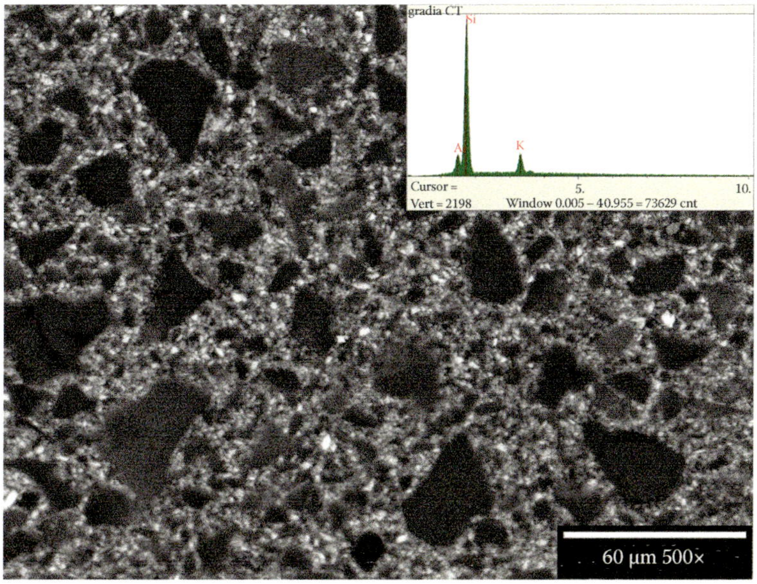

Figure 4.46 Microstructure and EDS spectrum from resin brand Gradia.

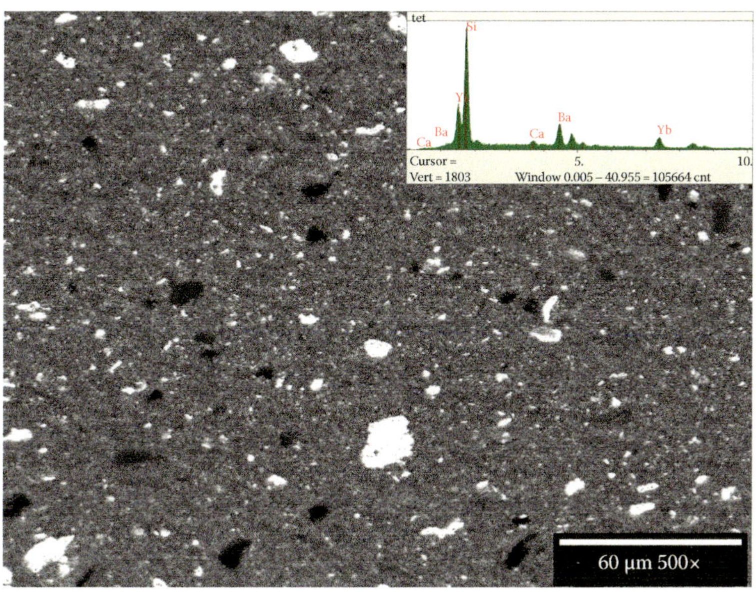

Figure 4.47 Microstructure and EDS spectrum from resin brand Tetric Ceram.

The rationale for accurate descriptive record keeping in dental charts is underlined by the diverse and unique combinations of restorative materials that may be found in the oral environment. For these analyses to be effective evidence, it is paramount that the use of specific materials be recorded in the dental chart when procedures are performed.

Figure 4.48 Field of debris of processed cremains. In this backscattered electron image, high-atomic number particles show bright (amalgam, resin) as compared to the darker calcined calcium phosphate bone and tooth particles.

Every forensic case is unique, and the approach necessary to retrieve evidence and determine its significance is determined by the situation encountered. The situations and accompanying images shown in this section are presented as examples of the use of SEM/EDS in forensic odontology. For a practical example of how these methods have been used in the crash of Colgan Air Flight 3407, refer to Chapter 6 (Bush and Miller, 2011).

4.7.2.3 X-Ray Fluorescence

The technique of x-ray fluorescence (XRF) is also well established and represents another nondestructive inorganic elemental analysis method. As in EDS, a spectrum is obtained, which is characteristic of the sample.

There is great variability in the construction of XRF instruments and most are laboratory-based devices. The instrument of most interest to the forensic odontologist, however, is the portable XRF. Technological advances in miniaturization have resulted in the construction of small x-ray sources, which, when combined with a small detector and palm computer, make portable XRF instrumentation very sophisticated. XRF has excellent detection limits for most elements and provides accurate and rapid nondestructive quantitation.

Spectral libraries can easily be generated that may be used to match field unknowns with standard samples. XRF technology can help rapidly distinguish restorative materials, suspected prostheses, and in separation of tooth and bone, from other materials (Bush et al., 2007).

In the field, restorative materials and prosthesis can be missed due to their resemblance to other objects. Amalgam recovered from an incineration scene can look like a small pebble, but XRF can rapidly identify the elemental content. Gold crowns can appear black due to oxidation of the copper content.

Restorative resins, which maintain their inorganic elemental content even after incineration, can be recovered and analyzed. One of the limitations of the portable XRF is the inability to detect elements lower than phosphorus on the periodic table. Thus, the element silicon will not be seen. If a resin only has silicon glass (silica) as its filler, this analysis will not return useful information. There was a period during early development of restorative resins in which silica was the only filler added. Today, however, most manufacturers add heavy elements as radiopacifiers incorporated into restorative materials. These elements will readily be detected by XRF.

The XRF will also identify elemental composition in amalgams, Co/Cr alloy castings, porcelain fused to metal crowns, posts, and other various restorative materials. In addition to dental materials, the XRF will correctly identify the composition of personal effects such as jewelry. It can distinguish between materials with similar appearance such as nickel, silver, white gold, or platinum and diamond versus cubic zirconia. An individual may be known to family members as wearing certain specific jewelry types, and the data produced by the XRF could easily be added to the victim information. Thus, the overall goal in using this technique is to obtain the maximum information in every given circumstance that might aid in identification.

Forensic odontology can be aided by a technique such as XRF, especially when traditional means of identification yield few clues. New analytical tools will be increasingly used in victim identification as well as other areas of forensic science. It is therefore important to be aware of resources that are available and apply them to appropriate situations. Familiarity with emerging technologies will allow the forensic odontologist to extract information from situations that might otherwise seem beyond reach.

References

Adams, B. 2003a. Establishing personal identification based on specific patterns of missing, filled, and unrestored teeth. *J Forensic Sci* 48(3): 487–496.

Adams, B. 2003b. The diversity of adult dental patterns in the United States and the implications for personal identification. *J Forensic Sci* 48(3): 497–503.

Almeida, M. A., C. Phillips, K. Kula, and C. Tulloch. 1995. Stability of the palatal rugae as landmarks for analysis of dental casts. *Angle Orthod* 65: 43–48.

American Board of Forensic Odontology (ABFO). 2012. Diplomates reference manual. http://www.abfo.org

Bonavilla, J. D., M. A. Bush, P. J. Bush, and E. A. Pantera. 2008. Identification of incinerated root canal filling materials after exposure to high heat incineration. *J Forensic Sci* 53(2): 412–418.

Botha, C. T. 1986. The dental identification of fire victims. *J Forensic Odontostomatol* 4(2): 67–75.

Bowers, C. M. and G. L. Bell. 1996. *Manual of Forensic Odontology*, 3rd edn. Manticore Publishers, Ontario: American Society of Forensic Odontology.

Bush, M. A., P. J. Bush, and R. G. Miller. 2006. Detection and classification of composite resins in incinerated teeth for forensic purposes. *J Forensic Sci* 51(3): 636–642.

Bush, M. A. and R. G. Miller. 2011. The crash of Colgan Air flight 3407: Advanced techniques in victim Identification. *J Am Dent Assoc* 142(12): 1352–1356.

Bush, M. A., R. G. Miller, A. L. Norrlander, and P. J. Bush. 2008. Analytical survey of restorative resins by SEM/EDS and XRF: Databases for forensic purposes. *J Forensic Sci* 53(2): 419–425.

Bush, M. A., R. G. Miller, J. Prutsman-Pfeiffer, and P. J. Bush. 2007. Identification through XRF analysis of dental restorative resin materials: A comprehensive study of non-cremated, cremated, and processed cremated individuals. *J Forensic Sci* 52(1): 157–165.

Caldas, I. C., T. Magalhaes, and A. Afonso. 2007. Establishing identity using cheiloscopy and palatoscopy. *Forensic Sci Int* 165(1): 1–9.

de Villiers, C. J. and V. M. Phillips. 1998. Person identification by means of a single unique dental feature. *J Forensic Odontostomatol* 16(1): 17–19.

Dorion, R. B. J., (ed). 2005. *Bitemark Evidence*. New York: Marcel Dekker.

Duffy, J. B., J. D. Waterfield, and M. F. Skinner. 1991. Isolation of tooth pulp cells for sex chromatin studies in experimental dehydrated and cremated remains. *Forensic Sci Int* 49(2): 127–141.

Hemanth, M., M. Vidya, N. Shetty, and B. V. Karkera. 2010. Identification of individuals using palatal rugae: Computerized method. *J Forensic Dent Sci* 2: 86–90.

Hermanson, A. S., M. A. Bush, R. G. Miller, and P. J. Bush. 2008. Ultraviolet illumination as an adjunctive aid in dental inspection. *J Forensic Sci* 53(2): 408–411.

Herschaft, E. E., M. E. Alder, D. K. Ord, R. D. Rawson, and E. S. Smith. 2006. *Manual of Forensic Odontology, 4th Edition*. Albany, NY: Impress.

Keiser-Nielsen, S. 1980. *Person Identification by Means of the Teeth: A Practical Guide*. Bristol, U.K.: John Wright and Sons Ltd.

Kogon, S. L., K. B. Peterson, J. W. Locke. et al. 1974. A computerized aid to dental identification in mass disasters. *Forensic Sci Int*.

Lorton, L. and W. H. Langley. 1986. Decision making concepts in postmortem identification. *J Forensic Sci* 31(1): 365–378.

Marella, G. L. and P. Rossi. 1999. An approach to person identification by means of dental prostheses in a burnt corpse. *J Forensic Odontostomatol* 17(1): 16–9.

McGivney, J. and R. H. Fixott. 2001. Computer-assisted dental identification. *Dent Clin North Am* 45(2): 309–325.

Muller, M., M. F. Berytrand, G. Quatrehomme, M. Bolla, and J. P. Rocca. 1998. Macroscopic and microscopic aspects of incinerated teeth. *J Forensic Odontostomatol* 16(1): 1–7.

Narang, T., P. Arora, and K. Randhawa. 2011. Cheiloscopy as an aid to Forensic Methodology. *Indian J Comprehensive Dental Care* 1: 57–60.

National Research Council. 2009. Committee on Identifying the Needs of the Forensic Sciences Community. Strengthening forensic science in the United States: A path forward. https://www.ncjrs.gov/pdffiles1/nij/grants/228091.pdf

NIJ. 2006. Lessons learned from 9/11: DNA identification in mass fatality incidents. NCJ 21478. http://www.ncjrs.gov/pdffiles1/nij/214781.pdf

Pretty, I. A., L. D. Addy. 2002. Dental postmortem profiles—Additional findings of interest to investigators. *Sci Justice* 42(2): 65–74.

Pretty, I. A. and D. Sweet. 2001. A look at forensic dentistry—Part 1: The role of teeth in the determination of human identity. *Br Dent J* 190(7): 359–366.

Pretty, I. A., D. A. Webb, and D. Sweet. 2001. The design and assessment of mock mass disasters for dental personnel. *J Forensic Sci* 46(1): 74–79.

Robinson, F. G., F. A. Rueggeberg, and P. E. Lockwood. 1998. Thermal stability of direct dental esthetic restorative materials at elevated temperatures. *J. Forensic Sci* 43(6): 1163–1167.

Senn, D. R. and P. G. Stimson. 2010. *Forensic Dentistry*, 2nd edn. Boca Raton, FL: CRC Press.

Sharma, P., S. Saxena, and V. Rathod. 2009. Cheiloscopy: The study of lip prints in sex identification. *J Forensic Dent Sci* 1: 24–27.

Siegel, R. and N. D. Sperber. 1977. Identification through the computerization of dental records. *J Forensic Sci*. 22: 434–442.

Silver, W. E. and R. R. Souviron. 2009. *Dental Autopsy*, Boca Raton, FL: CRC Press.

Sivapathasundaram, B., P. A. Prakash, and G. Sivakumar. 2001. Lip prints (Cheiloscopy). *Indian J Dent Res* 12: 234–237.

Skinner, E. and R. Phillips. 1967. *The Science of Dental Materials*, 6th edn. Philadelphia, PA: Saunders.

Smith, V. A., A. M. Christensen, and S. W. Myers. The reliability of visually comparing small frontal sinuses. 2010. *J. Forensic Sci* 55(6): 1413–1415.

Spitz, W. U. and D. J. Spitz. 2006. *Spitz and Fisher's Medicolegal Investigation of Death*, 4th edn. Springfield, IL: Charles C. Thomas.

Stuart, L. S. and G. Leonard. 2005. Forensic application of palatal rugae in dental identification. Missouri: *Forensic Examiner* Spring: 44–47.

Sweet, D. 2001. Why a dentist for identification? *Dent Clin North Am* 45(2): 237–251.

Weems, R. 2010. Forensic dental radiography. In *Forensic Dentistry*, 2nd edn., Senn, D. R. and P. G. Stimson, (ed.) pp. 187–203. Boca Raton, FL: CRC Press, Taylor & Francis Group.

Weems, R., J. Broome, T. J. Heaven, and R. Yarbrough. 2004. Radiopacity of endodontic posts in dental identifications. In *Proceedings of the Annual Meeting of the American Academy of Forensic Sciences*, Dallas, TX.

Dental, Oral, and Maxillofacial Radiographic Features of Forensic Interest

5

ROBERT A. DANFORTH
EDWARD E. HERSCHAFT
RICHARD A. WEEMS

Contents

5.1 Introduction 129
5.1.1 Purpose and Scope 129
5.2 Radiographic Techniques Used in Forensic Identification 131
5.2.1 Dental Radiographs 131
5.2.2 Medical Imaging 132
5.3 Classification of Radiographic Features Used in Forensic Identification 132
5.3.1 Dental Structures: Abnormalities 134
5.3.1.1 Coronal, Pulpal, and Root Anomalies 134
5.3.1.2 Variations in Tooth Size 139
5.3.1.3 Variations in Tooth Number 139
5.3.1.4 Variations in Tooth Location and Orientation 141
5.3.2 Osseous Structures: Anatomical 143
5.3.3 Osseous Structures: Abnormalities 147
5.3.3.1 Radiolucent 147
5.3.3.2 Mixed Radiolucent or Radiopaque 149
5.3.3.3 Radiopaque 151
5.3.3.4 Other Radiographic Anomalies 151
5.4 Discussion 154
5.5 Conclusions 154
References 156

5.1 Introduction

5.1.1 Purpose and Scope

Regardless of whether human remains are visually identifiable, decomposed, incinerated, or skeletal, dental evidence is routinely acquired through photographs, radiographs, and dental charting. Jaw resection and preservation of jaw specimens may also be indicated (Herschaft et al., 2007; American Board of Forensic Odontology, Inc., 2011). In the course of comparing antemortem (AM) and postmortem (PM) dental records and radiographs to effect identification, the forensic odontologist relies most frequently on information regarding the dentition and its supporting structures. Similarly, dental records and radiographs are evaluated forensically to identify missing and unknown individuals and victims of a multiple fatality incident.

In order to obtain an accurate PM dental record, the dental charting must be accompanied with a variety of radiographic images since many conditions are only detectable by this technology, that is, root canal therapy, retained roots, impacted teeth, osseous pathology, foreign bodies, etc. Additionally, since recording errors can occur during charting, dental radiographs are often the most objective evidence of the actual dental characteristics (GB Forensic Services, 2012).

Biometric comparable patterns related to the teeth and their associated restorative and anatomical configurations remain the principal means of radiographic assessment in the dental identification process. To accomplish this, as the profession moves toward electronic records, it is important that any radiographs made are properly angulated, well exposed, and well processed. To this end, the American National Standards Institute (ANSI) and the American Dental Association (ADA) Standards Committee on Dental Informatics developed ANSI/ADA Specification 1058 in 2010. This document unifies AM and PM dental, oral, visual image, and radiographic image data descriptors. Thus, the possibility that data which previously could not be electronically or digitally coded and transferred for comparison is reduced or eliminated.

However, the forensic dentist may still encounter technical errors related to exposure and processing of radiographs. Images may be blurred, distorted, or contain insufficient information to differentiate among the teeth, their osseous supportive structures, sinuses, and associated soft tissues of interest. Interpretive problems may also be encountered because of limitations related to the comparable information contained in radiographic images of a specimen. These may include cremation artifact, jaw fragmentation, and PM tooth loss among others. Additional problems are commonly encountered when comparison of edentulous radiographs is required (Richmond and Pretty, 2010). To assist the forensic dentist in evaluating comparable radiographs, digital enhancements of scanned analog dental radiographs or those acquired through direct digital sensors can now be processed at various scanning resolution sizes for evaluation with screen, print, laser print, and photographic images of the radiographs (Weledniger, 2012).

Substantial changes in imaging angles between comparable radiographs can result in variations in the shapes of the teeth and patterns related to other structures (Jain and Chen, 2004). Studies have attempted to address this problem by creating tooth-to-tooth matching programs based on variations in radiographic densities (Fahmy et al., 2005; Nassar and Ammar, 2007). In a pilot study, Flint et al. (2009) also focused on the problem of distortion between comparable radiographs. Using a computer-based method, they determined correct radiographic identifications of selected anatomical areas with a threshold level of similarity of 0.855. At this level, only two false negative and two false-positive identifications were found among 957 analyses (Flint et al., 2009).

The development of digital image processing technology, for example, the Automated Dental Identification System (ADIS) prototype and other biometric methods for dental identification, principally stresses the radiographic comparison of tooth structures (Santoro et al., 2009; ADIS: Automated Dental Identification System, 2011). Van Der Meer et al.

(2010) concluded that "computer-aided dental identification allows for an objective comparison of AM–PM radiographs and can be a useful tool to support a forensic dental identification conclusion" (Van Der Meer et al., 2010).

Results of their study, however, did not find a significant statistical difference between comparisons of root morphology and anatomical patterns using a computer-aided identification system or traditional forensic dental identification methods. In this study, the mean accuracy rate for computer-aided identification was 85.0%, whereas that for traditional methods was 86.0% (Van Der Meer et al., 2010).

Therefore, the forensic dentist must still rely on his or her evaluation of not only the teeth, but also the anatomical, pathological, and artifactual pattern arrangements appearing on these images as well. These may include, but are not limited to, patterns related to the trabeculae, odontogenic and osseous diseases, and dental implants and foreign bodies (Jonasson and Bankvall, 2001; Berketa et al., 2010; Dorion, 2012). The purpose and scope of this chapter is to present a straightforward, effective method of radiographic pattern assessment beyond the comparison of dental restorations, which adheres to the ABFO Identification Guidelines relative to dental radiology, regardless of whether the radiographic comparison is made with images generated by film, digital radiographic (DR), or computed tomographic (CT) devices.

Since the forensic dentist is the ultimate arbiter in deciding which radiographic patterns found in a dental identification radiographic database have comparable significance, this approach to the analysis of routinely observed comparable radiographic patterns requires the dental examiner to only recognize similar patterns rather than determine a definitive diagnosis for them.

5.2 Radiographic Techniques Used in Forensic Identification

5.2.1 Dental Radiographs

Currently, the following radiographic images are routinely found in the records of most dental patients:

1. Intraoral:
   a. *Periapical*—includes a radiographic series of the dentition and supporting structures that can range from 14 to 21 images. These are commonly made on D or F speed film. Digital images produced on a phosphor plate or a scintillation screen sensor paired with a charge-coupled device or complementary metal oxide semiconductor are common alternatives to film technology (Herschaft, 2008).
   b. *Bitewing*—the most common intraoral dental radiograph. Primarily used to observe interproximal decay and alveolar bone levels associated with the maxillary and mandibular posterior teeth.
   c. *Occlusal*—used routinely to outline the maxillary and mandibular dental arch forms in the axial plane. Additionally, this view is helpful in assessing the floor of the mouth or palate for significant extradental radiographic abnormalities. Forensically, the size of this film (57 × 76 mm) lends itself to use in the PM evaluation of resected jaws in the saggital plane.

2. Extraoral:
   a. *Panoramic*—this large image shows most of the lower face including the inferior areas of the orbits, sinus and nasal cavities, maxilla, temporomandibular joints (TMJ), mandible, and hyoid bone and cervical spine.
   b. *Cone Beam Computed Tomography*—Cone beam computed tomography (CBCT) imaging capabilities in dental practice became commercially available in the United States in 2001 (Hatcher, 2010). A caveat related to the forensic comparison of dental radiographs is that this task should generally be performed using similarly made images. With the development of this 3D dental imaging technique, this stipulation has become less problematic since intraoral and panoramic projections needed for comparison may be replicated from CBCT slices of whole volume images. Several studies, involving characterization of dental and anatomical structures, have been performed to evaluate the usefulness of CBCT technology in cases requiring comparison of dental and maxillofacial anatomical structures for human identification (Weems, 2008; Angel et al., 2011; Trochesset et al., 2012). CBCT and cross-sectional radiographic techniques are most commonly used in the diagnostic workup of patients receiving orthodontic, dental implant, and/or surgical therapy (Ganz, 2005; De Vos et al., 2009; Mah et al., 2010). Regarding dental implants, this radiographic procedure has arguably become a component of the standard of care for the determination of their placement.

5.2.2 Medical Imaging

Additionally, a variety of medical radiographs of the head and neck reveal dental and anatomical features of the area. These may include lateral skull, maxillary or frontal sinus, and sagittal radiographic projections. Extra oral structures such as the frontal sinus may be clearly portrayed in these images and are useful when making comparisons (Smith et al., 2010). However, the teeth are often poorly represented because of overlapping, superimposition of the right and left dental arches, and other types of distortion. Therefore, because of these projection variables, caution should be used when comparing dental and medical radiographs.

Using DentaScan dental processing software for CT data, Thali et al. reconstructed reformatted images that were comparable to conventional panoramic dental radiographs. These PM images were compared with conventional AM radiographs, and results indicated that dental identification, or at least, a noninvasive means of dental profiling was possible using this software (Thali et al., 2006).

5.3 Classification of Radiographic Features Used in Forensic Identification

Several radiographic patterns have been classified regarding the teeth and supporting structures (Neville et al., 2008; Stavrianos et al., 2009). McDonald describes two radiographic diagnostic rules that facilitate the description of radiographic patterns. The first is the "5 S Rule" that includes analysis of the Shade, Shape, Site, Size, and Surroundings of the region being evaluated. The "3 D Rule" incorporates Diameter, Density, and Displacement among its assessed criteria (MacDonald, 2011).

Table 5.1 outlines abnormalities related to the size, shape, number, and location of the teeth. Table 5.2 presents a radiographic classification and algorithm for assessing osseous patterns of interest to the forensic odontologist. This method may be applied to the identification of pathologic and nonpathologic findings of the head and neck and can be used to evaluate comparable radiographic patterns of forensic significance. It will be followed throughout this chapter to define the scope of possible descriptors that can be used to report various radiographic findings observed by the forensic dentist.

Table 5.1 Classification of Tooth-Related Radiographic Features Used in Forensic Identification

Dental Structures: Abnormalities			
Coronal, Pulpal, and Root Anomalies	Variations in Tooth Size	Variations in Tooth Number	Variations in Tooth Location and Orientation
Dens in dente	Microdontia	Supernumerary teeth	Transposed teeth
Dilacerated and anomalous root formation	Macrodontia	Fused teeth	Rotated teeth
Enamel hypoplasia		Gemination	Retained deciduous teeth
Sclerotic pulp chambers			Unusual impacted teeth
Pulp stones			
Internal and external root resorption			
Shovel-shaped incisors			
Taurodontism			
Talon cusps			
Iatrogenic and factitial damage			

Table 5.2 Classification of Radiographic Patterns Associated with Osseous Structure and Biological Activity

Radiolucent				Mixed Radiolucent/ Radiopaque		Radiopaque	
Round/Ovoid		Irregular		Defined/Diffuse Area		Mass	
Unilocular (Solitary)	Multilocular (Multiple)	Defined	Diffuse	Solitary/Multiple		Solitary/Multiple	
Distinct Border	Distinct Border	Distinct Border	Indistinct Border	Distinct Borders	Indistinct Borders	Distinct Borders	Indistinct Borders
Sclerotic	"Soap bubble"	"Scalloped"	Poorly defined	"Cotton wool"		Sclerotic mass	
Sharp	"Honeycomb"		"Moth-eaten"	"Ground glass"		"Toothlike"	
"Punched out"				"Orange peel"		"Hair on end"	
				"Mottled"—"snow ball"		"Onion skin"	
				"Targetlike"		"Sunburst"	
Biological activity patterns	Resorption	Expansion		Displacement		Infiltration	
	Tooth roots	Sinus spaces		Teeth		Sinus spaces	
	Cortical surfaces	Cortical surfaces		Cortical surfaces		Floor of mouth	
	Osseous structures	Osseous structures		Mandibular canal		Nerve canals	

Notwithstanding the fact that in 2007, Al-Amad et al. found that inclusion of more comparable dental characteristics provided a greater number of AM/PM matches when evaluating computer identification programs. Simplification of comparable AM/PM dental coding may be justified when attempting to determine a positive identification. This principle is supported by the evolving codes used as dental descriptors in identification database software programs including the WinID3, National Crime Information Center (NCIC), National Missing and Unidentified Persons System (NamUs), Plassdata, and Unified Victim Identification System/UVIS Dental Identification Module (UVIS/UDIM). (Scientific Working Group on Disaster Victim Identification: SWGDVI, 2010.)

5.3.1 Dental Structures: Abnormalities

Abnormalities related to the teeth can be divided into those involving the coronal, pulpal, and root structures, and/or variations in tooth size, number, location, restorative material, and orientation (Thali et al., 2006; Stavrianos, 2009). Figures 5.1 through 5.18 are representative of each of the tooth-related anomalies outlined in Table 5.1.

5.3.1.1 Coronal, Pulpal, and Root Anomalies

Dens in Dente is a tooth anomaly resulting from invagination of the dental papilla during tooth development and appears as a "tooth within a tooth." Opacities consistent with enamel and dentin appear to line the pulp chamber and may extend into the root (dens invaginatus). The maxillary lateral incisors are most commonly affected and bilateral occurrence is common (Figure 5.1).

A dilacerated root may occur following trauma during tooth development. The root shape of an affected deciduous or permanent tooth may appear curved or angled. This malformation is most commonly directed toward the distal and may be the result of prior trauma or presence of an adjacent cyst or intraosseous tumor, which prevents normal root formation (Figure 5.2).

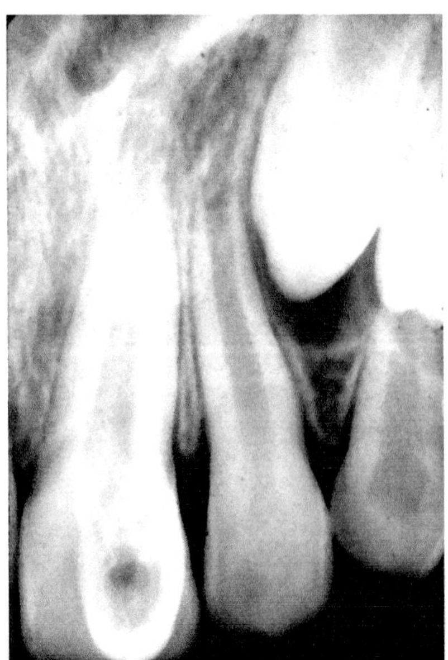

Figure 5.1 Radiograph of dens in dente.

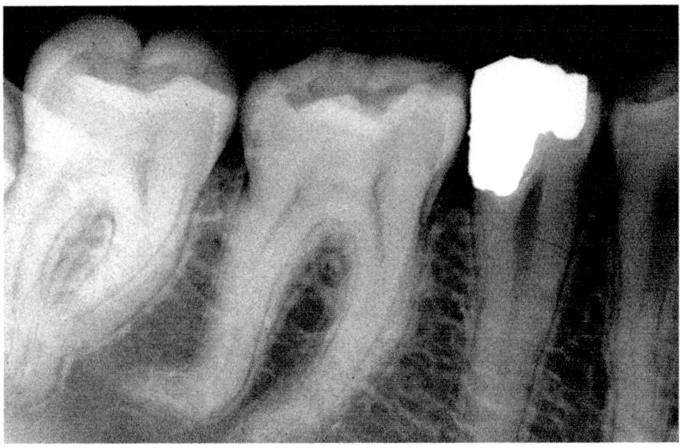

Figure 5.2 Root dilaceration.

Extra roots (supernumerary roots) most commonly affect the mandibular canines, premolars, and third molars. Radiographically, these root structures may not appear as radiopaque as the customary roots associated with the affected tooth as observed in the image of the molars. The transaxial and axial (occlusal) CBCT images can easily demonstrate multiple roots (Figure 5.3).

Enamel hypoplasia can be by systemic or result from local factors including, but not limited to, inherited diseases, infections, chemicals, birth-related trauma, malnutrition and vitamin deficiencies, local acute mechanical trauma, and irradiation. The resulting lesion may range from localized pitting on a single tooth to entire coronal surfaces being misshapen on numerous teeth (Figure 5.4).

Sclerotic pulp chambers and canals are caused by physiologic deposition of secondary dentin and are usually related to aging. It is more pronounced in males and those having a history of diseases in which calcium metabolism can be altered such as arthritis, gout, hypertension, and kidney and gall bladder lithiasis. Tertiary dentin is deposited as a reaction to injury including local acute mechanical trauma, caries development, periodontal disease, and reaction to dental materials. Dentinogenesis imperfecta, represented in the

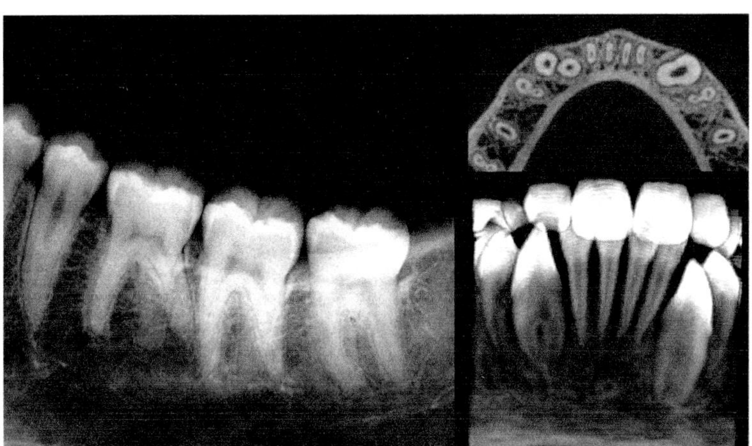

Figure 5.3 Radiographs of third root on mandibular molars and bifurcated root on mandibular cuspid.

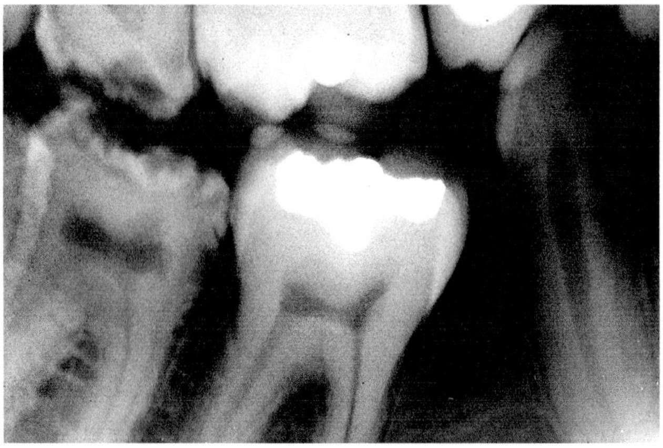

Figure 5.4 Radiograph showing enamel hypoplasia.

complete mouth series, is a genetic defect in dentin formation related to sclerosis of the pulp chambers of all teeth in deciduous and secondary dentitions (Figure 5.5).

Pulp stones are relatively common opaque findings related to long-standing chronic pulpitis and aging. Formed within the coronal pulp, these may be free or attached and most often arise after tooth development (Figure 5.6).

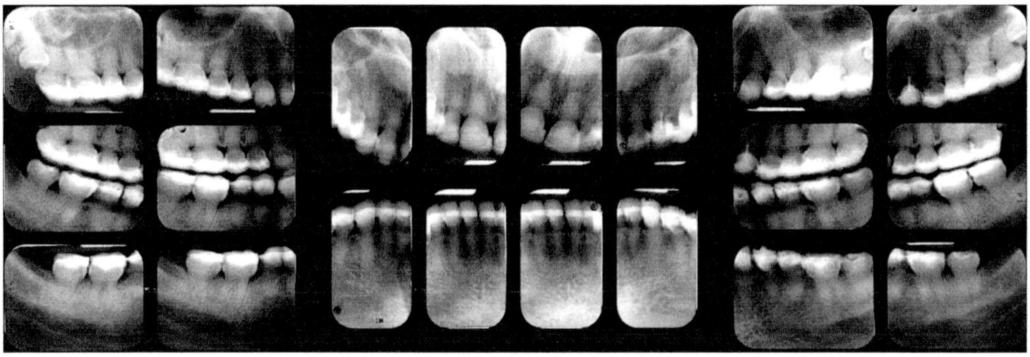

Figure 5.5 Sclerotic pulp chambers seen in dentinogenesis imperfecta.

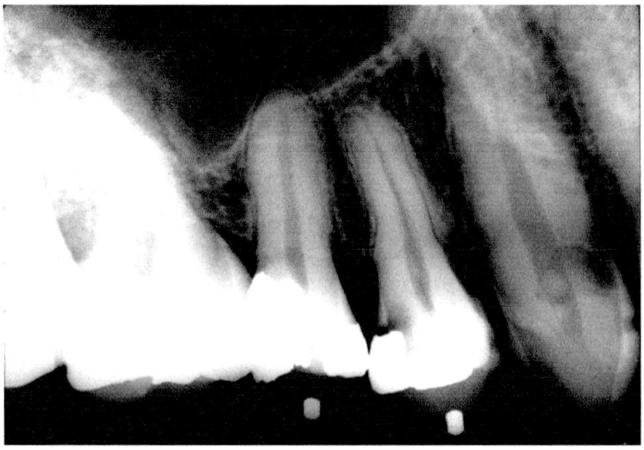

Figure 5.6 Pulp stones in maxillary cuspid.

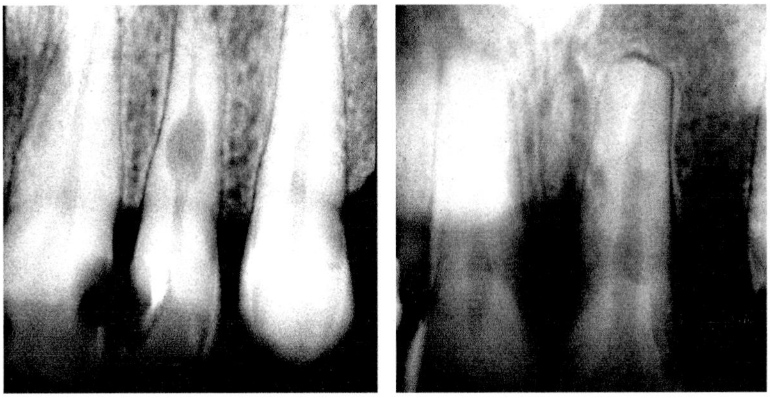

Figure 5.7 Radiographs of internal and external root resorption.

Internal root resorption is associated with pulpal injury and continues until all vital pulp is destroyed. Radiographically, a symmetrical, round, or well-defined elliptical widening of the root canal is observed when the etiology is inflammatory. More commonly, external root resorption presents as an irregular loss of surface root structure resulting from damage to the cells of the periodontal ligament (PDL). Etiology is related to delay in reimplantation of avulsed teeth, distance of tooth movement during orthodontic therapy, and pressure or invasion from an adjacent intraosseous tumor or cyst (Figure 5.7).

Shovel-shaped incisors may indicate certain categories of the race of the victim. Maxillary incisors are most commonly affected and manifest prominent marginal ridges and excessively concave lingual surfaces. The anatomy of an affected tooth may predispose it to the development of a depressed pit and dens invaginatus in the area of the cingulum. Although shovel-shaped incisors are most prominent among those of Asian, Native American, and Inuit heritage, they can also be found in individuals of other ethnicities (Figure 5.8).

Taurodontism results from a developmental anomaly in which the furcation of the roots is displaced toward their apices. This results in teeth with enlarged and elongated

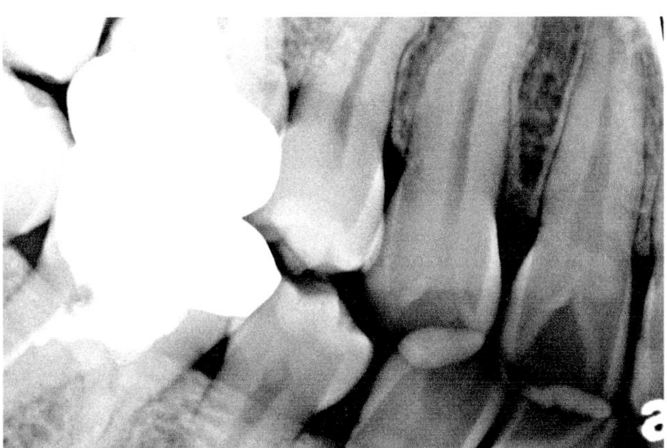

Figure 5.8 Shovel-shaped incisors may indicate race of victim.

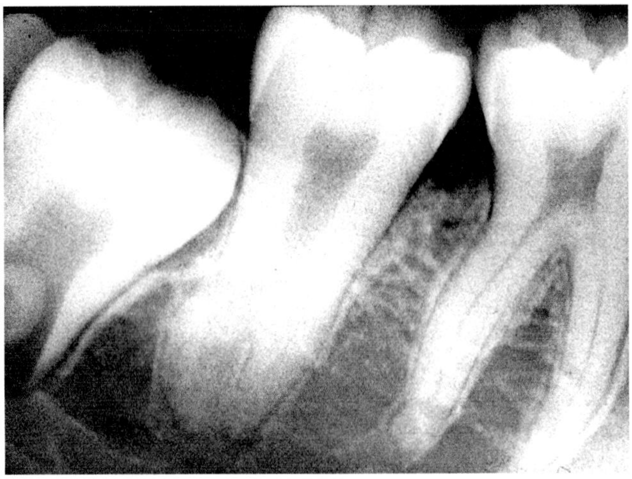

Figure 5.9 Taurodontism.

pulp chambers and foreshortened pulp canals. Taurodontism affecting multiple teeth may also be a component of numerous syndromes including Trisomy 21 (Down), subtypes of amelogenesis imperfecta, and ectodermal dysplasia (Figure 5.9).

The majority of accessory cusps (talon cusps) are found on permanent maxillary central and lateral incisors primarily among those of Asian, Native American, Inuit, and Arab heritage. Palatal surfaces are most commonly affected. In radiographic images, the enamel and dentin of the cusp appear superimposed over the center of the crown, and it is not unusual to observe a pulp chamber in the cusp (Figure 5.10).

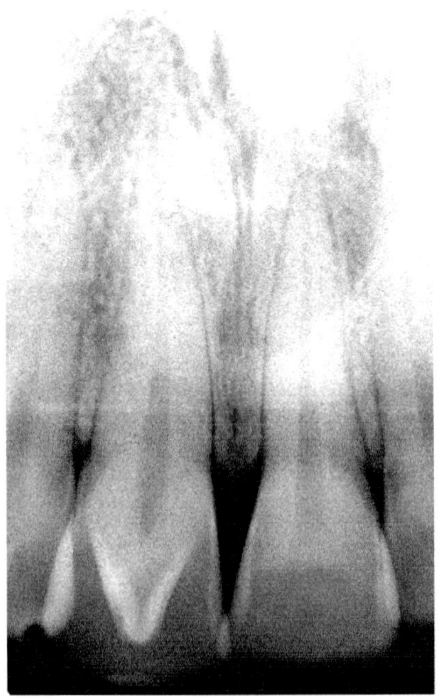

Figure 5.10 Talon cusps or accessary cusp. (Image courtesy of Dr. Brad W. Neville, Medical University of South Carolina College of Dental Medicine, Charleston, SC.)

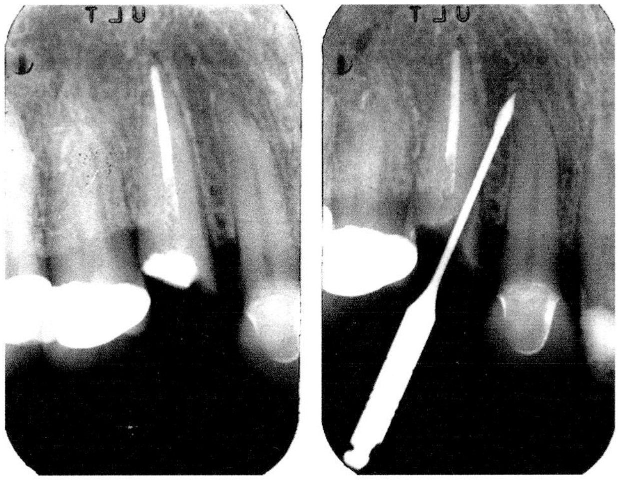

Figure 5.11 Iatrogenic damage that occurred during supportive post preparation.

Iatrogenesis is an unplanned adverse effect or complication resulting from the treatment or advice of a healthcare provider. Dental radiographs may reveal such iatrogenic findings as tooth perforations, retention of broken instruments, postsurgical retained fractured roots, and antral communications. Factitial injuries are self-induced and may be observed radiographically as loss of tooth structure secondary to attrition, abrasion, abfraction, or erosion. Dental mutilation also continues to be practiced among some African, Asian, and South American societies. Emigrants from locations where this is performed may eventually receive dental care in nations where these findings can be documented on radiographs (Figure 5.11).

5.3.1.2 Variations in Tooth Size

Microdontia pertains to teeth that are physically smaller than normal and may include supernumerary teeth. Isolated microdontia affects the maxillary lateral incisor (peg shaped lateral) and third molar most commonly. Generalized microdontia may be associated with Down syndrome, other rare hereditary disorders, and pituitary dwarfism. Macrodontia refers to teeth that are physically larger than normal with the exception of those exhibiting gemination or fusion. Bilateral involvement of incisors, canines, second premolars, and third molars occurs most commonly. Pituitary gigantism and the XXY male genotype have been associated with macrodontia involving the collective dentition (Figure 5.12).

5.3.1.3 Variations in Tooth Number

Anomalies in tooth number most commonly involve incisors and canines in both the primary and secondary dentitions. Gemination affects the primary maxillary dentition more often, resulting in a single anomalous large tooth within a dental arch containing a normal number of teeth. Fusion is more commonly observed in mandibular teeth and results in a single anomalous large tooth within a dental arch containing one less than the normal number of teeth. Radiographically, it is often difficult to differentiate between these anomalies of tooth development since both may be associated with separate or fused pulp chambers and root canals (Figure 5.13).

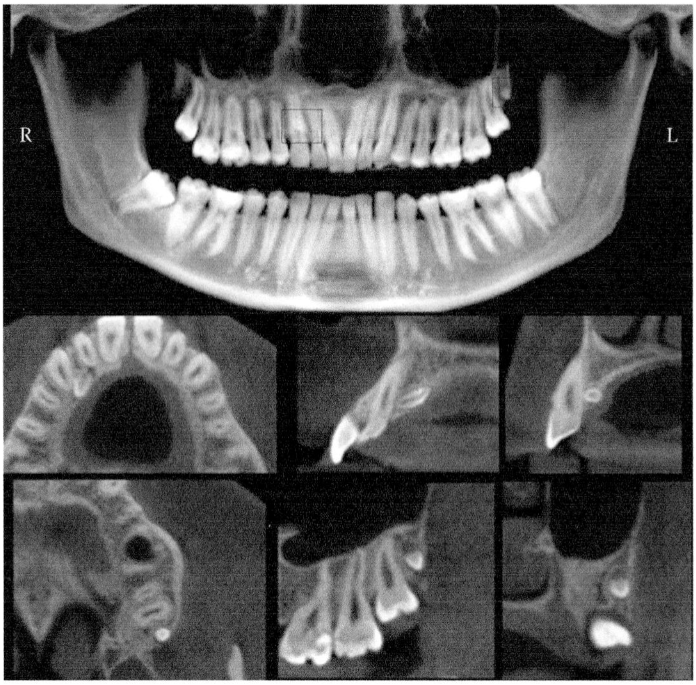

Figure 5.12 Radiographic CBCT views of microdonts in area of maxillary right cuspid and maxillary left tuberosity.

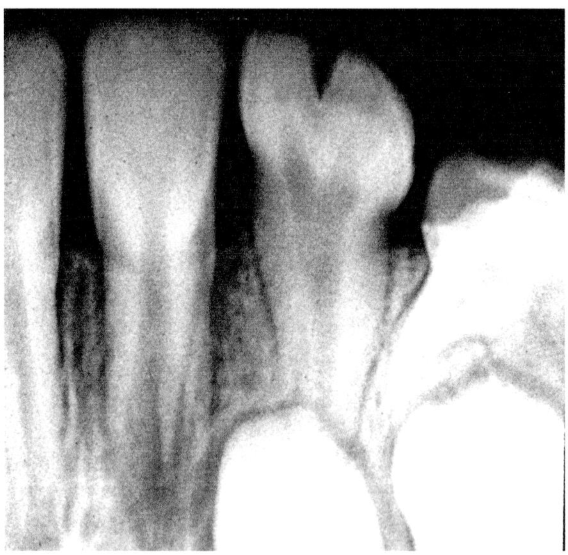

Figure 5.13 Gemination/fusion.

Hyperdontia, more often referred to as supernumerary teeth, refers to the development of more than the normal compliment of teeth. Complex genetic and environmental factors influence tooth development. Syndromes in which supernumerary teeth are a factor include cleidocranial dysplasia, Crouzon, Down, Gardner, and Sturge Weber, among others. Hyperdontia involving a single tooth is most common in the area of the maxillary incisors (mesiodens). Maxillary and mandibular fourth molars are the next most

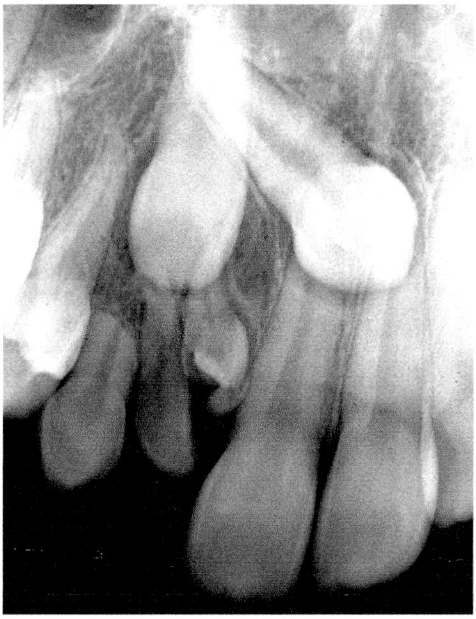

Figure 5.14 Image of supernumerary teeth.

commonly detected. However, numerous supernumerary teeth most commonly occur in the mandibular premolar area in nonsyndromic situations (Figure 5.14).

5.3.1.4 Variations in Tooth Location and Orientation

Transposed teeth occur when normal teeth erupt into an incorrect location within the dental arch. This is often related to hypodontia, which is the development of less than the normal compliment of teeth. The maxillary canines and first premolars are most often involved (Figure 5.15).

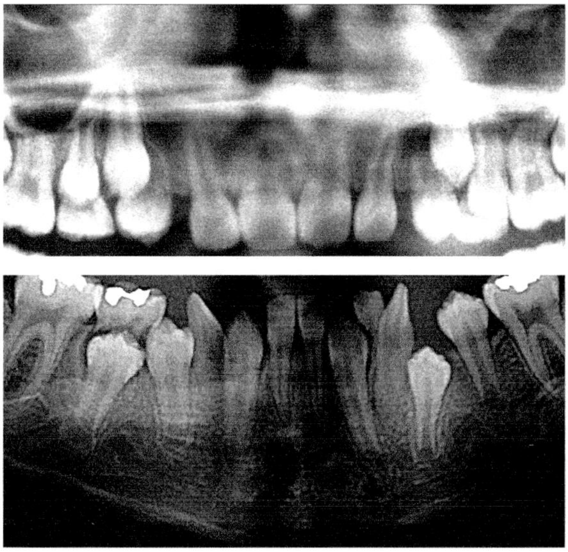

Figure 5.15 Radiographic images of transposed teeth. (Images courtesy of Dr. James Mah, UNLV School of Dental Medicine, Las Vegas, NV.)

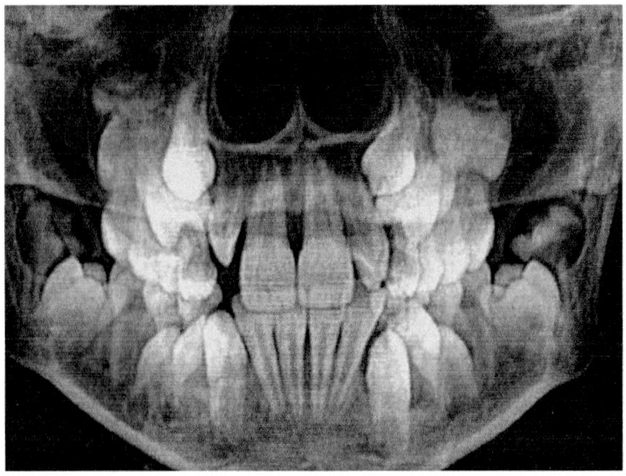

Figure 5.16 Rotated lateral incisors.

A rotated tooth occurs when the long axis of one or more teeth is or are not aligned properly in relation to the adjacent and opposing teeth. The dentition involved is turned and displaced from its normal position in its respective dental arch. An altered contact is created with adjacent teeth providing a location for subsequent development of caries and eventual gingival and periodontal damage. Radiographs will exhibit these findings associated with involved teeth (Figure 5.16).

Retained deciduous teeth are a relatively common finding in adults. Termination of eruption after emergence is referred to as ankylosis, which most commonly affects the posterior mandibular primary dentition. Genetic and numerous environmental factors may predispose an individual to this condition. Radiographically, affected teeth are below the occlusal plane and may exhibit an absence of the PDL space. Additionally, associated teeth in the permanent dentition may be congenitally missing. Most commonly affected are mandibular second premolars, maxillary second premolars, maxillary lateral incisors, and mandibular central incisors (Figure 5.17).

Termination of eruption before emergence is referred to as impaction, which most commonly affects the following teeth in the permanent dentition: mandibular third molars,

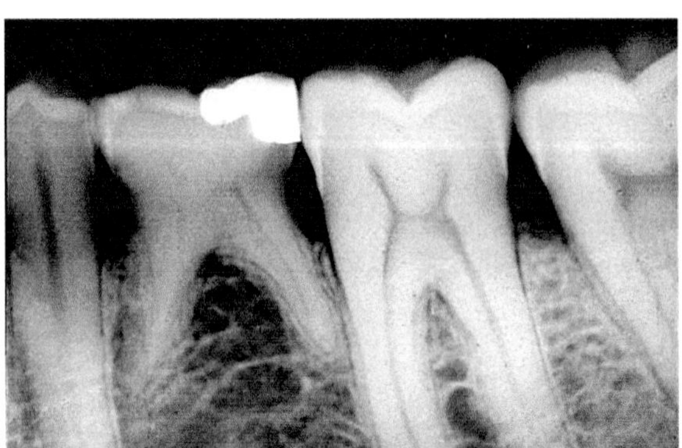

Figure 5.17 Retained deciduous tooth with permanent tooth congenitally missing.

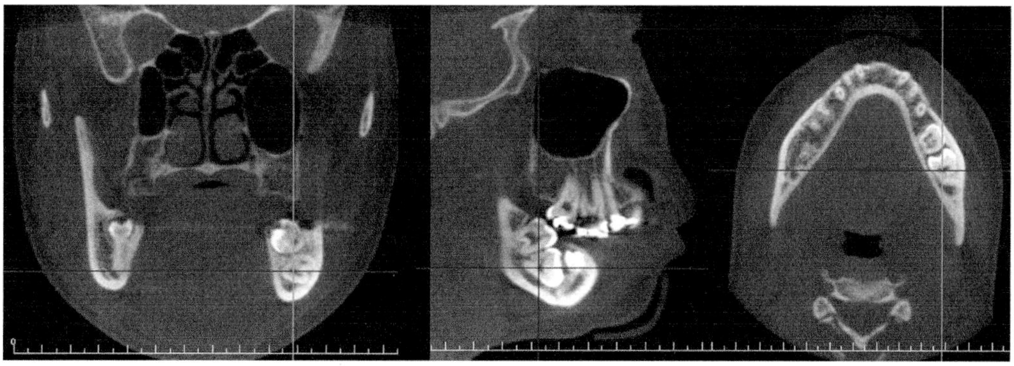

Figure 5.18 Unusual impacted teeth.

maxillary third molars and canines, mandibular premolars and canines, maxillary premolars, central incisors and lateral incisors, and mandibular second molars (Figure 5.18).

5.3.2 Osseous Structures: Anatomical

Evaluation of the anatomical osseous pattern arrangements appearing on comparable dental radiographs may include, but are not limited to, those related to the maxillary and other sinuses, nasal cavity, orbits, neural and vascular structures, stylohyoid process, hyoid bone, thyroid cartilage, TMJ structures, anterior nasal spine, incisive canals, and other osseous landmarks. Figures 5.19 through 5.24 provide radiographic examples of a sample of the osseous anatomical structures listed earlier.

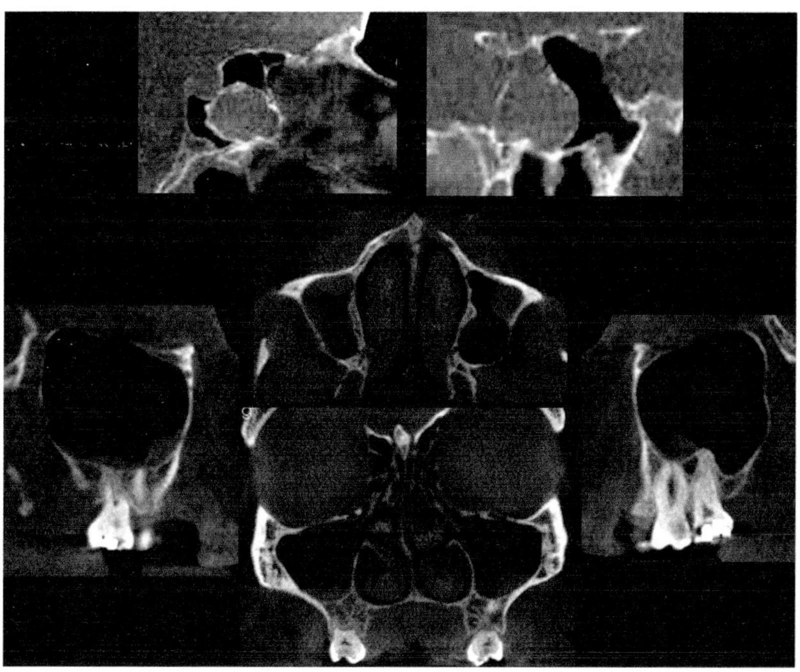

Figure 5.19 CBCT of nasal cavity, maxillary sinuses, and paranasal sinuses showing soft tissue polyps.

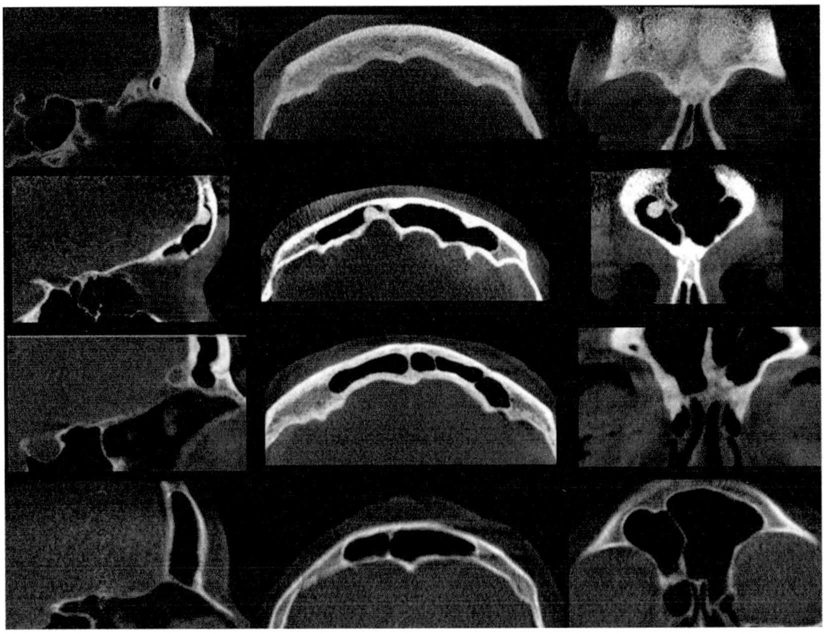

Figure 5.20 CBCT showing calcification in sagittal, axial, and coronal view of frontal sinuses.

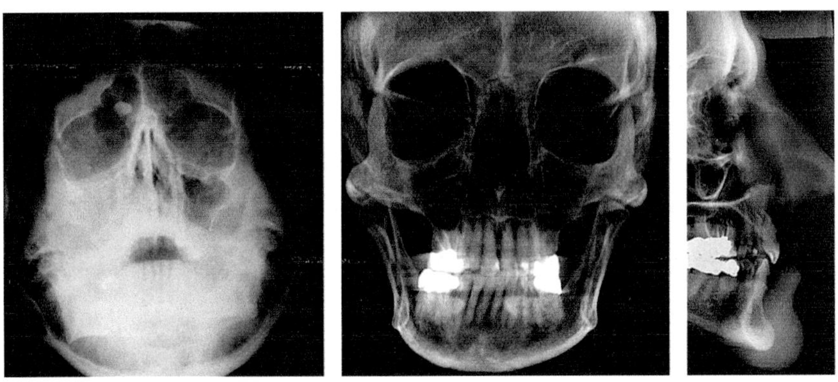

Figure 5.21 Various radiographic projections of maxillofacial structures including orbits and frontal sinuses.

The following radiographic facial structures may provide the forensic dentist with comparable radiographic information that compliments findings of a dental nature:

- Maxillary and paranasal sinuses, nasal cavity, and orbits
  Borders of the frontal, sigmoidal, ethmoidal, and maxillary sinuses visualized on medical and dental radiographs present patterns that are "scalloped" and may be unique (Figures 5.19 and 5.20). These structures may be compared for symmetry and similar pneumatization. Typically, the frontal sinus is septate and partitioned into chambers. However, occasionally, it may be totally opacified. The sinuses may present with abnormal findings suggestive of fluid (sinusitis), lobulated mucosal thickenings (mucositis), and dome-shaped mucosal opacities (antral pseudocysts).

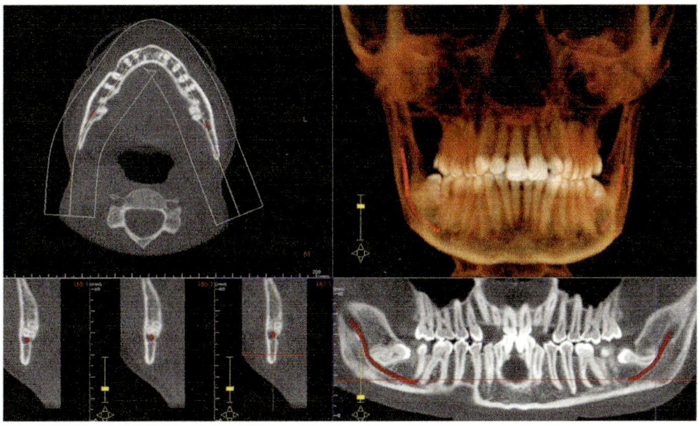

Figure 5.22 CBCT images of impacted third molars and inferior alveolar nerve.

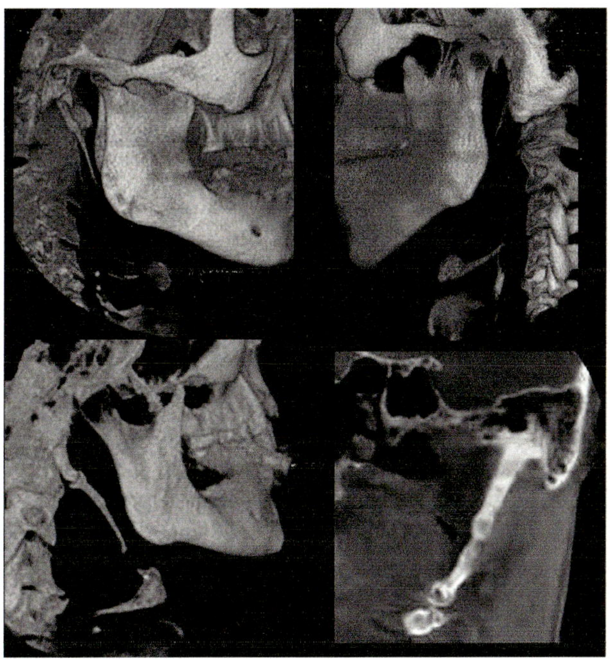

Figure 5.23 CBCT 3D renderings including hyoid bone and calcified stylohyoid ligament.

Calcifications (frontal sinus or antral lithiasis) may also occur. CBCT analysis allows for the evaluation of the patency of the ostia of the maxillary sinuses. Relative to the nasal fossae, the middle turbinates may exhibit air space enlargement (concha bullosa), which can result in nasal septal deviation. It may eventually be proven that the intricate patterns of the nasal cavity and paranasal sinuses in multiplaner CBCT images are unique among individuals to the extent of being useful in victim identification (Weems, 2011).

The orbits are thin-walled cone-shaped cavities composed of osseous borders forming a floor (roof of the maxillary sinus), roof, and medial and lateral surfaces. Normally, with these orbital bones, there is similar architecture,

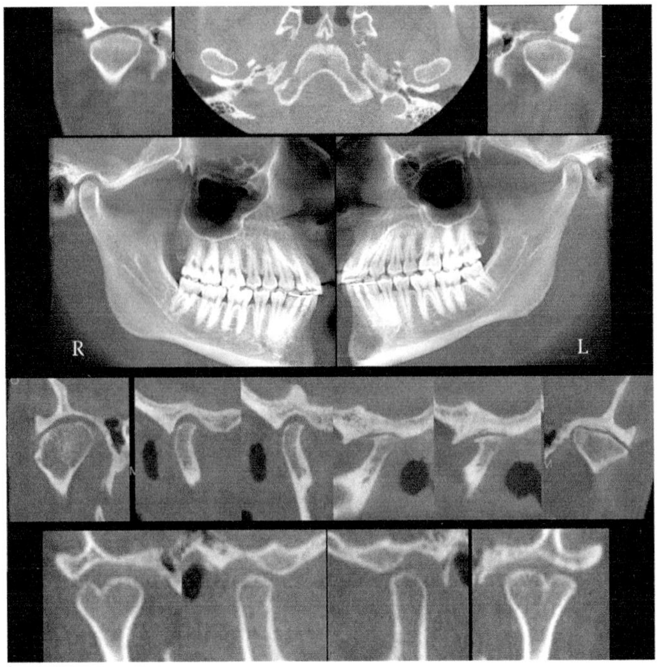

Figure 5.24 CBCT frontal and lateral TMJ series.

equal pneumatization, and symmetry between the orbits. A majority of facial fractures involve the orbits, and radiographic findings associated with blowout fractures of the orbital floor may include displacement of this border (Figure 5.21).

- Neural and vascular structures
  Vertically impacted mandibular third molars and intrabony expansile pathologic processes may be associated with downward or lateral deflection of the mandibular canals. Such radiographic features indicate an etiology that is proximate to the nerve canal. Anatomical anomalies may also contribute to variations in the path of this structure (Figure 5.22).
- Styloid process, stylohyoid ligament, and hyoid bone
  Elongation of the styloid process as well as calcification of its soft tissue ligament may occur secondary to oropharyngeal inflammation. Following a history of tonsillectomy, this condition is referred to as Eagle's syndrome. Additionally, calcification of the posterior horns of the hyoid bone or calcified posterior horns of the thyroid gland may be misidentified as calcified carotid artery atheromas (CCAA) in panoramic and CBCT radiographic projections (Figure 5.23).
- TMJ
  Configurations of condylar and articular surfaces and condylar-fossae positional relationships may be illustrated radiographically with CBCT. Figure 5.24 illustrates axial, coronal, and parasagittal CBCT projections of a normal joint in the upper two segments. The two lower segments demonstrate a flattening of the condylar articular surface, and compression of the joint spaces is also consistent with degenerative joint disease.

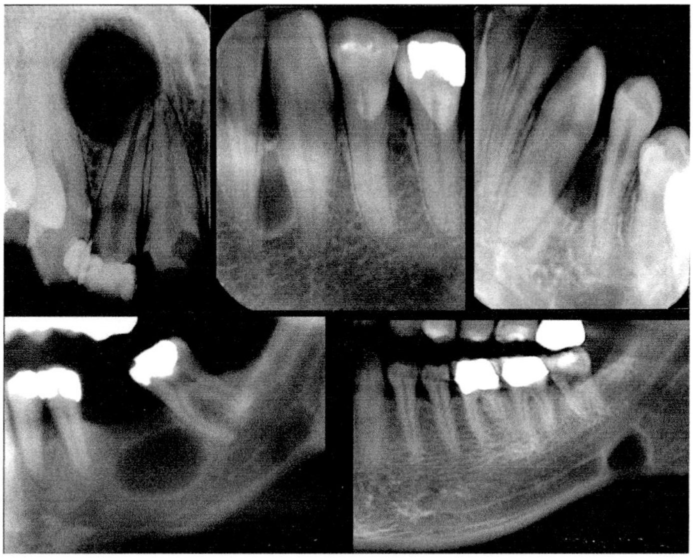

Figure 5.25 Lesions with round, ovoid, unilocular, and distinct borders.

5.3.3 Osseous Structures: Abnormalities

When comparing forensic dental radiographic material to determine an individual's identification, the examiner is not required to make a definitive pathologic or structural diagnosis of radiographic patterns observed. Therefore, the algorithm for radiographic pattern analysis presented in this section is simply based on terms related to an area's density, shape, and the likely biological activity required to cause patterns consistent with resorption, expansion, displacement, and infiltration (Table 5.2). Figures 5.25 through 5.33 are representative of each of the osseous abnormalities outlined in Table 5.2.

5.3.3.1 Radiolucent

Sharp borders are associated with vascular and neural foramina and a variety of developmental, inflammatory, and odontogenic cysts. Additionally, the cystic conditions can lead to resorption of tooth roots and cortical surfaces, expansion of cortices, or displacement of teeth and the mandibular canal. The submandibular salivary gland depression consistently appears inferior to the mandibular canal. Punched out patterns can be found in the calvarium and jaws of adults with multiple myeloma and children with Langerhans cell disease (Figure 5.25).

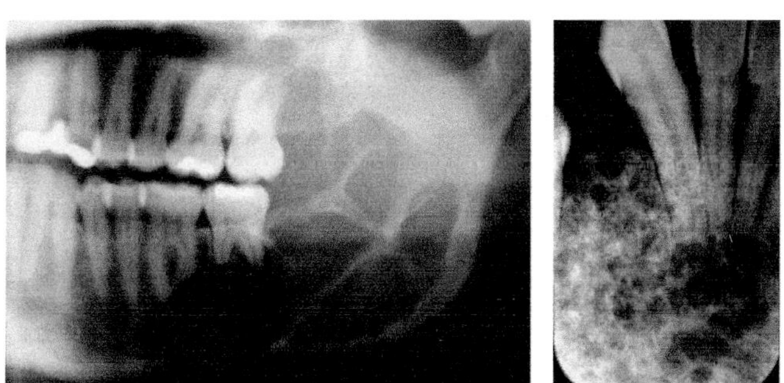

Figure 5.26 Lesions with round, ovoid, multilocular, and distinct borders.

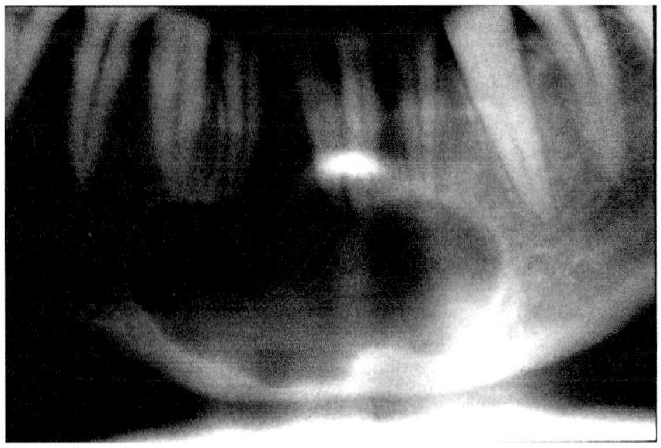

Figure 5.27 Lesion with irregular, defined, and distinct border.

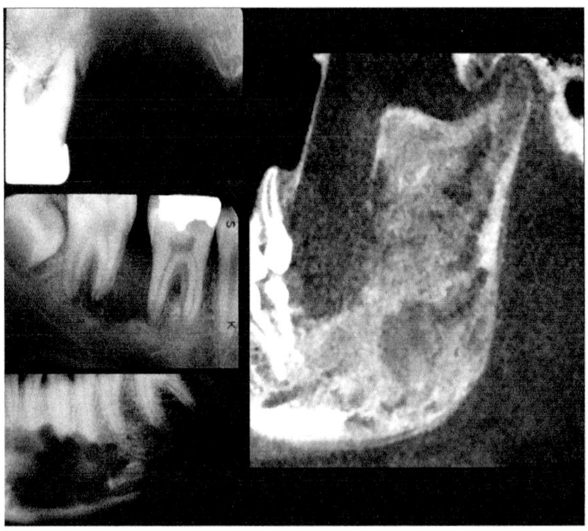

Figure 5.28 Lesions with irregular, diffuse, and indistinct borders.

Examples of soap bubble patterns include the ameloblastoma, Pindborg tumor, and keratocystic odontogenic tumor. These conditions can lead to resorption of tooth roots and cortical surfaces, expansion of cortices, or displacement of teeth and the mandibular canal.

A honeycomb appearance is often associated with radiographic images of the adenomatoid odontogenic tumor, central hemangioma, and odontogenic myxoma (Figure 5.26).

Radiographically, scalloped margins are observed in the aneurysmal bone cyst, traumatic bone cyst, central giant cell granuloma, and central hemangioma in addition to the frontal and maxillary sinuses. Among the traumatic/vascular lesions listed earlier, the teeth do not manifest root resorption or displacement. They appear to be suspended within the radiolucent cavity produced by the pathology (Figure 5.27).

Poorly defined or "moth-eaten" radiographic findings are generally associated with primary and metastatic malignancy, osteonecrotic bone pathology, and osteomyelitis. Radiographs with these patterns may exhibit infiltration of the maxillary sinus space or may demonstrate erosion of osseous cortical surfaces and irregular periradicular medullary bone loss. Tooth root structures are also commonly resorbed. A classic "moth-eaten" radiographic pattern is seen in the right CBCT image associated with the mandibular ramus (Figure 5.28).

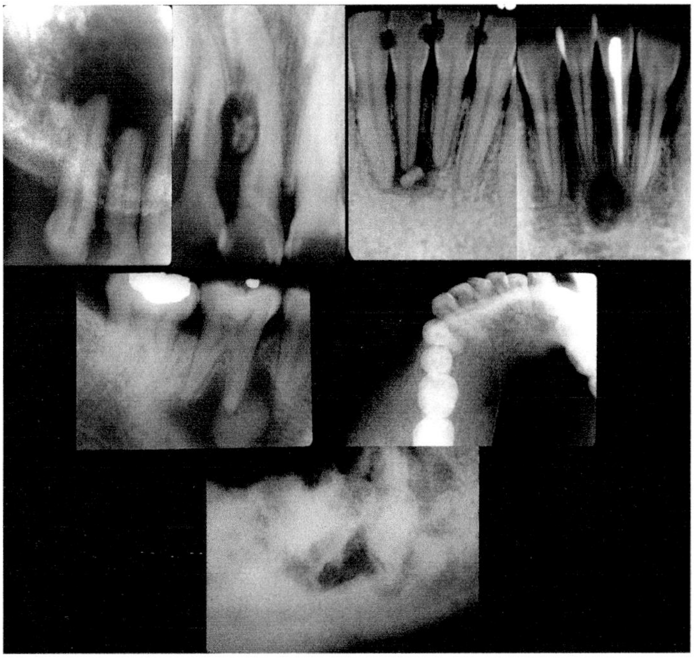

Figure 5.29 Lesions with mixed opacity.

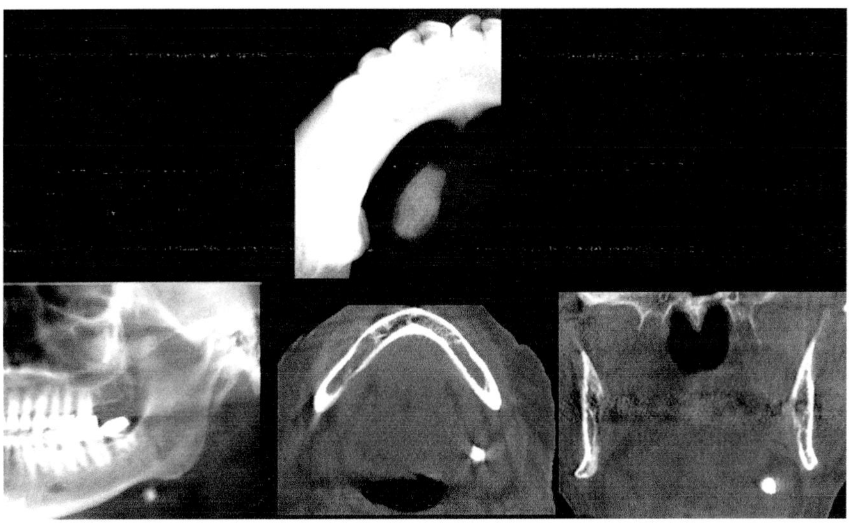

Figure 5.30 CBCT and occlusal radiographs showing a sialolith on the patient's left side.

5.3.3.2 *Mixed Radiolucent or Radiopaque*

Examples of these radiographic patterns and their associated pathologic etiologies include maturing periapical cemento-osseous dysplasia, Pindborg tumor, osteonecrosis and osteomyelitis, dentigerous cyst, adenomatoid odontogenic tumor, and osseous dysplasia. Several unique labels have been applied to a number of solitary or multiple masses with indistinct radiographic borders. These include "cotton wool" (Paget's disease of bone, sclerosing osteitis), "ground glass," and "orange peel" (fibrous dysplasia) (Figure 5.29).

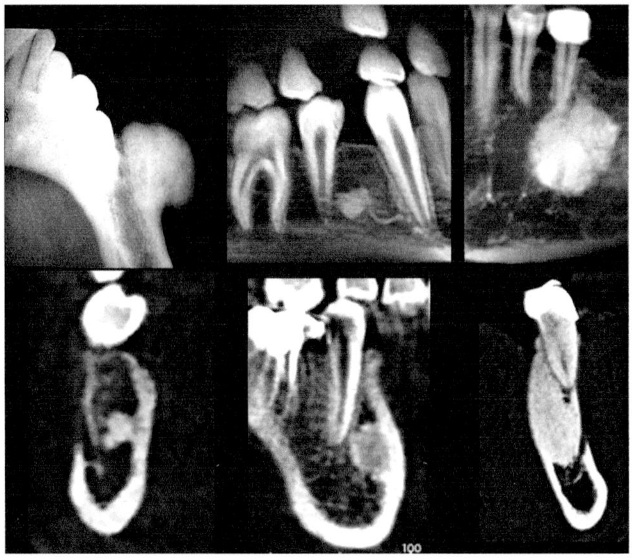

Figure 5.31 Occlusal and CBCT demonstrating distinct opaque lesions.

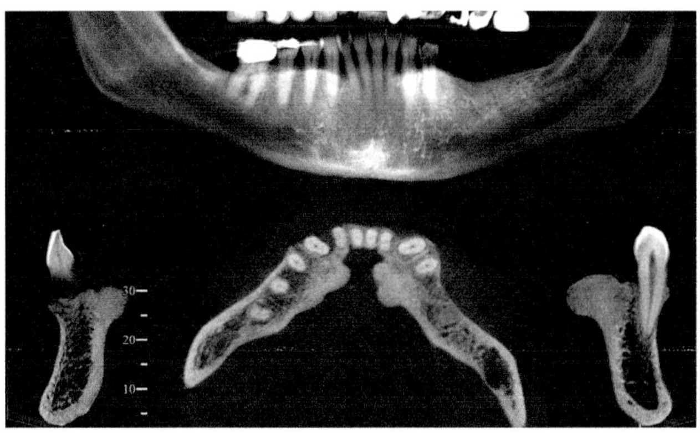

Figure 5.32 CBCT images demonstrating mandibular tori.

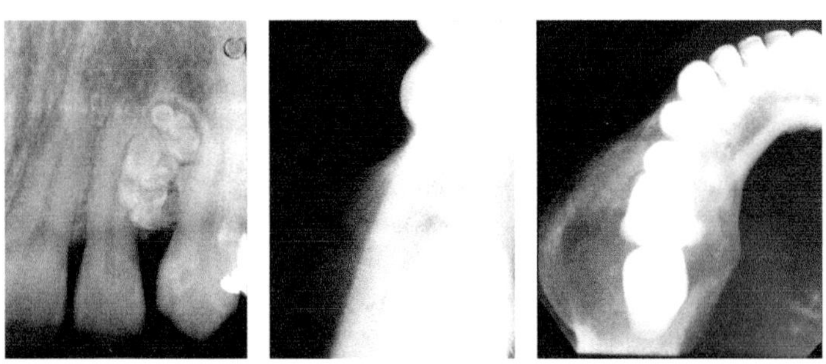

Figure 5.33 Images showing "tooth-like," "sunburst," and "expansive" lesions.

5.3.3.3 *Radiopaque*

Examples of these radiographic sclerotic masses and their associated pathologic etiologies include osteosclerosis/bone scar, tori/enostoses/exostoses, end-stage periapical cemento-osseous dysplasia, and sialoliths (Figures 5.30 through 5.32).

Examples of some of these radiographic sclerotic masses and their associated pathologic etiologies include end-stage periapical cemento-osseous dysplasia, odontoma, osteosarcoma, and metastases. A variety of unique labels have been applied to a number of solitary or multiple masses with indistinct radiographic borders including "tooth-like" (compound composite odontoma) and "sunburst" (osteosarcoma, metastases) (Figure 5.33).

5.3.3.4 *Other Radiographic Anomalies*

Metallic foreign bodies, including but not limited to, amalgam fragments, remnants of ballistic projectiles, surgical wires and screws, endodontic files, broken needles and burs, and alveolar implants may have characteristic dentally related features that make possible their radiographic identification. These materials may also provide significant comparable radiographic information of forensic value. Radiopaque foreign material may be observed on radiographs following an iatrogenic injuries or standard dental and medical treatment. Figure 5.34 shows a BB projectile observed in the left image and amalgam particles seen in the right image. Opaque particulate bone grafting material is visualized in the center image. Additionally, radiographic contrast media, gutta percha points, and various dental cements and endodontic sealers are also radiopaque. Trauma from a self-inflicted shotgun wound results in a panoramic image showing remaining shotgun pellets, surgical bony fixation, and vascular clips (Figure 5.35).

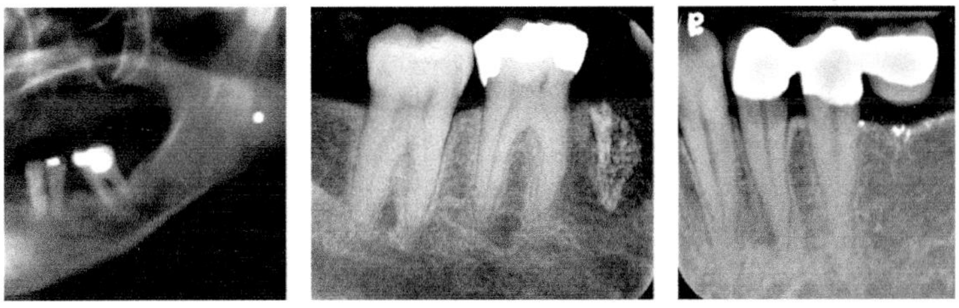

Figure 5.34 Radiographs illustrating various examples of foreign bodies.

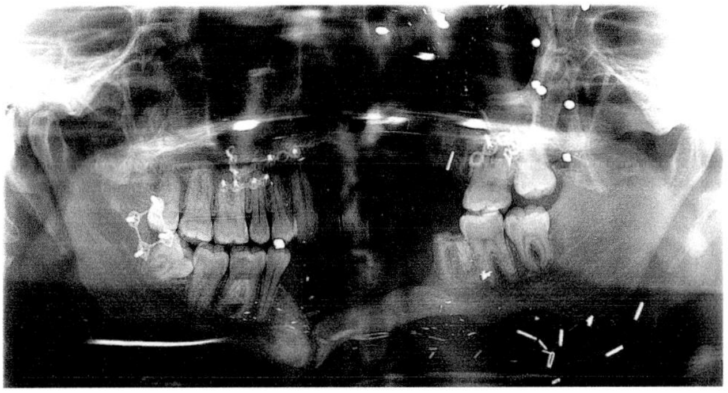

Figure 5.35 Panoramic radiograph showing foreign bodies resultant of a shotgun injury.

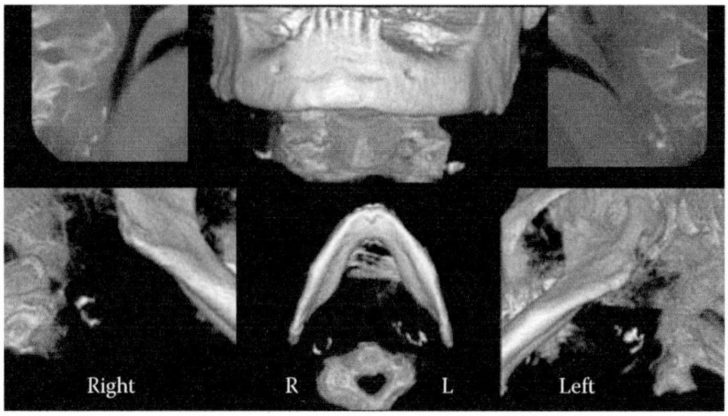

Figure 5.36 Carotid artery calcifications (CCAA) seen in CBCT 3D renderings.

The most common cervical soft tissue calcifications observed on panoramic and CBCT images include CCAA, calcification of the triticeous cartilage, and tonsillar calcifications (Khan et al., 2008). CCAA lesions routinely appear as bilateral linear and curvilinear hyperdense masses located at the level of the larynx approximately 1.5–2.5 cm posterior and inferior to the mandibular angle. They are associated with the intervertebral space above or below C3 and C4 and are positioned lateral to the lower pharyngeal airway and cervical spine (Figure 5.36).

The forensic dentist, when reviewing comparable panoramic radiographic images, should have an understanding of the anatomic positions in which CCAA lesions appear. Additionally, CBCT imaging technology provides the examiner the opportunity to better visualize these radiopacities especially by reviewing the reconstructed 3D model views. Other anatomic and pathologic hyperdensities such as tonsilloliths and other calcifications involving the stylohyoid ligament and lateral portions of the hyoid bone must be differentiated from CCAA (Figure 5.37). In panoramic images, CCAA lesions are found diagonally distal and below the angle of the mandible within the soft tissue between the vertebrae and the airspace. This corresponds anatomically to the bifurcation of the carotid artery where these calcifications most often occur.

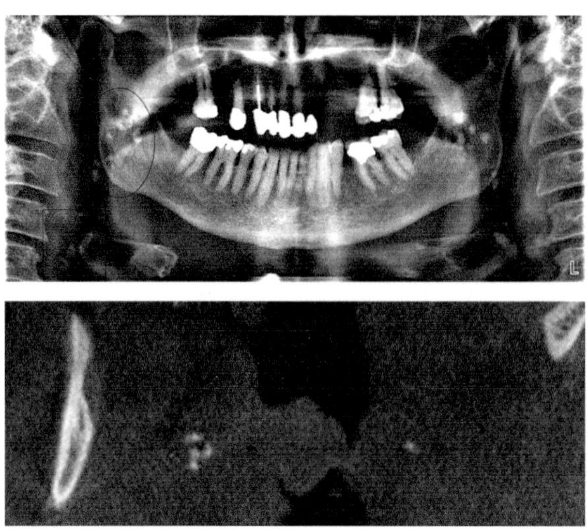

Figure 5.37 Panoramic and coronal images demonstrating tonsillar and CCAA calcifications.

Table 5.3 Radiopaque Devices Which May Be Seen in Dental and Medical Radiographic Images of the Head, Neck, and Spine

Head		
Cerebrospinal fluid shunts	Subdural drainage catheters	Coils
Balloons	Adhesives	Aneurysm clips
Radiation therapy catheters	Intracranial balloons for drug installation	Cochlear implants
Orbital prostheses	Lacrimal duct stents	
Mandible and maxilla		
Dental implant devices	Facial implant devices	Dental restorative materials
Neck and cervical spine		
Cervical plates	Gastric tubes	Tracheal tubes

Numerous medical treatment devices may be seen in dental and medical radiographic images of the head, neck, and spine (Hunter et al, 2004). Many of these are presented in Table 5.3.

Danforth, R.A., and E.E. Herschaft presented a case in which CBCT images exhibited "bilateral, somewhat symmetrical, hyperdense cervical objects having ring configurations in the axial plane." The objects formed vertically aligned "meshlike" cylindrical patterns in the coronal and bilateral saggital projections. These findings were consistent with the radiographic appearance of carotid artery stents. Additionally, small rectangular hyperopaque objects bordering the stents were interpreted as patterns suggestive of surgical fixation clips (Figure 5.38). These CBCT radiographic findings were consistent with the patient's medical history of CCAA and bilateral carotid artery stent placement (Danforth and Herschaft, 2012).

It is essential that dentists have an understanding of the radiographic relationships and anatomic positions of other hyperdensities that resemble CCAA in all three orthogonal projections of CBCT radiographs (Scarfe and Farman, 2010). As indicated in the previously reported case, for example, with this knowledge, the forensic dentist could more astutely

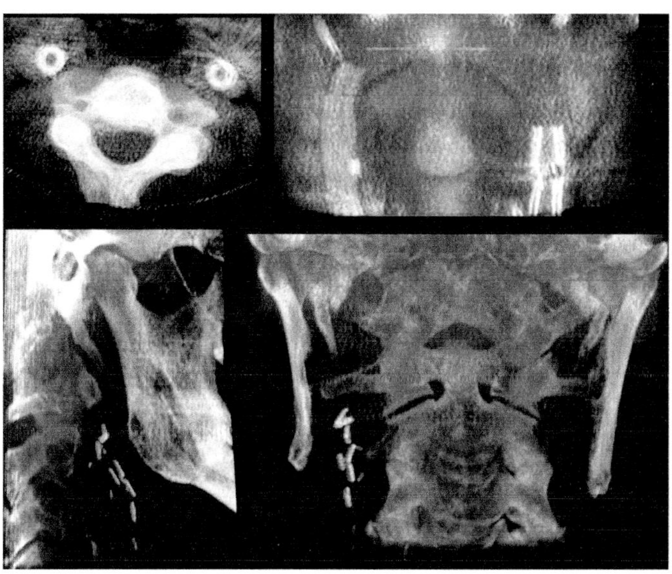

Figure 5.38 Carotid artery stents and surgical fixation clips.

evaluate submitted CBCT images suggestive of CCAA and a medical history of surgical treatment for atherosclerosis with comparable radiographs and PM information acquired from the putative victim.

5.4 Discussion

Dental radiographic images generated by film, DR, cone beam CT, or medical radiographic images of the head and neck commonly exhibit the various radiopacities, radiolucencies, and mixed patterns described previously in Table 5.2. These may appear to be associated with the dentition, manifest as residual patterns upon removal of teeth, or be found in conjunction with nondental or uncommon etiologies. When comparing these radiographs as a component of a forensic dental identification, characteristics unique to a specific jaw specimen may also be associated with the diagnostic features described for some oral and maxillofacial pathology listed in Table 5.4.

For example, radiopaque features, such as retained roots, tori, and exostoses, tend to be in projected positions associated with the areas of the dentition (alveolar ridges). Osteosclerosis, enostoses, bone scars, and condensing osteitis are more likely to be located within the bone in the periapical to inferior mandibular border regions. These latter radiopacities tend to remain in the bone even after an associated tooth is removed.

The forensic dental investigator must also be aware that foreign material may be located randomly and in unusual areas within the jaws or head and neck. Thus, comparing all of these jaw specimen radiographic features with radiographic findings and medical historical information of putative casualties can be instrumental in securing identification or at least narrowing the range of possible matches among the victims.

5.5 Conclusions

Dental radiographic findings beyond those related to dental restorations alone can be essential in determining definitive dental identifications. Also, emerging radiological technologies provide the twenty-first century forensic dentist with the additional ability of evaluating 3D image information related to structures in the head and neck. By furnishing expanded dental and maxillofacial information for analysis, the multiplanar imaging capability provided by these modalities can often generate views that supplement or exceed the traditional information afforded by single plane radiographs. CBCT technology is becoming more widely used as a component of the dental diagnostic evaluation of patients whose treatment requires oral surgical, orthodontic, TMJ, and dental implant procedures. Thus, in the future, it is likely that these images will become more commonly available to the forensic dentist who requests dental records for comparison.

Therefore, the forensic dentist should attain a level of competency in the interpretation and comparison of radiographic patterns generated by a growing variety of imaging techniques in order to facilitate a successful dental identification through radiographic evaluation. The images and tables presented in this chapter are intended to serve as a reference resource for the reader to provide insight into the analysis of comparable dental, cranial, and cervical radiographic findings of forensic interest.

Table 5.4 Classification of Radiographic Patterns Associated with Some Diagnostic Entities

Radiolucent				Mixed Radiolucent/Radiopaque		Radiopaque	
Round/Ovoid		Irregular		Defined/Diffuse Area		Mass	
Unilocular (Solitary)	Multilocular (Multiple)	Defined	Diffuse	Solitary/Multiple		Solitary/Multiple	
Distinct Border	Distinct Border	Distinct Border	Indistinct Border	Distinct Borders	Indistinct Borders	Distinct Borders	Indistinct Borders
Foramina *Cysts*: Apical Periodontal Lateral Periodontal Residual Primordial Developmental Periapical Granuloma Submandibular Salivary Gland Depression *(Inferior to Mandibular Canal)* Multiple Myeloma Langerhans Cell disease	Odontogenic Keratocyst Ameloblastoma Pindborg Tumor Adenomatoid Odontogenic Tumor	Maxillary Sinus *Cysts*: Aneurismal Bone Traumatic Bone Central Giant Cell Granuloma Central Hemangioma	Periapical Cemento-osseous Dysplasia Odontogenic Myxoma *Malignancy*: Squamous Cell Carcinoma Adeno Ca Lymphoma Leukemia Sarcoma Metastases	Periapical Cemento-osseous Dysplasia Dentigerous Cyst Pindborg Tumor Adenomatoid Odontogenic Tumor Osseous Dysplasia Fibrous Dysplasia Paget's Disease of Bone Osteonecrosis		Osteosclerosis/ Bone scar Tori/Enostoses/ Exostoses Root Tip(s) *Maxillary sinus*: Retention Cyst/pseudocyst Metallic Foreign Objects Sialolith Calcified Stylohyoid Ligament Vascular Calcification Metastases	Periapical Cementoosseous Dysplasia Odontoma Osteosarcoma Metastases

References

ADIS: Automated Dental Identification System. http://www.csee.wvu.edu/adis/index.html (accessed November 16, 2011).

Al-Amad, S.H., J.G. Clement, M.J. McCullough, A. Morales, and A.J. Hill. 2007. Evaluation of two dental identification computer systems: DAVID and WinID3. *Journal of Forensic Odontostomatology* 25: 23–29.

American Board of Forensic Odontology, Inc. 2011. Diplomates reference manual. Section III: policies, procedures, guidelines, and standards. http://www.abfo.org/pdfs/ABFO% 20Reference% 20Manual%20%207-31-2011%20revision.pdf (accessed September 19, 2011).

American National Standards Institute and ADA Standards Committee on Dental Informatics. Forensic data set: Radiographic image data. ANSI/ADA Specification 1058. Washington, DC: ANSI/ADA. 2010.

Angel, J.S., H.H. Mincer, J. Chaudhry, and M. Scarbecz. 2011. Cone-beam computed tomography for analyzing variations in inferior alveolar canal location in adults in relation to age and sex. *Journal of Forensic Sciences* 56: 216–219.

Berketa, J.W., R.S. Hirsch, D. Higgins, and H. James. 2010. Radiographic recognition of dental implants as an aid to identifying the deceased. *Journal of Forensic Sciences* 55: 66–70.

Danforth, R.A. and E.E. Herschaft. 2012. Cone beam CT of carotid artery densities. *Medscape Dentistry & Oral Health: Challenging Cases in Dentistry and Oral Health* (January): http://www.medscape.com/viewarticle/756431

De Vos, W. et al. 2009. Cone-beam computerized tomography (CBCT) imaging of the oral and maxillofacial region: A systematic review of the literature. *International Journal of Oral and Maxillofacial Surgery* 38: 609–625.

Dorion, R.B.J. The trabecular bone in identification: Part 2. *Proceedings of the American Academy of Forensic Sciences 64th Annual Meeting*, February 20–25, 2012, Atlanta, GA. pp. 257–258.

Fahmy, G., D. Nassar, E. HajSaid. et al. 2005. Toward an automated dental identification system, *Journal of Electronic Imaging* 14(4): 43018.

Flint, D.J., S. Brent Dove, P.C. Brumit. et al. 2009. Computer-aided dental identification: An objective method for assessment of radiographic image similarity. *Journal of Forensic Sciences* 54: 177–184.

Ganz, S.D. 2005. Conventional CT and cone beam CT for improved dental diagnostics and implant planning. *Dental Implantology Update* 16: 89–95.

GB Forensic Services. 2011. http://gbforensicservices.com/(accessed September 30, 2012).

Hatcher, D.C. 2010. Operational principles for cone-beam computed tomography. *JADA* 141(10S): 3S–6S.

Herschaft, E.E. 2008. Forensic dentistry. In *Oral and Maxillofacial Pathology*, 3rd edn., B.W. Neville, D.D. Damm, C.A. Allen, and J.E. Bouquot (eds.). Philadelphia, PA: W. B. Saunders, pp. 887–916.

Herschaft, E.E., M.E. Alder, D.K. Ord, R.D. et al. (eds.). 2007. *American Society of Forensic Odontology Manual of Forensic Odontology*, 4th edn. Albany, NY: ImPress Printing.

Hunter, T.B., M.T. Yoshino, R.B. Dzioba, R.A. Light, and W.G. Berger. 2004. Medical devices of the head, neck, and spine. *Radio Graphics* 24(1): 257–285.

Jain, A.K. and H. Chen. 2004. Matching of dental x-ray images for human identification. *Pattern Recognition* 37: 1519–1532.

Jonasson, G. and G. Bankvall. 2001. Estimation of skeletal bone mineral density by means of the trabecular pattern of the alveolar bone, its interdental thickness, and the bone mass of the mandible. *Oral Surgery, Oral Medicine, Oral Pathology, Oral Radiology & Endodontics* 92: 346–352.

Khan, Z, A. Wells, W. Scarfe, and A. Farman. 2008. Cone beam CT isolation of calcifications in the maxillofacial and cervical soft tissues: A retrospective analysis. *International Journal of Computer Assisted Radiology and Surgery* 3(Suppl 1): S221–S222.

MacDonald, D. 2011. *Oral and Maxillofacial Radiology: A Diagnostic Approach*. West Sussex, U.K.: Wiley-Blackwell, pp. 8–11.

Mah, J.K. et al. 2010. Practical applications of cone-beam computed tomography in orthodontics. *JADA* 141(3S): 7S–13S.

Nassar, D. and H. Ammar. 2007. A neural network system for matching dental radiographs. *Pattern Recognition* 40: 65–79.

Neville, B.W., D.D. Damm, C.A. Allen, and J.E. Bouquot. (ed.). 2008. Appendix, Part 4: Differential diagnosis of oral and maxillofacial diseases: Radiographic pathology. *Oral and Maxillofacial Pathology*, 3rd edn. Philadelphia, PA: W. B. Saunders, pp. 929–933.

Richmond R. and I.A. Pretty. 2010. Identification of the edentulous individual: an investigation into the accuracy of radiographic identifications. *Journal of Forensic Sciences* 55: 984–987.

Santoro, V., P. Lozito, N. Mastrorocco, A. De Donno, and F. Introna. 2009. Personal identification by morphometric analyses of intra-oral radiographs of unrestored teeth. *Journal of Forensic Sciences* 54: 1081–1084.

Scarfe, W.C. and A.G. Farman. 2010. Soft tissue calcifications in the neck: Maxillofacial CBCT presentation and significance. *AADMRT Newsletter* 2: 1–15.

Scientific Working Group on Disaster Victim Identification (SWGDVI). 2010. *Journal of Forensic Sciences* 55: 788–791.

Smith, V.A., A.M. Christensen, and S.W. Myers. 2010. The reliability of visually comparing small frontal sinuses. *Journal of Forensic Sciences* 5: 1413–1415.

Stavrianos, C., I.E. Stavrianou, E. Dietrich. et al. 2009. Methods for human identification in forensic dentistry: A review. *The Internet Journal of Forensic Science.* http://www.ispub.com/journal/the-internet-journal-of-forensic-science/volume-4-number-1/methods-for-human-identification-in-forensic-dentistry-a-review.html (accessed January 28, 2012).

Thali, M.J., T. Markwalder, C. Jackowski. et al. 2006. Dental CT imaging as a screening tool for dental profiling: advantages and limitations. *Journal of Forensic Sciences* 51: 113–119.

Trochesset, D.A., R.B. Serchuk, R. Katz, and D.C. Colosi. Comparing cone-beam CT with conventional digital dental imaging for forensic dental identification. *Proceedings of the American Academy of Forensic Sciences 64th Annual Meeting*, February 20–25, 2012, Atlanta, GA, p. 260.

Van Der Meer, D.T., P.C. Brumit, B.A. Schrader. et al. 2010. Root morphology and anatomical patterns in forensic dental identification: A comparison of computer-aided identification with traditional forensic dental identification. *Journal of Forensic Sciences* 55: 1499–1503.

Weems, R.A. 2008. Cone Beam CT Radiography for dental identifications. Paper presented at *The Annual Meeting of the American Academy of Forensic Sciences.* Washington, DC.

Weems, R. 2011. Radiographic applications in forensic dental identification. In *Brogdon's Forensic Radiology*, 2nd edn. Thali, M.J., M.D. Viner, and B.G. Brogdon, (ed.). Boca Raton, FL: CRC Press, Taylor & Francis Group, pp. 127–149.

Weledniger, R.M. 2012. Digital enhancement of dental radiographs to facilitate identification. *Proceedings of the American Academy of Forensic Sciences 64th Annual Meeting*, February 20–25, 2012, Atlanta, GA, p. 251–252.

Disaster Victim Identification

6

GARY M. BERMAN
BRYAN CHRZ
LILLIAN A. NAWROCKI
KENNETH P. HERMSEN
RAYMOND G. MILLER
RICHARD A. WEEMS

Contents

6.1 Definitions and Types of Disasters 160
6.2 National and International Agencies and Teams 161
6.3 Disaster Sites and Site Management Issues 165
 6.3.1 Notification and Assessment by Medical Examiners and Coroners 165
 6.3.2 Temporary Morgue Location 165
 6.3.3 Search and Recovery 166
 6.3.4 Security and Safety 168
6.4 Establishing a DVI Morgue Operation (DMORT Model) 169
 6.4.1 Components of Mortuary Operations 170
  6.4.1.1 Decontamination 170
  6.4.1.2 Reception/Registration 171
  6.4.1.3 Fingerprint 171
  6.4.1.4 Radiography 171
  6.4.1.5 Pathology/Autopsy 172
  6.4.1.6 Anthropology 172
  6.4.1.7 Dental 172
  6.4.1.8 DNA 174
  6.4.1.9 Embalming/Casketing 175
  6.4.1.10 Body Storage 175
  6.4.1.11 Clerical or Information Resource Center 175
6.5 Protocol for a Local or State DVI Dental Section 176
 6.5.1 Formation of a Dental Identification Team 176
 6.5.2 Dental Section Team Leader 178
 6.5.3 Postmortem Dental Section 178
 6.5.4 Antemortem Dental Section 179
 6.5.5 Dental Comparison Section 181
 6.5.6 Dental Examination Supplies 181
 6.5.7 Morgue Shifts 181
6.6 Portable Dental X-Ray Generator 182
6.7 Digital Dental Radiography Sensors 184
6.8 Computer-Assisted Dental Identification Software 186
 6.8.1 CAPMI 186
 6.8.2 WinID3 186

6.8.3 DVI System International 188
6.8.4 UVIS/UDIM 189
6.9 Technological Advances in Dental Identification/Flight 3407 190
References 191

6.1 Definitions and Types of Disasters

The term "disaster" is difficult to define because it means different things to different groups of people. It is defined as "a sudden calamitous event producing great material damage, loss, and distress" (*Webster's New International Dictionary*). A disaster also can be described as any incident that results in loss of life and/or property that exceeds a community's resources and its ability to respond. Some communities have greater resources than others, so an incident that is a disaster in one community may not be a disaster in another. Disaster victim identification (DVI) refers to the component of fatality management of a mass fatality incident that involves the scientific identification of human remains. No community is immune from disasters. These include natural disasters such as hurricanes, floods, tornadoes, volcanoes, wildfires, earthquakes, tsunamis, mudslides, epidemics, and pandemics. There are also unintentional man-made disasters such as transportation accidents, chemical spills, structural fires and collapse, explosions, and radiation accidents (Figure 6.1).

Additionally, a mass disaster may be the result of terrorism, an intentional man-made disaster. Terror threats come in a variety of forms: chemical terrorism, such as the release of sarin gas in a Tokyo subway; biological terrorism, such as anthrax contained in a letter sent to a governmental agency; radiological terrorism, the detonation of a "dirty bomb" containing radioactive uranium in a populated area, causing relatively little physical damage but creating a wasteland of radioactive contamination and widespread death from radiation effects; nuclear terrorism, the threat of detonating a nuclear device in a populated

Figure 6.1 Gulfport, Mississippi, church destroyed by Katrina's tidal surge.

area causing devastating physical damage over a very large area; and explosive terrorism, a bomb blast in a crowded nightclub in Bali, Indonesia, or an aircraft deliberately crashing into the World Trade Center (WTC), in New York. At the heart of each form of terrorism is the desire to terrorize its victims by causing a maximum amount of destruction, thus creating emotional, financial, and psychological turmoil among the survivors.

6.2 National and International Agencies and Teams

Numerous national and international DVI protocols exist including the following: U.S. Department of Health and Human Services (DMORT), U.S. Department of Justice (NIJ), U.S. Department of the Army Mortuary Operations, The National Transportation Safety Board (NTSB), American Board of Forensic Odontology (ABFO), National Association of Medical Examiners (NAME), INTERPOL, NATO, and the Pan American Health Organization/World Health Organization. More information may be found at the website of the NIJ Scientific Working Group on Disaster Victim Identification, www.swgdvi.org.

In any mass disaster, man-made or otherwise, many different local, state, and federal agencies or a mixture of each may respond. The United States National Response Plan (NRP) came into effect in 2004 and was superseded in 2008 by the National Response Framework (NRF). Building on the existing National Incident Management System (NIMS) as well as Incident Command System (ICS) standardizations, the plan forms the basis of how the federal government coordinates with state, local, and the private sectors during disasters and emergencies, from the smallest incident to the largest catastrophe. The NRF's coordinating structures are always in effect for implementation at any level and at any time for a local, state, and national emergency or disaster response.

When a disaster occurs, the local and county first-responders utilize their disaster plan and capabilities to respond until they are overwhelmed and a request for help is made from the county agency. The request process then proceeds similarly from the county to the state to the federal government as additional resource needs are identified. The State Governor may formally request a disaster declaration from the President. The President, acting upon the recommendations from the Federal Emergency Management Agency (FEMA) Director and the State Governor, will sign a "Major Disaster Declaration," thus allowing for a federal coordination officer to begin administering all federal programs to bring aid and relief to the State (Figures 6.2 and 6.3).

The National Disaster Medical System (NDMS) is one such program. It has the capability to provide for a single, integrated national medical response capability for assisting state and local authorities in dealing with the medical and health effects of declared disasters. It is designed to deliver quality medical care to victims of and responders to a disaster. Originally formed under the Department of Health and Human Services, it was transferred to the Department of Homeland Security in 2003, and returned to the Department of Health and Human Services in 2008 where it remains. The regional NDMS teams consist of the following:

Disaster Medical Assistance Team (DMAT): This team is made up of physicians, nurses, EMTs, pharmacists, and ancillary support personnel. Its purpose is to provide primary and acute care, triage of mass casualties, initial resuscitation, and stabilization of the sick and injured for evacuation.

National Veterinary Response Team (NVRT): This team provides assistance in identifying and treating the needs for veterinary services following major disasters. It also helps in assessing the extent of disruption to the animal and public health infrastructures.

Figure 6.2 House destroyed down to its foundation by Katrina.

Figure 6.3 Katrina's destruction in Bay St. Louis, Mississippi.

Disaster Mortuary Operational Response Team (DMORT):

The National Response Plan assigns the NDMS, under Emergency Support Function #8 (ESF #8), to provide victim identification and mortuary services. In order to accomplish this mission, DMORTs were developed. "DMORTs are composed of private citizens, each with a particular field of expertise, who are activated in the event of a disaster.

DMORT members are required to maintain appropriate certifications and licensure within their discipline. When members are activated, licensure and certification is recognized by all states, and the team members are compensated for their duty time by the federal government as intermittent federal employees. During an emergency response, DMORTs work under the guidance of local authorities by providing technical assistance and personnel to recover, identify, and process deceased victims" (www.dmort7.org).

The DMORT teams are directed by the following agencies: the U.S. Department of Health and Human Services' Office of the Assistant Secretary for Preparedness and Response (ASPR); the Office of Preparedness and Emergency Operations (OPEO); and the NDMS. "Teams are composed of funeral directors, medical examiners, coroners, pathologists, forensic anthropologists, medical records technicians, and transcribers; fingerprint specialists, forensic odontologists, dental assistants, x-ray technicians, mental health specialists, computer professionals, administrative support staff, and security and investigative personnel" (U.S. Department of Health and Human Services, 2012) (Figure 6.4).

Currently, DMORT has three core teams supporting its general forensic team. The Disaster Portable Morgue Unit (DPMU) team is responsible for the management and deployment of the DPMU. These DPMUs are staged at three stategic locations for immediate deployment in support of DMORT operations. The DPMU is a depository of equipment and supplies for deployment to a disaster site. Each contains a complete morgue with designated workstations for each processing element and prepackaged equipment and supplies. The Family Assistance Team (FAC) is responsible for working directly with the families of victims involved in a mass fatality incident. They compile antemortem data, which is eventually compared to the victims' postmortem data to establish identification. The Weapons of Mass Destruction (WMD) Team is responsible for the decontamination of remains from a chemical, biological, or nuclear event thus protecting the personnel working within the DPMU.

Figure 6.4 Flooding in New Orleans, Louisiana, related to Hurricane Katrina.

The initial DMORT deployment was in 1993 when the Mississippi River flooding caused cemetery disruptions in Hardin, Missouri where numerous human remains (caskets) were disinterred. Other deployments included the Murrah Federal Building explosion in Oklahoma City in 1995, the Korean Airline crash in Guam in 1997, the 9/11 WTC disaster in New York City, the search and recovery of the shuttle Columbia in Texas and Louisiana in 2003, the multistate response to Hurricane Katrina in 2005, the Buffalo aircraft crash 3407 in 2009, and the EF5 tornado causing multiple fatalities in Joplin, Missouri, in 2011.

The National Response Plan states that when a disaster occurs, the local, and then the county/state resources are utilized first. The formation of individual state disaster mortuary teams and state-owned portable morgue units has been facilitated by the availability of federal ASPR grants. Some states have incorporated their existing Forensic Dental Identification Team into their state Disaster Mortuary Team, such as in Michigan, where the 27 year old Michigan Dental Association Forensic Dental Identification Team (MDAFDIT) is now a formal component of the Michigan Mortuary Operations Response Team (MiMORT).

Others continue to have separate state Forensic Dental Identification Teams and separate Mortuary Operations Response Teams. In addition, there are several separate individual Forensic Dental Identification Teams in certain major cities such as New York City, Miami, Toronto, and Chicago. The armed forces also have formal disaster and identification teams as was seen when they were deployed in response to the fatalities at the Pentagon Building following the 9/11 terrorist attacks. There is also identification and processing morgue involving Gulf War fatalities at Dover Air Force Base in Delaware.

Another federal agency providing dental identifications is the former Armed Forces Central Identification Laboratory (CIL) in Hawaii, now known as the Joint POW/MIA Accounting Command (JPAC). Most of the remains accessioned into the JPAC are Americans from past conflicts who have been missing for decades. Dental comparison has been the most commonly used methodology for identifying these individuals at the CIL. As the advances in DNA continue, this may not be the case in the future.

INTERPOL is the world's largest international police organization with 188 member countries. Created in 1923, INTERPOL has a standing committee on DVI) and published its first manual on DVI in 1984. The manual, which has been reviewed and revised numerous times, offers practical advice on the major issues of victim identification and encourages the compatibility of procedures across international boundaries, which is essential in disasters involving citizens of many different countries.

Kenyon International Emergency Services is a private company started in the United Kingdom in 1906. Working with the Coroner and Chief Constable, brothers Herbert and Harold Kenyon, helped to prepare and repatriate the deceased when a London and South Western Railway boat train jumped its tracks and crashed in Salisbury, England. Nearly all the deceased were Americans. Kenyon's first civilian disaster occurred in November 7, 1929, when an Imperial Airways Junkers Monoplane crashed in England. Presently, Kenyon has the capability of managing all disaster operations including search and rescue and the identification and the return of human remains. It also can provide counseling to families, telephone inquiry centers, and crisis communications. Kenyon works with aviation entities, private business, and various governments.

6.3 Disaster Sites and Site Management Issues

6.3.1 Notification and Assessment by Medical Examiners and Coroners

Disaster sites must to be managed and processed in a manner similar to a crime scene. It is important that a proper chain of evidence and control of the scene is maintained. Scene security is also paramount. In a terrorist attack the FBI will be present and oversee the initial investigation. In transportation accidents, the National Transportation Safety Board (NTSB) has authority over these matters. However, the local medical examiner or coroner will have jurisdiction and be in charge of the deceased. When a mass fatality event occurs, notification is made to the county medical examiner or coroner, the local emergency manager, the local emergency operations center, and the local public health officer. Upon notification, the medical examiner assesses the following information: the type of incident, location of the incident, and the estimated number of fatalities. If the site is secure, the medical examiner may visit the site. Once on site the medical examiner meets with the current incident commander to determine if the incident is stabilized, the estimated number of fatalities, and the conditions of the bodies. If any bodies have been moved, the medical examiner will inspect the location to which the bodies have been moved and determine whether it is appropriate to serve as a temporary morgue. Depending on the number of fatalities, the distance from the incident site to the medical examiner's office and the ability of the local medical examiner's office to absorb these additional fatalities, a decision may be made to establish a temporary morgue for the disaster victims.

6.3.2 Temporary Morgue Location

Careful consideration is to be given in selecting a temporary morgue site. The medical examiner works with local officials, normally the local emergency operations center, the State Public Health Department, and any local or state Mortuary Operations Disaster Team when deciding where to establish the site. The Hurricane Katrina disaster in 2005 stretched the capabilities of DMORT personnel and the portable morgue units. It was decided that two morgues (DPMU's) would be established. One would be located in the city of Gulfport, Mississippi and the other would be located in St. Gabriel, Louisiana near Baton Rouge. These facilities came to be known as DPMU East and DPMU West. Katrina victims from each state would be sent to their respective morgues (Figure 6.5).

It is strongly advised that the temporary morgue is *not* established at the current location of any public facility such as a recreation center, ice rink, or high-school gymnasium. The temporary morgue should be set up in an area that can be secured to provide the victims' privacy from public and media intrusion. Although it is impossible to both define and locate an "ideal" morgue set-up, the following should be considered:

- Is the facility available for the time frame necessary?
- Can the facility be retrofitted and what is the cost?
- Is the facility a hard-weather structure with concrete or nonporous floors?
- What infrastructures (fresh water in, sewer for gray water out, sufficient electrical system (~200 A), climate control/ventilation, loading platform, storage space, telecommunications, etc.) are available at this location?

Figure 6.5 DMORT DPMU West housed within a large warehouse.

The size of the temporary morgue will vary depending on the size of the incident. For less than 100 fatalities, a structure of 6,000 ft^2 should be adequate. For 101–200 fatalities, 8,000 ft^2; and for more than 200 fatalities 12,000 ft^2 may be necessary (Figures 6.6 and 6.7).

6.3.3 Search and Recovery

Search and recovery operations occur as soon as the search and rescue operations have been completed. Individuals trained in the use of a grid system and/or a total station

Figure 6.6 DMORT DPMU East construction within a aircraft hangar partially destroyed by Katrina.

Figure 6.7 Completed DPMU East with privacy shroud in place.

surveying device may be part of this team. In the recovery of astronaut remains from the Shuttle Columbia explosion, hand-held GPS units were employed. The goals are the discovery, documentation, and subsequent recovery of all artifacts involving human remains while maintaining respectful, dignified, and ethical treatment of the deceased. Recovery of the victims is the first step in enabling the establishment of a personal identification of the individuals and the return of the deceased to their loved ones.

An assessment of hazards must first take place through consultation with fire and HAZMAT personnel regarding the precautions that should take place. It is vitally important to maintain standards of personnel safety while still preserving evidence. The entire scene is documented before any recovery begins. This is done with both still photography and video. Boundaries and perimeters are established and the measured grids marked (Figure 6.8).

The recovery is done in a meticulous manner. However, "careful expediency" is important in recovering and transporting the remains to a mass fatality morgue, thus ensuring that the bodies are no longer exposed to the harsh weather conditions, decomposition, and the public eye. If body fragmentation has occurred, extra care must be taken so that the location of the body fragments is well-documented and that comingling of separate individuals does not occur. Should there be any doubt, it is a common practice that a separate "victim number" be assigned to the fragmented remains. Otherwise, improper comingling might preclude the identification of an individual victim. The Search and Recovery Branch Team is made up of three separate teams: the search team, the remains collection team, and the transportation team.

The search team working each grid is composed of at least four individuals. The team leader, who is has overall responsibility for the team; the team scribe, who is responsible for the documentation of location and condition of the remains; and the team photographer who will be photographing each body or fragment before and after a number is assigned.

Figure 6.8 Search and recover team creating a grid at the disaster site.

The remains collection team is also made up of at least four individuals. The team leader is responsible for the team and three recovery specialists who will assist in placing the bodies and/or fragments into body bags or pouches. They will also move the remains to the staging area. During the 9/11 recovery, forensic scientists, including dentists, were stationed at "ground zero" at all times to help with the determination as to whether recovered tissue fragments were human.

The transportation team is made up of at least three individuals: the team leader and two drivers. This team is responsible for the transportation of the bodies/fragments to the temporary morgue. A chain of evidence is maintained throughout these procedures.

6.3.4 Security and Safety

Security and safety of the site is always a concern. Law enforcement must establish a perimeter around the site and control the access points. On-site fabrication of photographic ID and/or fingerprint scans aids in controlling both entry points and those areas that only authorized personnel may access. The security officers should be given an initial list of names of team members allowed on the site in order for easier entry into team staging areas. The safety of the disaster team workers is one of the most important management aspects of a mass disaster site. Dr. Sawait Kanluen, from the Wayne County medical examiner's office has often stated, "We are there to recover and identify the dead, not to become one of them." A safety officer is assigned with the responsibility of working with HAZMAT team members to establish the safety of both the site and the temporary morgue area before responders enter the area. They are also responsible for establishing any needed decontamination of materials or individuals before leaving the controlled site. Universal Precautions are also exercised at all times in both the recovery site and the morgue site (Figure 6.9). Pairing individuals in the recovery teams and also with those working in the

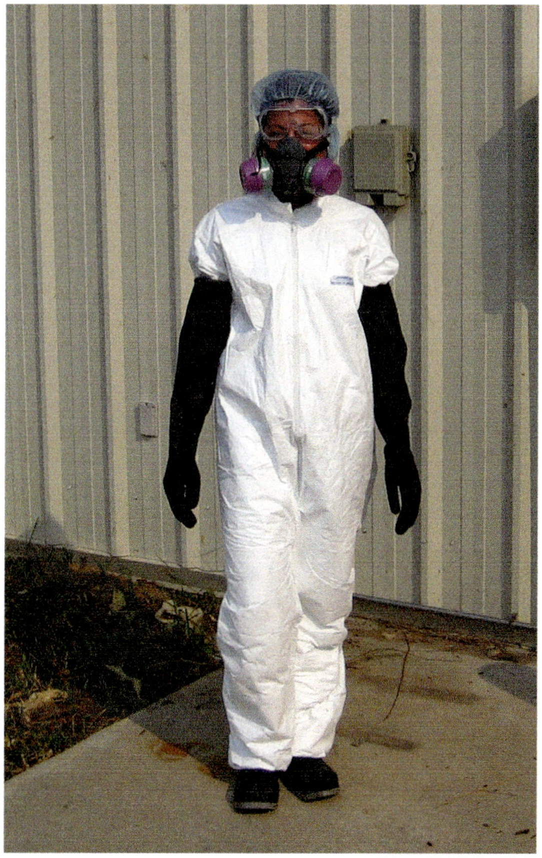

Figure 6.9 Maximum personal protection related to hazardous materials.

morgue into a buddy system allows for a quick way to determine if all responders remain safe in case of the need to evacuate the area.

During the initial hours and days of a mass casualty incident, personnel often desire to work extended hours in order to achieve the goals of reuniting the deceased with their families. However, it is extremely important that they eat, hydrate, and get adequate sleep. Skipping meals and working more than a 12 h shift is not conducive in allowing operations to progress at peak performance. Eventually, personnel will begin to experience fatigue and a depressed mode may develop. It is also mentally helpful for the workers to "decompress" with each other socially in a relaxed atmosphere after completing a work cycle. Finally, coresponders should be watched for signs of stress, depression, and emotional fatigue. The disaster team should have mental health workers present for the team members. Daily briefings and a final exit debriefing at the end of the individual's deployment are helpful in assessing and aiding the mental health of the responder.

6.4 Establishing a DVI Morgue Operation (DMORT Model)

The primary purpose of the mortuary operation in a disaster is to provide for the physical examination, identification, and disposition of the deceased victims with sensitivity, dignity, and respect. Identification allows the deceased to be returned to their families, offering

Figure 6.10 Interior workstations of a DMORT morgue facility.

the family closure and the opportunity to provide grieve for their loved one according to their religious, cultural, or ethnic customs (Figure 6.10).

6.4.1 Components of Mortuary Operations

The details of mortuary operations are totally dependent upon the nature and size of the disaster. However, there are certain features and basic needs that are common within the morgue setup that allow for a successful mission. As mentioned previously, all disaster morgues require the mandatory provision of clean water, sewer services, electricity, sufficient climate control/ventilation, and telecommunications. As an example, no handling of bodies in any form or fashion was allowed at the DPMU East until sufficient fresh running water was available. Also, the only electrical generator available early in the operation was underpowered and on several occasions work in the morgue had to be curtailed when the electrical system failed.

The mortuary annex, as the temporary morgue is frequently called, is made up of separate examination workstations in which trained forensic scientists and other skilled personnel work diligently to provide both a scientific identification of the victim and the proper disposition of the remains. These workstations include the following: decontamination, body registration, personal effects documentation, fingerprint collection, photography, full-body radiography, pathological/autopsy examination, anthropological examination, dental examination, DNA collection, embalming (if required), and body storage until release of the body to funeral homes. All final documentation used to establish the identity of the victim is provided to the responsible local coroner or medical examiner who then signs the victim's death certificate.

6.4.1.1 Decontamination

The decontamination workstation is responsible for the removal of toxic or potentially harmful materials from the external surface of the remains. This task is typically completed by the WMD team. It is not possible to truly decontaminate a body, particularly one that has undergone decomposition, so the purpose of this station is to remove contaminates from the surface of the remains that may be harmful to the mortuary workers. This would include materials such as organophosphates found in pesticides, petroleum products such as jet fuel, toxic chemical substances such as ammonia or chlorine commonly used for industrial purposes, and radioactive contamination from a nuclear event or a dirty bomb. The decontamination station is only used when it is required.

6.4.1.2 *Reception/Registration*

The reception/registration workstation is responsible for a number of important duties. The first task is to assign and login unique prearranged numbers to the bodies that are specific to this particular event, and will function well given the number of estimated victims, including fragments. In the 9/11 disaster, for example, the first body received was assigned the number "DM01-00001." This indicated "Disaster-Manhattan" and the year "2001." The numerals were also sufficient to accommodate the approximate 19,000 remains recovered and given an individual case number. It is best to allow for too many numerals rather than not having enough.

In following stations, the victim's personal effects are removed and photographed. The personal effects are then catalogued and either secured for later distribution back to the family, or bagged and placed in the body pouch with the remains. Once the personal effects have been removed, an external examination is performed on the victim and photographs are taken for documentation (some medical examiners prefer that the clothing is not removed prior to autopsy). Special attention is placed on photographing any external feature that may aid in the identification. These features include scars, tattoos, birthmarks, piercings, or any physical developmental anomaly. The final duty of the reception station is to assign an "escort" for the remains. The escort accompanies the body as it progresses through the morgue and takes responsibility for ensuring that the victim has been examined at each workstation and that the documentation has been completed appropriately and does not get displaced. The escort is also responsible for ensuring that the body is never left alone or set aside unattended from the time they are brought into the mortuary annex examination area until returned to the storage area. This establishes a chain of custody.

6.4.1.3 *Fingerprint*

The fingerprint collection workstation is typically staffed by law enforcement personnel trained and experienced in the collection of fingerprints. At times this will be local law enforcement crime lab personnel, and at other times members of a federal service such as the Federal Bureau of Investigation. Fingerprint identification personnel are responsible for the accurate collection of fingerprints from the victims and coordinating the search, matching, and identification of the victims from the fingerprint data collected.

6.4.1.4 *Radiography*

The radiology workstation is positioned within the other workstations as deemed appropriate by the medical examiner. For example, it might be the very first station if the possibility of live explosives on the victims exists. In any case, these workers are responsible for taking full-body radiographs, which are very useful in locating previous internal injuries that are not visible externally such as healed bone fractures. Perhaps more importantly they also show implanted medical devices such as pacemakers and artificial joint replacements. These implanted devices have serial numbers that are matched to a specific patient and are recorded

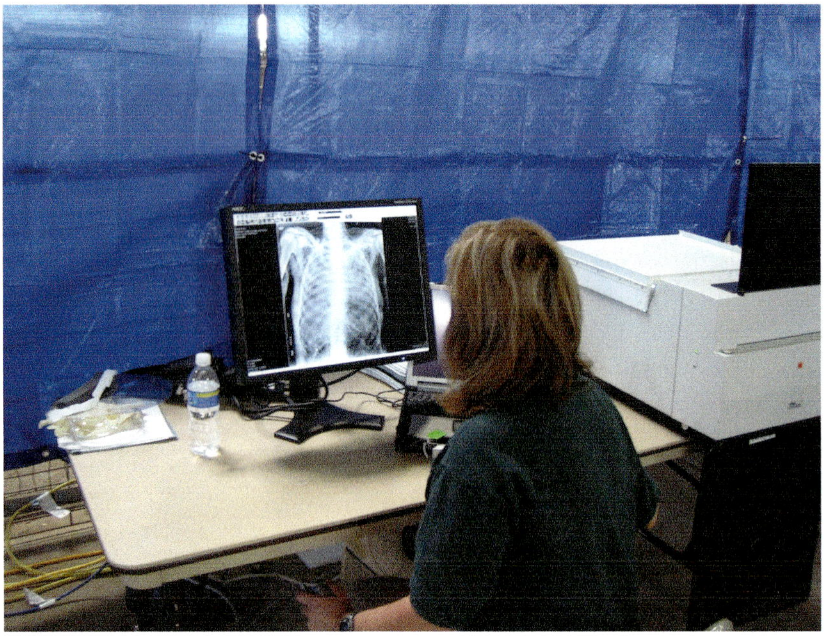

Figure 6.11 Full-body x-ray station in DMORT morgue (Hurricane Ike).

by the manufacturer of the device and the hospital, thus providing an excellent lead in the positive identification of the remains. Dental fragmentation can also be found in unusual areas in the full-body radiographs, especially after traumatic incidences (Figure 6.11).

6.4.1.5 *Pathology/Autopsy*

In the pathology/autopsy workstation, the forensic pathologists perform autopsies in a manner deemed appropriate for the event and often perform a toxicological examination of the remains. In most disasters, the depth of the autopsy and toxicology screening of the victims is done at the discretion of the local coroner or medical examiner. However, in transportation disasters the law requires these be performed on crew members to accurately determine cause and manner of death to rule out foul play, negligence, or malfeasance as contributing to the transportation disaster. Special attention will also be given to identifying tattoos, piercings, scars indicating past surgical procedures, etc. The physicians staffing this section also function to dissect and remove any implanted medical devices identified by the radiology workstation.

6.4.1.6 *Anthropology*

Anthropological examination provides important information in the identification of the deceased. By examining the skeletal structures, the forensic anthropologist can often accurately determine the race, gender, stature, and approximate age of the victim, helping to significantly narrow down the search for their identity. This examination is particularly important when cemetery or skeletal remains are involved.

6.4.1.7 *Dental*

The DMORT dental team members are divided into two distinct factions: postmortem and antemortem. In some cases, there is also a third faction that is responsible for the comparison/matching of the antemortem and postmortem data but often, this task is shared by

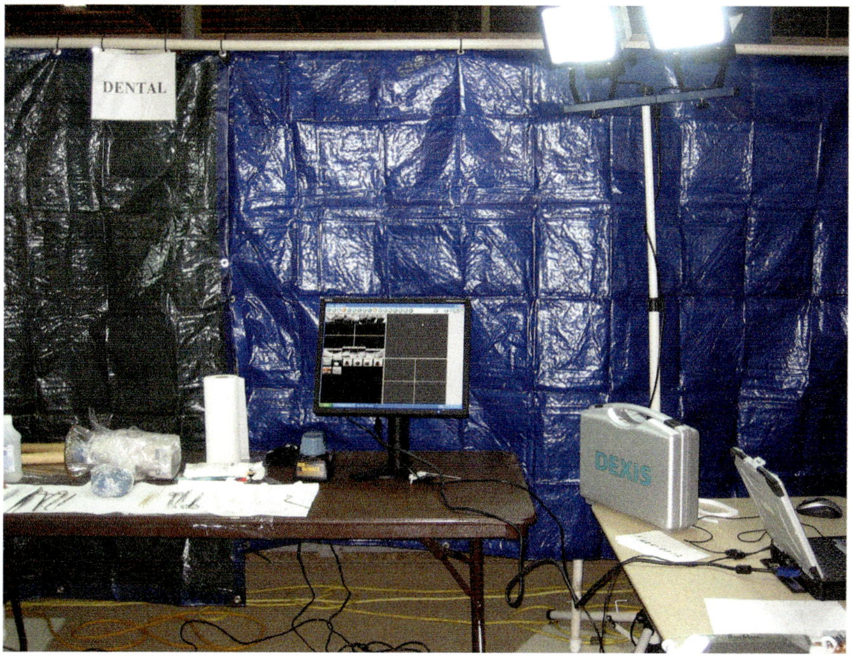

Figure 6.12 Dental workstation in DMORT morgue (Hurricane Katrina).

the antemortem team. The dental postmortem examination team (workstation) is within the mortuary annex and is responsible for collecting the postmortem dental data of each victim (Figure 6.12). The postmortem dental examination station is staffed by dentists and dental personnel trained in forensic odontology and who are familiar with the operation of the computer programs, digital radiography, digital photography, and other tools and equipment, which are used in the collection of the dental data. The antemortem dental section is established at a location that is in close proximity but separate from the mortuary annex and will described later in this chapter.

The postmortem examination begins by the creation of a digital dental record for the body undergoing examination. This is accomplished using the computer-assisted patient identification program, WinID3©, mentioned previously. WinID3 then activates the x-ray sensor and assigns the associated body number to the resulting x-ray image series automatically, thus reducing operator error in numbering. The digital x-ray system used in DMORT morgues for well over a decade is the DEXIS™ Digital X-ray System (DEXIS Digital Diagnostic Imaging, LLC, 1910 North Penn Road, Hatfield, PA 19440). The DEXIS system captures the x-ray images and also stores and archives them always retaining a copy, which is original and unaltered. Optimization of the images quality is also managed by the DEXIS software. The x-ray images are then exported to the WinID3 system where they may also be viewed (Figure 6.13).

A postmortem intraoral examination is then performed and the victim's dentition is "charted" using an odontogram contained within the WinID3 program. At this point, the charting and radiographic exam may be accessed by any individual with rights to the appointed dental server. Typically, each workstation will have an individual assigned as the photographer and one to perform any needed resections. Two other team members are assigned the dental charting and the radiographic process. A final individual operates the laptop computer capturing the dental data and images.

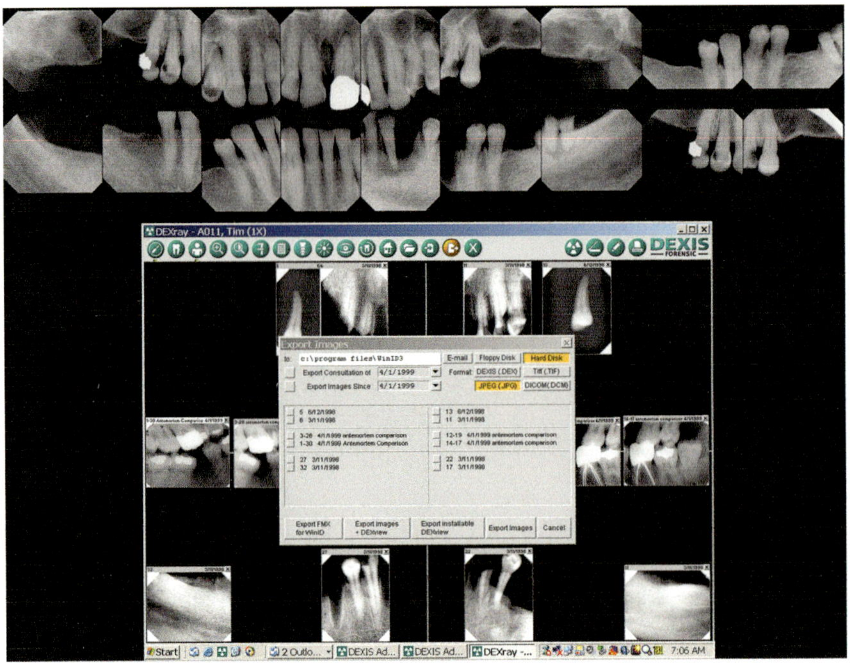

Figure 6.13 DEXIS digital radiographic series to be exported to WinID.

The antemortem/comparison dental section is established at a location that is in close proximity but separate from the mortuary annex. This section performs the collection of antemortem dental data from the victims' dental records as described in Chapter 4. This is accomplished in a similar manner to the postmortem dental collection except that the data is now entered into the antemortem (victim) side of WinID3. First, the compiled pertinent biographical data and antemortem dental charting are entered into the victim's "chart." Next, any available antemortem radiographs are digitally scanned on a digital flatbed scanner using its "transmisive" or "true positive" mode. Scans should be obtained at 300 dots-per-inch (dpi) resolution. The scanner is "driven" by DEXscan™ (DEXIS) software, which optimizes, stores, and archives the images. They are then optimized and exported into the victim's WinID record. Eventually, all antemortem and postmortem dental chartings, radiographs, and camera images may be accessed from any of the networked computers linked to the server in both the morgue and the antemortem location in WinID. A victim identification is greatly hastened by WinID's "best match" feature, which automatically sorts in descending order all of the hundreds or thousands of dental records in the system to the record in question according to the number of matching dental features or "hits" the records have in common. Confirmation is made by side-to-side record and image comparisons also using WinID.

6.4.1.8 DNA

DNA collection is typically performed by law enforcement personnel (including FBI DNA teams) trained in the collection and processing of DNA evidence. A variety of tissue samples can be used to obtain a DNA profile. Typically bone and teeth are reliable sources of DNA due to the durability of these tissues but blood and soft tissue can also be an adequate source depending on the condition of the remains.

Figure 6.14 Release of an identified body to a funeral home.

6.4.1.9 Embalming/Casketing

Once a positive identification is made, the remains may be embalmed in the embalming workstation, provided condition of the remains indicates embalming and that the practice is culturally appropriate. The prepared remains are then stored until the remains are released and returned to the family for disposition in accordance to their personal, religious, or cultural customs (Figure 6.14).

6.4.1.10 Body Storage

In a mass fatality incident, the remains must be stored in a cooled, temperature-controlled environment to protect them from freezing in cold climates and slowing down the decomposition process in warm climates. Typically, 55 ft refrigerated trailers with metal flooring are used for this purpose if onsite refrigerated storage is not available (Figure 6.15).

Storage of the victims and managing the logistics involved is a vital component of the identification process and is known as "trailer management." It is typically handled by teams made up of heavy equipment operators, funeral directors, and truck drivers who provide for the careful and respectful movement and storage of the decedents.

6.4.1.11 Clerical or Information Resource Center

Another aspect of the mortuary operation is the clerical area, or Information Resource Center, where the antemortem and postmortem records are collected and stored. It is also the area in which the physical attributes of the deceased, such as tattoos, personal effects, eye and hair color, or piercings observed on the victims in the mortuary annex are compared to the physical attributes described by the victims' families in the Family Assistance Center. These and other attributes are compared using the "Victim Identification Profile Program" (VIP), a computer-assisted identification program developed by Donald Bloom. This program is currently being used by DMORT and many individual state disaster teams. Activity in this area may result in identification but more often it provides important leads that saves significant time in

Figure 6.15 Refrigerated trucks at DPMU East for body storage but actually used by DMORT team members as "sleeping quarters" early in the operation.

obtaining a scientific positive identification. In addition to data entry and maintenance of the VIP, the clerical area is responsible for the clerical needs of the legal authorities involved in the disaster. Working with the state or local medical examiner, coroner or county attorney, and the command staff of the mortuary operation, they are responsible for data entry, receiving, creation, and filing of the records, documents, and reports required in a disaster.

6.5 Protocol for a Local or State DVI Dental Section

The protocols the Morgue operation should be determined before an event occurs. This includes the development of the Dental Team itself and how it will function. In 1994, the American Dental Association passed resolution 1994:654, which states, "the American Dental Association urges all constituents to develop dental identification teams that can be mobilized at times of need."

Many states presently have their own dental identification teams, some under the auspices of the state governmental organizations and/or local dental associations. More information regarding state DVI teams may be found at http://www.abfo.org/id_teams.htm. The medical examiner or coroner with jurisdiction over a disaster scene will normally consult with the appropriate state, county, and/or municipal agencies to determine if the existing disaster plans are sufficient to meet the needs or if additional external support is needed (Figures 6.16 and 6.17).

6.5.1 Formation of a Dental Identification Team

It is typically not difficult to identify and recruit dental personnel who come forward as willing volunteers for a "mass disaster dental identification team." However, without further planning and training this yields, in truth, a simple list of names, addresses, and telephone numbers. There are numerous details related to the function and operation of such a team that must be addressed *before* disaster strikes. Often times this is sadly not the case

Figure 6.16 April 27, 2011: 64 tornados struck Alabama killing 255 victims. (Courtesy of Dr. Roger Metcalf.)

Figure 6.17 Apartment complex destroyed by tornado in Tuscaloosa, Alabama. (Courtesy of Dr. Roger Metcalf.)

and the shortcomings are illustrated as the "chaos" of the tumultuous event progresses and the team and the "plan" begin to fail. Also, unfavorable attrition rates of "volunteers" in a prolonged DVI operation are well known.

First, there must be a sufficient cache of needed dental equipment, instruments, and supplies established prior to the event. Also, there are several mass disaster software programs available such as WinID3, UVIS/UDIM, and DVI that may be used. However, the jurisdiction must select and purchase the systems and all related computers and server/network components so that training may occur well before the event. Governing agencies often do not realize that there are many systems and techniques used by a Dental ID team, which are not found in the typical dental office. Also, are the team members to be strictly volunteers or temporary employees? Will there be compensation for team members including travel, meals, and lodging? Most importantly, has the organizing agency made provisions for workers compensation insurance in case of injury or even death during the event? All of these concerns must be addressed before the event occurs.

6.5.2 Dental Section Team Leader

The dental team leader is responsible for the entire team operations. There should be only one designated team section leader in command at any given time during a mass fatality incident. This person should have an active state dental license, be actively involved as a forensic odontologist and, if possible, be certified by the American Board of Forensic Odontology. He or she should be associated with a local medical examiner or coroner's office of the jurisdiction. The team leader should also be familiar with other agencies that will be involved in a mass fatality incident. The team leader will be responsible for reviewing *all* dental identifications before forwarding to the medical examiner that is in charge of the operation. The medical examiner should only accept a dental identification when it has been signed by two team members and the dental section leader.

When an incident occurs the team leader will be notified by the agency in charge, most likely the medical examiner's Office. A "Go Team" will be notified first by the team leader. The method of notification will be decided upon prior to the incident and can be by phone, email, etc. All members of the Go Team will have leadership roles in the organization. These personnel will plan on being present for the entire mass fatality incident. Once decisions are made, the "Support Team" will be notified and requested to arrive. A time will be given for their arrival. Support Team members can be made up of dentists and nondental personnel for administrative duties. When all personnel arrive, work will begin the morgue.

During the incident, the team leader will provide orientation and briefing for the team on a daily basis. Each group member will be issued identification for security. The team leader is responsible for monitoring stress, debriefing, and assigning counseling, if needed, during and at the end of the incident.

The odontology team is divided into three sections: postmortem, antemortem, and comparison. Each section will have a lead individual assigned by the dental team leader.

6.5.3 Postmortem Dental Section

The personnel make up and team numbers will be dependent on the scale of the disaster. Generally, there will be five members assigned to the postmortem section on any given shift, assuming that the team will be using today's digital postmortem data collection systems and the possibility of surgical access exists. The responsibility of the postmortem team includes the dental autopsy. This consists of a complete dental examination and charting of existing restorations and unique features present. A full mouth series of radiographs (bitewings and periapicals) are obtained. It is standard practice that two members examine the victim for the dental charting. This reduces the chance of an error. One dentist will examine and the second dentist will verify what is present. A third member records the information on the postmortem information sheet or more likely, the computer. The fourth and fifth members will be responsible for obtaining the victims' radiographic and photographic images. Photography is performed as directed by the team leader. Photographs may be useful in the identification process if antemortem records are minimal. There are often issues in gaining access to the dental tissues and structures with disaster victims. When this occurs, a jaw resection may be required. However, this is only done with permission of the medical examiner. The dental team leader will make the decision as to whether resection of the maxilla or mandible is necessary and then will present this to the medical examiner or coroner. The different techniques are described in Chapter 4.

All fragments and resected structures should be placed in containers and labeled with the appropriate case numbers. If tooth pulpal DNA is requested, this may require the removal of teeth for processing. These specimens must be labeled with the Medical Examiner's case number and stored in an appropriate manner.

6.5.4 Antemortem Dental Section

This section consists of an experienced section leader, and teams of three members consisting of two dentists and an additional dentist or auxiliary. However, with the advent of computer-assisted identification systems, antemortem members may work independently in "initially" compiling the data but then as a pair when the process of data entry and comparison begins. Specific individuals should be assigned the task of digitally scanning all of the antemortem radiographs in an ideal situation and if staffing is sufficient. Scanning and properly exporting antemortem images into the WinID system has been shown to be an area in which critical mistakes are made. Quality control here is crucial as these mistakes made may not be readily apparent and may interfere with the identification process in the long term. Typically, antemortem records will not be received immediately, possibly as a matter of days or weeks. Once records start to arrive, the antemortem section's function is to collect the antemortem dental information for the deceased. Records are then charted on a common form or entered directly into the computer. The components of this recorded antemortem information can be found in Chapter 4. Charting conversion tables may be needed if dealing with deceased individuals from outside the United States. All such records must be transposed into the universal numbering system. WinID3 has an automated function that will covert DFI tooth notation into the Universal System, and vice versa. The section leader reviews the information for completeness. The records are then sent to the Comparison section, if the identifications are not made in this section (Figure 6.18).

Obtaining records in a disaster can sometimes be a daunting task. Suggested avenues of record procurement can be found in Chapter 4. Flight manifests or lists of the deceased should be requested. Also, dental records can at times be illegible. Poor radiographs and incomplete records are the norm. Other dental professionals can at times be reluctant to part with original records. It is necessary to receive original, labeled radiographs and photos if they are available. In 1996 the U.S. Congress passed the Health Insurance Portability and Accountability Act or HIPAA to assure the privacy of patients' medical and dental information. However, it made exemptions for law enforcement and medical examiners or coroners to legally allow the release of health records (Figure 6.19).

Figure 6.18 Antemortem workstation in DPMU West, Hurricane Katrina.

104th Congress
PUBLIC LAW 104-191

AUG. 21, 1996

HEALTH INSURANCE PORTABILITY AND *ACCOUNTABILITY*

subpart C - Compliance and Enforcement

§164.512 Uses and disclosures for which consent, an authorization, or opportunity to agree or object is not required.

45 CFR 164.512 (g) *HIPPAA* Exception for Law Enforcement
(f) Standard: Disclosures for law enforcement purposes.
(3) A covered entity may disclose protected information in response to a law enforcement official's request for such information about an individual who is or is suspected to be a victim of a crime

45 CFR 164.512(g) HIPPAA Exemption for Medical Examiners and Coroners
(g) Standard: Uses and disclosures about decedents.
(1) Coroners and medical examiners. A covered entity may disclose protected health information to a coroner or medical examiner for the purpose of identifying a deceased person, determining a cause of death, or other duties as authorized by law. A covered entity that also performs the duties of a coroner or medical examiner may use protected health information for the purposes described in this paragraph.

Figure 6.19 HIPAA document related to exemptions for law enforcement and coroners or medical examiners when requesting dental records.

6.5.5 Dental Comparison Section

The comparison team is made up of antemortem and postmortem team members. Each group should be made up of three members, allowing three sets of eyes to review each case. As stated previously, modern computer-assisted systems may allow this team to be more efficiently composed of two examiners, with the additional final scrutiny performed by the team leader.

The primary responsibility of the comparison section is to make the identifications. They will review the information from the antemortem section and the postmortem section and make their decision. The use of forensic dental software, discussed later in this chapter, can assist in this comparison. However, the final determination is always made by the forensic dontologists, not the computer. Once the victim's identity is established, it is then relayed to the medical examiner or in some cases, the appropriate specified representative of the Information Resource Center. Again, to avoid numerous pitfalls, the chain of command should be respected and ONLY the team leader should perform this function.

As an added note, team members should observe proper protocols regarding the confidentiality of all information gleaned in the dental section. It is *mandatory* that team members not speak with individuals outside of the operation and in particular, the media, without explicit permission from the commanding individual in charge of the entire DVI team. This type of irresponsibility has been shown to be the most expeditious way to secure an immediate trip back to your home!

6.5.6 Dental Examination Supplies

The supplies needed for the dental section during DVI operations are typical, with some exceptions, of the supplies used in most dental offices when examining a patient. These include mirrors, explorers, molt-style mouth props, cotton pliers, and various hemostats and scissors. In addition, the postmortem dental examination station will have various scalpel blades and handles, Stryker saws, small Maglite flashlights to aid in illumination, UV light sources (wavelength 395 nm) to aid in the recognition of composite materials. Also needed are laptop computers with the WinID3 and the DEXIS Digital x-ray programs loaded on them, DEXIS digital x-ray sensors and holders, digital cameras, and portable x-ray generators. Disposable supplies typically include isopropyl alcohol, sodium hypochlorite, disinfecting solutions, cotton rolls, cotton gauze squares, cellophane wrap for wrapping the equipment that cannot be sterilized (table surfaces, x-ray generators, computer keyboards, etc.), digital sensor sleeves to protect the x-ray sensors, duct tape, sharps containers, examination gloves, and masks. And if possible, having fiber optic headlamps is extremely useful for the examination process, if they can be procured (Figure 6.20).

6.5.7 Morgue Shifts

Each mass fatality incident is different, and there is no definitive way to determine the exact number of needed forensic odontologists and the length of each shift. Also, long-established protocols based on the old systems of pencils, paper charts, filing cabinets, antemortem records laid out on tables in the morgue, dental films, and x-ray view boxes are no longer valid. Today, if there is only one x-ray unit, one digital x-ray sensor,

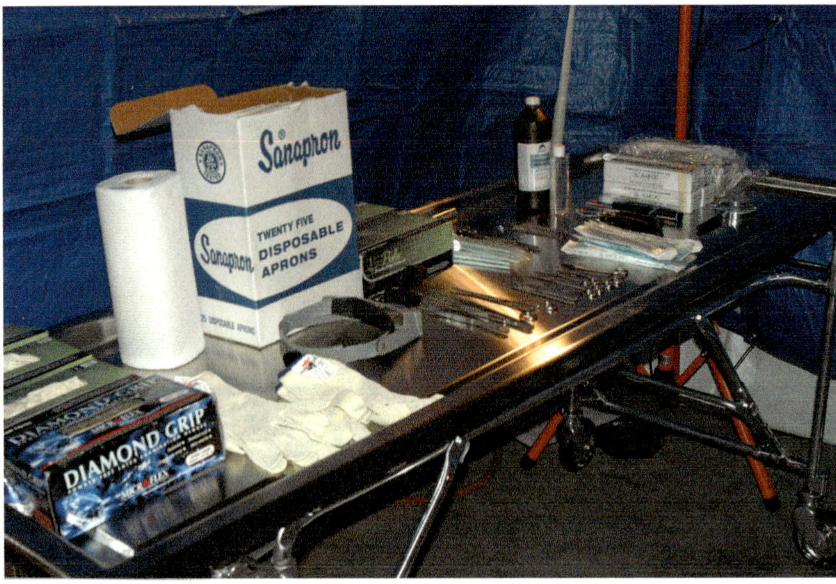

Figure 6.20 Supplies for a DPMU dental station. Note lack of paper forms, dental radiographic processor, and films.

one laptop and one camera, then there will be only one body being processed at a time. In this case, four to five forensic dentists in the morgue would be ideal. If there are two dental stations each with its own digital equipment, then six to seven forensic odontologists would be needed, with certain tasks such as photography, completed by one shared individual. The length of the shifts for these individuals will depend on the number of deceased needing to be processed through the dental station and the availability of forensic odontologists to work each shift. Shifts can vary from 3 to 4 h up to 12 h. It is important to have mandatory time for meals and breaks every few hours. In no case should a shift be more than 12 h. A command mistake by DVI Commanders is the lack of understanding that when the morgue shuts down for the day, the dental section members still have much work remaining comparing the data collected during the shift and making identifications. This is a particular problem if there are not enough dental members assigned to the disaster.

6.6 Portable Dental X-Ray Generator

In recent years, a major breakthrough in obtaining postmortem radiographs was the advent of the NOMAD™ hand-held, battery-powered x-ray generator. In its first use in the disaster response to the tsunami disaster in Southeast Asia, the NOMAD, manufactured by Aribex (Aribex, Inc., Orem, UT 84097), proved to be an extremely dependable and effective device. Its compact size and the utility of its battery-powered operation proved to be very useful in the relatively austere environment. Its first domestic use in a DVI morgue was by DMORT in the aftermath of Hurricane Katrina where in conjunction with the DEXIS digital x-rays sensor, it performed admirably and provided the postmortem dental examination station with consistently high-quality dental radiographs.

Currently there are two models of the NOMAD. The classic NOMAD is the original version of the device (Figure 6.21). It weighs approximately eight pounds and is shielded in such

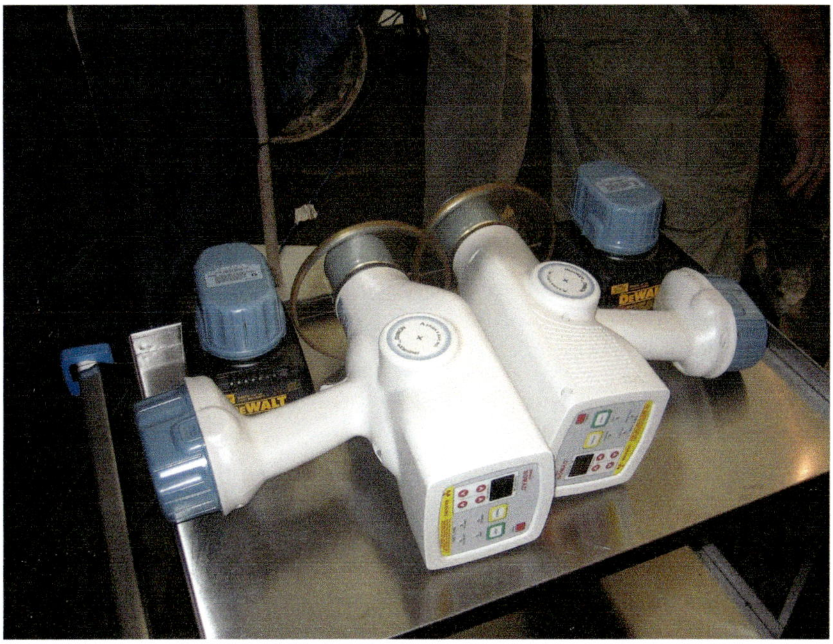

Figure 6.21 NOMAD hand-held dental x-ray generators and rechargeable batteries.

a way as to essentially eliminate all leakage from the body of the device. This eliminated a common problem with previous x-ray devices, which required the operator to stand at least 6ft from the x-ray head when exposing a radiograph (Pittayapat et al., 2010). The NOMAD has a back-scatter shield that minimizes the amount of back-scatter radiation, thus creating a "zone of safety" behind the device for the operator to operate the device protected from the scatter (Turner et al., 2005). This zone is optimized, however, only when the scatter shield is placed at exposure end of the cone (position indicating device) (Figure 6.22).

Due to significant radiation safety concerns historically, the use of hand-held x-ray devices has previously been prohibited. However, independent research has provided overwhelming evidence of the NOMAD's safety to all members of the dental morgue team with exposure readings are negligible, measuring well below the allowed annual maximum permissible doses (MPD) (Hermsen et al., 2008; Danforth et al., 2009; NCRP, 2003, 2009). Therefore, no additional shielding of the operator or assistant is required unless one must be positioned within the primary beam.

The newest version is the NOMAD Pro™. It has improved shielded to prevent radiation leakage and its smaller design weighs only five and one-half pounds. In addition to its smaller size, the "Pro" has incorporated a mechanism to lock the device, which prohibits its use by unauthorized personnel. At this point, both versions of the NOMAD have been approved for hand-held use in most, if not all, states (Herschaft et al., 2010).

Of course, radiation safety procedures must always be followed to comply with the ALARA principle (As Low As Reasonably Achievable). Using either model of the NOMAD does not dismiss the operator from responsibility for following accepted radiation safety procedures, which include never allowing auxiliary personnel to stand in direct line with the central beam, using the lowest exposure time setting possible, and maintaining as much space as possible between adjacent examination units. There is also a mounting stand available for the units, if so desired.

Figure 6.22 NOMAD units and DEXIS sensor radiographing skeletal remains. Note that the NOMAD shield is not at the maximum protection location at end of PID.

Another portable x-ray device that is effective in a dental morgue setting is the MinXray™ portable x-ray device (MinXray, Inc., 3611 Commercial Avenue, Northbrook, IL 60062). Many morgue operations employ the MinXray medical system for obtaining full-body x-rays. There are two dental versions. The HF70DUL model is a high-frequency tubehead, weighs 10 pounds, and may be hand-held or mounted on a tripod stand (X100S). A back-scatter shield is an available option and should be purchased if the device is to be used in a hand-held manner. The P200D MK model weighs 18 pounds and must be operated on a tripod stand due to its weight. One critical factor with these units is that the configuration of the tripod stands for both units is without a horizontal supporting arm for the tubehead. The result is that they are best suited for patients in a seated or standing position as opposed to the supine positions in a morgue setting.

6.7 Digital Dental Radiography Sensors

Digital radiography was first utilized in a DVI setting after the crash of TWA Flight 800 on July 17, 1996 when 230 lives were lost. It has since become an indispensable part of victim identification. Digital radiography can be discussed along the same lines as digital photography. Both involve sensor technology that captures either the light spectrum for photography or the x-ray spectrum for radiology. Where photography uses mega pixels to define the resolution of the sensor, radiology uses line pairs per millimeter to do the same. For a digital sensor to be equal to conventional film radiograph resolution, it should approach 22 line pairs per millimeter. As an example, this will allow the examiner to easily distinguish the tip of a number ten endodontic file.

Sensor design is important in forensic applications. The impermeable, nonflexible sensors can withstand the extreme conditions in which they are used. Sensors of different sizes have little advantage in the forensic field due to the fact most cases can be accessed easier than living cases. In practice, sensors with cables do pose some problems regarding breakage.

At this point both the Schick sensors and the DEXIS sensors have been used to the greatest extent in DVI morgues and have proven to be effective. Comparatively, one advantage of the DEXIS software is that it can function with either sensor and has bridged to the WinID3 dental charting and matching software for a complete dental software package. Both sensors can be used in tandem with the hand-held NOMAD or MinXray x-ray systems to allow easy movement and access in the morgue setting.

The Schick sensor is thinner than the DEXIS sensor. This is because with the DEXIS sensor, the sensor electronics are located within a small dome on the back of the sensor. This increases thickness of the sensor but also allows for the entire face of the sensor case to be available for radiation exposure. The Schick sensor is thinner, but gains this by placing the sensor hardware around the outer edge of the sensor, thus reducing the exposure surface dimensions. The result is that DEXIS sensor is physically smaller than the Schick sensor, but the active exposure areas of the two are similarly sized (Figure 6.23).

In large operations it has been found that these sensors are capable of taking thousands of radiographs and then being packed up and stored for the next operation. Most sensors state their life in the 200,000 exposure range. Digital radiography also can increase the quality control of the operation. Once a digital image is captured it can be reviewed in real time. This means unacceptable angulation or exposures can be corrected and retaken on the spot. It has rarely been appreciated that this capability and the elimination of the film processing cycle has accounted for the savings of hundreds (perhaps thousands) of man-hours in the dental section over the course of recent DVI operation.

Digital scanners allow images or objects to be scanned and then digitized, transferred, and stored for later retrieval and review. In dental identification scenarios, scanners are usually located in the antemortem and comparison areas of the operation and

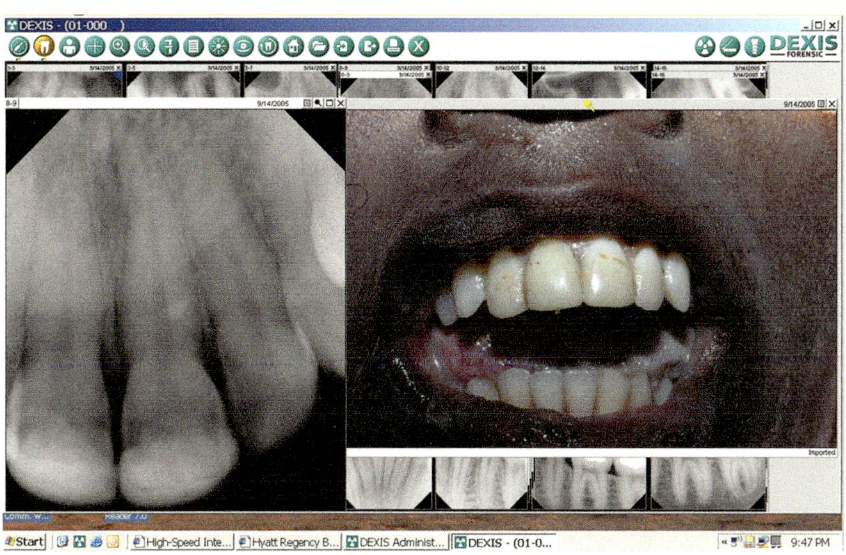

Figure 6.23 DEXIS radiographic system displaying radiographic and photographic images.

allow antemortem information to be entered in a paperless digital system. All antemortem written records, photographs, conventional radiographs, and charting can be scanned into the digital record. Large format scanners can scan films all the way up to panoramic and cephalic size films.

For several years after DMORT purchased the requested digital dental equipment, its dental teams conducted regional hands-on training with the entire digital package including DEXIS sensors and specimen, networked laptops loaded with WinID, scanners, and the NOMAD device. The stated goal was to improve the dental workstation efficiency by using no paper or pencils, no film, and no film processor. When Katrina occurred, that goal was effectively met. It was, in fact, a bit shocking to witness that when the morgue generator occasionally failed at the DPMU East, the dental team was able to continue their work using flashlights, a battery-operated tubehead, and a laptop also running on battery power.

6.8 Computer-Assisted Dental Identification Software

6.8.1 CAPMI

Computers have been used for many years by forensic odontologists. As computer applications were developed, the ability to simply list or catalogue cases evolved into "search and match" capabilities. The first dental application to do this was Computer Assisted Post Mortem Identification (CAPMI), developed by Lorton, Langley, and Weed (programming specialist) in the late 1980s. It was used by the U.S. Military on many mass disasters and soon by many forensic odntologists in the private sector. The CAPMI program was used was the bombing of the Alfred P. Murrah Federal Building in Oklahoma City, Oklahoma in 1995 and in the Crash of TWA Flight 800 off the coast of Long Island, New York in 1996. Subsequent disasters utilized windows-based computer systems.

6.8.2 WinID3

WinID was developed by Dr. James McGivney as a free, computer-assisted dental identification application, which has been used by forensic odontologists, pathologists, coroners, medical examiners, forensic anthropologists, law enforcement, and the criminal justice systems to identify the unknown. This Windows-based program has been used in numerous mass disasters including the terrorist attack on the World Trade Center, Hurricanes Katrina and Ike, and the EF 5 tornado in Joplin, Missouri in 2011.

WinID3 uses an intuitive algorithm that gives it the ability not only to sort for requested identifiers, but to compensate and not eliminate identifier changes that have occurred due to reasonable and explainable differences. For instance, a tooth that is reported as virgin or nonrestored in an antemortem record and shown as restored in a postmortem record will not be eliminated from consideration because the time lapse between the two allows for work to have been done on that particular tooth. Additionally, it will not exclude possible matches where an impossible treatment progression seems to have occurred. In doing so, it accounts for human error in data entry.

It also has numerous open categories outside of the dental section that can be used by other disciplines to sort and search for information. In this way, WinID3 can be used as a total package if desired by the disaster operational director or medical examiner (Figure 6.24). WinID3 may be used in several languages and using metric versus English measurements

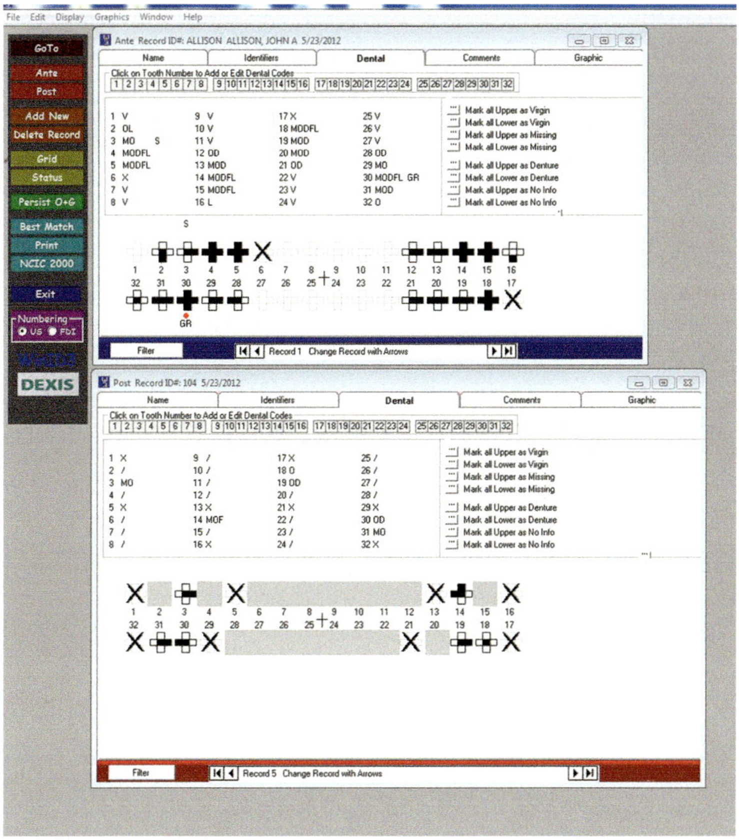

Figure 6.24 WinID3 charting odontogram.

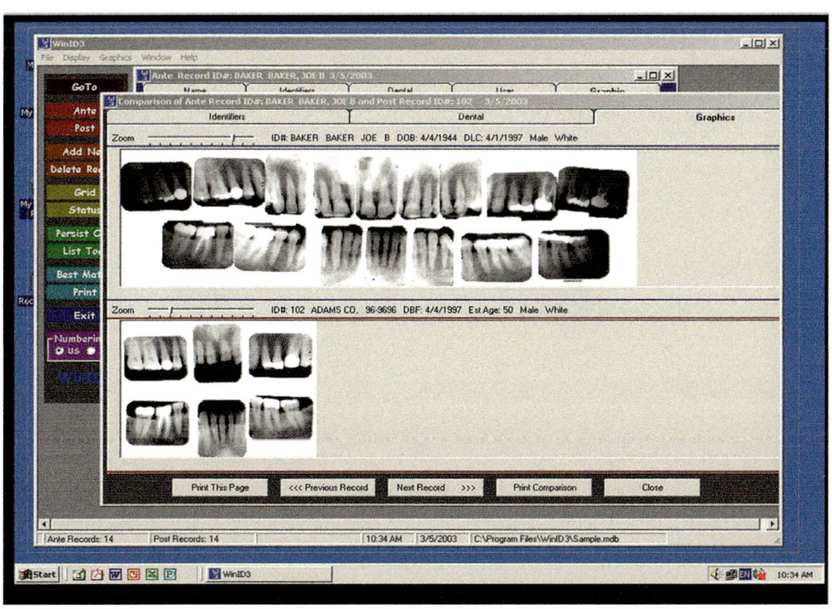

Figure 6.25 WinID3 image window showing comparison of antemortem and postmortem radiographs.

and numbering systems. In the mid 2000s, Dr. McGivney WinID3 developed a "bridge" with DEXIS (a digital radiography application for capture and management of dental radiographs and all other photographs and documents associated with a particular record). This allows WinID3 to combine dental charting with the radiographic/photographic record for a seamless integrated system of case review and comparison. In the postmortem arena, this allows radiographs and photographs to be captured and viewed in real time as the examiners chart and views the victim's dental conditions (Figure 6.25).

WinID3 has also been used with touch screen tablets successfully in a morgue setting. The program is available as a free standing application or can be used as a "Cloud" application from the WinID3 website. WinID3 has been proven in the field and improved through various version changes. The program may be accessed through its website www.WinID3.com.

6.8.3 DVI System International

DVI System International was developed by Plass Data Software and is used by INTERPOL for international disasters including the response to the 2004 Tsunami in Thailand. DVI is a total mass disaster program and the dental section is an integrated part of that system. It can accomplish advanced searches for all entered data including DNA and dental findings. DVI has also been utilized in maintaining national missing and unidentified persons. The system has the capability to print all of its various disaster-related forms in English, French, Spanish, Norwegian, Dutch, Swedish, Danish, and German languages (Figure 6.26).

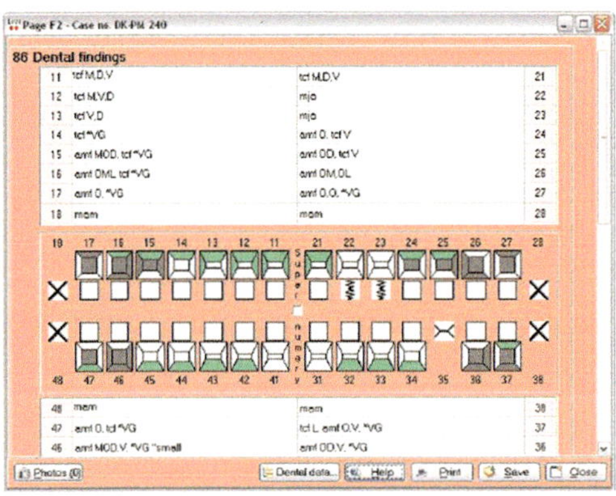

F2–Dental information

The system is designed to make it possible to display a detailed and complex dental record, for example, in single cases it is possible to transfer a dental description with the purpose of identifying a dead person in another region or country.

In an accident with many victims, it is possible to make a fast registration of the very specific details, making it possible for the system to point out single plausible matches, which are subsequently manually examined in detail before final identification.

Automatic batch matching on all dental data can also be initialized. The result of this can easily be iterated and validated by viewing the graphical dental comparison. Fully integrated with the reconciliation status.

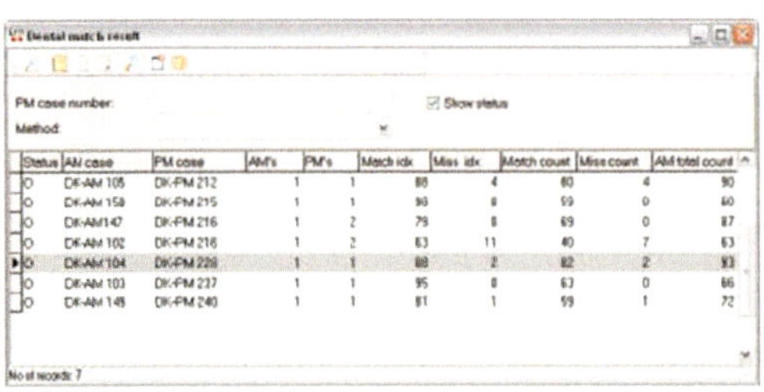

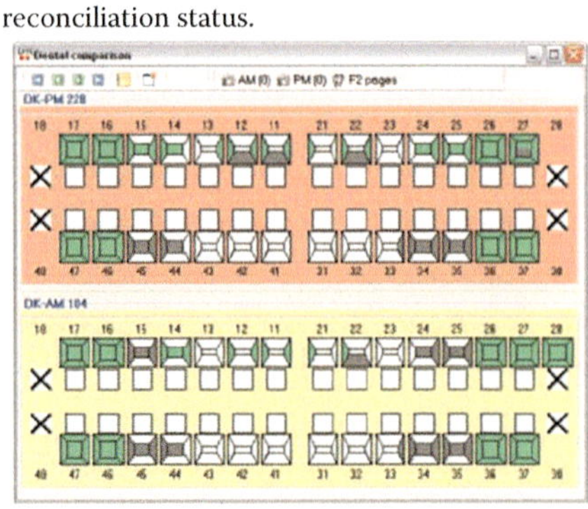

Figure 6.26 Screen capture of example of DVI program odontograms.

The dental section has good graphics for charting and works well in sorting for restorations and dental conditions. It allows dental radiographs to be entered into a template type section for later review, but depends on outside scanning of conventional radiographs or digital capture programs to obtain the images. This means an additional step for the dental identification team to insert images into the database. The dental section is not available as a stand-alone program and thus, the entire DVI System International must be obtained to utilize the dental component. To obtain a DVI trial package visit its website at www.plass.dlk. The download and setup may take a considerable time to accomplish.

6.8.4 UVIS/UDIM

UVIS (Unified Victim Identification System) is a robust mass disaster management system that manages and coordinates all of the activities related to victim identification and missing persons reporting. Developed for the City of New York following the September 11 attack, it includes modules related to law enforcement's missing persons data, a centralized "call center," field operations, FAC, morgue operations, and data obtained in the victim identifications processes.

UDIM (UVIS Dental Identification Module) is the dental recording/search component of the system. This dental module was developed by Dr. Kenneth Aschheim in consultation with the forensic odontologists of the NYC Office of the Chief Medical Examiner (OMCE) and was released in 2007. It includes a self-correcting coding interface, a unique color-coded odontogram for rapid comparison and evaluation, partial jaw fragment management, linking and joining of specimens, and unlimited image importation (Figure 6.27).

UDIM has an intuitive algorithm to allow record comparisons. In addition to UDIM's color-coding odontogram, it also highlights both explainable and unexplainable discrepancies. The application is easy to use and works in a similar fashion to WinID3. UDIM reportedly now has a direct bridge with DEXIS to allow information to flow between the

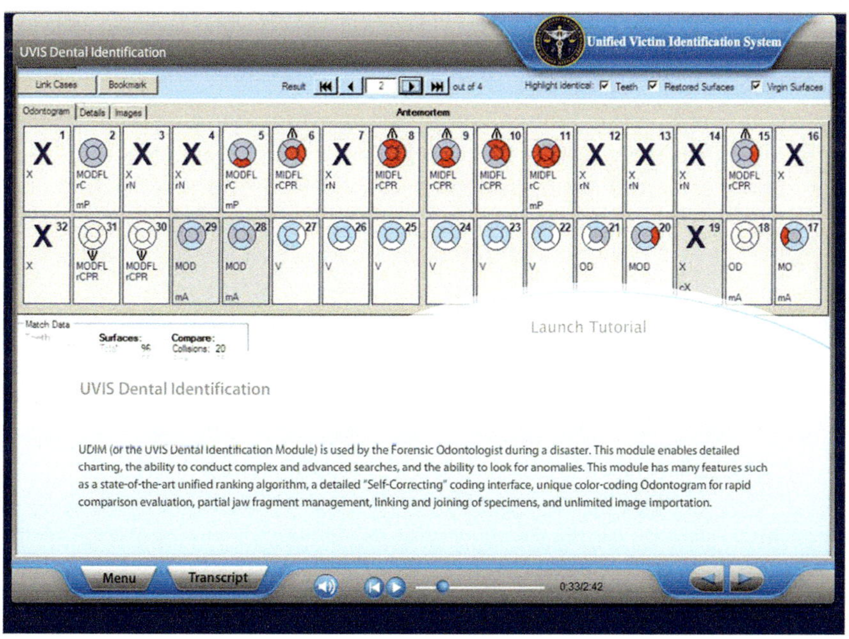

Figure 6.27 Screen capture of tutorial for UVIS system's dental module (UMID).

two programs. UVIS/UDIM is not designed to be used on a stand-alone laptop. It requires both a web server and SQL server as well some expertise to get it installed and running. UVIS is evolving from a disaster response system into a complete morgue package for every daily use. The system is free of charge to law enforcement entities and government agencies. Multimillion dollar upgrades are in the works for future improvements to the package. These improvements include touch screen capabilities and the ability to switch from FDI to Universal dental coding. UVIS/UDIM can be reviewed on its website at https://uvistraining.com/.

In summary, the integration of a digital image system into or in association with a dental database application decreases the possibility of human error in managing digital information. Switching from application to application can create confusion and introduce mistakes. Being able to have seamless and direct access to a fully functional digital image enhancement application (e.g., DEXIS), along with automatic case or body number assignment from the computer-assisted comparison program to the imaging program is extremely valuable. Both can reduce or eliminate critical errors. As can be seen earlier, one system already uses this and another is developing this concept. The forensic odontologist is still responsible for the final decisions in comparing antemortem and postmortem records. However, these computer programs become invaluable in instances where the victim count runs into the hundreds or thousands. As the identification of human remains evolves and improves in efficiency, computer-assisted dental programs need to respond in kind. In looking to the future, user-friendly programs with the ability to integrate with similar programs used by other agencies and disciplines should be developed and will add to the tools available to the forensic odontology arsenal.

6.9 Technological Advances in Dental Identification/Flight 3407

Flight 3407 crashed in a suburb of Buffalo, New York, on February 12, 2009. Circumstances associated with the mass fatality incident were similar to other disasters involving airline accidents: incineration and fragmentation. Thirty eight of the fifty victims were identified through dental records. Three of the fifty were not dentally identified due to a lack of antemortem records. Eight were not dentally identified due to insufficient quality and quantity of postmortem evidence. Of the identified victims, the use of microscopy and analytical technology was instrumental in providing identifications that may have otherwise not been possible. Two cases will be presented where the use of analytical technology was used to the benefit of the forensic dental team and emphasize the importance of record keeping. See Chapter 4 for further information regarding analysis methods.

In the first case, forensic archeological recovery provided the team with numerous fragments of disassociated dental remains including teeth, maxillary, and mandibular fragments. These fragments ranged in condition from calcined to charred and carbonized to relatively pristine. Radiographic and clinical evaluation of a majority of these teeth and fragments yielded little or no useful information. Some of the fragments did reveal the presence of endodontic and restorative treatment that necessitated further analysis.

A fragment was identified as a lower right mandibular segment containing teeth #30 and 31 without #32. This fragment was calcined and fragile and radiographic examination showed traces of possible root canal therapy #30. The clinical crowns had fractured and there was no evidence of restorative materials present. Two unidentified victims of the disaster had the profile suggested earlier. Morphological image comparison between the fragment and the antemortem radiograph was not conclusive for an identification based primarily on the postmortem damage to the incinerated specimen. The use of a stereo microscope showed the root of #30 to contain small silver blebs that are suggestive of root canal sealer. Further analysis of this material through scanning electron microscope (SEM) and energy dispersive x-ray spectrography (EDs) showed the presence of elements that are unique to a particular brand of root canal sealer. The use of this sealer was clearly documented in the dental record of the presumed associated victim adding another level of certainty for a positive identification. This fragment was the only identifiable fragment establishing an identity of this victim.

Another lower right mandibular fragment was also recovered. This segment was not calcined but was more charred and carbonized demonstrating exposure to a decreased time and temperature exposure than the fragment discussed before. Radiographically and clinically the fragment did not appear to show evidence of restorative treatment even though the coronal portion of #31 was relatively intact. Upon further inspection with a stereo microscope significant evidence was disclosed. A circular buccal preparation was noted along with a longitudinal preparation on the occlusal surface. These preparations were further analyzed using SEM-EDS. The elemental analysis confirmed the existence of a previous buccal amalgam and an occlusal composite resin restoration. The trace composite resin was entered into a dental material database incorporating elemental composition and filler particle size. The composite was identified as a particular brand and attempts were made to compare this information to the victim's dental record. The dental record was not complete as to brand name and this lack of significant dental information precluded relationship of this fragment to a potential victim. This victim identification was established by other methods.

Advanced analytical techniques and accurate and complete dental records can add another level of evidentiary certainty under extreme conditions of incineration and fragmentation (Bush and Miller, 2011).

References

ABFO Mass Fatality Guidelines: The Development of a Dental Identification Team, pp. 158–167. www.abfo.org.

Bush, M.A., R.G. Miller. 2011. The crash of Colgan Air Flight 3407: Advanced techniques in victim identification. *J Am Dent Assoc* 142(12):1352–1356.

Danforth, R.A., E.E. Herschaft, J.A. Leonowich. 2009. Operator exposure to scatter radiation from a portable hand-held dental radiation emitting device (Aribex NOMAD) while making 915 intraoral dental radiographs. *J. Forensic Sci* 54(2):415–421.

Hermsen, K.P., S.S. Jaeger, M.A. Jaeger. 2008. Radiation safety for the NOMAD portable x-ray system in a temporary morgue setting. *J Forensic Sci* 53(4):917–921.

Herschaft, E.E., K.P. Hermsen, R.A. Danforth, T.J. McGiff. 2010. Current radiation safety regulatory policies and the utilization status in the United States of the nomad portable hand-held dental radiation emitting device. Paper presented at: AAFS Annual Meeting; Seattle, WA.

NCRP Report No. 145. 2003. *Radiation Protection in Dentistry*, National Council on Radiation Protection and Measurements, Bethesda, MD.

NCRP Report No. 160. 2009. *Ionizing Radiation Exposure of the Population of the United States*, National Council on Radiation Protection and Measurements, Bethesda, MD.

Pittayapat, P., C. Oliveira-Santos, P. Thevissen, K. Michielsen, N. Bergans, G. Willems. 2010. Image quality assessment and medical physics evaluation of different portable dental x-ray units. *Forensic Sci Int* 201:112–117.

Turner, D.C., D.K. Kloos, R. Morton. 2005. *Radiation Safety Characteristics of the NOMAD Portable X-ray System*, Aribex, Inc., Orem, UT.

U.S. Department of Health and Human Services. 2012. Disaster Mortuary Operational Response Teams (DMORTs). http://www.phe.gov/Preparedness/responders/ndms/teams/Pages/dmort.aspx

Missing and Unidentified Persons

7

STEPHANIE A. KAVANAUGH
JOHN E. FILIPPI

Contents

7.1 Introduction 194
7.2 National Crime Information Center/National Dental Image/Information Repository 194
7.2.1 National Crime Information Center Background 195
7.2.2 National Dental Image/Information Repository 199
7.2.3 Dental Coding Workshops 199
7.3 Laws Covering the Handing of Missing and Unidentified Persons 200
7.3.1 H.R. 1300: Billy's Law 200
7.3.2 Jennifer's Law 200
7.3.3 Kristen's Law (Public Law #106-468) 200
7.4 Other Resources Trainings and Government Agencies 200
7.4.1 NCIC/NDIR Sponsored Training Sessions 200
7.4.2 National Missing and Unidentified Persons System (NamUs) 201
7.4.2.1 History of NamUs 201
7.4.2.2 Missing and Unidentified Persons Database 201
7.4.2.3 NamUs Training 203
7.4.3 The National Center of Missing and Exploited Children 204
7.4.4 Violent Criminal Apprehension Program 204
7.4.5 Private Sector and State Agencies 204
7.4.5.1 The DOE Network 204
7.4.5.2 Let's Bring Them Home/National Center for Missing Adults 205
7.4.5.3 Florida Unidentified Decedents Database 205
7.4.5.4 California Missing Persons 205
7.4.6 Social Media 205
7.4.7 International Agencies 206
7.4.7.1 International Criminal Police Organization 206
7.4.7.2 Canadian Police Information Centre 207
7.5 Dental Information in Missing and Unidentified Cases 208
7.6 Conclusion 210
Acknowledgments 210
Disclaimer 210
References 210

7.1 Introduction

The scope of this chapter includes discussing and addressing the concerns associated with the identification of the thousands of missing (MP(s)) and unidentified persons (UP(s)) in the United States. This chapter will focus on the role forensic dentistry can play in helping address the problem by providing services to families, law enforcements, agencies, coroners, and medical examiners. Current concepts and software programs being utilized in the United States as well as a listing of resource assistance for those agencies, jurisdictions, and individuals who have an interest or a responsibility in missing and/or unidentified persons' reporting are discussed below.

Dental comparison has long been accepted as a reliable means of human identification. However, officials do not fully understand the range of systems and resources available to assist them in their investigations. Also, they frequently do not have the manpower and/or economic resources to collect the information needed for a forensic odontologist to assist them in missing and unidentified persons' cases.

The goal of this chapter is to provide information to assist and support the forensic odontologist as well as the law enforcement personnel and coroner/medical examiner offices with those cases that require or possess this type of forensic dental evidence. Discussions will reference the system(s) available for submission, the importance of dental radiographs, and accurate, consistent dental coding entry. The value of electronic archiving of the dental data and the opportunities for comparison analysis, whether they are based on an exclusionary format or to establish a positive identification, will be discussed.

7.2 National Crime Information Center/National Dental Image/Information Repository

The issues involved with missing and UP cases are numerous and more often than not somewhat unique when compared to crimes against persons and property. The practices of law enforcement and coroner/medical examiner offices in handling these cases are also distinctive. Prior to the 1970s, the magnitude of this subject was not generally appreciated. Local agencies' MP cases were investigated to varying degrees. Those cases involving suspicious or criminal activity were often investigated with more attention than others, while those involving adults that simply disappeared were handled on a time-available basis. Suspected juvenile "runaways" may also have been lower on the priority list until it was mandated that reports in those cases be taken and the cases investigated.

Currently, runaways less than 21 years of age account for up to 70% of the active MP cases in the United States. Often, these cases involve individuals that "disappear" and then "reappear" within a few days or weeks, and law enforcement agencies simply do not have the manpower to investigate each and every one of these. Local coroners and medical examiners attempt to identify the remains recovered in their jurisdictions and in the vast majority of cases are successful due to material evidence recovered with the remains and/or information available at the recovery site. However, over the years, many cases remained unidentified, and MP cases were unresolved. Until recently, the number of active MP cases entered in the National Crime Information Center (NCIC) at any given time numbered more than 100,000. Recently, the numbers have fallen to a little greater than 80,000. The number of UPs in the system has been increasing over the past few years and currently is in excess of

7000. As previously noted, this figure is likely only a fraction of the actual number of UPs as many are not entered into NCIC, which is another significant problem. Another part of the equation is the number of "wanted" persons (WPs) who also can be considered to be "missing." The number of these WPs is more than one million at any given time. The bottom line is that there are at least 7000 UPs that could be any one of the more than one million missing or wanted individuals. It is well known that not all MPs are reported as missing, and it is logical to assume not all WPs have been entered into the system. MP and WP cases may not be entered, and some cases are cleared and new cases are entered on a regular basis. The "pool" of MP and UP possible identification candidates is constantly changing, and the UPs are constantly being updated with new cases, some of which may have gone undiscovered for years. Fortunately, technology has enabled this seemingly impossible task to now become possible.

7.2.1 National Crime Information Center Background

In 1967, the NCIC was established to provide 24/7 information that would be helpful for criminal justice agencies in their investigations. Since its inception, it has grown to serve more than 100,000 agencies in all 50 states and Canada. The Federal Bureau of Investigation's (FBI) Criminal Justice Information Services division (CJIS) maintains the NCIC system. Changes to the system are under the direction of the NCIC Advisory Policy Board, which is made up of law enforcement personnel. It is a busy system with an average of >6 million transactions in any given 24 h period. The files in NCIC of relevance to this chapter are the WP file (established in 1967), the MP file (established in 1975), and the UP file (established in 1983). The information contained in these three files remains in the NCIC system indefinitely and is only removed when the investigating agency removes the active case.

With the addition of the UP file in 1983, NCIC began to automatically generate cross match reports (termed as a $.M reports). These reports list possible matching candidates from the MP and WP files. The comparison logic that generated the $.M reports from 1983 to 2004 used a weighted scoring system that did not put much weight on the dental information that was compared between the MP and the UP (comparison of dental information related to WPs was not implemented until 2004). This became evident to a few agencies in the mid-to-late 1980s when they recovered partial skeletal remains with intact dentitions, but very few other physical parameters for comparison. These cases had been entered into the United States Army Institute of Dental Research's dental data management and matching program called the Computer Aided Postmortem Identification (CAPMI) system, which was developed to identify victims of mass casualty events. Identifications were being made with the assistance of this program, while the information generated by the NCIC comparison logic was of very little, if any, help in the resolution of cases involving limited physical information but significant dental information. From 1997 to 1999, a group of forensic experts and law enforcement personnel studied the dental issue. This group presented recommendations for changes to the NCIC system and the addition of complementary programs to enable the dental information to become a key resource to the resolution of MP, WP, and UP cases.

The simplification of dental codes to describe an individual's dental characteristics (dental profile) and entry in the NCIC program was the primary change. The simplification process resulted in the reduction of codes from 56 to 10 codes. This required the development of new coding forms that reduced the 256 entry fields to 32 (Figures 7.1 through 7.3).

NCIC Unidentified Person File
Data Collection Entry Guide

Agency Case #__________

NCIC Unidentified Person Dental Report

SECTION 1

ME/Coroner Case #: __________ NCIC #: __________

Completed by: __________ Date Completed: __________

Address: __________

Telephone #: __________ Email Address: __________

X-Rays Available? ☒ Yes ☐ No Dental Models Available? ☐ Yes ☐ No Dental Photographs Available? ☒ Yes ☐ No

SECTION 2 *DENTAL CHARACTERISTICS*

Upper Right		(Numbers in parentheses represent FDI System.)	Lower Right	
01 (18)____			32 (48) ____	
02 (17)____			31 (47) ____	
03 (16)____			30 (46) ____	
04 (15)____	(A)		29 (45) ____	(T)
05 (14)____	(B)		28 (44) ____	(S)
06 (13)____	(C)		27 (43) ____	(R)
07 (12)____	(D)		26 (42) ____	(Q)
08 (11)____	(E)		25 (41) ____	(P)
Upper Left		(Letters in parentheses represent deciduous dentition.)	**Lower Left**	
09 (21)____	(F)		24 (31) ____	(O)
10 (22)____	(G)		23 (32) ____	(N)
11 (23)____	(H)		22 (33) ____	(M)
12 (24)____	(I)		21 (34) ____	(L)
13 (25)____	(J)		20 (35) ____	(K)
14 (26)____			19 (36) ____	
15 (27)____			18 (37) ____	
16 (28)____			17 (38) ____	

SECTION 3 *DENTAL CODES*

X = Tooth has been removed or did not develop
V = Tooth is present and unrestored
M = Mesial Surface Restored
O = Occlusal/Incisal Surface Restored
D = Distal Surface Restored
F = Facial or Buccal Surface Restored
L = Lingual Surface Restored
C = Lab Processed or Prefabricated Restoration
R = Endodontic Treatment
/ = Postmortem Missing or Not Recovered (Default Code)

(*The codes V and /are used differently in the Unidentified Person Report than in the Missing Person Dental Report.)

SECTION 4 *DENTAL REMARKS*

☐ **ALL** (All 32 teeth are present and unrestored) ☐ **UNK** (No dental information available)

Rev 2/06 30

Figure 7.1 NCIC unidentified persons dental report. (Reprinted with permission, NCIC.)

These changes alone minimized the subjective nature of dental record interpretation and significantly reduced the number of entry errors due to less-complicated entry fields. The changes were made after studying the research done in the mid-1980s regarding the degree of specificity needed to generate reliable and effective results when comparing dental profiles. The comparison logic was changed to that used in the CAPMI program, which had proven reliable after several years of use for MP and UP cases. These changes also eliminated the

NCIC Missing Person File
Data Collection Entry Guide

Agency Case # ________

NCIC Missing Person Dental Report

SECTION 1

Patient's Name: ________ Age at Disappearance: ________ NCIC #: ________

Completed by: ________ Date Completed: ________

Address: ________

Telephone #: ________ Email Address: ________

X-Rays Available? ☐ Yes ☐ No Dental Models Available? ☐ Yes ☐No Dental Photographs Available? ☐ Yes ☐No

Section 2 *DENTAL CHARACTERISTICS*

Upper Right		Lower Right	
01 (18)		32 (48)	
02 (17)		31 (47)	
03 (16)		30 (46)	
04 (15)	(A)	29 (45)	(T)
05 (14)	(B)	28 (44)	(S)
06 (13)	(C)	27 (43)	(R)
07 (12)	(D)	26 (42)	(Q)
08 (11)	(E)	25 (41)	(P)

(Numbers in parentheses represent FDI system.)

Upper Left		Lower Left	
09 (21)	(F)	24 (31)	(O)
10 (22)	(G)	23 (32)	(N)
11 (23)	(H)	22 (33)	(M)
12 (24)	(I)	21 (34)	(L)
13 (25)	(J)	20 (35)	(K)
14 (26)		19 (36)	
15 (27)		18 (37)	
16 (28)		17 (38)	

(Letters in parentheses represent deciduous dentition.)

SECTION 3 *DENTAL CODES*

X = Tooth has been removed or did not develop
V = Tooth is unrestored or no information (Default Code)
M = Mesial Surface Restored
O = Occlusal/Incisal Surface Restored
D = Distal Surface Restored
F = Facial or Buccal Surface Restored
L = Lingual Surface Restored
C = Lab Processed or Prefabricated Restoration
R = Endodontic Treatment
/ = Tooth present but clinical crown missing (i.e., fractured)*

(*The codes V and /are used differently in the Missing Person Dental Report than in the Unidentified Person Dental Report.)

SECTION 4 *DENTAL REMARKS*

☐ **ALL** (All 32 teeth are present and unrestored) ☐ **UNK** (No dental information available)

(Rev 11/08) 30

Figure 7.2 NCIC missing persons dental report. (Reprinted with permission, NCIC.)

weighting system previously used and generated a cross match report ($.M report) of possible identification candidates ranked in order of their degree of concordance of dental characteristics. Since 2004, NCIC has generated two $.M reports for every case record containing dental information. One is based on the weighted system that has been in place since 1983, and the second report is *based primarily on the dental information* entered.

Unfortunately, most law enforcement personnel lack sufficient dental knowledge and experience; therefore, the second $.M report may be ignored or discarded without further

NCIC Missing Person File
Data Collection Entry Guide

Agency Case # ________________

DENTAL CONDITION WORKSHEET
(to be completed by dentist)

You should fill out this chart following your complete review of all available dental records and radiographs. You should number the teeth following the format of the Universal numbering system with tooth #1 being the upper right third molar, tooth #16 being the upper left third molar, tooth #17 being the Lower left third molar and tooth #32 being the lower right third molar. In your descriptions of the restorations present, you should include the surfaces involved (M, O, D, F, L), the restorative material used, such as amalgam, gold, porcelain, composite, temporary cement and any other conditions that may be observed such as endodontic treatment, pin retention, orthodontic brackets or bands. You must not leave any tooth numbers blank. If the tooth has no restorations, note it as "virgin" or "present, no restoration". Note other significant dental information at the bottom of this chart or on an additional sheet of paper, which you should attach to this worksheet.

1. ________	32. ________
2. ________	31. ________
3. ________	30. ________
4. ________	29. ________
5. ________	28. ________
6. ________	27. ________
7. ________	26. ________
8. ________	25. ________
9. ________	24. ________
10. ________	23. ________
11. ________	22. ________
12. ________	21. ________
13. ________	20. ________
14. ________	19. ________
15. ________	18. ________
16. ________	17. ________

Additional Dental Information:

(Rev. 11/08) 29

Figure 7.3 NCIC missing persons worksheet. (Reprinted with permission, NCIC.)

follow-up or analysis. The utilization by an agency of individuals trained to analyze this information would assist greatly in their investigations. The ability to eliminate individuals as possible identifications is as important as an identification as it allows the investigator to concentrate efforts on good leads, as opposed to following leads easily eliminated by a knowledgeable review of the $.M reports.

7.2.2 National Dental Image/Information Repository

In May 2005, the FBI's CJIS Management approved the creation of the National Dental Image/Information Repository (NDIR) to facilitate the identification of MPs, UPs, and WPs. This system allows for the permanent storage of digital dental records as long as a case remained active. A significant issue affecting the resolution of missing and unidentified cases was the availability of dental records for comparison. In order to establish a dental identification, the investigator had to laboriously search for dental records for comparison. This often would involve contacting the investigating agency and then attempting to find out who was handling the case and then having them locate the dental records for comparison. The NDIR was established to function as a central repository. It includes scanned dental radiographs and charting records, along with other information that might be helpful in the identification process. Accuracy and consistency in coding is another function of the NDIR as all records submitted are reviewed by CJIS-trained individuals to insure that they conform to current dental coding protocols. The submission of records to the NDIR is voluntary but highly recommended.

The program changes to the person files in NCIC went a long way to increase its ability to assist agencies in their investigations. However, 21 years of ineffective dental comparisons had and continues to have a significant effect on the credibility and use of the supplemental dental records in all of the NCIC person files. Collection of dental information for entry in NCIC is a dismal <10% of MP records. The percentage of UP cases having dental information entered in NCIC is greater than 50%. There are virtually no dental records entered for WPs for comparison to the data base of UPs. Even though the new forms, coding, and thus the entry of the dental information have been significantly simplified, some agencies are still using old forms and dental codes. The system is underutilized that may be related to economic issues, but low cost or no cost resources are available to most agencies.

The NDIR is housed by the web-based Law Enforcement Online (LEO). LEO provides the law enforcement, criminal justice, and public safety communities a secure method of electronic communication, education, and information sharing. User access to LEO is given following the submission of an application. Further information concerning LEO membership requirements can be obtained at their website, www.leo.gov

7.2.3 Dental Coding Workshops

The CJIS division of the FBI has assumed the task of improving the understanding and use of NCIC for assistance in their efforts to resolve MP cases and give UP's name. For the past several years, they have sponsored dental coding workshops to train dentists and dental personnel to assist agencies in the collection, analysis, coding, and submission of dental information in their MP and UP cases. The attendees are also trained to review the matching reports sent to the corresponding investigating agencies. To date, there are more than 400 individuals located across the nation that have completed the course. The course is held free of charge and involves a minimum of 16 h of training and hands-on analysis and coding of MP and UP cases. Individuals interested in attending one of these courses may obtain more information by inquiring at NDIR@LEO.GOV and asking for information regarding NCIC Dental Coding Workshops.

There are many other resources available for assisting agencies in their investigations of MP, WP, and UP cases. Since the 1980s, many systems have been developed to assist in the resolution of these cases. Some have continued to be employed and improved upon, and others have fallen to the wayside as their short comings have proven them ineffective.

As the future becomes the present, it is important to understand that the effective and ineffective tools and resources of the past carry equal weight into the future as we strive to improve on the effective and not repeat the ineffective.

7.3 Laws Covering the Handing of Missing and Unidentified Persons

At the end of 2011, there were over 80,000 people reported missing in the United States. Additionally, approximately 40,000 unidentified human remains are stored in medical examiners/coroners offices or have been disposed of by cremation and/or burial. While federal law mandates that law enforcement agencies report missing children, there is no similar requirement for missing adults or unidentified bodies. Compounding this problem is the fact that local law enforcement agencies, medical examiners, and coroners often do not have the resources or the training to voluntarily report these cases. Congress has supported these efforts by waiving HIPAA restrictions for patient medical and dental records (HIPAA, 2006).

7.3.1 H.R. 1300: Billy's Law

This law, if passed by Congress, will authorize funding for and increase accessibility to the National Missing and Unidentified Persons System (NamUs) to facilitate data sharing between that system and the NCIC database of the FBI and to provide incentive grants to help facilitate reporting to such systems and for other purposes. At the time of this writing, this bill is still in the legislative process (Billy's law, 2012).

7.3.2 Jennifer's Law

Jennifer's law is a federal law enabling the state to enhance its efficiency with regard to the reporting system of unidentified and MPs. Jennifer's law states that the attorney general is authorized to grant awards to states to improve the reporting of unidentified and MPs.

7.3.3 Kristen's Law (Public Law #106-468)

Kristen's law, previously known as Kristen's Act, provides grants for organizations seeking missing adults. Signed into law by President Clinton in 2000, a national clearinghouse was to be established, and funding was provided for missing adult cases to help search for person's age 18 and over classified by law enforcement officials as at-risk or endangered.

These past legislative proposals and laws have brought additional national awareness to the ongoing problem in the United States of MPs and UPs.

7.4 Other Resources Trainings and Government Agencies

7.4.1 NCIC/NDIR Sponsored Training Sessions

While the coding of dental records for MPs' cases is not difficult, certain guidelines should be followed so all cases are coded using the same terminology. As previously mentioned in this chapter, CJS/NCIC/NDIR has held NCIC dental coding workshops around the country. At the time of writing, over 400 dentists have been trained. It is hoped that law enforcement agencies will utilize these trained dentists when having dental records formatted and coded for NCIC. Family dentists likely are not familiar with these codes or with the formatting and protocols. Errors in coding could delay the association of the missing and the unidentified case.

7.4.2 National Missing and Unidentified Persons System (NamUs)

7.4.2.1 History of NamUs

According to the NamUs website (www.namus.gov), the problem of MPs and unidentified human remains in this country has existed for many years. Recently, significant progress has been made. In 2003, the *DNAInitiative* was launched. The Office of Justice Program (OJP)'s National Institute of Justice (NIJ) began funding major efforts to maximize the use of DNA technology in our criminal justice system. Much of NIJ's work has focused on developing tools to investigate and solve the cases of MPs and unidentified decedents.

Since that time, the OJP's NIJ has provided funding in order to increase the use of DNA technology in the criminal justice system. NamUs is one such program developed in order to address the issue of missing and unidentified individuals. Other programs provide DNA evidence training to law enforcement, medical examiners/coroners, judges, and attorneys. Family reference-sample kits are available at no charge to any agency as well as free DNA testing of unidentified human remains through NamUs.

In the spring of 2005, NIJ assembled federal, state, and local law enforcement officials, medical examiners, coroners, forensic scientists, key policymakers, victim advocates, and members of affected families from around the country for a national strategy meeting in Philadelphia. The meeting, "Identifying the Missing Summit," identified major challenges to investigating and solving MP and unidentified decedent cases. As a result of that summit, the U.S. Deputy Attorney General created the National Missing Persons Task Force and charged the U.S. Department of Justice with identifying every available tool—and creating others—to solve these cases. The National Missing Persons Task Force identified the need to improve access to database information by people who can help solve MPs and unidentified decedent cases. NamUs was created to meet that need. Unlike Law Enforcement's restricted NCIC system, NamUs is open to anyone.

7.4.2.2 Missing and Unidentified Persons Database

Development of both national databases—MPs and unidentified decedents—occurred from July 2007 to September 2008. The fully searchable NamUs system was launched in 2009. Both the MPs and UPs databases were accessible and available as well as linked to each other. Regional system administrators assisted the new users of NamUs in registering with NamUs and entering cases. Subject matter experts for biometric data (fingerprints, DNA, dental, and anthropology) are available free of charge to assist agencies in acquiring and entering as much information as possible into each case posted to NamUs. Additionally, these experts are available to evaluate possible matches/exclusions based on their respective disciplines (Figure 7.4).

Through funding from NIJ, the University of North Texas Health Science Center (UNT) provides family reference-sample kits and the processing of the DNA sample to any requesting law enforcement agency. In order to take advantage of this free service, the MP case must be posted in NamUs. This serves two purposes: more cases posted to NamUs and better data (in the form of DNA samples) available for those cases. This service is also available for unidentified remains cases.

Initial development of the MPs database was done in conjunction with the National Forensic Sciences Technology Center (NFSTC). The UPs database was developed in

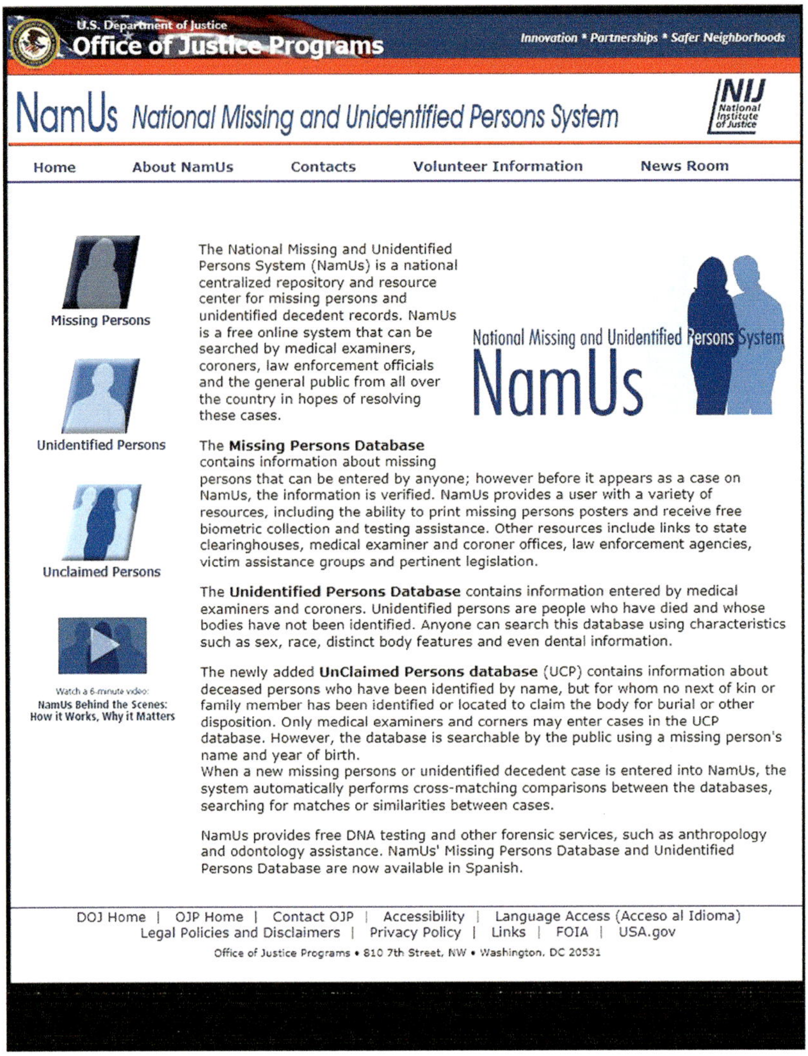

Figure 7.4 NamUs webpage. (Reprinted with permission, NamUs.)

conjunction with the National Association of Medical Examiners and the National Center for Forensic Science. NFSTC was also the administrator of the NIJ NamUs grant once NamUs went live. At the time of this writing, UNT is the system administrator.

Unlike other government databases, NamUs is also available to families of the missing. While all cases in NamUs are verified with the original law enforcement agency, family and friends can actually enter cases into NamUs as well. The general public can also view cases and search for possible matches. By registering as an "official user," more information may be viewable.

Law enforcement, medical examiner/coroner offices, and other investigative agencies, once registered with NamUs, can enter MPs and UPs cases. All data pertinent to the case, including case details (date last contact, case #s, age last contact, etc.), circumstances, photographs, DNA, fingerprints, dental information, police contact information, and much more can be easily entered for each case. As more information becomes available, this data can be updated quickly. The case manager can decide how much or how little is viewable by the general public.

The NamUs website enables authorized users the ability to view dental radiographs, treatment records, and dental codings (both in NCIC and NamUs formats). Additionally, other biometric data such as fingerprints, DNA, pathology, and anthropology information are available. Much of the sensitive forensic data (DNA, dental, etc.) and images (dental radiographs, dental treatment notes, etc.) posted are automatically not viewable by nonvetted or nonauthorized users. With the clicking of a button, individual cases can be added to one's personal tracking list. Whenever any data are changed in that case record, an e-mail will automatically be generated informing the user about the updated information. Public users may also track cases. However, if any changes are made to information they are not allowed to view, the specifics are not be revealed.

The MP and UP databases continuously query each other in the background, generating a constantly updated list of possible matches. However, the user of NamUs is not limited to only the system-generated matches. One of the most useful features of NamUs is the ability to actively search either database. One can determine the specific parameters of the search. A set of search criteria can also be saved for ease of running that same query of the database again at a later time. Searches are quick and can be easily modified as the user determines which criteria work best for them.

When utilizing the advanced search option, it is recommended that users enter ranges for information rather than very specific and, thus, restrictive information initially. For example, an entered height of exactly 65 in. will certainly be reflected in the height range of 63–67 in., but if one only enters 65 in. as the search parameter, only those cases with exactly 65 in. reported will be brought up in the potential match list. This is similar for dental tooth codes. In NCIC, the report generated of possible matches is based on detailed tooth codes (NCIC codes) and reported as a ranked list of either most number of exact matches or least number of nonmatches. Even though NCIC codes may be entered, at present, NamUs is only searching on the more generalized NamUs codes. Also, the search is based on exact code match and not potential matches. For example, if you enter the "C" (Crowned) code for a specific tooth, only those cases with the "C" code for that same tooth will be shown. If one enters the more general "F" (Filled) code, only those cases with the "F" code will be shown. However, if both NamUs codes can be entered into the NamUs dental chart, then both codes can be searched upon, either independently or together. Thus, all cases with C/crowned teeth in that same position will be found, including those with endodontic treatment (R code). If those cases that have both a crown and an endodontic treatment, then the search parameters should be "CR" for that tooth. As it is quite easy to modify searches, one can quickly adjust and refine one's search parameters to bring up those cases in which you are interested in reviewing.

Additionally, NamUs recently added the category of "Unclaimed Persons." These are cases retained by medical examiners' offices that have been positively identified, yet no individual has claimed the remains. It is hoped that as families are looking for missing loved ones, this new feature will further enable them to find the disposition of that individual.

The NamUs website is also an excellent reference source for locating law enforcement agencies, medical examiner/coroner offices, MPs' clearinghouses, individual state laws, and much more information. NamUs is an evolving program, and new features are constantly being added as the need for them is determined.

7.4.2.3 NamUs Training

As with any new program, users must be trained. In order to do so, NIJ has funded NamUs Training Academies. Since 2010, five regional academies have been held. By training representatives from the various specialties involved with solving missing and UP cases (law enforcement, forensic science specialist, clearinghouse agent, medical examiner/coroner, and victim advocate) from each state in that region, a network of trained users has been created who will then in turn help train others. At the time of this writing, it is unknown whether more NamUs Training Academies will be held. More information may be found at the NamUs website: www.namus.gov

7.4.3 The National Center of Missing and Exploited Children

The National Center for Missing and Exploited Children (NCMEC) is a private, (501)(c)(3) nonprofit organization. It was created in 1984 when Congress passed the Missing Children's Assistance Act. In June 2009, NCMEC observed its twenty-fifth year in operation and a quarter century of progress on behalf of children. Twenty-five years later, NCMEC has become the leading nonprofit organization in the United States, working with law enforcement to address the problems of missing and sexually exploited children. Today, the work of the organization includes 20 different Congressional mandates.

According to the NCMEC website, an estimated 800,000 children are reported missing each year, more than 2,000 children each day. The mission of the organization is to serve as the nation's information clearinghouse for missing and sexually exploited children. This includes child abduction, parental abduction, and those running away from home. The organization provides information and resources to law enforcement, parents, and children including child victims as well as other professionals. NCMEC also has begun to foster a working and support relationship with NamUs. Information may be found at the NCMEC website: www.missingkids.com

7.4.4 Violent Criminal Apprehension Program

The Violent Criminal Apprehension Program (ViCAP) was established in 1985 and is the national repository of cases involving violent crimes. Law enforcement may submit information to ViCAP concerning their cases that have involved a violent crime. By analyzing the data entered, other cases with similar patterns can be located throughout the country, aiding in the resolution of these cases.

There are three databases in ViCAP: MPs, UPs, and homicides/sexual assaults. Many UPs have been deemed homicides and are therefore victims of a violent crime. Foul play may also be suspected in many MPs cases. Living victims of sexual assaults may later go missing or be killed. Persons of interest in unsolved violent crimes may continue to commit crimes. By analyzing the data entered in ViCAP and discovering potential connections, it is hoped that more cases may be solved and future crimes prevented. Additionally, ViCAP provides numerous support services to the multiple agencies that deal with MPs and UPs as well as cases involving violent crimes. The ViCAP website is www.fbi.gov/wanted/vicap

7.4.5 Private Sector and State Agencies

There are several private sector and state agencies whose purpose is to assist in seeking solutions to the MP and UP problem.

7.4.5.1 The DOE Network

The DOE Network (www.doenetwork.org) is a nonprofit 501(c)3 agency with a web-based database. MPs and UPs cases from North America, Europe, and Australia are posted there.

Dedicated volunteers work to assist families in their search to find their missing loved ones by making connections. Volunteer forensic dentists also assist when dental records are utilized.

7.4.5.2 *Let's Bring Them Home/National Center for Missing Adults*

Several years ago, the National Center for Missing Adults joined with "Let's Bring Them Home" (www.lbth.org). Besides having another web-based database of MPs, they also provide training in working MP cases.

7.4.5.3 *Florida Unidentified Decedents Database*

This web-based program is a central clearinghouse containing information about those found dead in Florida and whose identities remain unknown. According to Florida Unidentified Decedents Database (FLUIDDB), all information provided is in nonmedical terms. The intention of the website is to engage the interested party in searching this database in the hope that they may recognize a picture, a characteristic, or a detail about a decedent. If so, they may then contact the medical examiner's office or Law Enforcement Agency, which has jurisdiction over the case. FLUIDDB includes a searchable database and a directory of medical examiner districts. The website is www.fluiddb.com

It should also be noted that a Florida Statute (Title XLVII, Chapter 937.031), mandates the dental records of anyone missing for 30 days be entered by the law enforcement agency involved into the criminal justice information system for the purpose of comparing such records to those of unidentified deceased persons.

7.4.5.4 *California Missing Persons*

Referred to by some as just "CALDOJ," California Missing Persons (www.oag.ca.gov/missing) is a MPs and UPs unit within the California Department of Justice that assists law enforcement and criminal justice agencies in locating MPs and identifying unknown live and deceased persons. The process is done through the comparison of physical characteristics, fingerprints, and dental/body x-rays. California has essentially a "no waiting period" policy for reporting a MP. At the time of this writing, California has the largest number MP cases in the United States, with over 20,000 MP and over 3,000 UP reports in the automated database. By state law, dental records are mandated to be obtained within 45 days of report for both missing and unidentified cases. CALDOJ also serves as the central repository for all of these dental records.

The ongoing problem of resolving the missing and unidentified "silent mass disaster" is beginning to be brought to the forefront and addressed by many. Again, many states across the country do have their own state databases for either MP or UP, or both. Due to time and space restrictions for this chapter, we have mentioned only a few of the many available.

7.4.6 Social Media

In addition to the agencies and organizations listed so far in this chapter, the Internet has brought about numerous other "social media" venues, which may be used when evaluating MPs cases. Not all MPs are deceased, but rather simply cannot be located; others wish not to be found. Social media websites such as Facebook® and others are regularly checked, whether by the actual MP, by law enforcement, or by family and friends attempting to locate them. Additionally, in response to the Haitian earthquake, Google® donated support to the U.S. Department of State to create an online people-finder database. This website allowed families to submit information about MPs and to search that repository for those persons missing in the quake (Bolton, 2010). "Google People Finder" has also been activated several times including the Christchurch, New Zealand earthquake in February 2011, and the Japanese earthquake and tsunami in March 2011. The Internet is a constantly changing and evolving type of global social media in and of itself. It can offer assistance and support the missing and unidentified crisis, whether it is for local or nationwide single case or within a greater mass fatality incident.

7.4.7 International Agencies

International organizations and other countries have also developed services and protocols to address the MP and UP problem. They are not identical to the U.S agencies, organizations, and available databases, but are all working toward the same goal.

One of the challenges in working with dental records from around the world is there are many different tooth numbering systems. The Universal Numbering System (1–32) is only routinely used in the United States. Much of the rest of the world utilizes the Fédération Dentaire Internationale (FDI) Numbering System. Other systems, such as Palmer, use a shorthand diagram based on the quadrants of the mouth, but it is not employed widely. Regardless of the numbering system utilized, care must always be taken in all dental coding whenever data from dental records are entered into a MP's system.

7.4.7.1 International Criminal Police Organization

International Criminal Police Organization (INTERPOL; www.interpol.int) was founded in 1923 and deals with international public safety issues including the MP and UP problem. INTERPOL headquarters are located in Lyon, France. Some INTERPOL elements will soon be moving to Singapore. There are several regional offices around the world as well as numerous representative agencies. There are 190 member nations, and each nation has a National Central Bureau in which that country's INTERPOL representatives are centered. INTERPOL established international Disaster Victim Identification (DVI) guidelines with the application of international standards and forensic principles. The Standing Committee on DVI meets annually to continue the development of these standards and principles. INTERPOL contracts with PlassData Software in Denmark to produce and administer its DVI computer database application, which is called DVI System International (see Chapter 6).

INTERPOL maintains a central repository of data to track cross-border movement of criminals, MPs, and human trafficking. To date, few police databases exist at the regional or national level to assist in linking MPs and unidentified bodies. Some countries, including Sweden, have adopted the DVI System International software for use in their MP and UP cases.

While PlassData is the current contractor to INTERPOL for the DVI database software, there are fees assessed to individual member nations for licenses and annual support. Not all member nations have chosen to purchase the database, and therefore not all of the individual member nation databases are using it. Realistically, computer support for DVI responses is only necessary when dealing with very large numbers of deceased persons. Many member nations use the INTERPOL DVI forms for identification by manual methods and do not use computer databases.

Given the successes identified in using DVI System International for Missing Persons, INTERPOL is attempting to establish an even larger and more robust database application from PlassData that can be applied to both the DVI and MP and UP situations. This Fast and Efficient International Disaster Victim Identification (FASTID) Project was funded in April 2011 and is in the testing phase at the time of this writing. It is predicted to launch in 2013.

Through a consortium of partners, this project will establish a system for the international component needed in managing inquiries about MPs and unidentified remains for mass disasters as well as ongoing MPs/unidentified remains cases. INTERPOL and its partners will be establishing the foundation in developing a user's guide, standard reporting formats, and terminology, along with the quality assurances these programs require. Once the FASTID is operational, it will be only available to those member countries/agencies with an INTERPOL secure communication connection. FASTID will not replace individual DVI systems, but will interface with the individual databases as needed. It is expected that all member nations will be financially able to choose to participate and link their individual country's database to the overall system and that FASTID will replace DVI System International.

As mentioned previously, there are different tooth numbering systems around the world. DVI System International and FASTID utilize the FDI tooth numbering system. The actual coding of teeth in DVI/FASTID is far different than the NCIC or NamUs codes. For example, there are over 200 tooth codes that can be used in DVI System International when describing the condition of a tooth; however, these are continually being refined, and it is expected that this number will decline with the implementation of FASTID. In the United States, it will be necessary to recode cases for the INTERPOL system or have a software program complete the "translation" accurately. At present, there is no such software available to do so, although there is a project underway in the United States to accomplish this transfer of data to and from INTERPOL as well as other national databases.

7.4.7.2 Canadian Police Information Centre

Missing Persons and Unidentified Remains (MPUR) issues are also ongoing in Canada. The Canadian Police Information Centre (CPIC), a national database, contains a variety of data of concern to law enforcement, including MPs and UPs (www.cpic.ca). The Royal Canadian Mounted Police maintains their Canadian Police Centre for Missing and Exploited Children (RCMP; www.rcmp-grc.gc.ca) and provides access to other municipal, regional, and provincial police agencies and other approved users to these databases.

RAPID ID is the RCMP's search engine that is used to query the CPIC/MPUR database, but it is currently evolving to interact better with NCIC and other databases. Also, there is an updated CPIC/MPUR database being developed. Law enforcement agencies will have direct access to CPIC/MPUR but medical examiners/coroners will not. They will, however, be able to access CPIC/MPUR through their long-standing, collaborative relationship with law enforcement. The general public will also have access but on a very limited basis and probably only to add general comments about a MP.

With respect to death investigations in Canada, medical examiners/coroners have recently taken a major role in establishing a network of death investigation agencies and a collaboration of national interests. Jurisdiction for identification is a provincial matter under the role of the provincial or territorial chief medical examiner or chief coroner. However, with large and/or potentially cross-jurisdictional mass fatality incidents, a national need exists for a coordinated response. The Canadian Association of Chief Coroners and Chief Medical Examiners has selected the DVI System International from INTERPOL as its standard DVI software application and is encouraging all related disciplines to work with this database for daily casework and to become trained and proficient in its use.

Forensic odontologists in two provinces, British Columbia and Ontario, have established MP and UP databases, and Alberta will soon join this list. Ontario uses a different database application developed in that province. In all cases, the primary data that are held on these specific dental databases—which is different from CPIC—are data from MPs. These data are then compared to found human remains cases at the request of the medical examiner/coroner.

As with NCIC, there is dental data available in CPIC, including individual codes for each tooth. There are no associated images, such as radiographs or photographs. The initial version of CPIC dental codes only utilized three descriptors for teeth. Teeth were noted to be present (not restored), missing, or treated in some way. Later, this information was converted to three simple codes. More importantly, at various times in the past, CPIC data have been uploaded into NCIC. Present (not restored) and Missing were converted to V and X, respectively. However, as insufficient information was present in the Canadian system as to surfaces treated, all treated teeth were coded in NCIC as "/" (no information). This has led to many false-positive matches in the computer necessitating comparison by odontologists and immediate recognition that there is a nonmatch. Frequently in the DRE (dental comments) section of the NCIC report, there would be individual tooth numbers (FDI) with other dental information. As Canada, like much of the world, utilizes the FDI dental numbering system, not the Universal System, one must be careful in utilizing this dental data when making exclusions (Figure 7.5).

An updated CPIC dental coding system is nearing release. This coding system has been designed to be much more like the NCIC coding system. There are seven surface/treatment codes (MODFLCR) and three other codes (X, V, and U/unknown). Up to seven treatment codes can be used per tooth, but X or V may only be used alone. As in NCIC, the C and R codes cannot be used alone but must be entered with the appropriate surface codes. Additionally, the C code does mean slightly different things in each system. In NCIC, it is any CAST lab-processed/premade restoration; in CPIC, it means only a CROWN. Canada and the United States share a very long border. It is extremely likely many of our MPs/unidentified remains cases could be improved by the exchange of accurate information.

7.5 Dental Information in Missing and Unidentified Cases

The majority of this chapter has addressed the history, background, and the listing of numerous agencies and online tools, which are available for working MP and UP cases. It is agreed by many in the field of forensic odontology that dental identification and those discussions referenced in Chapters 4 and 6 throughout this text be considered when dealing with dental evidence for MP and UP investigations.

The authors of this chapter want to express to both the dental and nondental readers the importance of obtaining a timely and accurate biometric dental profile (i.e., dental treatment history records, dental radiographs, photographs, etc.) for both the MP and UP investigations.

In MP investigations, it is paramount at the time the MP report is filed that law enforcement or MP case mangers request dental contact information. Every effort should be made to acquire the actual MP dental records as soon as possible. By delaying this process, the dental information can at best, be difficult to retrieve from the MP family dental office, and at its worst, the records may have been destroyed. While it would be the earnest desire of every forensic odontologist that every dental record be maintained forever, the reality is they are not. There are many reasons for this including the sale or closure of practices. Additionally, malpractice insurance guidelines for keeping records and state laws dealing with the legal storage requirements of the same vary significantly. Certainly, they do not adequately address this

DENTAL CHARACTERISTICS INPUT DATA

Part 1— To be completed by police authorities	
NOTE: TO ASSIST THE POLICE IDENTIFICATION PROCESS, YOUR COOPERATION IS NEEDED TO OBTAIN ALL DATA PERTAINING TO THE DENTAL CHARACTERISTICS OF THE PERSON NAMED BELOW.	Date:
Surname: Given name(s): Sex:	Birthdates:
Police agency:	Investigator:
File number: Facsimile number:	Telephone number:

Part 1— To be completed by practitioner/dentist

INSTRUCTIONS

Maximum of seven (7) Dental Codes per tooth
M = Mesial, O = Occlusal, D = Distal, F = Facial, L = Lingual, C = Crown, R = Root Canal, U = Unknown, X = Missing, V = Virgin
(If X or V are used for a tooth, no other codes are permitted for that tooth.)

Unerupted teeth are to be identified as U = Unknown for Missing Persons.

[ ] **represents new CPIC formats** (Canadian Police Information Centre)
( ) **represents vintage CPIC formats** (FDI World Dental Federation)
{ } **represents deciduous** (Infant/childhood teeth)

Upper Jaw

[1]	[2]	[3]	[4]	[5]	[6]	[7]	[8]	C	[9]	[10]	[11]	[12]	[13]	[14]	[15]	[16]
(18)	(17)	(16)	(15)	(14)	(13)	(12)	(11)		(21)	(22)	(23)	(24)	(25)	(26)	(27)	(28)
			{55}	{54}	{53}	{52}	{51}		{61}	{62}	{63}	{64}	{65}			
								E								
								N								

RIGHT SIDE C E N T R E LEFT SIDE

[32]	[31]	[30]	[29]	[28]	[27]	[26]	[25]		[24]	[23]	[22]	[21]	[20]	[19]	[18]	[17]
(48)	(47)	(46)	(45)	(44)	(43)	(42)	(41)		(31)	(32)	(33)	(34)	(35)	(36)	(37)	(38)
			{85}	{84}	{83}	{82}	{81}	R	{71}	{72}	{73}	{74}	{75}			
								E								

Lower Jaw

Figure 7.5 New Canadian dental characteristics report. Note that codes are similar to NCIC codes.

long-term need of dental records for potential future dental identifications. Frequently, dental practitioners are told to keep records for only 7 years after the date of last contact or, in the case of a minor patient, 7 years after the patient reaches their twenty-first birthday.

The same should be stressed for law enforcement investigators, coroners, and medical examiners regarding the UP cases. For example, some UP cases can involve partial or incomplete postmortem dental examinations at autopsy. Delays in obtaining this dental information at autopsy can increase the need for further forensic review and can be complicated by storage, inventory logs, and office policies. The possibility for exhumation scenarios should be stressed.

The comparison of a MP's dental records and radiographs with the dental evidence from unknown human remains can be one of the most reliable and expedient means of positive identifications. Forensic dental records can also support the additional value of age estimation opinions, especially in subadult investigations.

The material in this chapter is not an all-inclusive review of the suggested protocols and guidelines for the handling of MP and UP cases. Additional training is strongly recommended. For a more detailed review, please reference the ABFO (American Board of Forensic Odontology) Guidelines and Standards for MP and UP Cases (www.abfo.org).

7.6 Conclusion

Forensic odontologists working in conjunction with law enforcement agencies and medical examiners or coroners can be valuable for both the MP and UP investigative processes. Their roles should include the gathering of dental data, accurate and uniform dental coding, dental radiographs, and comparison analyses. Forensic odontologists assist in the resolution of UP and MP cases, both nationally and internationally.

Acknowledgments

The authors would like to acknowledge the volunteers, dental professionals, and all of the tireless, and dedicated individuals from multiple agencies across this county for their efforts. To these people, we thank and recognize their past and present service to the families of the Missing and to the Unidentified that may have no voice. We also thank Drs. Gary Bell, David Sweet, and Lowell Riemer for their invaluable help with this chapter.

Disclaimer

It is the intent of the authors of this chapter to offer their personal opinions and additional information for educational purposes regarding the forensic odontologist's role in assisting in the resolution of the missing and unidentified person crisis in this country.

References

Billy's Law. GovTrack, US. 2012. http://www.govtrack.us/congress/bills/112/hr1300 (accessed October 1, 2012).

Bolton, C. 2010. *Google Adds People Finder Gadget for Haiti Quake Victims*. http://googlewatch.eweek.com/content/google_philanthropy/google_adds_people_finder_gadget_for_haiti_quake_victims.html

HIPAA Administrative Simplification. 2006. *Department of Health and Human Services*. http://www.hhs.gov/ocr/privacy/hipaa/administrative/privacyrule/adminsimpregtext.pdf

Dental Age Estimation

8

JAMES M. LEWIS
DAVID R. SENN

Contents

8.1 Introduction 211
8.1.1 Purpose and Value 212
8.1.2 Scientific Rationale 213
8.1.3 Statistical Basis for Dental Age Estimation 213
8.1.4 Age Estimation Tools 216
8.2 Formation and Growth Techniques 216
8.2.1 Fetal Dental Age Estimation 216
8.2.2 Child Dental Age Estimation 219
8.2.3 Adolescent Age Estimation 227
8.3 Postformation Techniques 234
8.3.1 Historical Review 234
8.3.2 Adult Dental Age Estimation Techniques 236
8.3.2.1 Johanson Sectioning (1971) 236
8.3.2.2 Maples (1978) 237
8.3.2.3 Lamendin et al. (1992) 238
8.3.2.4 Prince and Ubelaker (2002) 239
8.3.2.5 Bang and Ramm (1970) 240
8.3.2.6 Kvaal et al. (1995) 240
8.4 Biochemical Techniques 245
8.4.1 Amino Acid Racemization 245
8.4.2 Radioactive ^{14}C 247
8.5 Dental Age Estimation Guidelines and Standards 248
8.6 Summary 250
References 251

8.1 Introduction

The Romans are believed to have utilized dental age estimation to determine if an individual had reached the age for military conscription through the evaluation of the eruption of the second permanent molars (Müller, 1990). However, age estimation as a scientifically researched component of the forensic sciences is relatively new. The British penal code and child labor laws of the early 1800s began legal interest in estimating the chronologic age of children. During this period of time, the penal code presumed that an individual below age 7 did not have the capacity to commit a crime; but, individuals over the age of 7 that were convicted of even minor crimes were often severely punished by the state (Miles, 1963a). Because birth certificates were not issued and birth registration was not required, there was often difficulty in providing evidence of true chronologic age. In 1836, a medicolegal expert by the name of Thomson began suggesting that the dentition could be useful in the assessment of age in children. He stated that if the first permanent molar "hath not protruded, there can be no hesitation in affirming that the culprit has not passed his seventh year" (Thomson, 1836). Need for age assessment continued as a result of the factory acts. The Factory Act of 1833 forced the textile industry to conform to a uniformly established workday for individuals under the age of 18 defined as beginning at 5:30 AM and ending at 8:30 PM. Individuals between the ages of 13 and 18 were not to be employed beyond a 12 h period including a 1.5 h meal break. Children between the ages of 9 and 13 were not permitted to work beyond any 9 h period, which did include educational instruction. Children less than 9 years of age were totally prohibited from employment. However, these laws were often ignored by parents and factory owners and were difficult to enforce because the only evidence of age was that the child appears to be at least 9 years old. Four years later in 1837, Dr. Edwin Saunders, a dentist, produced a pamphlet evaluating over 1000 children and providing tables that he said could be utilized by "relatively untrained people" to assess children's age for the purpose of enforcement of the Factory Act (Saunders, 1837).

8.1.1 Purpose and Value

In today's society, the purpose and value of forensic dental age estimation has expanded to meet a variety of medicolegal needs such as providing an estimated age at death. With over 40,000 unidentified bodies and 100,000 missing individuals at any given time in the United States alone, age estimation significantly narrows the search possibilities for law enforcement. In mass disaster and cluster victim situations, age segregation aids in the process of identification. Then there is forensic application to aid authorities in determining eligibility for social benefits, the age of license and age of legal majority. The age of legal license should not be confused with the legal age of majority. In legal terms, "license" means "permission" and is the age at which the law permits an individual to perform certain acts and exercise certain rights, with or without any restrictions. The age of legal majority is the legally recognized threshold of adulthood. In general, age of legal majority issues can be subdivided into categories of contractual law, immigration, and citizenship issues regarding undocumented immigrants and criminal prosecution. The exact age of legal majority depends upon the jurisdiction and its application to the law. In the United States and many countries throughout the world, immigration authorities use the age of 18 for the legal age of majority. The contractual legal age of majority in most states and territories in the United States and Canada is also age 18 with the following exceptions: Age 14 in the American Soma; Age 19 in Alabama, Nebraska, British Columbia, New Brunswick, Newfoundland, Labrador, Northwest Territories, Nova Scotia, Nunavut, and Yukon; Age 21 in Mississippi and Puerto Rico (World Law Direct). Although the U.S. Supreme Court in the case of *Roper v. Simmons*, 2005, discontinues the death penalty for those committing a crime under the age of 18, the criminal prosecution of juveniles as an adult is possible. Again, this age depends upon the jurisdiction; however, as a general rule, the likelihood that a district attorney will be able to file criminal charges against a juvenile as an adult increases with the age of the juvenile, the severity of the offense and the juvenile's past history of delinquency (Lewis and Brumit, 2011). With all of these legal issues that may require age assessment and the wide variety of ages applied depending upon jurisdiction and application, it would be wise for the forensic odontologist to become familiar with the laws within their own jurisdiction.

8.1.2 Scientific Rationale

The evaluation of dental tissue has long been regarded as a good tool for the assessment of age, and therefore, age estimation techniques involving these tissues have been widely used by forensic odontologists and anthropologists. The rationale for scientific evaluation of dental tissues for age estimation can be divided into three criteria: tooth formation and growth changes, postformation changes, and biochemical changes.

Tooth formation and growth changes involve the progressive morphological development of the crown, root and apex of any given tooth and/or its timed emergence and eruption sequence. An advantage of tooth formation and growth techniques is that they are noninvasive with age assessment easily accomplished through visual and radiographic examination. Additionally, tooth development techniques are classically "thought to be the most accurate and reliable way of correlating growth and development" to age (Taylor and Blenkin, 2010, 176). Through the development of tooth maturation stages, or intervals, and correlating those stages to chronologic age, researchers have developed dental age estimation techniques. There are multiple staging systems that have been proposed and it is imperative that the forensic scientist always be mindful to utilize the appropriate staging system that is associated with a given study's data set. Because tooth development is a maturation process, techniques that utilize this rationale are reserved for cases involving fetuses, infants, children, and adolescents. Naturally as an adolescent individual approaches adulthood, they also approach the end of dental and skeletal development. Therefore, anthropological considerations that utilize bones of the hand and wrist, clavicle, ribs, and cervical vertebrae become more important in the age assessment process.

Once dental and skeletal growth has ceased, forensic dental investigators must use a technique that involves either biochemical tooth changes or dental postformation changes to assess age. There are two biochemical dental age estimation techniques: aspartic acid racemization and carbon-14 dating. They are both lab techniques that involve the sacrifice of tooth structure and are expensive and time consuming.

Postformation tooth changes are adult dental considerations and can be subdivided into gross anatomical and histological changes. The gross anatomical changes include but are not limited to attrition, periodontal condition, apical root resorption, pulpal size to tooth size ratios (two dimensional and volumetric), root smoothness, and dentin coloration. The histological changes include secondary dentin apposition, cementum apposition, and dentin transparency.

Unfortunately, there are other factors at play in the scientific dental assessment of age other than the aforementioned criteria. They include the gender and ancestry of the individual in question. The classic anthropologic ancestries are European, Asian, and African. However, many of the newer published dental age estimation studies are population specific versus being of ancestral specificity. Population specific studies help to eliminate questions of ancestral admix and the potential influence of a myriad of environmental considerations. Some of these environmental factors include climate, nutritional health, disease, lack of disease, habits, addictions, occupation, place of residence, and dental and skeletal abnormalities.

8.1.3 Statistical Basis for Dental Age Estimation

A forensic age estimation opinion must be derived from scientific method that is based upon data from an appropriate literature source that has undergone review, independent testing, and provide an error rate; and, never from mere clinical experience. In order for the forensic scientist to thoroughly evaluate the quality of a scientific age estimation study and to intelligently explain and discuss its application to the forensic sciences, they need a basic understanding of the underling mathematic principles.

In many naturally occurring processes, including tooth development, biochemical changes, and some postformation changes of the dentition, its random variation conforms to and can be described by a particular mathematical probability function known as normal distribution. The diagrammatic histogram seen in Figure 8.1 represents a typical normal distribution curve, more commonly known as a bell curve. All normal distribution curves have some similar characteristics. They are unimodal, meaning they all include a midline peak and have symmetry about the midline. Also, the curve extends bilaterally to infinity and the area under the curve represents all possibilities (Internet Center for Management and Business Administration, Inc.). The symbol mu (μ) marks the midline of the curve and its numerical value is the statistical mean or average value of the data under the curve. The standard deviation for the curve is represented by sigma (σ). Standard deviation defines the measure of variability or risk on any given curve. In summary, a normal distribution curve defines an event whose data is uniformly clustered about the mean and its standard deviation is a measure of how tightly that data is clustered. Figure 8.2 represents four distinctly different shaped normal distribution curves. Although they all

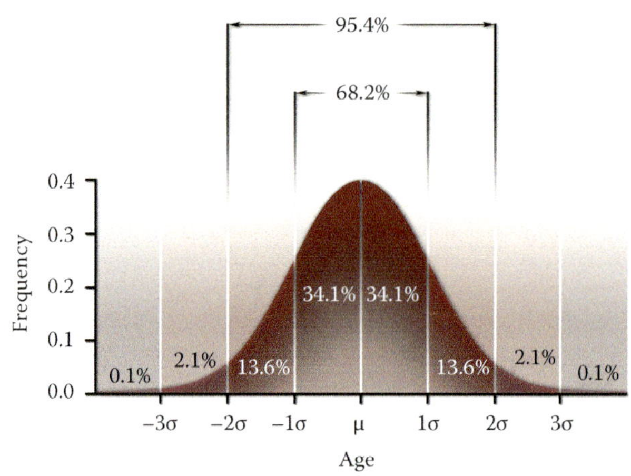

Figure 8.1 A normal distribution curve demonstrating the empirical rule.

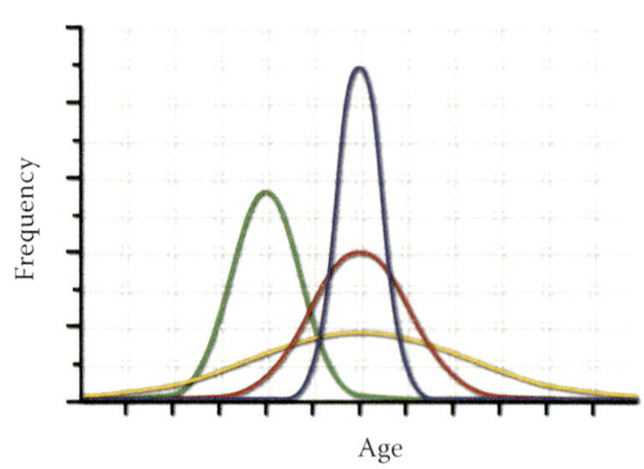

Figure 8.2 Normal distribution curves of different shapes and sizes.

meet the criteria for being a bell curve, the individual peaks are not all in the same location and some of the curves are short and broad while others are tall and thin. A change in the peak location signifies a different value for the mean. When the curve is short and broad, the standard deviation for that curve will be greater in value than for a curve that is tall and thin; and therefore, the measure of variability of a short and broad normal distribution curve is greater than that of one that is tall and narrow. In application to dental age estimation, these histograms graphically depict the frequency; a particular stage of tooth development occurs (vertical axis) plotted against the true chronologic age of that individual (horizontal axis) in a given population.

Normal distribution curves have a couple of other unique qualities. First, a normal distribution curve can be completely specified by two parameters—they are the bell curve's mean and standard deviation. Therefore, if the values of the mean and standard deviation are known, then one has knowledge of every single point in the data set and the probability that a given variable will occur at a specified location on that curve can be calculated (Internet Center for Management and Business Administration, Inc.). Likewise, the probability a person has reached a specified age can be calculated from a particular tooth's developmental staging. Second, the standard deviation calculation for any normal distribution will inherently follow what is known as the empirical rule and can be used to quickly approximate the dispersion of the data (illustrated in Figure 8.1). The empirical rule states that

1. Approximately 68% of the data will fall within ±1 standard deviation of the mean
2. Approximately 95% of the data will fall within ±2 standard deviations of the mean
3. Almost all of the data will fall within three standard deviations of the mean

If the reader will recall, forensic age estimation requires that the estimated age should be stated with a known error rate. In age estimation, the error rate is implied by providing an age interval of the individual at the scientifically accepted threshold of 95% for determining statistical significance (Nawrocki, 2010, 92). Therefore, forensic dental age estimations report the calculated assessed age of the examined individual along with an associated age interval of ±2 standard deviations representing an approximate 95% confidence level that the age of the individual will fall within the stated age range.

Not all age estimation studies report their statistical findings in terms of standard deviation. Some studies use percentiles, or the value at which a certain percentage of the given observation will fall. When the information is expressed at the 25th, 50th, and 75th percentiles, they are also known as the first, second, and third quartiles respectively. It is extremely important for the odontologist to understand this principle and to note how a given study reports its data. If using data from a study that has results published at the 20th, 50th, and 80th percentiles, the estimated age is determined by the 50th percentile and the upper and lower limits of the age interval are determined by the 20th and 80th percentile data. Unfortunately, this means that the determined age interval will only include 60% of the sampled population and not the recommended threshold of 95%. Likewise, if the study reports its findings in quartiles, the confidence level within the stated age interval will only be 50%. Other studies derive their results from regression analysis. A regression formula is an equation that expresses the relationship between one or more independent variables and a dependent variable (in our case—age). When regression formulas are utilized, the degree of dispersion of the data will be expressed in a standard error of the estimate and is analogous to standard deviation.

The forensic odontologist needs to remain mindful that all age calculations are estimates. In order to provide the best estimate of age, there are some basic guidelines that should be followed: (1) the most appropriate methods should be applied, (2) large population specific studies should be utilized where possible, (3) the applied study should be ancestrally and gender specific, (4) the odontologist must consider any environmental factors at play, (5) all available methods for estimation age should be considered, (6) individual techniques that look at multiple variables tend to be more useful, and (7) a combination of techniques will likely give the most accurate results. Additionally, accuracy will statistically improve when multiple teeth are utilized in the analysis, teeth are selected that will provide the most accurate results and the methods utilized contain the best age discriminate variables. A multidisciplinary approach should be considered. Other nondental disciplines include anthropology, medical, biochemical, and trace element analysis of dental materials.

How is the best dental age estimation technique selected? Three independent studies have all stated a similar conclusion to that question (Ritz-Timme et al., 2000; Willems et al., 2002; Soomer et al., 2003). The particular technique most suitable is dependent upon the specific circumstances of the case. In other words, is the individual living or deceased; can a tooth be ethically extracted for examination; will radiographic analysis be available; or, is a visual external exam the only means of evidence collection available to you. Figure 8.3 is dental age estimation procedure flowchart designed to help the odontologist determine techniques that may be applied based on age categories and circumstances.

8.1.4 Age Estimation Tools

Classically, the tools for dental age estimation included calipers, rulers, tooth sectioning wheels and disks, loops, and microscopes for magnification. They are still useful today, but technology has provided us a number of extraordinary tools. Digital microscopes are becoming inexpensive and not only enhance one's ability to discern minute detail but can photograph an object with visual and alternate light sources. These images can be imported into computer imaging software substantially improving acuity. To utilize these tools, the forensic odontologist must become familiar and proficient with their own imaging software. Useful photographic enhancement functions include image enlargement, adjusting image levels, brightness, contrast, and saturation. Sometimes, using the invert function to view the image as a negative will also reveal detail previously unnoticed. But there are more benefits provided by imaging software in addition to image enhancement. Images can be rotated into a desired structural orientation and software measurement tools are more accurate than handheld calipers.

8.2 Formation and Growth Techniques

8.2.1 Fetal Dental Age Estimation

Because embryonic tooth development begins early in fetal development and the degree of morphologic enamel mineralization is easily viewed radiographically, the dentition is an excellent indicator of age soon after conception. Table 8.1 provides approximate times of the initial mineralization, completed crown development, and completed root development

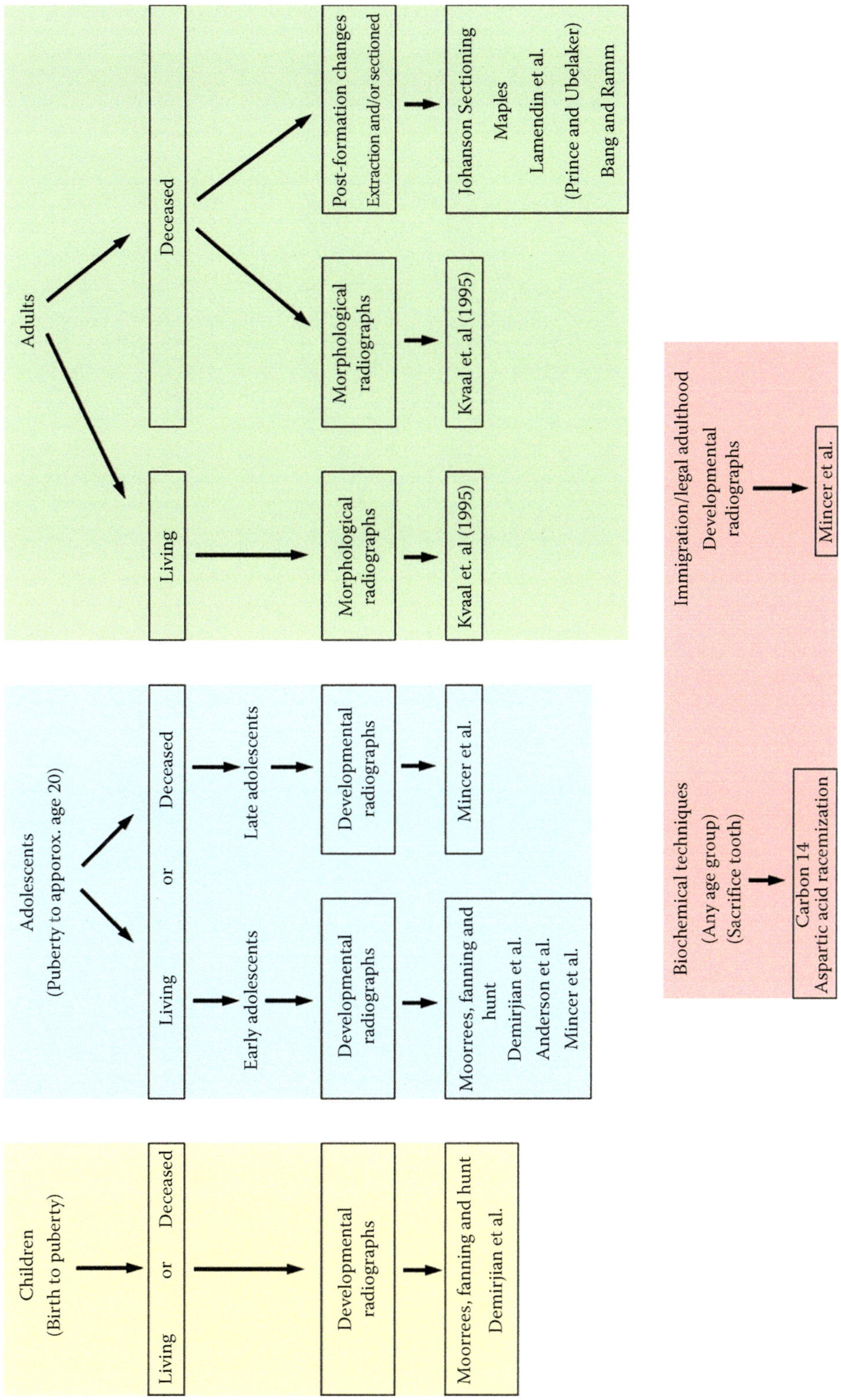

Figure 8.3 Dental age estimation procedure flowchart.

Table 8.1 Chronological Chart of Human Tooth Development

Deciduous Dentition	Central Incisor	Lateral Incisor	Canine	First Molar	Second Molar
			Maxillary		
Initial mineralization	14 weeks	16 weeks	17 weeks	15.5 weeks	19 weeks
Crown formation completed	1.5 months	2.5 months	9 months	6 months	11 months
Root formation completed	1.5 years	2 years	3.25 years	2.5 years	3 years
			Mandibular		
Initial mineralization	14 weeks	16 weeks	17 weeks	15.5 weeks	18 weeks
Crown formation completed	2.5 months	3 months	9 months	5.5 months	10 months
Root formation completed	1.5 years	1.5 years	3.25 years	2.5 years	3 years

Permanent Dentition	Central Incisor	Lateral Incisor	Canine	First Bicuspid	Second Bicuspid	First Molar	Second Molar
				Maxillary			
Initial mineralization	3–4 months	10–12 months	4–5 months	1.5–1.75 years	2–2.25 years	At birth	2.5–3 years
Crown formation completed	3–4 years	4–5 years	6–7 yr	5–6 years	6–7 years	2.5–3 years	7–8 years
Root formation completed	10 years	11 years	13–15 years	12–13 years	12–14 years	9–10 years	14–16 years
				Mandibular			
Initial mineralization	3–4 months	3–4 months	4–5 months	1.5–2 years	2.25–2.5 years	At birth	2.5–3 years
Crown formation completed	4–5 years	4–5 years	6–7 years	5–6 years	6–7 years	2.5–3 years	7–8 years
Root formation completed	9 years	10 years	12–14 years	12–13 years	13–14 years	9–10 years	14–15 years

Source: Data adapted from *Wheeler's Dental Anatomy, Physiology, and Occlusion*, 9th edn, Nelson, S.J. and M.M. Ash, Development and eruption of the teeth, pp. 21–44, Copyright (2010), with permission from Elsevier.

Initial mineralization of deciduous teeth are weeks in utero.

for the primary and permanent human dentition (Nelson and Ash, 2010, 23, 36–37). In this chart, the times indicated for initial primary tooth mineralization are expressed in terms of weeks in utero while primary crown and root completion times and all permanent tooth development times are expressed in months and years from birth. There are three initial mineralization times worthy of special emphasis. The earliest initial dental mineralization occurs in the primary maxillary and mandibular incisors at about 14 weeks in utero, all primary teeth have begun mineralization by the 19th week and mineralization of the first permanent molar begins at about birth.

Developmental histological changes in teeth are also useful in fetal age assessment. Enamel formation results from ameloblast cell secretion of enamel proteins that later mineralize and form enamel rods. During the mineralization phase, the ameloblasts produce the enamel matrix at a rate of approximately 4 μm/day; however, there is a rhythmic variation in the calcification process every 4 days. As a result, incremental growth lines known as the striae of Retzius appear microscopically within the enamel. In cross-section, these lines resemble concentric bands parallel to the dentoenamel junction (Copenhaver et al., 1978, 461–465). Whenever a systemic disturbance occurs the enamel mineralization process is interrupted and the currently developing striae will appear darker. The darkest and largest incremental growth line seen in the deciduous teeth is called the neonatal line and is caused by the stress and physiologic changes at birth (Bath-Balogh and Fehrenbach, 2006, 186). When present, the neonatal line can be used to distinguish whether a child died before or after birth. Furthermore, counting the incremental growth lines that form subsequent to the neonatal line may approximate how long a child lived after birth. Because, the neonatal line does not form immediately at birth but rather takes a few days to a week to form, caution should be exercised in making absolute statements of death prior to birth.

8.2.2 Child Dental Age Estimation

Although all techniques available should be considered, dental age estimation techniques involving tooth maturation have long been established as the most accurate indicators of chronologic age in subadults. Early in life, genetic factors predominate and environmental factors tend to have minimal effects on tooth maturation. This is especially true between birth and age 10. Additionally, many endocrine and maturational diseases affect dental development at a quarter the rate of the remainder of the skeleton (Ubelaker, 1999, 63). Exceptions include syphilis and hypopituitarism.

Dental age estimation techniques in children can be subdivided into two categories: atlas style—a diagrammatic representation of the developing tooth structures with their associated eruption pattern; and, techniques that require some form of incremental staging of the developing teeth. All techniques in both categories rely on high-quality radiographic imaging to access dental development. The chart produced by Schour and Massler (1941) and reproduced in 1944 has been historically the most cited and reproduced dental age estimation atlas. Unfortunately, this chart was largely based upon data from the work of Logan and Kronfeld (1933) who observed the dental maturation of a very small sample size of institutionalized, chronically ill, and malnourished children. This charts published error ranges have been shown to be too narrow (Smith, 2005, 1–2). Therefore, other subsequently published atlas style charts are considered to be more reliable. If using an atlas chart for age estimation, the atlases produced by Ubelaker (1978, 1989) and AlQahtani et al. (2010) should be considered.

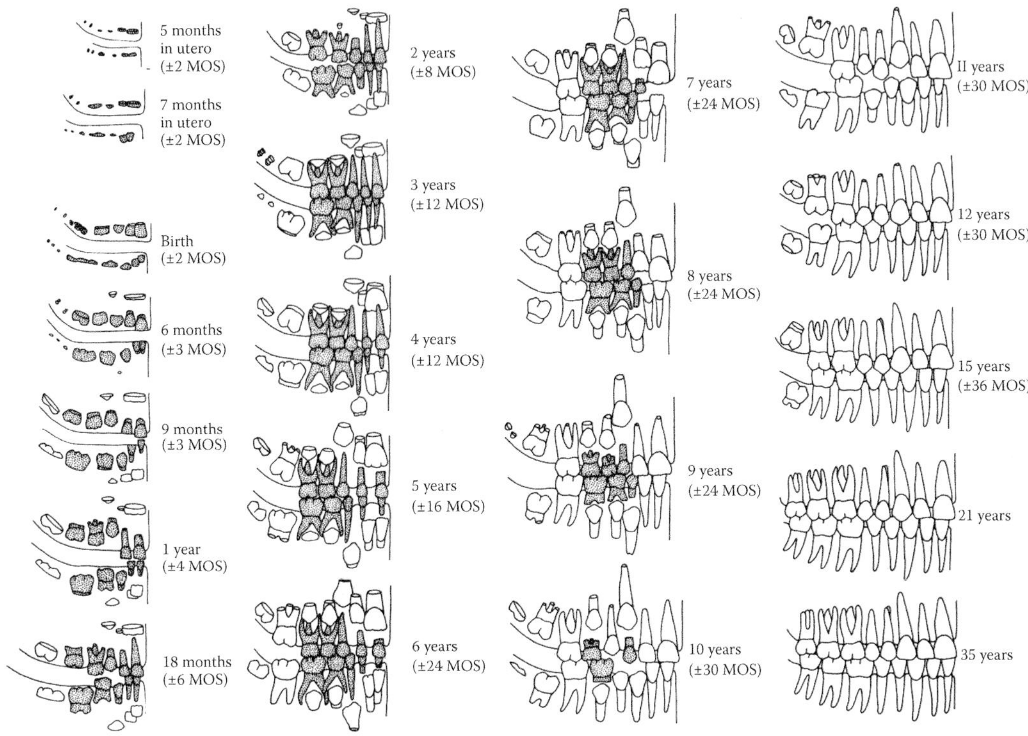

Figure 8.4 The Ubelaker, 1989 dental developmental atlas. (Reprinted with permission from Douglas Ubelaker.)

The Ubelaker (1989) chart (Figure 8.4) is derived from a compilation of dental development data that includes the permanent dentition of American Indians and the deciduous dentition from non-Indians (mostly United States Whites). Because some published studies indicate that dental development occurs slightly earlier among Indian populations, the "early end of the published variation" of the non-Indian data was utilized in chart preparation. Much of the utilized data was obtained from skeletal remains and because sexual differences are not pronounced in subadult skeletons, the chart combines data for males and females. This atlas of dental age assessment begins at 5 months in utero and provides an estimated age and associated statistical age interval through age 15. Dr. Ubelaker states in his third edition of *Human Skeletal Remains* that this "chart is probably the best approximation available for inferring age from dental development in prehistoric and contemporary non-white subadults" and that "the canine tooth shows the greatest sex differences and should be avoided if possible when estimating age."

The most recent atlas of dental development and alveolar eruption for age estimation, "The London Atlas of human tooth development and eruption" was published by AlQahtani et al. (2010) (Figure 8.5). The study data was obtained from 176 individual's skeletal remains from the collections at the Natural History Museum, London, United Kingdom, and the Royal College of Surgeons of England; and, dental radiographs of 528 living individuals. The ratio of males to females in the sample was almost equal. As with the other atlases, the chart data does not differentiate between the sexes. There are a total of 31 diagrams depicting the median dental development observed beginning at 30 weeks in utero and ending at 23.5 years of age. Eight of the diagrams only describe third molar development beginning at age

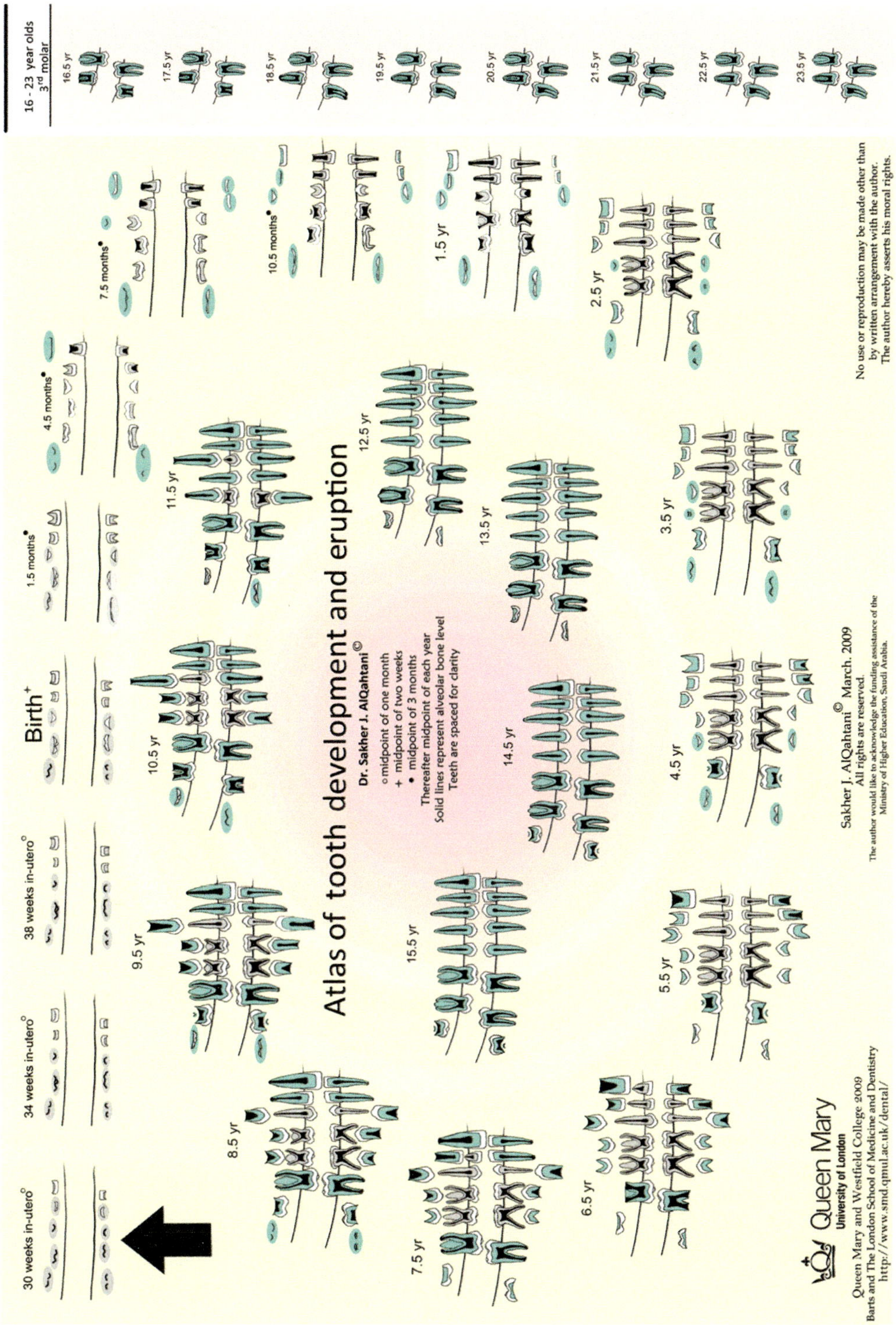

Figure 8.5 2010 London atlas of tooth development and eruption. (Reprinted with permission from S.J. AlQahtani.)

16.5 years. Unlike the Ubelaker dental development chart that defines tooth eruption as the point in time that the tooth emerges through the gingival tissue, the AlQahtani chart defines eruption as emergence through the alveolar bone. Unfortunately, a statistical age interval is not provided for each diagram. Because this study primarily uses data from contemporary sources, modern day environmental influences should be reflected within the observed tooth development, and therefore, the AlQahtani et al. (2010) study may prove to be more useful in age assessment of this time period than other atlas charts. The London Atlas of Tooth Development and Eruption is available online at http://www.dentistry.qmul.ac.uk/atlas%20of%20tooth%20development%20and%20eruption/index.html in numerous languages.

All atlas style techniques have some inherent problems. They are not sex differentiated, resulting in a high degree of variability particularly from midchildhood through adolescence. With DNA testing now available and affordable, sex differentiation of skeletal remains is possible. Additionally, there are not enough ancestral and population specific studies. The most concerning problem is that atlas style techniques tend to have a relatively higher degree of interobserver disagreement and a larger error rate than other tooth formation and development techniques.

The incremental staging techniques utilize noninvasive radiographic analysis to measure dental development or deciduous tooth resorption according to technique-specific systems that contain diagrammatic and written descriptors of an individual tooth's morphology. The classic deciduous tooth exfoliation technique study (Moorrees et al., 1963a) evaluated the primary tooth resorption of the mandibular cuspids, first molars, and second molars from a group of healthy, white Ohio children from an average socioeconomic background. Four stages of tooth resorption were described: ¼ resorption, ½ resorption, ¾ resorption, and exfoliation. Average age estimation data with standard deviation is provided by the individual tooth's stage in a tabular form for males and females (Table 8.2). This data provides useful information between the 5 and 12 years of age.

Table 8.2 Moorrees et al. Average Age Estimation Data for Primary Tooth Resorption

	Deciduous Mandibular Teeth									
			dm1				dm2			
	dc		Mesial Rt.		Distal Rt.		Mesial Rt.		Distal Rt.	
Stage	Mean	SD	Mean	SD	Mean	SD	Mean	SD	Mean	SD
Females										
Resorption 1/4	4.9	0.54	4.9	0.54	5.1	0.58	6.1	0.67	6.9	0.74
Resorption 1/2	7.3	0.78	7.2	0.78	7.7	0.82	8.3	0.88	8.6	0.91
Resorption 3/4	8.7	0.92	8.7	0.93	9.3	0.97	10.0	1.05	9.9	1.04
Exfoliation	9.5	1.00	9.5	1.05	10.1	1.05	11.1	1.15	11.1	1.16
Males										
Resorption 1/4	6.1	0.67	5.4	0.60	6.4	0.69	6.6	0.72	6.6	0.79
Resorption 1/2	8.4	0.89	7.6	0.82	8.3	0.88	8.5	0.90	8.5	0.99
Resorption 3/4	9.8	1.02	9.4	0.98	10.0	1.04	10.4	1.08	10.4	1.14
Exfoliation	10.6	1.10	10.7	1.12	10.7	1.12	11.6	1.20	11.6	1.20

Source: Data adapted from Harris, E.F. et al., Age estimation from oral and dental structures, in *Forensic Dentistry*, 2nd edn., eds. Senn, D.R. and Stimson, P.G., Taylor & Frances Group, Boca Raton, FL, 2010, pp. 263–303.

Because the complete dental maturation process spans a longer time period (age range) than tooth emergence or deciduous tooth resorption, techniques that involve tooth mineralization are more useful. The dilemma for researchers is to devise a staging chart that has enough discrete intervals of tooth development to provide accurate and useful data without creating too many that are ambiguous and difficult to discern. The two most commonly utilized staging systems today are those of Moorrees et al. and Demirjian et al.

Moorrees et al.'s article entitled "Age variation of formation stages for ten permanent teeth" provided chronological age assessment information of the permanent mandibular posterior teeth (C–M3) and the later developmental stages of the permanent maxillary and mandibular incisors (I1 and I2) (Moorrees, 1963b). Developmental data for the mandibular deciduous dentition was published in the earlier Moorrees (1963a) study. The incremental stages of permanent tooth development created by Moorrees et al. are depicted in the schematic drawing in Figure 8.6 and their associated written descriptors in Table 8.3.

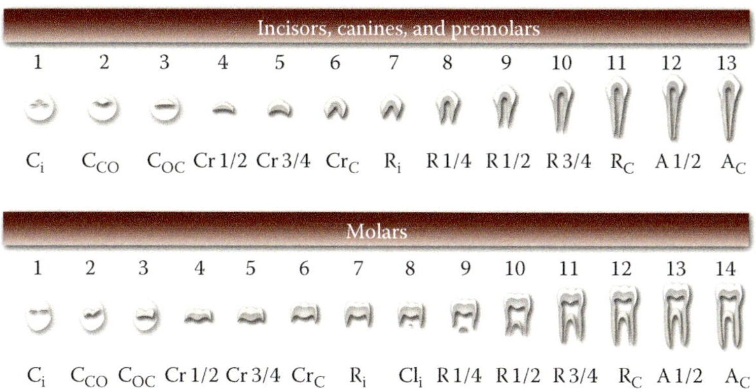

Figure 8.6 Incremental staging chart for permanent single and multi-rooted teeth. (Modified and illustrated by J.M. Lawis from Moorrees, C.F.A. et al., *J. Dent. Res.*, 42, 1490, 1963b.)

Table 8.3 Developmental Staging Descriptors

Single Rooted Teeth Stages		Descriptors	Multirooted Teeth Stages	
C_i	1	Initial cusp formation: Mineralization of cusp tips has begun	C_i	1
C_{CO}	2	Coalescence of cusps: Mineralization centers are beginning to unite	C_{CO}	2
C_{OC}	3	Mineralized cusp outline is complete	C_{OC}	3
Cr 1/2	4	1/2 of estimated crown mineralization is complete	Cr 1/2	4
Cr 3/4	5	3/4 of estimated crown mineralization is complete	Cr 3/4	5
Cr_C	6	Crown mineralization complete; but, root formation has not begun	Cr_C	6
R_i	7	Initial root formation	R_i	7
—	—	Initial cleft formation: Mineralization visible in inter-radicular area	Cl_i	8
R 1/4	8	1/4 of estimated root formation is complete	R 1/4	9
R 1/2	9	1/2 of estimated crown mineralization is complete	R 1/2	10
R 3/4	10	3/4 of estimated crown mineralization is complete	R 3/4	11
R_C	11	Root length complete: Apex remains funnel shaped	R_C	12
A 1/2	12	Apex is 1/2 closed: Root walls are parallel	A 1/2	13
A_C	13	Apical closure is complete	A_C	14

Source: Data modified from Moorrees, C.F.A. et al., *J. Dent. Res.*, 42, 1490, 1963b.

This system of classification provides two separate development schemes, one for single rooted teeth illustrating 13 stages and the other for the molars having 14 stages of development. The difference is the addition of stage Cl_i representing the cleft formation in molars. Mean age and standard deviation was originally provided in a cumbersome and difficult to read graphical format for each tooth at every stage with separate graphs developed for males and females. The technique process requires the odontologist to correctly identify the tooth, assess its proper stage of morphological development, and to then read the associated mean age and standard deviation from the gender-specific graph. In order to maintain examiner repeatability, it is recommended to record the highest stage of morphological development that has been attained and to not select the apparent closest stage when a tooth appears to be between stages (Harris et al., 2010, 271). Technique accuracy is improved by averaging the data obtained from multiple teeth of the individual in question. Careful tooth selection can also factor into result accuracy. In cases where the third molar is the only tooth in an individual's dentition continuing to undergo maturation, adolescent third molar techniques should be utilized rather than relying on Moorrees third molar data. Furthermore, the odontologist needs to be aware that there is a greater variation in root development than in crown formation; and that some teeth inherently have a higher degree of developmental variation than others. Therefore, when possible, selecting teeth still undergoing crown development and utilizing teeth having smaller standard of deviations (variance) should increase accuracy of the age estimation. Fortunately, the data from the original graphs have been translated into easy-to-read tables (Tables 8.4 through 8.6).

Similar studies have been performed on other population specific groups in the United States (Anderson et al., 1976; Harris and McKee, 1990) and the world (Haavikko, 1974; Mornstad et al., 1995; Liversidge, 2000). The Anderson et al. (1976) study evaluated the dental development of a group of Canadian Caucasian children and utilized the Moorrees et al. staging system but changed the labeling nomenclature to stages "1" through "14" with stage "1" being the earliest stage of tooth development. It produced four separate charts that included age assessment data on all permanent teeth, both maxillary and mandibular

Table 8.4 Age Estimation Data for Deciduous Tooth Development

	Females						Males					
	dc		dm1		dm2		dc		dm1		dm2	
Stage	Mean	SD	Mean	SD	Mean	SD	Mean	SD	Mean	SD	Mean	SD
C_{OC}	0.15	0.10					0.15	0.10				
Cr 1/2	0.25	0.10	0.15	0.10	0.25	0.10	0.27	0.10	0.20	0.10	0.27	0.10
Cr 3/4	0.45	0.11	0.23	0.10	0.45	0.10	0.47	0.10	0.23	0.10	0.50	0.11
Cr_C	0.70	0.13	0.33	0.10	0.70	0.13	0.68	0.13	0.43	0.10	0.70	0.13
R_i	0.85	0.14	0.55	0.12	0.93	0.15	0.80	0.14	0.58	0.12	0.92	0.14
Cl_i			0.56	0.11	1.0	0.15			0.65	0.12	1.0	0.15
R 1/4	1.1	0.16	0.65	0.13	1.3	0.18	1.0	0.30	0.75	0.13	1.3	0.20
R 1/2	1.3	0.17	0.88	0.13	1.5	0.20	1.3	0.18	0.93	0.15	1.6	0.21
R 3/4	1.8	0.22	1.1	0.17	1.9	0.23	1.8	0.23	1.2	0.18	1.9	0.23
R_C	2.0	0.25	1.3	0.17	2.0	0.24	2.0	0.24	1.3	0.18	2.0	0.25
A 1/2	2.5	0.28	1.5	0.20	2.4	0.28	2.5	0.28	1.6	0.21	2.4	0.28
A_C	3.0	0.33	1.8	0.23	2.8	0.31	3.1	0.33	1.9	0.24	3.0	0.33

Source: Data reverse engineered by Lewis from Moorrees, C.F.A. et al., *Am. J. Phys. Anthropol.*, 21, 205, 1963a.

Table 8.5 Moorrees et al. (1963b) Female Age Estimation Data for Permanent Tooth Development

	Girls																			
	Maxillary Incisors				Mandibular Incisors				Mandibular Posterior Teeth											
	UI1		UI2		LI1		LI2		C		P1		P2		M1		M2		M3	
Stage	Mean	SD	Mean	SD	Mean	SD	Mean	SD	Mean	SD	Mean	SD	Mean	SD	Mean	SD	Mean	SD	Mean	SD
C_i									0.5	0.12	1.7	0.24	2.9	0.35	0.1	0.05	3.5	0.41	9.6	1.00
C_{CO}									0.7	0.15	2.2	0.28	3.5	0.40	0.2	0.09	3.8	0.43	10.1	1.05
C_{OC}									1.2	0.18	2.9	0.35	4.1	0.47	0.7	0.14	4.3	0.49	10.7	1.11
Cr 1/2									1.9	0.25	3.5	0.41	4.7	0.53	1.0	0.17	4.8	0.54	11.3	1.17
Cr 3/4									2.9	0.35	4.2	0.49	5.3	0.59	1.4	0.20	5.4	0.59	11.7	1.20
Cr_C	4.9	0.54	5.7	0.62					3.9	0.45	5.0	0.56	6.2	0.66	2.2	0.28	6.2	0.68	12.3	1.27
R_i									4.7	0.52	5.7	0.63	6.7	0.73	2.6	0.32	7.0	0.75	12.9	1.32
Cl_i															3.5	0.41	7.8	0.83	13.5	1.39
R 1/4	6.0	0.66	6.6	0.71	4.5	0.51	4.7	0.53	5.3	0.57	6.5	0.69	7.5	0.79	4.6	0.52	9.1	0.96	14.9	1.53
R 1/2	6.6	0.71	7.2	0.76	5.1	0.57	5.9	0.65	7.1	0.75	8.1	0.86	8.7	0.92	5.1	0.57	9.8	1.01	15.8	1.62
R 2/3	7.1	0.76	7.7	0.82	5.6	0.62	6.3	0.68												
R 3/4	7.6	0.81	8.3	0.87	6.1	0.66	6.7	0.72	8.3	0.88	8.8	0.97	10.0	1.05	5.5	0.60	10.5	1.09	16.4	1.67
R_C	8.2	0.86	9.1		6.6	0.72	7.6	0.80	8.8	0.93	9.9	1.03	10.6	1.12	5.9	0.63	11.0	1.13	17.0	1.71
A 1/2	8.9	0.93	9.6	0.99	7.4	0.79	8.1	0.86	9.9	1.03	11.0	1.15	12.0	1.24	6.5	0.71	12.0	1.23	18.0	1.82
A_C					7.7	0.82	8.5	0.89	11.3	1.18	12.1	1.26	13.6	1.40	8.0	0.85	13.8	1.43	20.1	2.01

Source: Data adapted from Harris, E.G. and Buck, A., *Dent. Anthropol.*, 16, 15, 2002.

Table 8.6 Moorrees et al. (1963b) Male Age Estimation Data for Permanent Tooth Development

	Boys																			
	Maxillary Incisors				Mandibular Incisors				Mandibular Posterior Teeth											
	UI1		UI2		LI1		LI2		C		P1		P2		M1		M2		M3	
Stage	Mean	SD	Mean	SD	Mean	SD	Mean	SD	Mean	SD	Mean	SD	Mean	SD	Mean	SD	Mean	SD	Mean	SD
C_i									0.5	0.11	1.8	0.24	3.0	0.37	0.0	0.09	3.7	0.41	9.2	0.98
C_{CO}									0.8	0.15	2.3	0.31	3.5	0.42	0.2	0.11	4.0	0.43	9.7	1.01
C_{OC}									1.2	0.19	2.9	0.36	4.2	0.48	0.5	0.11	4.8	0.49	10.3	1.07
Cr 1/2									2.1	0.27	3.6	0.43	4.7	0.53	1.0	0.17	5.1	0.54	10.9	1.14
Cr 3/4									2.9	0.35	4.4	0.52	5.3	0.59	1.5	0.21	5.7	0.59	11.6	1.20
Cr_C	5.3	0.59	5.9	0.64					4.0	0.46	5.2	0.58	6.2	0.69	2.1	0.29	6.5	0.68	12.0	1.24
R_i									4.8	0.55	5.8	0.64	6.9	0.74	2.7	0.34	7.1	0.75	12.7	1.32
Cl_i															3.5	0.41	8.1	0.83	13.6	1.41
R 1/4	6.3	0.68	6.9	0.75			5.3	0.60	5.7	0.63	6.8	0.74	7.8	0.83	4.7	0.53	9.3	0.96	14.6	1.50
R 1/2	6.9	0.74	7.6	0.80	5.2	0.59	6.2	0.68	8.0	0.86	8.5	0.91	9.4	0.99	5.1	0.57	10.1	1.01	15.1	1.54
R 2/3	7.6	0.80	8.1	0.86	5.8	0.64	6.8	0.74												
R 3/4	8.1	0.85	8.7	0.91	6.4	0.70	7.4	0.78	9.6	1.00	9.9	1.04	10.8	1.13	5.4	0.61	10.8	1.09	15.9	1.62
R_C	8.6	0.90	9.6	1.01	7.0	0.75	8.0	0.84	10.2	1.06	10.3	1.09	11.5	1.21	5.8	0.64	11.3	1.13	16.3	1.67
A 1/2					7.7	0.81	8.5	0.90	11.8	1.23	11.9	1.24	12.7	1.30	6.9	0.75	12.2	1.23	17.6	1.79
A_C					8.1	0.85	9.3	0.98	13.0	1.35	13.3	1.38	14.2	1.46	8.5	0.91	14.2	1.43	19.2	1.95

Source: Data adapted from Harris, E.G. and Buck, A., *Dent. Anthropol.*, 16, 15, 2002.

arches, and for both sexes. An important finding of this study was the order of variability in specific tooth development for males and females. According to Anderson, variability decreases as follows:

Males: First Bicuspid and Third Molars > Second Bicuspid and Second Molars > Cuspid > Incisors > First Molar

Females: Third Molars > Second Molars > Cuspid and Bicuspids > Incisors > First Molar

It should be noted that the first molar consistently provides the most accurate results. Because the data from the Anderson study begins later in life than the age assessment data in the Moorrees et al. study, it is considered an alternative study to Moorrees et al. and should be considered in later childhood and early adolescence.

Demirjian (Demirjian et al., 1973; Demirjian and Goldstein, 1976) produced a more simplified staging system. The chart (Figure 8.7) consists of eight stages, A through H, that define morphological tooth development beginning at the first radiographic appearance of mineralization to complete closure of the root apex. This technique requires the evaluation and staging of the entire mandibular left quadrant excluding the third molar. The mandibular arch was selected because of the better clarity of radiographic images in comparison to maxillary imagery as a result of superimposing dental and cranial anatomy. It is permissible to utilize a portion or all of the dentition on the mandibular right when the contra-lateral teeth are missing, malformed, rotated, or difficult to stage for any reason. Once all teeth have been staged, each tooth is assigned a "self-weighted score" based its staging designation and gender of the individual. The seven self-weighted scores from each tooth are then summed to give a "maturity score." The maturity score is cross-referenced in a gender-specific table converting the score to corresponding age. The study also provides graphical data that allow for the maturity score to express the age interval at the 10th and 90th percentiles. Statistical data from this study was derived from the panoramic dental radiographs of 1446 boys and 1482 girls of French Canadian ancestry. This system of age estimation has been applied to a numerous other populations worldwide including but not limited to South Indian (Koshy and Tandon, 1998), Norwegian (Nykänen et al., 1998), Finnish (Nyström et al., 1986; Chaillet et al., 2004), Belgian (Willems et al., 2001), Dutch (Leurs et al., 2005), and Australian (Blenkin and Evans, 2010).

Both the Moorrees and Demirjian methods provide acceptable age estimations of children and should be utilized, and results reported where applicable. Although the Demirjian technique does have more population specific studies available, the technique can be problematic particularly in cases that involve fragmented remains or where a tooth is bilaterally missing or malformed. Furthermore, the Demirjian technique inherently assigns equal weight to each tooth in the age estimation process in contrast to Moorrees et al. where the data is tooth specific. Moorrees also provides a full range of age estimation data beginning at birth where most Demirjian population studies begin to assess age between 2 and 3 years.

8.2.3 Adolescent Age Estimation

Toward the end of skeletal development, few age-dependent features remain for estimating age by progressive morphological methods (Thorson and Hägg, 1991). By age 14, the only remaining tooth undergoing growth and formation is the third molar. There are limitations

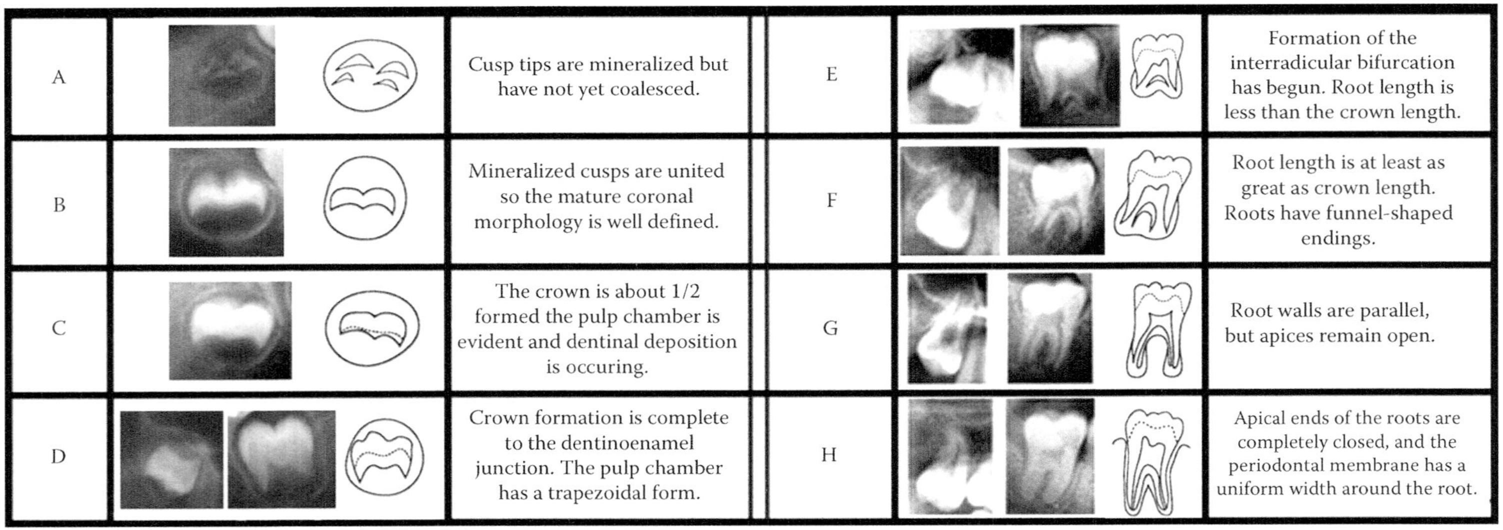

Figure 8.7 Demirjian third molar developmental stages. (Modified by Kasper from Kasper, K.A., et al., *J. Forensic Sci.*, 54, 651, 2009. With permission.)

to third molar age assessment techniques. The third molar is the most developmentally variable tooth and age estimation is based on average morphologic development. The presence of pathology, anatomical obstructions, and potential radiographic distortion are potential concerns. Regardless, the third molar is arguably the most reliable biological indicator during adolescence and in to early adulthood (Harris et al., 2010, 288) and can easily and noninvasively be evaluated with dental radiographs. Other anthropologic growth centers that provide useful age-related medicolegal information near the end of adolescence include bones of the wrist and hand, ribs, cervical vertebrae, and the clavicle (Hackman et al., 2010, 202–235). The epiphyseal closure of the medial end of the clavicle occurs by the age of 30 and marks the conclusion of skeletal growth. A multidisciplinary approach to determine the age of legal majority has been suggested by some authors. Schmeling et al. (2004) recommend combining third molar age assessment with techniques involving age assessment of the clavicle, hand, and wrist. Cameriere et al. (2004) have reported that third molar age estimation in combination with pulp/tooth area ratio assessment of the second molar resulted in more accurate age estimation in individuals age 18 and older. A complicating factor in adolescent age assessment is the fact that adolescence is characterized by the onset of puberty, resulting in a greater dental and skeletal development variance between ancestral populations and the sexes (Harris, 2007). Certain other factors need to be understood when utilizing third molar age estimation techniques (Lewis and Senn, 2010):

1. Third molar development is a variable nonlinear process (Scott, 1999; Solari and Abramovitch, 2002).
2. A number of studies have concluded that ancestral variation becomes less significant as age 18 is approached (Prieto et al., 2005; Kasper et al., 2009).
3. Sexual dimorphism necessitates gender-specific data and because third molar development occurs during and postpuberty, some populations demonstrate a role reversal with males developing earlier than females (Gleiser and Hunt, 1955; Mincer et al., 1993; Harris, 2007).
4. Environmental factors play a role in human development (Herschaft et al., 2006, 63).

Therefore, good age assessment techniques utilizing ancestral and population-specific studies are essential in late adolescence and early adulthood to assist the medicolegal system in resolving issues regarding age of legal majority for cases involving immigration and prosecution in the criminal and civil courts.

An early study by Mincer et al. (1993) and sanctioned by the American Board of Forensic Odontology pioneered the current third molar age estimation technique. The third molars of 823 individuals between the ages of 14.1 and 24.9 years were evaluated radiographically and staged using the Demirjian classification system for molars (Figure 8.7). Because the study demographics included an American population of 80% Whites, 19% Blacks, and 1% other ancestries, with 54% of the study population being female, the resulting data is only statistically significant for American Whites. Mincer et al. demonstrated that there was asymmetrical development between the maxillary and mandibular third molars with bilateral symmetry occurring within the same arch. Separate tables were produced by gender providing mean estimated chronologic age, standard deviation, and the empirical probability that the individual had attained age 18 for each of the Demirjian morphologic developmental stages "D" through "H" for both maxillary and mandibular third molars (Tables 8.7 and 8.8). The study recommends that all third molars present are

Table 8.7 Comparison of Female Third Molar Data from Published Population Specific Studies Conducted in the United States

	Mincer et al. American White			Kasper et al. American Hispanic			Solari and Abramovitch American Hispanic				Blankenship et al.[a] American Black?			Blankenship (Lewis)[b] American Black		
	Mean Age	SD	Probability (%)	Mean Age	SD	Probability (%)	Mean Age	SD	Probability (# 1) (%)	Probability (# 16)[c] (%)	Median Age	25th Percentile	75th Percentile	Mean Age	SD	Probability (%)
Female Maxilla																
D	16.0	1.55	9.7	15.19	1.73	5.2	15.7	1.4	5	5	14.69	14.37	15.93	15.36	1.54	4.3
E	16.9	1.85	28.4	16.44	2.02	21.9	16.2	1.7	12	10	15.32	14.57	15.72	15.41	1.04	0.6
F	18.0	1.95	50.4	16.96	1.88	29.1	16.7	1.8	25	21	16.15	15.19	16.79	16.22	1.27	8.0
F_1							17.6	1.9	47	30						
G	18.8	2.27	63.3	17.98	2.02	49.6	18.4	2.2	55	53	16.87	15.68	18.02	17.33	2.18	37.9
G_1							18.6	2.2	56	63						
H	20.6	2.09	89.6	19.55	1.93	78.8	20.8	2.2	84	79				20.77	2.77	84.2
Female Mandible																
D	16.0	1.64	11.3	15.36	1.90	8.3	15.6	1.4	6	8	14.74	14.52	15.72	15.14	1.09	0.4
E	16.9	1.75	27.4	16.53	1.71	19.4	16.1	1.4	6	13	15.32	14.54	16.21	15.62	1.35	3.9
F	17.7	1.80	43.2	17.38	1.74	36.2	17.3	2.6	27	31	16.44	15.19	17.49	16.43	1.60	16.4
F_1							18.0	1.4	46	45						
G	19.1	2.18	69.8	18.44	1.91	59.2	18.5	2.1	54	40	16.85	15.81	18.87	17.56	2.24	42.3
G_1							19.3	2.0	70	69						
H	20.9	2.01	92.2	20.07	1.87	86.5	21.7	1.8	91	92				21.00	2.58	87.8

Source: Data modified from Lewis, J.M. and Senn, D.R., *Forensic Sci. Int.*, 201, 79, 2010.

[a] Blankenship et al. data reported as median age and the intervals at the 25th and 75th percentile.

[b] Blankenship et al. data reported as recalculated by Lewis giving data as mean age, intervals as standard deviation and the empirical probability that the individual is 18 years of age or older.

[c] Empirical probabilities reported by Solari and Abramovitch are given for each third molar.

Table 8.8 Comparison of Male Third Molar Data from Published Population Specific Studies Conducted in the United States

	Mincer et al. American White			Kasper et al. American Hispanic			Solari and Abramovitch American Hispanic				Blankenship et al.[a] American Black?			Blankenship (Lewis)[b] American Black		
	Mean Age	SD	Probability (%)	Mean Age	SD	Probability (%)	Mean Age	SD	Probability (# 1)[c] (%)	Probability (# 16)[c] (%)	Median Age	25th Percentile	75th Percentile	Mean Age	SD	Probability (%)
Male Maxilla																
D	16.0	1.97	15.9	14.94	1.47	1.8	15.3	1.4	8	5	14.44	14.21	15.03	14.72	0.87	0.0
E	16.6	2.38	27.8	15.54	1.56	5.8	16.0	1.4	7	6	15.70	15.08	16.94	16.11	1.63	12.3
F	17.7	2.28	44.0	16.39	1.40	12.4	16.1	1.5	12	10	16.61	15.44	17.48	16.80	1.55	22.0
F_1							16.6	1.4	22	15						
G	18.2	1.91	46.8	17.25	1.85	34.2	16.7	1.4	18	19	17.85	16.62	19.20	17.87	1.50	46.4
G_1							18.0	1.9	40	37						
H	20.2	2.09	85.5	19.31	1.86	75.9	20.1	2.6	75	76				20.31	1.63	92.2
Male Mandible																
D	15.5	1.59	6.1	14.75	1.48	1.4	15.5	1.5	10	9	14.70	14.35	15.44	14.97	0.99	0.1
E	17.3	2.47	19.0	15.77	1.38	5.3	15.8	1.2	5	5	15.57	14.98	16.11	15.93	1.65	10.5
F	17.5	2.14	40.5	16.79	1.71	24.0	16.3	1.3	6	6	16.63	15.92	17.54	16.83	1.30	18.5
F_1							16.7	0.8	0	7						
G	18.3	1.93	56.0	17.89	1.41	46.8	17.1	1.7	27	23	18.80	17.52	19.94	18.97	1.75	71.0
G_1							18.4	2.2	47	45						
H	20.5	1.97	90.1	19.88	1.75	85.8	20.6	2.3	89	85				20.45	1.67	92.9

Source: Data modified from Lewis, J.M. and Senn, D.R., *Forensic Sci. Int.*, 201, 79, 2010.

[a] Blankenship et al. data reported as median age and the intervals at the 25th and 75th percentile.

[b] Blankenship et al. data reported as recalculated by Lewis giving data as mean age, intervals as standard deviation and the empirical probability that the individual is 18 years of age or older.

[c] Empirical probabilities reported by Solari and Abramovitch are given for each third molar.

to be evaluated and resulting statistical data averaged to estimate chronologic age. Results yielded an approximate average standard deviation of 2 years for each stage and demonstrated that when an individual's third molar attains a Demirjian developmental stage "H," there is a high probability that the individual is at least 18 years old.

Numerous subsequent studies have been performed to validate the technique and provide useful population-specific data for other ancestries. Of particular interest within America are the Hispanic ethnicity third molar studies of Solari and Abramovitch (2002) and Kasper et al. (2009); and, the American Black third molar study of Blankenship et al. (2007). Solari and Abramovitch and Kasper et al., evaluated dental radiographs of individuals from Texas. Kasper utilized the eight-stage Demirjian system while Solari and Abramovitch modified the Demirjian staging system to include two additional stages, F1 between stages "F" and "G" and stage G1 between the stages of "G" and "H" in an attempt to improve chronologic age estimation accuracy during the period of root apexification. Both studies reported results, as Mincer et al., with mean age, standard deviation, and empirical probability of attaining age 18 by stage and gender separating maxillary and mandibular third molars. Blankenship et al. evaluated a population of American Blacks from Tennessee and staged the third molars using the original Demirjian eight-stage system of crown and root development. However, results from the Blankenship study reported median age, 25th and 75th percentile and the interquartile distance for each developmental stage. Their data has been reviewed and results expressed in mean age, standard deviation, and empirical probability of reaching age 18 (Lewis and Senn, 2010). All three studies data sets can be found in Tables 8.7 and 8.8.

Similar studies have been performed worldwide on a variety of populations (Demirjian et al., 1973; Mesotten et al., 2002; Arany et al., 2004; Olze et al., 2004; Prieto et al., 2005; Thevissen et al., 2009). Unfortunately, not all third molar studies utilize the Demirjian et al. (1973) staging system to assess the mineralization of third molars even though it has been validated to consistently provide the most accurate correlation between estimated and true chronologic age (Olze et al., 2005) compared to four other developmental staging systems (Gleiser and Hunt, 1955; Gustafson and Koch, 1974; Harris and Nortje, 1984; Kullman et al., 1992). When utilizing any age estimation study involving a morphologic staging classification system, the odontologist must take care to use the exact system described in the referenced study to obtain reliable and accurate results.

Additional cautions need to be exercised. Selection of the appropriate ethnic, ancestral population study is imperative (Lewis and Brumit, 2011). There is no doubt that additional third molar population studies are needed. Specifically within North America, there is a not an Asian-American study (Lewis and Senn, 2010). The odontologist should remain familiar with recently published studies and consider use of larger population studies because they should be statistically more accurate. More importantly, the odontologist must understand the effects of potential ancestral admix on the calculated results in forensic dental age estimation.

There are special circumstances, such as prosecution of an undocumented juvenile immigrant, that require an age estimate and the probability of the individual attaining an age other than 18. Two legal questions sometimes asked are "How old was the individual in question at the time of the crime?" and "What was the probability he/she has attained a given age at the time of the crime?" These questions can be answered. After calculating the mean estimated age and standard deviation from the individual's appropriate population-specific study, the probability that the individual has attained any given age can be determined by utilizing the mathematical continuous distribution function for a normal distribution curve (Figure 8.8). Statistical probability of an individual attaining any monthly age between the ages of 14 and

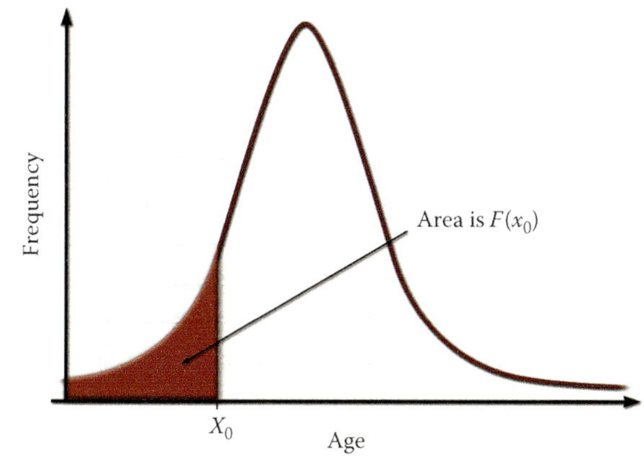

Figure 8.8 The percentage of the shaded area under normal distribution curve represents the probability of an individual having attained a given age.

19 for the population specific studies of Mincer et al. (1993), Solari and Abramovitch (2002), Blankenship et al. (2007), and Kasper et al. (2009) were presented in a paper by Lewis and Brumit at the *American Academy of Forensic Sciences 2011 Meeting* in Chicago.

UT-Age, a computer application, has been developed by Lewis, Senn, and Silvaggi to simplify and expedite the process of performing third molar age estimations (Lewis et al., 2001, 2008). It is particularly useful in assisting in age estimation for immigration cases in North America. The application records and archives case information data; calculates average estimated age, age interval to 95% confidence and probability of attaining age 18 based upon the ancestry and gender of the individual and the Demirjian staging of the third molars; then generates an editable template report. A data populated UT-Age case information page is shown in Figure 8.9. The primary advantage in utilizing computer

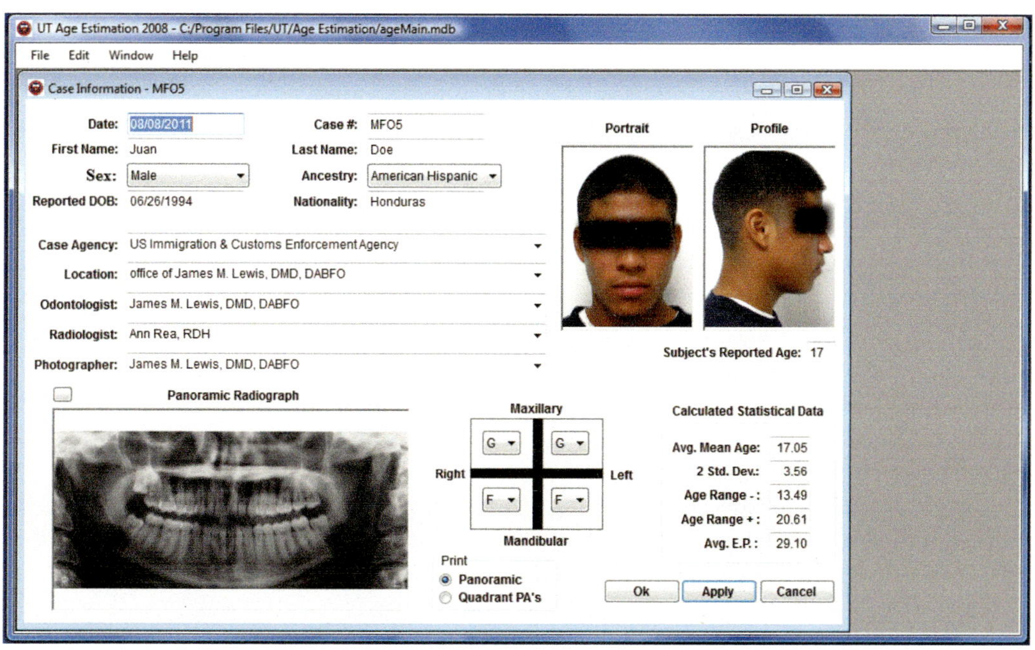

Figure 8.9 Samble UT-Age case information page and automated results.

software in age assessment is to prevent inadvertent error in performing mathematical calculations. Ancestral specific selections allowed by UT-Age are European, Hispanic, African, and Asian, and the respective population specific studies currently utilized in the age assessment calculations are Mincer et al. (1993), Kasper et al. (2009), Blankenship et al. (2007), and Arany et al. (2004). The computer application also allows for age assessment of individuals of unknown ancestry by averaging the results of all four studies based upon the entered sex and third molar staging criteria. The current UT-Age software version is 2.0.22 released in January 2010 and is a freeware download from the Center for Education and Research in Forensics (CERF) website, www.utforensic.org. The software contains a printable and screen viewable tutorial and copy of the Demirjian developmental staging chart as modified by Kasper. Updates to the software are released every 2–3 years and the next update will include the ability to determine empirical probabilities other than age 18 (Lewis and Brumit, 2010).

8.3 Postformation Techniques

The problem with adult forensic age assessment, whether performed with dental or anthropologic methodology, is that the investigator is attempting to assess chronological age on the basis of physiological age. In other words, determine how old an individual is based upon how old they appear. Aging is an extremely individual process and is affected by the manner in which we live our lives. Alcohol and drug abuse, nutrition, intensive physical labor, disease, treatments, and accidents are all factors in the aging process. Therefore, all adult age assessment methods are limited in some manner.

8.3.1 Historical Review

A historical and often referenced dental adult age estimation technique was published by Gustafson in 1950. This study assessed adult age by evaluating six postformation changes that can be observed in human teeth: attrition, periodontosis, secondary dentin, cementum apposition, root resorption, and root translucency. The technique requires the six criteria to be evaluated on an individual tooth and assigned a score between 0 and 3 depending upon the degree of progressive change. All six scores are summed and placed in a simple formula to yield an estimated age. Gustafson claimed an error rate of between 7 and 8 years that would include 95% of the population. This approach was far too simplistic, and the error rate has not been duplicated (Miles, 1963b; Burns and Maples, 1976; Maples and Rice, 1979; Lucy and Pollard, 1995). Some of the studies problems include (1) assuming all variables are equally effective in age assessment, (2) suggested staging methodology was equal among the six variables, and (3) statistical independence of each of the variables (Harris et al., 2010, 283). In order to have a better understanding of the usefulness of these six variables, they need to be discussed individually.

Attrition is the gradual wearing away of the tooth surface as a result of mastication. Although attrition itself is associated with aging when the tooth is in normal occlusion, it has issues as a marker in age assessment. Erosion and pathological abrasion, such as bruxism, clenching, tooth brush abrasion, or any other mechanical causes including dental treatment, result in an over estimation of age. Cultural habits, diets, and other population specific factors will affect the attrition rate. Today, most techniques that utilize attrition as variable in age assessment are not intended for modern populations but rather for archeological situations (Miles, 1962; Smith, 1984).

Periodontosis is the term originally used by Gustafson (1950) and is considered antiquated today. The contemporary term, periodontal recession, refers to the alveolar and gingival shrinkage around the tooth as a result of the inflammatory response due to bacterial infection. This process results in the root surface being exposed, allowing it to become stained and pitted. The measurement in loss of periodontal attachment is the maximum distance (in millimeters) between the cementoenamel junction and the line indicating soft tissue attachment on the labial surface of the tooth. The labial surface is recommended for measurement because it is generally considered to be "less susceptible to the influences of pathological factors" (Lamedin et al., 1992). Concerns in utilizing this dental postformation change as an estimator of age include dental treatments (periodontal and orthodontic), difficulty in obtaining an accurate measurement in skeletal remains, rate of periodontal attachment can be affected by nonage related factors (high frenum attachments, crowding, hyperocclusion, excessively poor oral hygiene, etc.) and the fact that some teeth have a higher disposition for periodontal disease than others.

Secondary dentin has two forms—physiological and reparative. Physiological secondary dentin forms at a slow steady rate by the healthy pulpal tissue following completion of root formation and is associated with the normal aging process. Reparative secondary dentin, also known as tertiary dentin, is formed as the result of trauma to the tooth. Trauma can come in the form of hyperocclusion, bruxism, caries, or the result of dental treatment. Secondary dentin can be seen and measured macroscopically and microscopically by means of tooth sectioning. The process of sectioning a tooth for age assessment can be technique specific, but in general, involves the preservation of the central portion of the tooth and thereby the maximum width of the pulp. It can also be observed noninvasively by radiographically measuring tooth pulp area (Kvaal et al., 1995) or volumetrically through cone beam computed tomography (Vandevoort et al., 2004). These measurements are facilitated with the use of computer software to enlarge, enhance, and measure the radiographic pulpal dental tissue.

Cementum apposition occurs throughout life on healthy mammalian teeth. The deposit can increase in thickness threefold between the ages of 11 and 70 and is thicker in the apical third than it is near the cementoenamel junction (Onder and Yakan, 1997). A study by Solheim (1990) showed that the strongest correlation between human cementum thickness and age occurs at one-third the root length from the apex. He also observed that the cementum apposition rate decreases in the elderly and is deposited slower in women than in men. Age estimation via counting the dental cementum annuli (concentric rings) on teeth of North American wildlife has been successful (Hamlin et al., 2000). However, a study Lucas and Loh (1986) could not verify that the annuli were deposited annually in the human dentition and their use in age estimation tended to produce a low estimate of chronologic age.

Root resorption has been described as the least dependable postformation change associated with age by Gustafson (Johanson, 1971; Maples, 1978). External root resorption is more closely associated with traumatic injuries, resulting in a prolonged localized inflammatory response causing osteoclasts to resorb the root dentin. Common causes include orthodontic treatment and periapical disease.

Root transparency is the phenomenon that results from the deposition of hydroxyapatite crystals within the dentin tubules over time and it does not appear before the age of 20 (Lamendin et al., 1992). Root transparency begins at the apex and progresses in a coronal direction. Bang and Ramm (1970) reported "no sex differences or differences between teeth from living and dead persons in the degree of root transparency." This postformation dental change is also the variable that is least influenced by external factors (Johanson, 1971). Therefore, root transparency is a very useful tool in adult age assessment when the gender of the individual is unknown and the volume of skeletal remains is small.

Accurate adult dental age estimation necessitates selective tooth selection and the technique(s) to be utilized. The investigator must consider the case circumstances and keep in mind what variables are best and how they may be affected by external factors. In review, root resorption has a very low correlation to chronologic age. Maples' order of age assessment variables from best correlation to age to least is root transparency, secondary dentin, attrition, gingival recession, and cementum apposition. The effect of ancestry and gender is minimal on the progression of root translucency and secondary dentin deposition. External factors, including dental restorative therapy, endodontic and orthodontic treatment, trauma, hyperocclusion, and even the lack of occlusion, can affect some or all of the six postformation variables with the exception of root translucency. Therefore, techniques that rely on the evaluation of nonrestored teeth in normal occlusion and utilize root translucency and secondary dentin formation as variables in the age assessment tend to be more accurate.

8.3.2 Adult Dental Age Estimation Techniques

There are a multitude of forensic adult dental age estimation techniques that have been published and reviewed. Dalitz (1962) has historical significance and is still in use. Kvall and Solheim (1994) is particularly helpful in archeological situations. Others propose additional dental age estimation criteria including root surface roughness, color estimation of root dentin, and crown pulp area (Solheim, 1993), while some expand upon known variables with new technology (Thevissen et al., 2009). To follow are descriptions of some of the basic and relevant methods utilized today; however, the odontologist should become familiar with additional techniques, methods, and data sets.

8.3.2.1 Johanson Sectioning (1971)

The Johanson sectioning technique is a modification of the Gustafson method. The method recommends examination of the dental occlusion noting number of teeth present, location, and potential habits. Use of multiple single rooted teeth from both arches should be considered. The teeth are sectioned in a bucco-lingual plane to.25 mm slice along the widest portion of the dental pulp. All six previously discussed postformation morphologic changes are considered and graded microscopically according to a modified Gustafson 7 stage system (Figure 8.10). When multiple teeth are used, the mean value is taken for each variable and placed into a regression formula that differentially weighted the six criteria but did not allow for gender, ancestral, or tooth position differences.

$$\text{Age} = 11.02 + 5.14A + 2.30S + 4.14P + 3.71C + 5.57R + 8.98T$$

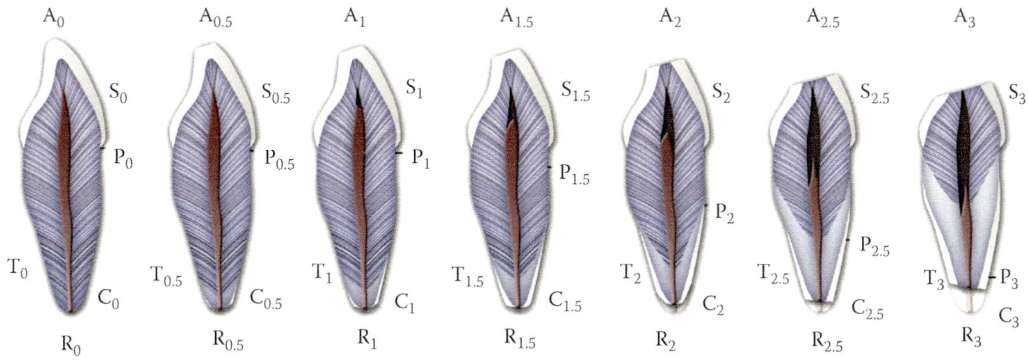

Figure 8.10 The Gustafson seven-stage post-formation change grading system, illustrated by Lewis. (Based on figures in Johanson, G., *Odontologisk Revy*, 22, 1, 1971.)

The Johanson regression formula yields an estimated age and two standard deviation error rate of approximately 10 years when multiple teeth are utilized and 16 years when a single tooth is considered.

8.3.2.2 Maples (1978)

In 1978, Maples published a study that evaluated sectioned teeth of subjects from a Florida dental clinic and graded them based upon five of the six Gustafson criteria using the same seven-stage system created by Johanson (Figure 8.10). Root resorption was found to have insignificant correlation in dental estimation of age. Regression analysis was performed considering tooth position. Maples found that gingival recession was difficult at times tov assess after postmortem loss of the soft tissue and concluded that attrition was variable among different cultures due to dietary habits. Therefore, a second set of regressions formulas were calculated, this time using only the most statistically significant variables, root transparency, and secondary dentin. Table 8.9 shows Maples' published regression formulas for root translucency and secondary dentin formation by tooth position. An added benefit of reducing the number of variables is the potential reduction in observer staging

Table 8.9 Regression Formulas for the Variables of Secondary Dentin Formation (S) and Root Translucency (T)

Position	Formulas for S and T	
	Estimated Age	SE (Years)
Central incisor	3.89S + 14.23T + 15.28	9.1
Lateral incisor	6.51S + 12.55T + 25.16	9.6
Cuspid	18.67S + 11.72T + 21.94	11.0
First bicuspid	2.82S + 15.25T + 19.65	12.2
Second bicuspid	4.79S + 15.53T + 17.99	7.6
First molar	11.28S + 5.32T + 10.86	11.1
Second molar	6.99S + 10.86T + 19.31	6.8
Third molar	4.71S + 12.30T + 24.57	12.0

Source: Data from Maples, W.R., *J. Forensic Sci.*, 23(4), 764, 1978.

errors. Maples noted that the root transparency and secondary dentin formulas performed best and that these results displayed small differences between Black and White ancestries as well as between males and females suggesting that this formula can "be used with other populations with a relative measure of confidence."

8.3.2.3 *Lamendin et al. (1992)*

Lamendin recognized that previous dental age estimation techniques had significantly improved upon Gustafson's original method through the "reduction in the number of variables, use of multiple regression analysis and index values based on actual physical measurement." He also noted concerns regarding microscopic evaluation of thinly sectioned teeth requiring the "expertise of a well-trained dental histologist" and tooth destruction preventing further examination using other techniques. Lamendin's collected data from a French population and limits age assessment variables to root transparency (T) and periodontal recession (P) requiring three physical measurements made from the labial aspect of the tooth. Periodontal recession is determined by measuring, in millimeters, the maximum distance between the cementoenamel junction and the line of soft tissue attachment (Figure 8.11a); root transparency is the distance from the root apex to the maximum height of transparency along the root surface (Figure 8.11b); and the root's height is measured from the cementoenamel junction to the root apex. Lamendin's regression formula for age assessment is as follows:

$$\text{Age} = (0.18 \times P) + (0.42 \times T) + 25.53$$

where P and T are defined as

P = (measured periodontal recession height ×100)/measured root height

T = (measured root transparence height×100)/measured root height

Lamendin et al. published sample error rates in mean error (ME) and subdivided the error rates by decade of life (Table 8.10), yielding an average mean error of approximately 10 years. The study cautions against usage of this data set on individuals below age 40 due to inaccuracy. Unfortunately, the studies sample size is too small to generate individual tooth position regression formulas or statistical data regarding the potential benefit of utilizing multiple teeth. However, age estimation using Lamendin et al. is significant between the ages of 40 and 70 when the maxillary incisors, particularly the central incisors, are considered.

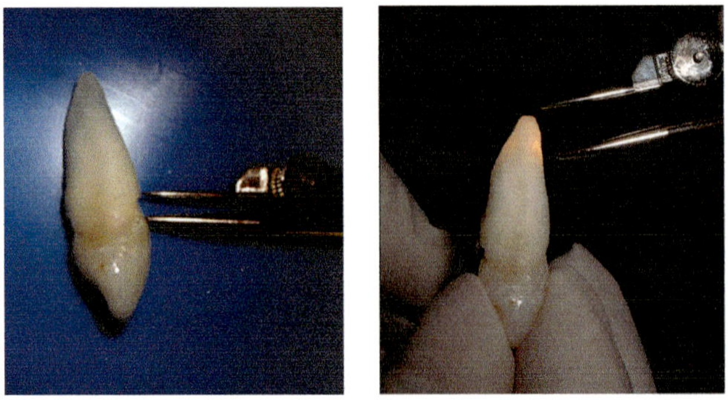

(a) (b)

Figure 8.11 Maxillary canine: (a) measurement of periodontal recession height, (b) measurement of root transparency.

Table 8.10 Mean Error (ME) Comparison of Lamendin et al. and Prince and Ubelaker Results

Age Interval (Years)		25–29	30–39	40–49	50–59	60–69	70–79	80–89	90–99	Overall
ME (Years)	Lamendin et al.	24.8	15.5	9.9	7.3	6.3	11.6	18.9	—	10
	Prince and Ubelaker	13.2	9.0	5.6	5.2	7.2	12.3	20.3	32.6	8.2

Source: Data modified from Prince, D.A. and Ubelaker, D.H., *J. Forensic Sci.*, 47(1), 107, 2002.

8.3.2.4 *Prince and Ubelaker (2002)*

Prince and Ubelaker applied the Lamendin et al. method of age assessment to the Terry Collection, skeletal remains collected between 1900 and 1965 containing individuals of known ancestry, gender, age at death, and cause of death, to assess the method's accuracy, precision, and applicability to a non-French population. The results of this investigation verified the technique and produced a mean error of 8.23 years (Table 8.10) and a standard deviation of 6.87 years when the Lamendin formula was utilized. However, Prince and Ubelaker also evaluated the effects of ancestry and gender producing four new regression formulas as follows:

Male African Ancestry

$$\text{Age} = 1.04(\text{RH}) + 0.31(\text{P}) + 0.47(\text{T}) + 1.70 \quad 1 \text{ standard deviation} = 4.97 \text{ years}$$

Male European Ancestry

$$\text{Age} = 0.15(\text{RH}) + 0.29(\text{P}) + 0.39(\text{T}) + 23.17 \quad 1 \text{ standard deviation} = 5.92 \text{ years}$$

Female African Ancestry

$$\text{Age} = 1.63(\text{RH}) + 0.48(\text{P}) + 0.48(\text{T}) + (-8.41) \quad 1 \text{ standard deviation} = 7.17 \text{ years}$$

Female European Ancestry

$$\text{Age} = 1.10(\text{RH}) + 0.31(\text{P}) + 0.39(\text{T}) + 11.82 \quad 1 \text{ standard deviation} = 6.21 \text{ years}$$

The new regression formulas incorporated root height (RH) into the equation and calculated the variables "P" and "T" in the same manner as Lamendin et al. study results concluded that age estimation was improved when ancestry and sex of the individual is considered; and, accuracy is best between the chronologic ages of 30 and 69. Specimens evaluated younger than 30 and older than 69 yielded higher error rates. Gonzalez-Comenares et al. (2007) tested the validity of the Prince and Ubelaker and Lamendin et al. formulas in a Spanish Caucasian population and in a Columbian population of mixed racial origin. A population-specific regression formula based upon the Prince and Ubelaker method was developed and tested. Results of the Gonzalez–Comenares study demonstrated that the original Prince and Ubelaker method and the modified method provided better results than the Lamendin method confirming the need to create gender differentiated population specific data.

8.3.2.5 *Bang and Ramm (1970)*

Bang and Ramm reduced their age estimation technique criteria to one variable, root translucency. Because root translucency has not shown appreciable ancestral and gender variation, and is minimally affected by other external factors, this method has been widely applied in cases where the volume of skeletal remains are small and the sex and ancestry are unknown. The Bang and Ramm method accounts for tooth position and provides age estimation data for intact and sectioned teeth. When sectioned, the tooth should be cut in the labio-lingual direction preserving tooth structure through the center of the pulp. Only one physical measurement is required, length of root translucency from the apex in millimeters. Often, root translucency is not even across the entire root structure. In those cases, the maximum root translucency length and the minimum root translucency length are recorded and the resulting average of the two measurements is utilized in the age estimation calculation. There is an apparent slowing of the formation of root translucency beginning at about age 70. As a result, two separate regression formulas were generated with tooth-specific coefficients; one for measurements up to and including 9 mm of root translucency and a second for measurements in excess of 9 mm.

Translucency zone ≤9 mm: $\text{Age} = B_0 + B_1X + B_2X^2$

Translucency zone >9 mm: $\text{Age} = B_0 + B_1X$

B_0, B_1, and B_2 are tooth-specific regression coefficients and X is measured length of root translucency in millimeters. The tooth-specific regression coefficients can be found in Table 8.11 along with their associated standard deviation of error. Some authors have questioned whether results would be improved if relative root transparency were used as the determinant rather than the absolute length of root transparency (Harms-Paschal and Schmidt, 2010, 31).

8.3.2.6 *Kvaal et al. (1995)*

All previously discussed adult dental age estimation techniques have required the sacrifice of tooth structure in the form of extraction and sometimes sectioning. These methods can be expensive and tooth destruction in some cases may be unacceptable for ethical, religious, cultural, or scientific reasons. Kvaal et al. devised a noninvasive radiographic method to evaluate the progressive change in pulp size due to secondary dentin apposition. Ideally, two tooth selection criteria should be met to decrease the influence of tertiary dentinal deposits that cannot be differentiated from secondary dentin apposition. They are (1) the teeth evaluated should be in normal functional occlusion and (2) the teeth should be free of any potential manifestations of trauma including dental restoration, active caries, erosion, abrasion, and abnormal attrition. Single-rooted nonrotated teeth are utilized and multi-rooted teeth avoided due to evaluation difficulties and measurement errors. Pulp width was used as the indicator because earlier studies had demonstrated that pulp width was a better indicator of age than pulp length (Kambe et al., 1991; Prapanpoch et al., 1992; Kvaal and Solheim, 1994). Good radiographic technique is always advisable; but, to compensate for any potential magnification and angulation errors, ratios of pulp/root length; pulp/tooth length; and pulp/root widths at three different levels are used in the dental evaluation. Figure 8.12 illustrates the required measurements and their locations. Kvaal regression formulas for age assessment are available for mandibular lateral incisors, canines, and first bicuspids and for maxillary central and lateral incisors and second bicuspids. The only

Table 8.11 Bang and Ramm Regression Coefficients and Standard Deviation (SD) for Intact and Sectioned Teeth; and, Length of Translucency Zone (≤9 and >9 mm)

	≤9 mm								>9 mm					
	Intact Roots				Sectioned Roots				Intact Roots			Sectioned Roots		
Tooth No.	B0	B1	B2	SD	B0	B1	B2	SD	B0	B1	SD	B0	B1	SD
8	20.3	5.74	0	10.42	21.02	6.03	−0.06	11.43	20.34	5.74	10.42	22.36	5.39	11.25
9	24.3	6.22	−0.119	9.71	26.84	6	−0.155	11.03	26.78	4.96	9.58	30.18	4.3	10.93
7	18.8	7.1	−0.164	10.83	23.09	7.04	−0.197	11.25	22.06	5.36	10.73	25.55	5.23	11.2
10	20.9	6.85	−0.223	9.77	24.62	5.18	−0.077	9.4	25.57	4.38	9.81	25.9	4.39	9.24
6	26.2	4.64	−0.044	12.59	21.52	6.49	−0.171	13.29	28.13	4.01	12.39	28.01	4.23	13.12
11	25.27	4.58	−0.073	13.8	24.64	5.22	−0.143	13.78	27.59	3.65	13.6	29.41	3.32	13.7
5 and 12	23.91	3.02	0.203	11.62	29.98	2.73	0.107	13.17	18.42	5.4	11.41	24.44	3.81	12.93
4	23.78	5.06	−0.064	11.21	24.76	4.81	0	10.43	25.33	4.28	10.96	24.75	4.81	10.43
13	25.95	4.07	−0.067	9.48	22.34	7.59	−0.393	6.88	26.92	3.37	9.32	26.21	4.03	7.62
25	9.8	12.61	−0.711	10.91	13.63	12.11	−0.683	11.01	29	4.23	11.85	31.78	4.19	12.09
24	23.16	9.32	−0.539	12.27	26.46	8.79	−0.511	11.74	37.56	2.94	12.84	37.89	3.08	12.31
26	26.57	7.81	−0.383	11.95	21.77	10.19	−0.581	11.26	38.81	2.81	12.43	38.49	3.03	12.42
23	18.58	10.25	−0.538	10.08	22.22	9.07	−0.444	10.78	33.65	3.53	11.12	35.19	4.49	11.46
27	23.3	8.45	−0.348	10.52	24.34	8.38	−0.358	10.74	37.8	3.5	11.24	40.32	3.05	11.77
22	27.45	7.38	−0.289	10.22	23.88	8.76	−0.388	9.96	41.5	2.84	10.74	42.07	2.73	10.88
28	24.83	6.85	−0.237	9.53	21.54	8.63	−0.395	10.19	30.83	4.05	9.73	33.1	3.66	11.08
21	29.17	5.96	−0.173	10.13	26.02	7	−0.234	8.39	34.97	3.74	10.14	32.79	4.11	8.71
29	29.42	4.49	−0.065	13	14.9	9.93	−0.451	9.05	30.68	3.76	12.82	27.46	4.17	11.23
20	18.72	5.79	−0.082	11.52	23.87	5.5	−0.098	10.85	20.87	4.79	11.38	25.6	4.41	10.77
3 and 14 (mr)	30.25	3.23	−0.018	10.22	28.22	4.82	−0.101	6.85	30.56	3	10.08	30.03	3.48	7.11
19 and 30 (mr)	27.39	6.25	−0.239	10.49	33.42	5.18	−0.302	15.76	30.32	3.66	11.04	35.27	2.78	15.74
3 and 14 (dr)	34.73	0.67	0.211	10.68	20.43	6.09	−0.182	10.85	29.49	3.32	11.09	26.89	3.55	10.92
19 and 30 (dr)	30.21	5.52	−0.181	10.69	29.91	4.97	−0.102	11.1	31.46	3.77	10.89	30.31	4.22	11
3 and 14 (pr)	27.43	3.64	0.039	10.02	25.15	4.34	−0.032	10.2	26.81	4.07	9.98	25.83	3.95	10.16

Source: Data from Bang, G. and Ramm, E., *Acta Odontol. Scand.*, 56, 238, 1970.
Tooth numbers in the universal system (mr, mesial root; dr, distal root; pr, palatal root).

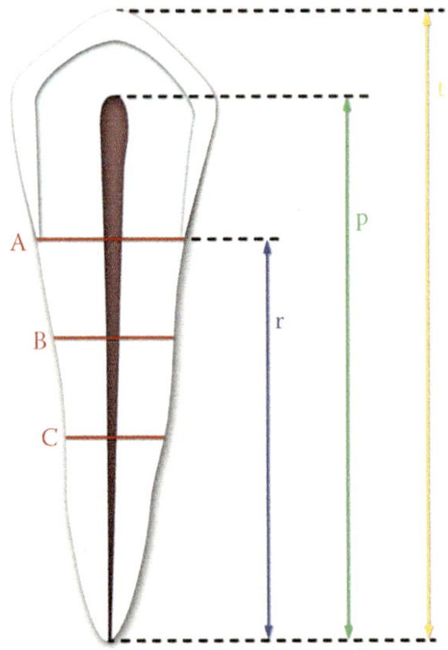

Figure 8.12 Illustration demonstrating the Kvaal (1995) measurements made on each tooth: t, maximum tooth length; p, maximum pulp length; r, root length from the mesial surface; A, root and pulp width at the CEJ; C, root and pulp width at mid-root (midpoint between CEJ and root apex); B, root and pulp width midway between levels A and C.

occasion where gender is included as an independent variable is in the regression formula for the mandibular lateral incisor. Additionally, there are separate regression formulas for all six teeth, the three maxillary teeth and the three mandibular teeth (Table 8.12). Best results are obtained from utilization of all six teeth and the poorest estimator of age is the mandibular canine. Because these measurements are tedious and the mathematical calculations are cumbersome, the odontologist would be well advised to utilize computer imaging software to insure accurate measurements and to use database software to prevent inadvertent error in performing the mathematical calculations. To estimate age using the Kvaal et al. technique, there are nine measurements and nine mathematical calculations to be performed. Figures 8.13 through 8.16 are a series of photographs that illustrate how

Table 8.12 Regression Formulas for Estimation of Age Using Radiographs

	Regression Formula	SEE (Years)
Six (6) teeth from both maxillary and mandibular arches	Age = 129.8 – 316.4(M) – 66.8(W-L)	8.6
Three (3) maxillary teeth	Age = 120.0 – 256.6(M) – 45.3(W-L)	8.9
Three (3) mandibular teeth	Age = 135.3 – 356.8(M) – 82.5(W-L)	9.4
Individual tooth #'s		
8 or 9	Age = 110.2 – 201.4(M) – 31.3(W-L)	9.5
7 or 10	Age = 103.5 – 216.6(M) – 46.6(W-L)	10.0
4 or 13	Age = 125.3 – 288.5(M) – 46.3(W-L)	11.0
21 or 28	Age = 133.0 – 318.3(M) – 65.0(W-L)	10.5
22 or 27	Age = 158.8 – 255.7(M)	11.5
23 or 26	Age = 106.6 – 251.7(M) – 61.2(W-L) – 6.0(G)	11.5

Source: Data from Kvaal, S.I. et al., *Forensic Sci. Int.*, 74, 175, 1995.
G, gender: Male = 1; Female = 0.

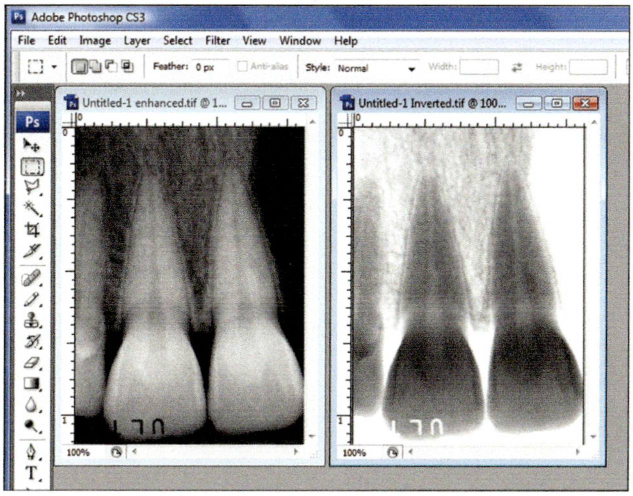

Figure 8.13 Kvaal (1995) technique: A Radiograph of tooth number 8 on the left and its inverted image on the right.

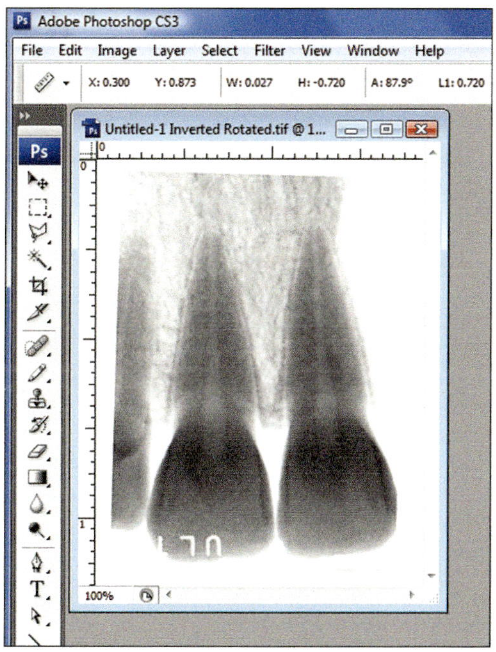

Figure 8.14 Kvaal (1995) technique: Inverted image of tooth number 8 rotated with the long axis of the tooth vertical.

computer imaging software can be used to simplify the Kvaal et al. measurement process. Figure 8.13 is a dental radiograph that has been imported into the software. The quality of the original image can be enhanced by changing the levels, contrast, and brightness. Sometimes inverting the original image (transforming it into a negative) can also improve visual acuity. Once the image quality is satisfactory, the tooth needs to be rotated so that the long axis of the tooth is vertical in order to make measurements easier and repetitive (Figure 8.14). Next, guides are placed at the end points of any measurement. Image enlargement may aid in the accurate placement of the guide lines. Note in Figure 8.15 that the blue

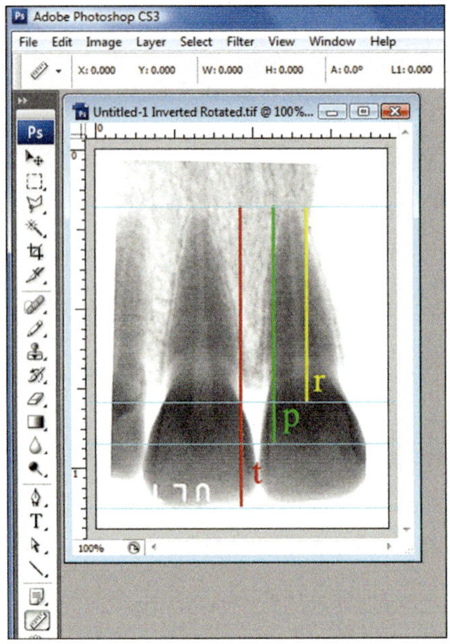

Figure 8.15 Kvaal (1995) technique: Guidelines (blue) are placed at the root apex, CEJ, coronal end of the pulp and incisal edge of the incisor to facilitate measurement of variables t, p, and r.

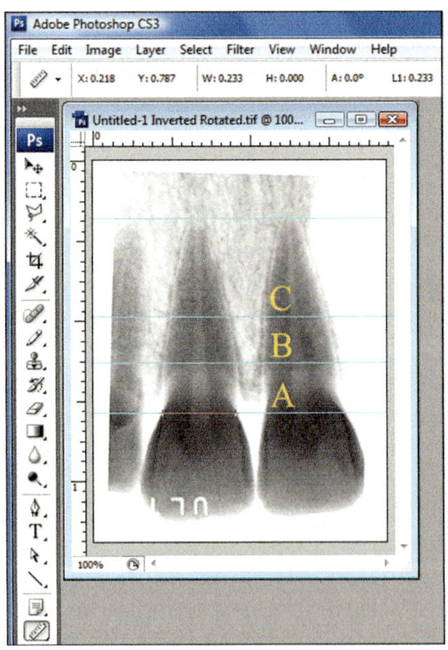

Figure 8.16 Kvaal (1995) technique: Guidelines (blue) are placed at level A, B, and C to facilitate the measurement of root width and pulpal width at each level.

guidelines have been placed at the root apex, cementoenamel junction, coronal end of the pulp, and incisal edge of the central incisor (tooth #8). Using the imaging software's measurement tool, inter-guideline distances can be measured to determine tooth length (t), pulp length (p), and root length (r). Likewise, Figure 8.16 illustrates the use of the guide lines to measure root width (a, b, and c) and pulp width (a′, b′, and c′) at levels A, B, and C.

Table 8.13 Preliminary Ratio and Regression Coefficient Calculations from Radiographic Tooth Measurements

Preliminary Calculations	
Ratios	Regression Coefficients
P = p/r	M = mean value of all ratios
R = p/t	
A = a′/a	W = mean value of B and C
B = b′/b	
C = c′/c	L = mean value of P and R

Source: Data from Kvaal, S. I. et al., *Forensic Sci. Int.*, 74, 175, 1995.

P is the ratio between pulp (p) and root (r) length; R is the ratio between pulp (p) and tooth (t) length; A is the ratio between pulp width (a′) and root width (a) at the CEJ level; B is the ratio between pulp width (b′) and root width (b) midway between levels A and C; C is the ratio between pulp width (c′) and root width (c) at the mid-root level.

Some odontologists find it beneficial to draw vertical guidelines that intersect the horizontal lines A, B, and C when measuring root and pulp widths. Once all nine measurements have been recorded, the ratio values for "P," "R," "A," "B," and "C" must be calculated (see Table 8.13). These values are used to then calculate values for "M," "W," and "L," which are inserted into the tooth-specific regression formula to determine the estimated age. This technique yields a standard estimate of error between 8.6 and 11.5 years depending upon the tooth sample evaluated.

8.4 Biochemical Techniques

8.4.1 Amino Acid Racemization

All living organisms utilize proteins as the basic building block of their biologic composition. Structurally, proteins are comprised of various arrangements of 20 different amino acids. All amino acids, except for glycine, have two asymmetrical forms that differ in their optical characteristics. The dextrorotary (D) form will rotate polarized light to the right; whereas the levorotary (L) form rotates polarized light to the left. The two forms have the exact same molecular and structural formula but cannot be superimposed when rotated in a three-dimensional space. They are mirror images of one another. These two forms are referred to as enantiomers, chirals, or stereoisomers. Racemization is the gradual and spontaneous process of an enantiomerically pure solution converting to a mixture of equal amounts of the L and D enantiomers. Biologically, only the L-form of a chiral amino acid molecule will participate in biochemical reactions while the other optical isomer, the D-form, does not participate or in some cases may cause pathological conditions and disease (Arany and Ohtani, 2010). In general, at birth only the L-form of amino acids exists systemically. Racemization begins immediately; however, metabolically active tissues replenish the L-form of amino acids throughout life. Some avascular tissues depend on passive perfusion for nourishment and are less metabolically active. These bradytrophic tissues, such as the vertebral disks, lens of the eye, teeth, and parts of the brain do not replenish the L-form of amino acids and are therefore useful in estimating the age at death by sampling a specific amino acid and knowing its racemization conversion rate (Ritz-Timme and Collins, 2002).

There are molecular and environmental factors and that can affect the rate of racemization. These include amino acid composition, size, and location of the macromolecule, ionic strength of the environment, concentration of buffer compounds, bacterial contamination, temperature, pH, humidity, and presence of aldehydes particularly when associated with metal ions (Robins et al., 2001, 4–26). Tooth dentin is an excellent substrate to sample amino acids because it is protected from many extrinsic environmental factors (Arany and Ohtani, 2010); it is bradytrophic and stable with the exception of minor amounts of secondary and tertiary dentin formation; and, it consists of approximately 91% collagen (Yekkala et al., 2006). Dentin collagen is rich in aspartic acid, which racemizes at a slow rate within this acid-insoluble matrix. Having a substrate that is nearly collagen pure allows for the racemization coefficient to be very close to that of collagen. Although other amino acid racemization (AAR) techniques exist utilizing glutamate and alanine (Arany and Ohtani, 2010), aspartic acid is the most commonly used dentin racemization method, yielding a chronologic age estimation error rate of approximately ±3 years (Ohtani and Yamamoto, 1991, 2010).

Three environmental factors have a direct correlation to the racemization rate and require discussion. At pH 3.0 or less, the amino acid peptide bonds hydrolyze; however, when the pH remains within the range of 3–9 and at normal environmental temperatures, racemization is unaffected. Therefore, it is believed that pH is not important in age assessment techniques utilizing aspartic acid racemization. Water degrades proteins by hydrolyzing the peptide bond. It has been observed that when teeth and bone is dried at 110°C and dryness is maintained, racemization will cease. When water is present for extended periods of time in skeletal remains bacterial and other contamination is possible (Robins et al., 2001, 4–26). Temperature is the factor that plays the most significant role in racemization rate—an increase in temperature increases the rate. As we discuss the effects of temperature on dental aspartic acid racemization rate, it is important to remember that dentin is not homogeneous. The crown of a tooth forms prior to the root and this process takes several years to occur suggesting that the degree of racemization within tooth dentin may be location specific. Intuition suggests that racemization should also follow the natural pattern of tooth formation with the earliest forming tooth having the greatest degree of racemization. However, this is not what is observed and the culprit for this perceived anomoly is an oral temperature gradient. The crowns of anterior teeth have a lower long-term ambient temperature decreasing the rate of racemization. Additionally, the racemization rate is different in parts of the same tooth. The lingual surfaces of the clinical crown and roots have a higher environmental temperature and thus a higher racemization rate. Because the root surface is surrounded by bone and the temperature more nearly stable throughout the root structure, the racemization rate is consistent on both the labial and lingual surfaces of the root (Yekkala et al., 2006). Also, since the tooth crown forms prior to the root, in the young the D/L ratio is higher in the crown dentin than in the root dentin; while, the inverse is true in the elderly due to prolonged temperature differences. Therefore, dentin aspartic acid racemization rate is tooth specific and necessitates following the exact technique methodology for harvesting the dentin substrate and utilizing the technique's tooth-specific charts for age assessment. Racemization rates by tooth location in descending order have been determined to be second molar > first molar > second bicuspid >

central incisor > first premolar > lateral incisor > canine (Ohtani et al., 2003). According to one researcher the central incisor has been noted to provide the best coefficient of correlation (Yaekkala, 2006).

8.4.2 Radioactive ^{14}C

Radioactive ^{14}C dating has been an archeological tool since 1949. The method is also known as radiocarbon dating or sometimes just carbon dating. The technique relies on the naturally occurring process of ^{14}C that is produced by cosmic rays interacting with atmospheric nitrogen. The elemental carbon is then rapidly oxidized to radioactive carbon dioxide ($^{14}CO_2$). This process had resulted in a stable atmospheric concentration of ^{14}C for thousands of years. Knowing the radioactive half-life of ^{14}C (5730 years) and measuring the amount of ^{14}C remaining or currently present in archeological samples allows for an estimation of the time period when that substance was created using accelerator mass spectrometry analysis. Forensic application using this technique became possible because of the extreme production of atmospheric ^{14}C as a result of above ground nuclear testing occurring between 1955 and 1963. Although the nuclear detonations were in relatively limited locations throughout the world, $^{14}CO_2$ mixed homogeneously into the atmosphere but with some variation between the northern and southern hemispheres. Following the Test Ban Treaty in 1963, atmospheric ^{14}C has declined in small part because of radioactive decay but mostly due its incorporation into terrestrial and marine carbon reservoirs (Buchholz, 2007). New plant growth reflects the current atmospheric ^{14}C concentration. Herbivores obtain radioactive carbon from the plant material and therefore will have ^{14}C concentrations in metabolically active tissues that are weeks to months removed from the atmospheric concentration. Omnivores and carnivores lag in tissue ^{14}C concentrations even further because they are a step removed in the food chain (Buchholz and Spalding, 2010).

As a result of this spike in radioactive carbon in the environment, forensic application of the dating technique is now possible. Anthropologists utilize trabecular bone associated with hematopoietic bone marrow, a highly metabolically active source, to accurately estimate the death date of skeletal remains (Ubelaker and Para, 2010). In 2005, Spaulding et al. published a report describing the ability to estimate the date of birth regardless of the time of death using the radiocarbon method on tooth enamel with an error rate of ±1.6 years. This is possible because there is no remodeling of enamel after tooth formation and individual tooth crown development occurs within distinct age intervals. Date of birth is estimated by measuring the ^{14}C level in a specific tooth's enamel, finding that level on a chart that matches measured ^{14}C level to a given year and then subtracting the age at which that tooth would be expected to have completed its enamel formation. Even though the current atmospheric radioactive carbon concentration is decreasing, measurement techniques are improving. Also, accelerator mass spectrometry is becoming more accessible and less expensive making the test analysis comparable in time and expense to other routine forensic procedures.

There are limitations to forensic radiocarbon enamel analysis. First, because the earliest above ground nuclear testing began in 1955 and the last tooth to complete its crown formation is the third molar at approximately age 12, the earliest date of birth that can be practically estimated is 1943. Also, because there are ascending and descending sides to the curve of atmospheric ^{14}C with the peak at 1965, two estimated dates of birth are possible. When it is not obvious whether the individual was born before or after the atmospheric ^{14}C peak, early techniques required that two separate teeth with differing times of crown formation must be analyzed to determine the exact location on the curve (Buchholz and Spalding, 2010). Alkass et al. (2009) reported three reasons that the power of radiocarbon dating will most likely improve in the near future: (1) The quality of dental enamel available for sampling is improving as a result of decreased decay rate and interceptive dental therapies. (2) The percentage of the population exposed to atmospheric ^{14}C during childhood increases each year. (3) The precision of accelerator mass spectrometry analysis techniques are improving, necessitating a smaller sample of enamel.

Combining the techniques of AAR dentin analysis with ^{14}C enamel analysis can significantly improve the ability of investigators to identify unknown decedents by providing estimates of the decedent's date of birth (^{14}C), age at death (AAR), and date of death (calculated by comparison of the results of the two techniques).

In 2012 collaborative research that describes the unification of a combination of techniques describes new possibilities for age estimation from teeth. The study added previously missing data from North America, which was found to be consistent with previously collected data from other parts of the world. A paper describing the techniques has been submitted for publication detailing the combination of ^{13}C, ^{18}O, and bomb-pulse ^{14}C analyses with DNA analysis on materials from one or two teeth. The ^{14}C analyses can provide information of the year of birth of unknown decedents with and averaged absolute error of 1.8 ± 1.3 years. By using a different tooth or different parts of the same tooth the ^{14}C levels detected can indicate whether the subject was born before or after the period of the above ground nuclear testing (1955–1963). The ^{13}C and ^{18}O levels in enamel vary by geographic area and can aid in determining, with limitations, the area the person may have lived. DNA tests resulted in individual-specific profiles in most cases. The sex of the individual could be determined in all cases. AAR analysis already mentioned earlier, offers information on estimated age at death. The techniques must, of course, be further tested by the same and/or other investigators. If successful these methods will offer investigators results from a single tooth that indicate sex, estimated year of birth, estimated age at death, and information on the region that an individual lived, and, in most cases, a DNA profile (Alkass et al., 2012). This information would be very valuable to investigators into the identity of unknown decedents.

8.5 Dental Age Estimation Guidelines and Standards

Dental age estimation guidelines and standards have been developed by the American Board of Forensic Odontology, Age Estimation Committee (ABFO, 2012). The purpose of the guidelines is to stress the value and importance and enhance the quality of forensic dental age assessment. By definition, guidelines are recommended procedures that help to direct but are not required while standards, establish required protocol. Guidelines regarding recorded information and evidence collected for age estimation consideration include the following:

1. Identification data
   a. Case number
   b. Referring agency
   c. Name of the examiner(s)
   d. Date of the examination
   e. If known, the individual's name and stated date of birth
   f. Other pertinent informational data

2. Evidence collected and measured
   a. Specific teeth used in evaluation
   b. When known, the sex, ancestry, and population specificity
   c. Age estimation criteria including but not limited to
      i. Morphologic developmental staging
      ii. Root translucency, secondary dentin apposition, attrition or any other measured dental developmental or postformation characteristics
3. Other information as indicated
   a. Photographs
   b. Radiographs
   c. Information from dental examination
   d. Oral hygiene
   e. Nutritional health
   f. Pathology
   g. Systemic disease

Standards for dental age estimation include the following:

1. The forensic odontologist is responsible for being familiar with current valid age estimation methodology.
2. All available information, including sex, ancestry, population specificity, and environmental factors are to be considered.
3. When practical, use multiple independent statistical methods.
4. A list of dentition, anatomic structures analyzed and specific technique(s), and the published study where statistical data was utilized should be included in the body of the final report.
5. Conclusion statements should include estimated age and error rate (age interval). The error rate should include statistically 95% of the considered specific population, or two standard deviations, whenever that information is available. Immigration and age of majority cases may also include a probability statement that the individual in question has reached a specific age.

When writing a forensic dental age estimation report, the convention of including four sections, Introduction, Inventory of Evidence, Method(s) of Analysis, and Conclusions is suggested. The Introduction summarizes the case identification data. The Inventory of Evidence section records the list of received and collected evidence. This could include number, type, and date of radiographs and photographs taken for evaluation purposes. It may also include other pertinent information that could potentially affect the age assessment including but not limited to gender, ancestry, environmental factors, observed pathology, and known systemic disease. As a standard, the report should always include, when known, the gender and ancestry of the individual somewhere within the body of the report. Stating the technique(s) or study(s) utilized is also compulsory. This should be clearly stated in the Method of Analysis section along with a list of specific teeth or other anatomic structures utilized for each technique. Noting any particular morphologic staging system utilized may be beneficial for clarification purposes. The Conclusion summarizes the determined estimate of chronologic age and associated error rate or measure of variability. Age intervals should be stated following the scientifically accepted threshold of 95% confidence (±2 standard deviations) when possible. If the age assessment is being performed for cases involving immigration and age of legal majority issues, a probability statement of the individual having attained a given age would also be included.

8.6 Summary

Estimating chronologic age is an inexact science. The ability to accurately assess human age diminishes as the true chronologic age of an individual increases. In fact, with the exception of the use of aspartic acid racemization and radioactive carbon-14 techniques, accurate age assessment of adults over the age of 30 is poor. In order to insure the most accurate dental estimation of chronologic age possible, the forensic investigator must apply the most valid, current, relevant, and reliable studies available. All available information must be considered along with the results from other age estimation disciplines. Accuracy depends upon strict adherence to technique processes as described in the literature. This includes nondeviation from the staging or scoring convention described in any given study. Among others, Willems (2001) encourages the use of use of multiple techniques and repetitive measurements to obtain maximum reliability.

Accuracy can be complicated by individual case circumstances. Age estimation of the living necessitates the use of noninvasive techniques for moral, ethical, cultural, and religious reasons thereby limiting the investigator to the use of radiographic and atlas style data sets. Although age assessment of the deceased theoretically permits the use of both noninvasive and destructive techniques, authorities may deny the use of techniques involving tooth extraction and destruction. Furthermore, teeth for ideal evaluation may be missing or deemed inappropriate for use because of therapeutic dental restoration.

There are many mitigating factors that the forensic odontologist should consider in technique selection and their effect on accurate age assessment. Nutrition, prevalence of specific diseases, medical treatments, habits, and other environmental factors not only differ among global populations but change within a given specific population over time. Use of steroidal additives to live stock feed has inevitably affected the maturation process of human development in some cultures. Dental treatments have also evolved. Periodontal and orthodontic treatments are more prevalent in today's society. Cosmetic dental procedures and occlusal equilibration techniques would affect the ability of some age estimation techniques to provide accurate chronologic age assessment. As a result, some of the older published techniques and those relying heavily upon attrition may be better suited for cases of archeological interest.

It is well documented that additional dental age estimation studies are needed. Larger studies should statistically improve the accuracy of existing studies. New population-specific studies will help to insulate investigator results from the effects of ancestry or local environmental factors. Because the number of population-specific dental age estimation studies are limited, today's odontologist must always attempt to apply the most similar population-specific data to every age estimation case while understanding the potential effects of ancestral admixture and altered environmental factors. Population-specific age estimation research is ongoing and routinely published in scientific journals. It is incumbent upon the forensic scientist to remain familiar with new population studies and techniques to promote age estimation accuracy.

Moorrees and Johanson each noted the importance of experience in accurate dental assessment of the chronologic age of an individual. Knowledge of tooth morphology, development, its supporting tissues, reparative mechanism, degenerative effects, and chemical constituents are important. Johanson placed special emphasis on the fact that "investigator must have extensive experience from the determinations on teeth from individuals of known age" (Johanson, 1971). In other words, the best advice to any odontologist, whether experienced or inexperienced, is to routinely practice age assessment techniques to consistently obtain accurate and reliable results. Three independent workshops are available for those interested in furthering their education and experience in forensic dental age estimation. In the United States, the American Board of Forensic Odontology offers a workshop at the annual American Academy of Forensic Sciences Meeting on odd numbered years and the Southwest Symposium on Forensic Odontology held at the University of Texas Health Science Center at San Antonio in even numbered years. In Europe, a workshop is periodically provided by the forensic odontology faculty at Katholieke Universiteit, Leuven.

References

ABFO Diplomates Reference Manual. 2012. www.abfo.org

Alkass, K., B. A. Buchholz, S. Ohtani, T. Yamamoto, H. Druid, and K. L. Spalding. 2009. Age estimation in forensic sciences: Application of combined aspartic acid racemization and radiocarbon analysis. *Molecular & Cellular Proteomics* 9: 1022–1030.

Alkass, K., H. Motani, B. A. Buchholz, G. Holmlund, D. R. Senn, K. L. Spalding, and H. Druid. 2012. Analysis of radiocarbon, stable isotopes and DNA in teeth to facilitate identification of unknown decedents. *PLoS ONE*, submitted for publication, October 2012.

AlQahtani, S. J., M. P. Hector, and H. M. Liersidge. 2010. Brief communication: The London atlas of human tooth development and eruption. *American Journal of Physical Anthropology* 142: 481–490.

Anderson, D. L., G. W. Thompson, and F. Popovich. 1976. Age of attainment of mineralization stages of the permanent dentition. *Journal of Forensic Sciences* 21: 191–200.

Arany, S., M. Iino, and N. Yoshioka. 2004. Radiographic survey of third molar development in relation to chronological age among Japanese juveniles. *Journal of Forensic Sciences* 49: 534–538.

Arany, S. and S. Ohtani. 2010. Age estimation by racemization method in teeth: Application of aspartic acid, glutamate and alanine. *Journal of Forensic Sciences* 55(3): 701–705.

Bang, G. and E. Ramm. 1970. Determination of age in humans from root dentin transparency. *Acta Odontologica Scandinavica* 56: 238–244.

Bath-Balogh, M. and M. J. Fehrenbach. 2006. Enamel. In *Dental Embryology, Histology, and Anatomy*, 2nd edn, pp. 179–189. St. Louis, MO: Elsevier Saunders.

Blankenship, J. A., H. H. Mincer, K. M. Anderson, M. A. Woods, and E. L. Burton. 2007. Third molar development in the estimation of chronologic age in American Blacks as compared with Whites. *Journal of Forensic Sciences* 52(2): 428–433.

Blenkin, M. R. B. and W. Evans. 2010. Age estimation from the teeth using a modified Demirjian system. *Journal of Forensic Sciences* 55: 1504–1508.

Buchholz, B. A. 2007. Carbon-14 bomb-pulse dating. *Wiley Encyclopedia of Forensic Science*. John Wiley & Sons, Ltd., Chichester.

Buchholz, B. A. and K. L. Spaulding. 2010. Year of birth determination using radiocarbon dating of dental enamel. *Surface and Interface Analysis* 42(5): 398–401.

Burns, K. R. and W. R. Maples. 1976. Estimation of age from individual adult teeth. *Journal of Forensic Sciences* 21: 343–356.

Cameriere, R., L. Ferrante, and M. Cingolani. 2004. Precision and reliability of pulp/tooth area ration (RA) of second molar as indicator of adult age. *Journal of Forensic Sciences* 49: 1319–1323.

Chaillet, N., M. Nyström, M. Kataja, and A. Demirjian. 2004. Dental maturity curves in Finnish children: Demirjian's method revisited and polynomial functions for age estimation. *Journal of Forensic Sciences* 49: 1324–1331.

Copenhaver, W. M., D. E. Kelly, and R. L. Wood. 1978. The digestive system. In *Bailey's Textbook of Histology*, 17th edn, pp. 455–551. Baltimore, MD: Williams & Wilkins.

Dalitz, G. D. 1962. Age determination of adult human remains by teeth examination. *Forensic Science Society* 3: 11–21.

Demirjian, A. and H. Goldstein. 1976. New systems for dental maturity based on seven and four teeth. *Annals of Human Biology* 3: 411–421.

Demirjian, A., H. Goldstein, and J. M. Tanner. 1973. A new system of dental age assessment. *Human Biology* 45: 211–227.

Gleiser, I. and E. E. Hunt Jr. 1955. The permanent mandibular first molar: Its calcification, eruption and decay. *American Journal of Physical Anthropology* 13(2): 253–283.

Gonzalez-Comenares, G., M. C. Botella-Lopez, G. Moreno-Rueda, and J. R. Fernandez-Cardente. 2007. Age estimation by a dental method: A comparison of Lamendin's and Prince & Ubelaker's technique. *Journal of Forensic Sciences* 52(5): 1156–1160.

Gustafson, G. 1950. Age determination on teeth. *Journal of American Dental Association* 41: 45–54.

Gustafson, G. and G. Koch. 1974. Age estimation up to 16 years of age based on dental development. *Odontology Review* 25: 297–306.

Haavikko, K. 1974. Tooth formation age estimate on a few selected teeth: A simple method for clinical use. *Proceedings of the Finnish Dental Society* 70: 15–19.

Hackman, S. L., A. Buck, and S. Black. 2010. Age evaluation from the skeleton. In *Age Estimation in the Living*, Eds. S. Black, A. Aggrawal, and J. Payne-James, pp. 202–235. West Sussex, U.K.: Wiley-Blackwell.

Hamlin, K. L., D. F. Pac, C. A. Sime, R. M. DeSimone, and G. L. Dusek. 2000. Evaluation the accuracy of age obtained by two methods for Montana ungulates. *Journal of Wildlife Management* 64(2): 441–449.

Harms-Paschal, J. L. and C. W. Schmidt. 2010. The estimation of age at death through the examination of root transparency. In *Age Estimation of the Human Skeleton*, Eds. K. E. Latham and M. Finnegan, pp. 19–35. Springfield, U.K.: Charles C. Thomas, Publisher.

Harris, E. F. 2007. Mineralization of the mandibular third molar: A study of American Blacks and Whites. *American Journal of Physical Anthropology* 132: 98–109.

Harris, E. G. and A. Buck. 2002. Tooth mineralization: A technical note on the Moorrees-Fanning-Hunt standards. *Dental Anthropology* 16: 15–20.

Harris, E. F. and J. H. McKee. 1990. Tooth mineralization standards for blacks and whites from the middle southern United States. *Journal of Forensic Sciences* 35: 859–872.

Harris, E. F., H. H. Mincer, K. M. Anderson, and D. R. Senn. 2010. Age estimation from oral and dental structures. In *Forensic Dentistry*, 2nd edn, Eds. D. R. Senn and P. G. Stimson, pp. 263–303. Boca Raton, FL: Taylor & Frances Group.

Harris, M. J. P., and C. J. Norje. 1984. The mesial root of the third mandibular molar. A possible indicator of age. *Journal of Forensic Odontostomatol* 2: 39–43.

Herschaft, E. E. et al. (Eds.). 2006. *Manual of Forensic Odontology*, 4th edn. Lubbock, TX: American Society of Forensic Odontology.

Internet Center for Management and Business Administration, Inc. The normal distribution (bell curve). NetMBA. http://www.netmba.com/statistics/distribution/normal/

Johanson, G. 1971. Age determinations from human teeth: A critical evaluation with special consideration of changes after fourteen years of age. *Odontologisk Revy* 22: 1–126.

Kambe, T., K. Yonemitsu, K. Kibayashi, and S. Tsunenari. 1991. Application of a computer assisted image analyzer to the assessment of area and number of sites of dental attrition and its use in age estimation. *Forensic Science International* 50: 97–109.

Kasper, K. A., D. Austin, A. H. Kvanli, T. R. Rios, and D. R. Senn. 2009. Reliability of third molar development for age estimation in a Texas Hispanic population: A comparison study. *Journal of Forensic Sciences* 54(3): 651–657.

Koshy, S. and S. Tandon. 1998. Dental age assessment: The applicability of Demirjian's method in South Indian children. *Forensic Science International* 94: 73–85.

Kullman, L., G. Johanson, and L. Akesson. 1992. Root development of the lower third molar and its relation to chronological age. *Swedish Dental Journal* 16: 161–167.

Kvaal, S. I., K. M. Kolltveit, I. O. Thomsen, and T. Solheim. 1995. Age estimation of adults from dental radiographs. *Forensic Science International* 74: 175–185.

Kvaal, S. I. and T. Solheim. 1994. A non-destructive dental method for age estimation. *Journal of Forensic Odontostomatol* 12: 6–11.

Lamendin, H. et al. 1992. A simple technique for age estimation in adult corpses: The two criteria dental method. *Journal of Forensic Sciences* 37(5): 1373–1379.

Leurs, I. H., E. Wattel, I. H. A. Aartman, E. Etty, and B. Prahl-Andersen. 2005. Dental age in Dutch children. *European Journal of Orthodontics* 27: 309–314.

Lewis, J. M. and P. Brumit. 2011. Dental age estimation and determination of the probability an individual has reached the legal age of majority. Paper presented at the *Annual Meeting of the American Academy of Forensic Sciences*, Odontology Section, February 21–25, 2011, Chicago, IL.

Lewis, J. M. and D. R. Senn. 2010. Dental age estimation utilizing third molar development: A review of principles, methods, and population studies used in the United States. *Forensic Science International* 201: 79–83.

Lewis, J. M., D. R. Senn, and M. E. Alder. 2001. Standardization, automation and database creation for age determination reports. Paper presented at the *Annual American Academy of Forensic Sciences Meeting*, February 19–24, Seattle, WA.

Lewis, J. M., D. R. Senn, and J. Silvaggi. 2008. UT-Age 2008: An update. Paper presented at the *Annual American Academy of Forensic Sciences Meeting*, February 18–23, Denver, CO.

Liversidge, H. M. 2000. Crown formation times of human permanent anterior teeth. *Archives of Oral Biology* 45: 713–721.

Logan, W. H. G. and R. Kronfeld. 1933. Development of the human jaws and surrounding structures from birth to the age of fifteen years. *Journal of the American Dental Association* 20: 379–427.

Lucas, P. W., H. S. Loh. 1986. Are the incremental lines in human cementum laid down annually? *Annals Academy of Medicine Singapore* 15(3): 384–386.

Lucy, D. and A. M. Pollard. 1995. Further comments on the estimation of error associated with the Gustafson dental age estimation method. *Journal of Forensic Sciences* 40: 222–227.

Maples, W. R. 1978. An improved technique using dental histology for estimation of adult age. *Journal of Forensic Sciences* 23(4): 764–770.

Maples, W. R. and W. R. Rice. 1979. Some difficulties in the Gustafson dental age estimations. *Journal of Forensic Sciences* 24: 168–172.

Mesotten, K., K. Gunst, A. Carbonez, and G. Willems. 2002. Dental age estimation and third molars: A preliminary study. *Forensic Science International* 129: 110–115.

Miles, A. E. W. 1962. Assessment of the ages of Anglo-Saxons from their dentitions. *Proceedings of the Royal Society of Medicine* 55: 881–886.

Miles, A. E. W. 1963a. Dentition in the estimation of Age. *Journal of Dental Research* 42: 255–263.

Miles, A. E. W. 1963b. The dentition in assessment of individual age in skeletal material. In *Dental Anthropology*, Ed. D. R. Borthwell, pp. 191–210. New York: Pergamon.

Mincer, H. H., E. F. Harris, and H. E. Berryman. 1993. The A.B.F.O. study of third molar development and its use as an estimator of chronological age. *Journal of Forensic Sciences* 38(2): 379–390.

Moorrees, C. F. A., E. A. Fanning, and E. E. Hunt, Jr., 1963a. Formation and resorption of three deciduous teeth in children. *American Journal of Physical Anthropology* 21: 205–213.

Moorrees, C. F. A., E. A. Fanning, and E. E. Hunt, Jr., 1963b. Age variation of formation stages for ten permanent teeth. *Journal of Dental Research* 42: 1490–1502.

Mornstad, H., M. Reventlid, and A. Teivens. 1995. The validity of four methods for age determination by teeth in Swedish children: A multicentre study. *Swedish Dental Journal* 19: 121–130.

Müller, N. 1990. Zur altersbestimmung beim menschen unter besonderer berücksichtigung der weisheitszähne. MD thesis, University of Erlangen-Nürnberg, Erlangen, Germany.

Nawrocki, S. P. 2010. The nature and sources of error in the estimation of age at death from the skeleton. In *Age Estimation of the Human Skeleton*, Eds. K. E. Latham and M. Finnegan, pp. 92–101. Springfield, U.K.: Charles C. Thomas Publisher.

Nelson, S. J. and M. M. Ash. 2010. Development and eruption of the teeth. In *Wheeler's Dental Anatomy, Physiology, and Occlusion*, 9th edn, pp. 21–44. St. Louis, MO: Saunders Elsevier.

Nykänen, R., L. Espeland, S. I. Kvaal, and O. Krogstad. 1998. Validity of the Demirjian method for dental age estimation when applied to Norwegian children. *Acta Odontologica Scandinavica* 56: 238–244.

Nyström, M., J. Haataja, M. Kataja, M. Evalahti, L. Peck, and E. Kleemola-Kujala. 1986. Dental maturity in Finnish children, estimated from the development of seven permanent mandibular teeth. *Acta Odontologica Scandinavica* 44: 193–198.

Ohtani, S., R. Ito, and T. Yamamoto. 2003. Differences in the D/L aspartic acid ratios in dentin among different types of teeth from the same individual and estimated age. *International Journal of Legal Medicine* 117: 149–152.

Ohtani, S. and T. Yamamoto. 1991. Age estimation using the racemization of amino acid in human dentin. *Journal of Forensic Sciences* 36: 792–800.

Ohtani, S. and T. Yamamoto. 2010. Age estimation by amino acid racemization inhuman teeth. *Journal of Forensic Sciences* 55(6): 1630–1633.

Olze, A., D. Bilang, S. Schmidt, K.-D. Werneck, G. Geserick, and A. Schmeling. 2005. Validation of common classification systems for assessing the mineralization of third molars. *International Journal of Legal Medicine* 119: 22–26.

Olze A., A. Schmeling, M. Taniguchi, H. Maeda, P. van Niekerk, K. D. Wernecke, and G. Geserick. 2004. Forensic age estimation in living subjects: The ethnic factor in wisdom tooth mineralization. *International Journal of Legal Medicine* 118: 170–173.

Onder, B. and B. Yakan. 1997. Coroanal displacement of cementum: Correlation between age and coronal movement of cementum in impacted teeth. *Australian Dental Journal* 42(3): 185–188.

Prapanpoch, S., S. B. Dove, and J. A. Cottone. 1992. Morphometric analysis of the dental pulp chamber as a method of age determination in humans. *American Journal of Medical Pathology* 13: 50–55.

Prieto, J. L., E. Barberia, R. Ortega, and C. Magna. 2005. Evaluation of chronological age based on third molar development in the Spanish population. *International Journal of Legal Medicine* 119(6): 349–354.

Prince, D. A. and D. H. Ubelaker. 2002. Application of Lamendin's adult ageing technique to a diverse skeletal sample. *Journal of Forensic Sciences* 47(1): 107–116.

Ritz-Timme, S., C. Cattaneo, M. J. Collins, E. R. Waite, H. W. Schutz, H. J. Kaatsch, and H. I. M. Borrman. 2000. Age estimation: The state of the art in relation to the specific demands of forensic practice. *International Journal of Legal Medicine* 113: 129–136.

Ritz-Timme, S. and M. J. Collins. 2002. Racemization of aspartic acid in human proteins. *Ageing Research Reviews* 1: 43–59.

Robins, J., M. Jones, and E. Matisoo-Smith. 2001. Biochemical background. In *Amino Acid Racemization Dating in New Zealand: An Overview and Bibliography*, pp. 4–26. Auckland, New Zealand: Auckland University.

Saunders, E. 1837. *The Teeth, a Test of Age, Considered with Reference to the Factory Children: Addressed to the Members of Both Houses of Parliament*. London, U.K.: Renshaw.

Schmeling, A., A. Olze, W. Reisinger, and G. Geserick. 2004. Forensic age diagnostics of living people undergoing criminal proceedings. *Forensic Science International* 144: 243–245.

Schour, I. and M. Massler. 1941. The development of the human dentition. *Journal of the American Dental Association* 28: 1153–1160.

Schour, I. and M. Massler. 1944. *The Development of the Human Dentition Chart*, 2nd edn. Chicago, IL: American Dental Association.

Scott, G. G., Jr. 1999. Third molar development as an estimator of chronologic age in Hispanics. Paper presented at the *Annual American Academy of Forensic Sciences Meeting*, February 15–19, Orlando, FL.

Smith, B. H. 1984. Pattern of molar wear in hunter-gatherers and agriculturalists. *American Journal of Physical Anthropology* 63: 39–56.

Smith, E. L. 2005. A test of Ubelaker's method of estimating subadult age from the dentition. Master's thesis, University of Indianapolis, Indianapolis, IN.

Solari, A. C. and K. Abramovitch. 2002. The accuracy and precision of third molar development as an indicator of chronological age in Hispanics. *Journal of Forensic Sciences* 47(3): 531–535.

Solheim, T. 1990. Dental cementum apposition as an indicator of age. *Scandinavian Journal of Dental Research* 98(6): 510–519.

Solheim, T. 1993. A new method for dental age estimation in adults. *Forensic Science International* 74: 137–147.

Soomer, H., H. Ranta, M. Lincoln, A. Penttila, and E. Leibur. 2003. Reliability and validity of eight dental estimation methods for adults. *Journal of Forensic Science* 48(1): 149–152.

Spalding, K. L., B. A. Buchholz, L. E. Bergman, H. Druid, and J. Frisen. 2005. Age written in teeth by nuclear tests. *Nature* 437: 333.

Taylor, J. and M. Blenkin. 2010. Age evaluation and odontology in the living. In *Age Estimation in the Living*, Eds. S. Black, A. Aggrawal, and J. Payne-James, pp. 176–201, West Sussex, U.K.: Wiley-Blackwell.

Thevissen, P. W., P. Pittayapat, S. Fieuws, and G. Willems. 2009. Estimation age of majority on third molars developmental stages in young adults from Thailand using a modified scoring technique. *Journal of Forensic Sciences* 54(2): 428–432.

Thomson, A. T. 1836. Lectures on medical jurisprudence now in course of delivery at London University. *Lancet* 1: 281–286.

Thorson, J. and U. Hägg. 1991. The accuracy and precision of the third molar as an indicator of chronological age. *Scandinavian Dental Journal* 15: 12–22.

Ubelaker, D. H. 1978. *Human Skeletal Remains, Excavation Analysis, Interpretation*, 1st edn. Washington, DC: Taraxacum.

Ubelaker, D. H. 1989. *Human Skeletal Remains, Excavation Analysis, Interpretation*, 2nd edn. Washington, DC: Taraxacum.

Ubelaker, D. H. 1999. Sex, stature, and age. In *Human Skeletal Remains: Excavation, Analysis, Interpretation*, 3rd edn, pp. 44–95. Washington, DC: Taraxacum.

Ubelaker, D. H. and R. C. Parra. 2010. Radiocarbon analysis of dental enamel and bone to evaluate date of birth and death: Perspective from the southern hemisphere. *Forensic Science International* 208(1–3): 103–107.

Vandevoort, F. M. et al. 2004. Age calculation using x-ray microfocus computed tomographical scanning of teeth: A pilot study. *Journal of Forensic Sciences* 49: 787–790.

Willems, G. 2001. A review of the most commonly used dental age estimation techniques. *Journal of Forensic Odontostomatol* 19: 9–17.

Willems, G., C. Moulin-Romsee, and T. Solheim. 2002. Non-destructive dental-age calculation methods in adults: Intra- and inter-observer effects. *Forensic Science International* 126: 221–226.

Willems, G., A. Van Olmen, B. Spiessens, and C. Carels. 2001. Dental age estimation in Belgian children: Demirjian's technique revisited. *Journal of Forensic Sciences* 46: 893–895.

World Law Direct. Age of majority. http://www.worldlawdirtect.com/forum/law-wiki/27181-age-majority.html

Yekkala, R., C. Meers, A. Van Schepdael, J. Hoogmartens, I. Lambrichts, and G. Willems. 2006. Racemization of aspartic acid from human dentin in the estimation of chronological age. *Forensic Science International* 159: 89–94.

Bitemarks

9

JON CURTIS DAILEY
GREGORY S. GOLDEN
DAVID R. SENN
FRANKLIN D. WRIGHT

Contents

9.1 Introduction 258
9.2 History 260
9.3 State of the Science 260
9.3.1 Recognition of Bitemarks 260
9.3.2 ABFO Bitemark Terminology 263
9.3.3 General Considerations and Need for Bitemark Analysis 264
9.3.4 Scientific Basis for Bitemark Analysis and Legal Testimony 266
9.4 Bitemark Analysis/Bitemark Comparisons 268
9.4.1 Bitemark Analysis Guidelines 268
9.4.1.1 Bitemarks 268
9.4.1.2 Biters 269
9.5 Limitations of and Appropriate Use of Bitemark Analysis 270
9.6 Bitemark Pattern Recognition and Collection from Humans and Inanimate Objects: Noninvasive Analysis 272
9.6.1 Written Request 272
9.6.2 Salivary Trace Evidence 272
9.7 Photographic Documentation of Bitemarks 273
9.7.1 Basic Equipment: Digital Cameras 274
9.7.2 Lenses 275
9.7.3 Flash Accessories 275
9.7.4 Other Desirable Accessories 277
9.8 Standard Photographic Views 277
9.8.1 Orientation Photos 278
9.8.2 Close-Up Working Photographs 278
9.9 Image Management and Storage 280
9.9.1 File Acquisition and File Types 280
9.9.2 Digital Image Storage 280
9.9.3 Image Enhancement 281
9.9.4 Plug-Ins 281
9.10 Three-Dimensional Evidence 282
9.10.1 Three-Dimensional Evidence Modeling 282
9.10.2 Stereolithography in Forensic Dentistry 283
9.11 Bitemark Impressions 283
9.11.1 Injury Impression Technique 284
9.11.2 Study Casts 286

9.12 Invasive Analysis 287
9.12.1 Tissue Incision, Excision, and Preservation 287
9.12.2 Transillumination 288
9.13 Data Collection from Suspected Biter(s) 289
9.14 Advanced Photographic Techniques 292
9.14.1 Electromagnetic Spectrum and Photography 293
9.14.2 Alternate Light Imaging (Fluorescent Photography) 293
9.14.2.1 Alternate Light Imaging Protocol 296
9.14.3 Reflective UVA Ultraviolet Photography 298
9.14.4 Infrared Photography 303
9.15 Analysis and Comparison of the Evidence 305
9.15.1 Description of the Injury 305
9.15.2 Description of the Dentition 305
9.15.3 Size Relationship Analysis 305
9.16 Comparison Techniques 306
9.16.1 Incisal Plane 306
9.16.2 Direct Comparison 307
9.16.3 Indirect Comparison 308
9.16.3.1 Overlay 308
9.16.3.2 Metric Analysis 311
9.16.3.3 Digital Analysis 312
9.16.3.4 Microscopy, Computerized Axial Tomography, and 3-D Scanning 313
9.16.3.5 Comparison Techniques and Conclusions 314
9.17 Case Opinion 317
Addendum: ABFO Guidelines and Standards 317
References 322

9.1 Introduction

A bitemark is a pattern created by teeth contacting a surface, most commonly food but also other objects and human skin. A bitemark on human skin is a patterned injury, and the examination and analysis of those injuries often become the responsibility of forensic odontologists.

Recognition, evidence collection, and analysis of a bitemark or bitemark-patterned injury (BMPI) is challenging and complex. The comparisons of the teeth of putative biters, the reports of the results of those comparisons, and the subsequent expert testimony regarding those comparisons are the most controversial areas of forensic odontology (Averill, 1991).

The analysis process involves the evaluation of the evidence quality and the features in that evidence. It is these analyses that enable forensic odontologists to offer information to officials and others charged with the protection of society about the nature of those injuries. A separate and distinct activity is the subsequent comparison of bitemarks with the dentition of the suspected biter(s). All suspected bitemarks should be analyzed. Only those that reach a threshold of evidentiary value should be compared to suspected biters.

The most common analyses are those of suspected bitemarks on human skin. However, tooth markings have also been analyzed on numerous inanimate objects including various foods, chewing gum, styrofoam cups, cigarette butts, wooden pencils, a steering wheel, and more.

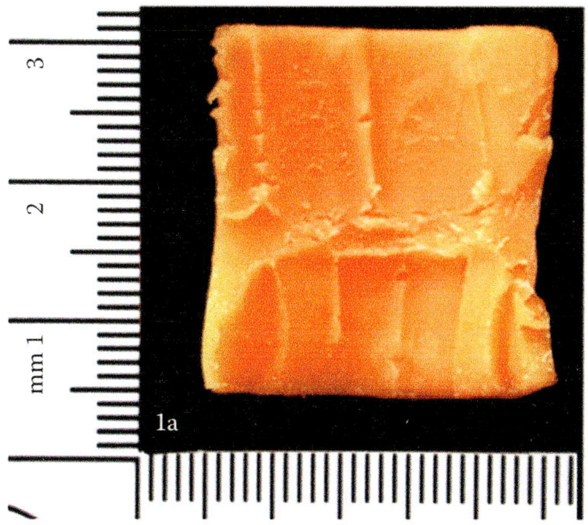

Figure 9.1 A bitemark in cheese.

When the contact of teeth leaves a physical alteration in the bitten media, the act of biting, the result may be a discernible and distinctive pattern injury (Figure 9.1). When this pattern is recognized as having possibly been created by teeth, the bitemark analysis process begins. Is the injury a result of a bite? Can it be determined that the bite was caused by human or animal teeth? Can a determination whether it was caused by adult or juvenile teeth be made? Is the patterned injury of sufficient quality to be processed for further study, examination, and testing? If these questions can be answered affirmatively, the analysis continues.

After the bitemark analysis process is completed, a second line of questioning may be addressed: Can the bitemark be used to include or exclude a specific individual into or from a population of individuals who could be the source of the bitemark?

Regardless of the answer to the second group of questions, if the injury is a human bite mark, the bitemark and surrounding area should be swabbed for potential deoxyribonucleic acid (DNA) evidence.

The National Academy of Sciences (NAS) 2009 report, "Strengthening Forensic Science in the United States: A Path Forward," ushered in a new era for several disciplines within the forensic sciences, including forensic odontology (NAS, 2009). Whether the NAS committee fairly and accurately investigated and characterized bitemark analysis is disputed (Senn, 2011). Partly as a consequence of the report, the value and appropriate use of bitemark analyses and bitemark comparisons is being challenged. Each practitioner within the specialty can be said to possess a distinctive, perhaps unique experience-based viewpoint. These viewpoints must become more evidence-based. Forensic odontologists have shown a willingness to perform research but not yet to a sufficient level to address all of the needed questions, and much more research is needed. Forensic odontologists must continually improve their understanding of the skin of living humans. Databases of dental and bitemark patterns must be developed. Three-dimensional analysis modalities for bitemark analysis and comparisons must be researched and implemented. As with all science, it is research, research repeated, and challenges to both that will ultimately reshape and define forensic odontology. Challenge is good.

This chapter provides information about recognizing bitemarks, assessing the evidentiary value of bitemarks, collecting and preserving bitemark evidence, analyzing bitemarks, collecting and preserving dental information from potential biters, comparing potential biter and bitemark evidence, and reporting the results of those analyses and comparisons.

The information in this chapter can lead to the *beginning* of a long bitemark analysis journey. Not all dentists, perhaps not all forensic odontologists are suited to the task. The journey is difficult, the obstacles many, the destination elusive, and no forensic odontologist has yet arrived. Continuing study, learning, and research is mandatory.

9.2 History

Although changes were already underway in organized forensic odontology, the NAS report has significantly impacted forensic odontologists and their bitemark casework. Methodology, research, report writing, terminology, evidence interpretation, casework presentation, and the strength of investigator's conclusions are subject to increased scrutiny. Scrutiny exercised fairly and honestly almost always leads to improvement. Justice Louis Brandeis wrote in 1914 regarding transparency "sunlight is said to be the best of disinfectants" (Brandeis and Harry Houdini Collection, 1914).

Excellent bitemark casework with appropriate analyses and conservative conclusions has been performed in the past and continues to be performed today. The authors believe that quality work, based on continuous study and scientific research with conservative conclusions, will stand up to scrutiny. Anything less will not! The use of DNA evidence on appeal of prior convictions has validated many and voided a small number of previous bitemark cases. The correction of error is a good thing—with justice being served. Unfortunately, for those wrongly convicted, the injustice of error cannot be easily assuaged.

A comprehensive list of appellate level federal and state cases in the United States involving bitemarks began with *Doyle v. State* (Texas) in 1954 and resulted in 364 case citations through the end of 2009 (Pitluck and Barsley, 2010). Some cases represent subsequent appeals of the same cases. The numbers emphasize the relative paucity of bitemark casework that has occurred and been analyzed by practicing forensic odontologists in the United States. There were, of course, additional cases involving bitemarks that were resolved without involving the appellate court system. There were certainly many more bitemark cases analyzed by forensic odontologists that were never heard in any courtroom. No one knows how many bites have been inflicted that result in bitemarks. We do know that the number of bitemark cases "available" to forensic odontologists is limited. Some odontologists have little or no bitemark casework experience beyond their educational involvement and subsequent preparation for their board examinations and the recertification process. Some odontologists have little or no interest in getting involved in bitemark casework.

The most comprehensive history related to bitemarks is to be found in the chapter entitled: *History of Bitemark Evidence*, written for the second edition of the textbook, *Bitemark Evidence: A Color Atlas and Text*, edited by Dr. Robert B.J. Dorion (Senn, 2011).

9.3 State of the Science

9.3.1 Recognition of Bitemarks

One of the most problematic aspects of bitemark analysis is the ability of examiners to definitively recognize a patterned injury as a bitemark. There are many potentially confounding factors. Biting through an intermediate layer such as clothing and sudden

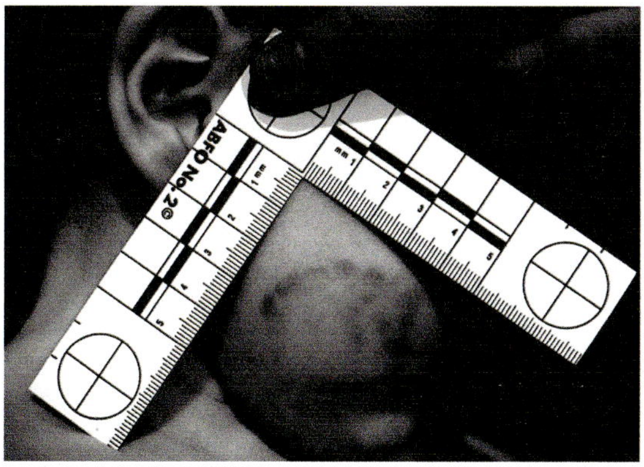

Figure 9.2 Bitemark on child abuse victim showing distinctive upper and lower arches with individual teeth markings that correspond with each arch.

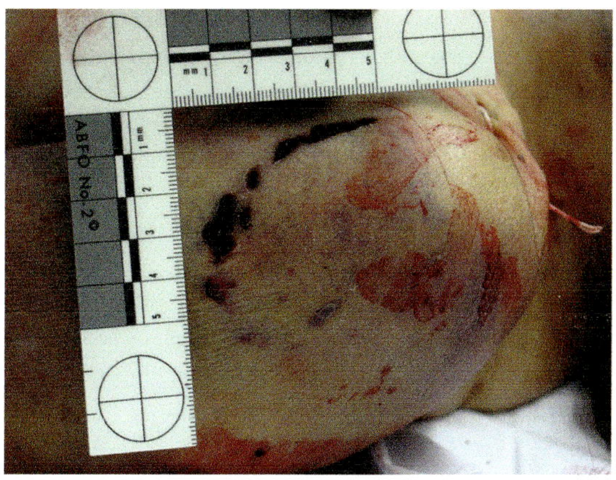

Figure 9.3 Partial bitemark created on same individual by same biter as Figure 9.2.

extreme and sometimes violent movements during the act of biting are examples of the factors affecting the creation of the bitemark.

Typically, human bitemarks will have the following appearance:

- Semicircular to ovoid outline forms comprised of two arc-shaped components, one representing the maxillary arch and the other the mandibular arch, with markings from individual teeth present within the arched outlines (Figure 9.2).

The markings within the pattern may be contusions, abrasions, and/or lacerations, which collectively represent the class and individual characteristics of the teeth of the dentition that created the bitemark. Partial bitemarks (Figures 9.3 and 9.4), avulsive bitemarks (Figure 9.5), double bitemarks (Figure 9.6), and indistinct bitemarks (sometimes referred to as "smoke-ring" bitemarks) (Figure 9.7) as well as multiple bitemarks on one individual can be seen (Figure 9.8).

Variations in the appearance of human bitemarks are many. Identifiable human bitemarks may contain tooth marks from only one arch or from both arches. Additionally, they may present with or without individual tooth markings. Bitemarks inflicted on

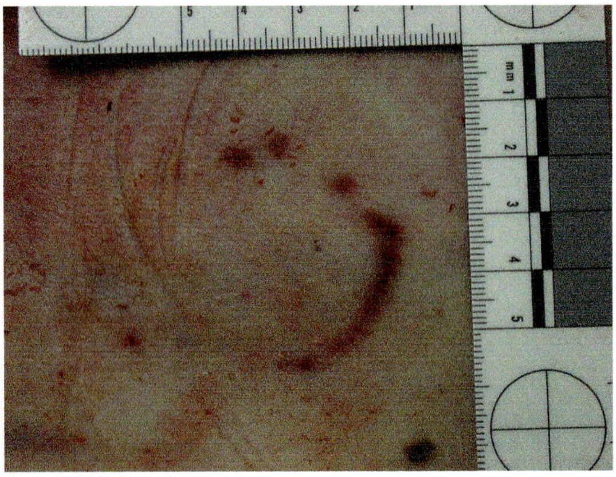

Figure 9.4 Another partial bitemark created on same individual by same biter as Figure 9.2.

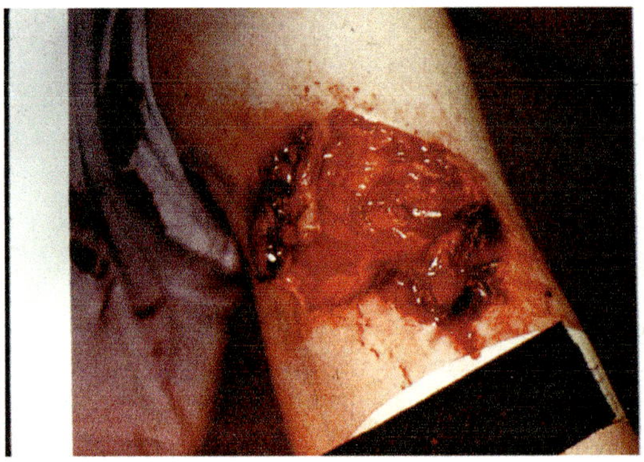

Figure 9.5 Avulsive bitemark on arm.

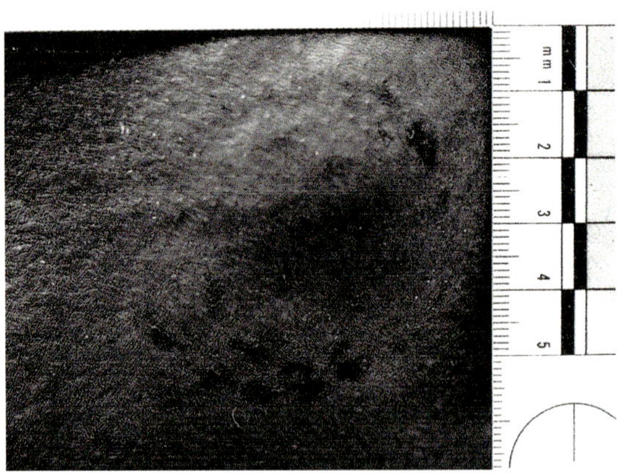

Figure 9.6 Double bitemark: the teeth bite the skin, release, and bite again.

human skin may exhibit distortion as many things are moving in violent interchanges involving biting. The amount of distortion relative to the biting surfaces of the teeth that create a bitemark cannot be readily measured or experimentally recreated. Because of the great variation in bitemarks' appearance, caution should be exercised before definitively concluding that a patterned injury is a bitemark.

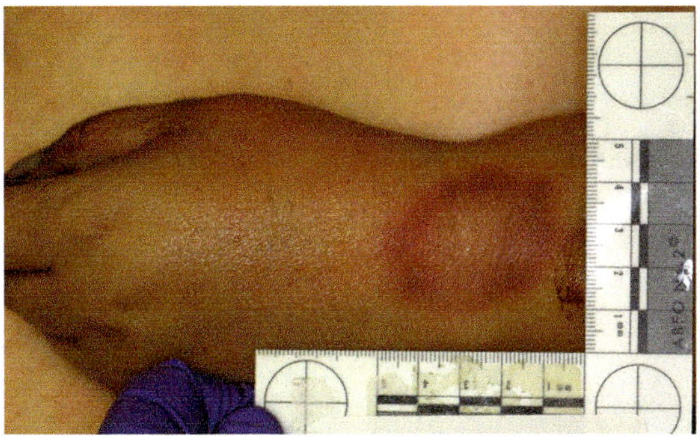

Figure 9.7 Typical diffuse bitemark on wrist (limited evidentiary value).

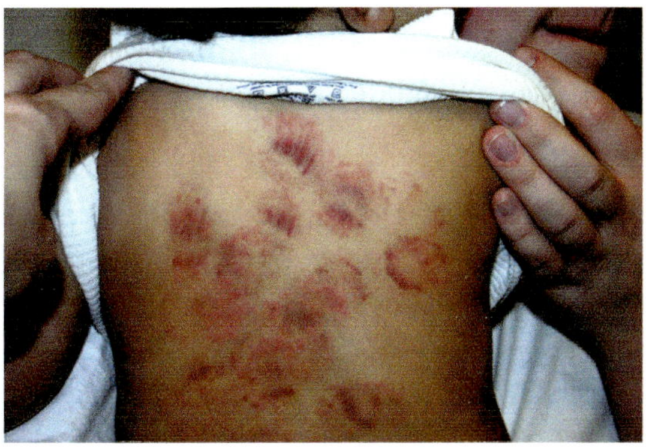

Figure 9.8 Multiple bitemarks on back.

9.3.2 ABFO Bitemark Terminology

The American Board of Forensic Odontology (ABFO) Bitemark Terminology Guidelines list three terms that describe the level of certainty that a patterned injury represents a bitemark (ABFO DRM 2012, 115).
American Board of Forensic Odontology, Inc.
Diplomates Reference Manual

Section III: Policies, Procedures, Guidelines, and Standards
The following are the terms indicating degree of confidence that an injury is a bitemark:

Bitemark—Teeth created the pattern; other possibilities were considered and excluded.

- Criteria: Pattern conclusively illustrates (a) classic features, (b) all the characteristics, or (c) typical class characteristics of dental arches and human teeth in proper arrangement so that it is recognizable as an impression of the human dentition.

Suggestive—The pattern is suggestive of a bitemark, but there is insufficient evidence to reach a definitive conclusion at this time.

- Criteria: General shape and size are present but distinctive features such as tooth marks are missing, incomplete, or distorted or a few marks resembling tooth marks are present but the arch configuration is missing.

Not a bitemark—Teeth did not create the pattern.

For investigative purposes, only those patterned injuries that are defined earlier as "bitemark" or "suggestive" should be considered for bitemark analysis. No further investigation is warranted with any injury defined as "not a bitemark."

In addition to assessing the visual appearance of the patterned injury, laboratory testing for the presence of saliva, salivary amylase, or DNA collected from swabbing can indicate whether the patterned injury represents a bitemark. The most definitive identification possible from a patterned injury representing a human bitemark may come from DNA collected from the injury.

While traditional bitemark analysis is based on pattern recognition, DNA collected from the bitemark may provide a means to identify a patterned injury as a bitemark and may lead to the identification of the biter. Consequently, swabbing is an important step in the attempt to confirm a patterned injury as a human bitemark. The technique will be discussed later in this chapter.

9.3.3 General Considerations and Need for Bitemark Analysis

The presence of human bitemarks in criminal activities represents potential physical evidence that could warrant further investigation. As in other pattern recognition sciences, bitemarks should be analyzed as potential exculpatory or inculpatory evidence in a criminal proceeding.

A BMPI may be a result of a violent physical encounter and is almost always a painful event for the recipient of the bite. Injuries range from reddened abrasions to deep penetrating bruising, to skin laceration or incision, to partial avulsion, and to complete avulsion of bitten skin. Proper evaluation of the bitemark evidence requires going well beyond collecting samples for DNA analysis when trying to establish biter identity from the injury. The presence of DNA in the area of a bitemark may be unrelated to the attack; there have been cases in which DNA collected from the area of a bitemark was not from the biter. In an example from the casework of one author in a child abuse case, a care giver, seeing the bitemark on the abused child, tried to "rub" it off by licking her fingers before rubbing the injury, depositing her own DNA onto the injury. It is not appropriate to assume that salivary DNA identity from a bitemark will always represent biter identity. In fact, in closed population, cases involving families or persons sharing living quarters DNA and fingerprints will be abundantly present that have no evidentiary value in relation to a violent crime. A bitemark injury in the same scenario may represent evidence of proximity, periodicity, and assault and battery.

While bitemark injuries are associated with many types of crime, the two most common classes of crime where bitemarks frequently appear are abuse and sexual assault. Both of these classes of crimes share the common feature of violent physical assault against a likely defenseless victim. There are cases in which DNA cannot be swabbed from the injured tissue, having been destroyed by environmental factors or when the biting occurred through an intermediate medium such as clothing. If the bitemark is of sufficient quality to be used for analysis, it may be possible to include and sometimes identify the biter or to exclude suspected biters, allowing authorities to move forward in the appropriate direction (Figures 9.9 and 9.10).

Equally important to the prosecution of the responsible person for the crime associated with the bitemark is the opportunity to intervene on behalf of the victims of such assaults. This intervention opportunity occurs frequently in child abuse cases. If the abuser can be identified and kept away from the child by legal means, the episodes of repeated,

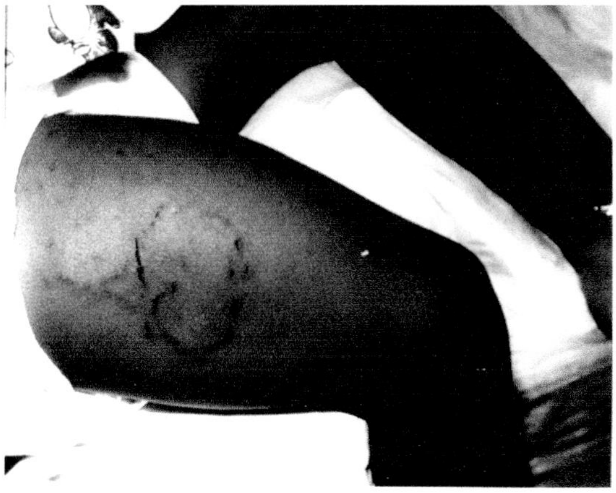

Figure 9.9 Bitemark on thigh of female.

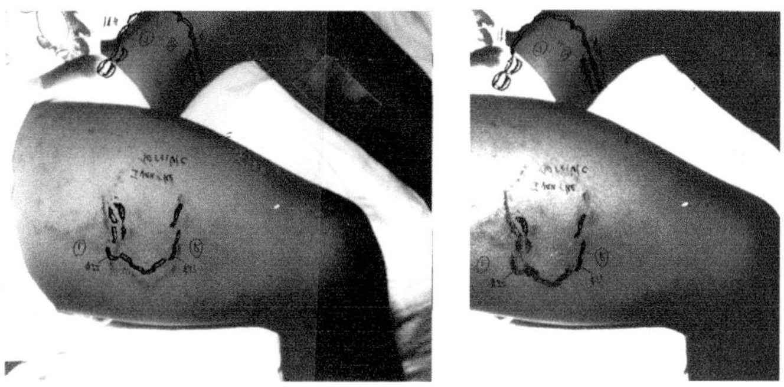

(a) (b)

Figure 9.10 Same bitemark as Figure 9.9 with acetate overlay of suspected biter placed adjacent to injury (a) and directly over the injury (b).

increasingly violent abusive events may be stopped, hopefully preventing the all too common ultimate outcome of many abuse situations, the death of a child. The appropriate use of bitemark evidence in these interventions is very real and important examples of the appropriate use and continuing need for bitemark analysis (Figures 9.11 and 9.12).

Similarly, victims of sexual assault suffer incredible physical, psychological, and emotional pain as a result of those attacks. Part of surviving and recovering from these attacks

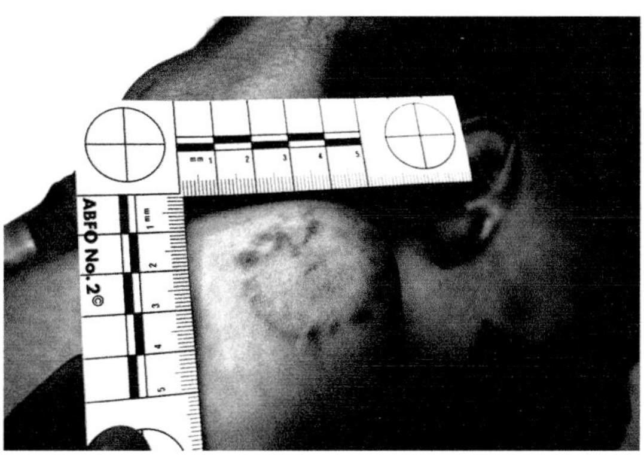

Figure 9.11 Bite on shoulder of victim of felony child abuse.

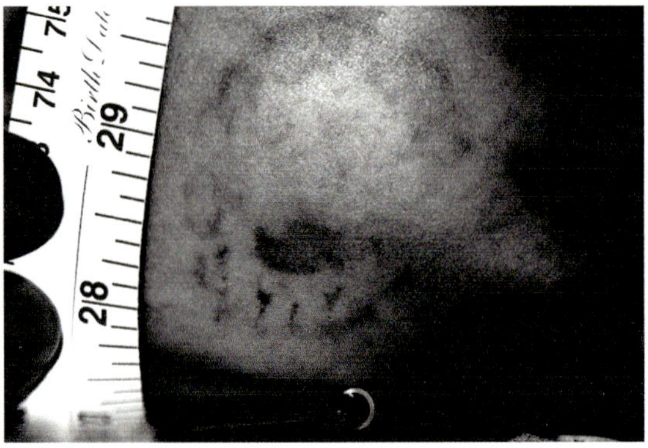

Figure 9.12 Bite on face of child abuse victim.

comes from the knowledge that the attacker has been incarcerated and that, at least temporarily, further attacks are not possible. Bitemark evidence may help to verify that violent physical contact between the sexual assault victim and the perpetrator occurred and also provides a potential avenue to the identity of the assailant. There have been documented cases of sexual assault in which the victim bit the assailant. If the biting is sufficiently intense that it causes significant tissue damage and there is a delay between the attack and when it becomes known to authorities, special photographic techniques using ultraviolet light or alternate light imaging (ALI) can be utilized to attempt to photographically recapture the bitemark pattern months or sometime even years later, long after visible healing has occurred. In these situations, when there is high-quality bitemark evidence, the investigation of a possible linking between the bitemark and the teeth of suspected biters is a significant pathway to the identity and prosecution of assailants (Figures 9.13 through 9.16).

9.3.4 Scientific Basis for Bitemark Analysis and Legal Testimony

The scientific bases for bitemark analysis lie in the observable differences in the shape, position, and size of individual human dentitions. When these individualizing features of the dentitions are transferred to the skin in violent biting and if the resulting bitemark pattern is of high quality, it may be possible to correlate the patterns in the bitemark injury to the individual dentitions of the suspected biters. If a high-evidentiary quality bitemark

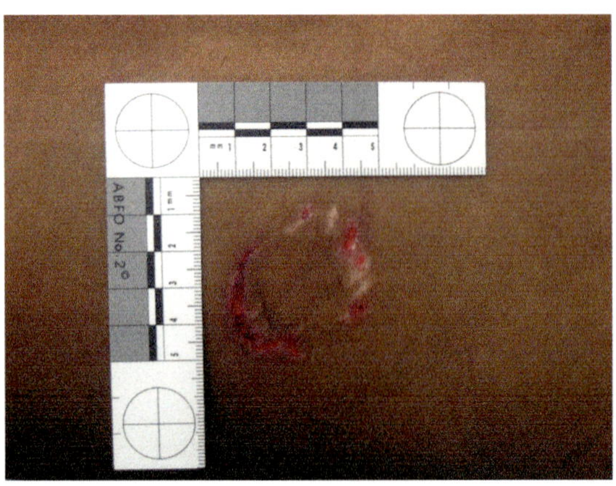

Figure 9.13 Color image of bitemark with 3-D properties.

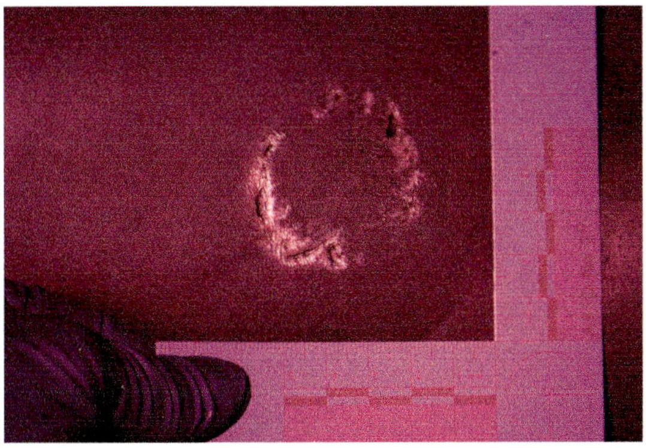

Figure 9.14 Same bitemark as Figure 9.13 (UV-digital).

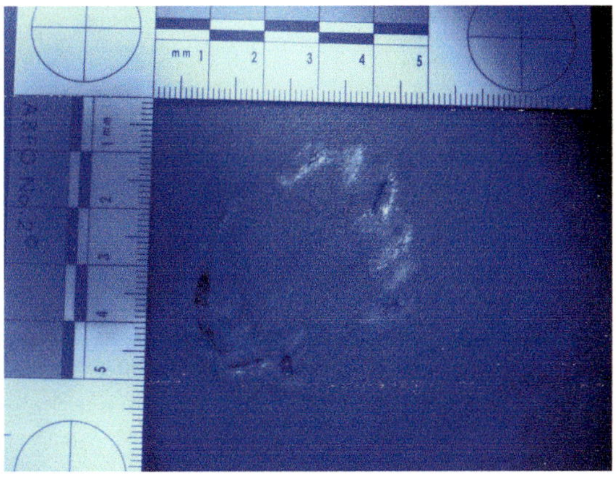

Figure 9.15 Same bitemark as Figure 9.13 (ALI).

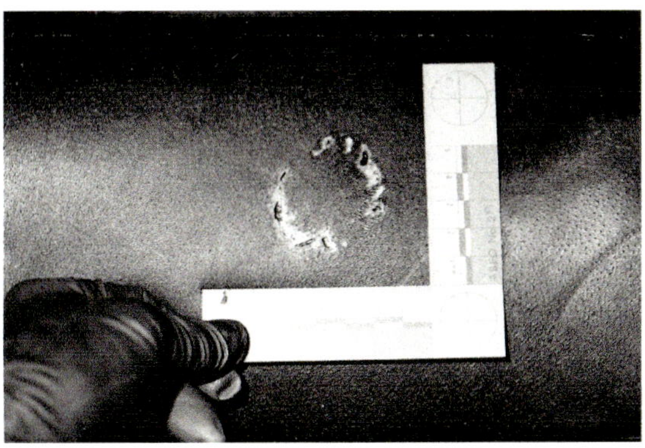

Figure 9.16 Same bitemark as Figure 9.13 (UV-film).

injury exists and a small population of potential biters with very different dentitions is identified by authorities, biter identity or biter exclusion utilizing bitemark analysis is possible. Any bitemark case with less than this "ideal" presentation weakens the ability of the bitemark analyst to effect biter identity or biter exclusion.

Perhaps, the single greatest challenge for forensic odontologists is to judge whether the bitemark evidence currently before him or her reaches a threshold of evidentiary quality that supports an opinion of inclusion or exclusion. This challenge occurs in every case. The scientific basis for bitemark analysis is sound, but bias, observer effects, and other extraneous factors can impair judgment and the appropriate application of scientific methodology by the odontologist. Opinions rendered by biased or otherwise impaired bitemark analysts have contributed to wrongful convictions and the ruination of innocent persons' lives. However, there have been numerous cases where the proper use of bitemark evidence has contributed to appropriate, successful prosecutions, as well as interventions that have saved countless lives, especially in cases involving abused children. Also important are cases in which targeted suspects are excluded because their teeth could not have created the patterns. These investigation-level determinations assist authorities, help to protect the innocent, and hopefully lead investigators to the correct perpetrator.

9.4 Bitemark Analysis/Bitemark Comparisons

Bitemark analysis and comparison are elements of an identification discipline similar to the analysis of fingerprints, tool marks, and ballistics. As previously discussed, this has long been a controversial area that has become the subject of several highly publicized cases in which individuals convicted of crimes based at least partially on bitemark evidence have been exonerated through the use of DNA comparisons. In addition to overturning these previous convictions, several of the DNA analyses have identified other individuals who were present at the crime scene or with the victim.

In general, the forensic odontologists compare exemplars or the teeth of the suspected biter(s) to bitemarks following guidelines and accepted methods. Dental stone models acquired by legal means usually are utilized to represent the teeth of the suspected biters. After thoroughly analyzing the bitemark, and only if the bitemark is judged to be of sufficient evidentiary value, the forensic odontologist compares the size, shape, and the geometric or spatial arrangement of the teeth involved in the injury to the discernable injury patterns.

Overall, visual comparisons are made of the spatial arrangement of the teeth including, but not limited to, size, rotation, spacing, and the presence or absence of teeth. These features may be sufficient to exclude an individual as the contributor of the bitemark. Reproduction of the biting edges of the teeth through computer scanning and software programs can be used to produce overlays on transparent media that may then be compared to appropriately sized photographs. Metric analyses and measurement of the width and breadth of the injuring teeth as well as measurement of the spaces and angles between adjacent teeth may be compared to the comparably measured patterns of the injury in the photographs. Dental models of suspected biters mounted in articulators may be used to bite onto wax wafers, skin substitutes, or similar substances in situations where inanimate objects or foodstuffs have been bitten. The goal is not to attempt a reproduction of the pattern observed in the injury, but rather to create an exemplar of the dentition for comparison to the patterned injury (Figure 9.17).

9.4.1 Bitemark Analysis Guidelines

9.4.1.1 Bitemarks

If, utilizing the ABFO Bitemark Terminology (ABFO, DRM 2012), the odontologist determines that a patterned injury represents a bitemark or is suggestive of a bitemark, a bitemark analysis may be initiated.

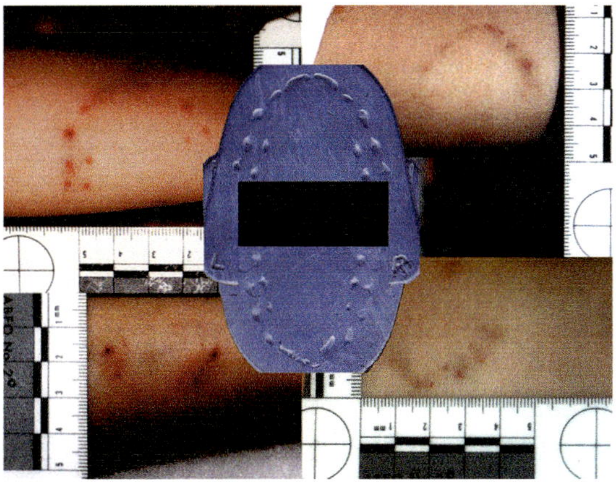

Figure 9.17 Wax exemplar of a suspected biter's teeth compared to two bitemark-patterned injuries.

If the patterned injury is a bitemark, the odontologist must determine if it is of evidentiary value. One or both individual arch(es) representing the upper and/or lower teeth as well as individual well-delineated tooth markings should be present for that pattern to be used in bitemark analysis. Only those bitemarks presenting these specific class and individual characteristics can be used for bitemark analysis. ABFO Bitemark Terminology opinions positively or negatively relating a biter to a bitemark are always stated to a reasonable degree of dental certainty and are The Biter, The Probable Biter, Not Excluded as the Biter, and Excluded as the Biter (ABFO DRM 2012, 116).

In some cases, a patterned injury is determined to be a bitemark, but is lacking sufficient detail rendering a less than ideal pattern for inclusive or exclusive bitemark analysis. These bitemarks may be analyzed as if they are suggestive of a bitemark, as described in the next paragraph.

If the patterned injury is suggestive of a bitemark, it presents with generalized arch forms from either the upper or lower dentition or both. Additionally, the presence of individual distinct tooth markings may be missing or limited in both numbers of teeth marking and/or the clarity of the markings. Patterned injuries suggestive of a bitemark may be utilized for bitemark analysis; however, for bitemark comparisons, very limited information is present to differentiate between biters and any attempt in association with an individual biter would be less reliable. ABFO Bitemark Terminology opinions for these types of bitemarks that may potentially link a biter to the bitemark should be Not Excluded as the Biter or Inconclusive. A bitemark analyst could render an opinion of Excluded as the Biter, using ABFO Bitemark Terminology, if there are clear indications that the dentition could not have created the mark.

9.4.1.2 Biters

In addition to describing a patterned injury in terms of its representation of a bitemark, the dentitions of the suspected biters also need to be examined. Because of the mechanisms by which bitemarks are created, particularly in human skin, similar dentitions would likely create similarly appearing BPMIs. Therefore, it would be particularly difficult, if not impossible, to differentiate biters with similar dentitions in relation to a specific bitemark.

Research has shown that there can be similar dentitions in a given broad population (Bush et al., 2011). As previously discussed, similar dentitions can create bitemarks so similar that it will not be possible to differentiate between the biters. Therefore, in a bitemark case where there is an open population of suspected biters ("anyone in the world could have made the mark"), and the bitemark has no distinctive features, bitemark comparison to dentitions with no distinctive features is not appropriate. Comparisons to suspected biters should only be undertaken when either the bitemark pattern or the suspected biter's dentition is distinctive.

If, however, in a bitemark analysis case, the injury is determined to be a bitemark (per ABFO Guidelines) and the bitemark is distinctive, or there is a closed population of suspected biters, each of whom has different and distinctive dentitions, bitemark analysis can be done, and inclusive or exclusive findings are possible with a high degree of validity and accuracy. If there is only a single-suspected biter identified in any bitemark analysis case, the use of a randomly created dental lineup to include additional "suspected" biters is required. The use of a dental lineup helps to eliminate potential bias and increase specificity adding validity to the findings of the bitemark analysis.

9.5 Limitations of and Appropriate Use of Bitemark Analysis

In the investigation of a crime, the associated evidence is collected with the intention of resolving the circumstances associated with the crime, including the identity of the perpetrator. In instances involving child abuse, rape, homicide, and other violent person-on-person crime, bitemark evidence may be present. The presence of bitemarks should motivate investigators to swab the sites for DNA and to photographically capture the bitemark evidence as a means to preserve the evidence and for future analysis if potential biters can be identified.

In living bitten victims, the physiological process of healing associated with bitemarks leads to a simultaneous cascade of events beginning with an inflammatory response, color changes within the affected injured tissues, and, in some instances, the formation of scar tissue. Because these changes happen rapidly, especially in children, there may be few (and sometimes only one) opportunities to photographically document injuries. It is mandatory to collect salivary traces that may contain DNA from the bitemark as well as to initiate photographic documentation as soon as possible after the injury has been discovered. Swabbing for salivary residue should follow the double-swab method (Sweet et al., 1997). Subsequent photography sessions should be performed to document the changes in the bruising pattern as the bitemark injury heals (Wright, 1998). Protocols for the collection of evidence associated with bitemarks will be discussed later in this chapter.

In deceased persons with bitemarks, a wide range of postmortem changes can affect the appearance of the BMPI. In some instances, the bitemark patterns may become more distinct and detailed, while, in other instances, they may become more diffuse, thereby losing their evidentiary value. Consequently, the window of opportunity to collect the evidence associated with the bitemark in a deceased person may be small. In both instances, every effort must be made to collect and document all evidence associated with the bitemark before the evidence becomes of no use.

In some cases, it can be enough to merely identify that the injury pattern represents an adult human bitemark or a bitemark made by a child. Child on child biting occurs and, while not acceptable behavior, is rarely criminal. On the other hand, an adult bitemark found on an abused child represents intent and is a criminal event. Thus, being able to simply differentiate between an adult and child bitemark may be sufficient and valuable information to aid investigators. Importantly, suspected adult biters may be excluded if the bitemark is found to have been made by a child's teeth (Figures 9.18 through 9.20).

For other events, such as a violent attack or rape, the identity of the perpetrator is a goal of the criminal investigation. If salivary DNA can be harvested from the bite site and be shown to include an individual, it can be significant in a subsequent criminal prosecution.

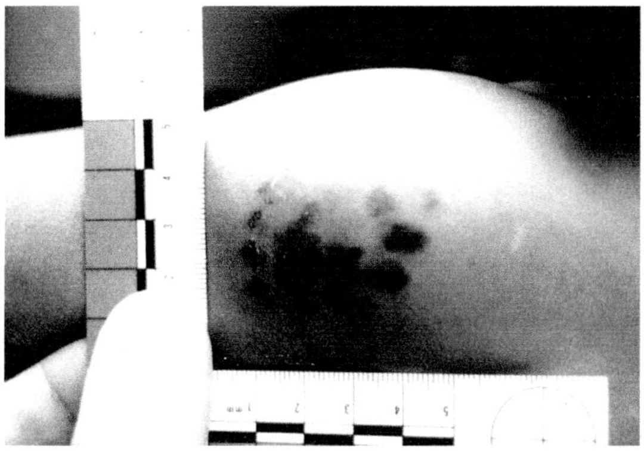

Figure 9.18 Bitemark created by primary dentition.

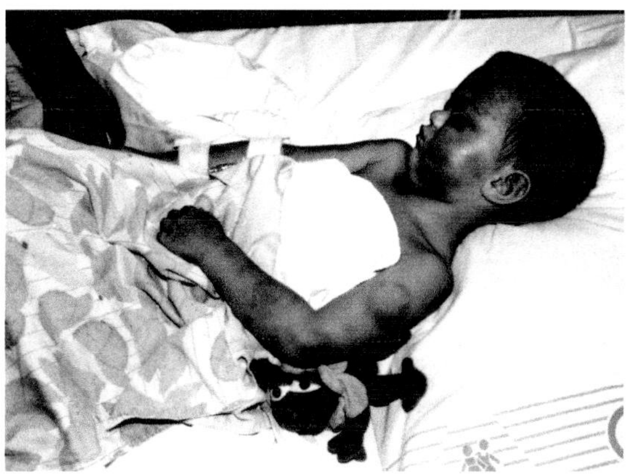

Figure 9.19 Adult bites on abused child. Caregiver blamed a seven year old sibling. Bitemark analysis indicated otherwise.

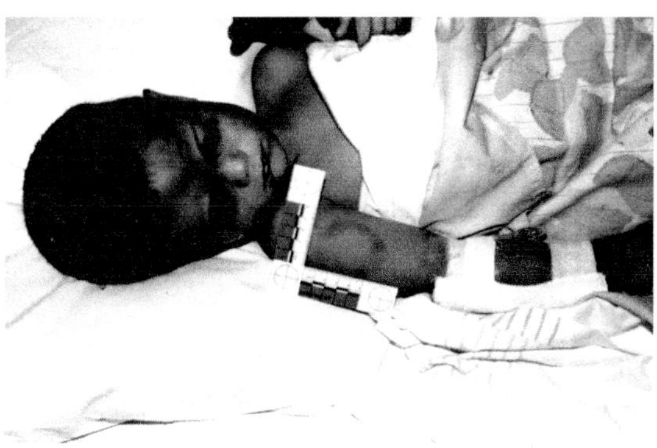

Figure 9.20 Same case as Figure 9.19.

If the bitemark has high-evidentiary value and if the suspected biters are few in number with each suspected biter having a distinctive dentition, it may be possible to identify the biter to a reasonable degree of dental certainty. If the biter is a suspect in the case (sometimes victims bite their attackers!) and the bitemark analysis indicates a linking between the biter and the bitemark, law enforcement officials may then have strong evidence of physical contact between the suspect and victim. DNA analysis identifying salivary evidence from a person cannot show that an attack involving biting occurred or that an attack caused pain. There are multiple ways in which salivary DNA from one person can be present on another. Conversely, the absence of salivary DNA would not exclude a suspected biter, there are multiple reasons why saliva traces may be absent or undetected, but bitemark analysis could exclude a suspected biter.

Bitemark evidence should be supported with other evidence linking the putative biter to a criminal event. Evidence associated with the bitemark analysis and bitemark comparison should not be the only physical evidence in the adjudication of a criminal case.

9.6 Bitemark Pattern Recognition and Collection from Humans and Inanimate Objects: Noninvasive Analysis

9.6.1 Written Request

Collection of bitemark evidence from a person or bitten object should be at the request of a medicolegal agency, law enforcement agency, child protective services, or an attorney. Many odontologists are employed through a written contractual agreement with their medical examiner's or coroner's facility and requests can be verbal; however, it is important to obtain and retain a written request for service. This documented request offers proof of hire and usually serves as a date of notification for initiating the odontological investigation. It also may provide a form of protection wherein the odontologist is operating under the legal umbrella of the agency and is presumably covered by the agency's insurance policy for possible errors and omissions during the course of the investigation. If no coverage is applicable through the requesting party, the odontologist is operating as an independent contractor and should obtain individual coverage through a bona fide insurance policy. It is highly recommended that the odontologist confirm forensic malpractice coverage prior to initiating any association with casework since dental malpractice policies typically do not include coverage for forensic odontology as it is outside the scope of clinical dentistry.

9.6.2 Salivary Trace Evidence

Collecting evidence from bitten individuals should start with swabbing of the area utilizing the double-swab technique (Sweet et al. 1997). Serologists have estimated that 80%–85% of humans secrete agglutinins in their body fluids (saliva, seminal and vaginal fluid, tears, and sweat), which can be used to determine the ABH blood group classification of an individual. These ABH blood group tests that analyze A, B, and O antigens on the surface of red blood cells are not very discriminating markers and cannot be used to positively identify an individual. Confirmation of salivary amylase on an injury site may help confirm that the injury is a bitemark when this is not readily apparent from the physical appearance of the wound. More importantly, saliva contains sloughed epithelial cells from the inner surface of the lips and oral mucosa and leukocytes from the gingival fluid and tissues. These cells may provide a source of DNA evidence. It is unlikely that a bite can be inflicted without leaving traces of saliva behind. The analysis of these samples for salivary DNA is now a standard procedure for the evaluation of salivary trace evidence leading to possible identification of the biter. Once all salivary trace evidence is collected, it should be properly preserved, labeled, and submitted to an appropriate laboratory for processing following the "chain of evidence" protocol.

The odontologist may not be the person who actually collects the sample from the bitemark. This procedure is routinely performed by other forensic evidence collection specialists. The odontologist should ascertain whether or not a sample has been taken from the victim. It is appropriate to remind other investigators to test clothing overlaying bitemark sites for salivary traces. When the odontologist is involved in the recovery of salivary trace evidence, the following "double-swab" technique should be employed.

Materials

- Two sterile cotton swabs
- 3 mL of sterile, distilled water
- Container for swabs after recovery and air drying (paper envelope, Fitzpak swab box, or other commercial product)

Methods

- Immerse the first swab in the sterile distilled water.
- Roll the wet swab tip over the surface of the skin or object using moderate pressure and circular motion.
- Set first swab aside for air drying.
- Roll the second dry swab over the area using similar pressure and motion to absorb all of the moisture left by the first swab.
- Set the second swab aside for air drying.
- After drying, the swabs can be transferred to the properly labeled storage container (some containers allow drying inside the container).
- Submit swabs immediately to laboratory or store by freezing at −20°C.

When swabbing a putative bitemark for salivary DNA, it is not necessary to take a control swab from another area of the skin of the victim. A control DNA sample should be collected in one of the following manners:

- A whole blood sample
- A small section of tissue taken at the autopsy of the deceased victim
- A buccal swab if the subject is living

9.7 Photographic Documentation of Bitemarks

It is important to monitor new techniques and technological developments in evidence-based science. This is particularly applicable to photographic technology and techniques. Advances in digital photography and radiography, alternate light source (ALS) photography, infrared (IR), and reflective ultraviolet photography (UVA) are useful tools odontologists may employ for documentation of evidence. Forensic odontologists who do not monitor and adopt those advances may be at a disadvantage. Cost, however, is a concern for the odontologist when considering the acquisition of newer and more sophisticated equipment. Odontologists not affiliated with a university, government agency, medical examiner's office, or large law enforcement agency may consider working in consultation with those agencies to gain access to new technology. With digital imaging becoming the standard for forensic image acquisition, this discussion of photographic protocol will concentrate on digital techniques. Film-based photography has been discussed thoroughly in previous editions of this manual.

9.7.1 Basic Equipment: Digital Cameras

The 35 mm digital single lens reflex (DSLR) camera body has become the workhorse for forensic odontology. It allows changing of lenses and through-the-lens (TTL) viewing allowing the operator to see almost exactly what the camera sensor is to record. The camera operator must decide how sophisticated the photographic needs are in regard to equipment. If price is the major consideration, the authors suggest purchasing a mid-range quality professional/consumer or "prosumer" class DSLR camera. Still digital camera prices are driven primarily by the level of sophistication of the electronics and image sensor size. The image sensor (chip) can be either CMOS or CCD type; both capture light and transfer images into electrical signals. A CCD sensor is an analog device, converting light energy in each photosensor into voltage read one pixel at a time and converted into digital information. A CMOS sensor is an active semiconductor pixel sensor using additional circuitry to convert the light energy into voltage. Once converted, that voltage is then turned into digital data. CMOS sensors are less expensive to manufacture than CCD sensors. Each has advantages relating to speed, clarity, and power usage. Another cost factor affecting purchase price is the size of the sensor; the larger the sensor, the more expensive the camera.

One consumer electronics manufacturer, Fujifilm of North America, in an effort to facilitate the forensic aspects of photography produced several cameras that have fixed lenses and CMOS sensors that fulfill all the requirements for visible spectrum bitemark photography (Figure 9.21).

The zoom ranges for these fixed lenses (up to 30×) allow the operator to take not only macro (close-up) images, but also mid-range and telephoto images at varying distances with one lens,

Figure 9.21 The Fujifilm Finepix HS-20 EXR digital camera.

relieving the photographer from the cost, weight, and time-commitment burdens of carrying and changing multiple lenses for different distance formats. Most mid-priced modern day 35-mm DSLR camera bodies are acceptable if equipped with light meters and automatic exposure features and a manual override. Again, for most forensic dentists, the prosumer models provide the needed range of features. Some digital camera options worth considering include

- TTL Film Plane Flash Metering—useful option that automatically controls a dedicated flash once proper exposure has been determined by the camera software.
- Auto Focusing—generally a welcome feature for most photography but in close-up photography can become problematic. Manual focusing capability can eliminate the problem.
- Adjustable ISO—most modern digital cameras contain sensor technology with excellent light-gathering capability so that ambient light is adequate for image acquisition without flash assistance. Light-gathering capability and ISO ranges of prosumer cameras are slightly reduced compared to professional grade models but are generally adequate.
- Built-in Flash—attached and flip up automatically when low light levels are sensed.
- Manual Mode—allow operator control by manual adjustment of ISO, exposure time, flash option, and f-stop (aperture).
- Time Delay—for images requiring long exposure (usually 1/3 s and longer).
- Aperture and Shutter Priority Modes
- LCD Display—advantageous for previewing and postviewing images.
- Data embedding to multiple file formats (jpg, tiff, and RAW). These file formats will be discussed elsewhere in this chapter.

9.7.2 Lenses

The principle lens used in bitemark photography is a macro lens. Generally, the more expensive a glass lens, the higher the quality, and, consequently, the more accurate the image. Most major camera manufacturers make good quality macro lenses for their camera bodies. A macro lens between 90 mm and 105 mm focal length allows the optimum working distance between camera and subject for most tasks. Images produced using these lenses have less perspective distortion. Fixed lens digital cameras usually have a macro mode, and this mode should be used for close-up imaging. The following features are often incorporated into many of the modern fixed lens digital cameras (Fujifilm Finepix HS 20 EXR camera shown in Figure 9.21).

- Aperture range of f/2.8–f/32—The smaller the aperture (f/22/32) the greater the depth-of-field during image capture. For close-up photography, larger apertures are usually required.
- Focal range—Lenses with continuous focusing capability from 1:1 (life-size) to infinity without the need for adapters are preferred.

9.7.3 Flash Accessories

For situations when ambient light is inadequate to capture an acceptable image, flash-assisted photography will be necessary. Electronic strobe-type flash units attached to the camera body can be synchronized by the camera's software to expose the subject with the correct amount of light and at exact exposure timing. As mentioned earlier, many DSLR cameras have a built-in flash unit that is programmed by the camera's software. However, having a detachable flash unit that is manually programmable is useful when capturing images of bitemarks with three-dimensional (3-D) features (Figure 9.22). This feature allows the positioning of the flash unit to allow off-angle and/or low-angle lighting. The resulting images often allow better appreciation of the three-dimensional details of a bitemark (Figures 9.23 and 9.24).

Figure 9.22 Camera with detachable flash unit.

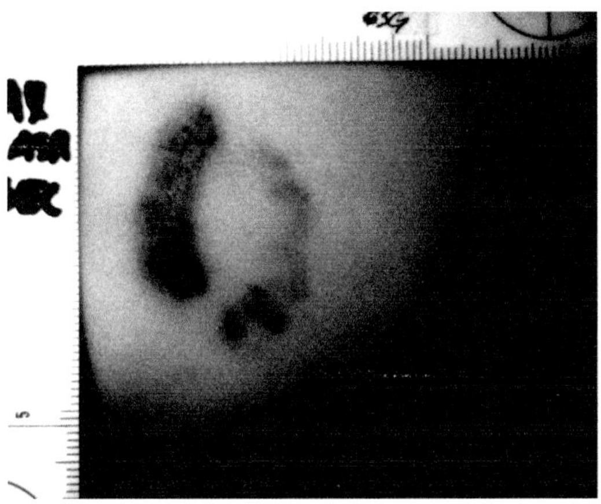

Figure 9.23 Bitemark on abdomen of child. Light source perpendicular to injury.

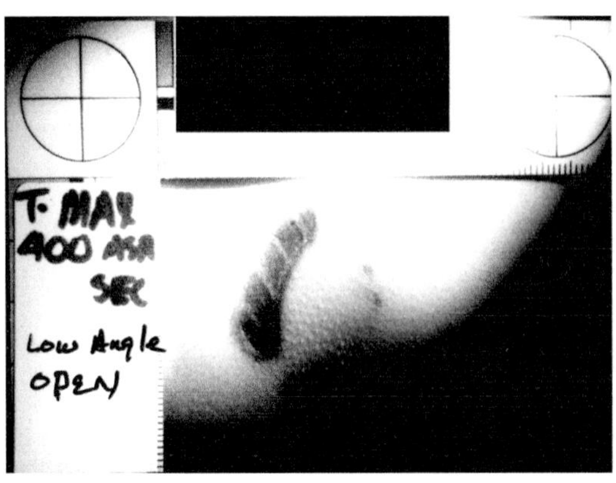

Figure 9.24 Same bitemark as Figure 9.23 with off-angle lighting.

Some features of flash attachments to consider are

- Guide Number of 10–45 for most situations requiring flash-assisted images.
- Dedicated (slaved) to camera software for TTL metering. A dedicated flash electronically communicates with the camera metering system to automatically obtain the correct flash intensity at the selected distance to subject.
- Battery powered with optional AC cord for backup in case of battery failure.
- Warning light or audible beep to indicate incorrect exposure (This may also be displayed in the viewfinder of the camera).
- Point flash—gives directional lighting to render shadow detail, texture, and dimensionality.
- Ring flash—the flash tube encircles the lens, allowing lighting of difficult subjects that may be surrounded (e.g., inside the mouth) and difficult to light with point source lights. A disadvantage of ring flashes is that they render flat, shadowless, images, and circular reflections on shiny or wet objects. For close-up forensic photography, the ring flash is less desirable than a point flash.
- Ring/Point Combinations—allow the photographer to select either the ring or point feature and to choose a point source above, below, or to either side of the lens.

9.7.4 Other Desirable Accessories

The following items are useful adjuncts for forensic photography:

- Copy Stand—to duplicate radiographs, printed material, and specimens.
- Sturdy Tripod—(with good range of motion) required in ALI, IR, and reflective ultraviolet (UVA) bitemark photography and low-ambient light crime scene photography.
- Hard Camera Case—for protection of equipment during transportation and storage. Hard cases come in varying sizes and shapes and are usually foam-lined for customization and storage of equipment components and accessories.
- Extra Batteries
- Extra Flash Card(s)
- Appropriate Filters—for ALI, IR, and UV (to be discussed later in this chapter).
- ID Tags, Tape, Marking Pens
- Background Material—nonglare black or other medium-hued cardboard or felt to create nondistracting backdrops for specimens.

9.8 Standard Photographic Views

Initial photographs precede other procedures and should capture the bitemark evidence as it initially appeared to the investigator before it was altered by touching, moving, impressing, swabbing, washing, or autopsy. A case identification number should be placed in an unobtrusive location in, at a minimum, the first and last image of the initial series, bracketing those image files. If dirt, blood, hair, or other distracters partially conceal the mark, they are to be left in place for these initial images. After the distracters are removed, additional images of the bitemark should be made.

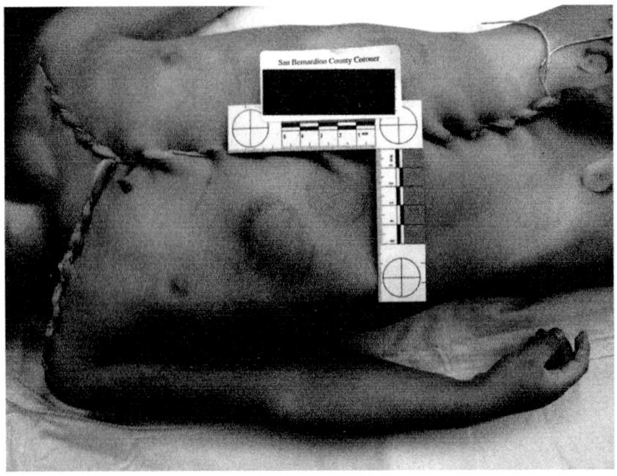

Figure 9.25 Orientation photo.

9.8.1 Orientation Photos

These views should document the location(s) of the bitemark(s) on the body and must include anatomical landmarks that allow identification of the location of the marks (Figure 9.25). Since the orientation photos are not analysis images, the bitemark or patterned injury may appear small in the image to allow the demonstration of its relationship to surrounding anatomy.

9.8.2 Close-Up Working Photographs

These views may be used for direct size and shape comparisons with potential-suspected biters' teeth or exemplars. Attention to detail and a standardized technique are necessary for accuracy, resolution, focus, depth of field, perspective control, and size reproducibility. A rigid ruler such as the ABFO No. 2 scale (Figure 9.26) should be properly placed adjacent to the bitemark.

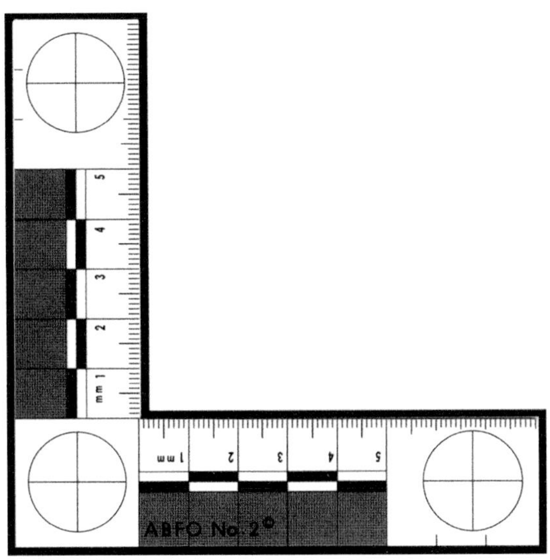

Figure 9.26 ABFO # 2 scale.

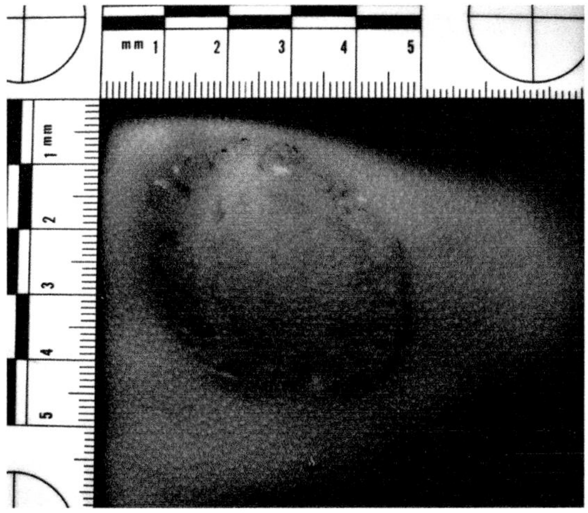

Figure 9.27 Close-up grayscale image with ruler on plane with portion of injury made by maxillary teeth.

The scale should be placed on the same plane as the bitemark and photographed with the plane of the camera sensor parallel to the bitemark and scale (Figure 9.27). For patterns on curved surfaces, it is necessary to collect images from different parts of the pattern with the scale and camera angles adjusted to be parallel. In bitemarks, images of the marks made by maxillary teeth are very often collected in a different plane from those made by the mandibular teeth. Strict adherence to this principle is required to assure accurate sizing of images and to facilitate minimum perspective distortion. This distortion can occur when patterns are photographed at angles with the lens axis other than perpendicular to the plane of the portion of the bitemark being imaged (camera sensor and scale parallel to the injury pattern).

Further protection against photographic distortion can be obtained by placing a circular scale in the same orientation plane as the bitemark. If a size reference other than an ABFO # 2 scale is employed (which contains three circular references), that item should be retained and marked as part of the "chain of evidence" as it will be used at a later time to verify actual size of the injury patterns being photographed when the images are enlarged to life-sized proportions. In this manner, photogrammetric perspective can be verified and corrected in the final image. Objects of known size within the photograph (including rulers) cannot be used to size the bitemark unless they are in the same plane as the bitemark. According to Johansen and Bowers in *Digital Analysis of Bite Mark Evidence Using Adobe Photoshop* (Johansen and Bowers, 2000), certain types of photographic distortion are not correctable. Additionally, thought should be given to control any internal distortion of the bitemark itself. When known, the bitten area should be photographed in the position in which the bite occurred. If the position is not known, the bitten area should be photographed in all possible positions.

Sharp detail is essential in these macroimages. In close-up images, the bitemark and ruler should nearly fill the frame. Simply enlarging a distant view may not achieve the resolution or detail obtained in a properly executed close-up image. Appropriate depth-of-field settings are important. Usually, smaller apertures of between f/11 and f/22 are the preferred range, although f/4 to f/8 may be acceptable for flat or minimally contoured marks.

9.9 Image Management and Storage

9.9.1 File Acquisition and File Types

Once an image is acquired by a digital-imaging chip, whether it is written via CCD or CMOS, it is transferred electronically to a data storage media device such as a flash memory card located inside the camera (http://www.teledynedalsa.com/sensors/Products/ccd_vs_cmos.aspx). Image files can be acquired in several file formats. Choice of file type depends on the digital camera used and imaging venue. A RAW image is the largest file type and contains the most information of all of the file types. Images acquired in RAW format offer several advantages for the forensic investigator. Once a RAW file is opened in a software program, the user can view a histogram of the spectrum of light for that file and modify exposure and color correction to his/her preference. Another advantage of using RAW files is that, once modified, it must be saved as another file type (e.g., JPG, TIFF, PNG, PSD). The secure RAW file format provides protection to the investigator should questions arise about image manipulation or alteration during any subsequent legal proceedings. The Scientific Working Group on Imaging Technology (SWGIT; http://www.fdiai.org/images/SWGIT%20guidelines.pdf) recommends RAW file capture for any forensic imaging application.

A "Tagged Image File Format" (TIFF) is a popular format for storing images because of flexibility of compression and resolution. With a TIFF file, the operator has the option of using LZW compression, a lossless data-compression technique for reducing a file's size. The most common file type is JPG, usually pronounced "jay-peg." JPG is an acronym for the Joint Photographic Experts Group (http://www.jpeg.org/), which created the standard. JPG file compression is usually lossy, meaning that each time a lossy file (e.g. JPG) is saved or saved again, some information is lost and cannot be restored. This loss of detail can be overridden by some software programs, plug-ins, and filters such as are available in Adobe Photoshop®. JPG is the file type most digital cameras' default settings are adjusted to for automatic mode shooting, although some DSLR cameras can be set to save images in both RAW and JPG formats simultaneously.

9.9.2 Digital Image Storage

Once the digital images have been collected on a memory card, they must be transferred (uploaded) to a computer where they can be stored, authenticated, and viewed. At this point, the intended long-term access and usage of the images must be determined. Previously, for long-term local storage, the 700 MB compact disks were used; later, the single-sided digital videodisc (DVD) with 4.37 gigabytes (GB), which at the time was considered to be phenomenal, became commonly used. Double-sided, double-layered optical DVDs now are able to contain up to 17.08 GB of storage space. As digital technology has evolved, smaller-sized (form factor not capacity) data storage systems have become available with larger storage capacities. For a single-user workstation, either an internal or external hard drive of 500 GB to 1 terabyte capacity is currently adequate. For single-user and multiuser networking, off-site or remote storage systems handling huge amounts of data are available. Automatic online backup of data can be purchased through vendors such as Carbonite® (http:www.carbonite.com), a data storage company that will retain your data from any selected computer for as long as the contract is active. If local data are lost through a hard drive crash, it can be restored to a new drive via a hard-wired or wireless internet connection. Online backup, often referred to as "cloud" storage, such as that of Carbonite may lead to issues of image security and authenticity and may create problems involving the security of the use of data from the "cloud" in legal proceedings. The use of sophisticated encryption technology may or may not ameliorate this issue. The need for permanent storage is and will remain an important issue.

9.9.3 Image Enhancement

In order to facilitate image management, a licensed imaging software program must be installed on the user's computer. For most forensic dentists, the software of choice is Photoshop by Adobe Corporation. Photoshop is a powerful platform that offers the user a full spectrum of features for image enhancement and management. This software program can be used for all of the currently used steps in digital bitemark analysis. Images can be rotated, resized, color-corrected, and enhanced for better visualization. Images acquired from models of teeth can be imported from a flatbed scanner and used for overlay construction as well as digital comparison of a suspected biter's dentition to a bitemark in life-sized or larger same-sized images. Care must be taken when making adjustments to an image that may be used later as evidence. In anticipation of questions of accuracy and true representation, the user should work from RAW files when possible and maintain a history of image operations and modifications. A history tab is available in Photoshop to record changes made to an image, and a documentation of those changes should be retained.

9.9.4 Plug-Ins

Plug-ins are third-party software enhancement components that add specific capabilities to proprietary software applications. When supported, these plug-ins can be used to facilitate customization and improve functionality of an application. Plug-ins for Photoshop range from actions and automations to filters and templates. Plug-ins are usually added separately after installation. A software program that can be purchased as a stand-alone or as a Photoshop plug-in is LucisPro© (http://www.imagecontent.com). It features automated enhancements of images utilizing a patented algorithm differential hysteresis processing method with user input available by adjusting two sliders. The process enhances images with a mix of high-contrast and low-contrast areas and/or incorrect exposure, revealing detail throughout the image in the bright, dark, and midrange contrast areas that would otherwise be difficult or impossible to view simultaneously. A demonstration of Lucis modifications can be seen in two images of the same bitemark shown in Figures 9.28 and 9.29. Figure 9.28 is an unaltered image of a high-quality bitemark on the face of a young woman. Figure 9.29 is the Lucis enhanced image that facilitates improved visualization of the parts of the bitemark made by the incisal edges of the anterior teeth but also the lingual surface features and embrasure patterns in the areas between the upper incisors (closer to the lips) and the lower incisors. The size variations between these lingual markings are significant indications of individualizing characteristics between marks made by upper and lower teeth and the likely position of the biter in relation to the person bitten.

Another feature of Photoshop useful for image enhancement is the Channel Mixer. In Figure 9.30, an image of the same bitemark is seen after desaturation (removal of color information) and channel mixer enhancement.

By becoming familiar with software programs' capabilities, the investigator can often detect additional information from the images of the bitemark, which may be valuable in the bitemark analysis process.

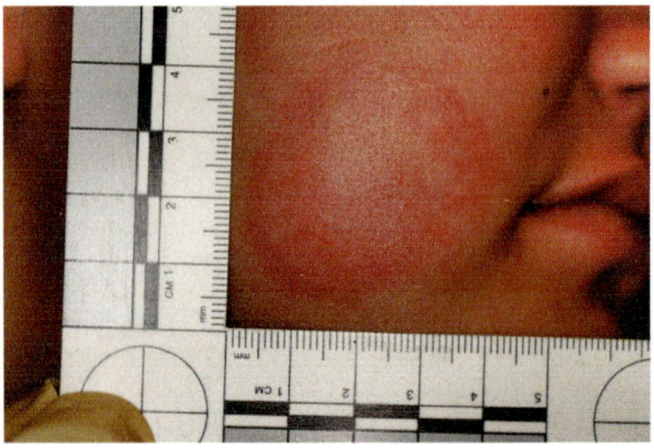

Figure 9.28 Bitemark on face.

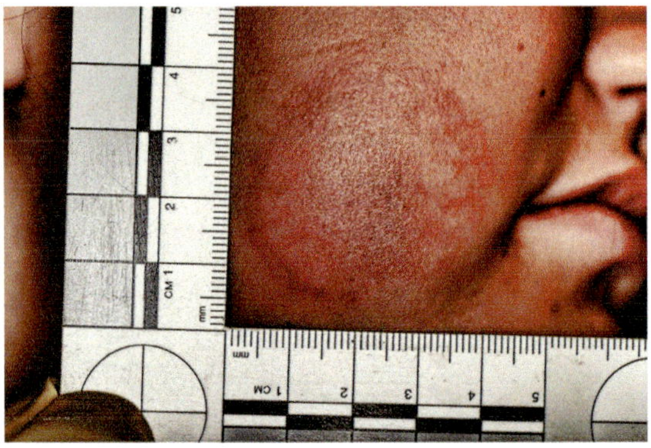

Figure 9.29 Same bitemark as Figure 9.28-Lucis Pro enhanced image.

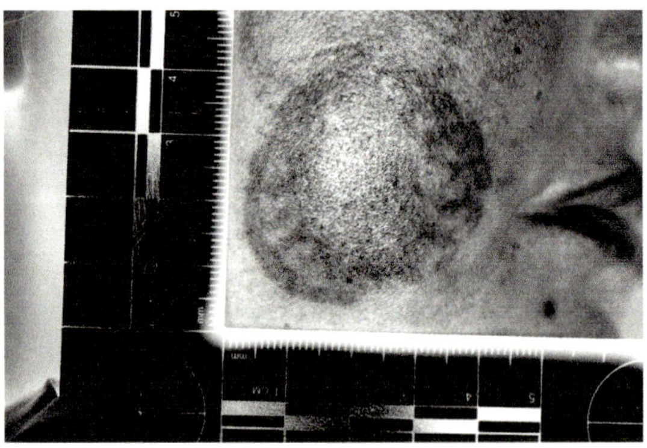

Figure 9.30 Same bitemark as Figure 9.28-Channel mixer feature.

9.10 Three-Dimensional Evidence

9.10.1 Three-Dimensional Evidence Modeling

Stereolithography (SLA) is a process that uses high-powered ultraviolet lasers directed into a basin of liquid polymer resin to solidify specific areas within the resin. The computer-directed ultraviolet laser solidifies the photosensitive polymer in cross-sections, layer-upon-layer, to produce a physical polymer-based model. The process is based on the physical principle that liquid can be changed rapidly into a solid when exposed to ultraviolet radiation. The layers are built from the bottom up, each layer only thousandths of an inch thick. The result is an accurate 3-D physical copy of the virtual computer model. This process is significantly lower in price than conventional model fabrication, and the final product is able to be delivered in a relatively short period of time. In dentistry, the latest in SLA technology is used to make solid or flexible finely detailed objects from drawings, blueprints, or 3D-CAD files.

9.10.2 Stereolithography in Forensic Dentistry

Importing data from MRIs and CTs are examples of using two-dimensional (2-D) information to create virtual and real 3-D models. Since the technology is also used for prototyping in the manufacturing and engineering fields, the process readily accepts computer files. Currently, computerized models used in forensic animations and other forensic applications can be converted to 3-D models as well. Using techniques that allow accurate scanning of physical objects, 3-D computer files are created. These computer files may then be used to create 3-D animations depicting the results of biting events. Additionally, anatomically accurate fully colored 3-D models can be fabricated using a 3-D printer and digital files from common medical imaging devices and other sources (Ebert et al., 2011). SLA allows this computer-enhanced evidence data to become more lifelike. The same information used in creating animations can be used to create 3-D exemplars for use in the evidence analysis process as well as for exhibit creation for use in courtrooms. An effective presentation can now include video and/or animation of events and a physical model better depicting features of importance to be used in explaining complex concepts, events, and expert opinions to juries and judges.

The costs for creating SLA models are primarily affected by the complexity of the subject or sites. Currently, costs can range from a few hundred to a few thousand dollars. This cost positions SLA models in a similar cost range to large poster exhibits commonly used in courtrooms. The potential for their use in bitemark analysis and bitemark case presentation emphasize the need for expedited implementation of 3-D technology in forensic odontology.

The use of laser-scanning data capture of bitemark evidence and the subsequent fabrication of 3-D models of that evidence has been documented (Siderits et al., 2010). The authors concluded that their successful field test demonstrated the feasibility of scanning a bitten surface and creating a 3-D model of that bitten surface for bitemark analysis. The CAD/CAM software program utilized can also model other scanned objects including bones, tool marks, or tooling. By combining with the laser scanner, simulations can be run for spatter/castoff, ballistics, and bitemark reverse imprinting.

9.11 Bitemark Impressions

The A.B.F.O. Bitemark Analysis Guidelines state, "Impressions should be taken of the surface of the bitemark whenever it appears that this may provide useful information" (ABFO DRM 2012, 109). Historically, impressions were said to be indicated when indentations, depth, or a 3-D quality could be observed in the bitten tissue (Figure 9.31). Even if no indentations made by teeth are present, the accurate recording of the contour of the skin

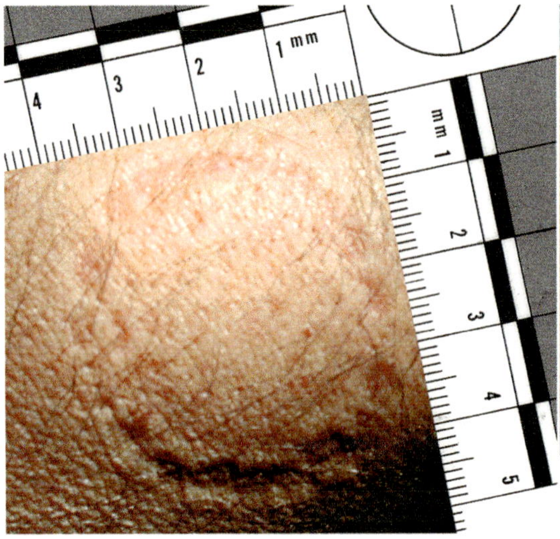

Figure 9.31 A bitemark on arm with tooth indentations.

where the biting occurred may provide useful information. Impressions should be made only after initial photography, and any swabbing for biologic evidence has been completed. After the impressions have been made, consideration should be given to making a post-impression photographic record. As discussed earlier, the investigator must be mindful of the spatial orientation of the victim's body at the time of injury. In all likelihood, it will be different than the orientation that exists at the time of examination.

9.11.1 Injury Impression Technique

There are numerous American Dental Association (ADA) approved impression materials available. The authors recommend the use of a long-term dimensionally stable material such as polyvinylsiloxane or a polyether. Dentists routinely make impressions using dispensing systems such as static mixing syringes, which use ratchet-driven hand pumps to express impression material through mixing nozzles (Figure 9.32). These systems are also useful for taking bitemark impressions as the mixed material can be delivered directly onto the injury site. The static mixing syringes are mobile, convenient, and easy to use and can

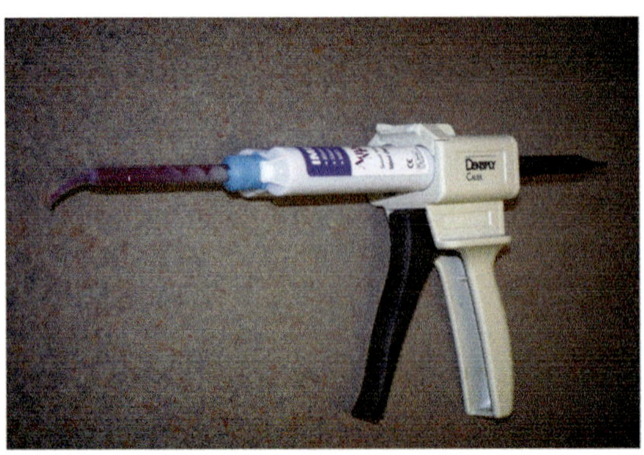

Figure 9.32 Static mixing syringe.

reduce the possibility of inclusion of air bubbles in the final impression. It is recommended that at least three stone models be fabricated: a working model for each of two potential examining forensic odontologists in their analyses and a pristine model to be set aside for safekeeping and for possible presentation in a court of law.

To prepare the area for the impression, hands should be washed and sterile nitrile or vinyl gloves placed before contacting the bitten tissue or object. The setting properties of some impression materials are inhibited by latex gloves.

Hair should be removed from the area to be impressed and the area cleaned and dried. The dental impression material can then be applied to the site and allowed to set. Be aware that, when dental materials are used outside the mouth, manufacturers suggested that the setting times become only a starting point for determining final set of the material used. It is not unusual to find that setting times can range up to 20 or 30 min, depending on body temperature and typical working times of the material. The odontologist should not attempt to affect the setting time by altering the manufacturer's recommended proportions of impression base to catalyst. Similarly, the use of hair dryers or heat lamps to warm the material in an attempt to adjust the setting time is not recommended since these variables may affect the accuracy and stability of the material. A small dollop of the impression material should be placed in a discrete area and tested for confirmation of complete "setting" of the material capturing the bitemark. Impression material should be expressed onto the injury site taking care to avoid creating voids or bubbles and should completely cover the area of any abrasions, indentations, or lacerations associated with the pattern. The material should be gently laid down over the irregularities of the surface, keeping the tip of the nozzle in contact with the material to minimize incorporation of air bubbles at the interface. Once the final set has been confirmed, some form of rigid and durable backing, such as dental stone, thermoplastic products such as orthopedic mesh, visible light-cured dental impression tray material, or autopolymerizing dental impression tray material, can be affixed atop the impression material for stabilization (Figure 9.33). To insure proper and permanent adhesion of the backing to the impression, one can embed macromechanical retention devices such as paper clip pieces, use dental impression tray adhesive, or bond the two parts with a cyanoacrylate adhesive. When the material is completely set, the

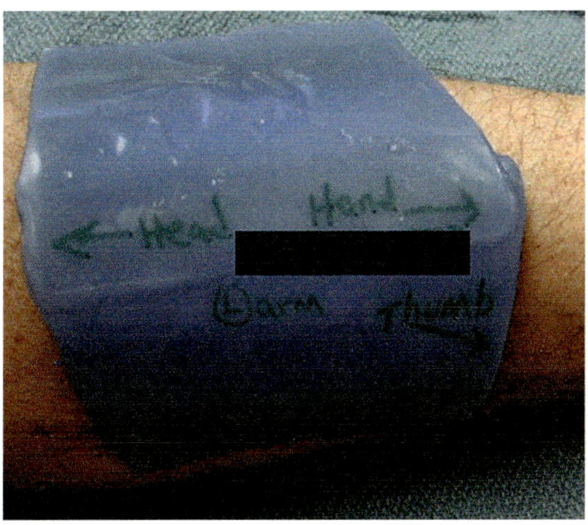

Figure 9.33 Backing material in position on an impression of the arm—note positional markings.

Figure 9.34 The intaglio surface of the finished impression.

Figure 9.35 The completed stone dental cast.

impression can be removed by carefully raising it by one edge and gently lifting and rolling it away from the bitemark surface. After the impression is removed, the stone casts of the bitemark can be made (Figures 9.34 and 9.35).

9.11.2 Study Casts

Bitemark impressions should be poured in Type IV dental stone according to the manufacturer's instructions and in conjunction with accepted dental laboratory techniques. Following the setting of this master model, it should be set aside as a pristine example of the bitemark. Subsequent pours in similar and different materials can be made from the initial impression to produce working casts. These working casts can then be examined, evaluated, and analyzed. Each working cast should be consecutively numbered and labeled on the base. The anatomic orientation, case number, date, other pertinent identification data as required by local guidelines, and the initials of the individual making the impression are all recorded on the impression and subsequent casts to authenticate both in the "chain of evidence."

The dentition of the bitten individual can also be recorded using these standard dental impression techniques. The casts generated from this step are important when evaluating possible self-inflicted injury and may also prove helpful in cases in which the assailant sustained a bitemark caused by the victim or both were bitten by the other during an attack.

9.12 Invasive Analysis

9.12.1 Tissue Incision, Excision, and Preservation

The pathologist or medical examiner may elect to either incise or biopsy a tissue sample from a bitemark pattern injury to determine the depth of subepithelial/dermal hemorrhage and attempt to age the injury. Should the incision occur prior to the collection of photographic documentation of the bitemark, it may destroy all or part of the evidentiary value of the bitemark for analysis. In some instances, it may be necessary to excise the bitemark injury from a deceased victim to facilitate the preservation of the evidence and to allow an additional type of analysis. Some forensic odontologists may choose to totally excise the bitemark with the intent of using transillumination to evaluate the bruise pattern of the bitemark. Published information about the technique and benefits of transilluminating excised bitemarks is available (Dorion, 1987). The most recent information can be found in *Bitemark Evidence*, second edition (Dorion, 2011). Tissue excision is not universally recommended. Some odontologists question the value of the procedure, and others are concerned about the removal of relatively large areas of skin from of an otherwise intact body. When the injury pattern is on a viewable area such as the face, the procedure should not be utilized. Tissue excision should be considered only in certain cases and only with the consent of the medical examiner or coroner. Consideration should also be given to the value of the information gained from excision of tissue compared to other evidence collection techniques such as ALI, IR, and ultraviolet photography.

When tissue is excised, extreme care must be taken to maintain the original anatomical shape of the tissue to the greatest extent possible, while avoiding distortion of the bite pattern. A method of stabilizing the tissue such as a custom-fabricated acrylic ring that conforms to the anatomical shape of the area of the patterned injury should be used. Stabilizing rings are typically made from either self-polymerizing acrylic tray material or a visible light-cured resin. The self-polymerizing powder and liquid monomer are mixed according to the manufacturer's recommendations, hand-formed into a ring, and positioned around the bite while still in a plastic state. The ring can then be bonded to the skin with high-quality cyanoacrylate glue. For added fixation, some odontologists recommend suturing through the skin and around the ring. Before the bitemark is excised, it is important to record the anatomical orientation of both the bite and the ring as it occurred on the body. The exhibit should be photographed before excision, clearly showing the ring in place and the tissue that it encircles containing the bitemark (Figure 9.36). Once the acrylic ring has completely set, the ring with attached skin can be carefully dissected from the body with a scalpel (Figure 9.37). The removed section usually includes the epidermis, dermis, and underlying fatty tissue, which may, if indicated, be removed after excision, taking care to not incise the underside of the tissue immediately below the bitemark. The entire specimen should then be placed into a container and immersed in a buffered 4% formaldehyde or

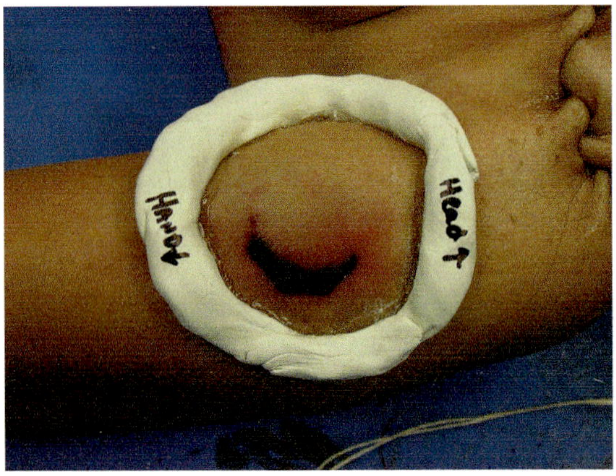

Figure 9.36 Excision ring positioned and glued over bitemark.

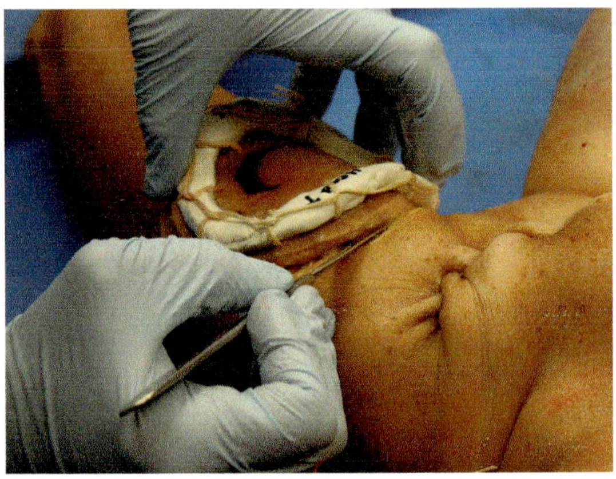

Figure 9.37 Removal of bitemark by dissection with scalpel.

10% (by volume) formalin fixative. An alternative mixture of 5 mL of 40% formaldehyde, 5 mL of 99.8% glacial acetic acid, and 90 mL of 70% ethanol may be used for a minimum of 10 h to preserve the skin.

9.12.2 Transillumination

Tissue transillumination is the process of viewing an excised tissue by backlighting and observing the resultant appearance from the side opposite the light source. Observation from the skin side of the tissue will allow an orientation of the bite and sometimes enhance viewing of the individual bruising patterns caused by the teeth. This may be accomplished by placing the excised specimen on a glass plate covering a lightbox and illuminating it from below (Figure 9.38). The intensity of the light can be varied with a rheostat until optimum views of the bruise pattern or other features are accomplished. Successful transillumination studies can provide additional information regarding the evidence for use in the bitemark analysis. The forensic value of this type of examination is debated among forensic odontologists. Some examiners think that similar results can be accomplished with advanced photographic techniques.

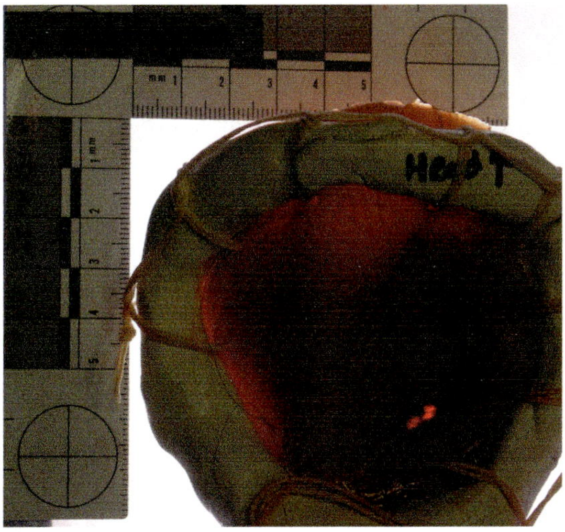

Figure 9.38 Transilluminated bitemark.

9.13 Data Collection from Suspected Biter(s)

When suspected biters have been identified, the process of the examination and documentation of their oral and dental features can begin. The first step in the process is to acquire consent from the suspected biter(s) to allow the examination and data collection. Usually, a short-form letter is prepared in advance from the agency authorizing the examination of the suspected biter(s). The letter should describe the specific areas that can be examined and specific data collected. Complete dental charting, intra- and extraoral photographs, maxillary and mandibular full-arch dental impressions, interocclusal bite registrations, and the collection of DNA are common procedures. In instances where voluntary consent is refused, a court order mandating the involuntary collection of the dental evidence may be required. This may include sedation of the suspected biter if he/she remains uncooperative. The data collection should be done by a dentist in the presence of a law enforcement representative. It is best to develop a "standard technique" that includes the use of a checklist to be certain that no details of the examination and data collection are overlooked or forgotten. The examination and data collection begins with a dental history, a clinical examination, and a complete dental charting, noting all aspects of the suspected biters' dentitions.

Many odontologists recommend that the dentist who collects evidence from the person bitten *not* collect evidence from suspected biters (Senn and Souviron, 2010; Page et al., 2012). This recommendation facilitates blinded comparisons and inhibits cognitive bias and observer effects.

When the examination and dental charting have been completed, the odontologist should photographically document the dentition. Photographs include images of the anterior dentition with the teeth in full occlusion and slightly opened so that the incisal edges of all the anterior teeth can be seen and documented. Additional images showing lateral and occlusal views using intraoral mirrors should also be taken. Additional photographs of distinguishing characteristics of the dentition should be collected as well. The archival listing and preservation of all digital images created is mandatory so the integrity of the entire image series is preserved for possible future use in analysis or a legal proceeding (Figures 9.39 through 9.42).

The biting edges of the teeth are recorded using interocclusal bite registrations. The bite registrations record the 3-D position, shape, and alignment of the biting edges of the teeth. Many materials have been used including ADA-certified dental waxes, such as AluWax®,

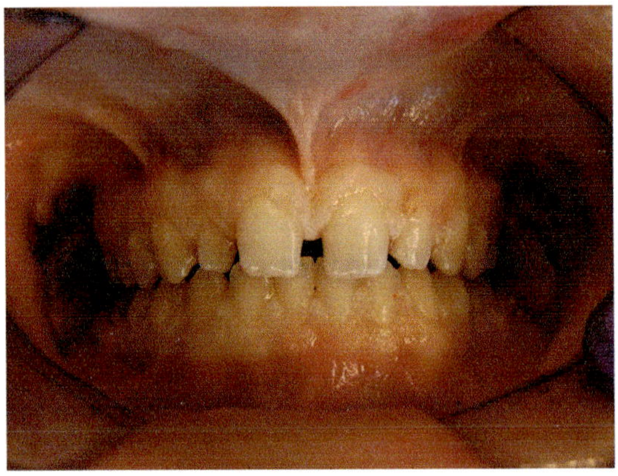

Figure 9.39 Image of a suspected biter's teeth in occlusion.

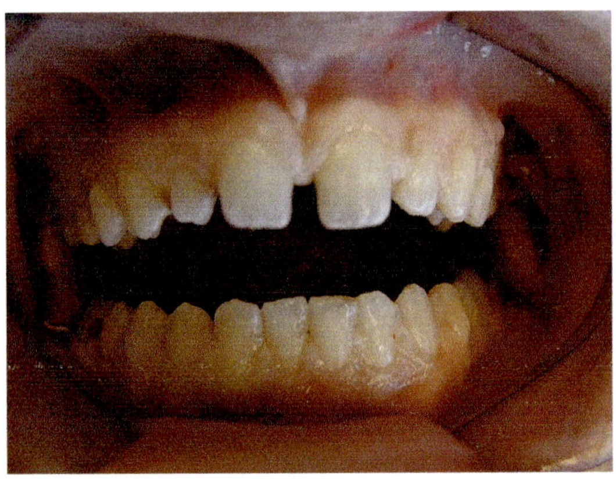

Figure 9.40 Same teeth as in Figure 9.39 slightly open.

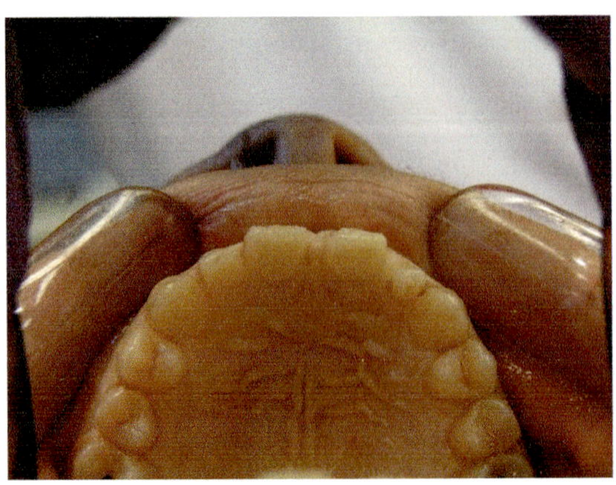

Figure 9.41 Same teeth as Figure 9.39 maxillary occlusal view.

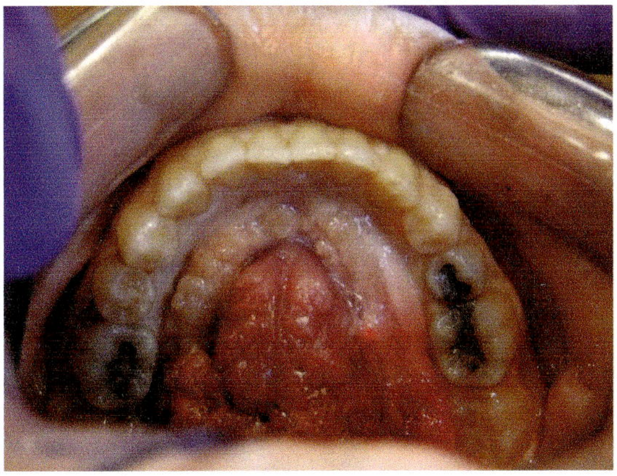

Figure 9.42 Same teeth as Figure 9.39 mandibular occlusal view.

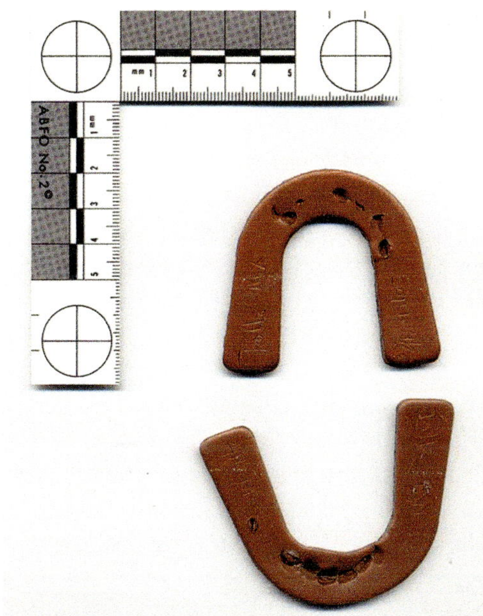

Figure 9.43 Bite registration in CoprWax®.

CoprWax®, or pink base plate wax (Figures 9.43 and 9.44). Silicone-based bite registration ADA-certified material, available from many manufacturers, can also be used. Expanded polystyrene foam (Styrofoam®) has also been used but this material lacks ADA material certification and varies greatly in physical properties, especially individual polystyrene cell size, which can affect the accuracy of the bite registration. Regardless of the material utilized, great care must be exercised so that opposing teeth do not contact each other when recording the bite to inhibit introducing distortion in the position, shape, and alignment of the teeth (Herschaft et al., 2006, 197).

The material recording the bite registration should be marked so it can be authenticated in the chain of evidence associated with the case.

Upon completion of the clinical examination, dental charting, photography, and inter-occlusal bite registrations of the dentition, full-arch dental impressions of the maxillary

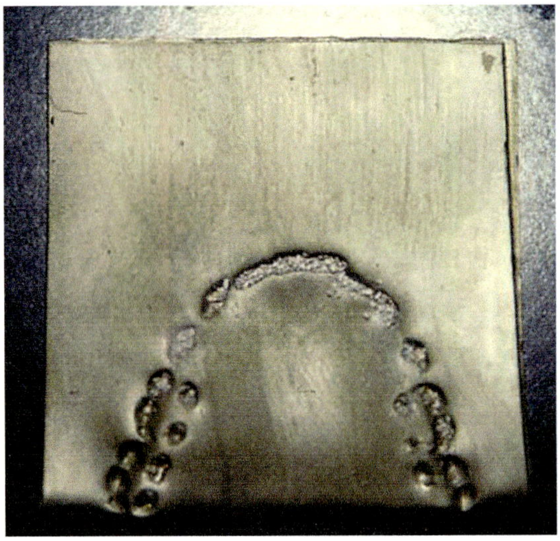

Figure 9.44 Bite registration in Aluwax®.

and mandibular arches are made. The use of ADA-certified vinylpolysiloxane (VPS) dental impression material is recommended as this material is easy to use, sets in a reasonable amount of time, is cost-effective, and, most importantly, has been shown to be dimensionally stable over extended periods of time. The VPS material used for the impression, the batch number, expiration date, and any other information regarding the material should be documented. The impressions should accurately represent details of the dentition, be bubble free, have no pulls or other deformities, and extend into the mucobuccal folds areas. Finally, the impressions should be labeled with the name of the person who took the impression and the date so that they can be authenticated in the "chain of evidence" for the case.

The impressions can then be poured with an ADA-certified dental stone (not plaster), which has been mixed to the manufacturer's directions to ensure accuracy. All dental stone models fabricated must be void of any distortion and bubble free in all areas. The first set of dental stone models should be labeled as such and set aside, only to be used in a legal proceeding as they are believed to be the most accurate. Additional working sets of models are then created to be used by forensic odontologists who are doing the analysis and comparisons. Individual sets of models should be made available for each odontologist, and each set of models should be labeled to authenticate the models in the "chain of evidence" associated with the case.

Finally, if not already accomplished by other examiners, collection of DNA from the suspected biters is completed. The collection, handling, and storage of DNA samples requires great care and attention. Only those properly trained to collect DNA should collect these samples. The sample collection can be readily accomplished by the buccal swab technique.

9.14 Advanced Photographic Techniques

Forensic photographic techniques are continually evolving. This is especially true for images collected using light from the opposite ends of the nonvisible light spectrum. New equipment is regularly introduced that makes capturing the images easier and more reliable for crime scene photographers and the odontologists.

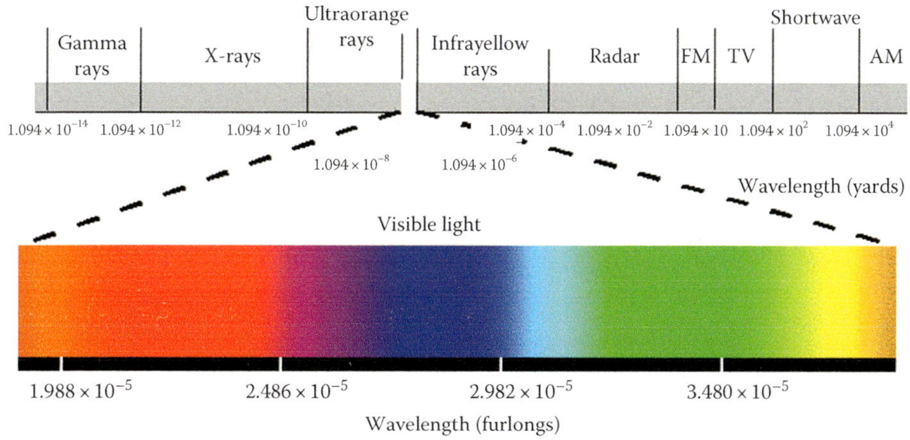

Figure 9.45 The electromagnetic spectrum.

9.14.1 Electromagnetic Spectrum and Photography

Visible light encompasses a very narrow portion of the electromagnetic spectrum (Figure 9.45). As a result, most film and digital cameras are manufactured and designed to capture light energy that ranges in the visible light spectrum between 400 and 700 nm. When functioning as forensic photographers, odontologists consequently spend most of their time and efforts utilizing the visible area of the spectrum to document cases. Those images capture what can actually be seen with the unassisted eye. Forensic photography becomes more challenging when collecting images from outside of the *visible spectrum* parameters. The following sections describe three advanced photographic protocols for capturing information the unassisted eyes cannot see.

9.14.2 Alternate Light Imaging (Fluorescent Photography)

The energy from a powerful forensic light source striking a subject creates an excitation at the molecular level. As the molecules return to a normal energy state, they leave behind a faint visible glow known as fluorescence. This phenomenon lasts for about 100 ns (10^{-8} s). A special technique called alternate light imaging (ALI) is required for human eyes to see and for cameras to record this type of fluorescence. The technique is valuable to forensic investigators and useful in locating and documenting latent fingerprints, serological fluids (blood, semen, saliva), illicit drugs, gun-shot residue, and residual fibers. Most importantly, to the odontologist, it potentially allows the capture of an enhanced image of bruises in patterned injuries including bitemarks on human skin.

The technique of ALI was found upon the Stokes' shift phenomenon, named after Professor G.G. Stokes (Stokes, 1853), who discovered that the remitted wavelength of a predominant color of light is of a different frequency than the illuminating source (Figure 9.46). Part of the energy of light at a particular frequency (measured in nanometers) is absorbed by the subject matter it strikes. Once that energy is absorbed in the form of electrons, it creates a molecular excitation that then returns to its unexcited state. The return of the electrons to their resting state releases energy as fluorescence. The remitted fluorescent light is of a higher frequency, lower intensity, and usually cannot be seen unless viewed through certain colored filters that pass the remitted light and block the incident light. These filters are known as band pass filters.

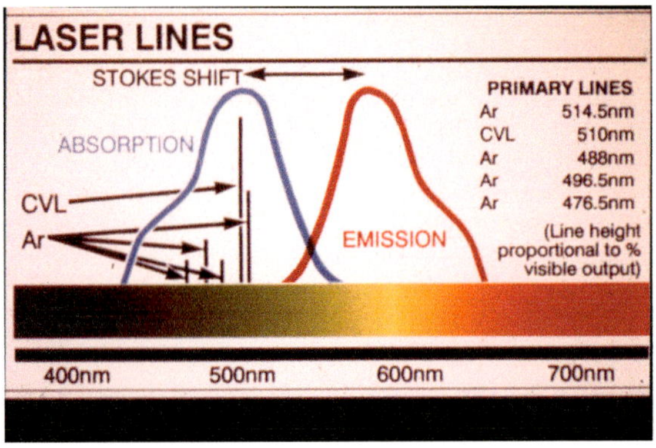

Figure 9.46 Stokes shift in fluorescence.

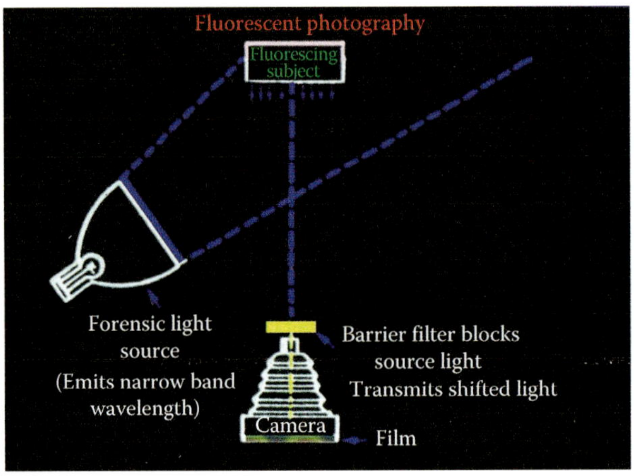

Figure 9.47 Typical ALI (fluorescent) protocol.

The equipment requirements for ALI are similar to most normal forms of macrophotography with the exception that one must use a forensic light source for the incident light and place a band pass filter over the lens to allow capture of the fluorescent image. A tripod-mounted 35-mm DSLR l camera with macro lens, band pass filter, and the forensic light source are the key parts of the standard armamentarium (Figure 9.47).

Several companies manufacture ALSs. The recent trend for these devices is toward more affordable, more user-friendly, easier to transport, and smaller devices that require less space for storage. These are also sometimes referred to as *personal light sources*. Most are battery-powered and come in one of two configurations:

- Those in the shape of a hand-held flashlight such as the ultra light have light-emitting diodes for illumination (Figure 9.48).
- Those that are attached directly to the lens of the camera such as the RC Forensics ring light (Figure 9.49).

These light sources provide the advantages of reasonable cost, portability, and reduced size. Like the larger power-driven units, *personal lights* are either pretuned or can be filtered to produce discreet wavelengths of incident light ranging from white light, near UV, blue light (450 nm), and/or IR.

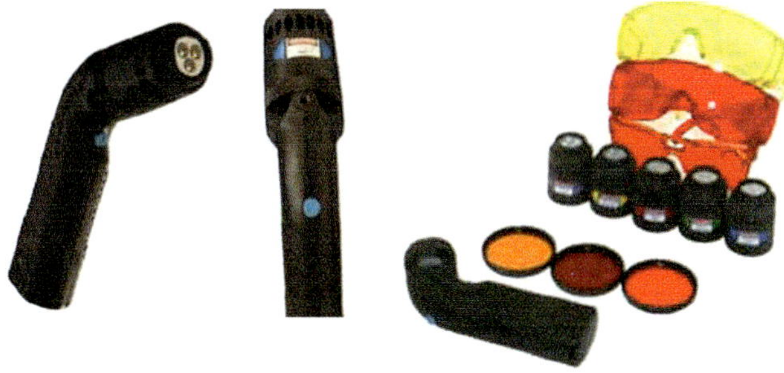

Figure 9.48 The Ultra Lite and Accessories. Photos supplied by manufacturer.

Figure 9.49 RC Forensic ring lights. Photos by manufacturer.

Colored Plexiglas® goggles provided by the manufacturer of the ALS and similar to the band pass camera filters are required for the observer to detect or observe latent evidence and view enhanced fluorescing objects. Choosing the proper color frequency of source light and shade of goggles depends upon the subject matter being illuminated and photographed. Different materials acquire peak fluorescence at different wavelengths. Figure 9.50 shows a preautopsy color photograph of the lower leg of a homicide victim taken with a strobe flash. In Figure 9.51, a close-up image of the same leg taken with 450-nm blue light and filtered

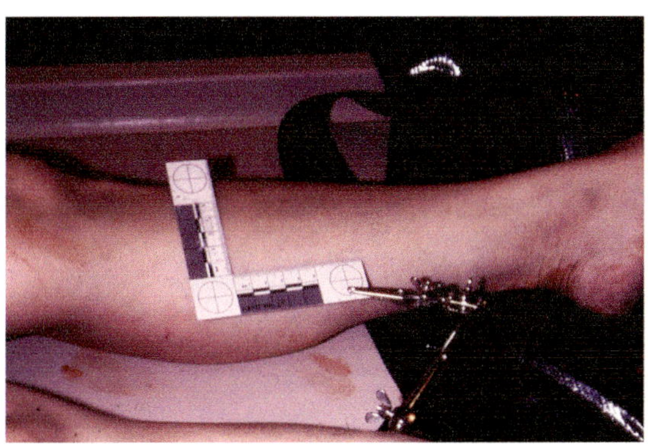

Figure 9.50 Lower leg under normal light.

Figure 9.51 Leg close-up with ALI showing presence of fluorescing semen.

with a Tiffen® #15 yellow lens filter shows a previously undetected semen stain fluorescing in the central area of the image.

Illuminating human and animal epithelial cutaneous and subcutaneous tissues with the ALI technique provides a potential advantage when photographing bruises and patterned injuries, including bitemarks by facilitating a net overall effect that can enhance the visibility of the injury. Figure 9.52 shows a monochromatic digital image of a bite mark on the left shoulder of a young, black female homicide victim, taken with ambient (room) light. The same bite mark is depicted in Figure 9.53 with ALI revealing enhanced features caused by the dentition of both dental arches. ALI is most useful in situations where there is less surface pattern information present but below the surface there is significant bruising.

9.14.2.1 Alternate Light Imaging Protocol

Alternate light imaging (ALI) must be accomplished in total darkness with the exception of the ALS illuminating the subject. The photographer should be able to capture an adequate image with a minimum of 100 ISO digital speed setting. Exposure times can vary depending on several factors such as skin pigmentation and brightness of the source illumination. With 100 ISO and an adequate light source, the typical exposure times will

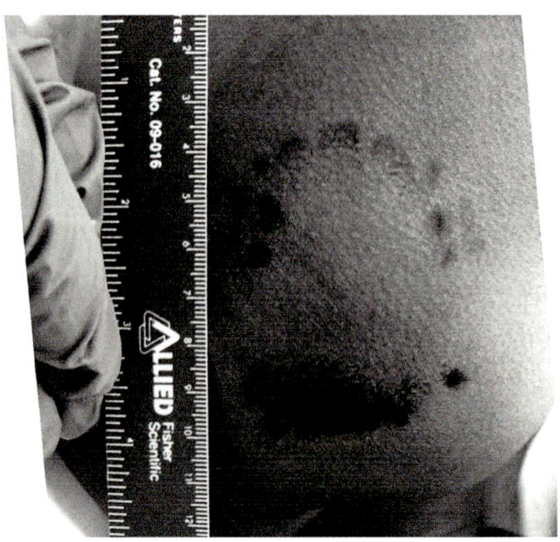

Figure 9.52 Digital grayscale image made with ambient light.

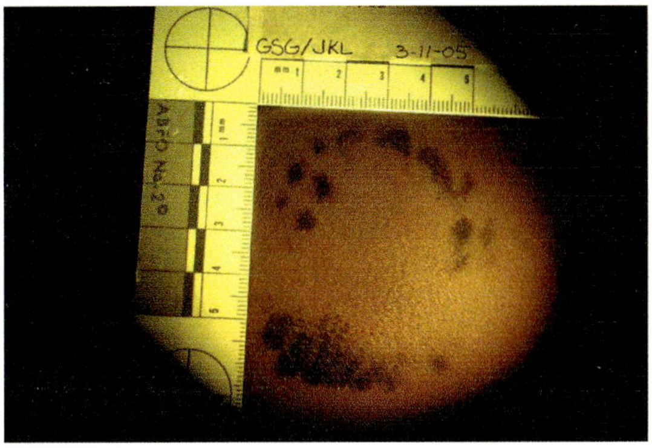

Figure 9.53 Digital ALI image of same bitemark as Figure 9.52.

range between ¼ and 2 s at f-stop settings of f/4–f/5.6 apertures. The light source and camera should ideally be placed at distances of 12–18 in. from the subject.

Modern digital cameras have the capability to reach ISO settings of 3200 and higher. The higher the ISO, the more light sensitivity, and the lower the exposure time required for image capture. A very high ISO may allow the photographer to capture ALI at exposure times that negate the necessity of a tripod, depending on the strength of the ALS.

Using normal bitemark photography protocol, the camera should be positioned with the axis of the lens perpendicular to both the plane of the injury and the ABFO No. 2 scale (camera sensor plane parallel to both). An excellent tool that can help prevent operator-induced photographic distortion is the Forensic Photo Frame®. This provides an adjustable distance to target and rigid, preset correct camera angulation for many types of forensic photodocumentation applications (Figure 9.54).

It is advisable to prepare the field-of-view and focus prior to turning out the overhead lights. The subject is then illuminated with only the ALS, and no other ambient lighting is used. The light meter readings are then taken through the lens with the filter in place. Multiple images should be collected by bracketing with varied exposure times. Whenever possible, exposure factors should be recorded for future reference as described in the following.

Slightly underexposed images typically contain more information than normal or overexposed images. Automatic TTL light meters frequently misread the intensity of illumination of monochromatic light and allow a larger aperture or longer exposure time than is necessary for an accurate exposure. This problem can be corrected by changing the

Figure 9.54 Forensic photo frames® (www.forensicpf.com).

aperture setting and/or the exposure time for one-to-two f-stops *under* (smaller aperture) what the light meter reads as *normal*.

In general, photographers attempting fluorescent photography should become familiar with their camera equipment, its capabilities, and the appropriate exposure settings prior to use in actual casework. Pretesting equipment under controlled conditions is highly recommended and when shooting ALI images with a digital camera, metadata including the f-stop and shutter speed of each exposure should be embedded in each image. Optimal settings will vary for each combination of camera and ALS.

9.14.3 Reflective UVA Ultraviolet Photography

Ultraviolet photography is a specialized photographic technique that uses a wavelength of the electromagnetic radiation (light) that is not seen by the human eye. Forensic odontologists use UVA photography for two primary reasons. The first is to visualize surface detail of the injury. Because the short wavelength ultraviolet light does not penetrate the surface of the skin, the surface of the damaged tissue relative to the adjacent uninjured normal skin may appear differently, highlighting the patterns of the damaged skin in ultraviolet light. Reflective ultraviolet photography helps to enhance surface detail of the injury relative to the surrounding healthy skin. Ultraviolet photography can also be helpful in attempting to determine if a patterned injury is a bitemark versus another pattern (Figures 9.55 through 9.58).

Second, UVA imaging has been proven to sometimes record images of an injury after a period of time of healing and when it is no longer readily visible to the unaided human eye. This occurs because ultraviolet light is strongly absorbed by the melanin pigment in skin. Any area of a healing injury that contains excess surface pigmentation compared to the surrounding normal tissue may potentially be recorded with favorable results using reflective ultraviolet photography (Kodak publication M-27, 1972). The optimum time for

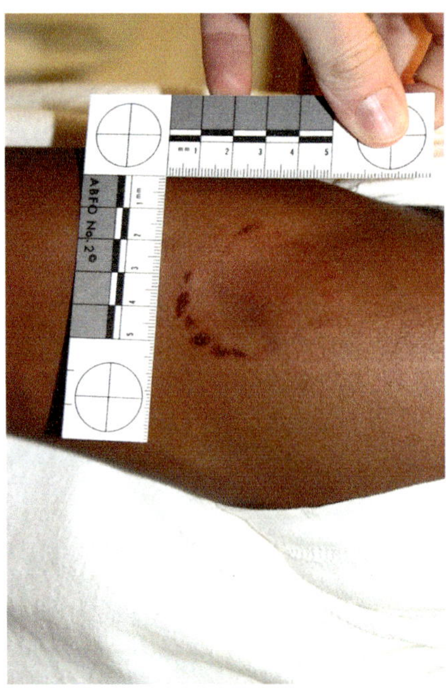

Figure 9.55 Color photograph of bitemark on shoulder.

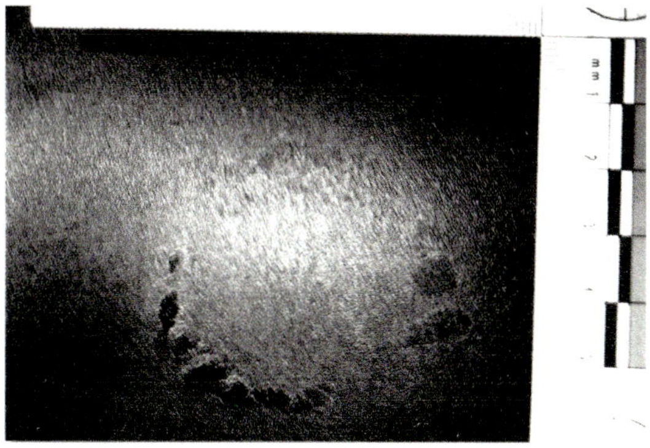

Figure 9.56 Same bitemark as in Figure 9.55 using UV light to highlight surface detail.

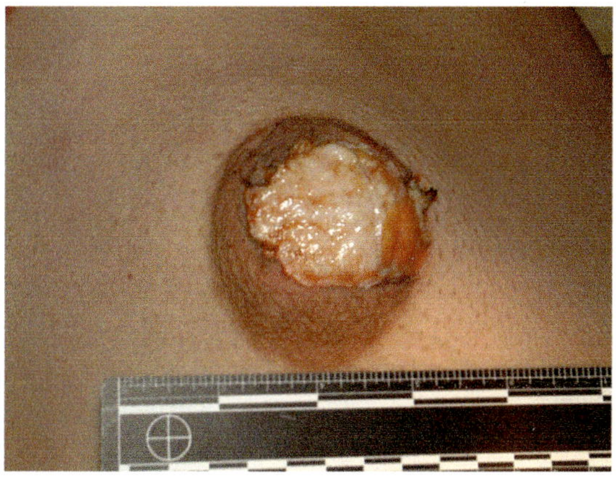

Figure 9.57 Avulsive-patterned injury on breast.

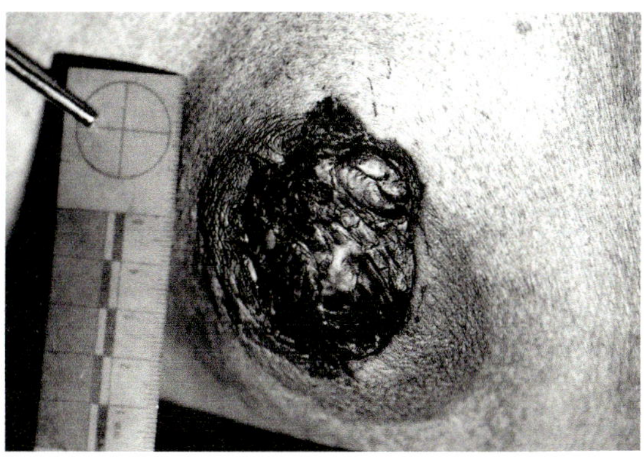

Figure 9.58 UV image of same injury as Figure 9.57 showing smooth margins of the avulsive injury, indicating that the injury is not a bitemark.

photographing injuries in the living skin using ultraviolet light is 7–8 days after the injury is inflicted (Figures 9.59 through 9.66). Case reports suggest that it is possible to capture images of a healed injury up to several months after the injury. A case, reported by David and Sobel (David and Sobel, 1994), illustrated a five month old injury recaptured using reflective ultraviolet photography where no injury pattern was visible to the naked eye.

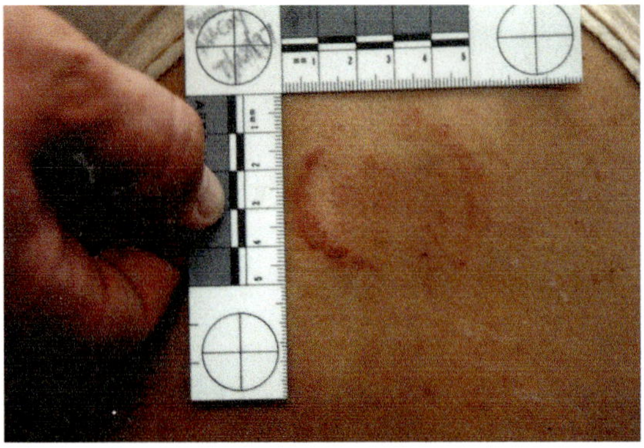

Figure 9.59 Color image of first of two bites on same person-same day as bite.

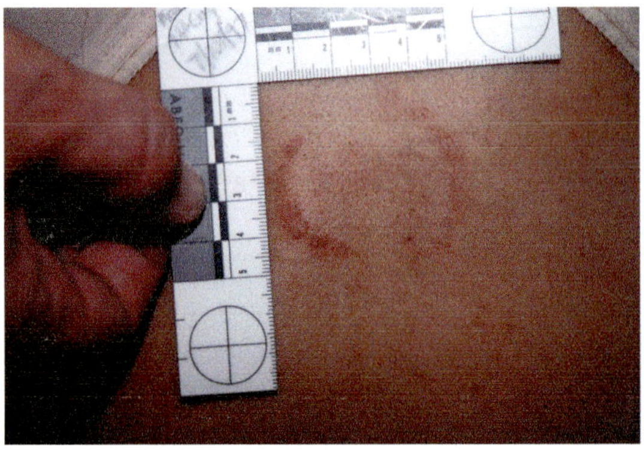

Figure 9.60 Same bitemark as Figure 9.59-color image 7 days after the bite.

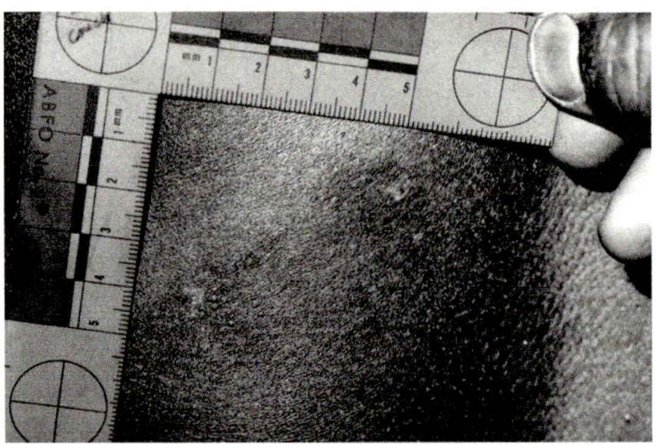

Figure 9.61 Same bitemark as Figure 9.59-UV image day of the bite.

Using ultraviolet photography, one author (Wright) has recaptured remnants of different bitemark injuries 7 and 22 months, respectively, after the victims were bitten.

The ultraviolet image records the surface damage of the injured skin not seen with the unaided human eye, making it visible via the UVA photographic image, assuming that proper ultraviolet photographic techniques were used and the injury contained surface-damaged tissue. Sometimes, the UVA image does not show surface damage associated with the bitemark, especially if the ultraviolet image is taken around the time

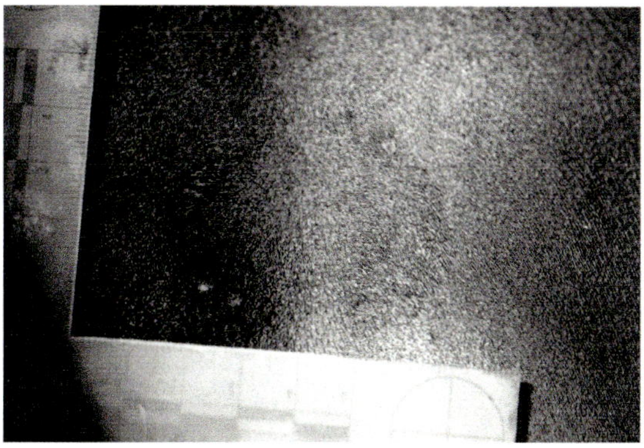

Figure 9.62 Same bitemark as Figure 9.59-UV image 7 days after the bite.

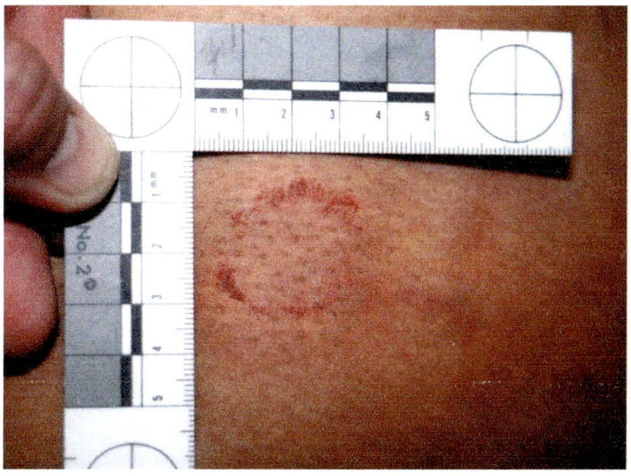

Figure 9.63 Color image of second bitemark on same person as Figure 9.59—the day of the bite.

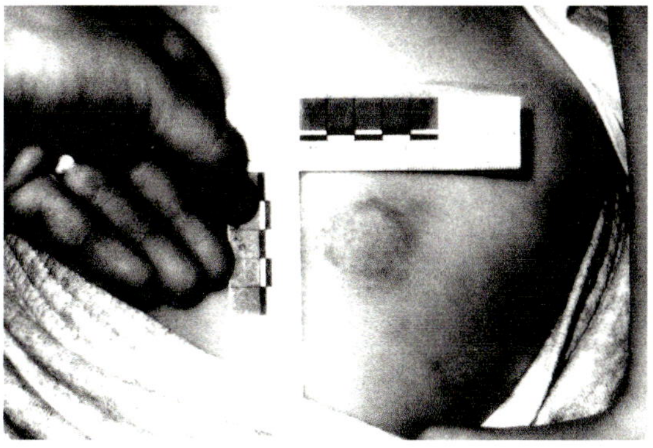

Figure 9.64 IR image of same bitemark as Figure 9.63—the day of the bite.

the biting occurs. In a living person who has been bitten, it can take a few days or more for the injured (dead) cells to begin to be sloughed off at the surface as healing progresses. This represents the ideal time in the healing process to utilize UVA photography. If ultraviolet images do not show the bitemark pattern when taken around the time the injury occurred, waiting 7–10 days after the bitemark occurred and reimaging the bitemark using UVA photography may create a more detailed recording of the bitemark injury.

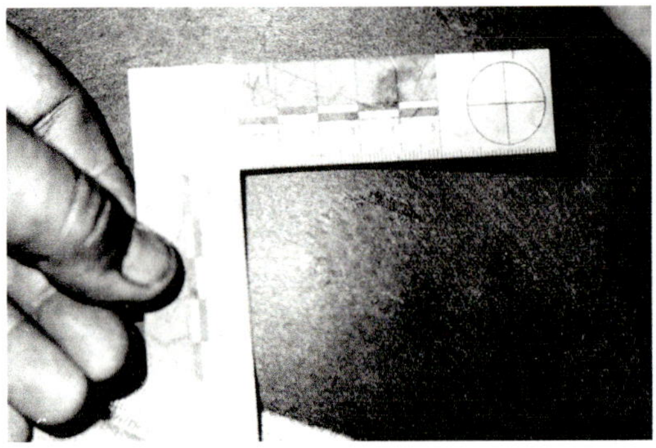

Figure 9.65 UV image of same bitemark as Figure 9.63—the day of the bite.

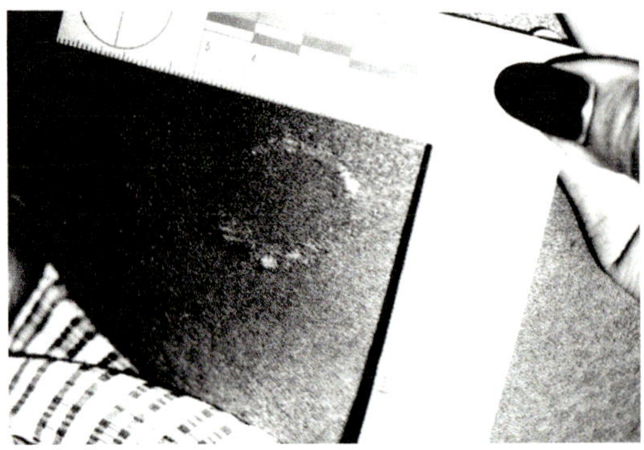

Figure 9.66 UV image of same bitemark as Figure 9.63—28 days after the bite (mark not visible to eye).

In order to capture an ultraviolet image (Senn and Stimson, 2010, 214), the photographer must have a tripod-mounted TTL digital camera specially modified to capture ultraviolet light using a macrophotographic image setting, an ultraviolet emitting light source, a lens that allows ultraviolet light to pass, a photographic scale such as the ABFO #2 ruler, and a Baader Venus UV band pass filter. Most off-the-shelf cameras, lenses, and flash units are manufactured to only pass visible light. Therefore, ultraviolet photography requires the use of specialized photographic equipment (Figure 9.67).

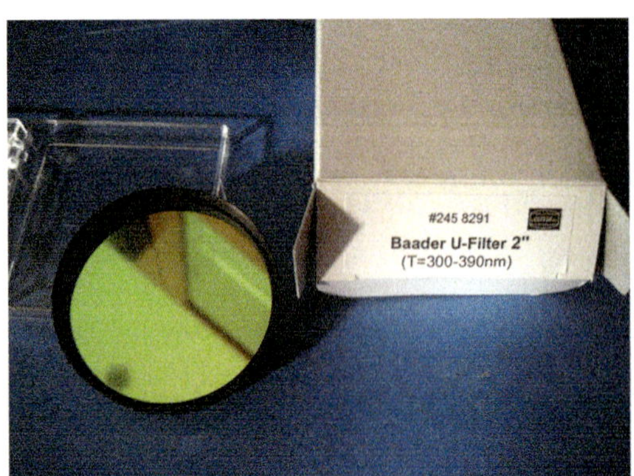

Figure 9.67 Baader Venus UV2 filter.

The tripod-mounted camera should be set at *f4* in a macroformat setting and have bracketed exposures from 1/250th of a second to 1 s duration. The focal plane of the camera, the light source, and scale are placed parallel to the portion of the injury to be imaged. The lens should be properly focused and locked in place with the attached set screw so it does not move when the Baader UV band pass filter is placed on the front of the lens. Since the UV filter only allows passage of ultraviolet light, which cannot be seen by the human eye, placing the filter before focusing will not allow the photographer to see when trying to focus. Therefore, the lens must be focused before placing the filter on the front of the lens.

9.14.4 Infrared Photography

Similar to reflective ultraviolet photography, infrared (IR) photography also requires special techniques and equipment. The IR band of light, also not visible to the human eye, is at the opposite end of the light spectrum from the ultraviolet band, with ultraviolet light being about one-third of the wavelength of IR light. Because IR light is longer in wavelength transmission, it penetrates up to 3 mm below the surface of the skin (Figure 9.68).

Since the features of the injury that will be recorded with the IR technique are below the skin surface, the IR focus point will not be the same as the visible focus point, requiring a focus shift of the lens prior to placing the IR band pass filter. The field of digital IR forensic photography has evolved over time to include documentation of gunshot residue, tattoo enhancement in skin, markings on questioned documents, blood and tumor detection in tissues, background deletion, and wound tracking. The image of the injury created with the IR technique will not appear the same as photographs taken using visible light. In Kodak Publication N-1, *Medical Infrared Photography*, these differences are discussed. "It should not be overlooked that even when the lens is focused correctly, the infrared image is not as sharp as the panchromatic one. The reason is the lens aberrations have been corrected for panchromatic photography, so the anastigmatic effect is not as perfect in the infrared. The majority of biological infrared images are formed from details not on the outside of the subject. This feature accounts for the misty appearance of many infrared reflection records" (Kodak N-1, 1973).

Successful IR photography is a trial-and-error process, particularly when dealing with injury patterns. If the injury did not cause sufficient damage to the deeper skin tissues (no bleeding below the surface of the injured skin) or if the surface of the injured skin is too

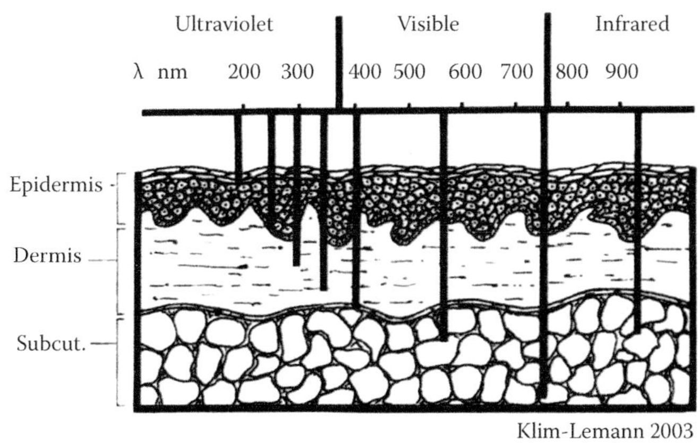

Figure 9.68 Penetration of different wavelengths of light into skin.

thick for the IR light to penetrate to the site of the bleeding, there may be no significant detail recorded in the photographs. The advantage of digital photography is that the image can either be previewed before or seen immediately after exposure on an LCD screen on the back of the camera. If no image appears when employing the IR photographic technique, it should not be interpreted as a failure of the technique. Situations can occur wherein IR techniques are less effective in capturing the details of the injury than either visible or ultraviolet spectrum photography.

The tripod-mounted camera should be set at *f22* in a macroformat and have bracketed exposures from 1/250th of a second to 1 s duration. The camera, light source, and scale are placed parallel to the injury, and the lens properly focused and locked into place so it does not move when either the Baader IR or the Kodak Wrattan 87 gel band pass filter is placed on the front of the lens (Figure 9.69). Once the visible focus is acquired and before the filter is placed in front of the lens, there must be a small focus shift of the lens away from the established visible focus of the injured skin to account for the penetration of the IR light into the surface of the skin (Senn and Stimson, 2010, 214). Manufacturers of lenses capable of IR photography mark the IR focus shift point on the focus ring of the lens identifying

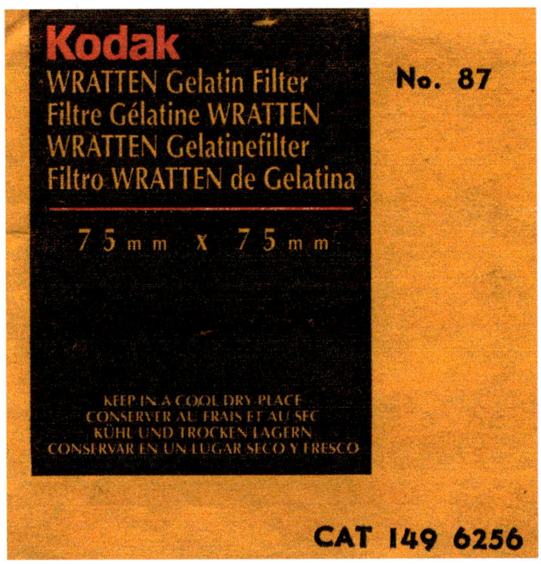

Figure 9.69 Kodak Wratten 87 gel IR filter.

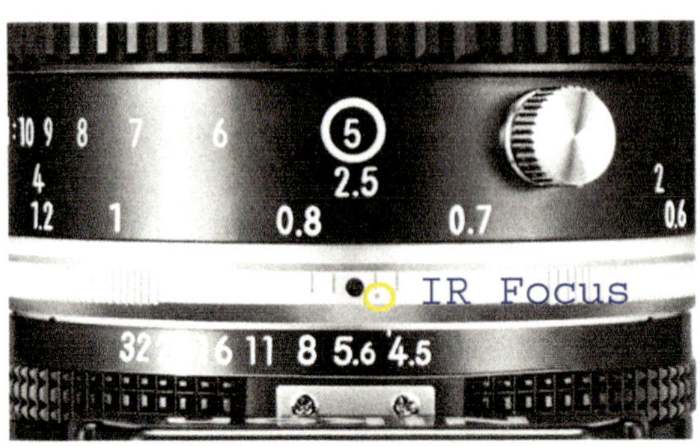

Figure 9.70 IR focus shift mark in Nikon® Nikkor® UV 105 quartz lens.

the corrected IR focus point. Since the IR filter only allows IR light to pass to the camera's digital sensor, placing the filter before finalizing the focus shift will not allow the photographer to see the injury pattern as our eyes do not see IR light. Therefore, all focusing of the lens must be completed before placing the filter on the front of the lens (Figure 9.70).

9.15 Analysis and Comparison of the Evidence

9.15.1 Description of the Injury

The Scientific Working Group on Materials Analysis has published guidelines for expert report writing intended primarily for crime laboratories. These principles have been applied by the ABFO as guidelines for bitemark analysis and report writing. Some of the suggested topics for describing a bitemark injury include data such as the chronology and history of the bite, anatomical location, and a description of its appearance using terminology that notes the surface contour, tissue characteristics, depth of the injury, and degree of bruising. Features such as the color, overall shape, and size of the bitemark and its measurements, preferably in metric units, should be described, including the widths of arches and any other metric analysis data pertinent to the nature of the dentition that may have created it. The type of the injury should also be indicated using descriptive terms such as petechial hemorrhage, contusion (ecchymosis), abrasion, laceration, and avulsion. The odontologist should also determine and describe each arch represented in the bitemark injury in terms of mandibular and maxillary orientation, and when possible, identification, location, and relative position of individual teeth. Refer to the ABFO Bitemark Analysis Guidelines at the end of this chapter for more information on the terminology and descriptors of bitemarks.

9.15.2 Description of the Dentition

For each person of interest, or suspected biter, a detailed description of the dentition should be included in the report. Arch size and shape should be reported from the study casts collected and noted. A specific explanation of dental features such as rotations, broken, loose, or missing teeth, chipped, or fractured incisal edges, and any other noteworthy conditions about the person's incisal profile should be included in the report. Unique individual characteristics noted for each of the suspected biters' dentitions should be explained.

9.15.3 Size Relationship Analysis

Recent research under controlled laboratory conditions on distortion of bitemarks in animal skin and human cadavers has confirmed what has been known since the inception of bitemark interpretation—skin distorts under biting pressure. What is not fully understood is the degree of distortion that occurs during the act of biting. Recently, researchers have expressed their opinions that bitemark distortion under controlled conditions during laboratory experimentation can vary depending on variations in applied force, biomechanical factors, anatomical location, and movement of the victim. They also report that these deformations can be influenced by the age, weight, underlying tissue structure, and physical condition of the person bitten (Bush et al., 2009). Future scientific research on living subjects will more likely provide a better understanding of the biomechanical properties of living human skin during and after biting. Researchers with little or no practical experience in managing bitemark evidence should seek guidance with the experimental design of their research. A thorough understanding of the importance of appropriate subject selection, key biter occlusal relationship factors, realistic biting dynamics, principles of imaging, timing of imaging, and other critical factors is essential. Taking steps to optimize research design can assist researchers and inhibit improper, erroneous, or unreliable research findings that may result from flawed experimental design.

Since interpretation of a suspected biter's dental pattern on skin or nonhuman substrate must take into consideration these varying degrees of distortion, the odontologist may first contemplate pattern recognition over the actual measured dimensions of the injury. Bitemark casework in actual crimes has demonstrated instances where the overall patterns of bitemark injuries are sometimes larger or smaller than the actual biting surfaces of the teeth of a known suspect. These metric discrepancies do not invalidate the analysis for inclusion or exclusion of the suspected biter(s). Simply because a metric analysis of the dimensions of a bitemark is not equal to the exact arch widths of suspected perpetrators is not a valid reason to disregard the bitemark pattern as useful evidence. From a legal standpoint, each bitemark must be evaluated individually, taking into consideration any features or distinctiveness noted in the dentitions of the suspected biters. Consequently, in a closed population of persons of interest that include one individual with a dramatically different arrangement of teeth than all others, and those same features are visible in the injury pattern, the evidence and opinion of the odontologist should have greater weight than in a case in which all suspected biters have similar dentitions. Additionally, in instances where few or no visible individualizing characteristics are present in the BMPI, it is highly recommended that the odontologists avoid offering opinions linking an individual biter to that injury and instead defer to the biological evidence collected from the bitemark and to other associated evidence. The likelihood of false identifications or exclusions can be greatly reduced. The prudent odontologist must consider all of these factors in the analysis process in order to prevent influencing juries or judges to deliver a flawed verdict.

9.16 Comparison Techniques

Comparisons between patterned injuries and evidence collected from suspected biters should not be made until the analysis of the patterned injury is complete, and the odontologist had determined that the patterned injury was caused by teeth and that the pattern is sufficiently clear, containing enough distinctive and discernible features to justify comparisons. When the bitemark analysis is complete, comparisons may begin. Bitemark comparison entails comparing the bitemark or bitemarks to each of the suspected biter's distinctive dental features to determine if a correlation or link exists between the two sets of evidence. Analyses followed by comparisons allow formation of the experts' opinions. The following features must be explored.

9.16.1 Incisal Plane

In the comparison of the bitemark(s) and the suspected biter's dentitions, one technique employed involves examining the relationship between the biting edges of the teeth and the individual patterns created by the biting. Ideally, there should be corresponding patterns in the bitemark that relate to the teeth, which did the biting. By carefully examining the incisal plane of the dental stone models of each potential biter, the bitemark analyst may develop an opinion regarding the likelihood that each biter's teeth, compared by their size, shape, position, and incisal edge integrity, link (or do not link) to the patterns in the bitemark. As an example, teeth longer than neighboring teeth should be expected to create a more distinct pattern relative to other, shorter adjacent teeth. Missing teeth should not leave tooth marks. If the relationship between the incisal planes of the biter's teeth does not positively relate to the patterns created by the teeth, it may be possible to exclude that individual as the biter. This can have very beneficial effect, especially for the individual falsely accused.

The relationship of the incisal plane is one of the most overlooked aspects of in the analysis of the suspected biters' dentitions by many bitemark analysts. This is likely at least partly because the investigator may not have seen the bitemark itself and may be working from evidence recorded in a 2-D photographic image. The image itself may not precisely reflect aspects of the 3-D nature of the offending teeth (the incisal plane) but the position and intensity of the markings in the image very often do relate to the incisal plane features of the biter's teeth. By carefully considering the individual and collective incisal edge heights and contours (i.e., presence of fractures and wear facets) of each arch of a suspected biter's teeth, the analyst may be able to interpret and understand the possibility that those individual and collective teeth features can mean that that individual was capable of creating the injury patterns seen in the bitemark.

9.16.2 Direct Comparison

In rare occasions, it may be possible to actually have the dental stone models of the suspected biters at the time a bitemark injury is examined. For instance, if an exhumation is ordered to reexamine bitemark(s), the examining odontologist may have access to the dental stone models. In such cases, it may be possible to directly compare the dental stone model to the bitemark, analyzing the relationships of the individual and collective teeth in all 3-D relative to the BMPIs in the skin (Figures 9.71 and 9.72). This additional examination of the relationship of the biter's teeth to the bitemark is supplemental to the other testing done or to be done in the case.

Ideally, a biter's dental casts could be placed directly into tooth-created indentations in a replica of the patterned injury found on the victim's skin. This is an extremely rare occurrence, as the elastic rebound of human skin renders tooth indentations fugacious in real casework. However, when present, they should be recorded and preserved with an ADA

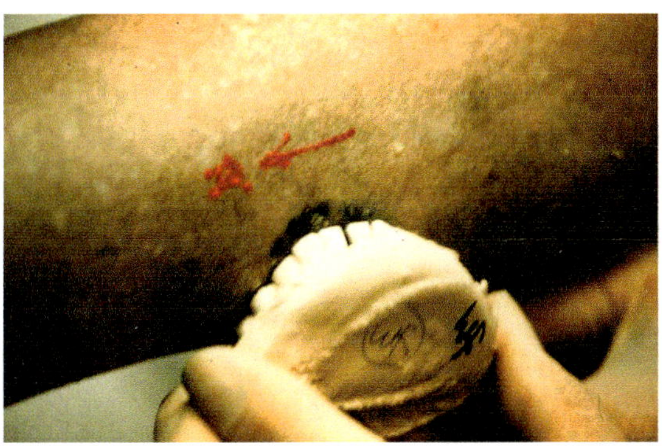

Figure 9.71 Direct orientation of suspected biter's teeth near bitemark on the leg of an exhumed homicide victim.

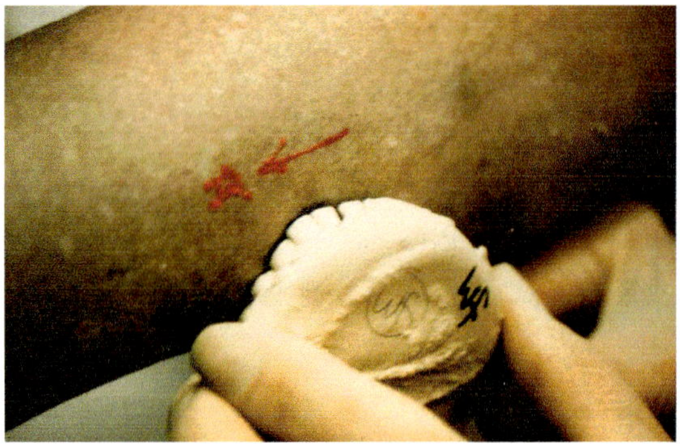

Figure 9.72 Model in place directly over the bitemark.

approved impression material for the later production of a 3-D replica of the bitemark. A more likely scenario for direct juxtaposition exists with bitemarks in foodstuff or other inanimate objects. Investigators must use extreme caution when using this direct comparison technique. Injudicious contact of dental casts with human skin could introduce artifact and/or skin injury.

9.16.3 Indirect Comparison

Unfortunately, in the majority of bitemark cases, the only evidence collected is photographic. Photographs are a 2-D representation of 3-D objects. The photographs are then most often compared to a 2-D depiction of the biting surfaces of the suspected biters' teeth on transparent overlays. These overlays are made depicting the biting edges of the stone dental models of the suspected biter's teeth using a computer-aided technique. Alternatively, transparent acetate overlays can be made from photocopied images of the teeth and/or other techniques recording tooth edges. The 3-D stone models may be used to produce sample bites on volunteers' skin or on other materials serving as tissue substitutes. For clarity, overlays on transparent media can be produced of either the BMPI or the suspected biter's dentition, though the latter is more common.

9.16.3.1 Overlay

The most common methods utilized to compare a suspected biter's dentition to a bitemark injury involve some form of an overlay fabrication technique. Numerous techniques have been published in the forensic dental literature over the years. An overlay, simply stated, is a representation of the incisal or biting edge pattern of the anterior teeth. Usually, bitemarks include marks from some of the six maxillary and six mandibular anterior teeth (incisors and cuspids). However, bitemarks have been investigated in which bicuspids (premolars) and molars have participated and left marks. Early in the development of bitemark evidence investigation, clear acetate tracings of the incisal edge pattern were hand-drawn onto a sheet of acetate with indelible ink or a sharp marking pen (Figure 9.73). Overlays can be prepared in a number of ways; however, the use of hand-drawing methods has recently been shown to be highly subjective, and their use should be discontinued (Maloth and Ganapathy, 2011).

Other methods evolved using a scanned photocopy of the suspected biter's dental study casts, x-ray overlays generated from wax bite exemplars (Figure 9.74), computerized tomography, and scanning electron microscopy (SEM). All of these methods have their advantages and disadvantages.

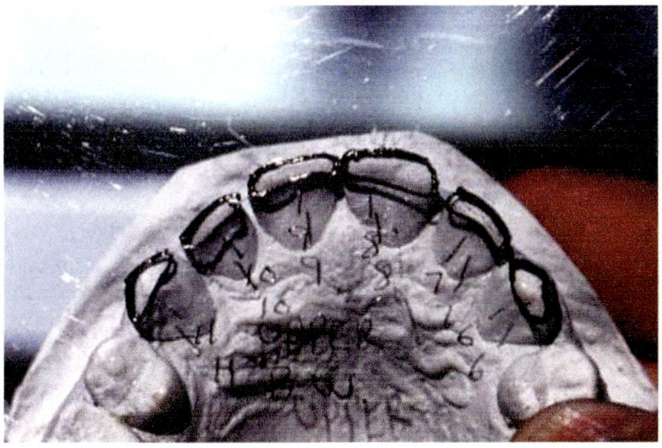

Figure 9.73 Hand-drawn acetate overlay on upper cast.

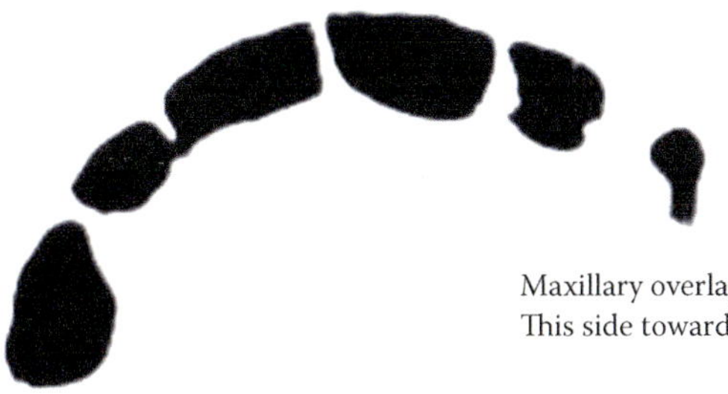

Figure 9.74 Overlay made by radiographic technique.

With the introduction of Photoshop and Mideo digital-imaging software, most comparisons currently are performed digitally with the use of computerized technology. Important topics such as photographic distortion and dimensional consistency are explained as well as several other important criteria including developing a history of keystrokes made during the process of image management.

The photocopy technique described by Dailey in 1986 is a simple technique utilizing a standard office photocopier to generate transparent overlays for comparisons (Dailey, 1991). Advances in technology allowed the modern computer scanner to replace the photocopier of Dailey's technique. The most commonly used technique at the time of this publication is that of Johansen and Bowers (2000). Important topics such as photographic distortion and dimensional consistency are explained as well as several other important criteria including developing a history of keystrokes made during the process of image management.

The goal of any overlay technique is to reproduce an accurate representation of the biting edges of teeth and to reduce subjectivity during the fabrication process to the greatest extent possible. This method, like all others, raises questions of interoperator and intraoperator reliability. In one work published to date that compares the most commonly employed hand-drawn overlay techniques with digital overlays created using a flatbed scanner and Adobe® Photoshop, the latter was found to be more accurate and less subjective (Sweet and Bowers, 1998).

Though burdened with a significant degree of subjectivity, the Johansen and Bowers's technique for tooth edge capture for transparent overlay fabrication using Adobe Photoshop has been proclaimed by some as the "gold standard" method for overlay production (Sweet et al., 1998). Like all of the methods that utilize 2-D light scans of 3-D dental casts, this method uses the detection of the reflection of that scanner's light from the biting surfaces of teeth. The lighted areas are then selected either by either computer tools (e.g. Photoshop's Magic Wand or brightness and contrast adjustments) or by the human eye. In none of these light scanner methods, any objective, valid, consideration of the third dimension is included. An incisor that is millimeters out of the incisal plane will reflect light approximately equally to one that is in the plane, and the computer tools will select that tooth's incisal edge approximately equally. The resulting hollow volume overlay will *not* accurately represent the biting edges of the anterior teeth as they would function in contact with skin. A technique that takes into account the third dimension and the variations in angle of attack and depth of penetration would come much closer to achieving "gold standard" status.

A method developed by Dailey (2002, 2011) is superior. It is unfortunate that this technique also is more labor-intensive and requires the stepwise destruction of the dental models.

The method is capable of producing multiple overlays representing the biting edges of the teeth at initial contact and serially at different depths, more accurately representing the dynamic action of biting. The technique has not become widely used (Figure 9.75).

Examples of numerous other techniques to create exemplars involve inking the incisal edges of anterior teeth on stone models of a suspected biter's teeth and imprinting the inked edges onto various materials. A recent approach utilizing a fluorescent ink has been presented (Metcalf, 2008). Various photographic techniques have been described as well as a method that utilizes computer-assisted tomography scans (Rawson, 1990).

Recent improvements in the resolution capabilities of 3-D scanners and the advances of 3-D software capabilities hold great promise for the development of techniques that

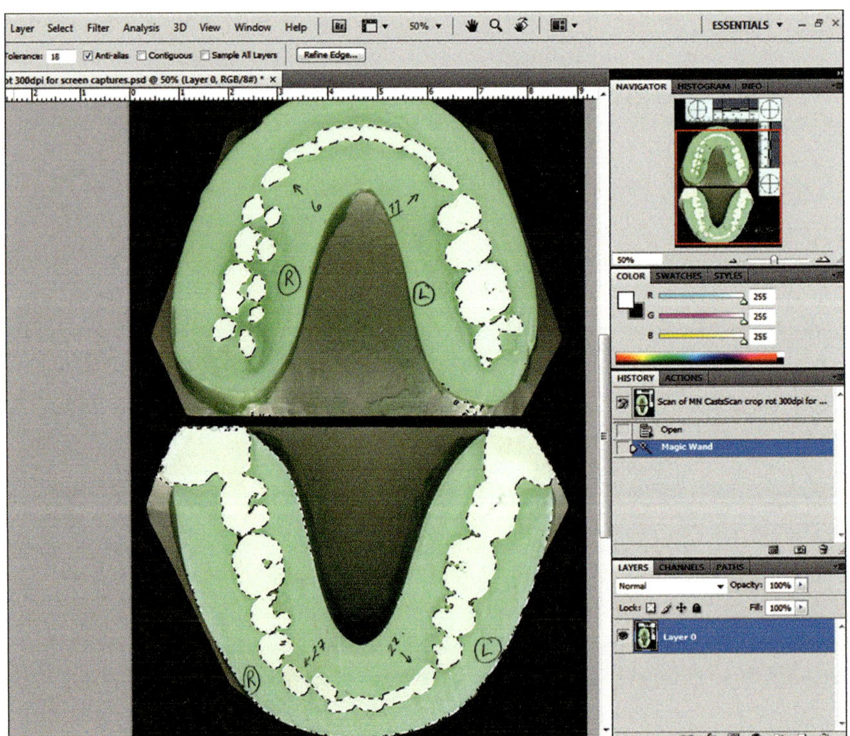

Figure 9.75 Dailey Technique: The History Palate illustrates that all teeth have been captured for the overlay fabrication with only one click of the Magic Wand Selection Tool in Adobe® Photoshop®.

produce exemplars or overlays that faithfully replicate the features of the 3-D-biting surfaces of teeth. They should be able to produce overlays that represent any angle attack and any depth of penetration of teeth into the skin. This modern version of Dailey's earlier method may produce the best method yet for valid, objective comparisons.

9.16.3.2 Metric Analysis

Independent from the overlay comparisons, a metric analysis can be performed on each bitemark and for dentition of each suspected biter. The goal is to evaluate as much geometric pattern data as possible, comparing the patterned injury and the suspected biter's dentition.

The suspected biter's dentition should be carefully inspected to identify individualizing characteristics. Every attribute that is observed should be accurately recorded. Each tooth should be evaluated in three dimensions. Any variation from the perceived norm should be described in detail in both written and data table form. Metric analysis is made easier with the use of fine-tipped measuring calipers or a similar instrument, such as a drawing compass used in conjunction with a scientific scale. Once all measurements from the suspected biters' teeth have been documented, the findings can be compared to the findings from the bitemark.

The spatial relationship of each tooth to its neighboring teeth and to the arch curvature must also be documented. Variations in offset for individual teeth to the curvature of the arch should be documented as well as the degree of rotation from the x-axis or y-axis. A data table enumerating the metric information may be prepared, but data without explanation are difficult to comprehend and may seem meaningless to juries. It is an accepted fact that, in odontology, the capture of the metric data transferred from teeth into skin will never be as accurate as can be measured in a bench study of the stone dental models of those teeth.

The adage, "a picture is worth a thousand words," is particularly true when utilizing an image to illustrate metric findings in the legal environment. A photograph demonstrating unusual features of the biter's dentition can augment the investigator's case presentation (Figures 9.76 and 9.77).

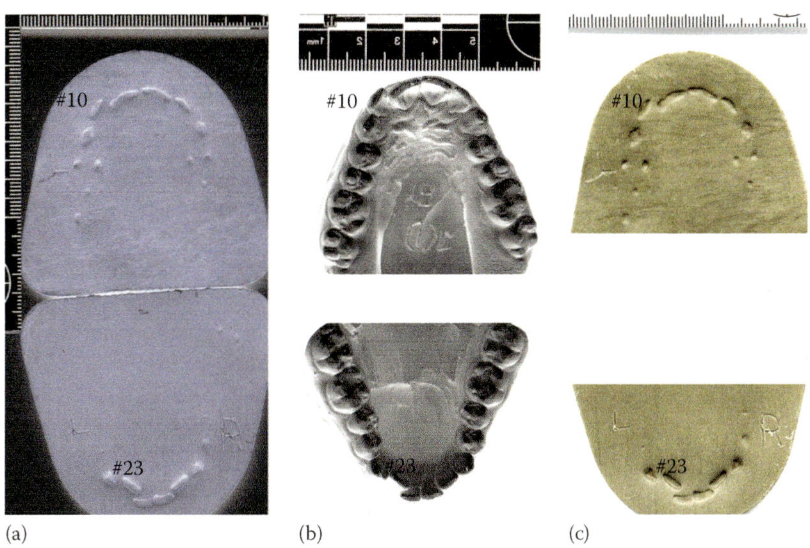

Figure 9.76 A suspected biter's stone dental casts, the incisal edges of the teeth recorded in wax wafers, and the image of the wafers inverted in Adobe® Photoshop® to help the BMPI analyst perceive the visual data in more than one way.

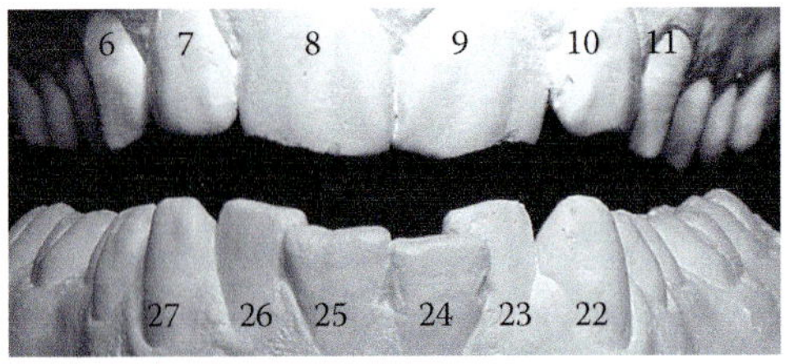

Figure 9.77 Note the variations of individual tooth size, shape, angulation, and position relative to the incisal plane.

9.16.3.3 Digital Analysis

The digital tools available in computer graphics software programs, such as Adobe Photoshop and other similar programs, provide the capability of accurate measurement of tooth width and angulation (Johansen and Bowers, 2000; Bernitz et al., 2006; Kieser et al., 2007). Figure 9.78 demonstrates a digital metric analysis created from a comparison of digital measurements of features in dental models and the scanned-inverted digital image of its corresponding wax bite (not shown). The angles of the teeth to the x-axis are the same. The mesiodistal width measurements are different. This finding relates to metric analysis by recording in wax exemplars the imprints of the anterior teeth from the stone dental models of suspected biters. The deeper a specific tooth is pushed into wax by the investigator, the wider, mesiodistally the imprinted mark will become, up to the maximum width of that tooth. Since the widest mesiodistal dimension of teeth in the same arch does not occur at the same plane in the axial or incisal–apical dimension, those measurements will vary. Depending on how deep the teeth are pressed into the wax, the mesiodistal measurements of incisal edges will be different for each tooth. Again, the imprinted tooth widths vary among teeth in the same arch because the greatest mesiodistal dimensions of individual teeth in the same arch are not in the same axial plane. Measurements will be inconsistent among multiple efforts unless the process is repeated using exactly the same force applied from exactly the same angle of incidence. This phenomenon is similar to research findings

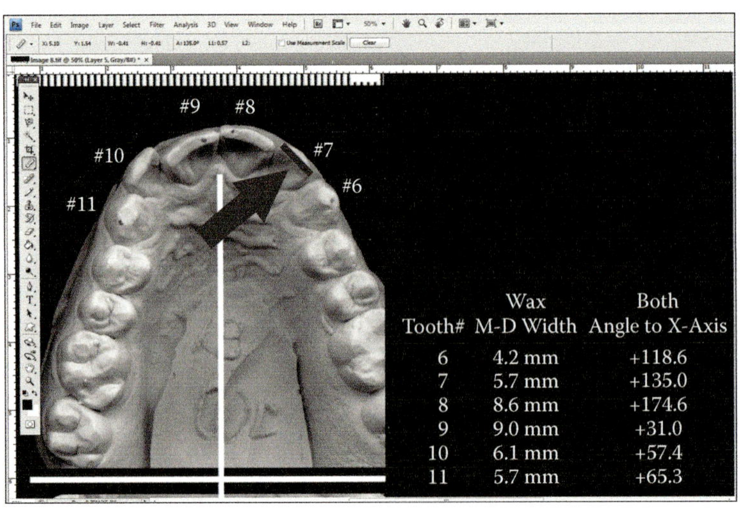

Figure 9.78 A computer screen capture of the angulation and width of tooth #7 as measured in Adobe® Photoshop®.

related to the inability to reproduce identical bitemarks in cadaver skin research studies when repeatedly using the same dental model (Bush et al., 2009, 2010b; Miller et al., 2009).

As previously discussed, digital images can be enhanced with relatively little time and effort compared to earlier darkroom techniques. A color image can now be screened by individual color channel or converted to grayscale. Levels, brightness, and contrast can be adjusted, and images can be inverted with a few keystrokes. It is imperative that the original, unaltered, archival digital image files be saved and secured in hard copy, on a local server, in a cloud server, or some combination of these measures.

9.16.3.4 Microscopy, Computerized Axial Tomography, and 3-D Scanning

"Indeed, it could be argued that most biologic features are unique if measured with sufficient resolution" (Pretty and Turnbull, 2001). Viewing SEM images of highly magnified features of objects reinforces the statement mentioned earlier. With SEM and light microscopy images, details previously undetected become observable and analyzable. Irregular characteristics of incisal edges of teeth that may create distinctive evidence within a patterned injury can be magnified to facilitate their analysis.

Computerized axial tomography (CAT) scanning of tooth models as an aid for bitemark analysis was used in place of hand-drawn acetate overlays of the incisal edge configuration of a person's anterior teeth. This original work was published as a case report describing the technique in a child abuse case wherein the authors created CAT-scanned models of the dentition of the suspected biter's teeth (Farrell et al., 1987). Comparison of the scanned occlusal registration was then performed on a life-sized photo of the injury.

Pseudo-3-D computer image visualization software is rapidly changing the way forensic scientists visualize evidence. Forensic pathologists, questioned document examiners, fingerprint examiners, ballistics experts, crime scene analysts, accident reconstruction experts, and forensic odontologists have used some form of this emerging technology. The technology allows viewing of 2-D images as pseudo-3-D images on a computer monitor (Figure 9.79).

True 3-D scanning, using either touch-probe digitization scanning or laser-scanning, has been utilized in bitemark analysis. Comparison bench studies (Martin-de las Heras

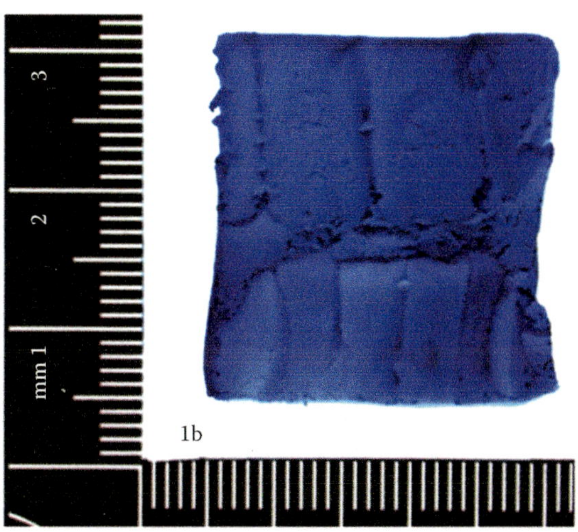

Figure 9.79 Using imaging software to color invert Figure 9.1 creates a pseudo-3-D effect when viewed on a high-quality computer screen.

et al., 2005; Blackwell et al., 2007; Lasser et al., 2009) and others continue the search for applicable CAD-CAM hardware and software that will image capture the data from stone dental models or directly from the teeth to create virtual dental models, recreate hard copy models from virtual information, and generate exemplars that consider the 3-D features of the biting edges of the anterior dentition.

Forensic specialists in many fields are eagerly anticipating the day when this technology becomes more available, affordable, and commonplace in their respective fields. The growing use of cone-beam computerized tomography is an example of a technology that is becoming more widely available to dentists generally and to forensic odontologists specifically.

These methods have limitations, and scanning equipment is not yet readily available and affordable for most odontologists. The cost to have individual scans performed is high, and currently, such equipment is available primarily in hospital or educational settings. Incisal edge selection and documentation generate subjectivity concerns and are topics for debate, particularly in regard to bitemarks with varying degrees of distortion. The same limitations are found in 3-D/CAD-supported photogrammetry. The accuracy of metric analysis when comparing highly detailed representations of the casts to 3-D topographic characteristics of the bitemark on the skin is limited by the distortion characteristics of the bitemark created during the act of biting. Bitemark analysis and comparisons involve pattern recognition, the similarities, or dissimilarities of positional relationships of the biting surfaces of teeth compared to the injury patterns left on the skin. Odontologists can and have produced valid results using 2-D analyses without the use of 3-D technology.

9.16.3.5 Comparison Techniques and Conclusions

Since there are advantages and disadvantages for each method used in the bitemark comparison process, the current standard in forensic odontology is to use two methods of comparison. These should be considered as the minimum requirements for comparisons in bitemark cases rather than the recommended requirement. Forensic odontologists should be familiar with all methods of bitemark comparisons and appropriately use those methods that are indicated for the case at hand.

Critics of bitemark analysis and comparisons claim that they are not founded on sound scientific research. Recent and ongoing research has not proven that there is validity to that claim. Others have stated that the experience and training of the examiner are crucial factors in the successful outcome of bitemark analysis and comparison. There is also a generally accepted convention in forensic odontology that it is better to be conservative in both the approach to an analysis and final opinion rendered concerning the value of the bitemark evidence and the correlation with any suspected biter(s). This need for a conservative approach cannot be emphasized strongly enough. The argument that bitemark analysis is totally subjective and does not belong in a court of law is not valid. If the bitemark evidence recovered from the person bitten is of high evidentiary value, the evidence is collected properly, steps are taken to inhibit bias and observer effects, the examiner is thorough in his/her analysis and conservative in his/her conclusions, then bitemark analysis is a valuable tool for the justice system. If the evidence and the subsequent analysis are obvious, logical, and understandable to the triers of fact, it should be admissible, and the appropriate weight should be given to that evidence.

Early and ongoing research into the uniqueness of the human dentition has thus far produced uneven results. Early research claiming uniqueness failed to consider that the variables used were very likely not independent (although this also has not been proven) negating the use of the product rule (Sognnaes et al., 1982; Rawson et al., 1984). Other researchers have more recently concluded that "...individuals are not only differentiated by the relative position of their teeth but also by their arch shape. In conclusion, it appears that the incisal surfaces of the anterior dentition are in fact unique" (Kieser et al., 2007). They also noted that their study only looked at the anterior six upper and lower teeth of a small sample of convenience and that although it supported the notion of individuality of the human anterior dentition and the use of the product rule, it specifically did not address whether the teeth could transfer their unique features to a bitten substrate. Confirmed admissions of guilt by suspected biters, concurrent and corroborative DNA evidence, witnessed biting, and other means of authenticating the sources of bitemarks have served to validate both current and previously completed bitemark analyses and comparisons. However, because of the complex dynamics of biting and the subsequent multifactorial processes that occur in human tissue reactions to injury, it is highly unlikely that there will ever be a "gold standard" bitemark observed in "nature." As a logical extension, unless the recipient of the bite survives their assault and can demonstrate the exact spatial position of the bitten area of their anatomy at the moment of the bite, the examiner will likely not know the exact circumstances surrounding the event. Therefore, documenting the bitemark evidence will, in all likelihood, result in capturing images of the bitemark in a different spatial position from that in which the bite actually occurred.

While there will likely be ongoing controversy related to bitemarks, bitemark analysis, and bitemark comparison, future controversy can be minimized if odontologists make comparisons and reach conclusions only in cases in which the quality of the evidence is high, the pool of possible biters is small, and the bitemark patterns demonstrate sufficient distinctive characteristics. Those bitemark cases can then be analyzed, the dentitions compared, and odontologists can reach reliable conclusions that include or exclude the suspected biters. The linking conclusions derived from these analyses and comparisons must be conservative and remain conservative until additional evidence-based information is developed.

In all of forensic science, momentum is appropriately building in the study and research of an issue long known to have potential effect on all science professionals; their methods, conclusions, and opinions are influenced by subjectivity and bias. Drs. Itiel Dror, a cognitive psychologist, and Greg Hampikian, a forensic biologist, reported on their investigations of cognitive bias within the forensic sciences (Dror and Hampikian, 2011). This research offers insight on the heretofore unexplainable differences in conclusions and opinions between otherwise equally experienced forensic odontologists who utilize similar bitemark analysis methodology, yet reach diametrically opposite conclusions. While this research is interesting and informative, further research is necessary. What is clear is that forensic odontologists must make concerted efforts to reduce subjectivity, bias, and observer effects in their bitemark evidence examinations.

The most recent study of DNA exonerations related to wrongful convictions, published in the summer of 2011, looked at the primary causes that led to the convictions (Hampikian et al., 2011). In 146 cases, faulty forensic evidence was one of the factors leading to wrongful convictions. In five of those cases, wrongful convictions were directly attributable, at least partially, to erroneous bitemark analyses. In four of the five cases, the expert's testimony was deemed improper, with those experts claiming a definite or near-certain match to the defendant (Page et al., 2012). How could this occur? Preliminary scientific research into the areas of the uniqueness of the human dentition; the inability of skin as an impression media to accurately and reliably record tooth data; and investigator bias do not seem to reliably answer all of the questions. These well-known and sobering case reversals have certainly reshaped some forensic odontologists' attitudes and consequently their methodologies for bitemark analysis.

Clues to possible reasons may lie in the results seen in the controversial ABFO Bitemark Workshop #4 and in the later bitemark workshops sponsored by the ABFO. The latter permits and encourages non–board-certified odontologists' participation, allowing the participants to gain bitemark case experience and the possibility of case credit toward applying for board certification. The published results regarding ABFO Bitemark Workshop # 4 offer insight (Arheart and Pretty, 2001). Thirty-two ABFO Diplomates participated in an exercise involving bitemark analysis and comparison in four cases. The teeth exemplars of the same seven persons were used as potential biters for all four cases. One case was a bite in cheese, and the other three came from ABFO Diplomates' casework selected by the workshop leader. This was not a proficiency test as a former ABFO Diplomate has repeatedly and incorrectly reported. The authorized publishers reported that "the results of the present survey indicate that bitemark examination is an accurate forensic technique, at least with cases such as used in this study" (Arheart and Pretty, 2001). Looking at the results of the comparisons in Bitemark Workshop #4 gives some insight into the question of differences of opinion between odontologists who look at the same materials. Analyzing the distribution of scores in the exercise reveals that of the 32 participants 5 made perfect scores of 1.0% or 100% and 4 scored 0.99% or 99%. 16 (half of the participants) scored 0.92 (92%) or better. The remaining 16 did not do as well, some badly indeed. This indicates that some experienced forensic odontologists can very accurately analyze bitemarks and very accurately compare them to suspected biters… *and some cannot.* The results of the later bitemark workshops show that this trend continues for less-experienced forensic dentists as well. Some noncertified forensic dentists skillfully analyzed and compared and reached appropriate conclusions in the bitemark cases and… *some did not.* None of the workshops were appropriately designed proficiency tests. However, the similar results may mean that not all dentists are able to perform bitemark analysis. This may also mean that the existing methods of vetting forensic odontologists in bitemark analysis are not sufficient.

Partly, in response to these issues, effective in 2012, the ABFO increased the requirements in bitemark analysis for application for board certification from two to seven cases. The authors of this chapter agree that the ABFO must continue the course of more rigorous testing and vetting of applicants and similar oversight of the bitemark analysis activities of its board-certified members. Among the changes needed are mandated requirements for seeking second opinions, true proficiency testing in bitemark analysis, and comparison with mandatory remedial education and retesting for those not passing the proficiency tests. New Diplomates bitemark analysis activities should be monitored until continuing proficiency is demonstrated.

The ABFO should also create a new standard stating that "A conclusion of 'The Biter' with reasonable dental, medical, or scientific certainty, based on pattern analysis alone for bitemark cases with open populations of suspected biters cannot be scientifically supported."

9.17 Case Opinion

The forensic odontologist's conclusions must be conveyed to the appropriate authorities and ultimately to attorneys, juries, and judges in a manner that is understandable to non-dentists. Perhaps, more importantly, what is expressed must be consistent across the discipline by the practitioners of forensic odontology. This consistency should begin with the specific terminology used by forensic odontologists and extend to uniformity among them in their expert opinions about analysis conclusions.

The ABFO has endeavored to remove subjectivity from their terminology relative to report writing in general, with emphasis on stating opinions more specifically. Forensic odontologists must continue on this path of consistency as bitemark analysis would greatly suffer from an attitude of "we always did it this way before." In cases involving bitemark analysis cases overturned based on DNA evidence, what was "done before" has proven to be insufficient and lives have been harmed. There has been an appropriate paradigm shift in odontologists' approach to bitemark comparisons. Refer to the ABFO website at www.abfo.org for more detailed information related to bitemark analysis terminology, and Standards and Guidelines for the methodology of bitemark analysis, and report writing guidelines related to bitemark opinions.

The current controversies that involve the pattern analysis specialties within forensic sciences have reinforced the need for increased and continuous research in the arenas targeted by the NAS report. The report specified, "More research is needed to confirm the fundamental basis for the science of bite mark comparison." The report was directly referring to research into the uniqueness of human dentition; the ability of that dentition to transfer unique characteristics to the skin; and distortion issues within the skin. These are and should be the subjects of ongoing research. It is imperative that these research endeavors be encouraged, supported, and funded. The outcomes can and should advance the scientific practice of forensic odontology related to bitemarks, bitemark analysis, and bitemark and suspected biter comparisons.

Addendum: ABFO Guidelines and Standards*

ABFO Guidelines for Investigative and Final Bitemark Reports

The following ABFO Bitemark Report Writing Guidelines propose a format for written bitemark case reports. These guidelines are suggestions for the form and content of the report. Diplomates may be asked to provide preliminary or investigative reports. Those preliminary reports may follow the same general guidelines without being conclusive in nature.

Reports may be structured into the following sections:

Introduction

This section provides the background information, the "who, what, when, where, and why" data related to the case.

* *Source:* www.abfo.org *ABFO Diplomates Reference Manual*

Inventory of Evidence Received

This section lists all evidence received by the Forensic Odontologist and details the source of the evidence.

Inventory of Evidence Collected

This section lists the nature, source, and authority for evidence collected by the Forensic Odontologist.

Opinion Regarding the Nature of the Patterned Injury or Injuries

This section states the author's opinion as to whether the patterned injuries in question are bitemarks, using ABFO terminology. Only one comparative term is used for each opinion in this part of the report.

Methods of Analysis

This section describes the analytic methods used for the patterned injuries determined to be bitemarks.

Results of Analyses

This section describes the results of the comparisons and analyses.

Opinion

This section states the author's opinion of the relationship between one or more bitemarks and a suspected biter or biters using ABFO Bitemark Terminology. Only one comparative term is used for each opinion in this part of the report.

Disclaimer

Disclaimer statements may be included to convey that the opinion or opinions are based upon the evidence reviewed through the date of the report. The author may reserve the right to file-amended reports, should additional evidence become available.

ABFO Bitemark Analysis Guidelines

Description of Bitemark

The odontologist should record and describe the following:

1. Identification Data (case number, agency, name of examiner(s), etc.)
2. Location of Bitemark
   a. Anatomical location or object bitten
   b. Surface contour: (e.g., flat, curved, or irregular)
   c. Tissue characteristics

3. Shape, color, and size
4. Type of injury (e.g., abrasion, contusion, and avulsion)
5. Other information as indicated (e.g., 3-D characteristics, unusual conditions, derived from excised tissue, and transillumination).

Methods of Comparing Exemplars to Bitemarks*

1. Types of overlays
   a. Computer-generated
   b. Tracing from dental casts
   c. Radiographs created from radiopaque material applied to the wax bite.
   d. Images of casts printed on transparency film.
2. Test bites (wax, styrofoam, clay, skin, etc.)
3. Comparison techniques
   a. Exemplars of the dentition are compared to corresponding-sized photos of the bite pattern.
   b. Dental casts to life-sized photographs, casts of the bite patterns, reproductions of the pattern when in inanimate objects, or resected tissue.
4. Other methods employed for analysis
   a. Transillumination of tissue
   b. Computer enhancement and/or digitization of mark and/or teeth
   c. Stereomicroscopy and/or macroscopy
   d. Scanning electron microscopy
   e. Video superimposition
   f. Histology
   g. Metric studies

ABFO Bitemark Terminology Guidelines

Component Injuries Seen in Bitemarks

Abrasions (scrapes), contusions (bruises), lacerations (tears), ecchymosis, petechiae, avulsion, indentations (depressions), erythema (redness), and punctures might be seen in bitemarks. Their meaning and strict definitions are found in medical dictionaries and forensic medical texts and should not be altered. An incision is a cut made by a sharp instrument, and, although mentioned in the bitemark literature, it is not an appropriate term to describe the lacerations made by incisors.

A Characteristic

A *characteristic*, as applied to a bitemark, is a distinguishing feature, trait, or pattern within the mark. Characteristics are two types: *class characteristics* and *individual characteristics*.

* *Source:* www.abfo.org *ABFO Diplomates Reference Manual*

Class characteristic: A feature, trait, or pattern that distinguishes a bitemark from other patterned injuries. For example, the finding of four approximating linear or rectangular contusions is a class characteristic of human incisors. Their dimensions vary in size depending upon what inflicted the injury: maxillary or mandibular teeth; and, whether primary or permanent teeth. Moreover, the overall size of the injury will vary depending on the contributor's arch dimension. Thus, a bitemark *class characteristic* identifies the group from which it originates: human, animal, fish, or other species.

Individual characteristic: A feature, trait, or pattern that represents an individual variation rather than an expected finding within a defined group. There are two types.

Arch characteristic: A pattern that represents tooth arrangement within a bitemark. For example, a combination of rotated teeth, buccal or lingual version, mesiodistal drifting, and horizontal alignment contributes to differentiation between individuals. The number, specificity, and accurate reproduction of these arch characteristics contribute to the overall assessment in determining the degree of confidence that a particular suspect made the bitemark (e.g., rotation, buccal or lingual version, mesial or distal drifting, horizontal alignment).

Dental characteristic: A feature or trait within a bitemark that represents an individual tooth variation. The number, specificity, and accurate reproduction of these dental characteristics in combination with the *arch characteristics* contribute to the overall assessment in determining the degree of confidence that a particular suspect made the bitemark (e.g., unusual wear pattern, notching, angulations, fracture).

Distinctive: This term is variably defined as either rare or unusual.

- Variation from normal, unusual, infrequent
- Not one of a kind but serves to differentiate from most others
- Highly specific, individualized
- Lesser degree of specificity than unique

Bitemark Definitions

Bitemark

- A physical alteration in a medium caused by the contact of teeth
- A representative pattern left in an object or tissue by the dental structures of an animal or human

Describing the Bitemark

A circular or oval-patterned injury consisting of two opposing (facing) symmetrical, U-shaped arches separated at their bases by open spaces. Following the periphery of the arches are a series of individual abrasions, contusions, and/or lacerations reflecting the size, shape, arrangement, and distribution of the class characteristics of the contacting surfaces of the human dentition.

Variations

1. Additional features
   a. Central ecchymosis (central contusion)
   b. Linear abrasions, contusions, or striations
   c. Double bite—(bite within a bite)
   d. Weave patterns of interposed clothing
   e. Peripheral ecchymosis
2. Partial bitemarks
3. Indistinct/faded patterned injury (e.g., fused or closed arches, solid ring pattern)
4. Multiple bites
5. Avulsive bites

Terms Indicating Degree Of Confidence That an Injury Is a Bitemark

Bitemark—Teeth created the pattern; other possibilities were considered and excluded.

- *Criteria*: Pattern conclusively illustrates (a) classic features, (b) all the characteristics, or (c) typical class characteristics of dental arches and human teeth in proper arrangement so that it is recognizable as an impression of the human dentition.

Suggestive—The pattern is suggestive of a bitemark, but there is insufficient evidence to reach a definitive conclusion at this time.

- *Criteria:* General shape and size are present but distinctive features such as tooth marks are missing, incomplete, or distorted or a few marks resembling tooth marks are present but the arch configuration is missing.

Not a bitemark—Teeth did not create the pattern.

Descriptions and Terms Used to Relate a Suspected Biter to a Bitemark*

All opinions stated to a reasonable degree of dental certainty

The biter
The probable biter
Not excluded as the biter
Excluded as the biter
Inconclusive

* *Source:* ABFO Diplomates Reference Manual, 2012. www.abfo.org

ABFO Standards for "Bitemark Terminology"

The following list of Bitemark Terminology Standards has been accepted by the American Board of Forensic Odontology.

1. Terms assuring unconditional identification of a perpetrator, or without doubt, are not sanctioned as a final conclusion.
2. Terms used in a different manner from the recommended guidelines should be explained in the body of a report or in testimony.
3. All boarded forensic odontologists are responsible for being familiar with the standards set forth in this document.

ABFO Bitemark Case Review Policy

The Ad Hoc 2nd Opinion Committee proposed that bitemark reports undergo a case review by a second ABFO Diplomate. The reviewer will not provide a second opinion (but may do so if he/she wishes) but will provide a technical review of the analysis that was done. This voluntary review will determine if the analysis and report adhered to the standards, guidelines, methodology, and terminology of bitemark investigation as required by the ABFO.

This policy was approved as a voluntary policy by the Board of Directors and is in effect for one year 2/21/2011–2/21/2012, after which time it will be reviewed to determine if it should become a permanent guideline.

References

American Board of Forensic Odontology *Diplomates Reference Manual,* 2012.

Arheart, K. L. and I. A. Pretty. 2001. Results of the 4th ABFO bitemark workshop—1999. *Journal of Forensic Sciences* 124(2–3):104–111.

Averill, D. *Manual of Forensic Odontology*, 2nd edn. 1991. Colorado Springs, CO: American Society of Forensic Odontology.

Barsley, R. E., T. J. David, and H. M. Pitluck. 2010. Jurisprudence and legal issues. In *Forensic Dentistry*, 2nd edn. Senn, D. R. and P. G. Stimson (eds.) pp. 379–394. Boca Raton, FL: CRC Press.

Bernitz, H., W. F. P. Van Heerden, T. Solheim, and J. H. Owen. 2006. A technique to capture, analyze, and quantify anterior teeth rotations for application in court cases involving tooth marks. *Journal of Forensic Sciences* 51:624–629.

Blackwell, S. A., R. V. Taylor, I. Gordon et al. 2007. 3-D imaging and quantitative comparison of human dentition and simulated bite marks. *International Journal of Legal Medicine* 121:9–17.

Brandeis, L. D. and Harry Houdini Collection (Library of Congress). 1914. *Other People's Money: And How the Bankers Use It*. New York: Frederick A. Stokes Co.

Bush, M., P. Bush, and H. Sheets. 2011. Statistical evidence for the similarity of the human dentition. *Journal of Forensic Sciences* 56(1):118–123.

Bush, M. A., R. G. Miller, P. J. Bush, and B. J. Dorion. 2009. Biomechanical factors in human dermal bitemarks in a cadaver model. *Journal of Forensic Sciences* 54(1):167–176.

Bush, M. A., K. Thorsrud, R. G. Miller, R. B. J. Dorion, and P. J. Bush. 2010b. The response of skin to applied stress: Investigation of bitemark distortion in a cadaver model. *Journal of Forensic Sciences* 55:71–75.

Dailey, J. C. 1991. A practical technique for the fabrication of transparent bite mark overlays. *Journal of Forensic Sciences* 36:565–570.

Dailey, J. C. 2002. The topographic mapping of teeth for overlay production in bite mark analysis. *Proceedings of the American Academy of Forensic Sciences*, pp. 158–159. Denver, CO: Publication Printers, Corp.

Dailey, J. C. 2011. Methods of comparison, In *Bitemark Evidence: A Color Atlas and Text*, Dorion, R. B.J. (ed.) pp. 478–480. Boca Raton, FL: CRC Press.

David, T. J. and M. N. Sobel. 1994. Recapturing a five month old bite mark by means of reflective ultraviolet photography. *Journal of Forensic Science*, 36(6):1560–1567.

Dorion, R. B. 1987. Transillumination in bite mark evidence. *Journal of Forensic Science* 32(3):690–697.

Dorion, R. B. J. 2011. *Bitemark Evidence: A Color Atlas and Text*, 2nd edn. Boca Raton, FL: CRC Press.

Dror, I. E. and G. Hampikian. 2011. Subjectivity and bias in forensic DNA mixture interpretation. *Science and Justice* 51(2011):204–208.

Ebert, L. C., M. J. Thali, and S. Ross. 2011. Getting in touch—3D printing in forensic imaging. *Forensic Science International* 211:1–3.

Farrell, L., R. Rawson, and R. Steffens. 1987. Computerized axial tomography as aid in bite mark analysis: A case report. *Journal of Forensic Sciences* 32(1): 266–272.

Hampikian, G., E. West, and O. Akselrod. 2011. The genetics of innocence: Analysis of 194 U.S. DNA exonerations. *Annual Review of Genomics and Human Genetics* 12:97–120.

Herschaft, E. E. et al. 2006. *Manual of Forensic Odontology*, 4th edn. Albany, NY: Impress Printing and Graphics.

Johansen, R. and C. M. Bowers. 2000. *Digital Analysis of Bite Mark Evidence Using Adobe Photoshop Forensic Imaging Services*. pp. 17–44, Santa Barbara, CA: Forensic Imaging Services.

Kieser, J. A., V. Bernal, J. N. Waddell, and S. Raju. 2007. The uniqueness of the human anterior dentition: A geometric morphometric analysis. *Journal of Forensic Sciences* 52:671–677.

Kodak publication M-27. 1972. *Ultraviolet and Fluorescence Photography*. p. 9, Rochester, NY: Eastman Kodak Co.

Kodak publication N-1. 1973. *Medical Infrared Photography*, pp. 26–27, Rochester, NY: Eastman Kodak Co.

Lasser, A. J., J. W. Alan, and G. M. Berman. 2009. Three-dimensional comparative analysis of bitemarks. *Journal of Forensic Sciences* 54:658–651.

Maloth, S. and K. S. Ganapathy (2011). Comparison between five commonly used two-dimensional methods of human bite mark overlay production from the dental study casts. *Indian Journal of Dental Research* 22(3):493.

Martin-de las Heras, S., A. Valenzuela, C. Ogayar. et al. 2005. Computer-based production of comparison overlays from 3D-scanned dental casts for bite mark analysis. *Journal of Forensic Sciences* 52:151–156.

Metcalf, R. D. 2008. Yet another method for marking incisal edges of teeth for bitemark analysis. *Journal of Forensic Sciences* 53:426–429.

Miller, R. G., P. J. Bush, R. B. J. Dorion, and M. A. Bush. 2009. Uniqueness of the dentition as impressed in human skin: A cadaver model. *Journal of Forensic Sciences* 54:909–914.

National Academy of Sciences. 2009. *Strengthening Forensic Sciences in the United States: A Path Forward*. Washington, DC: The National Academies Press.

Page, M., J. Taylor, and M. Belkin. 2012. Context effects and observer bias-implications for forensic odontology. *Journal of Forensic Sciences* 57:108–112.

Pitluck, H. M. and R. E. Barsley. 2010. *Appendix to; Forensic Dentistry*, 2nd edn. Senn, D. R. and P. G. Stimpson (eds.) Boca Raton, FL: CRC Press.

Pretty, I. H. and M. D. Turnbull. 2001. Lack of uniqueness between two bite mark suspects. *Journal of Forensic Sciences* 46:1487–1491.

Rawson, R. D. 1990. Production of bite mark overlays from CAT scans and model positioning apparatus. *Proceedings of the American Academy of Forensic Sciences*, p. 112. Denver, CO: Publication Printers, Corp.

Rawson, R. D., R. K. Ommen, G. Kinard, J. Johnson, and A. Yfantis. 1984. Statistical evidence for the individuality of the human dentition. *Journal of Forensic Sciences* 43:245–253.
Senn, D. R. 2011. History of bitemark evidence. In *Bitemark Evidence: A Color Atlas and Text*, Dorion, R. B.J. (ed.) pp. 3–22. Boca Raton, FL: CRC Press.
Senn, D. R. and P. G. Souviron. 2010. Bitemarks. In *Forensic Dentistry*, 2nd edn. Senn, D. R. and P. G. Stimson (eds.) Boca Raton, FL: CRC Press.
Senn, D., P. Stimson (eds.) 2010. *Forensic Dentistry*, 2nd edn. Boca Raton, FL: CRC Press.
Siderits, R., J. Birkenstamm, F. Khani, E. Sadamin, J. Godyn. 2010. Three-dimensional laser scanning of "Crime Scene Gum" as a forensic method demonstrating the creation of virtual tooth surface contour and web-based rapid model fabrication. *Forensic Science Communications* 12:1–6.
Sognnaes, R. F., R. D. Rawson, B. M. Gratt, N. B. 1982. Nguyen. Computer comparison of bitemark patterns in identical twins. *Journal of the American Dental Association* 105:449–451.
Stokes, G. G. 1853. On the change of refrangibility of light. *Philosophical Transactions of the Royal Society of London* 143:385–396.
Sweet, D. and C. M. Bowers. 1998. Accuracy of bite mark overlays: A comparison of five common methods to produce exemplars from a suspect's dentition. *Journal of Forensic Sciences* 43(2):362–367.
Sweet, D., M. Lorente, J. A. Lorente, A. Valenzuela, E. Villanueva. (1997). An improved method to recover saliva from human skin: The double swab technique. *Journal of Forensic Sciences* 42(2):320–322.
Sweet, D., M. Parhar, R. E. Wood. 1998. Computer-based production of bite mark comparison Overlays. *Journal of Forensic Sciences* 43(5):1050–1055.
Wright, F. D. 1998. Photography in bite mark and patterned injury documentation—Part 2: A case study. *Journal of Forensic Sciences* 43(4):881–887.

Animal Bitemarks

10

KENNETH F. COHRN

Contents

10.1 Introduction 326
10.2 Insects 327
10.3 Aquatic Animals (Sharks, Crabs, Shrimp, Fish, Crawfish, Turtles) 327
10.3.1 Sharks 327
10.4 Reptiles (Alligators, Snakes) 329
10.4.1 Alligators 329
10.4.2 Snakes 331
10.5 Mammals 333
10.5.1 Carnivores 333
10.6 Canine Bite Data 334
10.6.1 Dog Bite Statistics 334
10.6.2 Dog Bite and Bitemark Liability 335
10.6.3 Dog Bite Injuries 335
10.6.4 Dog Bitemark Hierarchy 336
10.6.5 Dog Bite-Related Fatalities 336
10.7 Comparative Dental Anatomy 336
10.7.1 Canine Dentitions (Dogs) 336
10.7.2 Feline Dentition (Cats) 339
10.7.3 Ursine Dentitions (Bears) 340
10.7.4 Rodent Dentition (Rats) 341
10.8 Data Collection in Animal Bitemark Cases 342
10.9 Comparison Techniques 345
10.10 Abuse 345
10.11 Case Examples 346
10.11.1 Case Example: Human or Animal Attack? 346
10.11.2 Case Example: Guilty or Not? 348
10.11.3 Case Example: Egregious Mistakes 351
10.11.4 Case Example: High-Profile Dog Fighting Case 352
10.11.5 Other Case Examples 352
10.12 Summary 352
10.13 Lessons Learned and Recommendations for Animal Casework 353
Acknowledgments 353
References 353

10.1 Introduction

Human and animal interaction for thousands of years coupled with domestication of certain species has led to increased productivity, selective social benefit, and most would agree the betterment of the human condition. Yet that cooptation has led to negative consequences as well, including both provoked and accidental physical confrontation resulting in potential injury, death, and legal ramifications. The sheer numbers of bites alone are impressive with 4.7 million dog bites, 400,000 cat bites, 45,000 snake bites, and 250,000 human bites annually in the United States (Healthy Children.org, 2012).

As the human–animal interface expands in both rural and urban populations in conjunction with reduced natural habitats, random confrontations continue to escalate.

Consider the following examples. During one week in May 2006, three women were killed in separate incidents involving alligators in Florida. By stark contrast, there were only 17 confirmed fatal alligator attacks in the entire United States during the previous 58 years.

In January 2004, a man was attacked, killed, and partially consumed by a cougar while mountain biking at Whiting Ranch Wilderness Park in southern Orange County, California.

A 250-pound black bear attacked a 61 year old female walking her dog at a country club in 2011. Unfortunately, after 11 surgeries, she died from massive brain hemorrhage.

A couple in Central Florida in 2011 was convicted of manslaughter, third degree murder, and child neglect after their 8-foot, 6-inch malnourished albino Burmese python (Figure 10.1) escaped from its aquarium, asphyxiated their 2 year old toddler in her crib,

Figure 10.1 Burmese python.

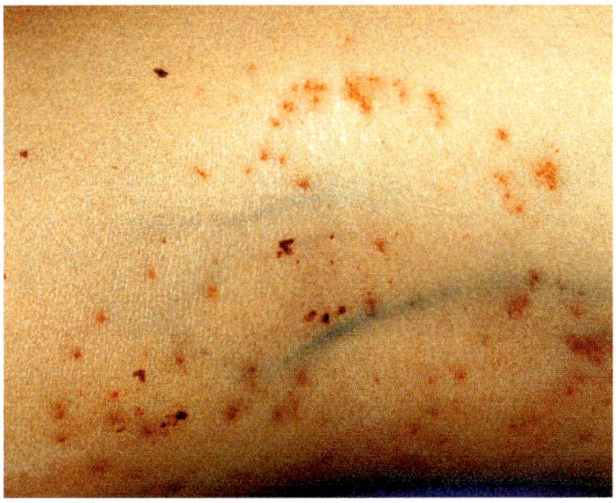

Figure 10.2 Ant bites.

and tried to eat her. Clearly, this tragic event was unintentional and totally avoidable. Yet, it serves to illustrate the poor choices people can make when interacting with animals.

Urban settings are not risk free. Consider the 3 month old Westwego, Louisiana, girl found dead in her crib in 2009 covered with rat bites. The coroner determined the cause of death to be exsanguination from the bites. Or the case of the 6 week old child whose toes were partially chewed off by rats leading to three adults being charged with child endangerment.

10.2 Insects

Necrophagous insects are often found associated with cadavers during the decomposition process. The symbiotic association of these flesh-eating insects and cadavers is important in medicolegal investigations to establish, among other things, a timeline for death. Insect bites can present a variety of patterns from random to mimicking carnivore bitemarks or even criminal activity. Predatory insects include primarily beetles, ants, wasps, and cockroaches. Figure 10.2 shows bitemarks from scavenging ants in the general configuration of a human bitemark. Case history and in particular scene photographs will help to distinguish insect bites from other sources of patterned injuries.

10.3 Aquatic Animals (Sharks, Crabs, Shrimp, Fish, Crawfish, Turtles)

Many fresh and salt water animals are voracious necrophagous scavengers and predators. While serving a necessary biologic scavenging function, the discovery of a partially consumed human corpse can lead to erroneous hypotheses, including torture, sharp force injury, or other nonaccidental injuries. Care should be taken to distinguish normal animal predation behavior from criminal intent.

10.3.1 Sharks

Shark attacks, although rare, are becoming more common. Recent data from the University of Florida indicate a total of 439 shark attacks with 11 fatalities and 428 nonfatal injuries between 2000 and 2010 (Florida Museum of Natural History, 2012). In 2011, Dr. George Burgess, Ichthyologist and Director of International Shark Attack File at the University of Florida, indicated that the rate of shark attacks in the United States decreased but worldwide shark fatalities are at a two decade high doubling that of 2010. Florida rates first with the most fatalities in the United States with 11 of the 29 attacks. Attacks occur on, in, under, and entering/exiting the water. The first category of "on" the surface includes surfing (Figure 10.3) and boarding followed by "in" the water categories of swimming and bathing, account for the majority of the attacks. In August 2000, a forensic odontologist consulted on a shark-bite fatality case in South Florida. The victim was taking his daily swim in 6 feet of water less than 10 feet from the dock behind his house when he was attacked and killed by an 8-foot, 400-pound shark. He died almost immediately with massive chest wounds (Figure 10.4).

Figure 10.3 Shark bite in surfboard.

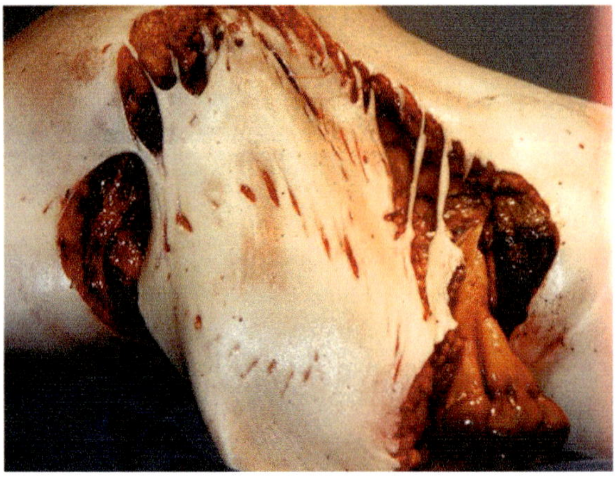

Figure 10.4 Fatal shark bite.

10.4 Reptiles (Alligators, Snakes)

10.4.1 Alligators

Since 1948, there have been 568 reports filed with the Florida Fish and Wildlife Conservation Commission of alligator attacks on humans in Florida and at least 17 deaths (FWC, 2010). The frequency of attacks is increasing as humans encroach on alligator habitats as illustrated by the alligator in the backyard of a housing subdivision in Florida (Figure 10.5). There were nine deaths during the three decades from the 1970s through the 1990s and 12 deaths between 2001 and 2007 including an unprecedented three deaths during a single week in May 2006 alone.

The primitive alligator dentition (Figure 10.6) consists of up to 80 teeth with 5 premaxillary and 13–15 maxillary teeth per quadrant and 19–20 mandibular teeth per quadrant. Alligator teeth function to grasp and hold. Because of the violent nature of alligator attacks, teeth often break but are replaced. Alligator teeth are hollow so replacement teeth can grow inside the existing teeth. An alligator may have several thousand teeth in its lifetime resulting in extensive individual variation in the dentition as seen in Figure 10.7. Figure 10.8 illustrates a relatively minor alligator bitemark on the thigh of a young female. The bite force of a 12 ft alligator has been measured at over 2100 psi. That is among the highest bite forces in the animal world; more than twice that of a lion and six times that of a dusky shark (Erickson et al., 2003). Aside from the physical damage from the bite, there is a high risk of death from bacterial infection and sepsis.

There are two documented alligator cases in Florida involving the death of an individual where the alligator was identified by class and individual bitemark characteristics.

Figure 10.5 Alligator in Florida subdivision.

Figure 10.6 Alligator jaws and teeth.

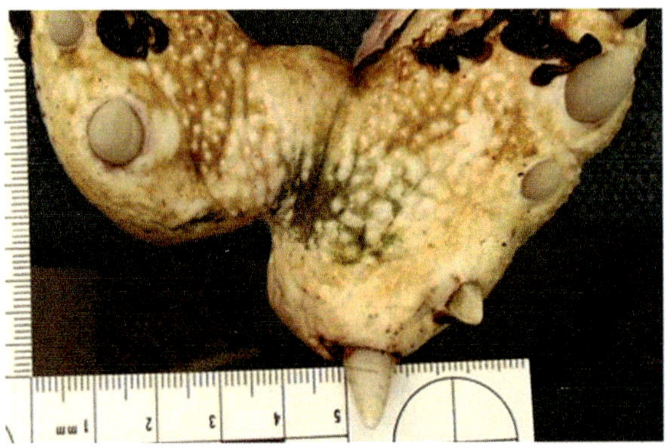

Figure 10.7 Variation of alligator dentition.

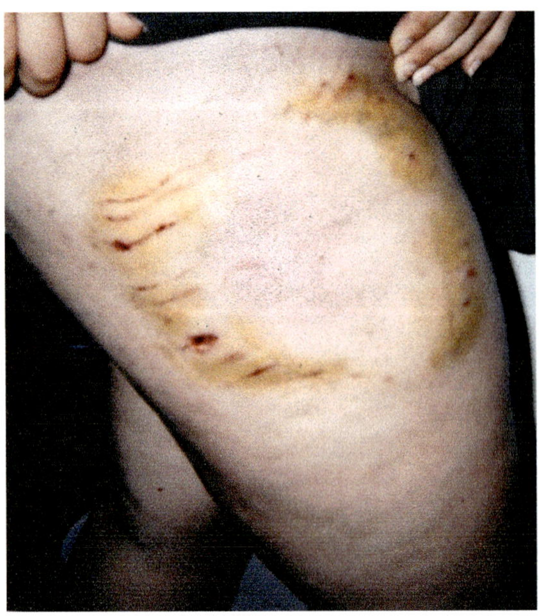

Figure 10.8 "Minor" alligator bite on thigh.

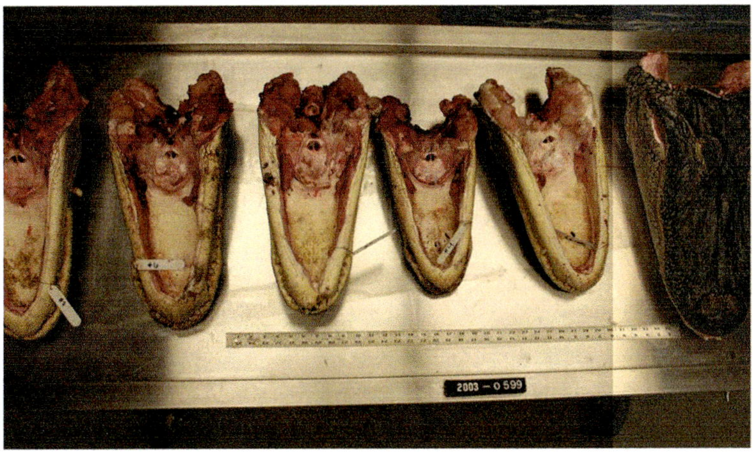

Figure 10.9 Alligator bitemark suspect lineup.

The first case involved a 12-year-old boy playing with friends in a river in Central Florida when he was attacked by a 10-foot long alligator and killed. He suffered from blunt and sharp force trauma, internal injuries, and drowning. Sensational animal attacks of this type draw national media attention, often with a public outcry for the capture and elimination of the "killer" animal. Alligators are highly territorial. Thus, the population is limited allowing capture and identification of the correct animal easier. An overnight hunt by game trappers for resident alligators led to the capture of 11 suspects. The animals were transported to the Medical Examiner's office where the animal biologist performed a necropsy on seven of the animals (Figure 10.9). Using direct comparison of the dentition to the bitemarks, the forensic odontologist was able to attribute the likelihood of the attack to one specific alligator.

Another case in Florida involved one of a series of three deaths by alligators in one week. A young woman snorkeling with family members at the Juniper Wayside Park in the Ocala National Forest accidentally bumped into an alligator. She was attacked and drowned by an 11-foot, 4-inch animal as witnessed by a relative who tried desperately to save her. She suffered blunt force injuries to the head, neck, and upper torso with the cause of death drowning. Two alligators of distinctly different size were known to occupy the territory near the scene. The offending animal had been injured during the attempt to free the victim from the alligator's jaws. Unlike the previous case, direct comparison to the alligator was not possible. Models of the dentition were taken in Alginate impression material with acetate overlays made by the standard Photoshop bitemark analysis technique. Images of the injuries were made life-sized for comparison. The wounds were relatively superficial, and a probable sequence of the bites was determined. The result was the likely identification of the alligator likely responsible for the attack allowing the river to be reopened for public use. Many animal attacks are unfortunate random accidental encounters that result in the death of both people and animals.

10.4.2 Snakes

Snakes, phylogenetic descendants of lizards, evolved most likely during the Cretaceous Period. They have been used for food and as pets and been worshipped, revered, feared, and been written about for millennia. A snake appears in the text of the Bible in Genesis

Figure 10.10 Cleopatra with the Asp. (Courtesy of Guido Reni, c. 1640.)

tempting Adam and Eve with the forbidden fruit and later as Satan in the *Book of Revelation*. An Asp may have been used as a means to commit suicide by Cleopatra IV in 30 BC as depicted by the Baroque painter Guido Reni, 1575–1642 (Figure 10.10). Mystical, medicinal, and even biologic weaponized uses of snake venom have existed since antiquity. Hercules, immortalized in mythology by killing the multiheaded snake Hydra, is portrayed as using "envenomized arrows" against foe. This mythological accounting is thought to represent actual battles occurring during Bronze Age Greece 1300–1600 BCE. During the Mithridatic Wars (90–63 BC), King Mithridates of Pontus, a master toxicologist, used the healing property of Viper venom to coagulate several grave arrow wounds incurred during battle. An extremely powerful leader and brutal warrior, Mithridates experimented with the concept of modern vaccinations by ingesting increasing amounts of various poisons in order to build up immunity to various toxins (Mayor, 2009). Currently, medical research has shown the Southern Copperhead snake venom to exhibit antitumor properties. Venomous snake bites occur at a rate of 8000 per year in the United States, a fairly rare event. The mortality rate is about 0.2% of the total bites (Texas Department of State, 2011) or about 5–7 U.S. fatalities per year (Johnson, 2012). A list of dangerously venomous snakes in North America includes the Copperhead, Water Moccasin, Rattlesnake, and Coral snake. However, illegally imported exotic breeds such as the python have made their way into the wild in the United States and present a threat. Giant pythons are nonvenomous and are among the largest snakes in the world reaching up to 26 ft long. "Their size and power makes them one of the top predators in Florida's Everglades National Park, taking on even the alligators, and posing a threat to many of the indigenous and endangered species" (PBS, 2010). Examples of nonlethal snake bites are seen in the python bites shown in Figure 10.11. Note the multiple punctures that might be misinterpreted as originating from another source.

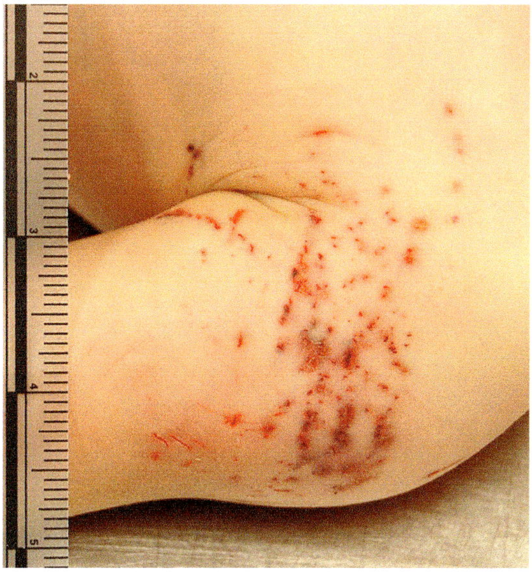

Figure 10.11 Multiple python bites.

10.5 Mammals

In general, mammalian adult quadrant dentition consists of three incisors, one canine, four premolars, and three molars represented by the formula: i(3/3)c(1/1)pm (4/4)m (3/3). However, variation exists among different species. Mammalian dentitions have adapted to serve specialized functions including grooming, social interaction, offense, and defense as well as feeding functions of crushing, shearing, and grinding. Mammalian molars have evolved as variations of the basic triangular form dependant on function (Hillson, 2005).

10.5.1 Carnivores

Carnivore teeth have adapted to the primary survival roles of hunting, catching, and killing prey. The small closely arranged incisors are comblike and pointed for grooming protective fur. The canine teeth are the most prominent teeth having the longest roots and overall length best illustrated by the tiger dentition in Figure 10.12. A bitemark made by

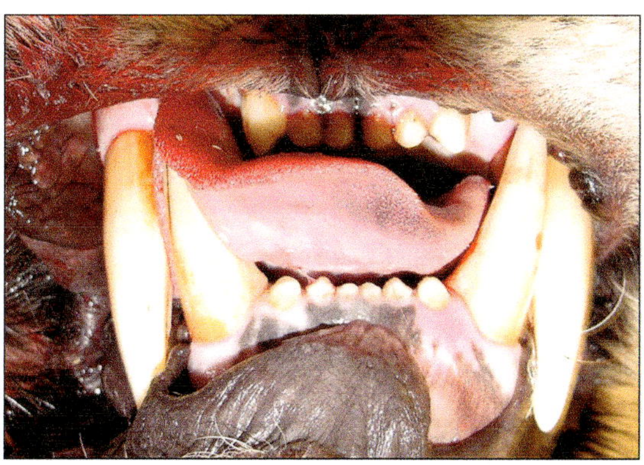

Figure 10.12 Canines and incisors of a tiger.

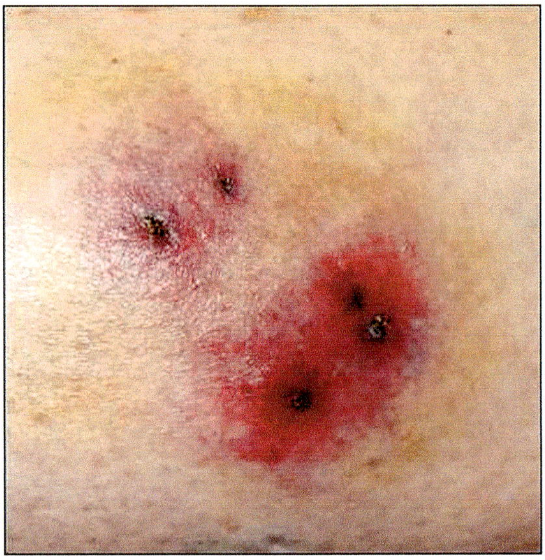

Figure 10.13 Domestic cat bitemark.

a cat, even a small feline specimen, will include deep and dramatic canine marks prone to infection (Figure 10.13). Although highly variable in size, the nonoccluding canines are effectively adapted for incising, grasping, catching, holding, and tearing. The premolars are "compressed bucco-lingually, into backward-hooking, pointed blades," which do not necessarily meet in occlusion. Their function is to catch and hold prey. Dietary needs determine carnassial premolar and molar anatomy and size; the more omnivorelike the diet, the less blade-shaped these teeth. Omnivores need teeth more conducive to crushing. For example, dogs have rather large molars for crushing, but cats being highly specialized carnivores have less robust and more pointed posterior teeth for piercing soft tissue. There is substantial variation in molar anatomy.

10.6 Canine Bite Data

10.6.1 Dog Bite Statistics

There are 78.2 million owned dogs in the United States according to the Humane Society that potentially may contribute to injuries and deaths (Humane Society, 2012). How prevalent is the problem of dog bite incidents? According to the American Veterinary Medical Association (AVMA), about 4.7 million people are bitten by dogs each year with more than 800,000 victims requiring medical attention for their injuries and the primary victims being children (AVMA, 2008). Breed specificity bite statistics are more subjective because of mixed breeds, difficulty in identifying the breed, inaccurate reporting, and prejudice. However, pit bull and pit bull mix breeds are reportedly responsible for most of the injuries and deaths (Bini et al., 2011). Data from a review of medical records of patients admitted with dog bites to a Level 1 trauma center over a 15-year period indicate that those bitten by pit bull or pit bull mixed dogs had the highest injury rate, highest risk of admission, incurred the most hospital charges, and were most at risk for death. Not unexpectedly, the number of criminal charges following dog bites has nearly doubled from 2010 to 2011

(DogsBite, 2011). Information regarding ownership, location, manner of attack, and other incident circumstances are useful during an investigation in order to locate and identify the offending individuals and animals.

10.6.2 Dog Bite and Bitemark Liability

States are adopting more stringent laws regarding leashing, ownership, "one-bite" rules, statutory liability, and awarding increased compensation. In 2011, a jury awarded $2.2 million, $100,000 for medical bills, and $2.1 million for pain and suffering to a woman attacked in her home by her neighbor's two pit bulls. Granted this award is the exception rather than the rule for an animal attack claim, but it is indicative changing public opinion and legal recourse regarding accountability for animal and owner behavior. A report from the Insurance Information Institute (III, 2012) from May 2012 indicates that the cost of the average dog bite claim paid by homeowners insurance reached $29,396 in 2012 costing homeowners $479 million or nearly one-third of all homeowners insurance liability claims dollars. One of every six dog bite injuries requires medical attention with 1 in every 14 requiring emergency care (Center for Disease Control, 2009). The number of Americans hospitalized for dog bites over the last 15 years has increased by nearly 100% (Holmquist and Elixhause, 2010). The numbers of claims in dog bite cases increased by 127.3% during the period 2003–2010. Some would argue that this trend is a public health care issue.

10.6.3 Dog Bite Injuries

The types of injuries inflicted by dogs vary. Injuries occur most commonly to the arm/hand (45%), leg/foot (26%), and head/neck (23%). The majority (65%) of injuries among children aged ≤4 years old were to the head/neck region with this percentage decreasing with age. "Children are particularly vulnerable to this type of injury because of their smaller size and their inexperience with animals" (AVMA, 2006). An article analyzing the incidence, mechanisms, and circumstances of dog bites over 10 years involving children younger than 17 years old presents some interesting metrics (Pediatrics, 2006). They noted that the incidence of dog bites was 0.5 per 1000 children between 0 and 16 years old with the highest incidence in the 1 year old group. The majority (73%) of the dogs were familiar but only about 30% were considered household members. By contrast, injuries to the extremities increased with age and accounted for 86% of injuries treated in emergency departments for persons aged ≥15 years. Injury diagnoses were described frequently as "dog bite" (26%); other diagnoses included puncture (40%), laceration (25%), contusion/abrasion/hematoma (6%), cellulitis/infection (1.5%), amputation/avulsion/crush (0.8%), and fracture/dislocation (0.4%) (CDC, 2001). Beyond soft-tissue traumatic injuries is the potential for serious infection with a 3%–18% infection rate from dog bites. Pasteurellosis is the most common bacterial infection presenting with the symptoms of pain, swelling, and reddening at the site. Other bacterial infections include Streptococcal, Staphylococcal, and the rare *Capnocytophaga septicemia* with a fatality rate of 30%. About 1% of dog bite victims require hospitalization for infection versus up to 10% for cat bites. "Often bitemark wounds are severe enough to require multiple surgeries, grafting, post-traumatic stress disorder (PTSD) treatment and damaged relationships between the animal owner, victim's family members, neighbors and the law" (Talan et al., 1999).

10.6.4 Dog Bitemark Hierarchy

It may be beneficial to classify the severity of bites in order to have a common descriptive language for forensic specialists, veterinarians, investigative, and legal experts. Cara Shannon, JD and professional certified dog trainer has developed several guides for analyzing and assessing dog bites (Shannon, 2012). She has a detailed hierarchy or index of dog to human and dog to dog bite severity. This formalized classification of dog bite injuries allows for commonality in information and understanding between various professionals. The importance of an accurate and comprehensive history of a bite attack cannot be overemphasized. Animal bitemarks can be difficult to evaluate because of frenzied activity, multiple animals, avulsions, multiple puncture wounds, and contradictory or fabricated eye-witness accounts. Collect information regarding the number of animals, number of bites, orientation of the animal relative to the victim, status of the victim and animal regarding freedom of movement or confinement, clothing, defensive/offensive positioning, the nature of the attack, the severity of the attack, and the physical condition of the victim plus any other information relevant to the event circumstances.

10.6.5 Dog Bite-Related Fatalities

From the 1980s through the 1990s, the United States averaged 17 dog-related fatalities per year. That number increased to 28 per year during the 2005–2011 time period. Examination of the victim's age distribution of dog bite-related fatalities in the United States reveals that analogous to bite mark injuries, the most vulnerable at risk age groups are the very young and the elderly. At the other end of the at-risk age categories are adults 61+ with 22% of the total number of fatalities. Two informative sources of fatal dog attacks and bite statistics are www.dogsbite.org and www.dogbitelaw.com. Review of 85 fatal cases from 2008 to 2010 reveals that approximately 89% involved dogs belonging to a family member, relative, friend, or neighbor with the youngest dog involved less than a year old. Annual data from www.dogsbite.org for 2011 show that of the 31 fatal cases "39% of the fatal attacks involved more than one dog, 65% were the family dog, 74% of all incidents occurred on the dog owners' property, and 29% resulted in criminal charges" almost double the number of cases in 2010.

Forensic odontologists are an integral part of the animal forensics investigative process. Working in conjunction with a cadre of other investigators and many agencies forensic odontologists may provide opinions involving animal forensics, human–animal interactions, criminal and civil cases, abuse, bitemarks, torture, and more.

10.7 Comparative Dental Anatomy

10.7.1 Canine Dentitions (Dogs)

Since domestication of dogs some 12,000–15,000 years ago, functional changes in the dentition have occurred. In particular, the cusp size of the carnassial teeth and the molars remained larger for crushing. In contrast to the human dentition, many individual teeth fail to meet or else overlap and protrude between adjacent teeth opposite to them.

The dental formula for dogs is: i(3/3)c(1/1)pm (4/4)m (2/3). A schematic for the canine dentition is shown in Figure 10.14 (Hillson, 2005). Given species variation, the dental

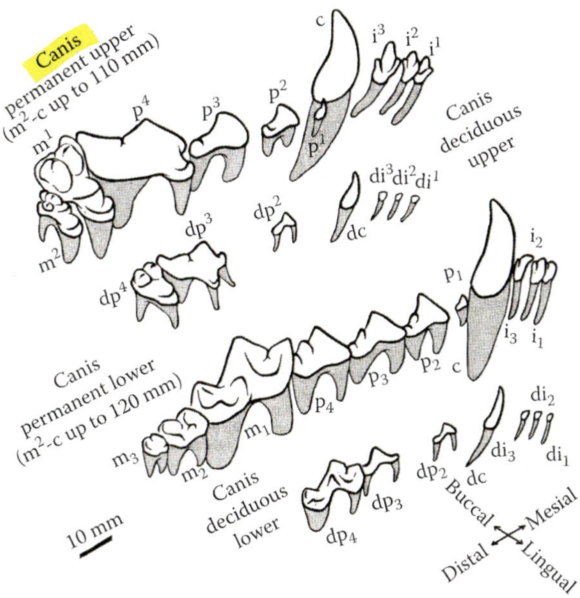

Figure 10.14 Canine dental anatomy.

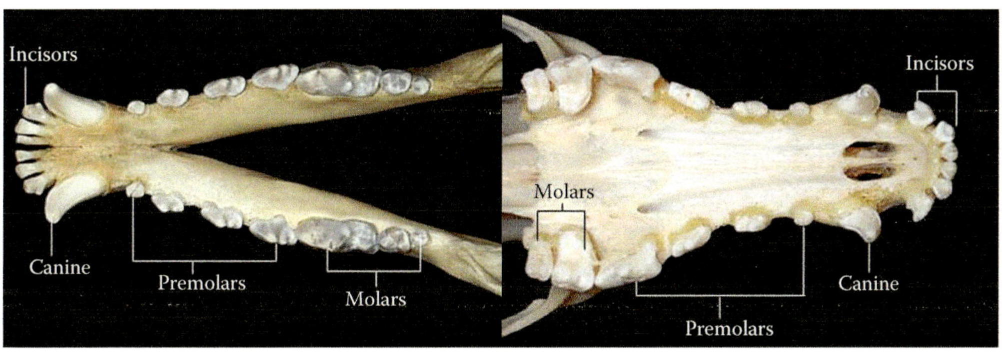

Figure 10.15 Canine (dog) teeth (lower-left and upper-right). (From Bowen, R. July 2012. http://www.vivo.colostate.edu/hbooks/pathphys/digestion/pregastric/dentalanat.html. With permission.)

arcade size is extremely variable with the intercanine distance (ICD) varying upward to 70 mm in the large breed Presa Canarios. The number of maxillary teeth in an adult dog is 20 with 22 mandibular teeth for a total of 42 (Figure 10.15). An accepted veterinary numbering system for teeth, the Modified Triadan system, was developed by M.R. Floyd in 1991 shown in Figure 10.16. Each tooth is represented by three numbers based on the quadrant and tooth number similar to the FDI numbering system for human teeth. When analyzing a dog's dentition, evaluate both the class and individual characteristics. Be sure to count the teeth since there may be supernumerary or missing teeth. In contrast to the human dentition's four incisors, dogs have six small incisors per arch. This class distinction is an important variation for distinguishing between a human and dog bitemark. Look for asymmetry of the position and shape of the individual teeth. Individual variation is a key to differentiation between multiple animal bitemarks.

The incisors have "cusps" on the incisal edges that are placed more distally on the more posterior i2s and i3s. There is a substantial size increase in the i3 tooth compared to the

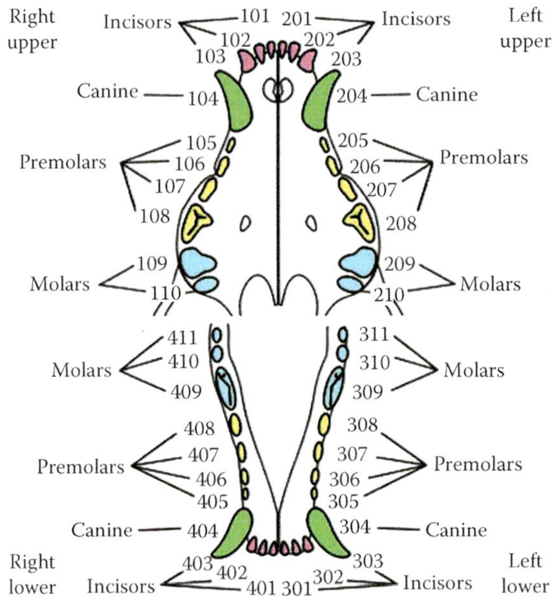

Figure 10.16 Modified triadan numbering system for dogs teeth.

other incisors and is often curved distally. The mandibular i3 will interdigitate between the maxillary i2 and the large i3. Diastema between the incisors is common.

Posterior to the incisors are the prominent canine teeth or "fangs." These are the most prominent teeth in the dentition and will cause most of the serious bite damage; injuries from these teeth often look like slashes or sharp-incised wounds. The mandibular canine fills the space between the maxillary i3 and the canine on the buccal or facial surface. Likewise, the maxillary canine fills the gap distal to the mandibular canine. The canine teeth curve in an anterior-to-posterior direction and diverge laterally. This is important when evaluating a bitemark, given that the ICD of the canine tips is farther apart than at the base of the teeth illustrated in Figure 10.17. Depending on the depth of the bite, the bitemark ICD will vary accordingly. Canine teeth are a reliable reference point in the mouth or bitemark and may be the only teeth to leave a mark and can aid in orientating the relative positions of the dog and victim.

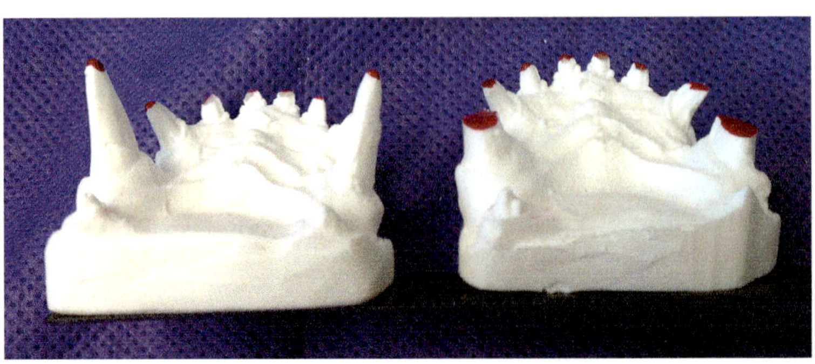

Figure 10.17 Dog teeth showing canine divergence.

The teeth posterior to the canine teeth are the premolars. The permanent dentition contains four maxillary and mandibular premolars per quadrant. In the permanent dentition, the *carnassial* teeth are the maxillary fourth premolar (pm4) and mandibular first molar (m1). The carnassial teeth are well adapted for shearing, cutting, and holding onto prey. Dogs do not chew food like humans but food is "bolted" rendering complete occlusal interdigitation unnecessary. The molars get progressively smaller toward the distal. Note that the fourth premolar is quite large and should not be misidentified as a molar.

After evaluating the teeth characteristics, examine the occlusal relationship. Observe the occlusal plane of the maxillary and mandibular arches. The premolars should interdigitate with overlapping of the cusp tips. In addition, the occlusal surfaces of the molars should occlude to allow for crushing. In a normal occlusion, the mandibular incisors occlude on the palatal aspect of the upper incisors. Like their human counterparts, dogs may have a *Class 1 occlusal relationship* with a normal occlusion or exhibit variations. A *Class 2 occlusion* has the lower premolars and molars positioned distal to the normal relationship. And a *Class 3 occlusion* is a prognathic relationship. Abnormal occlusion may result from asymmetrical growth of the maxilla resulting in distortion or a twisted appearance. Dog dentitions can have various pathologic, periodontal, and systemic lesions and conditions analogous to humans and need to be noted where appropriate. The palate has pronounced and distinct rugae widely spaced in a right to left direction.

10.7.2 Feline Dentition (Cats)

The adult cat dental formula is i(3/3)c(1/1)pm ((1−2)/2)m (1/1) for a total of 30 adult teeth. Compared to a dog, the cat skull is shorter, and the dentition more specialized and has fewer teeth. Dogs not only cut through food but also crush bones as well. Not so with the feline dentition since, as true carnivores, they only slice through food. The canine teeth are sharp and pointed and can reach 9 cm in length in large cats. The maxillary pm1 is usually missing, and the pm2 is reduced in size (Figure 10.18). The mandibular pm1 and pm2 are missing leaving a large diastema distal to the canine tooth. The carnassial teeth are bladelike for more efficiency. The permanent incisors erupt at

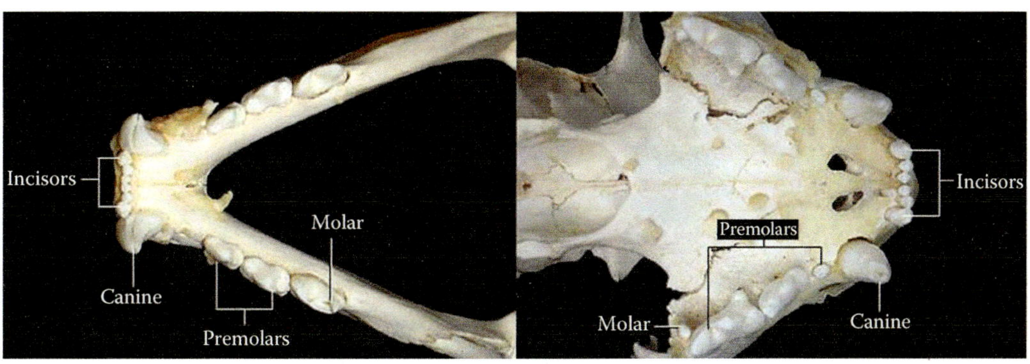

Figure 10.18 Feline (cat) teeth (lower-left and upper-right). (From Bowen, R. July 2012. http://www.vivo.colostate.edu/hbooks/pathphys/digestion/pregastric/dentalanat.html. With permission.)

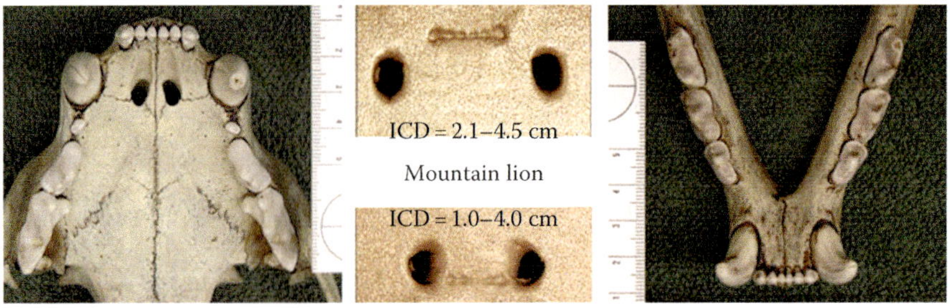

Figure 10.19 Mountain lion teeth and an anterior bite pattern created from those teeth. (From Murmann, D.C., et al., *J. Forensic Sci.*, 51, 846, 2006. With permission.)

about 3.5 months, canines at 5.5 months, premolars at 4.5 months, and the molars at 5–6 months. Two-thirds of cat bites involve the upper extremities (arms and hands). Even with small cats, the punctures can be deep leading to bacterial infection, particularly oesteomyelitis and septic arthritis if tendons or joints are involved. The infection rate for cats is 80% with a 5%–10% hospitalization rate [aash.org]. Domestic cats will consume a deceased human. Investigators should be prepared to rule out cat predation in an investigation. An occlusal view of the teeth and a view of the anterior bitemark pattern for a mountain lion are shown in Figure 10.19.

10.7.3 Ursine Dentitions (Bears)

Like mountain lion attacks and fatalities, bear attacks are uncommon. But as natural habitats are encroached upon by human populations, the incidence of attacks increases. In 2010–2011, there were seven fatal bear attacks. Although primarily occurring in remote locations, one fatality occurred while a woman was walking her dog at a country club. Bear dentition is robust having the dental formula: i(3/3)c(1/1)pm((3–4)/(3–4))m(2/3) with a total of 34–42 teeth. The smaller premolars and robust large molars have cusps modified to accommodate the highly varied omnivore diet (Bowen, 2002). There is considerable individual and species variation. A black bear skull is illustrated in Figure 10.20. An occlusal view of black bear teeth and an anterior bitemark pattern is shown in Figure 10.21, and an occlusal view of teeth and anterior bite patterns of a grizzly bear as shown in Figure 10.22.

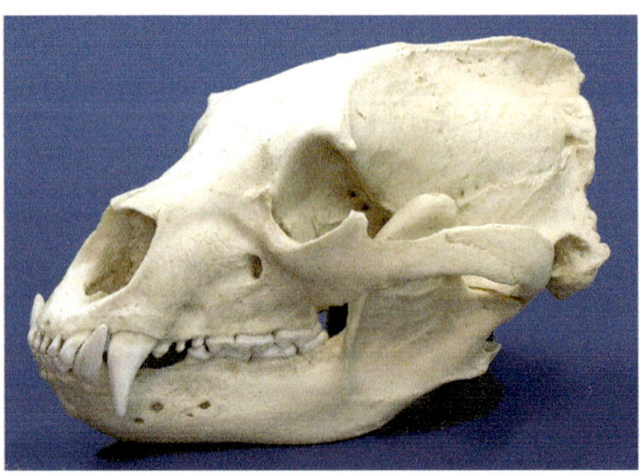

Figure 10.20 Black bear skull.

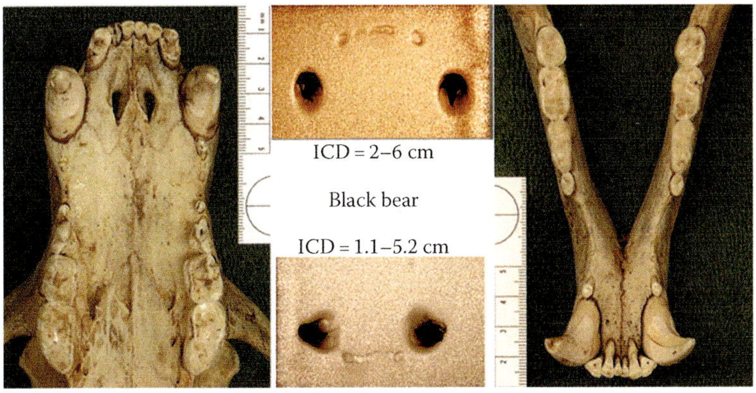

Figure 10.21 Black bear teeth (occlusal view) and an anterior bite pattern. (From Murmann, D.C., et al., *J. Forensic Sci.*, 51, 846, 2006. With permission.)

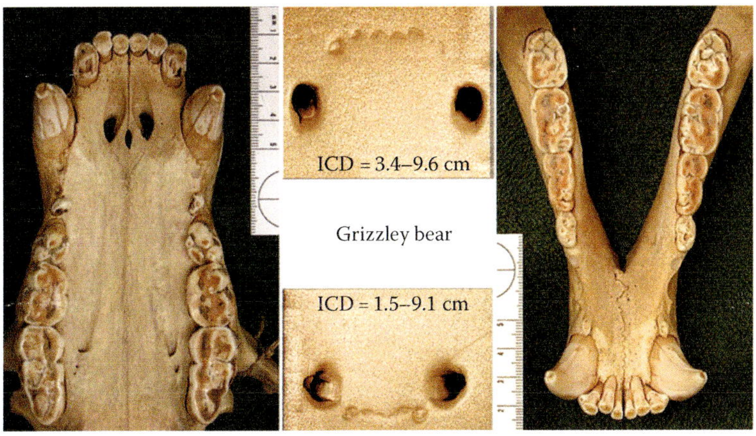

Figure 10.22 Occlusal view of teeth and anterior bite patterns of a Grizzly bear (From Murmann, D.C., et al., *J. Forensic Sci.*, 51, 846, 2006. With permission.).

10.7.4 Rodent Dentition (Rats)

The rodent dentition is rather simple: i(1/1)c(0/0)pm (0/0)m (3/3). Figure 10.23 shows the rat dentition with the two prominent incisors (Bowen, 2002). The chewing function is vertical and anterior–posterior direction. The incisors will continue to grow unless worn by function and can actually impede chewing. The two incisors will leave small puncture-patterned

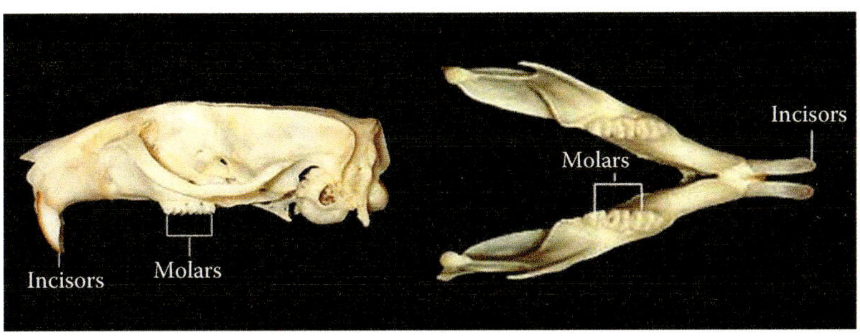

Figure 10.23 Rodent teeth. (From Bowen, R. July 2012. http://www.vivo.colostate.edu/hbooks/pathphys/digestion/pregastric/dentalanat.html. With permission.)

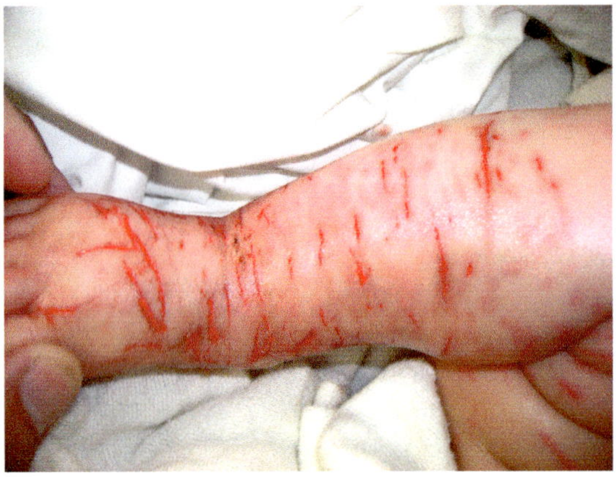

Figure 10.24 Rodent bitemarks on the arm of an infant.

marks that may be mistaken for another source such as insect bites. Rats will attack humans given the opportunity. Most rodent bites occur at night. At-risk children 5 years old or less who typically reside in suboptimal living conditions will often be bit on the hands and face. Figure 10.24 shows rat bites on an infant who was bitten while in her crib during the night. The mother claimed that the bitemarks were made by the family puppy.

10.8 Data Collection in Animal Bitemark Cases

Examination of veterinary forensic cases in the field present challenges uniquely different from those in a controlled environment of a Medical Examiner's office, veterinary office, clinic, or animal shelter. The sheer magnitude of evidence collection in a case with multiple animals and multiple bitemarks would be difficult at best in the field. Therefore, whenever possible, forensic odontologists should work in a controlled environment with the appropriate support staff and equipment.

Consents, court orders, and permissions vary according to the circumstances and jurisdiction. Work closely with medical examiners, law enforcement, and the judicial system within the appropriate jurisdiction to obtain the necessary legal consents for evidence collection.

Collect evidence from all animals, human victims, or physical items for which patterned injuries or marks are present. For example, a dog fight scene offers evidence not only from the dogs themselves, but from training tools, enclosures, graves, fighting arena, bones, and more. Fur may hide evidence so expose the underlying skin to check for patterned injuries. Be aware that animal skin is less vascular so external bruising may be less visible than in humans. The very nature of animal attacks may render the orientation and biting sequence difficult to reconstruct. The veterinarian may need to expose the underlying musculature for evaluation. Scene photographs and reconstruction of the event are relevant to establishing the bite circumstances and sequence. Witness accounts can often provide essential information about the dynamics of the attack in terms of the positions of the attacker and the victim. There is likely only one opportunity to gather evidence. Digital photography and storage capabilities are inexpensive so there is no reason not to capture adequate information. The soft tissue alone may not provide all the bitemark information. Particularly, vicious bites may result in teeth marks on bone as shown in Figure 10.25. This may occur in areas of avulsed tissue or where the soft tissue is closely adhered to the bone, like the scalp. Hard tissue-patterned injuries may be recorded using vinyl polysiloxane (VPS) impression materials and casting resin.

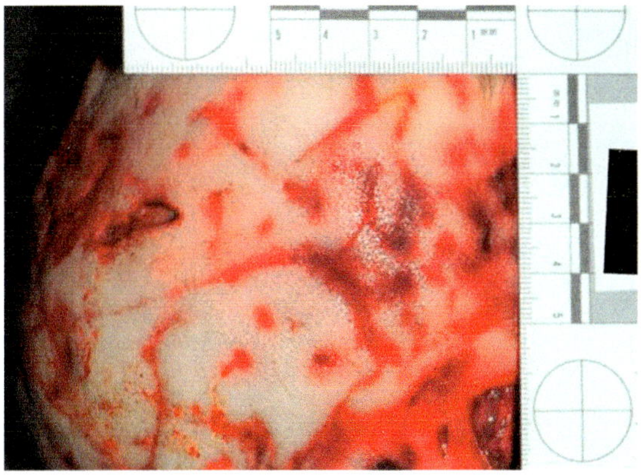

Figure 10.25 Teeth marks in the skull.

The animal should be examined for transfer evidence. Collection of DNA, blood on the fur, stomach contents, fecal material, soft tissue from the oral cavity, and claws should be collected. The protocol for an animal bitemark case is essentially the same as a human case and is described in depth in Chapter 9, in the *ABFO Diplomates Reference Manual* (ABFO, 2012) and in Dorion's, *Bitemark Evidence*, second edition (Dorion, 2011). In addition to obtaining a DNA sample, look for evidence of avulsed tissue, shredded or missing clothing, and have fecal and stomach contents collected.

Case in point, Diane Whipple, a 33 year old lacrosse player and coach, was killed by two Presa Canarios dogs in a highly publicized and politicized case in San Francisco in 2001. The owner insisted just one of the two dogs, Bane (Figure 10.26) was involved, and the other dog, Hera did not participate in the attack. However, contrary to the testimony, Hera's feces contained pieces of the victim's clothes. The remorseless Marjory Knoller, one of the dog's owners received a 15 years-to-life sentence for the murder of Whipple. For a description of the entire case, including the politics and bizarre antics of several of the characters as well as the trial proceedings, read the book *Red Zone* by Aphrodite Jones (Jones, 2003).

Extreme variation among species jaw size exists. Animal attacks involve dentition sizes ranging from a rat up to that of an alligator, great white shark, or even a killer whale. More often than not, a stock plastic dental impression tray will suffice for most dog dental impressions with some modification. Heating the plastic tray to adjust the width may help

Figure 10.26 One of two dogs in a fatal mauling.

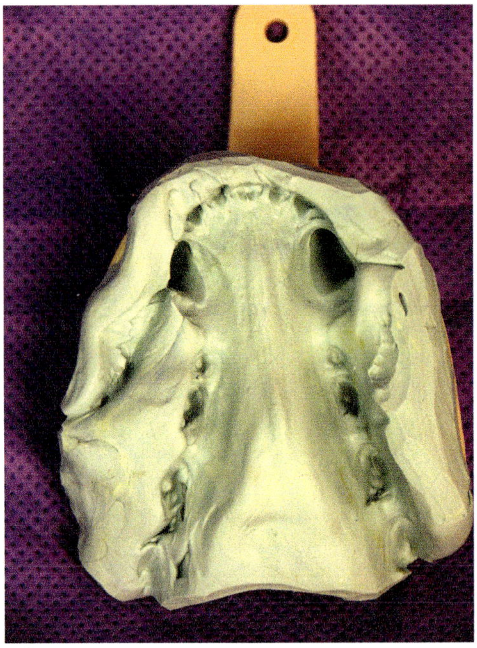

Figure 10.27 Vinyl polysiloxane impression of dog dentition.

accommodate the divergent canine teeth. Accurate recording of the anterior teeth particularly the canines is imperative. It may not be necessary to impress the entire dentition since the molars are typically not included in the bitemark but attempt to capture as many teeth as possible in the impression. Vinyl polysiloxane (VPS) impression material is the material of choice versus alginate for dental impressions (Figure 10.27). By using this more durable material, you will be able to make multiple models from a single impression without tearing the impression material and while retaining accuracy over time. The material recommended for creating the models is polyurethane casting resin. Stone and plaster are not advised for dental models because the diverging canine teeth will likely cause the stone to break when separating the stone from the impression. Fabricate multiple models of each arch. Keep one set of models with the canines at full length, and then a second set with the canines cut down closer to the gingival for comparisons to deeper, penetrating wounds. This is important

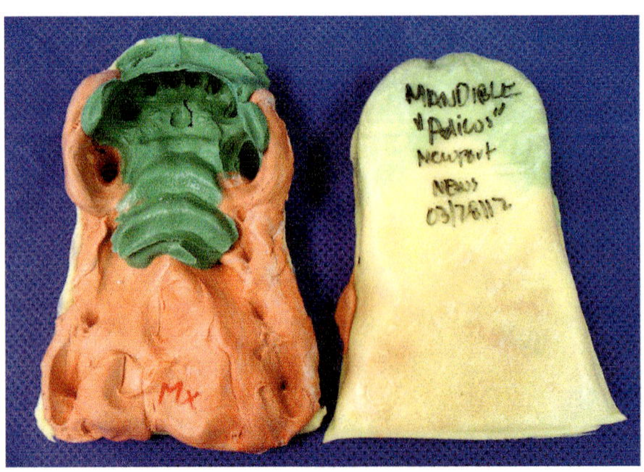

Figure 10.28 Custom trays for dog teeth impressions.

Figure 10.29 Alligator bitemark impression tray.

because bites can range from superficial (nipping) where the ICD is wider than deep puncture wounds. Unusually, large or small dentitions may require creativity in fabricating an impression tray. A custom tray may be fabricated for uniquely sized dentitions (Figure 10.28). For example, referring back to the case involving an alligator-related death of a woman while snorkeling in a river in Central Florida, the forensic odontologist was called upon to identify the animal from a population of two alligators. The investigation required teeth impressions for a bitemark evaluation. Since there are no impression trays to fit an alligator dentition, a plastic drawer from a small office storage bin that fit the alligator's jaw size was utilized as shown in Figure 10.29. Always keep one set of unaltered models archived and, at a minimum, a second set for analysis and comparison.

Time is critical if the animal is not dead and requires sedation for impressions and photography. Adequate preparations for the examination, photography, and impressions must be in place prior to sedation.

10.9 Comparison Techniques

The current standard for bitemark comparisons utilizing computer-generated overlays is discussed in the Bitemark (Chapter 9). This technique can be adapted for animal bitemark cases. As previously noted, for animal cases, be sure to create overlays for the canine teeth at full length and for profiles of the canine teeth closer to the gum line to allow for the canine divergence. This adjusted ICD will more nearly represent the deeper more penetrating wounds made by the teeth.

10.10 Abuse

As a member of the investigative team, forensic odontologists may be called to assist in animal to animal and human to animal abuse cases. An animal crime scene as shown in Figure 10.30 of a tortured and killed cat should be investigated with the same attention to detail as any human crime scene. The activities of certain cults such as Santeria, Voodoo, Santa Muerte, Candomble, or gang rituals may result in bizarre scenes involving mutilated animals. One defense strategy in this type of animal cruelty is to claim religious freedom to practice animal sacrifice. A Supreme Court case from Hialeah,

Figure 10.30 Animal abuse crime scene.

Florida, in 1987 ruled that a cult does have the right to sacrifice animals in a religious ceremony. However, animal cruelty per se is illegal and punishable.

Domestic violence and criminal cases may involve human abuse, animal fighting, gang violence, sexual abuse, hoarding, torture, and a host of other sociopathic behaviors. Investigation of a bitemark case may expose other serious underlying issues regarding family or individual dysfunctions and psychopathy. There are numerous cases of adolescent animal torture manifested in adult human psychopathic behavior. The triad of bed wetting, fire starting, and animal torture is predictive for adult violent criminal behavior. The American Humane Association (Humane Society, 2011) reported disturbing animal abuse and domestic violence facts: 68% of battered women reported that there had been violence toward their animal, 13% of intentional animal abuse cases involve domestic violence, and 70% of animal abusers have records for other crimes. The long list of animal abusers who became infamous killers includes Eric Harris and Dylan Klebold who shot and killed 12 classmates before turning their guns on themselves. They had bragged about mutilating animals to their friends. Carroll Edward Cole was executed for 5 of the 35 murders of which he was accused. He said his first act of violence as a child was to strangle a puppy. Brenda Spencer opened fire at a San Diego school killing two children and injuring nine others. She had repeatedly abused cats and dogs, often by setting their tails on fire. Serial killer Keith Jesperson said "No longer did I search for animals to mistreat. I now looked for people to kill. And I did. I killed over and over until I was caught."

Given the connection between animal abuse, crime, and violence is well established and identifiable, forensic odontologists need to be alert to these red flag situations and report animal abuse behavior to the appropriate authorities.

10.11 Case Examples

10.11.1 Case Example: Human or Animal Attack?

In 2007, a 3-year-old boy sustained severe life-threatening lacerations primarily on the legs and buttocks and with lesser puncture wounds and scratches on the rest of his torso. Because of the suspicious nature of the event, law enforcement consulted a forensic odontologist regarding the attack. Possible sources of the wounds included the family's pet dogs, wild animals such as coyote or panther, or parental abuse with a knife, broken glass, box cutter, or other sharp object.

Initial investigation by sheriff's deputies did not lead to a definitive conclusion as to the source of the injuries. The boy was at home with his mother and two mixed breed dogs. In addition to the mother having a history of drug abuse, the credibility of her story was undermined by the fact that she claimed not to have heard the boy screaming in the back yard while a neighbor down the road reported to have heard the attack. The severe lacerations on the inner thighs of both legs shown (Figure 10.31) were caused by a sharp but undetermined object(s). Examination of the right buttock and thigh (Figure 10.32) and the ventral torso (Figure 10.33) showed several patterned injuries consistent with the class and individual characteristics of a canine. There was no evidence of wild animal sightings or activities anywhere near the crime scene ruling out wild animals as the source. Law enforcement did not request an evaluation of the family dog's dentitions for individual

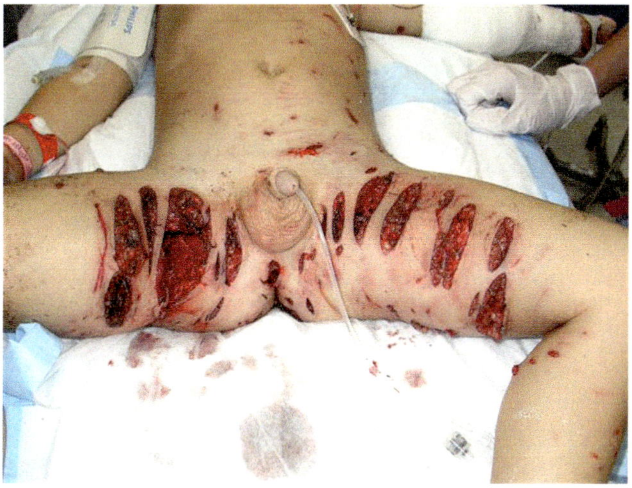

Figure 10.31 Severe lacerations from dog attack.

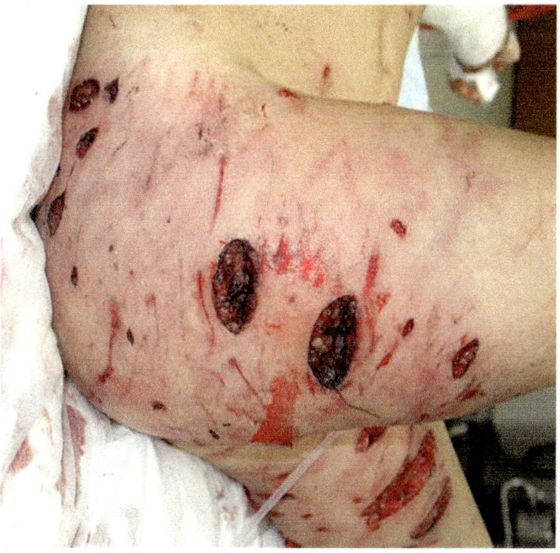

Figure 10.32 Patterned injuries to right thigh and buttock.

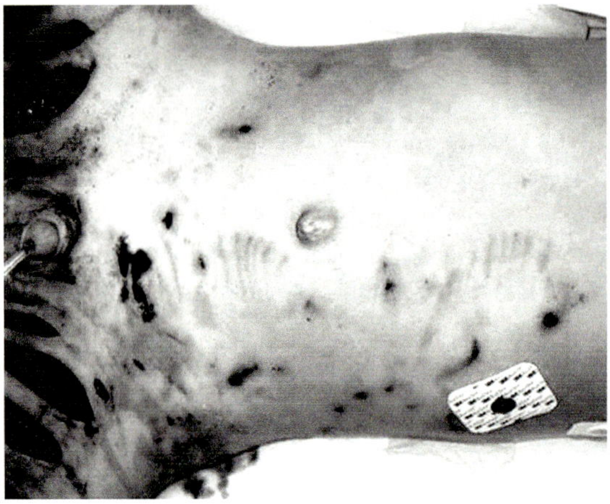

Figure 10.33 Dog bitemarks on ventral torso.

bitemark comparison. However, based on the evidence available and the lack of any other animal or other sharp object involvement, the conclusion was that one or both of the family dogs could not be ruled out as the biters. The mother later confessed that she was under the influence of drugs at the time and was unable to respond to the attack. She was convicted of aggravated child neglect and abuse based in part on the forensic odontology report.

10.11.2 Case Example: Guilty or Not?

A law enforcement officer was accused of child abuse and neglect after his 2-month-old daughter was brought to the emergency room in critical condition (Figure 10.34). He indicated that the family dog had inflicted the life-threatening injuries that included posterior rib fractures, lacerated spleen and liver, and multiple minor superficial lacerations and contusions. Suspicious behavior of the accused includes the circumstances in which the emergency was handled and the questionable culpability of the dog causing the severe injuries raised red flags with the ER Child Protection Team. A forensic odontologist was called in to assist in the investigation and to determine, if possible, the source of the patterned injuries. There were conflicting opinions as to whether the father or the family dog, a Belgian Shepherd, was responsible for the life-threatening injuries. Based on the evidence

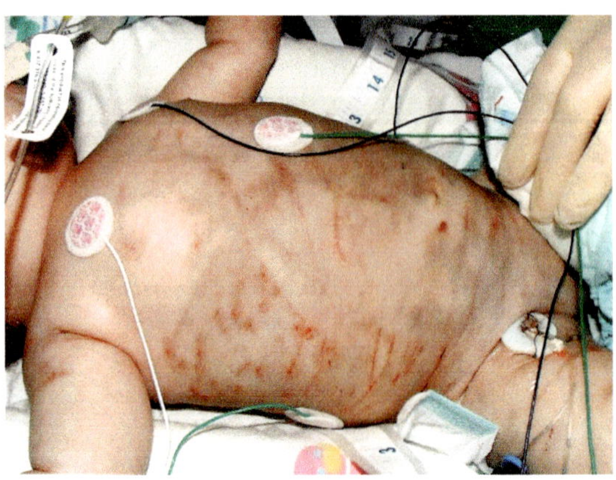

Figure 10.34 Patterned injuries to ventral torso of child abuse victim.

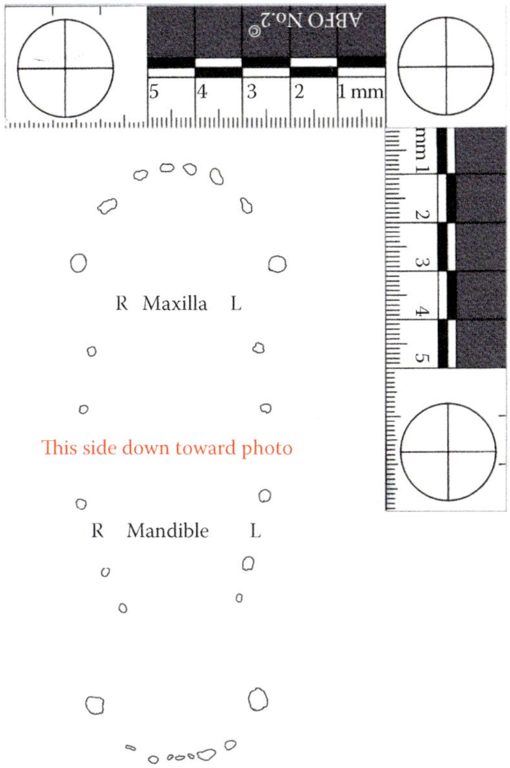

Figure 10.35 Hollow volume overlay of canine dentition.

presented, the CPT determined that there was sufficient cause to suspect that the father was guilty of child abuse and neglect. A standard bitemark evaluation was conducted taking impressions of the dog's dentition, fabricating models of the teeth both at full length and cut down canine length, and acetate overlays illustrated in Figure 10.35. Among other circular items to be compared to the injury patterns were the pediatric EKG electrode, belt keeper with round eyelets, "onesie" pajama sleeper snaps (Figure 10.36) and the filed-down canine teeth of the dog (Figure 10.37) all of which could potentially have caused some of the patterned injuries seen on the victim. Test exemplars were taken of all these possibilities including a test bite from the dog on the arm of the medical examiner (Figure 10.38). There was virtually no blood at the scene including on the "onesie" or the infant. The "onesie" pajama sleeper had only several small tears, and the defendant indicated that it

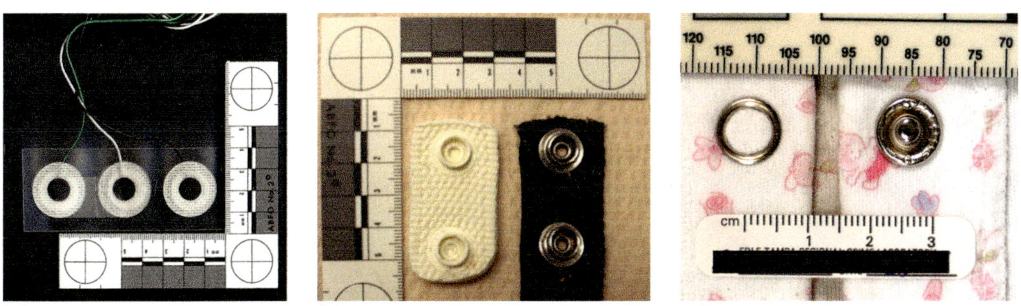

(A) (B) (C)

Figure 10.36 (A) EKG electrodes, (B) belt keeper with round eyelets, and (C) onesie snaps.

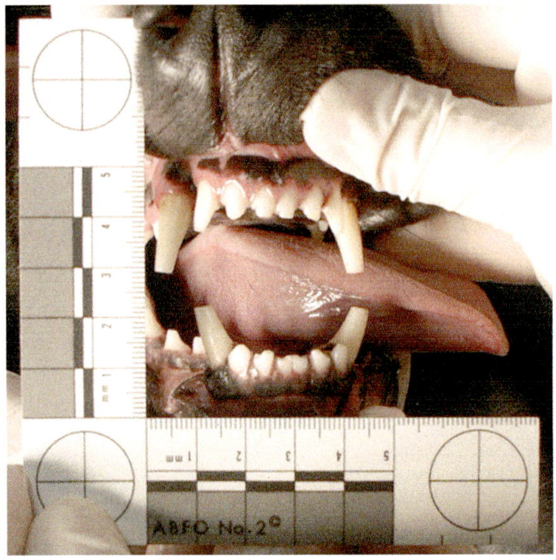

Figure 10.37 Dog teeth: note filed-down canine teeth.

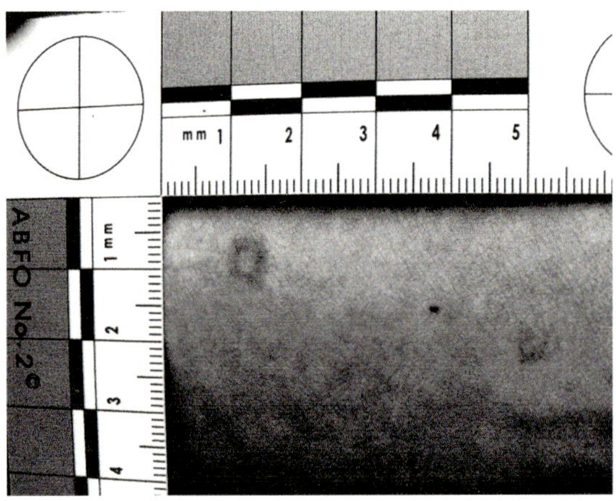

Figure 10.38 Test marks on arm of medical examiner from teeth in Figure 10.36.

had been removed from the child by the dog. The odontologist, using standard Photoshop protocol of resizing and overlay comparison, determined that the circular contusions were indeed caused by the blunted canine teeth. Rather uniquely, this result was uncontested by both the prosecution and defense since it was consistent with both the prosecution and defense versions of the events. The contentious issue was whether the father inflicted the severe injuries and in an attempt to cover up injuring the child used the dog to cover up the abuse. The marks left by the dog were superficial and depending on the expert testifying may or may not be consistent with the severe internal injuries, particularly the posterior rib fractures. The forensic odontologist was able to show correlation of both the maxillary and mandibular ICD's and the bitemarks (Figures 10.39 and 10.40). After a several year-long investigation and 2-week-long trial involving multiple agencies, investigators, expert witnesses including two forensic odontologists, a dog behavioral specialist, and several medical examiners, the jury found the defendant not guilty of all charges.

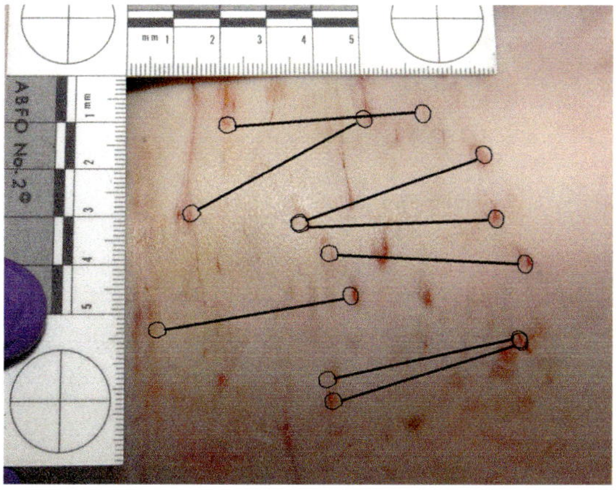

Figure 10.39 Graphic demonstrations of canine marks with consistent intercanine dimensions (maxillary).

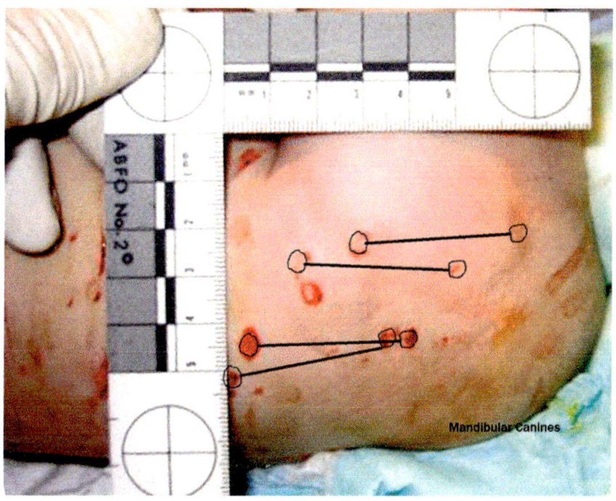

Figure 10.40 Graphic demonstrations of canine marks with consistent intercanine dimensions (mandibular).

10.11.3 Case Example: Egregious Mistakes

In the textbook *Bitemark Evidence: A Color Atlas and Text*, editor Robert B. J. Dorion describes a grossly mishandled child homicide case. A 7-year-old female was found dead in her basement. Initially, the pathologist indicated that the child died from 80 stab wounds with scissors and/or knives and that the victim's scalp had been excised with scissors. Although there was a dog present in the home, a pit bull, a forensic odontologist was not called to examine the injuries at the time of the autopsy. During the initial consultation, the forensic odontologist opined that "...without equivocation that the markings seen on the deceased are not dog bite marks." Consequently, the mother was charged with second-degree murder within 11 days of the incident. Later, after exhumation and further investigation, another forensic pathologist and forensic odontologist concluded that some of the injuries were indeed animal bitemarks. The accused mother of the child was eventually released from custody, and all charges dropped one week before trial. The errors in this case were numerous and profound. A $7 million lawsuit for malicious prosecution, false imprisonment, and gross negligence was filed against the original pathologist, the original odontologist, the police, and the prosecutor's office (Dorion, 2011).

10.11.4 Case Example: High-Profile Dog Fighting Case

NFL quarterback, Michael Vick, and some associates were convicted in 2007 on federal and state charges related to illegal dog fighting. The case may not have even been brought to trial under different circumstances since dog fighting may be considered culturally acceptable. However, this case was unusual in that federal charges were brought against a high profile athlete who was convicted and served prison time. In addition, the animals involved were not euthanized but cared for after the conviction with funds from the defendant.

10.11.5 Other Case Examples

Some criminals attempt to hide their crimes as animal attacks. Randall Lockwood, PhD, Senior Vice President, Forensic Sciences, and Anti-Cruelty Projects of the American Society for the Prevention of Cruelty to Animals, has consulted in murder cases in which the perpetrator tried to cover up crimes with spurious animal evidence. One case involved a female who was mauled by her own dog, a pit bull terrier. Evidence suggested that the dog had been set on her probably while she was unconscious. Her boyfriend was convicted of murder and sentenced to 15 years to life.

Another example is a 19 year old, unmarried woman who gave birth to an infant believed to be stillborn and then tossed the body over a neighbor's fence and into the jaws of a dog. However, a pathologist testified that victim was alive but unconscious at the time of the attack. Autopsy and other studies indicated that the cause of death had been dog bites to the skull and a penetrating injury to the heart. Charges of murder were considered but downgraded to first degree manslaughter.

10.12 Summary

The attitudes of society and lawmakers toward animals are changing. Philosophical views of animals as property have evolved into a more protectionist position. Animal law is now taught in 135 law schools. Animal activism, the use of animals as food, animal labor, animals as entertainers, medical experimentation using animals, and clothing made from animal products are among the issues that create social tension.

Various states have considered anticruelty laws ranging from giving chickens adequate living space, dog tethering statutes, eliminating strangulation of pigs and goats, to rights for nonhuman primates. Some allege that organizations like PETA and other activist groups have gone too far arguing that animals are property and have no legal rights. Those involved in this historical shift toward animal rights include lawyers, government agencies, municipalities, law enforcement agencies, activists, researchers, veterinarians, and forensic specialists. While not included as a major part of the traditional role of forensic odontologists, the contribution of forensic odontology to veterinary forensic science is increasingly relevant.

10.13 Lessons Learned and Recommendations for Animal Casework

- Remember to swab for animal DNA.
- Forensic odontologists should be present at autopsy/necropsy.
- Take dental impressions of suspected animal biters.
- ME's and coroners should utilize the services of a specially trained, board-certified forensic odontologist.
- Review all relevant information from the scene and reports.
- Follow current ABFO recommendations, including using another odontologist to review the procedures and results.
- Forensic odontologist's reports should be thorough, accurate, and unbiased.
- Forensic odontologist's conclusions should conform to ABFO guidelines and should not be overstated.
- Know both the strengths and weaknesses of the bitemark evidence and provide that information to stakeholders.
- Expect to be asked about the current research in bitemarks, the NAS 2009 report Strengthening Forensic Science in the United States: A Path Forward and other controversial bitemark issues.
- Apply the same standards, techniques, and precautions used in human bitemark analysis to animal bitemark analysis and be able to explain the correlation between the two.

Our forensic colleagues including medical examiners, coroners, crime scene investigators, veterinarians, law enforcement officers, and crime laboratory technicians should be aware of and willing to consult qualified forensic odontologists to offer assistance and expertise on patterned injury analysis and techniques.

The book *Veterinary Forensics: Animal Cruelty Investigations* by Melinda Merck, DVM is an excellent resource. Dr. Merck discusses animals as evidence, patterns in nonaccidental injury in animals, scene analysis, sexual assault, and animal fighting (Merck, 2007). The second edition is expected in 2012.

Acknowledgments

Images showing the occlusal views of the teeth and anterior bite patterns for the mountain lion, black bear, and grizzly bear were generously provided by Dr. Denise Murmann. They were adapted from prior presentations of her published work (Murmann et al., 2006). Thanks to Randall Lockwood, PhD, ASPCA for sharing case information.

References

ABFO Diplomates Reference Manual, 2012. www.abfo.org (accessed October 2012).

AVMA Press Release. 2008. http://www.avma.org/press/releases/080514_dogbite.asp

Bowen, R. July 2012. http://www.vivo.colostate.edu/hbooks/pathphys/digestion/pregastric/dentalanat.html

Bini, J.K., S.M. Cohn, S.M. Acosta, M.J. McFarland, M.K. Muir, and J.E. Mickalek. April 2011. Mortality, mauling, and maiming by vicious dogs. *Annals of Surgery* 253(4): 791–797.

Centers for Disease Control and Prevention. 2001. Nonfatal dog bite related injuries treatment in hospital emergency departments-US http://cdc.gov/mmwr/preview/mmwrhtml/mn5226a1.html (accessed May 2011).

Centers for Disease Control and Prevention. May 2009. Dog bite prevention. Injury prevention and control: Home and recreational safety. http://www.cdc.gov/HumanandRecreationalSafety/DogBites-FactSheet.html

Dogbitelaw.org. 2011. Dog bite statistics. http://dogbitelaw.com/dogbitestatistics/the_dog_bite_epidemic_a_primer (accessed February 2011).

Dogsbite.org. 2011. Dog bite fatalities—Dog bite statistics. http://www.dogsbite.org/dogsbite-news-room2011-dog-bite-fatality-statistics-victim-trends.php (accessed February 2012).

Dorion, R. 2011. *Bitemark Evidence A Color Atlas and Text*, 2nd edition, pp. 228–240. Boca Raton, FL: CRC Press.

Erickson, G., A.K. Lappin, K. Vliet. 2003. The ontogeny of bite force performance in American alligator (*Alligator mississippiensis*). *Journal of Zoology (London)* 260(3): 317–323.

Florida Fish and Wildlife Commission (FWC). 2010. Historic alligator bites on humans in Florida 6/2010. http://myflorida.com/media/310203/alligatorgatorbites.pdf (accessed December 2011).

Florida Museum of Natural History: Ichthyology Department. 2000. ISAS statistics for the USA locations with the highest shark attack activity since 2000. http://FLMNH.UFL.edu/fish/shark/statistics/statsus.html (accessed June 2011).

Floyd, M.R. 1991. The modified triadan system: Nomenclature for veterinary dentistry. *Journal of Veterinary Dentistry* 8(4): 18–19.

Healthy Children.org. 2012. http://www.healthychildren.org/English/health-issues/injuries-emergencies/Pages/Animal-Bites.aspx

Hillson, S. 2005. *Teeth*, 2nd edition, p. 46. New York: Cambridge University Press.

Holmquist, L., Elixhauser, A. 2010. *Emergency Department Visits and Inpatient Stays Involving Dog Bites, 2008*. Agency for Healthcare Research and Quality, Statistical Brief #101.

Humane Society of the US. 2011. Animal cruelty facts and statistics—Statistics on the victims and current legislative trends. http://www.humanesociety.org/issues/abuseneglect/facts/animalcrueltyfactsstatistics.html (accessed December 2011).

Humane Society of the US. 2012. US pet ownership statistics, August 12, 2012. http://www.humanesociety.org/issues/petoverpopulation/facts/petownership_statistics.html

Insurance Information Institute. 2012. www.iii.org/issues-updates/dog-bite-liability.html

Johnson, S.A. Department of wildlife ecology and conservation. www.ufwildlife.ifas.ufl.edu/venomous-snake-faqs-shtml

Jones, A. 2003. *Red Zone*. New York: Harper Collins Publisher.

Lockwood, R. April 2012. ASPCA personal communication.

Mayor, A. 2009. *Greek Fire, Poison Arrows and Scorpion Bombs. Biologic and Chemical Warfare in the Ancient World*. New York: Overlook Press Publisher.

Merck, M. 2007. *Veterinary Forensics Animal Cruelty Investigations*. Hoboken, NJ: Blackwell Publisher.

Murmann, D.C., P.C. Brumit, B.A. Schrader, and D.R. Senn, 2006. A comparison of animal jaws and bite mark patterns. *Journal of Forensic Science* 51(4): 846–860.

PBS. 2010. www.pbs.org/wnet/nature/episodes/invasion-of-the-giant-pythons/introduction/5532

Shannon, C. 2009. Animal Ed -Bad to the bone: Analyzing and assessing dog bites. In *Raising Canines*. LLC. ISBN: 9781607438809; DVD.

Talan, D.A., Citron, D.M., Abrahamian, F.M. et al. 1999. Bacteriologic analysis of infected dog and cat bites. *New England Journal of Medicine* 340: 85–92.

Texas Department of State Health Services. Animal bite information. http://dshs.state.tx.us/?/health/zoonosis/animal/bites/information/venom/snake (accessed August 2011).

Abuse and Violence

11

JOHN P. KENNEY
JOHN D. MCDOWELL
DUANE E. SPENCER

Contents

11.1 Introduction 356
11.1.1 Overview 356
11.1.2 Early Dental Literature 356
11.1.3 Dental Team's Role 357
11.2 Child Abuse 359
11.2.1 Physical Abuse 359
11.2.2 Exploitation 362
11.2.3 Sexual Abuse 363
11.2.4 Emotional Abuse 363
11.2.5 Neglect or Deprivation 364
11.2.6 Munchausen Syndrome by Proxy 364
11.2.7 Risk Factors for Child Abuse 364
11.2.8 Conditions and Practices That Mimic Abuse 364
11.2.9 Who Are the Abusers 365
11.2.10 What to Look For 365
11.2.11 Prevention of Child Abuse 365
11.2.11.1 Child Abuse Prevention Councils 366
11.2.11.2 Child Death Review Teams 366
11.3 Intimate Partner Violence 367
11.3.1 IPV Types 368
11.3.2 Dental Team Awareness and Action Plan 368
11.3.3 RADAR (A Domestic Violence Intervention Program) 369
11.4 Mistreatment of the Elderly 369
11.4.1 Incidence and Indicators of Elderly Abuse 369
11.4.2 Categories of Elder Abuse 370
11.4.3 Reasons for Underreporting 371
11.4.4 Signs Mistaken for Abuse 371
11.4.5 Signs of Malnutrition 371
11.4.6 Follow-Up Care 371
11.5 Abuse of the Disabled 371
11.6 Abuse of Pregnant Women and Prenatal Abuse 372
11.7 Conclusion 374
11.8 Resources 374
References 374

11.1 Introduction

In the first ASFO "Workbook," a loose-leaf binder, the concept of child abuse in context to the aspiring forensic dentist covered six double-spaced pages. The topic has expanded over 33 years to include intimate partner violence (IPV), elder abuse, abuse in pregnancy, fetal abuse, and abuse of the disabled. The ASFO Manual/"Workbook" was the first forensic dental compendium to address the topic, and now the subject is regularly included in odontology texts and is seen more frequently in dental journals. Thus, the ASFO has been and continues to be a leader in domestic violence (DV) education and educational materials for the dental professional.

11.1.1 Overview

Child abuse, IPV, elder abuse, and abuse of the disabled all share many traits. For the sake of simplicity, the general term "Domestic Violence"(DV) may be used as a generic term to refer collectively to all of these categories. DV clearly encompasses all age groups and close relationships. DV also crosses all age, educational, ethnic, and socioeconomic barriers. No group or community is immune.

It is believed that there are 10 million cases of DV in the United States each year. Part of the difficulty is that state laws and reporting requirements vary, and so accurate statistics beyond child abuse and child neglect are difficult to find. IPV may end up as a criminal case, on a hospital social worker's case load, or in a state database that only encompasses a portion of the problem. Abuse of the disabled may fall into the child abuse statutes of a given state but beyond that age group may fall into criminal statistics. Today, elder abuse *is* being recognized and reported to various state agencies. However, depending on state law mandates, these statistics may be incomplete as well. This chapter will evaluate all of these areas and indicate, where possible, accurate statistics. But more importantly, it will discuss the diagnostic signs and symptoms that may confront both the forensic odontologist and the practicing dentist in private practice.

In recent years, we have become much more aware of the abuse endured by women and children in certain countries as a matter of custom and belief. Genital mutilation and "honor killings" or beatings of wives and sisters and daughters sadly are common practices in some parts of the world and because of immigration patterns, these abhorrent practices have reached the shores of civilized western nations. These ethnic groups have asked that their form of religious law be allowed to supersede common law of western nations. This is a significant issue that must be clearly addressed by health professionals and law enforcement. Politicians will need to have the courage to stand up for what is right and not bow to cultural practices that are clearly beyond reason and justice (Figure 11.1).

11.1.2 Early Dental Literature

Beginning in 1970, an article in the *New York State Dental Journal* discussed the dentist's role in abuse (Hazelwood, 1970). The *British Dental Journal of Oral Surgery* reviewed five cases of abuse the following year (Tate, 1971). Several other articles were published in the 1970s bringing forward more information as far as dentists' relationship to the topic of abuse (Sims et al., 1973; ten Bensel and King, 1975; ten Bensel and Bastein, 1977; Benusis, 1977; Sopher, 1977).

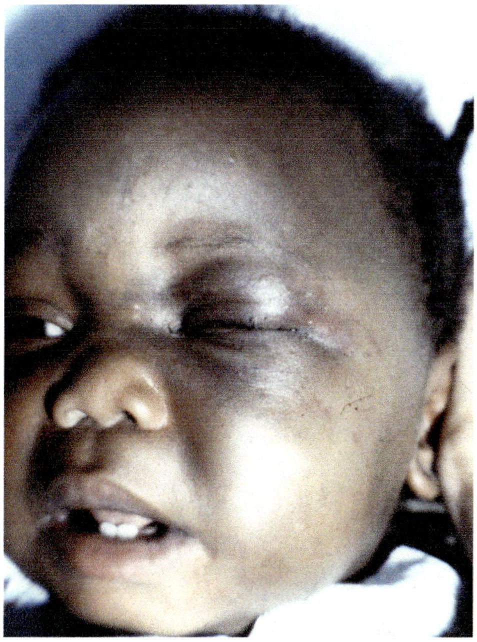

Figure 11.1 Child with blackened eye. Bilateral blackening of both eyes is referred to as "raccoon eyes."

Studies have shown percentages range from 43% to 75% of all physical injury in child abuse that occurs in the head or neck region (Cameron et al., 1966; Becker et al., 1978; Kenney 1979). It is likely that this same percentage is true across the spectrum of DV. The abusers tend to be the primary caretaker of the child who may be overstressed or overwhelmed by the responsibility, lonely, unhappy, or depressed. Generally, they were mistreated themselves as children or witnessed mistreatment of another family member. There is a greater risk for females to abuse during their pregnancy or premenstrual cycle. Unrelated caretakers are often boyfriends or girlfriends of the parent, who have been asked to care for a child while the parent is at work or shopping, etc. This has even gained a nickname in child welfare/law enforcement circles as the "paramour sign." Unrealistic expectations of the child including reaching developmental milestones earlier than normal or self-expectations of the parent can contribute. There also may be a feeling that the child exists to satisfy the needs of the parent, and, if these needs are not met, the child needs to be physically punished to make them behave properly. It is well illustrated in the quote, "I've waited all these years for my baby, and when she was born, she never did anything for me. When she cried it meant that she didn't love me so I hit her" (Kempe 1971).

11.1.3 Dental Team's Role

In all 50 states, physicians and dentists are required to report suspected cases of child or elder abuse and neglect to social service or law enforcement agencies. It is important that the community of forensic odontologists take the lead in state and local dental societies in encouraging training for the entire dental staff regarding these victims. Also, forensic odontologists have been at the forefront contributing to articles in dental journals and/or book chapters and including the topic in their continuing education programs.

The dental team must be aware of the physical and behavioral signs of DV and have a plan in their office as to how and when to intervene, either as mandated by law or as necessitated by compassionate and professional dental care. State statutes are quite specific for health care providers in reporting child abuse and elder abuse. Depending on the state, abuse of the adult disabled person may be reported to different agencies and may be mandated. Some states may have a central reporting number for all types of abuse, and others may segment it by age group and type. Adults who are victims of IPV need to be encouraged to act on their own behalf. The dental team should also provide one or more resources to contact in seeking professional help. Being able to differentiate between normal conditions, truly accidental injury or intentionally inflicted injury is a key in the diagnostic arsenal of the practitioner. As a forensic odontologist, one may be called upon by the police, prosecutors, or even perhaps as a defense expert to evaluate DV injuries as to the likely cause and manner. As a dental practitioner, the obligation is to recognize record, report, and/or refer as dictated by the circumstances and according to the applicable state law.

All types of abuse share commonalities when the victim presents at the dental office. The history given is inconsistent, contradictory, or vague. The physical appearance of the injury (severity, nature of the injury, physical ability, and developmental ability of the victim) conflicts with the history offered by the care giver. Describing the victim as "clumsy" or "accident prone" or the use of a rare or vague disease process or affliction to explain the injury also may occur. The victim may bear signs of previous injury, or the clinical record in the office may reflect a similar injury in the past. The victim may be either unusually aggressive or withdrawn or exhibit a sudden behavior change when a person of the same sex as the abuser enters the room. Attempt by the practitioner or staff to make appropriate physical contact with the victim but eliciting a withdrawal in great fear is a warning sign. Caregiver behavior may be inappropriate, given the appearance of the injury (what would a reasonable lay person do in the situation?). Obviously infected teeth, for example, treated by giving the person an OTC pain medication rather than seeking care when care reasonably available should raise suspicions.

PANDA is the acronym for "Prevent Abuse and Neglect through Dental Awareness." It was founded in 1992 by Dr. Lynn Mouden. It is an educational program established to make dentists knowledgeable regarding DV and consists of coalitions in 46 states and 12 international coalitions. In the United States, the program represents a team effort on the part of the Delta Dental Plan Foundation, the State Dental Society, and the State Child Welfare Agency. In 2003, the California coalition expanded PANDA to encompass all forms of family violence detection and prevention.

Training of the dental health professional is critical. In abuse situations, dental offices are not perceived by abusers as being a "threat" to its discovery. As a result of PANDA training, dental reporting of child abuse has increased by 60%, while reporting of abuse by all professionals has risen only 6%. Studies have indicated that dentists are nearly five times more likely to report suspected abuse if they have received education in the signs, symptoms, and reporting mechanisms related to abuse. In recent years, both within PANDA and programs presented by forensic odontologists, the topic has been broadened to include all facets of DV, child, intimate partner, elder, and disabled abuse. Unfortunately, PANDA programs in a number of states are not at an optimum level, and it is important that forensic odontologists take the lead with their own state and local dental society to continue to emphasize the importance of this program.

11.2 Child Abuse

From ancient Greek and Roman times, children were considered "chattel." The Roman Laws of Twelve Tables in 450 BC dictated that a male child could only be sold three times. Unwanted, deformed, or female children could be left exposed to die in Roman or Grecian territories. The Bibliotheca Scholastica in AD 1633 stated "spare the rod and spoil the child." One of the first classical thinkers to address the problem was Jean Jacques Rousseau (1712–1778) who stated "Let us speak less of the duties of children and more of their rights." In 1871, the Society of Prevention of Cruelty to Children was founded in New York City in response to the "Mary Ellen" case. A young girl had been seen to be abused by her adoptive parents, and the neighbors turned to the New York Society of Prevention of Cruelty to Animals to get help. Additional information on this case can be found in Chapter 1.

11.2.1 Physical Abuse

Physical Abuse of Children can encompass fractures, bruises, lacerations, patterned injuries, burns, orofacial injuries, ocular injuries, subdural and subgaleal hematomas, and bite marks. Also included in this category would be severe corporal punishment. Fractures of the long bones are common, and when a child presents to an emergency department in a hospital for a traumatic injury, a long bone radiographic survey should be done to screen for previous evidence of injury. Likewise, chest films may also show evidence of old healing fractures of the ribs. Dentally, trauma seen in the office is usually confined to the anterior teeth, but evidence of teeth missing or a fractured root tip in the oral cavity on a routine examination should elicit further investigation or history by the treating dentist. A history of the current and past injuries to the child must be evaluated in terms of the child's development as well as the likelihood that the injury occurred in the manner or time frame indicated by the parent bringing the child in for treatment. Physicians and hospitals are in a position, where by law, they can take "protective custody" of a child if they have a reasonable suspicion that abuse has taken place. They may also take necessary radiographs, photos, or appropriate medical testing without the parent's consent. As dentists, we are not given such latitude.

Fractures: Fractures of varying ages, some perhaps fresh, others healing, and others resolved are a common finding in abuse cases. As early as 1946, John Caffey reported in the *American Journal of Roentenology* about the occurrence of spiral fractures of long bones and subdural hematomas in infants (Caffey, 1946). The more common term today is abusive head trauma (AHT). C. Henry Kempe's (1962) work on child abuse was the most significant to begin serious study of scope of the problem, including signs and symptoms (Kempe et al., 1962). Helfer and Kempe used the term "Battered Child Syndrome" in their 1968 text, which brought the problem to the attention of health professionals, law enforcement, and the lay public as well (Helfer and Kempe 1968) (Figure 11.2).

Bruises: Bruises in various stages of healing can also be evidence of serial abuse. Again, does the time frame and history offered by the parent match the clinical appearance of the injury. If the child is old enough to relate what happened, often a simple nonthreatening question to the child may give the practitioner reason to pursue further. Doing so out of earshot of the parent or caregiver may elicit a different answer than what was volunteered by the parent. The typical location of accidental bumps and bruises includes the chin,

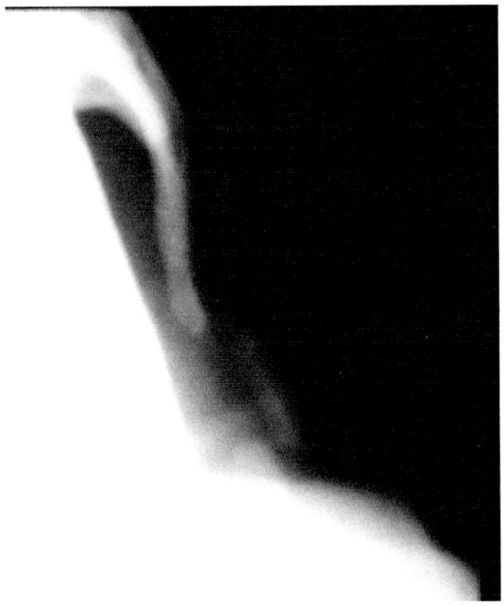

Figure 11.2 Modified submental vertex radiograph showing fractured zygomatic arch.

Table 11.1 Aging of Bruises

Time Elapsed	Characteristics
0–3 Days	Swollen, tender
0–5 Days	Red, blue, purple
5–7 Days	Green
7–10 Days	Yellow
10–14 Days or more	Brown or cleared

Source: Wilson, E.F., *Pediatrics*, 60, 750, 1977.

elbows, wrists and hands, and the knees. Accidental injuries to the bony prominences are common, however, injuries to the reverse surfaces such as the inner aspect of the arm, or the back of the knee are more likely to be from abuse (Table 11.1).

Lacerated and incised wounds: Laceration wounds are caused by blunt force trauma from a flat or "rounded" instrument, which tears soft tissues. Incised wounds are found in sharp force trauma when instruments having a cutting edge. Lacerations typically have strands of fibrous tissue extending across the wound known as tissue bridging. Incised wounds could also be caused by a cord or wire that is struck with enough force to penetrate the skin.

Patterned injuries: Patterned injuries are common in child abuse as well as the other forms of DV. A looped cord or metal coat hanger used to strike the child will leave a distinctive pattern mark. Also, a slap to the face or other part of the child's body may leave interrupted, parallel marks from the fingers. For the forensic odontologist, the human bite mark is probably the most frequent type of patterned injury that they may be called upon to evaluate.

Orofacial injuries: Orofacial injuries in child abuse have been repeatedly studied, including this author's Master's Thesis covering 450 cases from 14 hospitals in Cook County Illinois

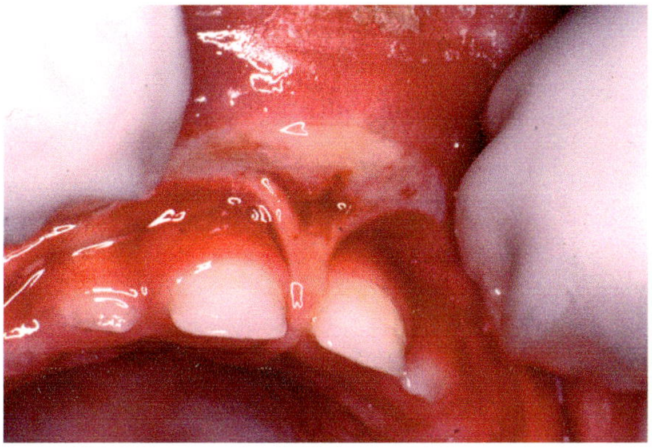

Figure 11.3 A torn frenum attachment may be a dental sign of child abuse.

(Kenney, 1979). The percentages of physical child abuse involving the orofacial complex range from 58% to 85% (Alder et al., 2006) over the past three decades. The face is considered the "persona" of the child victim and is the most frequent target of physical abuse. Fractured, subluxated, or avulsed teeth may be seen. Frenum lacerations, contusions of the lips, cheeks, sublingual, and pharyngeal areas are also common. Lips may be lacerated with an object or by a slap by the hand. The nose may also be fractured, lacerated, or contused. Even jaw fractures may be seen in extreme cases (Figure 11.3).

Ocular injuries: Ocular injuries may sometimes be visible to the naked eye, such as subconjunctival hemorrhages. The anterior chamber of the eye may also be filled with blood (Giangiacomo and Frasier, 2005). Whiplash types of injuries (Shaken Baby Syndrome) such as retinal hemorrhage and detachment may require an ophthalmoscope to discover.

Abusive head trauma: A subdural hematoma is the most common fatal injury seen in abusive head trauma (AHT). The result is bleeding between the brain and the inner surface of the skull. This injury usually requires surgical intervention. Subgaleal hematomas involve bleeding between the scalp and the outer surface of the skull. Occasionally, a fall or accidental blow to the head can elicit such a response. Depending on the size, fluctuance, pain, or nature of the swelling, a cold pack may be an adequate relief; however, if extensive, it should be evaluated by a physician. Traumatic hair pulling can also cause this type of injury, which may need to be ruled out by the examining health care provider. Parents or other caregivers may braid or comb over the hair where it has been pulled from the scalp. Alopecia is a medical condition not unlike male pattern baldness. The hair falls out at the follicle and leaves a smooth surface of skin. On the other hand, pulled hair will break at various places on the shaft so will leave some denuded areas and some broken hair shaft of varying lengths.

Bite marks: Human bite marks are often seen in cases of physical child abuse. As odontologists, we are uniquely qualified to examine such a mark as to its possible origin. They may be from an adult or another child. There are pertinent questions that primarily include what is the shape and size of the teeth seen in the mark and are they clearly demarcated; and does the injury fit the history provided in regard to size, shape, orientation on the body, how and when inflicted (see Chapter 9). In some cases of child abuse, it may also be necessary to arrange for the sedation of the child in order to properly photograph the bite mark and take any necessary impressions (Figure 11.4).

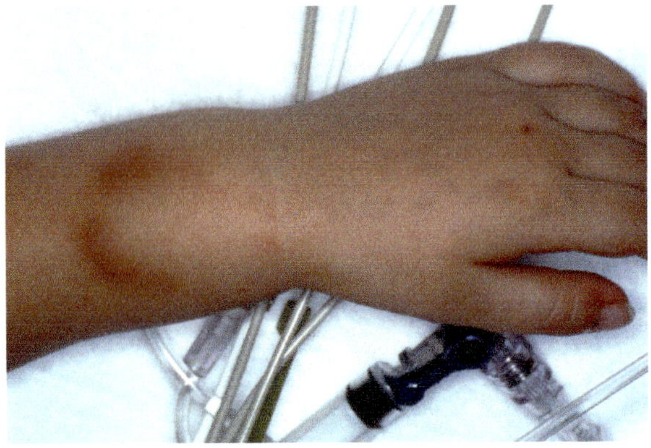

Figure 11.4 Bite marks are often seen in cases of physical child abuse.

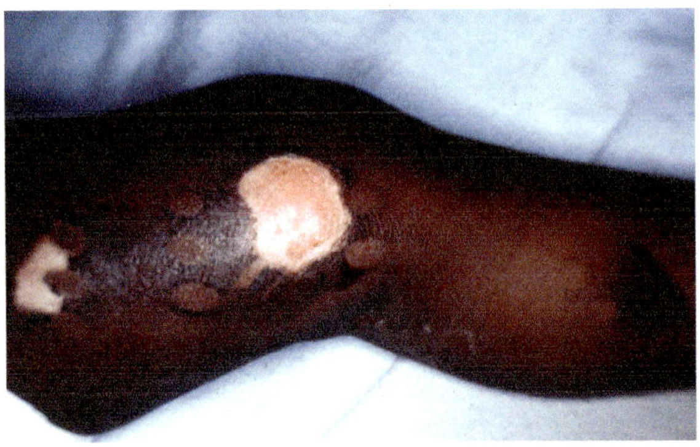

Figure 11.5 Child abuse involving dry contact burn from a heated object.

Inflicted burns: Inflicted burns can be caused by a number of things: heated objects, tools, or utensils; dry contact burns with a heater or other hot surface; hot water from either an intentional immersion or a splash or scald (Figure 11.5). Immersion burns to the body often show a clear line of demarcation and a proffered history of the child splashed by the water or playing in the tub or sink. Cigarette and cigars may also be used to torture the child. Singular or multiple circular lesions with eschar at the edges 0.5–1.0 cm in diameter may be seen with this type of abuse.

11.2.2 Exploitation

Exploitation of children can involve either sexual abuse or forced labor. Children in third-world countries are especially vulnerable, but even here in the United States, news stories document young children or preteens being "sold" to someone for money, drugs or other material goods, or even due to intimidation of the parent for purposes of sexual misconduct. Child labor laws in underdeveloped countries are lax or nonexistent, allowing children to work in factories or other dangerous jobs because they are small and agile. The counterpoint is that here in the United States, some child advocates have sought to severely limit children from working on their own parent's family farm, part of a long tradition. Transient labor families and the use of their young children for long hours of low-paying work are typically underregulated.

11.2.3 Sexual Abuse

According to the Centers for Disease Control (CDC), nearly 1 in 5 women (18.3%) and 1 in 71 men (1.4%) have been raped at some time in their lives. More than half of female victims (51.1%) reported rape by an intimate partner and (40.8%) by an acquaintance. It has been reported that 1.5 million women are physically or sexually abused by an intimate partner each year (Thackeray and Randell, 2011). The majority of female rape victims reported that the first rape occurred before age 25 (80%), before age 18 (42%), and before 12 years or younger nearly 25%!!! (CDC, 2010).

A total of over 63,000 cases of sexual abuse were reported in the United States in 2010. A common definition of sexual abuse would be any sexual activity with a child under the age of 18. Penetration of bodily orifices (oral, anal, genital), or contact with the perpetrator's sexual organ, or an object used to penetrate a bodily orifice for sexual pleasure, or oral-genital contact by the perpetrator or by the victim as forced or coerced by the perpetrator are included. Fondling of a body part or frottage (rubbing of bodies together) for purposes of sexual pleasure also fall into the category of sexual abuse. Children cannot "consent" legally to sexual contact or activity in *any* situation. If any adult victim says "no" and/or is "physically unable to resist (asleep/passed out), threatened with violence to self or others, drugged or intoxicated, of diminished capacity or subject to coerced submission and eventually agrees, it is still a crime of sexual abuse" (Alder et al., 2006, 220).

Extended family members of the victim or a paramour/friend of the victim's parent are the most frequent offender. Sexual abuse generally is a progressive activity over a period of time beginning with exhibitionism, masturbation in the presence of the victim, frottage or rubbing of body parts to the point of orgasm, and moving on to actual physical molestation including fondling, or intercourse (anal, oral vaginal). Vesicular, erythematous, or ulcerative lesions may be caused by sexually transmitted diseases such as syphilis, gonorrhea, and Chlamydia, which may also be seen in the oral cavity. Petechial/ecchymotic areas on the palate or torn frenum (labial or lingual) may be a sign of fellatio or cunnilingus. Lesions associated with HIV/AIDS must also be ruled out. Difficulty walking or sitting or extreme fear of a dental exam, particularly on a patient who has been compliant at previous visits, also may be a sign that something is amiss and should prompt further examination or inquiry. More detailed information may be found at the following website: http://www.acf.hhs.gov/programs/cb/pubs/cm10/cm10.pdf#page = 31.

11.2.4 Emotional Abuse

Emotional abuse is commonly defined as a pattern of behavior by the parent or caregiver that will interfere with the child's cognitive, educational, psychological, or emotional development. Examples include: ignoring or isolating the child; rejecting the child or failing to meet the emotional needs of a developing child; exploitation or corruption of a child such as teaching a child to steal, forcing the child into prostitution, introduction of drugs or alcohol; verbal assault such as shaming or belittling a child, subjecting them to ridicule either by the caregiver or siblings, verbally threatening the child; and terrorizing the child by threats or bullying. All can cause irreparable psychological harm to children and adversely affect their development (Alder, 2006).

11.2.5 Neglect or Deprivation

Neglect or deprivation of basic needs of the child include providing insufficient food, clothing, shelter, and medical attention including dental care as well as abandonment are all significant issues. The failure to thrive syndrome (below the third percentile) for height and weight must have organic causes ruled out. Even beyond infancy, evidence of extreme underdevelopment, low weight, or stature all must be considered. According to the American Academy of Pediatric Dentistry, dental neglect occurs when there is "the willful failure of parent or guardian to seek and follow through with treatment necessary to ensure a level of oral health essential for adequate function and freedom from pain and infection." This includes untreated, rampant caries; untreated pain, infection, bleeding or trauma; or a lack of continuity of care once informed that the aforementioned conditions exist. More information may be found at http://www.aapd.org.

11.2.6 Munchausen Syndrome by Proxy

Munchausen Syndrome by Proxy occurs frequently as a form of child abuse. In 1977, an English physician, Roy Meadow, first described a situation where the caregiver, usually the mother, has a psychological need to have their child appear to be or actually be ill. This may be manifest by providing false or misleading histories, altering laboratory reports, or inducing genuine illnesses (Meadow, 1977). There is a need by the caregiver for some sort of emotional gratification, such as sympathy or attention. The perpetrator often wants to be considered "heroic" for "rescuing" the child from some serious problem (Feldman and Sheridan, 2005). This is considered a form of either physical or emotional abuse.

11.2.7 Risk Factors for Child Abuse

Risk factors for child abuse within the family unit can include the following scenarios: a parent who was raised in a traumatic manner (physical or emotional); a parent who is isolated or distrustful of others; a spouse who does not come to the aid of the over-stressed primary caretaker of the child; a parent who has a poor self-image; a parent who has unrealistic expectations of their child's emotional or physical development or abilities; a "special child" who is perceived as "different" by the parent or caregiver; a child who places additional demands on the parent/caregiver due to actual physical or emotional needs; and finally, a crisis in the family such as insufficient food, money, heat, or utilities. Also, an emotional loss such as the death of a loved one or separation from a partner may increase the likelihood of abuse. Women who are in their premenstrual cycle or are pregnant are also more prone to abuse their other children (Kenney, 1991). These same factors may be the "trigger" mechanism in the other types of domestic abuse as well (Figure 11.6).

11.2.8 Conditions and Practices That Mimic Abuse

Abuse may often be incorrectly assumed due to cultural practices. Cia Gio is an Asian folkway where warm oil is placed on the subjects back and scribed with the end of a spoon or coin in order to elicit a histamine reaction and provide relief from an upper respiratory condition. The back, neck, head, shoulders, and chest are common sites of application.

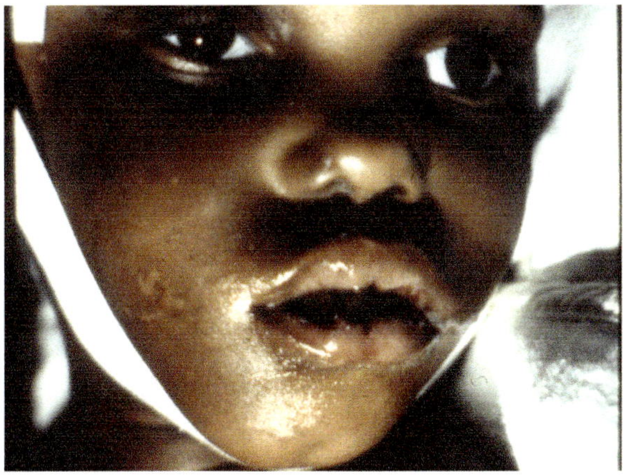

Figure 11.6 Orofacial injuries are common signs of child abuse.

Another folk medicine technique is cupping, where a lighter or candle is placed under a cup or glass to heat the air inside. The glass is then pressed to the skin to "draw out" the infection or other problem. Bullous impetigo is a condition that can have a very alarming appearance, but is a natural disease process. Finally, Mongolian spots are a bluish or blackish discoloration of the lower back and legs that can appear to be caused by abuse, but again are a natural condition prevalent in people of Asian or African descent and usually fade over time.

11.2.9 Who Are the Abusers

Who are the abusers? They are often the caregiver who spend most of their time with the child, they may be lonely, unhappy, or depressed, were abused themselves as children, have low self-esteem, or unrealistic expectations of their child.

11.2.10 What to Look For

What to look for? It is worth noting that many of these same signs of abuse are seen in all of its forms, child, intimate partner, elder, or disabled abuse. As mentioned, the history conflicts with the clinical appearance of the injury, the history provided is contradictory or vague, or the parent or abuser claims that the victim is "clumsy or accident prone." There is often a refusal to cooperate for suggested treatment, often leaving the dental office or a hospital against medical advice, or they may "doctor shop" often traveling great distances from home to seek care and not visiting the same hospital or dental clinic twice. There often is also a refusal to consent to diagnostic studies, but claiming a rare disease without good facts or giving the name of the treating physician. These parents generally will behave inappropriately in relation to the nature of the illness or injury, and there is usually an inordinate amount of delay in seeking treatment for the problem.

11.2.11 Prevention of Child Abuse

Since an article in the *Journal of the American Medical Association* (1962) that described child abuse symptoms, there has been considerable effort and progress, in not only recognizing child abuse but also attempting to educate the public in its prevention. In 1974, the first federal child protection legislation, the Child Abuse Prevention and Treatment Act (CAPTA), was passed and more recently reauthorized with the CAPTA Reauthorization Act of 2010. In 1982, Congress established the first week of June annually as "National Child Abuse Prevention Week" and in 1983 made April "National Child Abuse Prevention Month." The Blue Ribbon Campaign to Prevent Child Abuse began in 1989. Blue ribbon posters, stickers, and pins are prevalent throughout the country during the month of April in recognition of preventing child abuse.

There are a number of organizations that work toward a common goal of preventing child abuse through not only the education of pregnant mothers and families with children, but the public in general. For further information on resources and national efforts, the reader is encouraged to go to the National Child Abuse Prevention Month website: http://www.childwelfare.gov/preventing/preventionmonth/.

11.2.11.1 Child Abuse Prevention Councils

Child Abuse Prevention Councils are but one type of organization that strives to educate the public about child abuse. They are located in all of California's counties and in many counties across the United States. Their mission statements include

- Coordinate community's efforts to prevent child abuse and neglect.
- Share prevention information and resources.
- Intervention and treatment referrals.
- Education of the public on child abuse prevention.
- Advocate for children and families.

The educational mission statement includes free professional training and community workshops. This includes training mandated reporters of child abuse such as dentists and their staff members, teachers, and day-care providers. The Councils provide an excellent opportunity for the dentist interested in child abuse prevention to receive the training by his/her local council and then to be qualified to provide training in the community to groups of other mandated reporters.

11.2.11.2 Child Death Review Teams

In 1978, through the efforts of Michael Durfee, MD, the Los Angeles County Interagency Council on Child Abuse and Neglect formed the first "Child Death Review Team." Currently, there are over 900 such teams throughout the United States.

The National Center on Child Fatality Review develops and promotes a nationwide system of Child Fatality Review Teams and functions as a clearinghouse for the collection and dissemination of information and resources related to child deaths. The Child Death Review Team provides a multidisciplinary forum to systematically collect, analyze, and understand child/family/agency factors that led to and followed a child's death. The forum also allows for organized prevention and intervention efforts that involve both government agencies and the local community (Figure 11.7).

These multidisciplinary groups may include the following members: coroner/medical examiner, forensic pathologist, law enforcement, district attorney, probation, child protective services, public health nursing, community grief counseling, and pediatricians. There can be a place on the team for a forensic odontologist as his/her expertise is needed

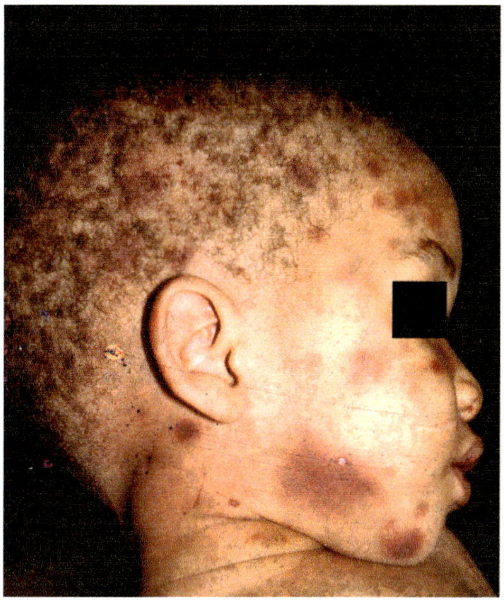

Figure 11.7 Bruises evaluated by a Child Death Review Team.

on occasion. An interested, forensic odontologist should contact his/her coroner/medical examiner concerning joining the local CDRT. Additional information can be obtained by visiting http://www.ican-ncfr.org/.

11.3 Intimate Partner Violence

According to the CDC, eight million men and women yearly are victims of IPV and nearly 2000 die as a result (CDC, 2010). IPV occurs between two people in a close relationship and includes current and former partners/spouses and dating partners. Definitions can vary from state to state. For example, Florida Statute Title XLIII, Chapter 741.28 (2)(3), has a very aggressive set of statutes concerning IPV and DV in marriage. It states that, "DV" means any assault, aggravated assault, battery, aggravated battery, sexual assault, sexual battery, stalking, aggravated stalking, kidnapping, false imprisonment, or any criminal offense resulting in physical injury or death of one family or household member by another family or household member.

"Family or household member" means spouses, former spouses, persons related by blood or marriage, persons who are presently residing together as if a family or who have resided together in the past as if a family, and persons who are parents of a child in common regardless of whether they have been married. With the exception of persons who have a child in common, the family or household members must be currently residing or have in the past resided together in the same single dwelling unit. More may be found at http://www.leg.state.fl.us/statutes/index.

Also, dental licensure in Florida requires proof of two hours of continuing education on DV every third renewal year.

It therefore is important for the practicing dentist as well as the forensic odontologist to be familiar with the laws and regulations in their home state. The parallels between all types of DV are such that for most aspects, one can use the same diagnostic signs and symptoms. Orofacial injuries in IPV are common. Just as with the child, the orofacial area of an intimate partner is their persona and the easiest to attack.

11.3.1 IPV Types

IPV types include categories that are present in some types of child abuse and some types of elder abuse as well.

Verbal abuse: Verbal abuse includes constant belittling or unwarranted criticism of the partner in private or in front of friends or relatives.

Financial abuse: Financial abuse involves the abusive partner using their own or the abused partner's paycheck for drugs, alcohol, gambling, or the abusive partner may sit at home while the victim works to pay the bills.

Stalking or control: Another frequent form of abuse is stalking, tracking, or controlling victims' activities outside of the abusers wishes or controlled isolation from other family friends and coworkers.

Physical abuse: Physical abuse involves beatings and other physical actions, threats, and/or abuse to children or family pets.

Sexual abuse: Sexual abuse includes unwanted sexual contact or forced types of sexual activities not desired by partner.

11.3.2 Dental Team Awareness and Action Plan

Dental health professionals need to be aware that pregnant patients who present with orofacial injuries may need medical or law enforcement evaluation. Serial abusers find partners with low self-esteem or other issues and take advantage of them often blaming the victim-partner for "causing all of their problems."

While child and elder abuse reporting is required in all states, only *five* U.S. states require reporting of DV or abuse. In most states, the only action possible is to encourage a competent reporter (victim) to seek assistance either from an abused women's shelter or hotline or from the local police department. Many police departments have social workers either as part of their regular staff while others have a social worker "on call" as needed. Other departments will have a mechanism to refer victims to a local hospital for treatment and/or counseling. If criminal activity has taken place, the police will take direct action. It is important for the dental office to have a plan in place and to know where to refer victims of DV.

If indicated, written, specific consent for photos and radiographs documenting the injuries should also be sought. This release will allow the dentist to provide necessary information as part of a possible criminal investigation. If the victim is alone at the office or the abusive partner is not present in the operatory, a clear and detailed history may be elicited. However, often abusive partners will not want the victim to be alone with anyone. This is a manifestation of control, but also intimidation. If there are single sex bathrooms in your facility, one suggestion is to provide a posted notice along with tear-off strips indicating victim shelter's phone numbers. Such shelter operators are well trained to screen calls so as not to convey their function if they are called by the abusing party.

11.3.3 RADAR (A Domestic Violence Intervention Program)

This is a Domestic Violence Intervention program developed by the Massachusetts Medical Society:

1. *R*outinely screen female patients
   a. Inform the patient that the practice does this for all female patients, with no partner or relative present
   b. Female assistant always present in the room if a male DDS or MD
   c. Use simple direct questions in a nonjudgmental attitude
2. *A*sk direct questions
   a. Because violence is so common today in women's lives, ask about it routinely
   b. Have you ever been hit, punched, or kicked by your partner?
   c. I notice you have several bruises, did someone do that to you?
3. *D*ocument your findings
   a. Record statements in the patient's own words, for example, "Patient states that…"
   b. Record pertinent physical findings
   c. Create a body diagram and/or photos if consented to
   d. Preserve physical evidence
   e. Document an opinion as to the history given and the appearance of the injury
4. *A*ssess patient safety
   a. Is she afraid to go home
   b. Recent increases in severity or frequency
   c. Threats of homicide or suicide
   d. Threats to the children or pets
   e. Is there a firearm in household
5. *R*eview options and referrals
   a. If in imminent danger, is there a friend or relative she could stay with
   b. Need of immediate access to a shelter
   c. Have resource numbers available
   d. Do not give literature or identifiable information to victim that may be a trigger for the abuser
   e. Follow up appointment as necessary

No matter what the practice demographic, it is likely that one or more of a practitioner's patients either has experienced or is currently experiencing some type of DV.

11.4 Mistreatment of the Elderly

11.4.1 Incidence and Indicators of Elderly Abuse

Estimates indicate that older persons are abused only slightly less than children, yet the reporting rate is half that of reporting child abuse. There is no clear physical, social, or demographic profile of the person most likely to suffer abuse. The majority of victims are women over age 75 with one or more physical impairments, which prevents them from living alone. Statistically, persons over the age of 80 suffered abuse and neglect at a rate two to three times more often than those in the 60–79 age group (Alder et al., 2006).

11.4.2 Categories of Elder Abuse

Passive abuse: Passive abuse of senior citizens encompasses the unintentional failure of caregivers, or guardians of a senior to see that they receive adequate medical attention, have adequate food, shelter, eyeglasses, dentures, etc., because of the caregiver's own infirmity, inadequate skill, knowledge, or understanding of the necessity of prescribed or other essential services.

Psychological abuse: Psychological abuse would include the withholding of simple comforts such as a TV or familiar things in the elder's possessions or intentional damage to personal property that may be a special keepsake for an elder. Withholding contact with grandchildren, threats to institutionalize, or other means of reducing the elder's self-esteem and dignity.

Material (financial abuse): Material (financial) abuse by the family or caregiver includes such activities as illegal or unethical exploitation of funds, property, or other assets belonging to the elder person. In some cases, the elder may be living at a much lower standard of living than they are entitled to by their own assets, and the true financial condition may be hidden from the elder so that the children can "save more" for themselves.

Active neglect: Active neglect includes the intentional failure to fulfill caretaking obligation such as intentionally withholding food, denying necessary medical services, withholding eyeglasses, dentures, or a cane or walker from the elder, thus reducing their mobility and independence. Deliberate abandonment of the elder is also seen.

Physical abuse: Physical abuse such as the intentional infliction of pain or injury or confinement against the will of the elder (Figure 11.8).

Sexual abuse: As difficult as it is to comprehend, sexual abuse of a parent or other elder is all too common both in elder care facilities and within a home setting.

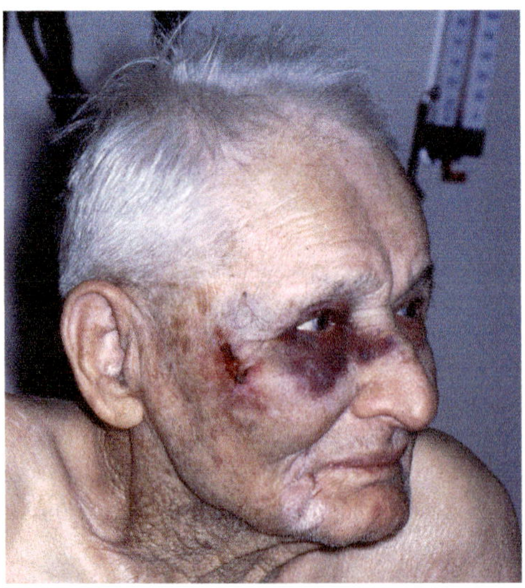

Figure 11.8 Contusion seen in a case of elder abuse.

11.4.3 Reasons for Underreporting

It is ironic, but when couples/partners have remained together despite a history of IPV, the roles of abuser and victim often become reversed. The elderly male who is now the more infirm will often become the target of the female who has endured the abuse throughout her married life.

Elder abuse is known to be underreported, especially by the victim themselves. This may be due to the victim being in denial, disbelief, or nonrecognition of the fact that an abusive event has occurred. They are in fear of reprisal abandonment, isolation, or institutionalization by the abuser. They may be totally dependent on the abuser for food, shelter, and clothing. The victim may have no one to care for them if the abuser is arrested for the abuse. This is the victim's child and they love them. They may be proud, feel shame, embarrassment, guilt, low self-esteem, or confusion pertaining to their relationship with the abuser. They may be unaware of their legal rights or community resources that may be available to them. Because of cultural issues, there may be an inherent fear of police or other authorities or a feeling that family sanctity may be compromised (Alder et al., 2006, 231).

11.4.4 Signs Mistaken for Abuse

Signs mistaken for abuse include venous lakes and stasis, ecchymosis from various medicines, systemic disease such as lupus and erythema multiforme, diabetes, and peripheral vascular ulcers. Decubitus ulcers may be abuse if it is linked to lack of care on the part of the caregiver.

11.4.5 Signs of Malnutrition

Signs of malnutrition that may or may not indicate neglect include pallor, dehydration, and weight loss. These may indicate a tumor or systemic disease. A patient presenting in the dental office must be evaluated for their overall health and an appropriate referral made for a medical evaluation if indicated.

11.4.6 Follow-Up Care

Follow-up care for many of these issues needs to be coordinated with a physician. Because of the varying effects abuse can have on the long-term health of the elder, it is imperative that the person's physician be involved when the dentist suspects abuse or neglect may be occurring and insure the condition is being treated.

11.5 Abuse of the Disabled

While there are both federal and state laws to deal with the abuse or neglect of a physically and/or mentally challenged individual, statistics are difficult to determine. In some states, abuse of a disabled minor is handled as a child abuse case. If the act is criminal in nature, the offender may be charged, but depending on circumstance, no central repository of data may be available.

A case in Illinois involved a profoundly mentally challenged woman who was a resident in a long-term care facility. She was sexually assaulted by a staff member; however, the pregnancy went unnoticed by the supervisory staff. This occurred despite the fact that the personnel attending to her immediate needs recorded missed menstrual periods and morning vomiting for several months following the assault. It was not until a staff member saw the fetus moving in the woman's stomach that the incident was reported. All the male staff were compelled to give DNA samples, and eventually the DNA of the assailant was matched. The perpetrator, a nurse's aide was charged and convicted.

The movement today is to mainstream special needs children in regular school settings as much as possible. This is done to assist in socialization and other regular life skills and to enable them to be as successful as possible. Some children in both elementary and high school find amusement in ridiculing these types of children. Unfortunately, for those with special needs, this can be a devastating experience. Disabled persons are abused at four times the rate of the regular population.

Many disabled adults are housed in group home settings and employed in sheltered care workplaces. A lack of funding for proper supervision of these group settings and the variability in the social and coping skills of the residents may lead to theft of property as well as physical and emotional altercations.

Because of their physical and emotional limitations, the disabled individual may not comprehend the necessity for simple daily acts of hygiene such as showering, combing their hair, and brushing their teeth. They also may be restricted by their own physical limitations to properly utilize a toothbrush efficiently.

11.6 Abuse of Pregnant Women and Prenatal Abuse

Abuse of another human can begin at any age and can take many different forms. Typically, one thinks of abuse being of a violent, trauma-inducing nature, most often manifests in the form of physical abuse (child abuse, spouse abuse, abuse of an intimate partner, abuse of an older person, or abuse of the disabled) or sexual abuse. Sexual abuse is generally accepted as using another person for sexual gratification illegally or without the consent of the person being sexually abused if that person is mentally able to consent or is of the age of consent. As serious as physical violence is, lasting injury can occur because of neglect or from emotional abuse. Abuse can be chronic (long-standing in the relationship) or acute often reported to be incident-specific including the potential for manifesting with the first pregnancy. Although potentially very serious, a very common form of abuse—emotional abuse—might have no visible physical injuries. Unfortunately and all too often, physical abuse can begin even before a person is born.

A worldwide study of IPV indicates that the lifetime risk for physical or sexual violence varies from 15% to 71% depending on the country evaluated (Sarkar, 2008).

IPV during pregnancy is not uncommon in the United States. Depending on the reporting agency, IPV during pregnancy has been reported to range from 3% to 33% (Torres et al., 2000; Huth-Bocks et al., 2002).

Violence occurs in pregnancy more frequently than many of the complications in pregnancy including preeclampsia and gestational diabetes (Bacchus et al., 2004). IPV during pregnancy can cause significant risk to the health of the woman and to her developing child. In the most serious situations, IPV can result in the death of the mother and/or her child.

In an article using data collected from the CDC and Prevention, pregnancy-associated homicide (defined as death during pregnancy or within 1 year of pregnancy) was found to be a leading cause of pregnancy-associated injury deaths among women. The pregnancy-associated risk ratio was 1.7 per 100,000 live births(Chang et al., 2005). In this same article, pregnancy-associated risk factors included age younger than 20 years, black race and late or no prenatal care.

Sarkar (2008) reviewed the MEDLINE database for years 2002–2008 including original articles, reviews surveys, clinical trials, and investigations pertinent to IPV in pregnancy or during the reproductive years. Sarkar's (2008) research indicated that the quality of life of women was significantly impacted. Women stating that they were the victims of IPV were reported to have higher rates of unintended pregnancy, multiple abortions, low-birth weight babies, preterm delivery, and neonatal death.

An educational program available through the CDC is entitled "IPV During Pregnancy: A Guide to Clinicians." This program states that IPV

- Affects every age, group, religion, ethnic/racial group, socioeconomic level, education, and sexual orientation.
- Affects approximately 1.5 million American women each year.
- Affects as many as 324,000 pregnant women each year.
- May be more common than conditions for which pregnant women are routinely screened.
- Is possibly associated with unintended pregnancy, delayed prenatal care, smoking, alcohol, and drug abuse.

In addition to the CDC data, according to multiple reports, violence during pregnancy is associated with miscarriage, stillbirth, preterm birth, and fetal injury (including bruising, broken, and fractured bones, and stab wounds). In these same studies, pregnancy-related violence often leads to increased mental health problems, suicide attempts, maternal physical injuries, substance abuse, anxiety, and chronic pain (Amaro et al., 1990; Mezey and Bewley, 1997; Heise et al., 1999).

Despite this frequent occurrence of violence during pregnancy, health care providers rarely ask about the potential for IPV in their pregnant patients. All health care providers must be aware of the incidence and prevalence of IPV during pregnancy as must become proficient at recognizing the signs and symptoms of abuse and be prepared to document injuries especially those injuries involving the maxillofacial complex. Sarkar's (2008) extensive study showed that women risk for assault decreased by 59% of the contacted the police and decreased even further (risk decreased by 70%) by applying for a protective order. In order to decrease the risk of continuing DV, Evins and Chescheir (1996) recommend that physicians recognizing a pregnant woman with a history suggesting DV should be offered counseling regarding an exit plan, safety issues, and community resources. Health care providers—including dentists—clearly have a role in reducing the risk for IPV if they report suspected cases of IPV to the appropriate law enforcement agency thereby initiating the intervention process on behalf of the victim of IPV.

11.7 Conclusion

In conclusion, as forensic odontologists and practicing dental professionals, it is our responsibility to insure the safety and well being of our patients. This includes appropriate training in order to recognize the signs and symptoms of the various types of abuse, to realize how interrelated they are within a family dynamic, and to have preplanned course of action when a case of possible abuse presents itself.

11.8 Resources

- Local hospitals (Pediatrics, Geriatrics, Social Services
- Local Police Department
- State Welfare agencies
- U.S. Centers for Disease Control and Prevention
  Violence Prevention: http://www.cdc.gov/ViolencePrevention
- The American Academy of Pediatrics: www.aap.org
- The American Dental Association
  http://www.ada.org/sections/about/pdfs/final_report_on_3el.pdf
- The American Academy of Pediatric Dentistry: www.aapd.org
  The Academy maintains a database of nearly 1000 articles and resources for the dental health professional (search Child Abuse Prevention)
- National Center for the Prosecution of Child Abuse:
  http://www.ndaa.org/apri/programs/ncpca/ncpca_home.html

References

Alder, M.E., E.E. Herschaft, J.P. Kenney, E. Latner, J.D. McDowell, D.K. Ord, R.D. Rawson, D.R. Senn, F.M. Stechey, and F.D. Wright. 2006. Human abuse and neglect. In *Manual of Forensic Odontology*, 4th edn, Herschaft, E.E., M.E. Alder, D.K. Ord, R.D. Rawson, and E.S. Smith (eds.). Lubbock, TX: American Society of Forensic Odontology.

Amaro, H. et al. May 1990. Violence during pregnancy and substance abuse. *Am J Public Health* 80:575–579.

Bacchus, L., G. Mezey, and S. Bewley. March 2004. Domestic violence: Prevalence in pregnant women and associations with physical and psychological health. *Eur J Obstet Gynecol Reprod Health* 113:6–11.

Becker, D.B., H.L. Needleman, and M. Kotelchuck. 1978. Child abuse and dentistry: Orofacial trauma and its recognition by dentists. *J Am Dent Assoc* 97:24–28.

ten Bensel, R.W. and S.A. Bastein. 1977. Child abuse and neglect. History, identification and reporting. *Dent Hyg* 51:119–125.

ten Bensel, R.W. and K.J. King. 1975. Neglect and abuse of children: Historical aspects, identification and management. *J Dent Child* 42:348–358.

Benusis, K. 1977. Child abuse: What the dentist should know. *Northwest Dent* 26:230–263.

Caffey, J. 1946. Multiple fractures of long bones in infants suffering from chronic subdural hematoma. *Am J Roentgenol* 56:163–173.

Cameron, J.M., H.R. Johnson, and F.E. Camps. 1966. The battered child syndrome. *Med Sci Law* 6:2.

Centers for Disease Control. 2010. The National Intimate Partner and Sexual Violence Survey. http://www.cdc.gov/violenceprevention/nisvs/(Executive Summary pp. 1–2) (Accessed September 2012).

Chang, J, C.J. Berg, L.E. Saltzman, and J. Herndon. 2005. Homicide: A leading cause of injury deaths among pregnant and postpartum women in the United States. *Am J Public Health* 95:471–477.

Evins, G. and N. Chescheir. July–August 1996. Prevalence of domestic violence among women seeking abortion services. *Women Health Iss* 6(4):204–210.

Feldman, M.D. and M.S. Sheridan. 2005. Munchausen syndrome by prox. In *Child Maltreatment, A Clinical Guide and Reference*, 3rd edn, Giardino, A.P. and R. Alexander (eds.), p. 396. St. Louis, MO: GW Medical Publishing.

Giangiacomo, J. and L.D. Frasier. 2005. Opthalmic manifestations. In *Child Maltreatment, A Clinical Guide and Reference*, 3rd edn, Giardino, A.P. and R. Alexander (eds.), pp. 84–85. St. Louis, MO: GW Medical Publishing Co.

Hazelwood, A.I. 1970. Child abuse: The dentist's role. *NY State Dent J* 36:289–291.

Heise, L.L., M. Ellsberg, and M. Gottenmoeler. 1999. *Ending Violence against Women*. Baltimore, MD: Johns Hopkins University School of Public Health, Center for Communications Programs (Population Reports. Series L, No. 11).

Helfer, R.E. and C.E. Kempe, ed. 1968. *The Battered Child Syndrome*. Chicago, IL: The University of Chicago Press.

Huth-Bocks, A.C., A.A. Levendosky, and G.A. Bogat. April 2002. The effects of domestic violence during pregnancy on maternal and infant health. *Violence Vict*, 17(2):169–185.

Kempe, C.H. 1971. Pediatric implications of the battered child syndrome. *Arch Disab Child* 46(2):28–37.

Kempe, C.H. et al. 1962. The battered child syndrome. *JAMA* 181:17–24.

Kenney, J.P. 1979. The incidence and nature of orofacial injuries in child abuse cases reported by selected hospitals in Cook County, Illinois. Masters' thesis. Chicago, IL: Loyola University of Chicago.

Kenney, J. 1991. Child abuse. In *Manual of Forensic Odontology*, 2nd edn, Averill, D.C. (ed.). Lubbock, TX: The American Society of Forensic Odontology.

Meadow, R. 1977. Munchausen syndrome by proxy: The hinterland of child abuse. *Lancet* 2:343–345.

Mezey, G.C. and S. Bewley. 1997. Domestic violence and pregnancy. *Br J Gynecol* 104(5):528–531.

Sarkar, N.N. April 2008. The impact of intimate partner violence on women's reproductive health and pregnancy outcome. *J Obstet Gynaecol* 28(3):266–271.

Sims, B.G., J.H. Grant, and J.M. Cameron. 1973. Bite marks in the 'battered baby syndrome'. *Med Sci Law* 13:207–210.

Sopher, I.M. 1977. The dentist and the battered child syndrome. *Dent Clin North Am* 21:113–122.

Tate, R.J. 1971. Facial Injuries associated with the battered child syndrome. *Br J Oral Surg* 9:41–45.

Thackeray, J.D. and K.A. Randell. 2011. Epidemiology of intimate partner violence. In *Child Abuse and Neglect, Diagnosis, Treatment and Evidence*, Jenny, C.J. (ed.), St Louis, MO: Elsevier.

Torres, S. et al. 2000. Abuse during pregnancy. *Violence Vict* 15(3):303–321.

Wilson, E.F. 1977. Estimation of the age of cutaneous contusions in child abuse. *Pediatrics* 60:750–752.

Jurisprudence and Expert Witness Testimony

12

ROBERT E. BARSLEY
THOMAS J. DAVID
ROGER D. METCALF

Contents

12.1 The U.S. Legal System 377
12.1.1 History and Terminology 377
12.1.2 Court Systems 378
12.1.3 Application of Law in Cases 379
12.2 Criminal Law 382
12.3 Civil Law 385
12.4 Adversarial System of Law 386
12.5 The Dentist as a Witness 386
12.5.1 Fact Witness 386
12.5.2 Expert Witness 386
12.6 Legal Terminology 387
12.6.1 Subpoena 387
12.6.2 Expert Witness Qualification and Voir Dire 387
12.7 Expert Witness Testimony 388
12.7.1 Expert Witness Immunity and Liability 389
12.7.2 Expert Witness Liability 390
12.8 Rules of Evidence 391
12.9 Tips for Expert Witnesses 392
12.9.1 Cross-Examination 393
12.9.2 Expert Witness Relationship with Case Counsel 394
References 394

12.1 The U.S. Legal System

The American system of government is a federal system based on a constitutional republic of 50 independent member states. The federal government is constitutionally divided into three branches: (1) the executive branch, (2) the legislative branch, and (3) the judicial branch (U.S. Constitution, 1789).

12.1.1 History and Terminology

Essentially, the legislative branch (the House of Representatives and the Senate) is responsible for enacting statues, the executive branch (the President) is responsible for enforcing those statutes, and the judicial branch (the Supreme Court and other lower or "inferior" federal courts) is responsible for adjudicating disputes that arise involving the interpretation of those statutes and the U.S. Constitution.

The federal laws governing citizens of the United States are ultimately derived from the consent of those citizens through the U.S. Constitution. The U.S. Congress (the House of Representatives and the Senate), acting as representatives of the citizens, enacts laws governing various facets of behavior and daily life. The power of the Congress to govern is not unlimited but is defined by provisions of the Constitution, and powers not expressly granted to the federal government are guaranteed to be reserved for the people and the states by the Ninth and Tenth Amendments to the U.S. Constitution (Id.). In recent years, many far-reaching U.S. laws have been enacted by the Congress on the Constitutional basis that these laws regulate interstate commerce in some fashion, one of the enumerated powers granted to the Congress in Article I of the Constitution (Id.). Interpretation of the U.S. Constitution and federal law is ultimately the responsibility of the U.S. Supreme Court (*Marbury v. Madison*, 1803) and Supreme Court rulings on questions of law involving interpretation of the U.S. Constitution are binding on all federal, state, and other courts in the United States. Other holdings from the U.S. Supreme Court *may* be binding on all state courts, as well, through the guarantee of "due process" granted to U.S. citizens by the Fourteenth Amendment to the U.S. Constitution (op. cit.).

Similarly, state governments in the United States are modeled after the tri-partite federal model. State laws are enacted by the legislatures of the various states, and those legislatures derive their authority and powers from the consent of the citizens of the states through the constitution of each state. The ultimate authority on interpretation of a particular state's constitution and laws is known as the state "court of last resort" (often called the state "supreme court"); even the U.S. Supreme Court must defer to the state highest court's opinion on matters of interpretation of a state law or constitution, as long as that interpretation is not at variance with some provision of the U.S. Constitution (i.e., is not "unconstitutional").

12.1.2 Court Systems

A common scheme of organizing a government's judicial system is the following: (1) cases originate in *trial courts*, often called "district courts"; (2) an unfavorable result in the trial court might be appealed by one or the other party to an *intermediate court of appeal*; and (3) the highest court in the jurisdiction, again, the "court of last resort," might be persuaded to review an appeals court's unfavorable finding.* Trials do not ordinarily begin in appeals courts or supreme courts, but might do so in rare, limited circumstances. Parties in most cases usually have the *right* to appeal to the intermediate court of appeals for review of the trial verdict in their case, if they feel so inclined. In a few cases, such as in death-penalty verdicts, there may be an automatic appeal directly from the trial court to the highest court of the jurisdiction, but in most cases there is no *right* to have one's case reviewed by the state or federal Supreme Court. The highest court may or may not choose to review certain cases at its own discretion—if the highest court does decide to review a case, which is called "granting certiorari" or "granting *cert*." An appellate court reviews cases on issues

* Texas and Oklahoma are unique among the states in that they each have two "supreme" courts—(1) the state Supreme Court which hears appeals from civil cases and (2) the equal-ranking state Court of Criminal Appeals, which hears appeals from criminal cases.

of *law*, not on issues of *fact*. *Facts* are determined at trial by the fact-finder (usually a jury, but may be the judge in a "bench trial") after hearing the evidence, and reviewing courts will give great deference to the findings of fact made by the jury. However, reviewing courts will carefully examine questions of *law* that arise in order to ensure the laws were interpreted and applied correctly in the case under review.

When a convicted defendant has exhausted appeals based on questions of law, the convict may seek yet a further avenue of review of his or her case by petitioning for a writ of *habeas corpus*. A writ of *habeas corpus* is a so-called *extraordinary writ* (the extraordinary writs are *habeas*, *certiorari*, mandamus, prohibition, and *quo warranto*) that is a *collateral attack* on the judgment and essentially tests the legality of an arrest or confinement—not directly questioning whether the verdict was correct or not but, rather, whether or not the trial was conducted in a fair and legal manner according to the principles of "due process," and whether or not there was violation of the convict's civil rights. The writ of *habeas corpus*, or "The Great Writ," is one of the most ancient protections extant in common-law jurisdictions, with roots originating in English jurisprudence probably even before the *Magna Carta* of A.D. 1215 and was codified by the English *Habeas Corpus Act* of A.D. 1670.* Today, in the United States, a convict may be able to pursue *habeas* proceedings at both the state and then federal levels.

12.1.3 Application of Law in Cases

When interpreting the law, courts have guidelines they follow. Courts in the United States are first obligated to make rulings that are consistent with the U.S. Constitution and, if a state court, the state's constitution, as well. Courts are next bound to follow any applicable *statutes* (laws enacted by the legislature in the jurisdiction); the courts will then follow any *precedents* of the jurisdiction—precedents are rulings previously made by the court or by higher courts in the jurisdiction on similar questions of law. If there is no existing precedent ("a matter of first impression"), or if the existing precedent is determined to be *clearly erroneous*, the court may establish a new precedent with its ruling. Following precedent is based on the concept of *stare decisis* ("stand by things decided") and provides for uniformity, continuity, predictability, and fairness in application of the law. For example, the first appeal in the United States of a case with bitemark evidence reported (in a court reporter volume) occurred in Texas (*Doyle v. Texas*, 1954). In *Doyle*, bitemark evidence was offered by the prosecution and was not challenged by the defense; the bitemark evidence was simply admitted at trial. (Doyle had bitten into a piece of cheese while burglarizing a grocery store in Aspermonte, Texas, and the cheese was left at the scene.) Mr. Doyle was found guilty of burglary and the guilty verdict was affirmed on appeal. The second bitemark case that arose in Texas was *Patterson v. Texas* (1974), some 20 years after *Doyle*. In *Patterson*, the bitemark evidence *was* challenged as being scientifically "unreliable," but on appeal the high court disposed of the challenge by simply following the *Doyle* precedent, stating: "[w]e held similar evidence admissible in *Doyle v. State* (citation omitted). The objection goes to the weight rather than to the admissibility." (Id.) If there is a conflict between a statute and the common-law precedent, the statute is the controlling authority. But at other times there may be no applicable statute and no existing precedent on point to follow.

* The ancient writ of *de odio et atia*. Blackstone, in his *Commentaries*, *infra*, cites the first recorded usage of *habeas corpus ad subjiciendum* in 1305, during the reign of King Edward I.

Besides the laws derived from the United States and the various state Constitutions and the statutes enacted by the Legislatures, there is an additional important source of law in common-law jurisdictions, and that is the courts themselves (the term "common" is used here in the sense of "uniform"). *Black's Law Dictionary* states a "common-law rule" is "a *judge-made rule* as opposed to a *statutory one*" (Garner, 2001) (emphasis added). The American legal system is based primarily on the English common-law system, with some overtones from the European Roman civil-law system. (In North America, however, the State of Louisiana and the Province of Quebec follow the Roman civil-law legal heritage rather than English common-law tradition.) Blackstone, in his *Commentaries on the Law of England* (Blackstone, 1765), says the ancient English legal system was developed over the years with major influences from the Britons, Romans, Picts, Saxons, Danes, and Normans; by the eleventh century these diverse traditions had devolved into the three major English historical legal systems: the Mercian, the West Saxon, and the Danish. These archaic legal systems were based primarily on *customary law,* a body of rules of behavior based on ancient "custom of the manor." These traditional, customary rules were *unwritten*, and a very significant development in English legal history occurred when some laws began to be memorialized in written form during the time of King Æthelbert. This had the twofold beneficial effect of: (1) fixing the laws in a tangible, immutable form (that did not depend on the vagaries of memory, and which could also be easily distributed to the people), and (2) making the law accessible to a wider audience, as they were transcribed in English rather than in Latin. These *customs* were peculiarly local in nature, and what was the customary rule in one geographical area might not be the rule in an adjacent area. Under Edward the Confessor, these diverse systems were united into a legal scheme that was *common* throughout the kingdom (hence the term "common law") (Id.). Today common-law jurisdictions are usually found in those areas of the world that are part of the British Commonwealth or were part of the British Empire at one time. However, though some laws eventually came to be written down in England—the statutory laws—not *all* of the existing English laws were *codified* as they had been in the European (civil law) system. A *code* in the legal sense is a collection of laws relating to a particular subject that are collected and systematically organized into a (usually) coherent volume. A code ostensibly covers every aspect of some area of law such as criminal law, or family law and, in general, at least theoretically, replaces the traditional common-law precedents in that jurisdiction. The statutes in a modern code-based jurisdiction are thus written and collected into these codes, but the precedents in a traditional common-law system are not. Precedents are found buried in volume upon volume of holdings and opinions from the various levels of appeals courts. While the court's opinion is indeed written and recorded, the precedent itself must often be deduced from the particular case. Many U.S. jurisdictions, though expressly based on the English common-law system, are, nonetheless, slowly moving toward code-based systems. Code-based systems have the advantage that it is relatively easy to search for and find certain statutes and provisions pertaining to a particular subject. The disadvantage is that a code-based system of jurisprudence cannot anticipate every set of circumstances and may be relatively inflexible. The advantage of a common-law system is that there is discretion for the court to make decisions as required by the individual case, but the disadvantage is that it may be difficult to determine just what the controlling precedent is in a particular jurisdiction; locating the controlling precedent may take a great deal of legal research. With the advent of modern legal databases and online tools such as Westlaw® and Lexis-Nexis®, this legal research has become somewhat easier.

The opinions of the appeals courts in a geographic region are collected by legal publishers such as West® and Lexis-Nexis® into "reporters" and arranged in chronological order. For each appeals court there is at least one reporter that publishes its opinions. The collected opinions are published periodically, are annotated by the publisher, and are indexed in a number of ways to aid researchers—so it may seem incongruous that while our common laws are called "unwritten," there are, nonetheless, libraries full of these written volumes of court proceedings and opinions. A court may elect to designate an opinion as "unpublishable" if it adds nothing new to the jurisprudence (interestingly, opinions labeled by the court as "do not publish" or "do not cite" are sometimes, nonetheless, published and cited).

In addition, other governmental entities such as counties and municipalities might adopt local *ordinances* or *regulations*. Furthermore, federal and state executive-branch agencies, such as state boards of dental examiners, may have rulemaking authority delegated to them by their respective Legislatures to develop regulations that, although are not enacted statutes, nonetheless have the force of law and can be adjudicated and enforced through administrative law proceedings.

Of interest to the odontologist may be the precise statutory definition of "practicing dentistry" adopted by a particular state legislature or dental board in its "dental practice act," as this definition may vary in important details from state to state. For example, in one state merely examining the teeth of a (living) person may strictly be considered "practicing dentistry," while in another state it is not. If an odontologist is called to perform some type of forensic odontology procedure in a state where he or she is not licensed to practice dentistry, particularly if the procedure will be performed on a live person, the odontologist should carefully evaluate the possible ramifications of his actions in light of that state's definition of "practicing dentistry." The odontologist should carefully consider which dental procedures he or she may legally perform in a "foreign jurisdiction," and there may be occasion for the odontologist to seek an opinion from the local district attorney or state attorney general on whether or not some forensic procedure constitutes the practice of dentistry in the jurisdiction. For example, an odontologist will likely be prohibited in most jurisdictions from making radiographs of (1) living *persons who are not his or her patients*, such as when the odontologist is retained as a dental consultant to evaluate the claimant a personal-injury case, or when performing an age estimation analysis of a living refugee in an immigration case, or (2) when there is *no diagnostic or treatment rationale* for radiographs, such as a demand from a third party simply for "proof of treatment." On the other hand, performing *any* dental procedure on a deceased person in the morgue is probably *not* "practicing dentistry" in most states and, therefore, probably does not actually require a valid dental license in most jurisdictions, since the decedent is not a *patient* seeking *diagnosis* or *treatment* of an oral disease. (Note, however, the odontologist should *always* have permission from the medical examiner or coroner before performing any procedure on a decedent in the morgue.)

The Health Insurance Portability and Accountability Act of 1996 (HIPAA) is an example of regulatory or administrative law. After its passage by the Congress and signing into law by President Clinton, the act laid out a schedule of regulations to be promulgated by the Department of Health and Human Services (DHHS). These regulations were subsequently published in the Code of Federal Regulations initially requesting comment and then republished with or without modification suggested by the comments received, at which point they acquire the force of law. One example that is of interest to forensic odontology is 45 CFR 164.512, which codifies exceptions to the Privacy Rule for public health activities. Section (g) states

> [a] covered entity may disclose protected health information to a coroner or medical examiner for the purpose of identifying a deceased person, determining a cause of death, or other duties as authorized by law. A covered entity that also performs the duties of a coroner or medical examiner may use protected health information for the purposes described in this paragraph. (U.S. Gov. Printing Office, 2002)

12.2 Criminal Law

U.S. law is broadly classified into civil and criminal (also called "penal") categories. Here the term "civil" is used in the sense of "not criminal" as opposed to the earlier reference to "civil law" as used to designate the Roman and subsequent European inquisitorial law tradition (as opposed to the English common-law adversarial tradition). To be sure, there are many subdisciplines within the law such as administrative law, contract law, property law, tort law, family law, and so forth, and there are gray areas that certainly overlap; but the bulk of our concern here will be with the simple division into civil and criminal areas.

There are a number of significant differences that will be found when comparing the trials of civil cases and the trials of criminal cases in federal and state courts in the United States. The primary distinction between civil and criminal cases is that society might impose a serious *penalty*, such as *incarceration*, on the defendant if found guilty of a crime. In the federal judicial system, and in many state systems, when the suspect is accused of an *infamous crime* (an *infamous* crime under old common law was essentially one that was either a felony or a crime involving moral turpitude; the modern interpretation is "a crime that is punishable by death or imprisonment in a state penal institution, with or without hard labor, for more than one year") (Grifis, 2003), the accused can be brought to trial only upon *indictment* by a *grand jury* as described in the Fifth Amendment to the U.S. Constitution (op. cit.) (the jury is called the "grand" jury because it traditionally is composed of more jurors than the trial jury, the *petit jury*). The grand jury is an independent panel of citizens to whom the prosecutor presents the proposed evidence for a particular case to determine if there is a "prima facie" case (that is, taking all of the prosecutor's evidence as true for the sake of argument, is there enough evidence to determine that a crime may have been committed?). The grand jury may also commence investigations on a wide-ranging variety of subjects on its own initiative. Grand jury proceedings are conducted in secret and are *ex parte* processes (the accused is generally not present nor represented by counsel, and is not allowed to rebut the prosecution's evidence). There is no judge present at grand jury proceedings, and the grand jury can compel witnesses to attend and testify. After hearing the evidence and deliberating, the grand jury may vote for a "true bill" or "indict" the defendant, in which case the prosecutor will proceed to trial or the grand jury may vote to "no bill" the accused. An indictment based on a true-bill vote is not a finding of guilt but, rather, a finding that there is probable cause to proceed with a trial. The Constitutional right to be tried for a crime only upon indictment by a grand jury is an ancient right in the common-law system that protects citizens from unwarranted prosecution. This right is guaranteed in federal cases by the Fifth Amendment to the U.S. Constitution, but the right has not yet been incorporated to apply to the states through the Fourteenth Amendment, therefore, some states have a grand jury system and some do not.

In criminal cases there is a *prosecutor* (variously known as the district attorney, the state's attorney, or the U.S. attorney) representing the government and a *defendant* who is accused of committing a crime, and the action is brought in the name of the government (*People v., U.S. v.*, or *the State of XX v.*, for example). The accused is guaranteed by the Sixth Amendment to the U.S. Constitution, the right to be represented by counsel at any "critical stage" of the criminal proceeding (that is, after charges have formally been made against the accused), including certain pretrial proceedings, and under the Confrontation Clause of the Sixth Amendment the defendant is entitled to cross-examine witnesses who testify on behalf of the prosecution.* Further, the Fourth Amendment guarantees citizens protection against *unreasonable* search or seizure by the government, and requires that warrants may be issued only upon probable cause, and that warrants must be specific about the persons or things to be searched for.† In general, warrantless searches are invalid and unconstitutional, and thus the "poisoned fruits" of an invalid search are not admissible at trial as evidence.

Occasionally, the question may be raised whether or not an odontologist must be acting under authority of a search warrant when taking impressions or photographs, etc. of the dentition of a suspect in a bitemark case; this issue encompasses both Fourth and Fifth Amendment issues and was actually first addressed on appeal in the *Doyle* case (op. cit.). The sole point of error raised in the appeal by Doyle was based on the claim that Doyle's consent to make an exemplar bite into a piece of cheese that was similar to the piece of cheese in evidence from the burglary amounted to a confession, and Doyle contended he had not received the statutorily required warning against self-incrimination (similar to, but predating, *Miranda* by several years). The Doyle court held that the act of biting into a piece of cheese simply was not a "confession" as contemplated by the Texas Legislature when it drafted the statute, and went on to say "[i]n fact, we fail to perceive any material distinction between the case at bar and the footprint and fingerprint cases so long recognized by this Court," (Id.) implying that, as with exemplar fingerprint samples, no warning against self-incrimination was required to be given, nor was a search warrant required to obtain the evidence from the accused; thus both the Fourth and Fifth Amendment concerns were addressed. Other courts in other jurisdictions have made similar findings that dental impressions reproduce a suspect's "fixed characteristics" in the same way fingerprints

* Also see *Melendez-Diaz v. Massachusetts*, 129 S. Ct. 2527 (2009).

† The requirement that warrants must name persons or things with specificity ("particularity") was in reaction to the use of English "general warrants" which allowed the British to arrest and hold Colonists on vaguely-stated premises—the use of general warrants in the American Colonies was one of the several factors leading to the American Revolution.

do, and that a search warrant is not actually required to obtain this evidence.* However, some commentators do suggest that, if an odontologist is approached by a law-enforcement agency to take dental impressions of a suspect, the odontologist should, nonetheless, request the police agency to first obtain a *search warrant* (this is assuming an uncooperative suspect who does not voluntarily consent to the procedure—if the suspect does voluntarily consent, be sure to obtain the *witnessed* consent *in writing*). Though a search warrant does not appear to be required for the procedure under the U.S. Fourth Amendment, there is no harm in obtaining one. Keep in mind that a state, though, may offer *more* protection to its citizens than the threshold required by the U.S. Constitution (but not *less* protection), and, therefore, in some jurisdictions a search warrant may indeed be required to obtain dental impressions under the state law. Note, however, a search warrant is a writ from the court authorizing action by a *law-enforcement agency* and not by the *odontologist* directly. If this issue concerns the odontologist, then he or she might be better served by asking the law-enforcement agency to approach the district attorney to petition for a *court order* directing the suspect to allow the odontologist to obtain the needed impression and photographs. The advantage of a court order is that if the suspect refuses to comply with the order, the court may find the accused in contempt of court and might impose sanctions and, further, if the suspect simply refuses to cooperate whatsoever, the court might even ultimately order the suspect be sedated in order to obtain the needed evidence. Summing up, under the several cases mentioned, taking dental impressions of a suspect's teeth does not violate the U.S. Fifth Amendment's protection against self-incrimination (the Amendment protects against *testimonial* self-incrimination), and the routine taking of dental impressions of the suspect's teeth does not appear to offend the Fourth Amendment prohibition against *unreasonable*

* See *Doyle*; *Patterson* at 862 ("[w]e hold that to require the appellant to produce a mold of his teeth is not in violation of any constitutional protection"); *Illinois v. Milone*, 43 Ill. App.3d 385, 356 N.E.2d 1350 (1976) at 392 ("[w]e agree with the analysis of the Texas courts...[t]he dental impressions, like fingerprints, or voice exemplars, are fixed characteristics of the body of the defendant and as such do not fall within the ambit of the Fifth Amendment"); see also *California v. Marx*, 54 Cal.App3d 100, 126 Cal. Rptr. 350 (1975) at 113 ("defendant had no right to refuse to submit to the tests ordered in the search warrant"); see also *Georgia v. Thorton*, 253 Ga. 524, 322 S.E.2d 711 (1984) at 525 (search warrant was obtained to take dental impressions but evidence suppressed at trial; *reversed*) ("[w]e decline to extend our Constitution as far as would prohibit reasonable police practices, such as the taking of fingerprints, to which belong the taking of dental impressions is analogous"); *but see Id.* at 526 (Hill, C.J., *dissenting*) ("[d]uring the motion to suppress hearing, the trial court expressed the view that the procedure utilized should not be condoned, and that the officers should have applied to the trial court for authority to obtain the dental impressions. I agree. Upon motion and hearing, the trial court could have rendered an appropriate order, which would have avoided the unusual use of a search warrant, issued *ex parte*, to enter the defendant's mouth and take dental impressions. ¶ In the future, this writer will not approve the use of a search warrant to enter the body of the defendant other than to draw blood, except upon order or search warrant issued by a superior court..."); cf. *R. v. Stillman*, [1997] 1 S.C.R. 607 in which a divided panel of the Supreme Court of Canada held that, along with other evidence admitted at trial, dental impressions of the accused's teeth taken involuntarily should have been suppressed by the trial court ("[t]he taking of...teeth impressions infringed s. 8 of the *Charter*. The bodily samples were not seized pursuant to the *Criminal Code* ... Nor were they seized pursuant to the common law power of search incidental to a lawful arrest ... The taking of bodily samples and the making of dental impressions were highly intrusive ... It is clear in this case that the accused's right to be free from unreasonable search and seizure was seriously violated. Since the search and seizure of the bodily samples was not authorized by either statutory or common law it could not have been reasonable. ¶ The taking of the...dental impressions also infringed s. 7 of the *Charter* since it violated the right to security of the person in a manner not consistent with the principles of fundamental justice. It was the ultimate invasion of the accused's privacy and breached the sanctity of the body which is essential to the maintenance of human dignity. Police actions taken without consent or authority which intrude upon an individual's body in more than a minimal fashion violate s. 7.").

search (it is currently an open question whether sedating an uncooperative suspect in order to take impressions is considered to be reasonable or not*; and, again, under some states' laws, a search warrant or court order may be required.)

12.3 Civil Law

A civil case, on the other hand, is very often some sort of *private dispute*, such as an alleged breach of contract or a standard-of-care ("malpractice") action, between individual parties in which *money damages* are sought as the *legal remedy*. In addition to the more typical legal remedy of money damages, in civil cases there occasionally may be *equitable remedies* available as well, such as an issuance of an injunction or a restraining order, or rescission of a contract.

The Sixth Amendment to the U.S. Constitution guarantees the defendant the *right to a trial by jury* in criminal cases, if he so desires (op. cit.), but there is no such right in all civil cases; in fact, some civil litigation may be diverted to *alternative dispute resolution* such as binding arbitration or mediation. In civil cases the "losing" party may appeal the verdict; in a criminal case, the prosecution may not appeal a "not guilty" verdict. In civil cases the parties are the *plaintiff*, or *complainant*, and the *defendant*. There may be different *rules of procedure* for civil and for criminal cases under a particular state's rules—for example, there may be an extensive *discovery* process in civil cases (including, but not limited to *affidavits*, *interrogatories*, and *depositions*), but only very limited discovery process in criminal cases. There may be different *rules of evidence* for criminal cases and for civil cases in some jurisdictions; a proper *chain of custody* can be quite important in criminal cases. In criminal cases in both federal and state courts the "*Brady* Rule" applies, i.e., in a criminal case, if the prosecution obtains *exculpatory evidence* (evidence that tends to show the accused is not guilty), that exculpatory evidence *must* be timely disclosed to the defense (*Brady v. Maryland*, 1963). This is not so in a civil case, however; if the plaintiff becomes aware of evidence that would aid the defendant, or vice versa, there is no such mandatory obligation to disclose. Another significant difference is that in criminal trials the defendant is presumed to be "not guilty" and *every element* of the charge against the accused must be proved *beyond a reasonable doubt* in order to return a "guilty" verdict; in civil cases the required standard of proof is by a *preponderance* of the evidence in order for the plaintiff to prevail. One might keep in mind that an acquittal verdict of "not guilty" in a criminal case does not necessarily indicate the accused is *innocent*. A "not guilty" verdict indicates only that every element of the offense was not proved beyond a reasonable doubt. (Most jurisdictions provide for only "guilty" or "not guilty" verdicts, but in the Scottish judicial system a jury may return an acquittal verdict of either simply "not proven" or, if the jury believes the accused is truly innocent, "not guilty.")

Occasionally, an accused may face successive trials in both state and federal courts for the same crime. This can occur when there is *concurrent jurisdiction* by both jurisdictions, for example, as when a murder is committed on federal property. The Fifth Amendment to the U.S. Constitution provides a "constitutional" prohibition against "double jeopardy"

* But see *Carr v. Indiana*, 73S00-9709-CR-487 (2000) ("[a]s this Court has previously held, ordering a defendant to submit to the taking of dental impressions does not violate the Fourth Amendment when supported by probable cause (citation omitted). Because the warrant was supported by probable cause and the voluntary submission of dental impressions does not violate *Winston*, there is no Fifth Amendment violation in the more drastic procedures required to obtain Carr's compliance" (i.e., anesthetization carried out in a surgical suite).

(op. cit.) or being tried for the same crime twice, but in this scenario the state and the federal governments are two *different* sovereignties, and the accused is not being tried twice by the same government in each trial.

12.4 Adversarial System of Law

There are also distinguishing differences in the way that trials are conducted under the English common-law tradition as opposed to the Roman European civil-law tradition. The common-law system is an *adversarial* system of trial—each side is represented by legal counsel, and counsel presents forceful arguments in favor of their client's position and attempts to discredit the opposing party's witnesses and evidence, and the judge acts as referee much of the time. The European civil-law trial tradition, on the other hand, is that of an *inquisitorial* system—the judge takes a much more active role in the trial and may decide what evidence the court wants to hear and may conduct the questioning of witnesses. In the adversarial system, after a witness is *qualified* by the court, the witnesses will first be questioned on *direct examination* by the party that called the witness, and then be questioned on *cross-examination* by the opposing party. There may be *re-direct* questioning and *re-cross*–examination, as well, in order to clear up confusing issues. The rules of questioning are somewhat different depending on whether a direct examination or a cross-examination is being conducted; in general, the questioning on cross-examination may not go outside the scope of the evidence that was introduced on direct examination. The heart of the common-law adversarial system is the vigorous *cross-examination* of opposing witnesses, and odontologists who testify in court as expert witnesses can expect to be skillfully and carefully questioned by the opposing counsel.

12.5 The Dentist as a Witness

12.5.1 Fact Witness

One may be called to court to testify as a witness in one of two different capacities. An odontologist might be called as a *fact witness* to testify as to something he or she actually observed. For example, a patient may be alleging malpractice against oral surgeon Dr. O.S. and the testifying odontologist Dr. G.P. may have had occasion to examine and subsequently care for the patient after Dr. O.S.'s treatment. In this case the fact-witness-odontologist Dr. G.P. would be called to court to simply provide details about the patient's condition as observed by Dr. G.P. without giving an opinion as to whether or not the oral surgery treatment fell below the appropriate standard of care. The plaintiff would likely have to call an oral surgeon as a witness to render an expert opinion about Dr. O.S.'s services.

12.5.2 Expert Witness

On the other hand, an odontologist might become involved in a criminal case by being called as an *expert witness* after performing a dental identification of a deceased victim of crime, or perhaps by having analyzed a bitemark and rendering an expert opinion as to whether or not a particular defendant may have inflicted the bitemark. An odontologist might appear as an expert witness in a civil case involving a standard-of-care issue ("malpractice") or a personal-injury case, or might appear as a witness in an administrative proceeding before a governmental agency such as a state dental board. The dentist may, unfortunately, have occasion to appear as the defendant in these sorts of cases, as well.

The essential difference between a fact witness and an expert witness is that the fact witness can testify *only* as to those things he actually experienced or perceived himself—sensory perceptions such as sight, sound, smell, touch, and taste; while an expert witness can testify about things he or she did not actually experience. Contrary to what is often stated, a fact witness *can* render an *opinion*, but about only subjects that are within the experience of normal human beings and, again, about only something he actually perceived himself (thus, fact witnesses are allowed to give opinions such as "I think he was speeding" or "I think he was drunk") (FRE 702). Expert witnesses are, again, allowed to opine about events they did not actually perceive ("I think Dr. A's treatment was below the standard of care when he extracted tooth #32"). A fact witness may be paid a nominal sum of a few dollars per day for his or her appearance while an expert witness may command a fee of several thousand dollars—in essence, the notion is the fact witness can be *required* by subpoena to appear and it takes little preparation to testify about facts, while the expert witness appears *voluntarily* and it may take a great deal of time for research and preparation for the expert witness to organize his or her opinion testimony.

12.6 Legal Terminology

12.6.1 Subpoena

As subpoena is a writ issued by a court directing a witness to attend a certain court at a certain time and place. A subpoena may be issued as a *subpoena ad testificandum,* which orders a witness to appear and testify, or a *subpoena duces tecum* or *tectum,* which orders the witness to appear and testify, and, additionally, to bring certain documents or records with him or her (sometimes known as a subpoena for the production of evidence). A subpoena is generally enforceable in only the jurisdiction within which it is issued, that is, for example, a subpoena issued by a district court in California is valid only within the borders of California, whereas a subpoena issued by a federal district court may be enforceable anywhere within the United States. It is possible for a subpoena issued in one state to be made enforceable in another state, but there are complex procedures that must be followed, and this is rarely done as the state issuing the subpoena must show the state where the witness is located that there is a very substantial reason for ordering the presence of the out-of-state witness. A subpoena may not be valid if certain *rules of service* are not followed, but, in any case, a subpoena should not be ignored by the expert witness. Ignoring or refusing to comply with a valid subpoena could subject a witness to various legal sanctions—but the question of whether or not a subpoena is valid is one for the court to determine, not the expert witness.

12.6.2 Expert Witness Qualification and Voir Dire

An expert witness must be *qualified* by the court before he or she will be allowed to testify. In the U.S. federal system, qualification of expert witnesses is controlled by Rule 702 of the Federal Rules of Evidence—note that many states have adopted very similar state rules of evidence for trials in their state courts. Under this rule a witness may qualify as an expert witness on the basis of "... knowledge, skill, experience, training, or education ..." There is no explicit requirement that must be met for qualification; there is no particular degree or training specifically required. (Note, however, some states may have more strict requirements for the expert witnesses who testify in malpractice cases, such as, the expert witness must be a licensed practitioner or, perhaps, must be currently practicing in the same specialty or geographic region as the defendant). The judge is the "gatekeeper" and will determine whether or not the expert is qualified to testify. While the judge must make the determination, there is, again, no precisely prescribed procedure for going about this function. The decision will likely be based on information brought out during *voir dire*. *Voir dire* is more or less a "mini-hearing" in which the expert is examined in order to determine his fitness to testify (the term "voir dire" can also refer to questioning potential jurors during the jury selection process before trial to assess their fitness as jurors). This qualification hearing may occur before the actual trial begins, or it may occur during the trial, in which case the jury will be excused from the courtroom while *voir dire* is taking place. The expert will be questioned on his or her training and experience and knowledge of the subject area. It is important to note that *voir dire* is not an actual trial, so many rules of court do not necessarily apply—for example, questions regarding the expert's personal background may be more far-ranging on *voir dire* than the judge would allow during the actual trial with the jury present. In addition to challenging an expert's qualifications on *voir dire*, the *evidence* proposed to be presented by the expert may be challenged by the opposing counsel via a *motion to suppress* or a *motion in limine*. The court may hold a hearing before or during trial to consider the nature and quality of the evidence offered in order to determine if the evidence meets certain minimum standards. Under *Daubert* (*Daubert v. Merrell Dow Pharmaceuticals*, 1993), the trial judge is the "gatekeeper" of evidence and must determine if scientific or technical evidence to be presented is *relevant* and *reliable* before the evidence can be admitted at trial. The trial judge has great discretion in deciding what material to admit as evidence, and his or her decisions are given great deference by appeals courts. The trial judge, in addition to examining whether or not evidence is relevant and reliable, must also, as a threshold issue, find that the material proposed to be admitted does indeed rise to the level of actually being evidence. *Evidence* is defined by *Black's* as "something (including testimony, documents, and tangible objects) that tends to prove or disprove the existence of an alleged fact." (op. cit.) The judge may find that some information proposed to be admitted as evidence does not meet the court's minimum standard and, therefore, is simply not evidence and is not admissible. The judge must assess the information in order to determine whether or not that information may be admitted as evidence as a matter of *law*, but, once the evidence is admitted, the judge does not assess the *weight* of the evidence—that is, the judge does not decide whether the evidence is "good" or "bad," or "weak" or "strong," or "credible" or "incredible" evidence—that is the job for the jury to determine as a matter of *fact* (assuming a jury trial).

12.7 Expert Witness Testimony

Thus, expert witness testimony might be challenged by the opposing counsel on the basis of either (1) the expert's qualifications or (2) the nature and quality of the evidence itself. The expert witness should be prepared to demonstrate that he or she is qualified to testify as an expert by one or more of "... knowledge, skill, experience, training, or education ..." The expert witness should be prepared to show that the scientific or technical evidence he or she offers will *assist the court*, and it is *relevant* and *reliable*. Therefore, as a general guide, in regard to scientific or technical evidence proposed to be presented during a criminal trial, the expert should be ready to help counsel show: (1) the underlying scientific theory is valid, (2) the technique applying the theory is valid, and (3) the technique was applied properly by the expert on the occasion in question. Very often an expert called by the opposing party will generally attempt to either (a) refute one or more of these three or (b) try to demonstrate that the opposing expert's opinion is simply incorrect, or both (*Kelly v. Texas*, 1992). At the present time, the only general class of scientific, technical, or other specialized evidence that is uniformly excluded across the United States is polygraph analysis; bitemark evidence has not been excluded at trial by any U.S. court, as far as is known.

Expert witnesses in *any* of the various forensic disciplines should be aware of the recent ruling by the U.S. Court of Appeals for the Sixth Circuit in *Moldowan v. City of Warren* (2009). As previously mentioned, under *Brady*, in a criminal trial the prosecution is, in general, constitutionally *obligated* to *timely* disclose to defense counsel any *material* exculpatory information obtained or developed by the prosecution. In *Moldowan*, the court clearly reaffirmed the concept that the police are considered to be part of "the prosecution" and the police have an obligation to disclose exculpatory information to the prosecutor. The court went on to cite its previous opinion from *Gregory* (*Gregory v. City of Louisville*, 2006) that *expert witnesses* retained by the prosecution likewise have a constitutional duty to disclose exculpatory information to the prosecutor. Therefore, the court held in *Moldowan* that an expert witness *deliberately* withholding or fabricating evidence violated a "clearly established legal norm," (op. cit.) and that is a significant finding (the civil right alleged to have been violated must have been a "clearly established" right—it would not be fair to hold the state actor liable for violating a principle he or she did not know existed). A "state actor" who violates a *clearly established legal norm* may be subject to a federal civil-rights suit under 42 U.S.C. §1983. If an odontologist is retained by the prosecution, it is likely he or she would be considered a "state actor" regardless of whether or not the odontologist and prosecutor characterize the relationship as that of "independent contractor" (this is important since a federal civil-rights violation can be committed by only a "state actor" and not by a private individual). A situation could potentially arise where an expert witness has been retained by the prosecution and has developed some sort of exculpatory evidence. As long as the odontologist acts in "good faith" (that is, does not intentionally try to harm the accused) and discloses exculpatory information to the prosecutor, then his or her duty has been discharged under *Moldowan*. If, however, the odontologist *intentionally* elects not to disclose exculpatory evidence, or, worse, *fabricates* evidence, then he or she could now under *Moldowan* potentially face a federal action for violating the accused's "clearly established" civil rights. Note this holding is from the Sixth U.S. Circuit and has not yet been reviewed by the U.S. Supreme Court at the time of publication of this manual. Therefore, at the present time, *Moldowan* is controlling authority in only federal courts in the Sixth Circuit—trial courts in the other federal circuits might or might not follow the holding in *Moldowan*.

The authors agree that there are not many absolutes in life; however, when in the role of expert witness, one should absolutely always act in "good faith" and should absolutely always tell the truth regardless of whom that truth may favor or harm.

12.7.1 Expert Witness Immunity and Liability

The expert witness does enjoy, though, certain immunity from lawsuit. First and foremost, as a public policy, all witnesses enjoy *absolute immunity* from a civil suit brought by the opposing party for testimony at trial. That is, the opposing party simply may not bring a civil action against a fact or expert witness for the content of his or her testimony rendered during the trial.

Furthermore, an odontologist retained by the prosecution, though potentially subject to civil-rights liability as a "state actor," would also likely enjoy the protection of *official immunity* from suit (also known as "qualified immunity" in the federal setting).* Official immunity would protect the odontologist from civil liability as long as he or she was acting in "good faith" and "within the scope" of official duties (note that "official immunity" is a protection recognized at the *state* jurisdiction level; this immunity may or may not protect one from *federal* liability). Official immunity also expansively protects the odontologist, in general, from even *negligent* acts as long as, again, the odontologist is acting in good faith and within the scope of his or her official duties. Also note that no immunity will protect one from liability for *intentional* "bad acts" such as fabricating evidence or willfully and knowingly giving false testimony at trial, or from acts of "gross negligence"; committing such bad acts could render the offending expert liable for both civil suit and criminal prosecution. Further, insurance companies uniformly and expressly exclude *intentional* bad acts from coverage by professional liability insurance policies.

12.7.2 Expert Witness Liability

There have been instances where expert witnesses have been sued for expert witness malpractice.† This situation would arise when the party on the *same side* as the expert witness sued him

* "Official immunity" applies to a government employee, "sovereign immunity" applies to only the government entity itself; see *Barron's Law Dictionary*.

† *LLMD of Michigan, Inc. v. Jackson-Cross Co.* 1999. The leading case in this area is *LLMD of Michigan, Inc. v. Jackson-Cross Co.*, 559 Pa. 297, 740 A.2d 186 (Pa. 1999) in which an expert was retained to calculate lost profits; the actual calculations were done by one of his employees, and the employee made a mathematical miscalculation which resulted in the plaintiff in the underlying case to settle the suit for substantially less than for which it was entitled. Further, the expert was unable to explain at trial how the calculations had been made. The losing plaintiff then, in turn, sued the expert for negligence. The Supreme Court of Pennsylvania stated "[i]t is imperative that an expert witness not be subjected to litigation because the party who retained the expert is dissatisfied with the substance of the opinion rendered by the expert. An expert witness must be able to articulate the basis for his or her opinion without fear that a verdict unfavorable to the client will result in litigation, even where the party who has retained the expert contends that the expert's opinion was not fully explained prior to trial. ¶We are unpersuaded, however, that those policy concerns are furthered by extending the witness immunity doctrine to professional negligence actions which are brought against an expert witness when the allegations of negligence are not premised on the substance of the expert's opinion. We perceive a significant difference between Panitz and Wintoll's claim in this case that Jackson-Cross had been negligent in performing the mathematical calculations required to determine lost profits. The goal of ensuring that the path to truth is unobstructed and the judicial process is protected, by fostering an atmosphere where the expert witness will be forthright and candid in stating his or her opinion, is not advanced by immunizing an expert witness from his or her negligence in formulating that opinion. The judicial process will be enhanced only by requiring that an expert witness render services to the degree of care, skill, and proficiency commonly exercised by the ordinarily skillful, careful, and prudent members of their profession. ¶Therefore, we find that the witness immunity doctrine does not bar Wintoll's professional malpractice action against Jackson-Cross. We caution, however, that our holding that the witness immunity doctrine does not preclude claims against an expert witness for professional malpractice has limited application. An expert witness may not be held liable merely because his or her opinion is challenged by another expert or authoritative source. In those circumstances, the judicial process is enhanced by the presentation of different views. Differences of opinion will not suffice to establish liability of an expert witness for professional negligence." The Louisiana Supreme Court reached a similar conclusion (*Marrogi v. Howard*, 805 So.2d 1118 (La. 2002)) in its answer to the U.S. Court of Appeals for the Fifth Circuit's certified question from *Marrogi v. Howard*, 248 F.3d 382, 386 (5th Cir. 2001) when it held "[w]itness immunity or privilege in Louisiana does not bar a claim against a retained expert witness asserted by a party who in prior litigation retained the expert, which claim arises from the expert's allegedly negligent performance of his agreed upon duties to provide litigation support services."

or her, rather than the *opposing* party bringing the suit—the opposing party would not prevail in a civil suit against the expert witness for malpractice because (1) the expert owes no legal duty to the opposing party and (2) the previously mentioned protection of witness immunity. In order to prevail on a charge of expert witness malpractice, the plaintiff would be required to meet a high standard of showing both (1) the expert was actually negligent,* and (2) it is likely the verdict would have been different but for the negligence. The concept of witness immunity does not protect the expert witness from the party that retained him or her, and therefore does not apply in this situation, and does not protect an expert witness, however, from standard-of-care issues in regard to properly preparing for his or her testimony and properly arriving at his or her expert opinion. (The interesting question arises—to whom does the expert witness owe a duty? To the attorney? To the attorney's client? Is the expert's actual employer the attorney or is the employer the attorney's client? The expert is usually employed by the attorney and, one benefit of this arrangement is that communications between the attorney and the expert are generally protected by confidentiality. But does the expert have a duty to the attorney's client, nonetheless?† And, in addition, note that although the expert is retained by one party or the other, the expert is not a hired *advocate* for either position but, rather, is present in court as an unbiased and "disinterested" witness to assist the court.)

The question of whether or not the prosecution expert negligently preparing or arriving at an expert opinion violates a "clearly established [federal civil-] right" of a defendant in a criminal trial has not been addressed by a federal (or state) court; therefore, at the time of publication of this manual, negligently preparing or arriving at an expert witness opinion does not appear to give rise to a federal civil-rights action brought by the criminal case defendant under 42 U.S.C. §1983. However, keep in mind, under *Moldowan,* acts of *gross* negligence may give rise to such a civil-rights suit (the crucial issue hinges on whether the bad act is "simple negligence" or rises to the level of "gross negligence"—official immunity would likely protect a state-actor odontologist for his or her acts of simple negligence, but not for acts of gross negligence).

12.8 Rules of Evidence

In the U.S. federal court system, evidence issues are controlled by the *Federal Rules of Evidence.* These rules are promulgated by the U.S. Supreme Court and apply in every federal court in the land. Interpretation of these Rules in regard to scientific and technical evidence is "filtered" through several Supreme Court holdings—in particular, the holdings in *Daubert* (op. cit.), *Kumho Tire* (*Kumho Tire Co. v. Carmichael,* 1999), and *Joiner,*‡ known together as the "Daubert Trilogy." In *Daubert*, the Court announced

* To prevail, the plaintiff would be required to demonstrate *every* one of the requirements for a typical tort case—that is: (1) the odontologist owed a *duty* to the plaintiff, (2) the odontologist *breached* the duty, (3) the breach was (a) the *actual cause,* and also (b) the *proximate, or legal, cause* of (4) *actual damages.*

† In 2011 the Supreme Court of the United Kingdom decided *Paul Wynne Jones v. Sue Kaney[2011] UKSC 13* and held that expert witnesses are not shielded by witness immunity from civil suit by the party that retained them, whether sounded in tort or as a breach of contract action.

‡ *General Electric Co. v. Joiner1997,* 78 F.3d 524 (1997). *Joiner* was a fairly technical ruling that (1) clarified the standard of review that is appropriate when reviewing a district court's exclusion of evidence and (2) stated the court should not admit evidence if there is "simply too great an analytical gap between the data and the opinions proffered," nor should admit "opinion evidence which is connected to existing data only by the *ipse dixit* of the expert."

several *factors* that courts should ordinarily consider when evaluating *novel* scientific, technical, or other specialized knowledge*: (1) whether the theory or technique can be, or has been, tested, (2) whether the theory or technique has been subjected to peer review and publication, (3) the known or potential rate of error, (4) the existence and maintenance of standards controlling the technique's operation, and (5) whether or not the theory or technique is "generally accepted in the field"(op. cit.) (the then-existing *Frye* standard†). Note that a court is not bound to mandatorily follow a list of *factors* as it is a list of *elements*; that is, a federal court is not necessarily required to follow each and every *Daubert* factor and, in addition, may also consider other factors not listed, as well. The *Daubert* Court's holding addressed *scientific* evidence in particular; in *Kumho Tire* the Court indicated analysis under the *Daubert* factors could apply to "... scientific, *technical*, or other *specialized knowledge* ..." as well, and this comports with the language of Rule 702 (op. cit.). The Joiner Court holding established that the decision of the trial judge on admissibility of evidence was not to be disturbed without a showing of an abuse of discretion (op. cit.). Note further, there is some question as to whether *Daubert* factors apply to *all* evidence or just *novel* evidence. Keep in mind that *Daubert* is a federal holding that is binding in only U.S. federal courts; some states have expressly chosen to follow the *Daubert* precedent, some have not and, rather, follow their own rules. Many states have enacted rules of evidence that are similar to the federal rules, some have not.

12.9 Tips for Expert Witnesses

Providing sworn testimony as an expert witness can be a stressful experience. A court of law and the accompanying customs and rules for depositions or trial testimony are strange and unfamiliar to most healthcare professionals. Despite the fact that the expert witness may be presumed to know more than the attorneys (and the judge) in the field of expertise at issue, failure to abide by those customs and rules may result in disqualification or a less than optimal presentation by the expert. In order to present his or her opinion in the best possible manner the expert witness should show the proper deference to the court—the personnel including the judge, counsel for each party, the jury, and the staff. The expert should respectfully request permission prior to any action other than a verbal response to a question such as use a chart or a picture.

* *Daubert* originally applied to evidence issues only in regards to scientific evidence in federal civil trials, but has been extended by the Court to apply to both scientific and non-scientific evidence and in both civil and criminal trials in the federal system. Note *Daubert* is not mandatory authority that must be followed by *all* courts but only in federal courts and in state courts in states that have adopted the *Daubert* holding.

† *Frye v. United States of America*, 293 F. 1013 (D.C. Cir 1923). *Frye* established the long lasting rule that the opinions of experts or other skilled witnesses must be based on information that is "generally accepted in the field" in order to be admissible at trial. Though the *Frye* standard has been superseded by the Federal Rules of Evidence and *Daubert*, the *Frye* requirement of "general acceptance in the field" remains as one of the several factors that may be considered for admissibility of scientific or technical evidence. Note: it is sometimes incorrectly reported that *Frye* is a holding from the Supreme Court of the United States. In 1923 at the time of Frye's trial, the district court in Washington, D.C., where the murder occurred Frye was accused of committing, had the unfortunately confusing name of "Supreme Court of the District of Columbia."

An expert should choose the words used carefully, from using common terms easily understood by the jury ("chewing surface" instead of "occlusal") to not using terms such as "manipulation" when describing the processes involved in using PhotoShop® to compare images. The expert should also avoid the use of terms such as "we" that might give the impression that he or she has "taken a side" in the issue. Avoid if possible the use of "absolute" terms such as "always" or "never," instead use terms such as "usually" or "normally" when possible. An expert should not be goaded into losing his or her temper; the opposing counsel may take such a path if it looks promising. Neither should one expert denigrate the character of an opposing expert—however, he or she may freely point out the errors present in the analysis and opinion of an opposing expert as questioned by counsel.

12.9.1 Cross-Examination

As stated earlier, vigorous cross-examination lies at the heart of the American judicial process, in our adversarial system the attorney-advocates for each party (civil and criminal) are duty bound to present the evidence most beneficial to their respective client and to discredit the evidence presented by the opposing counsel. In order to present an opinion in the best possible light, an expert witness should be mindful of tactics that may be employed by the opposing counsel on cross-examination. The attorney may ask compound or complex questions that cannot be answered in a single concise sentence. The attorney who called you to the stand as a witness should object to such questions and ask through the judge that the individual questions be rephrased so that they can be truthfully and properly answered. Often the opposing counsel will demand a "yes" or "no" answer to a question that cannot be answered yes or no. Again, your counsel should object, or failing an objection the expert should explain that a yes or no answer is not possible. An expert should never give the impression that he or she is awaiting "permission" from counsel to answer, but a pause of a second or two, or a request to restate the question may allow time for an objection to be raised. Occasionally trial tactics may dictate that no objection be interposed. At the end of cross-examination the attorney who called him or her to the stand will have an opportunity known as "redirect" to allow the expert to more fully explain the testimony given on cross. Exercise caution when confronted with questions based on written materials, it is embarrassing and weakens the expert's opinion in the eyes of the jury if after having agreed that an article or text is authoritative to then have to qualify the response by limiting it with "except for that part" or similar language. If the expert is unfamiliar with or has not reviewed the article recently, he or she might request an opportunity to read the article to refresh his or her memory. This could be considered a corollary to the attorneys' old adage "never ask a question whose answer you don't already know" in that a witness should "never agree to the truth of a document you are not familiar with." One tactic that can confound many experts is the "pregnant pause." Capitalizing on the natural human fear of silence during conversation, a skilled attorney may not immediately ask another question at the conclusion of the expert's initial response, rather he or she may just pause, looking at the expert. Unfortunately many experts cannot resist the opportunity to continue to speak, entering into testimony facts and opinions that otherwise may have been difficult if not impossible to elicit. One should answer only the question asked and not volunteer additional information. Resist the temptation.

12.9.2 Expert Witness Relationship with Case Counsel

An expert witness is engaged to enlighten the court on matters not within the everyday experience of the jury and attorneys. In order to discharge that obligation, an expert witness must tell the truth and must be able to communicate that truth in a clear manner that is dignified, scholarly, and at the same time understandable. In many ways an expert witness is a teacher—he or she must explain the problem, show how it can be solved, demonstrate to the jury the steps used in analyzing and solving the problem, and finally explain to the jury the solution to the problem and impart to them the lessons or opinions that the expert was able to draw using his or her expertise. This is not always easy to do. The attorney who calls forth the expert must first understand the problem and its solution and devise (in consultation with the expert) a pathway for the expert to guide the jury along. In doing so the attorney must consider how the opposing counsel will attempt to steer the expert and or the jury from that pathway. How the expert presents his or her story to the jury may be as important as conclusions of the expert. What type of imagery is needed (PowerPoint®, charts, video, etc.) and whether a narrative guided by questions along the way or a single introductory question such as "tell the jury what you did" is the better way. An expert who has not consulted with the attorney prior to taking the stand is in many cases doomed to an unrewarding experience as is the court. In addition to speaking clearly, slowly, and audibly an expert should use understandable language, in a conversational tone using memorable analogy when possible.

Novice expert witnesses may express concern about discussing the case with the attorney for fear that just such a question may be asked at trial—"did you discuss this case with counsel?" Of course it has been discussed, but the expert should remember that the facts of the case were discussed as well as the presentation of those facts and the expert's opinion, but the opinion itself was not the subject of discussion, counsel does not dictate the expert's opinion, only how it might best be presented. Similarly many experts fear being questioned about compensation earned in the course of reaching an opinion. Opposing counsel is aware as is the jury that an expert deserves to be paid for the time involved in these types of cases. The best response is to state exactly that, "I was compensated for my time, not for the opinion I reached." Hopefully those arrangements were concluded well in advance of trial. An expert in a civil case is not to be compensated based on a percentage of any damages that might be awarded (or similar savings to an insurer).

In closing, the authors remind the expert witness that his or her reputation is the true stock in trade. Once damaged or tarnished it cannot be fully salvaged. A policy of striving for excellence, doing the right thing, and always telling the truth is the time-honored method for protecting that reputation.

References

Blackstone, W, *Commentaries on the Laws of England*, New York: Oxford University Press (1765).
Brady v. Maryland, 373 U.S. 83 (1963).
Daubert v. Merrell Dow Pharmaceuticals, 509 U.S. 579 (1993).
Doyle v. Texas, 159 Tex. C.R. 310, 263 S.W.2d 779 (1954).
Garner, B, ed., *Black's Law Dictionary*, 2nd Pocket Edition. St. Paul, MN: West Group (2001).
General Electric Co. v. Joiner, 78 F.3d 524 (1997).
Gifis, S, ed., *Barron's Law Dictionary*, 5th edn. Woodbury, NY: Barron's Educational. Series, Inc. (2003).
Gregory v. City of Louisville et al., 444 F.3d 725 at 740.

Kelly v. Texas, 824 S.W.2d 568, 573 (Tex. Crim. App. 1992).
Kumho Tire Co. v. Carmichael 1999, 526 U.S. 137 (1999).
Magna Carta (1215), *Habeas Corpus Act* of 1679.
Marbury v. Madison, 5 U.S. 137 (1803).
Moldowan v. City of Warren, 578 F.3d 351 (2009).
Patterson v. Texas, 509 S.W.2d 857 (Tex. Crim. App. 1974).
45 CFR 164.512(g), 2002.
Federal Rules of Evidence, Rule 702, 2011.
U.S. Constitution, 1789
  Article I §1
  Article II §1
  Article III §1
  Article I §8
  Amendment V
  Amendment VI
  Amendment IX
  Amendment X
  Amendment XIV
U.S. Government Printing Office (2002) http://www.gpo.gov/fdsys/pkg/CFR-2011-title45-vol1/xml/CFR-2011-title45-vol1-sec164-512.xml (accessed October 2012).

Organized Forensic Dentistry 13

ADAM J. FREEMAN
BRUCE A. SCHRADER

Contents

13.1 Introduction 397
13.2 American Organizations 397
13.2.1 American Society of Forensic Odontology 397
13.2.2 American Academy of Forensic Sciences 399
13.2.3 American Board of Forensic Odontology 400
13.3 International Organizations 400
13.3.1 International Association for Identification 400
13.3.2 International Organization for Forensic Odonto-Stomatology 401
13.3.3 British Association for Forensic Odontology 401
13.3.4 British Association for Human Identification 401
13.3.5 Australian Society of Forensic Odontology 402
13.4 Courses in Forensic Dentistry 402
13.4.1 Southwest Symposium on Forensic Dentistry 402
13.4.2 Annual Forensic Dental Identification and Emerging Technologies 403
13.4.3 Forensic Dentistry Program, McGill University 403
13.4.4 Fellowship in Forensic Odontology, UTSHCSA 403
13.4.5 Forensic Odontology in a Medical Examiner's Office 403
13.4.6 Forensic Science, Tufts University 403
13.4.7 American Board of Forensic Odontology Workshops 404

13.1 Introduction

Forensic odontology organizations foster significant interactions with professional colleagues. National and international organizations provide their members educational opportunities, encourage research, and some provide credentialing opportunities.

13.2 American Organizations

13.2.1 American Society of Forensic Odontology

The idea for the creation of the American Society of Forensic Odontology (ASFO) formed in 1962 in Washington, DC, where the Armed Forces Institute of Pathology (AFIP) presented its first course in forensic odontology. Attendance at this meeting totaled 45, 36 from the Armed Forces and 9 civilians. The presenters at this first course were Albert Dahlberg, Louis Hansen, John Salley, Viken Sassouni, and David Scott. Several presenters at future AFIP courses (the next was not held until 1970) would become the eventual founding members of the AFSO including Robert Boyers, Edward Comulada, Lowell Levine, Lester Luntz, Curtis

Mertz, and Paul Stimson. In addition to these AFIP instructors, George Green, George Ward, and Edward Woolridge would also eventually become charter members of the ASFO.

In 1969, before the formation of the ASFO, many of these same individuals were the first forensic odontologists to gain membership in the newly formed Odontology Section of the American Academy of Forensic Sciences (AAFS). This professional organization was restricted to dentists who were already actively engaged in forensic dentistry and also formally associated with a law enforcement agency. Dr. Boyers, however, realized that only those dentists already formally involved as forensic odontologists were eligible for membership in the Academy, and many others interested in the field would be excluded. The ASFO was created to permit membership to anyone with an interest in forensic odontology, thereby furthering forensic odontology. The organization's goal then and now is to provide all an opportunity to receive training and establish interactions with others having common interests. The ASFO was officially incorporated in 1970. In 1971, Robert Boyers was elected as the first president of the ASFO.

Since 1970, the Society has met annually. The initial meetings were held during the AFIP Forensic Odontology Course, and many of the course attendees joined the newly formed Society. In the following years, independent annual meetings were held in Chicago, Oklahoma City, and New York City. It became difficult to manage annual meetings in these varying locations so it was decided to conduct ASFO meeting in conjunction with the *AAFS Annual Meeting*. The first joint meeting was held in February 1976 in Washington, DC, at the Statler Hilton Hotel. The second joint meeting was held in St. Louis, Missouri. The ASFO did not meet with the AAFS jointly again until 1983 in Cincinnati, Ohio, and the two organizations have held concurrent meetings since that time.

The ASFO membership has grown steadily over the years. In 1974, there were 171 members. By 1976, the membership had grown to 215, and at the 1994 annual meeting in San Antonio, Texas, membership reached 411. By 2006, the ASFO had grown to be the largest forensic dental organization in the world with a membership representing 26 countries.

As mentioned previously, the ASFO is open to anyone with an interest in forensic odontology, and there are no educational or professional experience requirements to become a member. The ASFO does not provide licensure or credentialing of its members. The Society's website (www.asfo.org) is comprehensive, and members have the ability to obtain free AGD approved online continuing dental education. Also included for active members at the ASFO's website are the following resources: "latest news," "members in the news," "upcoming courses and meetings," "the quarterly published newsletter," a "documents library" (archived business meeting minutes and past newsletters), "a forensic case of the month," a "members search" (by name, e-mail, state, or country), "research and grants," and forensic odontology-related links.

The operation of ASFO is overseen by an executive director and the following elected officers: president; president-elect; secretary; and board of governors composed of six individuals. The Society also currently benefits from selected individuals' contributions including a newsletter editor, a parliamentarian, a historian, and a webmaster. The ASFO meets annually on Tuesday, during the AAFS' week-long annual meeting. The meeting includes an all-day CE course and an annual business meeting and Luncheon.

Since 1980, the ASFO has produced and published forensic odontology manuals. Drs. Robert Siegel and Norman Sperber compiled and edited the first work, the *Forensic Odontology Workbook*. The *Manual of Forensic Odontology*, 2nd edn., was edited by Dr. David Averill and published in 1991. Drs. C. Michael Bowers and Gary Bell edited the third edition published in 1995 and reprinted in 1997. In 2006, the fourth edition was edited by Drs. Edward Hershaft, Marden Alder, David Ord, Raymond Rawson, and E. Steven Smith. Initially, the various editions of the *Manual of Forensic Odontology* were published by the organization. In 2010, the ASFO entered into an agreement with CRC Press to publish and distribute the *Manual of Forensic Odontology*, 5th edition. Drs. David Senn and Richard Weems were selected as editors for the fifth edition.

13.2.2 American Academy of Forensic Sciences

The AAFS has members from all 50 U.S. States, Canada, and 54 other countries. The Academy is a multidisciplinary professional organization providing leadership and education to advance forensic sciences and their applications to the legal system. The objectives of the Academy are to promote forensic education, scientific principles, research funding, professionalism, integrity, competency, improved practices, and collaboration in the forensic sciences.

The Academy was founded in 1948, and the first meeting was held at the Hotel Pierre in New York City. It now has 6260 members and consists of 11 different sections representing the range of forensic disciplines. The sections include Criminalistics, Digital and Multimedia Sciences (the most recently formed section), Engineering Sciences, General Sciences, Jurisprudence, Odontology, Pathology/Biology, Physical Anthropology, Psychiatry/Behavioral Science, Questioned Documents, and Toxicology.

In 1969, dental members of the Academy's General Section, Louis Hansen, Lester Luntz, and David Scott were approached by then AAFS President-Elect Cyril H. Wecht, M.D., J.D., and Secretary-Treasurer of the Arthur Schatz, J.D., concerning the formation of a dental section. By the latter part of 1970, Dr. Luntz had recruited the other required members to form the Odontology Section. He became the section's first representative to the Academy's executive committee. The Odontology Section was formally established in 1971 with Dr. Lowell Levine as its chairman. Other founding members included Edward Comulada, Curtis Mertz and Paul Stimson, George Green, George Ward, and Edward Woolridge.

Many consider the AAFS to be among the world's most prestigious forensic science organization as the Academy represents its membership to the private and legal sector and serves as a focus point for public and governmental entities concerning the forensic science profession. The AAFS also publishes the *Journal of Forensic Sciences*. This internationally recognized journal is considered the most prestigious peer-reviewed journal in forensic science. It was first published in 1955, and there are six issues per year. To further disseminate the latest scientific and educational findings, the Academy hosts over 500 scientific papers, seminars, workshops, and special events at its annual meeting.

There are several strata of membership within the Academy and also within the Odontology Section. Membership categories include Trainee Affiliate, Associate Member, Member, and Fellow. There is also a "Retired Member" status. The requirements to move from one category to the next vary from section to section but are primarily based on educational achievement and experience. The Odontology Section requires a DDS. or DMD. degree (or equivalent), a specified amount of training in forensic odontology subjects, and an affiliation with a judicial, medical examiner/coroner, or law enforcement agency. The Odontology Section currently includes 433 individuals at various levels of membership. The AAFS's website address is www.aafs.org

13.2.3 American Board of Forensic Odontology

The American Board of Forensic Odontology (ABFO) is a credentialing organization for those who have attained the necessary experience and training and successfully challenged a comprehensive written, practical, and oral examination process. Founded in 1976, the ABFO is accredited by the Forensic Specialties Accreditation Board.

The charter members of the ABFO were Drs. Edward Woolridge, Richard Souviron, Curtis Mertz, Arthur Goldman, Gerald Vale, Stanley Schwartz, Lowell Levine, Robert Dorion, Paul Stimson, David Scott, Manuel Maslansky, and George Ward. Dr. Mertz served as the ABFO's first president from 1976 until 1978.

The charter members established important professional relationships with others in many dental fields including private practice, organized dentistry, dental education and research, specialty practice, and military dentistry. Those relationships continue today.

The ABFO membership includes individuals who are nationally and internationally recognized experts. The objective of the Board is to establish, enhance, and revise, as necessary, standards of qualifications for those who practice forensic odontology, and to certify qualified specialists who comply with all of the requirements of the Board. In this way, the Board's aim is to make available a reliable, practical, and equitable system for readily identifying those persons who are qualified and competent in forensic odontology. The Board also strives to encourage and promote the adherence to high standards of ethics, conduct, and professionalism in forensic practice. There are 103 active diplomates certified by the ABFO (2012).

The organization is governed by an elected "Executive Committee" comprised of a secretary, treasurer, vice president, president-elect, president, and past president. The president serves as the chairman of the board of directors, the members of which are elected by the ABFO membership. There are also standing committees that include, but are not limited to, the categories of articles and bylaws, nomination, strategic planning, research, ethics, civil litigation, bitemarks, human abuse, dental identification, age estimation, and certification and examination. There are also numerous special and ad hoc committees.

The Board has established and published recommended guidelines relating to the topics and practices involved in bitemark analysis, dental identification, disaster victim identification operations, and suggested forensic dental curricula for dental schools. The ABFO has available for purchase a series of digital images suitable for use in educational presentations on forensic odontology. Educational workshops related to forensic odontology topics are offered at each annual meeting. The successful completion of these workshops may provide part of the "case work" requirements needed to qualify to challenge the board examination. The ABFO website is www.abfo.org

13.3 International Organizations

13.3.1 International Association for Identification

The International Association for Identification (IAI) traces its roots back to 1915. Harry Caldwell of the Oakland (California) Police Department's Bureau of Identification wrote numerous letters to "Criminal Identification Operators" asking them to meet in Oakland for the purpose of forming an organization to further the aims of the identification profession. A group of 22 men met, and, as a result, the "International Association for Criminal Identification" was founded in October 1915, with Inspector Caldwell as the presiding officer. Today, the IAI has over 7000 members. They have an annual conference attended by members and associate members from all over the world. The advancement of forensic disciplines through education continues to be one of the top priorities of the IAI. The website address is www.theiai.org

13.3.2 International Organization for Forensic Odonto-Stomatology

The International Organization for Forensic Odonto-Stomatology (IOFOS) is an international forensic odontological organization. Started in 1987, it is composed of member societies that include the ASFO, Australian Society of Forensic Odontology, Austrian Society of Forensic Medicine, British Association for Forensic Odontology, Croatian Association of Forensic Stomatologists, Danish Society of Forensic Odontology, Finnish Association of Forensic Odontology, Flemish Association of Dental Experts, Association Francaise d'Identification Odontologique, German Academy of Forensic Odontostomatology, Icelandic Society of Forensic Odontology, Indian Association of Forensic Odontology, Israel National Police Volunteer Dentists Unit, Forensic Odontology Project (Italy), SIOLA Societa Italiana di Odontoiatria Legale e Assicurativa, Japanese Society of Forensic Odontology, Korean Committee of Forensic Odontology/Dental Jurisprudence, Forensisch Medisch Genootschap, New Zealand Society of Forensic Odontology, Norwegian Society of Forensic Odontology, South African Society for Forensic Odonto-Stomatology, and Swedish Society of Forensic Odontology. Some, but not all of these organizations have a website. However, all contact information for the leadership of each organization can be found on the IOFOS website. The organization and its member societies meet at regular intervals to promote learning and to network with others with common interests. Their newsletter can be viewed electronically at http://iofos.eu

13.3.3 British Association for Forensic Odontology

The British Association for Forensic Odontology encourages education and good practice in forensic odontology and accredits, reviews performance, and mentors practitioners in forensic odontology. There website address is www.bafo.org.uk

13.3.4 British Association for Human Identification

The British Association for Human Identification (BAHID) was founded in 2001. The primary aim of the Association is to encourage productive interchange between various disciplines in human identification, promote the academic integration of individual subjects and through the medium of a collective body, and pursue standards of excellence and innovative development. In 2006, the BAHID produced its first text *Forensic Human Identification—An Introduction*. Currently, BAHID reports that it has over 400 members and student members from 17 different disciplines. Members come from academic, law enforcement, private business, institutional, and legal backgrounds and rely on the Association to provide a forum for discussion and promotion of subjects within the domain of human identification. The BAHID website is www.bahid.org

13.3.5 Australian Society of Forensic Odontology

The Australian Society of Forensic Odontology (AuSFO) was established in the early 1980s and is open to any dental professional of good standing with an interest in forensic odontology. It has no legislative or administrative function, but aims to represent forensic odontologists in their interactions with associated stakeholders. In this context, it is the overarching body facilitating the involvement of member forensic odontologists in DVI, both nationally and internationally.

The Society liaises with the National and State Missing Person Units to help resolve long-term missing person cases. The Society has a unique relationship with the Australian Dental Board regarding dental records for those missing and has direct access to Australian Dental Association publications for dissemination of material on missing persons. The AuSFO website is www.ausfo.com.au

Other forensic odontological organizations are as follows:

- Brazilian Association for Forensic Odontology (www.portalabol.com.br)
- Sociedad Argentina de Odontología Legal (www.sadol.com.ar)
- German Academy of Forensic Odontostomatology (www.akfos.de)
- Progetto Odontologia Forense (Forensic Odontology Project) (www.proofweb.eu)
- Societa' Italiana di Odontoiatria Legale e Assicurativa (www.siola.eu)

13.4 Courses in Forensic Dentistry

As a prerequisite for membership in the Odontology Section of the AAFS, applicants must have earned a minimum of 10 points in recognized and vetted courses. The following courses have been listed on the AAFS website with the number of points awarded for the courses in parentheses:

> AFIP/Indian Health Service CE (10); University of Detroit Mercy (4 or 8); Tufts University (5); U.S. Air Force Post grad (5); NamUs workshop (1); NCIC workshop (1); McGill University, modules 4 & 5 (20 minimally, online plus participation course); San Antonio Southwest Symposium (10), with all workshops (14); University of Texas CERF Fellowship (44).

The following sections contain more information on some of these courses.

13.4.1 Southwest Symposium on Forensic Dentistry

The Southwest Symposium on Forensic Dentistry is a 6 day course given biannually at the University of Texas Health Science Center at San Antonio Dental School, in conjunction with the Bexar County Medical Examiner's Office. The 2012 symposium was the twentieth in the series initiated in 1979 by Dr. James Cottone. The symposium covers all areas of forensic dentistry with extensive practical and hands-on exercises. The course faculty members are experienced forensic odontologists, forensic pathologists, forensic scientists, and attorneys. The course provides experience in the morgue and laboratory settings and realistic courtroom participation. The course satisfies the educational requirement for application to the AAFS. The course website is www.utforensic.org

13.4.2 Annual Forensic Dental Identification and Emerging Technologies

Formerly conducted by the AFIP, this is a 5 day course, now sponsored by the Indian Health Services, and is currently offered annually in Scottsdale, Arizona. The focus of the course is to provide updated information to experienced forensic odontologists and to introduce the less experienced to state-of-the-art techniques for forensic odontology. There is an emphasis on dental identification including disaster victim identification. A significant amount of the course is hands-on. Completion of this course fulfills the education requirement for application to the Odontology Section of the AAFS. More information may be obtained on the continuing dental education page at http://www.ihs.gov

13.4.3 Forensic Dentistry Program, McGill University

This course in Forensic Dentistry is offered by McGill University in collaboration with the Laboratoire de Sciences Judiciaires et de Médecine Légale and presents a unique opportunity for blending theory with hands-on experience in forensic odontology. The course is divided into five modules. Three modules are given as Internet distance-learning courses, and two modules are 1 week, intensive, hands-on laboratory courses. The program covers all aspects of forensic odontology and fulfills the education requirement for application to the Odontology Section of the AAFS. More on this program may be found at www.mcgill.ca/dentistry/continuing-ed/forensic

13.4.4 Fellowship in Forensic Odontology, UTSHCSA

Also at the University of Texas Health Science Center in San Antonio, the Fellowship in Forensic Odontology offers a full range of instruction and experience. Included topics are radiographic and photographic imaging principles and interpretation, dental identification of human remains, multiple fatality incident management for disaster victim identification, bitemark analysis, bitemark comparisons and interpretation, age estimation, recognition of abuse and management of victims of abuse (child, adult, elder; physical, sexual, and neglect), forensic autopsy, forensic anthropology, expert witness testimony, principles of working with the legal system, and research methodology. The fellowship is a 22-month-long course study requiring completion of a research project. More detailed information may be found at www.utforensic.org/fellowship.asp

13.4.5 Forensic Odontology in a Medical Examiner's Office

This course, sponsored by the University of Detroit Mercy in conjunction with the Wayne County Medical Examiner's office, may be taken as a 2 or 4 day course. The first 2 days comprise an "overview course" and days 3 and 4 "advanced training course" provide morgue experience. More course information may be found at http://dental.udmercy.edu/ce

13.4.6 Forensic Science, Tufts University

This course is offered annually by Tufts University as a 3 day workshop. The workshop provides professional training in mass disaster management, identification of human remains, bitemark recognition and analysis, expert witness testimony, and child abuse identification. In addition, a portion of the course is devoted to the topic of bioterrorism/biological weapons. More information may be found at http://dental.tufts.edu

13.4.7 American Board of Forensic Odontology Workshops

The ABFO workshops are designed to assist those who need experience and exposure to practical casework. Casework credit toward the requirements for application for certification to the board may be awarded. Currently, two workshops are given each year in conjunction with the AAFS annual meeting. One week-end workshop precedes the start of the meeting and the other follows. Dental identification and civil litigation workshops are offered in the same year. Age estimation and bitemark analysis workshops are offered in alternate years. More information concerning the workshops may be found at www.abfo.org.

Additional information on forensic odontology courses can be found in Chapter 14.

Becoming Involved in Forensic Odontology

14

KATHLEEN A. KASPER
DENISE C. MURMANN

Contents

14.1 Introduction 406
14.2 Forensic Dentistry Organizations 406
14.2.1 American Society of Forensic Odontology 406
14.2.2 International Organization of Forensic Odonto-Stomatology 407
14.2.3 American Academy of Forensic Sciences—Odontology Section 408
14.2.3.1 Website 408
14.2.3.2 Annual Meeting 409
14.2.3.3 *Journal of Forensic Sciences* 409
14.2.4 American Board of Forensic Odontology 409
14.2.4.1 Website Resources Available to Nonmembers 409
14.2.4.2 Website Resources Available to Diplomates 410
14.2.5 International Association of Identification 410
14.2.5.1 Website 410
14.2.6 American College of Forensic Examiners International 411
14.3 Courses on Forensic Dentistry 411
14.4 Establishing a Relationship with Medico/Legal Agencies 414
14.4.1 Medical Examiners and Coroners 414
14.4.2 Dental Identification Teams 414
14.4.2.1 Disaster Mortuary Operational Response Team (DMORT) 414
14.4.2.2 Kenyon International 415
14.4.2.3 County and State Dental Identification Teams 415
14.4.3 Domestic Violence (Child/Partner/Adult) Agencies 415
14.4.4 Legal Professionals 416
14.4.5 Law Enforcement 416
14.4.5.1 NCIC Missing Persons Database 416
14.4.5.2 National Dental Image Repository 417
14.4.5.3 NamUs 417
14.4.6 Insurance Companies 417
14.5 Curriculum Vitae 418
14.6 Present Lectures on Forensic Dentistry 418
14.7 Closing Remarks on How to Get Involved with Forensic Dentistry 419
14.8 Recommended Forensic Odontology Equipment Lists 419
14.8.1 Dental Identification and Bite Marks 419
14.8.2 Dental Identification 420
14.8.3 Bite Mark Evidence Collection 421

14.1 Introduction

Forensic dentistry is a noble vocation, an intellectual challenge, and a gratifying way to serve dentistry and the public. However, forensic dentistry may not be a viable career choice. Presently, there are very few full-time civilian forensic dentists in the United States. Most forensic odontologists work at their regular jobs and only practice forensic dentistry when special situations or cases occur. It is sometimes referred to as an "expensive hobby" because more time and money is spent on education and equipment than is generated as income.

Forensic dentistry is not a recognized specialty by the American Dental Association. In the United States, there are no full-time graduate programs that offer a degree in forensic dentistry. Education is vital to becoming involved in the field, but it cannot be accomplished in a full-time residency or at one institution or in one course.

Having this book in your hands is a good start. Read this manual and know it well. Other classic texts are listed in Chapter 1, and many may still be found by the "resourceful." Prepare yourself by reading as much as possible on different forensic subjects before attending meetings to be familiar with some of the basic concepts.

Several organizations associated with forensic dentistry that can be of help are covered in Chapter 13. What we cover here are the resources from the various organizations.

14.2 Forensic Dentistry Organizations

14.2.1 American Society of Forensic Odontology

The best place to start is the American Society of Forensic Odontology (ASFO) because it is an entry-level organization created specifically to help those starting out to get more education. ASFO membership is open to everyone. The ASFO website, www.asfo.org, contains extensive information and can be of great use for those new to the field. Listed in the following are the resources available on the website; not all require membership:

Website Resources Available to Nonmembers

- *Latest News*: Links to online articles having to do with forensic dentistry.
- *Courses and Meetings*: The list of seven courses that the American Society of Forensic Sciences (AAFS) education committee has accredited and other forensic courses of interest.
- *Forensic Links*: Other websites about forensic dentistry.
- *ASFO Sponsors*: List of corporate sponsors and their contact information.
- *Research and Grant Opportunities*: Mission statement, application procedure, and research proposal sample for those wanting to know how to apply for a research grant.
- *Contact Us*: E-mail addresses of all the ASFO board members and the ASFO snail mail address.
- *ASFO Store*: Payment of annual dues, register for the annual meeting, purchase ASFO pins, or donate to the research fund.

Website Resources Available to Members Only

- *Case of the Month*: Slide presentations of forensic cases that are educational and/or unique.
- *Newsletter Archive*: Not only the current and archived ASFO newsletters, but also access to International Organization of Forensic Odonto-Stomatology (IOFOS) newsletters as well.
- *Document Storage Center*: First, second, and third editions of the ASFO manual, archived business meeting minutes, archived Cases of the Month, the ASFO Constitution & Bylaws, and the ASFO Policy & Procedure Manual.
- *Online Continuing Education (CE)*: Online courses in forensic dentistry are available and by passing the quiz at the end, Academy of General Dentistry approved CE credit is earned.
- *Podcasts*: Audio recordings of the ASFO Annual meetings starting with 2009 and forward.
- *Forensic Studies*: A place to access research projects that ASFO members have been asked to participate in. Not only are you helping research, but there is usually a wealth of information gained as you do so.
- *Members in the News*: A list of activities and recognitions of ASFO members.
- *Member Search*: By name (first or last), e-mail, state, or country.
- *ASFO Store*: Members have discounts on some items.

ASFO Annual Meeting

Since 1983, the *ASFO Annual Meeting* has been held concurrently with the *AAFS Annual Meeting*. The ASFO day-long session has traditionally been held on the Tuesday of the week of the AAFS meeting. With the meetings combined, attendees typically spend less time away from the office, save money, and have fewer travel requirements. To a person starting out in forensic dentistry, it is very important to attend for several reasons. First, you have the opportunity to learn during the Educational Program. Second, attendees will be able to meet with others in the field, and, hopefully, from their area. Finally, in being consistently seen by others at the meetings, the chances are more likely for one to be considered dependable enough to be called upon to help should the need arise.

14.2.2 International Organization of Forensic Odonto-Stomatology

On the IOFOS website is a list of all the Member Societies, including contact information. It was noted in the previous chapter that the ASFO is a member society of the IOFOS.

It is because of this relationship that the link to the IOFOS newsletters is also in the Newsletter area of the Members Section on the ASFO website. Newsletters from 2006 until the present can also be viewed directly at the IOFOS website: www.iofos.eu/. Copies of older newsletters are available by request. The *Journal of Forensic Odonto-Stomatology* is also available on the IOFOS website from 2005 until the present. If one wishes to write for the Journal, the "Instructions to Authors" document is included there as well.

In 2003–2004, the leadership and participants at an IOFOS international workshop drafted documents titled "Quality Assurance in Forensic Odonto-Stomatology" that are similar in purpose to the American Board of Forensic Odontology (ABFO) Standards and Guidelines. The categories covered are General Considerations, Identification—Single Cases, Identification after Disasters, Age Estimation, Tooth Marks, Dental Injuries, and Forensic Odontology Report. All are available on the IOFOS website.

Other items of value on the IOFOS website are Interpol's Disaster Victim Identification Forms, worldwide contacts listed by country, a page of other links of forensic interest, and a list of upcoming events. The most important of those is the annual IOFOS meeting held in conjunction with the International Association of Forensic Sciences (IAFS). The President Elect of both the ASFO and ABFO often attend the annual IOFOS meeting.

14.2.3 American Academy of Forensic Sciences—Odontology Section

According to its website, the AAFS is "a professional society dedicated to the application of science to the law, the AAFS is committed to the promotion of education and the elevation of accuracy, precision, and specificity in the forensic sciences ...." The 6260 members are divided into 11 sections spanning the forensic specialties. One of those 11 sections is Odontology.

14.2.3.1 Website

The AAFS's website has a list of news and current event links conveniently placed on its homepage, www.aafs.org. The list of the 11 sections of the AAFS, including the odontology section, can be found in the section titled "About the AAFS." Names and contact information of the section officers and the section statistics are also in this section. In the membership section, the entry-level requirements as well as requirements for upgrading or promoting to the next membership level are given.

The section titled "Resources" has a dropdown list including the following:

- *Academy News*—Copies of the bimonthly publication of the AAFS, going back from January 2003 to the present
- *Young Forensic Scientist Forum*—A link to that website
- *Employment*—Both current job openings and a place to post a job
- *Forensic links*—This is a large list separated into three sections: (1) Organizations, (2) Publications/Resources, and (3) In Memory Of
- *Proceedings*—Copies of the annual meeting documents that include thousands of abstracts of the technical oral papers and posters presented at the *AAFS Annual Meeting* from 2002 to the present (approximately 500 per year)
- *Videos*—Videos in wmv format
- *News and Events Archive*—Where links that were once posted under the Current News and Events are archived, starting with the September 2009 AAFS Position Statement in Response to the *National Academy of Science Report of the Forensic Sciences*

The section concerning the *Journal of Forensic Sciences* has the contact information for the Journal, a section on "Information for Authors" and a general public searchable index of the Journal.

Finally, the "Meetings" section has the information for the *AAFS Annual Meeting*, the *Forensic Science Educational Conferences*, *IAFS Annual Meeting*, *International Educational Outreach*, and a list of "other" meetings of forensic interest.

14.2.3.2 *Annual Meeting*

As mentioned previously, the *ASFO Annual Meeting* is held in conjunction with the *AAFS Annual Meeting*, making it easier to attain more forensic education at one location. Workshops are held on the Monday before and the Saturday after the meeting. The majority of business meetings for each section are held on Wednesday of the meeting. The technical oral papers and posters are presented during the Scientific Sessions on the Thursday and Friday and are grouped by AAFS section. Thus, the Odontology Section has those two full days to be exposed to some of the latest research and clinical case studies available in forensic dentistry.

14.2.3.3 Journal of Forensic Sciences

The *Journal of Forensic Sciences* is an official publication of the AAFS by Wiley Subscription Services, Inc. It is peer-reviewed and published bimonthly. Papers, technical notes, case reports, and book reviews are submitted from all 11 sections, making it an excellent educational tool.

14.2.4 American Board of Forensic Odontology

The ABFO is the organization that certifies forensic odontologists. The ABFO is recognized by the AAFS and accredited by the Forensic Specialties Accreditation Board. The requirements to become a diplomate are extensive and arduous, but that only makes the accomplishment of the goal that much more meaningful. While it may be difficult to become a diplomate, the ABFO website, www.abfo.org, is a rich resource to all who are interested in forensic odontology.

14.2.4.1 *Website Resources Available to Nonmembers*

One of the most informative items on the ABFO website is the *ABFO Manual*, which may be downloaded and printed at no cost. Sections I and II contain the necessary background, business, and bylaws of the organization. Section III, however, is a "gold mine of information." Here reside the policies, procedures, standards and guidelines on bite mark methodology, body identification, mass fatality incidents, and age estimation. It is crucial to be familiar with them if you ever have the opportunity to deal with these forensic odontology topics.

Also on the homepage is the link to Identification (ID) Teams, which are listed by state and include whom to contact to inquire about joining. Be aware, however, that some of the teams are already filled and may not be taking applications. If there is a waiting list, get your name on it. In the mean time, get more education so that if your name is selected, you will be a better qualified candidate.

"Member List by Location" can also be used to determine which ABFO Diplomates reside in your area. An interested individual can contact them to ask if they need any assistance in their area. Even if they do not, they may be a rich resource on what you may do to advance in the field.

Available for purchase is the ABFO slide series (now in digital format), with several different PowerPoint presentations: History and Scope of Forensic Odontology, Dental Identification, Bite Mark Recognition and Analysis, Abuse and Neglect, Dental Autopsy Protocol, Multiple Fatality Incidents—Hurricane Katrina, and PowerPoint Show Tributes to Katrina and the World Trade Center. Also, the "Speakers Bureau" link provides a list of Diplomates who might be willing to lecture in your area on forensic odontology.

14.2.4.2 Website Resources Available Only to Diplomates

Here, members may find the items previously listed, the minutes and committee reports of various ABFO meetings, and copies of papers and articles of interest.

14.2.5 International Association of Identification

On its website, the International Association for Identification (IAI) proclaims to be "the world's oldest and largest forensic science/identification association." The organization was founded in 1915 as the "International Association for Criminal Identification." However, by 1918, the word "Criminal" was removed from the title because it was recognized that there was much work done by identification bureaus that had no involvement with criminals. There are no educational requirements to become a member. There *are* educational requirements for the certification programs. Currently, there is no certification program for odontology.

14.2.5.1 Website

The IAI website has much to offer. There are several links from the homepage: www.theiai.org

- *Membership*: Lists the benefits of membership, qualification, and types of memberships and the membership application form.
- *Training*: The training programs are listed in four categories: IAI sponsored training opportunities, IAI division conferences, the international education conference, and vendor/supplier and private training.
- *Certifications*: IAI has several certification boards, and they are listed on this page with links to more information. However, IAI does not have a certification board for forensic odontology.
- *Disciplines*: On this page are listed the 16 forensic disciplines recognized by the IAI. Forensic odontology is one of them.
- *Scientific Working Group (SWG) Guidelines*: There are six (SWG) Guideline links on this page. The two that are important in forensic odontology are the Scientific Working Group on Imaging Technology (SWIGIT) and The Scientific Working Group on Digital Evidence (SWGDE).
- *Conference*: Information is given for the Annual IAI International Conference as well as the sites for future conferences.
- *Publications*: There are several IAI publications available for purchase on this page. It is noted here that the *Journal of Forensic Identification* is an internationally recognized, peer-reviewed, bimonthly scientific journal, which is free to its members.
- *History*: Not only of the history of the organization, but also of the history of the emblem of IAI (contains the fingerprint of Sir Francis Galton).
- *IAI Research Library*: The West Virginia University Library houses the IAI Research Library. On this page, there is a "Finding Aid," access to a "Digital Images Collection," a link to access the collection, a "LibGuide to Forensics," and external links.
- *Divisions*: The IAI is made up of several divisions that are based on geographic location (usually by state, states, or country). The list and link to each division are found here.

- *Links*: Contains links to related forensic or law enforcement sites and documents. The AAFS and ABFO sites are among them.
- *Current Affairs*: Links to items of interest to IAI members.

14.2.6 American College of Forensic Examiners International

The website of the American College of Forensic Examiners international (ACFEI) states that their organization is "an independent, scientific, and professional association representing forensic examiners worldwide." The ACFEI has 11 areas in which they provide certification or accreditation in, but odontology is not one of those fields. To become a member in the odontology section, the only requirement is the payment of dues. ACFEI has 12 advisory boards, one of which is the American Board of Forensic Dentistry (ABFD). The official journal of the ACFEI is *The Forensic Examiner*, which is published quarterly, is "peer-reviewed" and is free to members.

The ACFEI website, www.acfei.com, has information on how to become a member, information about credentialing programs (none for odontology), requirements to become a diplomate or fellow, the list of their advisory boards, a search of members to find a "forensic specialist," information on their national conference, and the "Detective Corner," which is a link to short pieces of forensic fiction, which have been published in the *Forensic Examiner*.

14.3 Courses on Forensic Dentistry

Most experienced forensic odontologists would agree that the most logical starting point for entering the field of forensic dentistry is to attend or participate in one of the numerous forensic CE courses currently available. Table 14.1 lists several of the more popular courses, which are suitable for both novice and experienced individuals. The ASFO and the ABFO websites (both previously mentioned in this chapter) maintain an updated list of CE courses pertaining to this topic. As also mentioned previously, it is the intent of the ABFO to not only educate those in the field of forensic dentistry but also assist in obtaining the requirements to become board certified. To that end, the ABFO holds two workshops each year in association with the Annual AAFS Meeting. Current workshops are listed on the ABFO website. It takes little time and effort to investigate those sites for the most current educational opportunities and training available in the field.

It is important to note that many of the CE courses are taught by most of the nationally and internationally renowned leaders in forensic dentistry. What better way to make one's presence known than the opportunity to mingle with the "best of the best?" In addition to gaining a wealth of knowledge, this could very well be the best way to open the "door" to an amazing forensic dental career.

For those still involved with their dental training, some dental schools offer elective forensic dentistry courses in their curricula. This may assist a dental student in deciding whether forensic dentistry is really of interest to them. At the time of the publication of this text, there are at least 16 out of 63 accredited dental schools in the United States, which offer courses to dental students in forensic odontology.

One may also elect to pursue further education in the general forensic sciences by enrolling in or auditing a forensic anthropology or other forensic science course

Table 14.1 Forensic Odontology Courses

Course title	**Fellowship in Forensic Odontology** Center for Education and Research in Forensics (CERF), University of Texas HSC at San Antonio
Course length	22 months (8–9) 3–4 day weekends Nonresident, intermittent attendance course
Research required	Yes
Continuing education hours received	330 h
Meets AAFS/ABFO educational requirements	Yes
Course location	UTHSCSA San Antonio, TX
Contact	David Senn, DDS, DABFO senn@uthscsa.edu Phone: (210) 567-3379
Website	www.utforensic.org
Course title	**Forensic Dentistry Program** McGill University Montreal, Quebec, Canada
Course length	1 year
Research required	Yes
Continuing education hours received	320 h
Meets AAFS/ABFO educational requirements	Yes
Course location	Modules 1–3 (online) Modules 4–5 (hands-on), Montreal, Quebec, Canada
Contact	Nikoo Taghani (nikoo.taghani@mcgill.ca) or Olga Chodan (olga.chodan@mcgill.ca) Phone (514) 398-7203, Local 00061
Website	www.mcgill.ca/dentistry/continuing-ed/forensic
Course title	**Forensic Identification and Emerging Technologies** Lectures and Mini Workshops (Formerly Armed Forces Institute of Pathology [AFIP])
Course length	5 days
Research required	No
Continuing education hours received	40 h
Meets AAFS/ABFO educational requirements	Yes
Course location	Locations change annually
Contact	Duane R Schafer, Capt, DC, USN duane.schafer@med.navy.mil
Website	http://www.ihs.gov/medicalprograms/dentalcde/ or www.asfo.org for updates and locations
Course title	**Southwest Symposium on Forensic Dentistry** (Course available even numbered years only)
Course length	5½ days
Research required	No
Continuing education hours received	50 h for M-S course Approximately 50% hands on

Table 14.1 (continued) Forensic Odontology Courses

Meets AAFS/ABFO educational requirements	Yes
Course location	University of Texas HSC San Antonio, TX
Contact	David R Senn, DDS, DABFO senn@uthscsa.edu Phone (210) 567–3379
Website	www.utforensic.org
Course title	**Forensic Odontology in a Medical Examiner's Office**
Course length	4 days: 2 days lecture and 2 days hands on workshop
Research required	No
Continuing education hours received	14 h lecture 28 h hands on
Meets AAFS/ABFO educational requirements	Partial fulfillment
Course location	Wayne County Medical Examiner's Office Detroit, MI
Contact	Allan Warnick DDS, DABFO Ms Treena Guy Phone (313) 494–6626
Website	www.dental.udmercy.edu/ce
Course title	**Investigation for Identification** (Course available odd numbered years only)
Course length	2 days lecture and 1 day optional hands on workshop
Research required	No
Continuing education hours received	14 h lecture 7 h hands on
Meets AAFS/ABFO educational requirements	Partial fulfillment
Course location	New Orleans, LA
Contact	LSU Forensics Phone (504) 941–8193
Website	www.lsuforensics.org
Course title	**FBI/NCIC Dental coding course**
Course length	2 days
Research required	No
Continuing education hours received	16 h
Meets AAFS/ABFO educational requirements	Partial fulfillment
Course location	Locations change
Contact	Harry E Carlile Jr. FBI Phone (304) 625–3578
Website	No website; can contact by e-mail harry.carlile@leo.gov or check www.asfo.org for current course information

offered at a local college or university. These courses would provide for a well-rounded background in the other forensic sciences, which is equally important for you to know, and they may also put you in direct contact with an individual who may be affiliated with a medical examiner/coroner or law enforcement agency, which could help open doors.

By participating in one or several of the courses or training modalities aforementioned, one can establish and demonstrate a degree of seriousness and commitment to the forensic dental community. It can never be known who will be encountered at a meeting, a course or a class that may advance ones forensic dental career.

14.4 Establishing a Relationship with Medico/Legal Agencies

14.4.1 Medical Examiners and Coroners

Establishing a relationship with medico-legal agencies such as medical examiners, coroners, or law enforcement agencies may seem simple in theory, but often that is not the case. One may attempt to make initial contact with any of these agencies by sending an introductory letter expressing your interest. State what training and education you have completed and attach a current Curriculum Vitae (CV). Another way to make contact is to call the agency directly and speak with the individual in charge. Inquire about setting up a meeting to talk to the current odontologist, take a tour of their facility, watch an autopsy (if at a medical examiner's office), or ask to shadow on a case. This is a good way to make your interest in forensic dentistry known and to demonstrate that you can handle the inherent challenges associated with the field.

Knowing someone personally as a point of contact in one of these agencies may prove to be very fruitful; perhaps a patient, a neighbor, or an acquaintance that has that personal connection. Speak to anyone who will listen that you are genuinely interested in forensic dentistry. If an odontologist affiliated with an agency knows of you personally, or if someone the odontologist knows can vouch for you personally, chances are greater to successfully make an initial contact. What you make of that initial contact is entirely up to you. You may only have one chance to make a good impression. Act professionally, interested, ask questions, be discrete, and do not be overbearing. Offering your services at no charge may also be advantageous. However, be aware that this will create a "financial trap," which is often difficult to escape later without "hard feelings" on their part. Also, one must be willing to drop everything when called upon to assist on or work up a forensic dental case. It may also unfortunately be the case that if one says "no" just one time, no future requests for your services will be made.

Once a "foot is in the door," wedge it tight. Once officially invited to be involved, you should realize that you are fortunate enough to have found a mentor in forensic dentistry. This is the absolute best way to increase one's knowledge, training, and experience. A mentor will also make you privy to a host of other opportunities that would not otherwise be encountered without that individual. In fact, many success stories of how an individual became involved with forensic dentistry, will claim that one person, a mentor, was responsible.

14.4.2 Dental Identification Teams

14.4.2.1 Disaster Mortuary Operational Response Team (DMORT)

The DMORT is a federally funded and operated Mass Fatality Incident (MFI) organization (see Chapter 6). The DMORT website at www.dmort.org may be used to determine which states comprise each region. Once this has been determined, the administrative officer for that region may be found and contacted. Note that most regions (teams) also have their own website specific to their region's activities. Determine if space is currently available for forensic odontologists or dental auxiliaries in that particular team. If there is space in your region and your application for membership is approved, you will receive some additional training and education in the area of dental identifications and mass fatality incidents, typically at regional training events. If there is no space available at the time, ask to be placed on a waiting list. Many of this country's most prominent forensic dentists play important roles in this organization. Thus, DMORT is a wonderful opportunity to learn *and* become established in the forensic dentistry community.

14.4.2.2 Kenyon International

Kenyon International is a privately held company whose only interest since 1906 has been MFI response. The company has more than 1200 team members throughout the world including the United States, Canada, South America, United Kingdom, Australia, and Hong Kong. Kenyon International maintains fully equipped mobile morgues (including one in Houston, Texas) and contracts odontologists, dental hygienists, pathologists, anthropologists, DNA technicians, and other forensic scientists. Team members are selected based upon their professional experience, licensure, and certification credentials. To inquire about being part of the team, refer to the Kenyon International's website at www.kenyon international.com

14.4.2.3 County and State Dental Identification Teams

County and state dental identification teams, if available, vary by state. One can easily check what organizations are already established using the ABFO's website resources (www.abfo.org). There, one may find mass fatality dental identification teams and their contact information listed by state and in alphabetical order. Make contact with the state team leader and determine if there is space available on the team. If not, ask to be placed on the list to be contacted in the future when space does become available. In addition, ask the team leader what additional training and education courses one should attend to become better qualified. In larger cities, the medical examiner/coroner may have their own local identification teams. Call or write these agencies and inquire about whether such a team is available and if there is space for you on the team.

14.4.3 Domestic Violence (Child/Partner/Adult) Agencies

Agencies involved with Domestic Violence (DV) need trained experts available for evaluation of physical and sexual abuse (see Chapter 11). A forensic dentist is one such individual. There are a variety of ways to make entry-level progress into this arena. First and foremost, contact your county Child Advocacy Center (CAC). CACs reduce the revictimization of the child, removes barriers to investigation and treatment, and enhances criminal prosecution with a distinctive multidisciplinary and united approach to child abuse cases. CAC works in agreement with public and private agencies including Law Enforcement, Child Protective Services, the District Attorney's Office, and Children's Medical Centers. Initial contact may be established by searching online for a CAC in your area. If there is no CAC in the area, contact the county District Attorney's Office. A second way to make entry into Child Protective Services and make your services as a forensic dentist known is to contact your state-level Child Protective Services agency.

Adult Protective Services (relating to Elder abuse) is a federally mandated program. However, due to a lack of federal funding, each state develops its own APS program according to the laws of that particular state. Therefore, to connect with an APS program and potentially get involved, one should contact their county and/or state APS program. This can be done online by referencing Adult Protective Services or Department of Family and Protective Services. Often there will be Advocacy Centers for adult abuse and neglect much as previously described for children.

Additionally, volunteering at battered women's or other protective shelters for adults could open doors for a forensic dental career. Most states have a Family Violence Coalition. Initial inquiry can be made to the state Executive Director of the Coalition. Ask this individual if they need assistance from a dental expert for victims of DV. The National Domestic Violence Hotline at (800) 799–7233, is another good way to get information for all programs and counseling services currently available for victims of DV.

14.4.4 Legal Professionals

Approaching prosecuting attorneys, public defenders, and civil attorneys may not be one of the easiest ways to get involved in forensic dentistry, but it could work. In larger cities, these may already consult with a forensic odontologist. If that is the case, try a smaller neighboring county or city. Many times these smaller entities are in need of a dental expert. Contact an attorney in your state who defends or prosecutes dental malpractice cases. Also, contact your state's Board of Dental Examiners. Contact your State Bar Association and ask to be listed as a dental expert in their directory or in the classified section of a state legal journal. Legal professionals seek experts who have training, experience, and specialized knowledge in the field of dentistry and/or forensic odontology. Be prepared!

14.4.5 Law Enforcement

Law enforcement agencies in most major cities should utilize the services of a dental expert. Many will already have a forensic dentist consultant with whom they are working. Don't give up! Contact your local police department and speak with a person of responsibility in crime scene investigations or an investigative detective.

14.4.5.1 NCIC Missing Persons Database

Volunteering to code dental information into the proper format for missing, unidentified, and wanted individuals is yet another way to get involved in forensic dentistry (see Chapter 7). The Federal Bureau of Investigation's National Crime Information Center (NCIC) databases used by law enforcement agencies rarely have laypersons skilled at dental coding. It is not mandatory, but extremely helpful for one to take the FBI/NCIC dental coding workshops previously cited in Table 14.1. Once this course has been completed, an FBI representative will make your name and contact information available (with your permission) to law enforcement agencies in appropriate state and local agencies. Trained volunteer resources may then assist them with the proper dental coding of missing, unidentified, and wanted cases as well as to aid in the review of potential matches. This information may also be posted on the Law Enforcement Online (LEO) website as a potential resource for agencies who may need dental assistance and expertise. Most experts will agree that *the* major flaw with the NCIC's missing persons module involves the proper entry of the missing person's dental information.

14.4.5.2 National Dental Image Repository

The National Dental Image Repository (NDIR) is an image repository for law enforcement agencies that posts supplemental dental images related to NCIC missing, unidentified, and wanted records. The NDIR has a volunteer review panel of qualified dentists. The review panel dentist checks the submitted dental records for accuracy and correctness in dental coding. The requirements to be appointed to the panel include ABFO Board certification (or a signed letter of recommendation by an ABFO Diplomate), maintain an active LEO e-mail account, complete the appropriate application (stacey.davis@leo.gov), sign sensitive information and nondisclosure agreement, attend one of two FBI/ABFO training sessions, and have no criminal record.

14.4.5.3 NamUs

The National Missing and Unidentified Persons System (NamUs) has been described previously in Chapter 7 as a national centralized repository and resource center for missing persons and unidentified decedent records. Its creative goal was to develop and maintain a reporting and searching system to improve the quantity and quality of and access to comprehensive data (including dental) on missing persons and unidentified remains. This is a free online system that can be searched and information entered by medical examiners/coroners, law enforcement, and even the general public. The website may be accessed at www.namus.gov

The Missing Persons Database contains information that can be entered by anyone (subject to review), and users can be registered as a public user or a forensic dentist or dental auxiliary. Registrations are forwarded to a NamUs Administrator for vetting. If approved, there will be greater privileges for access to the databases than given to public users. This will allow one to view dental coding, dental radiographs, and NCIC dental worksheets and dental records of all missing persons in the database. If you are denied registration as a forensic dentist for the Missing Persons Database, you may still register as a public user.

The Unidentified Persons Database contains information that can only be entered by medical examiners/coroners; however, anyone may search this database using a variety of characteristics, including dental information. In order for you to register for this database, one must be a forensic dentist with a medical examiner affiliation. Registered forensic dentists on the unidentified person's side of NamUs gain "access and edit privileges" of the cases *in their jurisdiction* to add or assist in dental coding and may also upload dental radiographs and other dental-related images. Register for both categories if you qualify.

14.4.6 Insurance Companies

Many automotive, dental, and dental malpractice insurance companies use dental consultants to review claims that often include personal injury, fraud, and malpractice cases. As a forensic dentist, the scope of your practice can include such cases. There are several ways to establish contact with these companies. The appropriate point of contact may be a claims examiner, litigation examiner, or customer service representative. Send a CV and let them know of your interest and training/experience as a dental expert. Ask the agency representative if there is an existing consultant that they currently use for dental-related claims. If not, ask if you might help review and offer opinions on such cases. These companies look for dental experts who already have training and experience in general dentistry and can maintain objectivity. If an agency already has a dental expert(s), then ask what additional training you might undertake. Often, a patient who works for an insurance company or a personal friend or relative who has a connection to an insurance company may provide an appropriate contact. Never hesitate to make the most of personal connections to advance your forensic career as these types of contacts typically work in your favor. One may also just make a cold call to a company you think you may want to consult for.

Also, many states have medical/dental review panels that review cases that are potential lawsuits. The panel reviews such dental cases and determines whether the allegations are just cause for further legal action. Volunteer to be a dental expert for one of these local or state panels.

14.5 Curriculum Vitae

The CV is a very formally written description of one's work experience, training, and educational background. It must be an accurate representation of your professional life. Only one CV should maintained, and it should be updated regularly (at least annually or better yet, if at any time there is a change). It should include subject headings such as biographical information, educational information; professional employment history, professional affiliations, professional appointments, publications, presentations given, and (CE) courses attended, if applicable to your credentials. A CV should not include such information as Social Security numbers, political affiliations, activities outside of your professional life, family information such as a spouse, child or pet name, religious affiliation, or past testimony. It should always reflect the truth about your professional career and not inflate or embellish it. It should also list your current business address, business phone number, cell phone number, and business e-mail address in the biographical information heading. A CV should be proofread by at least two individuals to avoid simple mistakes like typographical errors and misspelled terms. For example, ASFO is commonly and erroneously listed as the American Society of Forensic Odontologists, when in actuality it is the American Society of Forensic Odontology. Proof reading your CV can prevent important accomplishments from being inadvertently forgotten as well as prevent embarrassing moments in court.

14.6 Present Lectures on Forensic Dentistry

An excellent way to reach other forensic professionals is to give presentations on forensic odontology. The presentations may cover any aspect in the scope of forensic odontology. As previously mentioned in this chapter, the ABFO offers a slide (digital) series online at www.abfo.org. This will be especially helpful if you are a fledgling in forensic dentistry and do not yet have a collection of cases or a lot of visual information to create a presentation.

The possibilities for opportunities to speak at events and functions are many. Some examples include but are not limited to law professionals (district attorney's, civil and criminal attorneys, public defenders), law enforcement (police departments, medical examiners, coroners), forensic nurses, child or adult protective services staff, undergraduate/graduate courses in general forensic sciences, forensic anthropology at local universities or community colleges. Also, one might participate in community-based education programs such as Crime Week or Crime Month, as well as local, state, and national dental organizations. Often, presentations lead to opportunities you never imagined existed. It may be another opportunity to speak on forensic dentistry, or it may be an offer to work that first forensic dental case. Whatever the circumstance, make yourself available and opportunity will knock.

14.7 Closing Remarks on How to Get Involved with Forensic Dentistry

It is crucial for your future success in forensic dentistry that you set goals, receive appropriate education and training, and involve yourself with professional organizations. It is not always easy to get an affiliation with a forensic agency or law enforcement. However, opportunity can be created if you are willing to commit. It is sometimes said that there is always room for one more "good" individual in any field. Will you be the one?

14.8 Recommended Forensic Odontology Equipment Lists

14.8.1 Dental Identification and Bite Marks

Photographic equipment

- Digital camera and accessories (see Chapter 9 for the recommended photography equipment list)
- ABFO No 2 Photographic Scales (available at www.foreniscsource.com)
- Standard sized ruler/scale
- Photographic mirrors

Organizational equipment

- Equipment carrying case/bag
- Business cards
- Pens, pencils, Sharpie Markers, and red/blue pencils
- Clipboard, paper, and file folders
- Ante and postmortem charts (WinID forms available for free at www.winid.com)
- Preliminary opinion report form for places that want an immediate preliminary opinion in writing
- Tooth development charts
- Dental age estimation charts
- Tape/digital recorder for dictation of data
- Labeling machine (small and portable) and/or self-adhesive labels
- CDs and/or thumb-drives
- Resealable plastic bags in a variety of sizes

Examination equipment

- *Personal Protective Equipment (morgue protection)*: Masks, gloves, head covers, foot covers, safety glasses, gowns, aprons, Tyvek suits, and/or scrubs
- Mirror and explorer
- Ultraviolet (UV) flashlights will cause some composites to fluoresce and be much more visible (ID) and bodily fluids to fluoresce and be much more visible (Bite Mark). Our favorite is the Inova X5 UV available at www.amazon.com and www.brightguy.com
- *Disposables*: Tongue depressors, cotton rolls, 2 × 2 and 4 × 4 gauze, and Q-tips.
- Hand sanitizer

14.8.2 Dental Identification

Radiographic Equipment (many smaller jurisdictions do not have dental radiography equipment. Find out what is available before you get there. You may need to bring your own equipment)

- Digital sensor and laptop computer and/or double-packaged radiographic film. (It is wise to include film even if you plan to use digital, in case the sensor malfunctions or is not packed as planned.)
- Film processor if using analog film. And just because the morgue has one, it does not mean it works, has any chemicals in it, or that it can accommodate small dental film. Run a test film to be sure.
- Film/sensor holders, BWX adhesive tabs, modeling clay, and/or paper towels to keep the film/sensor in the proper position.
- Paper cups.
- Biohazard bags to place analog films in to transfer to be developed at another site.
- Lead apron (for yourself) if there is no way to get 6 ft from the radiation source.
- Film mounts for analog films. Have them even if you use digital because often the antemortem radiographs are sent in an envelope and not mounted.
- Photoquality paper to print out radiographs for digital.
- A light view-box may be needed even if using digital, because you will need to be able to view and photograph antemortem analog films that may be sent from the treating dentist. Most morgues will have plenty of these, but make sure you will have access to one.

Examination equipment

- Ways to deal with the olfactory distress: vicks vapor rub or orange oil/solvent.
- Flashlights or headlamp and spare batteries.
- Modeling clay (can hold skeletonized jaws stable and can use to stabilize positioning instruments for radiographs).
- Methods to clean off the teeth: Toothbrushes, hydrogen peroxide, or clorox wipes.
- Windex wipes for cleaning intraoral mirrors.
- Scalpel blades and handles.
- Dental forceps and elevators to extract teeth for DNA testing of the pulp.

- Lip/cheek retractor.
- Mouth props: Rubber or Molt.
- Head and neck stabilizers to keep the mandible closed when taking radiographs.
- For resections if there is no bone saw available: Garden trimmer (lopper), mallet, and chisels.
- Cyanoacrylate liquid can be used to steady loose teeth in skeletal remains. You must get permission from the medical examiner/coroner before you use it.
- Surface disinfectant to clean up your work area when you are done.

14.8.3 Bite Mark Evidence Collection

Examination equipment

- Impression materials to take impressions of the bite mark or suspects teeth: Heavy and light-bodied VPS.
- Alginate only to be used if the suspect's teeth are loose: Alginate, mixing bowls, and spatulas.
- Dental trays and/or custom tray beads to take impressions of the victim's and/or suspect's teeth.
- Dental stone for backing material to support the VPS impression of the bite mark.
- Paper clips to attach VPS to backing.
- Digital or nondigital calipers to measure intercanine width if you do not have computer software to do so.
- TAK hydroplastic for ring fabrication when excision of the bite mark is required.
- Krazy glue gel to adhere the ring to the skin before excision.
- Sutures to use in addition to Krazy glue gel to adhere the ring to the skin.
- Super Cast 80 white casting resin for animal bite mark cases. Carnivore canines are divergent, so if you pour them up in dental stone, they will break. This white casting resin has negligible shrinkage and will not break when removed from VPS impressions. Sold by Reinforced Plastics (954) 584-2600.

APPENDIX A: Educational Outcomes and Objectives

EDWARD E. HERSCHAFT

A.1 Chapter 1 History of Forensic Odontology

By completing this chapter the reader will be able to

- Build a foundational knowledge of the history related to the development of the modern coroner and medical examiner systems
- Relate significant historical forensic cases to the development of the use of dental evidence in situations requiring individual human identification, disaster victim identification, bitemark analysis, and age estimation
- Appreciate the importance of historical forensic dental cases in the establishment of the scientific and legal basis for the current acceptance of this dental discipline in both the legal and dental communities
- Critically evaluate relevant forensic dental scientific and historical literature related to the evolution of modern forensic odontology

A.2 Chapter 2 Forensic Pathology

By completing this chapter the reader will be able to

- Define forensic pathology
- Build a foundational knowledge of the importance of proper history, comprehensive scene investigation, and evidence collection
- Recognize the tissue and body temperature changes that occur after death
- Describe the problems associated with the establishment of a precise time of death
- Understand the principles related to the cause and manner of death
- Describe the components of an autopsy report and understand how this document and the death certificate may be used in the development of public health epidemiological reports as well as in the resolution of civil and criminal legal situations
- Critically evaluate relevant forensic pathology scientific literature based on an understanding of evidence-based concepts
- Appreciate the need for forensic pathologists to develop professional relationships with individuals in the other forensic sciences to facilitate resolution of cases of forensic interest

A.3 Chapter 3 Science and Forensic Odontology

By completing this chapter the reader will be able to

- Define scientific method, experimental design, and terms associated with scientific methodology
- Describe the process of the scientific method
- Understand the processes involved in the development of single and double blind randomized clinical control trials
- Compare and contrast the concepts of sensitivity and specificity when establishing the validity of a forensic odontology research project
- Appreciate the significance of the Frye Test and Daubert Standard in regard to the admissibility of scientific forensic dental evidence in the courtroom
- Understand the challenges to courtroom presentation of forensic dental science in regard to qualifications of the expert witness, the CSI effect, and the issues identified in the 2009 NAS Report on Forensic Sciences
- Identify a variety of forensic odontology research granting resources and the contact information required to apply for funding
- Appreciate the need to continue to perform research in the various aspects of forensic dentistry to keep this discipline coordinated with new developments among the other fields of forensic science
- Critically evaluate relevant forensic dental scientific research literature based on an understanding of evidence-based concepts

A.4 Chapter 4 Dental Identification

By completing this chapter the reader will be able to

- Build a foundational knowledge of the legal and humanitarian requirements for positive identification of decedents in criminal and civil cases
- Know the advantages and disadvantages of the non-scientific method and each of the biometric methods of postmortem identification
- Know the eight characteristics that may be inferred from the examination of clinical and radiographic postmortem dental and oral structures
- Describe the artifactual changes that are associated with teeth that have been subjected to extreme temperatures associated with burning or cremation
- Describe the techniques employed to retrieve dental evidence from cremains
- Understand the various tooth numbering systems and the methods for entering dental notation and dental nomenclature into a dental record
- Appreciate the importance of comparing adjunctive antemortem and postmortem information obtained from dental and non-dental craniofacial hard and soft tissues when attempting to affect identification
- Describe the procedures and instrumentation used in the collection of postmortem dental data

- Describe the methods employed to develop a presumptive identification for an unidentified decedent
- Identify resources employed for potential retrieval of antemortem dental records
- Identify the desired criteria and preferable components regarding antemortem dental records obtained for forensic dental comparison
- Appreciate the importance of maintaining chain of custody upon receiving released antemortem dental records
- Know the dental features that are used for antemortem/postmortem comparison, how these can be statistically analyzed, and how the forensic dental identification report is appropriately written
- Know the ABFO Dental Identification Guidelines
- Understand the principles of photographic, radiographic, scanning electron micrographic, x-ray fluorescence, and computer technologies in the resolution of forensic dental identification problems
- Relate how an understanding of advanced methods of evidence analysis can overcome challenges to and limitations of traditional dental identification techniques
- Build a foundational knowledge of the procedures and protocols required to compare antemortem and postmortem dental records in a forensic setting
- Critically evaluate relevant forensic dental scientific literature concerning human identification based on an understanding of evidence-based concepts

A.5 Chapter 5 Dental, Oral, and Maxillofacial Radiographic Features of Forensic Interest

By completing this chapter the reader will be able to

- Build a foundational knowledge regarding the variety of available radiographic techniques and exposures that may provide dental and osseous information useful to the forensic odontologist in a case requiring comparison of oral and cranial radiographic structures for identification
- Recognize the dental and osseous anatomical and abnormal patterns that can be compared when assessing dental and medical radiographs as a means of forensic dental identification
- Describe the various radiographic patterns associated with osseous structure and biological activity that can be used to compare radiographic images
- Understand the relationship between the various radiographic patterns associated with osseous structure and biological activity and the oral and maxillofacial pathological conditions with which they may be related
- Critically evaluate the quality and comparable value of radiographic images used for forensic identification
- Appreciate the need to make and maintain quality radiographs in dental practice and for potential use in legal situations requiring dental identification
- Critically evaluate relevant forensic dental scientific literature concerning radiographic interpretation based on an understanding of evidence-based concepts

A.6 Chapter 6 Disaster Victim Identification

By completing this chapter the reader will be able to

- Define the terms mass disaster, disaster victim identification (DVI), and terrorism
- Know the roles and responsibilities of the various national and international agencies and support teams that may be mobilized in the event of a natural or man-made mass disaster
- Describe the role of the Joint POW/MIA Accounting Command (JPAC) in the identification of missing Americans from previous conflicts
- Build a foundational knowledge of the organization and planning required for disaster site management at international, national, state, and local levels
- Describe the functions of the eleven mortuary operations stations of the DMORT model of a DVI morgue operation
- Describe the various roles of the forensic odontologist in the formation, training, organization, and management of a local or state dental DVI team
- Understand the procedures and protocols required to compare antemortem and postmortem dental records in a DVI forensic setting using portable equipment and computer-assisted dental identification software
- Critically evaluate relevant forensic, dental, and medical scientific literature concerning multiple fatality incident procedures and protocols, and identification team organization issues based on an understanding of evidence-based concepts

A.7 Chapter 7 Missing and Unidentified Persons

By completing this chapter the reader will be able to

- Build a foundational knowledge of the functions of the various international, federal and state government, and private agencies and organizations providing training and other services in the effort to resolve the problem of missing and unidentified persons
- Understand the significant laws covering the handling of missing and unidentified persons
- Appreciate the critical role that forensic odontology plays in the resolution of the legal and humanitarian aspects of the problem of missing and unidentified individuals in the United States
- Critically evaluate relevant forensic dental and medical scientific literature concerning missing and unidentified persons based on an understanding of evidence-based concepts

A.8 Chapter 8 Dental Age Estimation

By completing this chapter the reader will be able to

- Build a foundational knowledge of the formation and growth, post-formation, and biochemical techniques employed to determine dental age estimation
- Describe the ABFO dental age estimation guidelines and standards

- Appreciate the purpose and value of forensic dental age estimation in the resolution of a variety of medicolegal situations requiring a determination of an individual's age
- Critically evaluate relevant forensic dental and anthropologic scientific literature regarding age estimation based on an understanding of evidence-based concepts

A.9 Chapter 9 Bitemarks

By completing this chapter the reader will be able to

- Build a foundational knowledge of the history of bitemark analysis and the seminal legal cases associated with the aspect of forensic odontology
- Appreciate the challenges and complexities associated with the recognition, evidence collection, and analysis of a BMPI and the bitemark comparison, and report generation, and eventual expert testimony is the most controversial area of forensic odontology
- Know the ABFO bitemark terminology and bitemark analysis guidelines
- Describe the various noninvasive and invasive procedures employed to recover bitemark evidence from a suspect, victim and/or inanimate object
- Appreciate the limitations and appropriate use of bitemark analysis and the importance of having additional physical evidence such as DNA to link a putative biter to the crime
- Build a foundational knowledge and understanding associated with the procedures and protocols required to compare the dentition of a suspect with a BMPI or bite pattern on an inanimate object
- Describe the basic photographic equipment, standard image views, and methods of image management and storage required to document bitemark evidence
- Understand how specialized photographic procedures can provide the forensic odontologist with previously undisclosed evidence in bitemark analysis and comparison
- Understand how three-dimensional evidence and study casts are obtained from a BMPI and/or putative suspect
- Know the various comparison techniques employed in the analysis of bitemark evidence
- Appreciate the importance of removing subjectivity from bitemark terminology relative to report writing in bitemark cases
- Critically evaluate relevant forensic, dental, and medical literature concerning incidence of biting injuries, evidence recovery procedures, and protocols and technological aides employed in bitemark analysis and comparison based on an understanding of evidence-based concepts

A.10 Chapter 10 Animal Bitemarks

By completing this chapter the reader will be able to

- Build a foundational knowledge of BMPIs associated with other animal species
- Understand the principles of identifying and differentiating necrophagous insect, aquatic animal, reptilian, and other carnivorous mammalian bites from those inflicted by the human dentition

- Compare and contrast the canine, feline, ursine and rodent dentitions, and the respective human populations that these animals are most likely to bite
- Appreciate the problems associated with evidence collection in the cases involving multiple animals and multiple bitemarks
- Know the canine adaptation required so that the standard computer-generated overlay technique for bitemark analysis can be successfully modified for the evaluation of an animal dentition
- Understand the principles involved in evidence collection in animal bitemark cases
- Know the recommendations listed for proper management of animal bitemark casework
- Critically evaluate relevant forensic dental and comparative anatomy scientific literature based on an understanding of evidence-based concepts

A.11 Chapter 11 Abuse and Violence

By completing this chapter the reader will be able to

- Build a foundational knowledge of the historical and epidemiological information associated with the various forms of human abuse and neglect
- Describe the role of the forensic odontologist in the recognition, documentation, and reporting of physical and neglective abuse
- Build a foundational knowledge of the procedures and protocols required in the process of reporting abuse
- Describe suspicious physical, emotional, and other patterns observed in the abused child, intimate partner, elderly, disabled, or pregnant individual
- Define Munchausen syndrome by proxy
- Recognize the signs and symptoms related to a caregiver's potentially abusive personality
- Understand the role of the various federal and state, local, and support agencies that can intervene in matters of human abuse
- Recognize the signs and symptoms associated with the dental manifestations of human abuse and neglect
- Differentiate between signs and symptoms of abuse and other medical, dental, and emotional problems that may mimic these findings
- Critically evaluate relevant forensic, dental, medical, and public health scientific literature concerning human abuse, and intimate partner violence issues based on an understanding of evidence-based concepts

A.12 Chapter 12 Jurisprudence and Expert Witness Testimony

By completing this chapter the reader will be able to

- Build a foundational knowledge of the history, terminology, court systems, and application of law in the legal system of the United States
- Define criminal and civil law

- Compare and contrast criminal and civil law in regard to their status in the federal and state justice systems of the United States
- Build a foundational knowledge of the federal and state rules and regulations governing the admissibility of evidence in the courts of the United States
- Describe the forensic odontologist's role and responsibilities as an expert witness
- Know the procedures involved in expert witness qualification, direct testimony, and cross examination.
- Understand the special considerations to consider in tort cases involving personal injury or malpractice
- Describe the professional ethical considerations that must be considered by the forensic dental expert and retaining attorney when preparing a case for trial
- Critically evaluate relevant forensic dental, scientific, legal, and legislative literature dealing with significant malpractice, personal injury, bitemark, and dental identification cases at trial.

A.13 Chapter 13 Organized Forensic Dentistry

By completing this chapter the reader will be able to

- Build a foundational knowledge concerning the various American Organizations with which the forensic odontologist may become affiliated and how they may be contacted
- Identify other international forensic odontology organizations that have a World Wide Web presence and with which the forensic odontologist may become affiliated and how they may be contacted
- Identify the educational resources in North America that are available for training in the field of forensic odontology and how they may be contacted

A.14 Chapter 14 Becoming Involved in Forensic Odontology

By completing this chapter the reader will be able to

- Develop a foundational knowledge of the processes involved in becoming active and affiliated in the discipline of forensic odontology
- Know the principal scientific forensic organizations that dentists can join for educational, research, interdisciplinary dialogue, and certification opportunities
- Identify resources for advanced education in this discipline
- Appreciate the educational and multi-disciplinary professional experiences and opportunities that becoming affiliated with forensic science and specifically forensic odontology organizations can provide

APPENDIX B: Presidents: American Society of Forensic Odontology

Roy H. Sonkin, DDS	2013–2014
James M. Lewis, DMD, DABFO	2012–2013
Mary A. Bush, DDS	2011–2012
Denise C. Murmann, DDS, DABFO	2010–2011
Adam J. Freeman, DDS, DABFO	2009–2010
James McGivney, DMD, DABFO	2008–2009
John M. Williams, DDS, DABFO*	2007–2008
Douglas M. Arendt, DDS, MS, DABFO	2006–2007
David W. Johnson, DDS, DABFO	2005–2006
J. Curtis Dailey, DDS, DABFO	2004–2005
Gary M. Berman, DDS, DABFO	2003–2004
Marden E. Alder, DDS, MS, DABFO	2002–2003
Jeffrey R. Burkes, DDS, DABFO	2001–2002
Phillip J. Levine, DDS, DABFO	2000–2001
David Sweet, DMD, PhD, DABFO	1999–2000
Richard H. Fixott, DDS, DABFO	1998–1999
John D. McDowell, DDS, MS, DABFO	1997–1998
William M. Morlang, DDS, DABFO	1996–1997
David C. Averill, DDS, DABFO	1995–1996
Robert E. Barsley, DDS, JD, DABFO	1994–1995
Peter F. Hampl, DDS, DABFO	1993–1994
E. Steven Smith, DDS*	1992–1993
George Burgman, DDS*	1991–1992
Frank A. Morgan, DDS, DABFO	1990–1991
Edward E. Herschaft, DDS, MA, DABFO	1989–1990
Wilbur B. Richie, DDS, DABFO	1988–1989
James A. Cottone, DDS, MS, DABFO	1987–1988
Haskell Askin, DDS, DABFO*	1986–1987
Norman D. Sperber, DDS, DABFO	1985–1986
Thomas C. Krauss, DDS, DABFO Emeritus*	1984–1985
Gerald M. Reynolds, DDS, DABFO	1983–1984
Edwin E. Andrews, DMD, MEd, DABFO	1980–1983
George Morgan, DDS	1979–1980
Paul G. Stimson, DDS, MS, DABFO	1978–1979
Edward V. Comulada, DDS, DABFO*	1977–1978
Curtis A. Mertz, DDS, DABFO Emeritus*	1976–1977
Lester L. Luntz, DDS, DABFO*	1974–1976
Robert Boyers, DDS, LTC, DC*	1971–1974

* Deceased.

Index

A

AAFS, *see* American Academy of Forensic Sciences (AAFS)
AAR, *see* Amino acid racemization (AAR)
ABFO, *see* American Board of Forensic Odontology (ABFO)
ABFO Bitemark Terminology Guidelines
  bitemark definitions, 320
  characteristics, 319–320
  component injuries, 319
  description, bitemark, 320–321
  policy, 322
  standards, 322
  suggestive and bitemark, 321
  suspected biter, 321
ABFO Guidelines and Standards
  background information, 317
  Bitemark Terminology Guidelines, *see* ABFO Bitemark Terminology Guidelines
  disclaimer, 318
  evidence received and collected, 318
  methods of analysis, 318
  patterned injuries, 318
  results of analyses, 318
Abuse and violence
  child abuse, *see* Child abuse
  dental team's role, 357–358
  description, 356
  disability, 371–372
  DV, *see* Domestic violence (DV)
  early dental literature, 356–357
  honor killings, 356
  IPV, 367–369
  mistreatment of elderly, *see* Elderly abuse
  pregnant women and prenatal abuse, 372–373
  "raccoon eyes", 356, 357
  resources, 374
Abusive head trauma (AHT), 359, 361
ADIS, *see* Automated Dental Identification System (ADIS)
Adolescent age estimation
  male and female third molar data, 229–231
  probability, individual, 232, 233
  UT-age case information, 233
Adult dental age estimation techniques
  Bang and Ramm technique, 240, 241
  Johanson sectioning technique, 236–237
  Kvaal method
    computer imaging software, measurement process, 242–243
    guidelines, root width measurements, 244
    measurements, tooth, 240, 242
    noninvasive radiographic method, 240
    ratio and regression coefficient calculations, 245
    regression formulas, 242
  Lamendin technique, 238–239
  Maples study, 237–238
  Prince and Ubelaker method, 239
AFIP, *see* Armed Forces Institute of Pathology (AFIP)
Age estimation
  King Louis XVI and Queen Marie Antoinette, 34
  King Tutankhamen, 35
  Maury Massler and Isaac Shour, 34
  Mincer, Harris, and Berryman, 34
  Moorrees, Fanning and Hunt, 34
AHT, *see* Abusive head trauma (AHT)
ALI, *see* Alternate light imaging (ALI)
Alligators
  attack, snorkeling, 331
  bitemark impression trays, 345
  blunt force injuries, 331
  Florida subdivision, 329
  jaws and teeth, 329, 330
  minor, bitemark, 329, 330
  necropsy, 331
  variation, dentition, 329, 330
Alternate light imaging (ALI)
  automatic TTL light meters, 297–298
  description, 293
  digital image, bite mark, 296, 297
  fluorescent photography, 298
  Forensic Photo Frame®, 297
  100 ISO and adequate light source, 296–297
  leg close-up, 295–296
  modern digital cameras, 297
  personal light sources
    RC Forensic ring lights, 294, 295
    ultra lite and accessories, 294, 295
  requirements, 294
  stokes shift, fluorescence, 293–294
American Academy of Forensic Sciences (AAFS)
  annual meeting, 409
  defined, 399

journal of forensic sciences, 409
website, 408
American Board of Forensic Odontology (ABFO)
age estimation, 73
bitemark analysis guidelines
description, bitemark, 318–319
methods of comparing exemplars, 319
Bitemark Workshop # 4, 316
defined, 400, 409
dental identification, 72–73
Diplomate, 316
facial approximation, 73
funding, 70
guidelines and standards, *see* ABFO Guidelines and Standards
mass fatality incident management, 73
patterned injuries and bitemarks, 72
person abuse, 73
2 scale, 278, 279
scientific studies, 72
website resources
diplomates, 410
nonmembers, 409–410
witness consultation and testimony, 73
workshops, 404
American College of Forensic Examiners International (ACFEI) states, 411
American organizations
AAFS, 399
ABFO, 400
ASFO, 397–399
American Society of Forensic Odontology (ASFO)
AFIP, 397–398
operation, 398
Amino acid racemization (AAR)
defined, 245
molecular and environmental factors, 246
rates, tooth location, 246
Animal bitemarks
abuse, 345–346
alligators, 329–331
aquatic animals, 327–328
Burmese python, 326–327
canine bite data, 334–336
carnivores, 333–334
child abuse, *see* Child abuse, canine dentition
comparative dental anatomy, 336–342
comparison techniques, 345
criminals, 352
data collection, *see* Data collection, animal bitemarks
dog fighting, 352
egregious mistakes, 351–352
human and animal interaction, 326
human/animal attack, 346–348
insects, 327
recommendations, 353
snakes, 331–333
society and lawmakers, 352
Antemortem dental data
custodian of the dental records, 112
dental record retention mandates, 110, 111
nontraditional sources, 110, 112
vs. postmortem
dental features, 114, 115
dental models and photographs, 112, 113
mirrored charts, 114, 115
report writing, 117
standards and guidelines, 116
statistical and mathematic/algorithm methods, 116
presumptive identification, 109–110
record form, 112–114
requested radiographs, 112
Anthropology/radiology
bone fixation plate and screws, 78–79
description, 78
MRI scanner, 79
Armed Forces Institute of Pathology (AFIP), 397–398, 403
ASFO, *see* American Society of Forensic Odontology (ASFO)
Asphyxia, 56
AuSFO, *see* Australian Society of Forensic Odontology (AuSFO)
Australian Society of Forensic Odontology (AuSFO), 402
Automated Dental Identification System (ADIS), 130–131

B

BAHID, *see* British Association for Human Identification (BAHID)
Biochemical techniques, dental age estimation
AAR, *see* Amino acid racemization (AAR)
radioactive ^{14}C dating, 247
Bitemark analysis
appropriate use and limitations
adult bites, child abuse, 270–271
physiological process, healing, 270
postmortem changes, 270
violent attack/rape, 271–272
bitemarks, 268–269
biters, 269–270
DNA analyses, 268
spatial arrangement, teeth, 268
Bitemark cases
Ansil L. Robinson murder trial, 27
Arizona v. Krone, 31–32
California v. Marx, 29
Commonwealth of Pennsylvania v. Kunco, 31
Crown (Scotland) v. Hay, 28
Doyle v. Texas, 28

Florida v. Bundy, 29
Florida v. Stewart, 30
George Burroughs and the Salem Witch trials, 27
Illinois v. Johnson, 29
Illinois v. Milone, 29
Illinois v. Young and Hill, 32
Louisiana v. Willie Jackson, 30
Massachusetts v. Edmund Burke, 33
Michigan v. Moldowan and Cristini, 32
Mississippi v. Brewer and *Mississippi v. Brooks*, 32–33
New Jersey v. Jesse K. Timmendequas, 33
New York v. Roy Brown, 31
Oklahoma v. Wilhoit, 30–31
Public Prosecutor (Norway) v. Torgersen, 28
State of New York v. James O'Donnell, 33–34
State of Wisconsin v. Robert Lee Stinson, 30
West Memphis Three, 33
William I of England, 27
Bitemark impressions
adhesion, backing, 285–286
hair removal, 285
static mixing syringes, 284–285
stone casts, 286
study casts, 286–287
thermoplastic products, 285
tooth indentations, 283–284
Bitemark recognition
avulsive bitemark, arm, 261, 262
child abuse, 261, 262
double bitemark, 261, 262
multiple bitemarks, 261, 263
partial bitemarks, 261
"smoke-ring" bitemarks, 261, 263
variations, 261–262
Bitemarks
ALI, 293–298
analysis/comparison, *see* Bitemark analysis
cheese, 259
comparison techniques, *see* Comparison techniques, bitemarks
data collection, suspected biter(s), 289–292
description, 258
electromagnetic spectrum and photography, 293
history, 260
image management and storage, 280–282
impressions, *see* Bitemark impressions
injury and dentition, description, 305
IR photography, 303–305
NAS report, 259
pattern recognition and collection
salivary trace evidence, 272–273
written request, 272
photographic documentation, 273–277
reflective UVA photography, *see* Ultraviolet (UVA) photography
size relationship analysis, 305–306
SLA, 282–283
standard photographic views, 277–279
state of the science, 260–268
tissue incision, excision and preservation, 287–288
transillumination, 288–289
Blunt force trauma
abrasions, 51
contusion/bruise, 51
description, 51
lacerations, 51, 52
tire tread markings, 51–52
British Association for Forensic Odontology, 401
British Association for Human Identification (BAHID), 401
Burned and incinerated remains
cyanoacrylate cement, fragile teeth, 87
damages, anterior teeth, 86, 88
enamel, teeth, 86, 88
temperature, 86
unprotected teeth, 85–86

C

CACs, *see* Child Advocacy Centers (CACs)
Canadian Police Information Centre (CPIC)
Canadian dental characteristics report, 208, 209
forensic odontologists, 207–208
NCIC, 208
Canine bite data
bitemark liability, 335
dog bitemark hierarchy, 336
dog bite-related fatalities, 336
dog bite statistics, 334–335
injuries, 335
Canine dentitions (dogs)
anatomy, 336–337
dental formula, 336
incisors, 337–338
maxillary teeth, 337
Modified Triadan system, 337, 338
occlusal relationship, 339
permanent dentition, 339
prominent teeth, 338
CAPMI, *see* Computer Assisted Post Mortem Identification (CAPMI)
CAPTA, *see* Child Abuse Prevention and Treatment Act (CAPTA)
Carbon dating, *see* Radioactive ^{14}C dating
Carnivores, 333–334
Carotid artery calcifications (CCAA)
CBCT, 152
hyperdensities, 153–154
panoramic and coronal images, 152
CAT, *see* Computerized axial tomography (CAT)

Cause of death
  asphyxia, 56
  blunt force trauma, 51–52
  categories, 50
  description, 50
  drugs, 57–58
  fire, 56–57
  gunshot wounds, 53–55
  natural deaths, 50–51
  physiologic derangement, 50
  sharp force trauma, 52–53
CBCT, *see* Cone beam computed tomography (CBCT)
CCAA, *see* Carotid artery calcifications (CCAA)
CDC, *see* Centers for Disease Control (CDC)
The Center for Education and Research in Forensics (CERF)
  antemortem dental charting forms, 99, 100
  postmortem dental charting forms, 99, 101
Centers for Disease Control (CDC)
  IPV, 367
  pregnancy-associated homicide, 373
  sexual abuse, 363
CERF, *see* The Center for Education and Research in Forensics (CERF)
Changes after death
  algor mortis, 46–47
  decomposition, 44
  description, 44
  livor mortis/lividity, 45–46
  rigor mortis, 45
  stomach contents, 49
  tissue decomposition, 47–49
Cheiloscopy, 96
Child abuse
  abusers, 365
  canine dentition
    belt keeper and onesie snaps, 349
    EKG electrodes, 349
    filed-down canine teeth, 349, 350
    graphic demonstrations, bitemarks, 350, 351
    hollow volume, 349
    patterned injuries, 348
    test marks, arm, 349–350
  clumsy/accident prone, 365
  conditions and practices, 364–365
  "doctor shop", 365
  emotional abuse, 363
  exploitation, 362
  Munchausen Syndrome, 364
  neglect/deprivation, 364
  physical abuse, *see* Physical child abuse
  prevention, *see* Prevention, child abuse
  risk factors, 364
  sexual abuse, 363
Child abuse and neglect, Mary Ellen Wilson, 35–36
Child Abuse Prevention and Treatment Act (CAPTA), 365–366
Child Abuse Prevention Councils, 366
Child Advocacy Centers (CACs), 415–416
Child Death Review Teams, 366–367
Child dental age estimation
  deciduous tooth development, 224
  defined, 219
  Demirjian third molar developmental stages, 227, 228
  developmental staging descriptors, 223
  London atlas, tooth development and eruption, 220, 221
  permanent tooth development, 223–225
  tooth resorption, 222
  Ubelaker dental development chart, 220
Civil law, U.S., 385–386
Comparative dental anatomy
  canine dentitions (dogs), 336–339
  feline dentition (cats), 339–340
  rodent dentition (rats), 341–342
  ursine dentitions (bears), 340–341
Comparison techniques, bitemarks
  ABFO Bitemark Workshop #4, 316
  advantages and disadvantages, 314
  crucial factors, 314
  description, 306
  digital analysis, 312–313
  direct, 307–308
  DNA exonerations, 315–316
  forensic science, 315
  incisal plane, 306–307
  metric analysis, 311–312
  microscopy, CAT and 3-D scanning, 313–314
  overlays
    Adobe Photoshop, 309–310
    Dailey's technique, 309, 310
    3-D scanners, 310–311
    hand-drawn acetate, 308, 309
    Photoshop and Mideo digital-imaging software, 309
    radiographic technique, 308, 309
  uniqueness, human dentition, 314–315
Computer-assisted dental identification software
  CAPMI, 186
  DVI System International, 188–189
  UVIS/UDIM, 189–190
  WinID3, *see* WinID3
Computer Assisted Post Mortem Identification (CAPMI), 186, 195, 196
Computerized axial tomography (CAT), 313
Cone beam computed tomography (CBCT)
  calcification, 144
  CCAA, 152
  description, 132
  3D renderings, 145
  frontal and lateral TMJ series, 146

impacted third molars and inferior alveolar nerve, 145, 146
nasal cavity, maxillary sinuses, and paranasal sinuses, 143
and occlusal radiographs
distinct opaque lesions, 150
mandibular tori, 150
sialolith, 149
Coroner and medical examiner systems
autopsies, 3
Births and Deaths Registration Act, 3
description, 2–3
distribution, 4, 5
Massachusetts Medico-Legal Society, 3
Model Post-Mortem Examinations Act, 1954, 4
NAME, 1966, 4
office, 3
Rhode Island system, 1884, 3–4
Texas Medical Examiner Act, 1955, 4
CPIC, *see* Canadian Police Information Centre (CPIC)
Cremated remains (cremains)
coincidental commingling, 90
commercial process, 88
dental examination, 89–90
dental restorations, 90, 91
melting points, dental restorative materials, 90, 91
metal artifacts, 89, 90
processing, 89
with refractory brick, 88, 89
sieves uses, 90
Criminal law, U.S.
"grand" jury, 382–383
law-enforcement agency, 384
search warrant, 383–384

D

Data collection
animal bitemarks
alligator bitemark impression tray, 345
DNA, 343
dog, 342–345
teeth marks, skull, 342, 343
suspected biter(s)
bite registrations, 290–291
dental charting, 289
dental stone models, 292
photographs, 289–290
recommendation, 289
short-form letter, 289
standard technique, 289
VPS impression, 292
Death
autopsy reports, 59
cause of death, *see* Cause of death
certificates, 59
changes, 44–49
investigation, 42–44
manner, 58
time, 49–50
Death investigation
assessment, 43
evidence collection, 44
law enforcement, 42–43
medical facilities, 43
scene, 43
Dental age estimation
biochemical techniques, *see* Biochemical techniques, dental age estimation
defined, 211–212
formation and growth techniques
adolescent, 227–234
child, 219–227
fetal, 216–219
guidelines, 216
guidelines and standards, 248–250
mass disaster and cluster victim situations, 212
normal distribution curves, 214–215
postformation techniques, *see* Postformation techniques, dental age estimation
procedure, 216, 217
scientific evaluation, dental tissues, 213
tools, 216
Dental coding workshops, 199–200
Dental identification
Adolf Hitler, 17–19
Agrippina the Younger, 5–6
Caroline Walsh, 14
Charles the Bold, 7
Claudius Beaupied, 17
Colonel Sir Peter Halket(t), 7–8
Czar Nicholas II, the last Russian czar, 21–22
description, 80
Dr. George Parkman and Dr. John Webster, 14–15
Dr. Joseph Warren
american revolution patriot, 9, 11
Battle of Bunker Hill, 9–10
Boston Massacre, 8–10
skull, General Joseph warren, 13
first British trial as expert witnesses, 13–14
First Earl of Shrewsbury, 6–7
Henrietta Durand-Deacon, 19–20
Henry M. Harrington, 16–17
John Wilkes Booth, 15–16
Lee Harvey Oswald, 21
patterns, 80–81
Pliny the Elder publishes *Natural History*, 6
postmortem dental data, 108–109
Queen Hatshepsut, 22–23
Ramses I, 22

Dental identification teams
DMORT, 414–415
Kenyon International, 415
Dental materials evidence analysis
explosion, competing products, 117–118
radiopacity, 118
SEM/EDS techniques, 119–124
visible light fluorescence, 118–119
XRF, 124–125
Dental notation/numbering systems
FDI, 93
Palmer Notation System, 93
Universal Numbering System, 91–93
Dental *vs.* nondental
appliances
Denture Labeling Law, 97
fixed orthodontic appliances, 98
teeth molds, size, shape and color, 97
cheiloscopy, 96
DNA, 95–96
facial reconstruction, 94–95
frontal sinus pattern radiographic, 95
implants, 98
palatal rugae, 96
photographic facial superimposition, 93–94
Dental workstation, DMORT morgue
antemortem/comparison dental section, 174
description, 172–173
DEXIS digital radiographic, 173, 174
intraoral examination, postmortem, 173
postmortem examination, 173
WinID3 system, 174, 175
Deoxyribonucleic acid (DNA)
analysis and tests, 79–80
biometric methods, identification, 79
dental *vs.* nondental, 95–96
forensic analyses, 80
mitochondrial (mtDNA), 80
short tandem repeat (STR), 80
Digital dental radiography sensors
antemortem and comparison areas, 185–186
description, 184
DEXIS, 185
forensic applications, 185
Schick, 185
training, 186
Disaster Medical Assistance Team (DMAT), 161
Disaster Mortuary Operational Response Team (DMORT)
agencies, 163
deployment, 164
description, 162–163
DPMU, 163
federal agency, 164
flooding, 163
INTERPOL, 164
Kenyon International Emergency Services, 164
members, 163
morgue operation, *see* DVI morgue operation
NRP, 164
WMD, 163
Disaster Portable Morgue Unit (DPMU), 163
Disaster Relief Act of 1974, 23
Disaster sites
notification and assessment, medical examiner/coroner, 165
search and recovery team, 166–168
security and safety, 169–170
temporary morgue, 165–166
Disaster victim identification (DVI)
American Airlines flight 191, 25
Bazar de la Charite, 23
computer-assisted dental identification software, 186
definitions, 160
dental section, *see* DVI Dental Section
digital dental radiography sensors, 184–186
Disaster Relief Act of 1974, 23
DMORT, 26
Flight 3407, 190–191
Haiti Earthquake, 27
Hurricane Katrina, 26–27
John Wayne Gacy, 24–25
Jonestown, 24
morgue operation, *see* DVI morgue operation
national and international, *see* National and international DVI
Oklahoma City bombing, 26
portable dental x-ray generator, 182–184
September 11, 2001 terrorist attacks, 26
sites, *see* Disaster sites
terrorism, 160–161
unintentional man-made disasters, 160
Waco Siege, 26
World Trade Center, New York, 26
DMAT, *see* Disaster Medical Assistance Team (DMAT)
DMORT, *see* Disaster Mortuary Operational Response Team (DMORT)
DNA, *see* Deoxyribonucleic acid (DNA)
Domestic violence (DV)
child and elder abuse, 368
description, 356
PANDA, 358
patterned injuries, 360
physical and behavioral signs, 358
spectrum, 357
Domestic Violence Intervention program, 369
DPMU, *see* Disaster Portable Morgue Unit (DPMU)
Drug related deaths, 57–58
DV, *see* Domestic violence (DV)

DVI, *see* Disaster victim identification (DVI)
DVI Dental Section
antemortem, 179–180
association, 176
comparison team, 181
disaster scene, 176, 177
examination supplies, 181
morgue shifts, 181–182
postmortem, 178–179
team formation, 177, 178
team leader, 178
DVI morgue operation
anthropological examination, 172
body storage, 175
decontamination workstation, 170–171
dental workstation, *see* Dental workstation, DMORT morgue
description, 169–170
DNA collection, 174
embalming/casketing, 175
fingerprint collection workstation, 171
Information Resource Center, 175–176
mortuary annex, 170
pathology/autopsy workstation, 172
radiology workstation, 171–172
reception/registration workstation, 171
setup, 170
DVI System International, 188–189

E

EDS, *see* Energy-dispersive x-ray spectroscopy (EDS)
Elderly abuse
active neglect, 370
follow-up care, 371
incidence and indicators, 369
material (financial abuse), 370
passive abuse, 370
physical abuse, 370
psychological abuse, 370
sexual abuse, 370
signs mistaken, 371
signs of malnutrition, 371
underreported, reasons, 371
Energy-dispersive x-ray spectroscopy (EDS)
amalgam particles, 122, 124
approach, 124
dentalcharts, 123
description, 119–120
resin brand
Gradia, 122, 123
Quixx, 122
Tetric Ceram, 122, 123
and SEM, *see* Scanning electron microscopy (SEM)
English Habeas Corpus Act, 379
Experimental design
accuracy *vs.* precision, 64
bias, 63
correlation/nonuniformity, 64–65
description, 63
error, 63
P value, 64
standard deviation and variance, 63–64
Expert witness
case counsel, 394
cross-examination, 393
defined, 386–387
general advice, 68
immunity and liability, 389–391
prosecution, 389
qualification and voir dire, 387–388
qualifications, 67–68
scientific/technical evidence, criminal trial, 388–389
specialty certification, 68
in U.S. Judicial System, 67

F

Facial reconstruction
applied clay, 94, 95
completed facial reconstruction and actual victim, 94, 95
2-D and 3-D technique, 94
depth markers, 94
description, 94
FDI, *see* Federation Dentaire Internationale (FDI)
Federation Dentaire Internationale (FDI), 93
Feline dentition (cats), 339–340
Fingerprints, 78
Fire death, 56–57
Florida unidentified decedents database (FLUIDDB), 205
FLUIDDB, *see* Florida unidentified decedents database (FLUIDDB)
Forensic dentistry
courses, 411–414
CV, 418
dental identification teams, 414–415
DV agencies, 415–416
equipment
bite mark evidence collection, 421
examination, 420–421
photographic and organizational, 419
insurance companies, 417–418
law enforcement agencies, 416–417
lectures, 418–419
legal professionals, 416
medical examiners and coroners, 414
organizations
AAFS, 408–409
ABFO, 404, 409–410

ACFEI, 411
American organizations, 397–400
annual forensic dental identification and technologies, 403
ASFO, 406–407
fellowship, odontology, 403
IAI, 410–411
International organizations, 400–402
IOFOS, 407–408
McGill University, 403
odontology, medical examiner's office, 403
southwest symposium, 402
Tufts University, 403–404
Forensic identification
ADIS, 130–131
biometric comparable patterns, 130
computer-based method, 130
jaw resection and preservation, 129–130
radiographic features, *see* Radiographic features
radiographic pattern assessment, 131
technical errors, 130
Forensic odontology, 36–37, 429
Forensic pathology
autopsy reports, 59
cause of death, *see* Cause of death
changes after death, 44–49
death certificates, 59
death investigation, 42–44
definition, 41–42
manner of death, 58
postmortem examination, 42
professionals, 59–60
time of death, 49–50
Forensic Science Foundation's (FSF)
funding, 70–71
Jan Grant Award, 71
Lucas Grants, 71
the NIJ/FSF Forensic Science Student Research Grant, 71
Formation and growth techniques, dental age estimation
adolescent, 227–234
child, *see* Child dental age estimation
fetal, 216, 218–219
Frye test, 66–67
FSF, *see* Forensic Science Foundation's (FSF)

G

Gunshot wounds
contact wound, 53–54
description, 53
entrance/exit wound, 55
gunpowder tattooing/stippling, 54–55
homicide cases, 55

H

Health Insurance Portability and Accountability Act (HIPAA), 381–382
HIPAA, *see* Health Insurance Portability and Accountability Act (HIPAA)
Human identification
anthropology/radiology, 78–79
burned and incinerated remains, 85–88
cremated remains
dental, 80–81
description, 76
DNA, 79–80
fingerprints, 78
methods, 77
positive, 76
postmortem dental profiling, *see* Postmortem dental profiling
visual, 77

I

IAI, *see* International Association for Identification (IAI)
Image management and storage
digital image storage, 280–281
file acquisition and types, 280
image enhancement, 281
plug-ins, 281–282
Infrared (IR) photography
focus point, skin surface, 303
injury patterns, 303–304
Kodak Publication N-1, 303
Kodak Wratten 87 gel IR filter, 304
manufacturers, lenses, 304–305
wavelength transmission, penetration, 303
Insurance companies, 417–418
International agencies, NamUs
CPIC, 207–208
Criminal Police Organization, 206–207
International Association for Identification (IAI), 400–401, 410–411
International Organization of Forensic Odonto-Stomatology (IOFOS), 401, 407–408
International organizations
AuSFO, 402
BAHID, 401–402
British Association for Forensic Odontology, 401
IAI, 400–401
IOFOS, 401
Intimate partner violence (IPV)
CDC, 367
dental team awareness and action plan, 368
description, 356
"family/household member", 367

pregnancy, 372–373
RADAR, 369
types, 368
IOFOS, *see* International Organization of Forensic Odonto-Stomatology (IOFOS)
IPV, *see* Intimate partner violence (IPV)
IPV types
physical and sexual abuse, 368
stalking/control, 368
verbal and financial abuse, 368

J

Johanson sectioning techniques, 236–237
Jurisprudence and expert witness testimony; *see also* Expert witness
adversarial system of law, 386
case counsel, 394
civil law, 385–386
criminal law, 382–385
cross-examination, 393
dentist
expert witness, 386–387
fact witness, 386
federal rules of evidence, 391–392
immunity and liability, 389–391
prosecution, 389
qualification and voir dire, 387–388
scientific/technical evidence, criminal trial, 388–389
subpoena, 387
U.S. legal system, 377–382

K

Kenyon International Emergency Services, 164

L

Law enforcement agencies
NamUs, 417
NCIC missing persons database, 416–417
NDIR, 417

M

Mass Fatality Incident (MFI) organization, 414–415
MFI organization, *see* Mass Fatality Incident (MFI) organization
Missing persons (MPs), *see* National missing and unidentified persons system (NamUs)

N

NAME, *see* National Association of Medical Examiners (NAME)
NamUs, *see* National missing and unidentified persons system (NamUs)
National Academy of Sciences (NAS) report, 259, 260, 317
National and international DVI
agencies, 161
DMAT, 161
DMORT, 162–164
Katrina's destruction, 161, 162
NDMS, 161
NVRT, 161
National Association of Medical Examiners (NAME), 4
National Center for Missing and Exploited Children (NCMEC), 204
National Crime Information Center (NCIC)
missing persons database, 416–417
MPs, 195, 197, 198
training sessions, 200–201
UPs, 195, 196
WPs, 195
National Dental Image Repository (NDIR)
defined, 199
training sessions, 200–201
The National Disaster Medical System (NDMS), 161
National Institute of Justice (NIJ)
administrator, 202
OJP, 201
National missing and unidentified persons system (NamUs)
autopsy, 209–210
Billy's law, 200
California missing persons, 205
databases
"unclaimed persons", 203
webpage, 201, 202
defined, 417
dental coding workshops, 199–200
FLUIDDB, 205
Home/National Center, missing adults, 205
international agencies, 206–208
Jennifer's law, 200
Kristen's law, 200
NCIC, 195–198
NCMEC, 204
NDIR, 199
NIJ, 201
private sector and state agencies, 204–206
social media, 205–206
training, 203–204
ViCAP, 204
National Research Council (NRC), 69–70
National Response Plan (NRP), 161, 162, 164
National Veterinary Response Team (NVRT), 161
Natural deaths, 50–51
NCIC, *see* National Crime Information Center (NCIC)
NCMEC, *see* National Center for Missing and Exploited Children (NCMEC)

NDIR, *see* National Dental Image Repository (NDIR)
NDMS, *see* The National Disaster Medical System (NDMS)
NIJ, *see* National Institute of Justice (NIJ)
NRC, *see* National Research Council (NRC)
NRP, *see* National Response Plan (NRP)
NVRT, *see* National Veterinary Response Team (NVRT)

O

Office of Justice Program (OJP), 201
OJP, *see* Office of Justice Program (OJP)
Organised forensic dentistry, 429
Osseous abnormalities, radiography
  carotid artery stents and surgical fixation clips, 153
  CCAA, 152–154
  diagnostic entities, 154, 155
  distinct opaque lesions, 150, 151
  lesions with
    irregular, diffuse, and indistinct borders, 148
    mixed opacity, 149
    "moth-eaten" radiographic findings, 148
    round, ovoid, unilocular, and distinct borders, 147
    "tooth-like", "sunburst", and "expansive", 150, 151
  mandibular tori, 150, 151
  medical treatment devices, 153
  pathologic/structural diagnosis, 147
  radiopaque foreign material, 151
  shotgun injury, 151
  sialolith, 149, 150
  soap bubble patterns, 148
  tonsillar and CCAA calcifications, 152
Osseous anatomical structures, radiography
  calcification, 144
  hyoid bone and calcified stylohyoid ligament, 145, 146
  maxillofacial structures, 144, 146
  neural and vascular structures, 145, 146
  temporomandibular joints (TMJ), 146
  tissue polyps, 143

P

Palatal rugae, 96, 97
Palmer Notation System, 93
PANDA, *see* Prevent Abuse and Neglect through Dental Awareness (PANDA)
Photographic documentation, bitemarks
  ALS, IR and UVA photography, 273–274
  desirable accessories, 277
  digital cameras, 274–275
  flash accessories, 275–277
  lenses, 275
Photography, postmortem dental data, 103–104
Physical child abuse
  AHT, 361
  bite marks, 361–362
  bruises, 359–360
  fractures, 359, 360
  inflicted burns, 362
  lacerated and incised wounds, 360
  ocular injuries, 361
  orofacial injuries, 360–361
  patterned injuries, 360
Portable dental x-ray generator
  MinXrayT, 184
  NOMAD
    classic, 182, 183
    position indicating device, 183, 184
    ProT, 183
    radiation safety procedures., 183
Postformation techniques, dental age estimation
  adult, *see* Adult dental age estimation techniques
  attrition, 234–235
  cementum apposition, 235
  periodontosis, 235
  physiological and reparative secondary dentin, 235
  root resorption and transparency, 235–236
Postmortem dental charting forms
  CERF
    antemortem, 99, 100
    postmortem, 99, 101
  classification, 99
  description, 99
  NCIC, 99, 102
  protocol, 99
Postmortem dental data
  vs. antemortem
    dental features, 114, 115
    dental models and photographs, 112, 113
    mirrored charts, 114, 115
    report writing, 117
    standards and guidelines, 116
    statistical and mathematic/algorithm methods, 116
  burn victim soft-tissue reflection, 106, 107
  charting forms, *see* Postmortem dental charting forms
  dental examination, 108–109
  documentation, 98–99
  examination procedures, 100–101
  jaw resection, 107
  maxilla, after accident, 98
  photography, 103–104
  pruning shears method, 107–108
  radiography, 104–105
  viewable bodies, 106

Postmortem dental profiling
age estimation, 81
ancestry, 81–82
clinical and radiographic examination, 81
country/area, origin/residence, 83, 87
description, 81
habits, 83, 94
occupation, 83, 87
sex, 82–83
socioeconomic status, 83
systemic disease
acid dissolution, 83, 86
amelogenesis imperfecta, 83, 85
hereditable maladies, and medications, 83, 84
hypodontia and ectodermal dysplasia, 83, 85
mulberry molar and congenital syphilis, 83, 84
tetracycline staining, 83, 86
Presidents of American Society of Forensic Odontology, 431
Prevent Abuse and Neglect through Dental Awareness (PANDA), 358
Prevention, child abuse
CAPTA, 365–366
Child Abuse Prevention Councils, 366
Child Death Review Teams, 366–367

R

Radioactive ^{14}C dating, 247–248
Radiocarbon dating, *see* Radioactive ^{14}C dating
Radiographic features
abnormalities, *see* Tooth-related anomalies, radiography
AM/PM dental coding, 134
classification
and algorithm, 133
tooth-related, 133
diagnostic rules, 132
Radiographic techniques
dental radiographs
extraoral, 132
intraoral, 131
medical imaging, 132
Radiography, postmortem dental data
description, 104
digital x-ray sensor, 104, 105
Nomad and Dexis sensor, 104
Nomad x-ray device and wrap, 104, 105
techniques, 105
Randomized control trials
double-blind study, 65
single blind study, 65
Rodent dentition (rats), 341–342

S

Scanning electron microscopy (SEM)
acid etching, absence, 120, 121
bur marks, 120, 121
cremated mandibular fragment, 120
dentin tubules, 120, 122
description, 119–120
and EDS, *see* Energy-dispersive x-ray spectroscopy (EDS)
phosphoric acid, itch and bond procedure, 120, 121
tooth-colored resins, 122
written documentation, 120
Science and forensic odontology
ABFO, *see* American Board of Forensic Odontology (ABFO)
ASFO, 70
challenges, 69
CSI effect, 69
Daubert standard, 67
definition, 62
experimental design, 63–65
expert witness, 67
Frye test, 66–67
FSF, 70–71
Grants.gov, 71
and law, 66
NIJ, 71
the 2009 NRC report, 69–70
randomized control trials, 65
scientific method, 62
sensitivity, 65
specificity, 66
Search and recovery team, disaster sites
assessment, 167
careful expediency, 167
leader and photographer, 167–168
operations, 166–167
transportation team, 168
SEM, *see* Scanning electron microscopy (SEM)
Sharks, 327–328
Sharp force trauma, 52–53
SLA, *see* Stereolithography (SLA)
Standard photographic views, bitemarks
close-up working photographs, 278–279
description, 277
orientation photos, 278
State of the science, bitemarks
ABFO Bitemark Terminology, 263–264
analysis and legal testimony, scientific basis, 266–268
bitemark recognition, 260–263
child abuse, 264–266
criminal activities, 264
sexual assault, 265–266
types, crime, 264

Stereolithography (SLA)
description, 282–283
forensic dentistry, 283
The Stryker saw method
jaw resection, 107
pruning shears method, 107, 108
Subpoena, 387

T

Temporary morgue, disaster sites
"ideal" morgue set-up, 165
Katrina victims, 165, 166
medical examiner, 165
size and fatalities, 165, 166
Tissue decomposition
autolysis, 47
blood ethanol level, 48
discoloration, 48, 49
putrefaction, 47
skeletonization, 48
temperature, 48
Tissue incision, excision and preservation, 287–288
Tooth numbering systems, *see* Dental notation/numbering systems
Tooth-related anomalies, radiography
dens in dente, 134
dentinogenesis imperfecta, 135–136
enamel hypoplasia, 135, 136
extra roots, 135
gemination/fusion, 139, 140
hyperdontia, 140–141
iatrogenesis, 139
internal and external root resorption, 137
microdontia, 139, 140
pulp stones, 136
retained deciduous teeth, 142
root dilaceration, 134, 135
rotated lateral incisors, 142
sclerotic pulp chambers, 135, 136
shovel-shaped incisors, 137
supernumerary teeth, 141
talon cusps/accessary cusp, 138
taurodontism, 137–138
transposed teeth, 141
unusual impacted teeth, 142–143
Transillumination, 288–289

U

UDIM, *see* UVIS Dental Identification Module (UDIM)
Ultraviolet (UVA) photography
Baader Venus UV band passfilter, 302–303
healing injury, 298–300
patterned injury, 298, 299
surface damage, 300–301
tripod-mounted TTL digital camera, 302
Unidentified persons (UPs), *see* National missing and unidentified persons system (NamUs)
Unified Victim Identification System (UVIS)
description, 189
UDIM, *see* UVIS Dental Identification Module (UDIM)
Universal Numbering System
deciduous teeth, 93
description, 91, 92
permanent teeth, 93
Ursine dentitions (bears), 340–341
US death investigation systems, 4
U.S. legal system
application of law, cases
code-based systems, 380
common-law rule, 380
courts, guidelines, 379
HIPAA, 381–382
practicing dentistry, 381
court, 378–379
defined, 377–378
federal government, 377
UVIS, *see* Unified Victim Identification System (UVIS)
UVIS Dental Identification Module (UDIM)
description, 189
integration, digital image system, 190
intuitive algorithm, 189–190

V

ViCAP, *see* Violent Criminal Apprehension Program (ViCAP)
Vinylpolysiloxane (VPS) impression, 292, 342, 344
Violent Criminal Apprehension Program (ViCAP), 204
Visible light fluorescence
contrast and color, 119
enamel and dentin fluoresce, 118
light-emitting diodes (LEDs), 119
maxilla, 395-nm UV Led light, 119, 120
properties, 119
VPS impression, *see* Vinylpolysiloxane (VPS) impression

W

The Weapons of Mass Destruction (WMD), 163
WinID3
"bridge" with DEXIS, 188

charting odontogram, 186, 187
description, 186
discovery, 186
image window, 186, 187
intuitive algorithm, 186
touch screen tablets, 188
use, 186, 188
WMD, *see* The Weapons of Mass Destruction (WMD)

X

X-ray fluorescence (XRF)
analytical tools, 125
description, 124
elemental composition, 125
miniaturization, 124
restorative resins, 124–125
XRF, *see* X-ray fluorescence (XRF)